A Guide to the Sources of United States Military History

EDITED BY

ROBIN HIGHAM

ARCHON BOOKS
HAMDEN, CONNECTICUT
1975

Library of Congress Cataloging in Publication Data

Main entry under title:

A Guide to the sources of United States military history.

1. United States—History, Military—Bibliography. I.
Higham, Robin D. S.
Z1249.M5G83 [E181]   016.355′00973   75-14455
ISBN 0-208-01499-3

First published 1975 as an
Archon Book, an imprint of
The Shoe String Press, Inc.
Hamden, Connecticut 06514

Printed in the United States of America

A Guide to the Sources of
United States Military History

Dedicated to
LEW WIGGIN,
who thought of the idea

CONTENTS

EDITORIAL NOTE

The authors of each of the chapters in this book were given the following instructions:

> Each chapter is to be 20 double-spaced text pages and 300 entries. Each author should provide a section on general references, background surveys, and useful periodicals which will be added to the Introduction. Then he should survey first the broad literature and monographs that apply in general to the whole period or field. After that he should proceed logically to cover policy, strategy, tactics, planning, logistics and operations, as applicable. Special attention may be given to incidents that have been controversial. Robin Higham, *A Guide to the Sources of British Military History* (1972) should be used as a reference. Each essay should end with information in the book list on the various applicable archives, their location, and any restrictions or prior application for their use which are necessary (but do not give the name of the person to whom to apply, only his title), and the whole should conclude with suggestions for further research.

Coverage of the Civil War was restricted both because it is already well handled and so as not to unbalance the book. The authors also received instructions on arranging entries—to use the Library of Congress citation form so that entries would generally be found in card catalogues where LC put them. This raises occasional problems as, for instance, in the case of the U.S. Army "green volumes", the official history of World War II, where the LC main entry is under the authors and not under "U.S. Department of the Army, Office of the Chief of Military History," etc. The alphabetical/numerical list at the end of each chapter is designed for easy checking by librarians.

This book differs from *A Guide to the Sources of British Military History* (146). That volume did not include material on museums. It probably should have.

By agreement with Archon Books, each author is keeping a file of new materials with the expectation that at the end of each quinquennial period a supplement to the volume will be issued. Suggestions for additions, corrections, and comments may be sent either to the Editor or directly to the authors of the chapters.

Most chapters were completed before May 1974.

R. H.

Kansas State University

AUTHORS

Dean C. Allard, Head of the Operational Archives of the U.S. Naval History Division in Washington, served in the USN from 1955 to 1958, when he joined the Division. A graduate of Dartmouth, he received his Ph. D. from George Washington University and is a frequent panelist at professional meetings as well as a contributor to scholarly journals such as *The American Neptune*.

Daniel R. Beaver, professor of history at the University of Cincinnati, was educated at Heidelberg College and received his Ph. D. from Northwestern University. A former infantryman, he is the author of *Newton D. Baker* (1966) and of *Some Pathways in Twentieth Century History* (1969).

William R. Braisted, professor of history at the University of Texas at Austin is a graduate of Stanford and received his Ph. D. from the University of Chicago. A military intelligence analyst for the U.S. Army in World War II, he has since been a Fulbright fellow in Japan. His publications include *The United States Navy in the Pacific, 1897-1909* (1958) and *The United States Navy in the Pacific, 1909-1922* (1971).

James O. Breeden is professor of history at Southern Methodist University. A graduate of the University of Virginia, he obtained his Ph.D. from Tulane University in 1967. He is the author of a number of articles and of *Joseph Jones, MD—Scientist of the Old South* (1974).

Calvin L. Christman, associate professor of history at William Penn College in Iowa, got his A.B. at Dartmouth and his Ph.D. at The Ohio State University in 1971. His specialty is modern American diplomatic history and relations with Latin America, while his dissertation was on the economic mobilization for World War II.

Robert W. Coakley, Deputy Chief Historian, Center for Military History, Department of the Army Washington, D.C., was graduated from William and Mary and received his Ph. D. from the University of Virginia. He was both a field artilleryman and a military historian in World War II. He is the co-author of a number of official volumes including two on global logistics and strategy in World War II and is also with Stetson Conn responsible for the forthcoming CMH study, *The War of the American Revolution: Narrative, Chronology and Bibliography*.

B. Franklin Cooling III, is both Chief of the Historical Research and Reference Branch, U.S. Army Military History Research Collection, Carlisle Barracks, and member of the faculty, U.S. Army War College. In the Army Reserve, 1956-1963, he graduated from Rutgers and received his Ph. D. from the University of Pennsylvania. He is co-compiler of the annual dissertations in *Military Affairs* and is the author of *Benjamin Franklin Tracy: Father of the Modern American Fighting Navy* (1973) and *Symbol, Sword, and Shield: Defending Washington during the Civil War* (1975).

Richard N. Ellis, professor of history at the University of New Mexico, received his Ph. D. from the University of Colorado in 1967. He has contributed a large number of articles to a variety of periodicals and is the author of *General Pope and the U.S. Indian Policy* (1970), *New Mexico, Past and Present* (1971), and of *The Western American Indian: Case Studies in Tribal History* (1972).

Edward C. Ezell, a NASA contractor with the University of Houston, graduated from Butler University, had a Hagley Museum Fellowship and received his Ph.D. from the Case Institute of Technology. He specializes in arms procurement and has contributed articles to a number of journals in the field and was in 1975 awarded the AMI's Moncado Prize.

Robert Frank Futrell, a graduate of the University of Mississippi, received his Ph.D. from Vanderbilt. He joined the USAAF Historical Office in Washington in 1946 and the staff of the Air University Maxwell AFB, in 1950, retiring in 1974 after serving with the Project Corona Harvest staff evaluating the air war in Southeast Asia. He served in the field artillery and in the USAAF in World War II. He is the author of a large number of official monographs and of *The United States Air Force in Korea, 1950-1953* (1961) and of *Ideas, Concepts Doctrine: A History of Basic Thinking in the United States Air Force, 1907-1964* (1971).

Kenneth J. Hagan, a graduate of the University of California at Berkeley, receive his Ph.D. from the Claremont Graduate School in 1970. He is currently an associate professor of history at the United States Naval Academy and the author of *American Gunboat Diplomacy in the Old Navy 1877-1889* (1973) and is the contributor of articles to a number of journals and to the USNI's *America Spreads Her Sails* (1973).

Robin Higham, professor of history at Kansas State University and Editor of both *Military Affairs* and of *Aerospace Historian*, is the author of a number of books and articles, edited *A Guide to the Sources of British Military History* (1971) and *Bayonets in the Streets* (1969). He is the author of *Air Power: A Concise History* (1973) and of *The Compleat Academic* (1975). He served in the RAFVR, 1943-47.

Douglas Edward Leach received his A.B. from Brown University and his Ph.D. from Harvard. Currently professor of history at Vanderbilt University, he has been a Fulbright lecturer at the Universities of Liverpool and Auckland. His publications include *Flintlock and Tomahawk: New England in King Philip's War* (1958), *The Northern Colonial Frontier, 1607-1763* (1966), and *Arms for Empire: A Military History of the British Colonies in North America, 1607-1763* (1973).

Philip K. Lundeberg, Curator of Naval History at the Smithsonian Institution, received his A.B. from Duke and his Ph.D. from Harvard. He joined the Smithsonian staff in 1959, after serving in both World War II and the Korean War in the USN. He has contributed to numerous books and is the author of *The Continental Gunboat Philadelphia* (1966) and of *Samuel Colt's Submarine Battery* (1975) as well as since 1968 writing the "Museums Perspective" in *Military Affairs*. He was president of the American Military Institute, 1971-73.

Grady McWhiney received his B.S. from Centenary College and his Ph. D. from Columbia. He is Chairman of the Department of History at the University of Alabama and is the author of the Prize-winning *Braxton Bragg and Confederate Defeat* (1969). Often a visiting professor, he is also the author of *Southerners and other Americans* (1973) and co-editor of *Robert E. Lee's Dispatches to Jefferson Davis* (1957) and of *To Mexico with Taylor and Scott* (1969), and editor of *Grant, Lee, Lincoln and the Radicals* (1964).

Roger L. Nichols, professor of history at the University of Arizona, graduated from Wisconsin State College, La Crosse, and received his Ph. D. from the University of Wisconsin. He is the author of *The American Indian: Past and Present* (1971), *The Missouri Expedition, 1818-1820* (1969), and of *General Henry Atkinson: A Western Military Career* (1965), as well as of some 50 articles.

Carroll W. Pursell, Jr. received both his A.B. and his Ph.D. from the University of California at Berkeley. Co-editor of *Technology and Western Civilization* (1968), he is the author of *Early Stationary Steam Engines in America* (1969) and editor of *The Politics of American Science*. He is professor of history at Lehigh University and secretary of the Society for the History of Technology.

Hugh F. Rankin, professor of history at Tulane University, graduated from Elon College and received his Ph.D. from the University of North Carolina at Chapel Hill. A former superintendent of highway construction he served in the Corps of Engineers, USA, in World War II. Co-author of *Rebels and Redcoats* (1957) and author of *North Carolina in the American Revolution* (1959) and of *Pirates of Colonial North Carolina* (1950), *The American Revolution* (1964), and of *Francis Marion: Swamp Fox* (1973), he is well known in his field.

Russell F. Weigley, professor of history at Temple University, graduated from Albright College and received his Ph.D. from the University of Pennsylvania. Editor of *Pennsylvania History*, 1962-1967, he is the author of *Quartermaster-General of the Union Army: A Biography of M. C. Meigs* (1959), *Towards an American Army: Military Thought from Washington to Marshall* (1962), *History of the United States Army* (1967) and *The American Way of War* (1973), a multiple book-club selection.

I

INTRODUCTION

Robin Higham
(with the assistance of the contributors)

This *Guide* to the sources of American military history is shorter than the 1971 *A Guide to the Sources of British Military History* from which it sprang for the field is smaller and the activities covered less diffuse. In contrast to British history as a whole, American history is far better served with up-to-date reference tools.

Apart from the few topical fields—the European background, science and technology, military and naval medicine, and museums as historical sources—the arrangement is chronological. Thus there may be some overlap between chapters, or a need to consult one or more sections. The essays should be used as introductions and the lists of titles considered selective rather than definitive. No bibliography can hope to be up to date. Most essays in this book were finished before May 1974, so that the important periodicals in the field should be surveyed since that date for new works.

It was only in World War II and then with a sharp acceleration in the 1950s that military affairs came under constructive scrutiny from amateurs, professionals and politicians at the same time that business administrators were developing new management tools for cost-accounting. The importance of this work for historians lies in the new concepts and tools it has made available. Similarly, World War II is the first war in U.S. history to be well covered by official histories, adding a new dimension to research and documentation since then, too.

GENERAL REFERENCE AND BIBLIOGRAPHY. Scholars in U.S. history are very fortunate in that the field is well covered by up-to-date references. Researchers must start with the revised *Harvard Guide to American History* (134). Its weakness is that it provides little guidance as to the value of the works cited. A comparison of the *Harvard Guide*'s lists in the military, naval, and aeronautical fields will show that the authors of this *Guide* have chosen, quite rightly, to omit some of the broad general histories and even some specialist studies which they consider of little value. In this respect, researchers should remember that the newest book is not always the best, though recent monographs usually provide up-to-date references.

1

In addition to the *Harvard Guide*, the Goldentree bibliographies in American History (119) may also be helpful as these paperback volumes cover a number of topical areas such as economic and social history. Of a more specialized nature is Hardin Craig, Jr's., international chronological list of military encyclopedias and dictionaries (83) which helps when wanting a contemporary title through which to identify a technical term; Albion's naval and maritime bibliography (8), is of course, an indispensable standard guide; Kurt Lang's *Military Institutions and the Sociology of War* (188) has interesting introductory chapters and a well-balanced survey of the literature from around the world. Also of specialized interest are Arthur D. Larson's *Civil-Military Relations and Militarism* (192); the Dupuys' *Encyclopedia of Military History* (99), which is both a chronology and a bibliography; and Trevor Dupuys' *A Documentary History of the American Armed Forces* (101) (due to appear as this went to press and which can be valuable). More specialized is Ziegler's *World War II: books in English* (393) and its supplements.

In the modern field are Greenwood (123) and Burt (62), which started out to be more comprehensive than they have ended up—the original bibliography by Greenwood being broken into several additional volumes and the historical perspective vitiated. Lastly, the Conference on British Studies *Current Research in British History* (73) indicates tangential research in one other country.

The *Library of Congress Catalog* is a useful bibliographical tool especially for checking citations, and has subject indices. However, entries are at times erratic. If in doubt or if only part of a series is listed, a letter to the LC Reference Division may turn up an answer or a full listing of all items.

Over and above these the British Ministry of Defence (Central and Army) Library (Old War Office Building, London S.W.1, England) provides a very comprehensive acquisitions list free of charge and also has compiled over 2200 subject bibliographical lists which include U.S. topics. An index to these is available (121). Another basic set of bibliographies are those of the U.S. Army Military History Research Collection at Carlisle Barracks (336). By 1975 ten had appeared. It should be noted, however, that they cover only the MHRC's own collections. On the other hand, this makes them exceptionally useful for interlibrary loan or for ordering photocopies. Another similarly vital work is the *West Point Library Catalogue*, a $450 item which reproduces the card-catalogue entries for that special collection (352).

Certain special service libraries have excellent collections of books. Notable is the U.S. Navy War College Library at Newport, R.I., the Army Library in the Pentagon, and the U.S. Air Force Academy Library, to name just a few. As clearance may sometimes be needed for access to these facilities, it is wise to write ahead. Faculty of state universities and colleges are government employees and their official I.D. card is often a key to doors which do not have classified material behind them.

There is now a large collection of worldwide *Who's Who's* (379). Though not much help for the period before 1900, after that date they are a gradually increasing resource. It must be noted, however, that the subjects provide their own material and that they change the emphasis as they advance in years. As an adjunct to the series, there are also *Who Was Who* volumes (four for the U.S. currently) which give death dates. For guidance see *The Marquis*

Who's Who Bibliographical Library of Indispensible Reference Works, now issued annually.

In 1973/74 Xerox University Microfilms produced a 37-volume index of virtually all 400,000 doctoral dissertations, many of which deal with military affairs, accepted in American Ph.D. programs since they started in 1861, to which will be added annual supplements. More concisely usable is Allan R. Millett and B. Franklin Cooling's *Doctoral Dissertations in [in the field of] Military Affairs* (228), first published in 1972 and updated annually in the April 1973 *Military Affairs*, and thereafter in the February issue. It covers all known dissertations in English.

A research aid is the Library of Congress *Subject Collections* which lists the special holdings of 15,000 libraries and museums in the US and Canada with entries arranged by LC headings. The major source for U.S. Government materials outside USGPO catalogues is the National Archives which has recently reorganized the Military Archives Division along more funtional lines. The Military Projects Branch will produce finding aids and microfilm; the Navy and Old Army Branch will handle all Navy and Army records to 1940; the Modern Military Branch will handle all records from 1940 to 1954 (as of 1975) as well as captured records.

An increasingly important source will be TV materials, as yet unsystematized. Vanderbilt University started to tape the daily news broadcasts during the Vietnam War and this led to a suit in 1974 by the Columbia Broadcasting System, which then decided, before the issue was resolved, to give its tapes to the National Archives.

The catalogues of a number of companies specializing in reprinting and microfilms or microfiche may be well worth perusing: NCR Microcards, Arno, Bell & Howell, Xerox University Microfilms, for instance. In addition, University Microfilms has an extensive out-of-print (OP) service as well as controlling the reproduction of dissertations in the United States. (In this last respect, some universities, such as Harvard and Kansas State, allow candidates to have their works sequestered for a number of years until they can have them published.) A librarian knows how to order almost any dissertation on film for a fee (in 1974 it was $4.00).

Another publisher whose list merits careful perusal is the United States Naval Institute which has marketed many of the main contributions to naval history since 1945. The wise researcher learns, in fact, which presses consistently produce good books and to note everything applicable in their catalogues as well as spotting which journals make the widest contribution to the field in terms of both articles and books noticed.

The United States is ill-served as compared to Britain with bookshops devoted to military materials. The Soldier Shop (1013 Madison Ave., New York City, NY, 10021) lists many interesting bibliographic and model items in its catalogue and also publishes a specialized quarterly (508). Recently the Military History Bookshop opened (29A Grove St., Boston, Mass., 02114) and its catalogues are a succinct bibliography in themselves.

JOURNALS. The field of U.S. Military history in general is served by two types of journals—current and historical. In the first category are all those like *Military Review*, *Cavalry/Armor*, *Marine Corps Gazette*, *Infantry*

Journal, United States Naval Institute Proceedings, Air Force Magazine, and the masses of Department of Defense (DOD) and other official and semi- or quasi-official publications which are so useful for historians for their information on contemporary service developments. A partial listing is included at the end of this chapter (397-).

On the other side are the historical journals, of which relatively few publish articles on military affairs. This is in part because for many years few scholars wrote in the field, though each war has caused some noted historians to jump on the bandwagon. But since World War II the ranks of military historians have been swelling until in 1974 they represented some five percent of the American Historical Association's membership and number, according to memberships in the American Military Institute, close to 1000 strong.

The historical journals publishing military history may be divided into six groups. First there are the few journals such as *Civil War History*, *Military Affairs*, and *Aerospace Historian* which do scholarly historical articles; then there are the publications for the buffs such as *The Military Historian and Collector*, *Warship International*, the *Journal of the American Aviation Historical Society*, and the Council on Abandoned Military Posts (CAMP)'s *Periodical*, which concentrate on rather narrow, often technological pieces. Third come the service-oriented publications such as *Army*, the *USNI Proceedings*, *Military Review*, *Air University Review*, *Air Force Magazine*, the *Marine Corps Gazette* and others, which occasionally publish such pieces, usually without notes. Fourth, there are the state historical journals and the regional and topical magazines, such as *Journal of the West*, which from time to time print excellent articles of limited scope, and, fifth, there are the standard journals like *American Heritage* and *American History Illustrated*, and sixth, the standard scholarly journals such as the *American Historical Review* and the *Journal of American History*.

The USAF *Air University Library Index of Military Periodicals* lists service journals available to the public as well as private magazines, such as *Aerospace Historian*, to which regular subscriptions may be obtained. It is not, however, reliable for. coverage varies from issue to issue with current usefulness the criterion. The Naval War College at Newport, R.I., 02840, has a wide collection of periodicals and will make available on request a list of what it receives. Many of these are new specialist journals, such as *Data*, and others are house organs of particular companies, such as *Exxon* (formerly *Esso) Air World*, which nevertheless sometimes contain technical and historical work by experts designed to be read by the average intelligent reader.

Occasionally, journals not in the field will run special issues which may be of interest, such as "The Military after Vietnam: The Search for Legal Controls," *Indiana Law Journal*, summer 1974. Or a government research division will do a study in order to bring expertise to bear, i.e., *Military Blood Banking, 1941-1973: Lessons Learned Applicable to Civil Disasters and Other Considerations* (335).

The series, *Academic Writer's Guide to Periodicals* (2), tells a good deal not only about the journals in any geographical field, but also indicates their editorial biases in the early 1970s.

A not-to-be-neglected source are the indices (526-) for periodicals, where these exist. Recently completed are those for *Aerospace Historian* (7), *American Heritage* (15), *The Cavalry Journal/Armor* (65), *Military Affairs* (223),

Military Review (224), and on microfilm, the *USNI Proceedings* (362).

The general field of article bibliography has become overwhelming with the proliferation of journals. What makes this especially difficult has been the failure of the major journals to recognize military history as a field, and a very broad one at that.

A good example is *Writings on American History* (19) which began in 1902 with a first volume in 1903. As the amount of materials increased, its production fell farther and farther behind so that the *Writings . . . 1961* appeared in 1975. The missing *Writings . . . 1962-1973* were then consolidated into four volumes and published by the AHA with Kraus in 1975. At the same time the AHA finally created a new system and *Writings on American History, 1973-74*, it was hoped, would be the first of a series which would cover from June to June each year. It provided an alphabetical list by author of most writings in American history with eighteen columns devoted to military and naval history, while the volume itself also contained an author index. Starting in 1976 the AHR will excise the "Recently Published Articles" from the journal and issue these instead thrice yearly as separates instead of, as at present, producing them in the February, June, and October *AHR*'s. Better bibliographical control has been obtained, in part through exchanges between the AHR and other scholarly journals. The first volume, however, did not cover *Aerospace Historian* articles, though the journal was listed as being indexed. The *Recently Published Articles* series is expected to be worldwide in scope. *The Journal of American History* (463) has a similar compilation in each issue. An additional source is *Historical Abstracts* (152) which not only gives citations, but summarizes the article.

In the military history field, guides to articles are also found in the "Recent Journal Articles" in *Military Affairs* (476) and a similar, but variable listing of books and articles in the *United States Naval Institute Proceedings* (522) (including in the December issue each year an article on notable naval books, actually written in September), and the *Air University Library Index to Military Periodicals*. Each of these listings suffers some over the years from the different interests and breadth of vision of the compilers.

An additional bibliographical aid, coming late for the historical as compared to the scientific fields, is computerized bibliography. One such system is Nexus (247). How useful it is for the price will depend on how well the key-word system works and how much trouble it is to check the numeric for a journal against its name on another list.

OTHER SOURCES. *Brassey's Naval Annual*, later *Armed Forces Yearbook* and now the *RUSI and Brassey's Defence Annual*, though a British publication, has frequently had a number of interesting articles on the US forces.

The Brookings Institution, whose primary concern is economic, produces staff papers and full-length studies which tackle many defense problems, such as *U.S. Reserve Forces: the problem of the week-end warrior* (41). *The Brookings Bulletin* provides summaries of these findings.

A MAJOR OVERVIEW. The broadest attempt to write a military history of the United States is, of course, the current Macmillan Wars of the United States Series (209), edited by Louis Morton. This will eventually cover all three services. The volumes so far produced are scholarly, but readable, and in many cases will be definitive for some time to come. As is inevitable in cooperative or contributed efforts, there have been changes of authors, and not all the authors first contacted could or would join the project. Each volume has its own bibliography.

SERVICE BIBLIOGRAPHIC AND OTHER SOURCES. Each of the services has provided some direct bibliographical aid to its students. The Army has Maurice Matloff's volume, *American Military History* (214), which has a well-planned bibliography, while the book itself, designed as an ROTC instructional text, is an inexpensive one-volume guide, but lacking, of course, the detail of the Macmillan set (209).

On the Army a beginning may be made with Bernardo and Bacon, *American Military Policy* (34); Walter Millis, *American Military Thought* (229) and *Arms and Men* (230); O'Connor, *American Defense Policy in Perspective* (251); Russell F. Weigley, *The American Way of War* (214), and T. Harry Williams, *Americans at War* (382). Beyond these general scholarly syntheses lie a plethora of monographs, biographies, reports, guides, regulations and manuals, reports, hearings, periodicals, and collections of original documents which must be patiently mined. Two additional official bibliographies are on the Reserves (333) and the Army and National Guard (332).

The Navy's equivalent to Matloff is the privately published Potter & Nimitz, *Sea Power* (265), which covers the whole of naval history and has a reasonable bibliography. The Naval History Division has produced two useful lists (356, 357), the first of which covers books and the second of which indicates sources in the Washington area. The best work on naval strategy is that by Brodie (56).

In addition Myron J. Smith, Jr.'s *American Naval Bibliography* series (294) has recently been published. It marks a new era in naval historiography. Nothing like it has been attempted in over a half century and the interested student can now find entries for almost every conceivable topic. Smith's contribution should make possible a new general history of the period 1789-1890. The best coverage at present is in Dudley Knox, *A History of the United States Navy* (185), which is over twenty-five years old.

As Smith's bibliography makes evident, the most valuable periodical source for American naval history is the *U.S. Naval Institute Proceedings*. That journal began publication in 1874, and thus it is in some respects a primary source as well as a collection of useful secondary articles. The next most useful journal is *Military Affairs*, which has published articles on a variety of naval subjects.

The U.S. Marine Corps has long had an active historical program, one of the latest of whose products is *The Marines in Vietnam, 1954-1974* (346), and Hilliard's annotated reading list (151). A labor-of-love bibliography on the Corps is Capt. John B. Moran's *Creating a Legend* (231), a mammoth descriptive catalogue of writings on the USMC.

Nor is the Coast Guard to be forgotten; it has produced recently its own annotated source list (341).

The U.S. Air Force has yet to produce a satisfactory, generally available text, though one is in process by Colonel Hurley (209) in the Macmillan series. Until then, Higham's *Air Power: A Concise History* (144) will have to fill the niche.

The recently formed Office of Air Force History has only started to turn out such materials, starting with *United States Air Force History: An Annotated Bibliography* (320) and continuing with *United States Air Force History: A Guide to Documentary Sources* (321). Many specialized studies have been done by the historians at Maxwell AFB, a list of whose work may now be obtained from the Albert F. Simpson Center at the Air University there as the list in *Official Histories* (147) is incomplete due to classification problems in the 1960's. Little (201), suggests a handbook for military institutions while Rodberg and Shearer, *Pentagon Watchers* (279) gives, perhaps, the best single tool to researchers through an appendix, "How to Research the Military," surely to remain basic for the future.

The United States government is a tremendously large activity and over even the short life so far of the country has generated great quantities of material, all of which are uncopyrighted and in the public domain, though not all ever will be fully declassified. These resources consist of both printed and achival sources. Chapter XIX contains a guide to the materiel collections, while our individual authors have noted the documentary resources available for research in a particular period.

LOCAL SOURCES. In addition to contemporary journals, there are also newspapers of the national, state and local genre, not to mention post and base papers. Care must be taken in the use of these materials. Journalists are not always accurate, artists may have been nowhere near the scenes they depict, and what, for instance, appears on the front page may not be the story which "Shipping Intelligence" tells (149). The best guides to these sources are the *Harvard Guide*, and the specialized newspaper and serials reference works found in any standard college library collection.

Other than these items, base or post archives are a rarity owing to a lack of historical sense in most officers with the result that unless there is a strong local or state historical society with an interest in these materials, they have usually been thrown out, or they only show up in odd places outside the National Archives. For instance, in addition to the Kansas City Records Center, The Eisenhower Library at Abilene, Kansas, had at one time 275 foot lockers of World War II army records including a set of divisional scrapbooks from a training base on the West Coast now, in 1975, being processed for public use.

Two helpful items in this area are Cumming's *Guide to the Writing of Local History* (86) and Murray's *Brief Guide to Research on Army Posts (238).*

OTHER DOCUMENTARY SOURCES. Corporate and labor records are equally mysterious. General Motors says it gave its wartime records for the 1941-45 period for aircraft production to the Army. But numerous inquiries have failed, so far, to locate these. Yet they could be a useful source for a fresh look at wartime technology, procurement, and industrial management and production. The best guide to business materials is that produced at the Graduate School of Business Administration at Harvard by Lorna Daniells (88).

A surprising number of business and other public and private records have found their way to state historical and other society archives, which should be consulted. Usually the curators are extremely knowledgeable and can quickly indicate what they hold.

Much harder to track down, but sometimes valuable, are the collections of private materials still not in archives or historical societies, though clues to their whereabouts may be in state historical journals or those for retired personel. With the current large number of military men, regular and temporary, in the United States today, this sort of material may provide additional insights.

A lot has been done in the last twenty years with oral history in this respect. Columbia University maintains a large archive (72, 39). A combined program operated by the U.S. Army War College and the Command & General Staff College is beginning to interview retired generals (See Chapter XVII). The value of this material depends on a number of factors—the attitude of the person being interviewed, the knowledge of the person doing so, and the transcription and editing of the end result. Thus interviews long after the event should be approached with something of the same skepticism that Edmund G. Love mentions in regard to post-battle debriefings in *War is a Private Affair* (202). Sample questionnaires may be found in the back of the USAMHRC *Spanish-American War Era*, part I (336).

The best guide to manuscripts is Philip Hamer, ed., *A Guide to Archives and Manuscripts in the United States* (130). There is also an LC catalogue (345). Some individual research libraries also have published guides to their holdings, but Hamer is certainly the place to start. Major university libraries, state historical societies, and private research institutions such as the Newberry Library and the Huntington Library and Art Gallery all have extensive manuscript collections. The Manuscript Division of the Library of Congress also houses the papers of many national leaders—including leading political and military figures.

TECHNICAL KNOWLEDGE. A good way to pick up an intimate knowledge of what servicemen at the time were required to know is to browse the used bookstores for *The Bluejacket's Manual* (365), *Knight's Modern Seamanship* (184), instructional manuals for artillery officers (14), and what have you. Yet another way is to seek out the weapons volumes in the now discontinued Ballantine series on World War II and on the Violent Century. Both these series were illustrated with contemporary photographs and line drawings and were written for the 15-32 age-group, many of whom had never been in the service. For older weapons there are numerous useful volumes, while a wealth of detail is also to be found in books on uniforms and equipment such as those listed in *The Soldier Shop Quarterly* (508).

The identification of modern naval vessels and information as to their characteristics is to be found in either *Jane's Fighting Ships* (169) or for World War II there are Fahey's *Ships and Aircraft of the USN* (105), and Silverstone's *U.S. Warships of World War II* (292). Special studies of the development of aircraft-carriers, a major US weapon are by MacDonald (206) and Polmar (263).

In addition, for guns there are works by Harold L. Peterson of the National Park Service (259, 260), Lewis (198), and others and of Ian Hogg on artillery

(154, 155). For the modern period Smith & Smith's *Small Arms of the World* (295), the older editions of which trace weapons back to approximately the mid-19th century, is comprehensive. Tanks are well served with the Profile series on armoured fighting vehicles (266), with Chamberlain and Ellis on British and American tanks (66) and on tanks in general (67) and with the excellent general approach to the topic by Macksey and Batchelor (208).

There is no source for American aviation comparable to the Putnam series on British aircraft and the companies who made them. However, the series also contains *United States Navy Aircraft since 1911* (313) and *United States Military Aircraft since 1908* (312). Both provide a wealth of information arranged by producing companies. Equally useful is Ray Wagner's *American Combat Planes* (370), which has the advantage that it shows the development of various types, including all experimental models. How aircraft actually were flown is the subject of *Flying Combat Aircraft of the USAAF-USAF* (145).

And lastly, in the modern day, the May issue of both *Air Force Magazine* and the *USNI Proceedings* and the October issue of *Army* carry annual reports which usually include the structure of the service with the names of the officers and civilians in charge of major departments, divisions, and units.

Old or contemporary runs of specialized periodicals read with attention provide both knowledge and the vocabulary which allows intelligent research and fluent writing.

For help in locating cartographic materials, start with Bowker's *International Maps and Atlases in Print* (47). The single most useful collection of maps is probably *The West Point Atlas of American Wars* (351) which was compiled for the use of the instructional staff and cadets. Other map collections are to be found in Adams (5) and Paullin (257) and in the various archives.

For a start on the environment in which the American military spent much of its time, see *Climates of North America* (60).

PHOTO SOURCES. There are a number of excellent sources for photographs such as the Bettman Archive of New York (35), the Library of Congress, the Presidential Libraries (395), and the National Archives. The latter especially gradually acquires the bulk of official photos as they are disposed of by the Washington agencies. Unfortunately, many valuable collections are not treated so systematically. Thus those at test facilities, in station, base, and post photo sections may have been discarded and the negatives destroyed or have been squirrelled away in some private collection. Since about 1900 many officers and some enlisted men collected pictures and had cameras of their own. Again, some warning words: pictures may be miscaptioned and great care should be taken to cross-check that they are what they purport to be and not some Hollywood set; second, most historians have had no training in photo identification. This is where knowledgeable curators of post museums or at the Smithsonian can be very helpful as can experts on weapons and uniforms, who can at least give the chronological parameters and sometimes the units within which the picture must have been taken.

Each of the services has its own photographic collections for the modern period. The Army Still Photo Library in the Pentagon (337) contains a large collection of pictures from the World War II era and before, including Air

Corps pictures from the days when the Signal Corps took all photos. It is an easy-to-use collection, but there is a searching fee if the researcher cannot visit the library. It is also the only photo collection that requires cash or a certified check with the order for prints. The Navy Photographic Center (353) is easy to use by mail. The user merely has to describe approximately what he or she wants, and information will be forthcoming as to what shots exist; these may be ordered and a personal check sent. All USAF photos are currently held in the 1361st Photo Squadron (324). The collection here runs back to the First World War and is indexed in a variety of ways. Not only does the collection hold a large number of USAAF-USAF shots, but also copies of pictures taken by US aircraft, including, for instance, those of foreign warships visiting Hawaii. It is possible that some of these collections may be transferred to the National Archives.

MILITARY FICTION. Military fiction has been explored by Wayne C. Miller in *An Armed America* (226), by Russell Spindler for the U.S. Armed Forces Institute self-study series (326), and for the USAF alone by Colonel Gatlin of the USAF Academy English Department (116).

NOTE. By no means everything in the list at the end of this chapter has been noted in the foregoing discussion. Nor has any attempt been made to make it comprehensive since many of the items that could be listed are to be found in the bibliographies of those works which are mentioned in the text.

SUGGESTIONS FOR FURTHER RESEARCH. Although the authors of each of the chapters have provided their own lists of suggestions for further research, there are also broad fields that remain wide open, which is one of the reasons that military history is still such an exciting field.

Very little has yet been done to see American military history in the main stream of comparative history, to talk about the patterns of military evolution within any society and to see how well the U.S. fits the general model. We are just getting profiles of American generals of the nineteenth century that will enable us to measure careers against a norm, that look at the American frontier experience against that of troops on other such borders. We still need to make real inroads into the mountains of recruiting and medical materials that are available, to use works like Stouffer *et al.*, *The American Soldier in Combat and After* (309) as a tool with which to explore other eras, as Pete Maslowski has done for the Civil War Soldier (211). Samuel Huntington has looked at *The Soldier and the State* (162) and Arthur Larson has provided a bibliography on civil-military relations (192), but there is still lots of room for further exploration in this area and perhaps for a new look at the man-on-horseback in America. Those interested could look more closely at the relationships between state governments and military forces including the matter of defending National Guardsmen in court as a consequence of their official actions.

While Kenneth J. Hagan and Peter Karsten and others have broken the ground on the naval side of diplomatic and imperial action (see chapters VI and XIII), little has yet been done to look at Army and Marine officers outside of some specific actions such as the occupations of Dominica and the like. Political scientists have explored some of the more recent cases, but historians could begin to look at service thinking behind bases overseas in political, economic, military, social (including familial) and ideological terms. There is as yet no scholarly history of Annapolis.

The military-industrial complex has generated a lot of heat in recent times, but it is not a new topic and arguments over weapons procurement and military costs need to be seen against a larger backdrop.

The whole ideological-educational area also could be more widely explored. The services have of necessity pioneered the teaching of masses of men and women in short order, but little has been written of this by military historians, yet it is one area in which the military have had a great impact on civilian society. Could much of the civilian electronic business have made a profit if the military had not trained its technicians for nothing?

Whole areas lie open to someone using new tools to look at the attitudes of active and retired military personnel of various ranks. Do they all commonly veer to the right politically, or are other patterns to be observed? What has been the relationship between the flying services and the airline and general aviation industries?

The history of veterans organizations has not been much attempted yet, but these are an important link in civil-military relations.

Women in the military has been a largely neglected subject except for some studies of nursing (331, 334) and of the World War II ferry pilots (175) and of the Women's Army Corps (314, 319). It is interesting to note that even the feminists have largely neglected, or are ignorant of, the role of their sex in military affairs. A bibliographic essay on women in the military is expected for *Military Affairs* for 1976.

The problem of minorities, which historiographically came earlier, has followed much the same pattern. Lee's (196) and Dalfiume's (87) volumes on the Army and the blacks and on desegregation in the forces were for a long time little known and there were only a few studies like Dudley Cornish's (77).

The area of medical history—since the Crimean War—is one in which much material has been collected by investigators and practitioners, often with at least as good an education as the historians of the day. Yet modern military historians have neglected these sources, which frequently throw new and sometimes different light onto past events.

And lastly, one of the areas to which military historians have paid very little attention is that of martial and military law. Currently about the only books of consequence on the subject are Wiener's *Civilians under Military Justice* (380) and Bishop (43), though *The Military Law Review* (460) contains excellent articles and some others are to be found in the *Index to Legal Periodicals*.

BIBLIOGRAPHY

1. Abrahamsson, Bengt. *Military Professionalization and Political Power*. Beverly Hills, California: Sage, 1972.
2. Academic Writer's Guide to Periodicals edited by Alexander S. Birkos and Lewis A. Tambs.

    a. *Latin American Studies* (1971)
    b. *East European and Slavic Studies* (1972)
    c. *African and Black-American Studies* (1975)
    d. *Middle Eastern Studies*
    e. *Asian Studies*
    f. *West European and Scandinavian Studies*
    g. *American and Canadian Studies*

3. Ackley, Charles Walton. *The Modern Military in American Society: A Study in the Nature of Military Power.* Philadelphia: Westminster Press, 1972.

4. Adams, F. D. *National Aeronautics and Space Administration Aeronautical Dictionary.* Glenview: Anthony Maita, 1959.

5. Adams, James Truslow, ed. *Atlas of American History.* New York: Scribner's, 1943.

6. Adams, James, Truslow, ed. *Dictionary of American History.* 2nd rev. ed. New York: Scribner's 1942-1961. 5 vols. J. G. Hopkins and W. Andrews, eds. vols. 6, *Supplement One.* New York: 1961.

7. *Aerospace Historian. Aerospace Historian Cumulative Index by Author, Title and Subject, 1954-1973.* Manhattan, Kansas: *Aerospace Historian,* 1974.

8. Albion, Robert Greenhalgh. *Naval & Maritime History: an annotated* bibliography. Mystic Seaport, Connecticut: 4th ed. 1972.

9. Ambrose, Stephen E. *Duty, Honor, Country: A History of West Point.* Baltimore,: Johns Hopkins Press, 1966.

10. Ambrose, Stephen E., and James Alden Barber, eds. *The Military and American Society,* New York: Free Press, 1972.

11. American Association of Railroads. *Railroads in Defense and War: A Bibliography.* Washington: AAR, 1953.

12. American Committee on the History of the Second World War. *The Second World War: A Bibliography; A Selected List of Publications Appearing since 1968.* Gainesville, Florida: American Committee on the History of the Second World War, 1972.

13. American Economic Association. *Index of Economic Articles in Journals and Collective Volumes.*

14. American Expeditionary Forces, Headquarters France. *Artillery Firing,* translated from the French edition of November 19, 1917. France: HQ, AEF, March 1918.

15. American Heritage. *A Chronological Subject Guide to American Heritage Magazine, December 1954 - October 1966: A Listing for Teachers and Students of the Articles in the First Twelve Years of The Magazine of History. Classified by Subject within Fourteen Major Periods of American History.* New York: American Heritage, 1967.

16. *American Heritage Pictorial Atlas of United States History.* New York: American Heritage, 1966.

17. *The American Historical Association's Guide to Historical Literature.* New York: Macmillan, 1961.

18. American Historical Association. Service Center for the Teachers of History. *Writings on World War II* by Louis Morton. Washington: AHA, 1967, pamphlet series.

19. American Historical Association. *Writings on American History: A Subject Bibliography of Articles.* Washington: AHA, 1903-

20. *America: History and Life: A Guide to Periodical Literature.* Santa Barbara: Clio Press, 1964.

21. American Library Association. *The Allied Occupation of Japan, 1945-1972: An Annotated Bibliography of Western-Language Materials,* compiled and edited by Robert E. Ward and Frank Joseph Shulman. Chicago: American Library Association, March 1974.

22. *American Reference Books.* Littleton, Colorado: Libraries Unlimited, 1970- . Annual.

23. *Armed Forces Journal. A Dictionary of American Military Anniversaries from 1775 to the Present.* New York: Macmillan, 1974.

24. *The Army Almanac: A Book of Facts Concerning the United States Army.* 2nd ed. Harrisburg: Stackpole, 1959.

25. Athearn, Robert G. *Forts of the Upper Missouri.* Lincoln: University of Nebraska Press, 1972.

26. *"The Atlas of the American Revolution*—Story behind the Book," *Publishers Weekly,* 8 December 1974, 38.

27. Bailey, Thomas A. *A Diplomatic History of the American People,* 7th edition, 1964. New York: Appleton-Century Crofts, 1940 and numerous successive editions.

28. Banks, Arthur. *A World Atlas of Military History,* I, *to 1500.* New York: Hippocrene, 1973.

29. Beadnell, C. M. *An Encyclopaedic Dictionary of Science and War* (1943). Detroit: Gale Research, reprint, 1974.

30. Beebe, G. W. *Battle Casualties: Incidence, Mortality and Logistic Considerations.* Glenview: Anthony Maita, 1952.

31. Beers, H. P. *Guide to the Archives of the Confedderate States of America.* Washington: G.P.O., 1968.

32. Beers, Henry P. *The Western Military Frontier, 1815-1846.* Philadelphia: University of Pennsylvania, 1935.

33. Berg, F. A. *Encyclopedia of Continental Army Units; Battalions, Regiments and Independent Corps.* Harrisburg: Stackpole, 1972.

34. Bernardo, C. Joseph, and Eugene H. Bacon. *American Military Policy: Its Development since 1775.* Harrisburg: Military Service Publishing Co., 1955.

35. Bettman Archive, 136 East 57th St, New York, NY 10022.

36. Billias, George Athan, and Gerald Grob. *American History, Retrospect and Prospect.* New York: Free Press, 1971.

37. Billings, J. D. *Hardtack and Coffee: Or the Unwritten Story of Army Life* (Reprint of 1887 ed.). Glendale, New York: Benchmark Publishing Corp, 1970.

38. Billington, Ray Allen. *Soldier and Brave: Indian and Military Affairs in the Trans-Mississippi West, Including a Guide to Historical Sites and Landmarks* (National Park Service). New York: Harper & Row, 1963.

39. Bilstein, Roger. "Sources in Aerospace History: Oral History Collections at Columbia University," *Aerospace Historian,* March, 1975.

40. Binkin, M. *Support Costs in the Defense Budget; the Submerged*

One-third. Washington: Brookings Institution, 1972.

41. Binkin, Martin. *U.S. Reserve Forces: The Problem of the Weekend Warrior.* Washington: Brookings Institution, 1974.
42. Birkos, Alexander S. "A Bibliographical Introduction to Foreign Military Periodicals," *Military Affairs*, December 1969.
43. Bishop, Joseph W. *Justice Under Fire: A Study of Military Law.* New York: Charterhouse, 1974.
44. Blum, Albert A. *Drafted or Deferred: Practices Past and Present.* Ann Arbor: University of Michigan Press, 1967.
45. Boehm, Eric H., and Lalit Adolphus, eds. *Historical Periodicals: An Annotated World List of Historical and Related Serial Publications.* Santa Barbara, California: Clio Press, 1961.
46. Bourne, P. G. *Men, Stress, and Vietnam.* Boston: Little, Brown Co., 1970.
47. Bowker, R. R., Co. *International Maps and Atlases in Print.* Compiled by Kenneth Winch. Ann Arbor, Michigan: R. R. Bowker, 1974.
48. Bowker, R. R., Co. *Oral History Collections.* Edited by Alan Meckler and Ruth McMullin. Ann Arbor, Michigan: R. R. Bowker, 1975.
49. Bowker, R. R., Co. *The Puerto Ricans: An Annotated Bibliography.* Edited by Paquito Vivo. Ann Arbor, Michigan: R. R. Bowker, 1973.
50. Bowker, R. R., Co. *Who's Who in American Politics, 1973-1974.* 14th Edition. Edited by Paul A. Theis and Edmund L. Henshaw, Jr. Ann Arbor, Michigan: R. R. Bowker, 1973.
51. Bowker, R. R., Co. *Subject Collections.* 4th edition. Edited by Lee Ash. Ann Arbor, Michigan: R. R. Bowker, 1974.
52. Brigham, Clarence S. *History and Bibliography of American Newspapers, 1690-1820.* Worcester, Massachusetts: American Antiquarian Society, 1947. 2 vols.
53. Brinckerhoff, Sidney B. *Metal Uniform Insignia of the Frontier U.S. Army 1846-1902.* Phoenix: Arizona Historical Society, 1973.
54. Brock, Peter. *Pacifism in the United States: From the Colonial Era to the First World War.* Princeton: Princeton University Press, 1968.
55. Broderick, John C. "Locating Major Resource Collections for Research in American Civilization," *American Studies*, Spring 1972, 3-10.
56. Brodie, Bernard. *A Guide to Naval Strategy.* Princeton: Princeton University Press, 1944.
57. Brodie, Bernard. *Strategy in the Missile Age.* Princeton: Princeton University Press, 1959.
58. Brodie, Bernard. *War and Politics.* New York: Macmillan, 1973.
59. Brodie, Bernard, and Fawn Brodie. *From Crossbow to H-Bomb.* Revised edition. Bloomington: Indiana University Press, 1973.
60. Bryson, R. A., and F. K. Hare, eds. *Climates of North America.* World Survey of Climatology, Vol. 11, 1974.
61. Buchan, Alastair. *War in Modern Society.* London: Watts, 1966.
62. Burt, Richard. *Congressional Hearings on American Defense Policy, 1947-1971: A bibliography.* Lawrence: University Press of Kansas. 1974.
63. Cagle, M. W. *The Naval Aviation Guide.* 2nd ed. Naval Institute, 1969.

64. Cartwright, William H., and Richard L. Watson, Jr, eds. *The Reinterpretation of American History and Culture*. Washington: National Council for the Social Studies, 1973.

65. *The Cavalry Journal/Armor Cumulative Indices, 1888-1968*. Compiled by Walter E. Young and arranged by John J. Vander Velde. Manhattan: Kansas State University Library Bibliographical Series No. 12, 1974.

66. Chamberlain, Peter, and Chris Ellis. *British and American Tanks of World War II: the complete illustrated history of British, American and Commonwealth tanks, 1939-1945*. New York: Arco, 1970.

67. Chamberlain, Peter, and Chris Ellis. *Pictorial History of Tanks of the World, 1915-1945*. Harrisburg: Stackpole, 1972.

68. Chapelle, H. I. *The Search for Speed Under Sail 1700-1855*. New York: Norton, 1967.

69. Chatfield, Charles. *For Peace and Justice: Pacifism in America, 1914-1941*. Knoxville: University of Tennessee Press, 1971.

70. Clark, David Sanders. *Index to Maps of the American Revolution in Books and Periodicals Illustrating the Revolutionary War and Other Events of the Period, 1763-1789*. Westport, Connecticut: Greenwood, 1974.

71. Cochran, Charles L., ed. *Civil-Military-Relations: Changing Concepts in the Seventies*. Glencoe, Illinois: Free Press, 1974.

72. Columbia University. Oral History Association, Box 20, Butler Library, Columbia University, New York, 10027.

73. Conference on British Studies. *Current Research in British History*. Various publishers (1975 edition, Manhattan, Kansas: *Military Affairs*, 1975).

74. Contributions to Military Sociology, Rotterdam University Press, 1972-
    1. *The Perceived Role of the Military* edited by M. R. van Gils (1971)
    2. *On Military Intervention* edited by Morris Janowitz. (1973)
    3. *On Military Idelogy* edited by Morris Janowitz (1972)
    4. Teitler, G. *The Professionalization of the Military Leadership: a sociological and historical analysis*.

75. Cook, A. A., and J. P. White. *Estimating the Quality of Air Force Volunteers*. Santa Monica: Rand Corp, 1970.

76. Cook, A. A. *The Supply of Air Force Volunteers*. Santa Monica: Rand Corp, 1970.

77. Cornish, Dudley. *The Sable Arm: Negro Troops in the Union Army, 1861-1865*. New York: Norton, 1966.

78. Council on Foreign Affairs. *Documents on American Foreign Relations*. New York: 1939-   . Annual.

79. Council on Foreign Relations. *Foreign Affairs Bibliography (1919-1962)*. 4 vols. New York: 1933-1964.

80. Council on Foreign Relations. *Foreign Affairs 50-Year Bibliography: New Evaluations of Significant Books on International Relations, 1920-1970*. New York: R. R. Bowker, 1972.

81. Council on Foreign Relations. *The United States in World Affairs*. New York: 1932-   . Annual.

82. Cox, Harvey, ed. *Military Chaplains*. Philadelphia: Pilgrim Press, 1974.

83. Craig, Hardin, Jr. *A Bibliography of Encyclopedias and Dictionaries Dealing with Military, Naval and Maritime Affairs, 1577-1971*. Houston, Texas: Dept. of History, Rice University, 1971.

84. Cuff, Robert D. "Newton D. Baker, Frank A. Scott, and "The American Reinforcement in the World War," *Military Affairs*, February 1970, 11-13.

85. Cullum, George W. *Bibliographical Register of the Officers and Graduates of the U.S. Military Academy*. 1868, 2 vols.

86. Cumming, John. *A Guide to the Writing of Local History*. Detroit: Michigan American Revolution Bicentennial Commission, 1974.

87. Dalfiume, Richard. *Desegregation of the U.S. Armed Forces: Fighting on Two Fronts, 1939-1953*. Columbia: University of Missouri Press, 1969.

88. Daniells, Lorna. *Studies in Enterprise: A Selected Bibliography of American and Canadian Company Histories and Biographies of Businessmen*. Boston: Baker Library, 1957 and later.

89. Dargan, Marion. *Guide to American biography*. Albuquerque: University of New Mexico Press, 1949-1952. 2 vols.

90. David, Jay and Elaine Crane. *The Black Soldier: from the American Revolution to Vietnam*. New York: William Morrow & Co., 1971.

91. Davis, Kenneth S., ed. *Arms, Industry and America*. The Reference Shelf, Vol. 43, No. 1. New York: H. W. Wilson Co., 1971.

92. Dickson, Paul. *Think Tanks: America's Newest and Most Ambitious Industry*. New York: Atheneum Publishers, 1971.

93. *Dictionary of American Biography*. Allen Johnson et al., eds. New York: Scribner's, 1928-1973, 20 vols. and 3 supplementary vols.

94. DiMona, Joseph. *The Great Court Martial Cases in American History*. New York: Grosset and Dunlap, 1972.

95. Dornbusch, Charles E. *Unit Histories of the United States Air Force including Privately Printed Personal Narrations*. Hampton Bays, New York: Hampton Books, 1958.

96. Dunner, Joseph (ed.). *Handbook of World History: concepts and issues*. New York: Philosophical Library, 1967.

97. Dupuy, Trevor N., and Wendell Blanchard. *The Almanac of World Military Power*. 2nd ed. New York: R. R. Bowker, 1972.

98. Dupuy, Trevor (ed.). *A Documentary History of the American Armed Forces*. New York: Random House, 1975.

99. Dupuy, R. Ernest, and Trevor N. Dupuy. *The Encyclopedia of Military History from 3500 BC to the Present*. New York: Harper & Row, 1970.

100. Dupuy, Col. R. Ernest, and Maj. Gen. William H. Baumer. *The Little Wars of the United States*. New York: Hawthorn, 1969.

101. Dupuy, R. E., and T. N. Dupuy. *Military Heritage of America*. New York: McGraw-Hill Book Co., 1973.

102. Ekirch, Jr., Arthur A. *The Civilian and the Military: A History of The American Anti-Militarist Tradition*. Colorado Springs, Ralph Myles Pub., 1973.

103. Ellis, John, and Robert Moore. *School for Soldiers: West Point and the Profession of Arms*. New York: Oxford, 1974.
104. Evans, Charles, comp. *American bibliography: A Chronological Dictionary of All Books, Pamphlets, and Periodical Publications Printed in the United States of America from the Genesis of Printing in 1639 down to and including the Year 1800*. Chicago: 1903-1934. 12 vols. Several supplementary volumes have been published starting in 1955. See also C. K. Shipton and J. E. Mooney, comps., *National index of American imprints through 1800: the short-title Evans*. Worcester, Massachusetts: American Antiquarian Society, 1969. 2 vols.
105. *Fahey's Ships and Aircraft of the U.S. Fleet*. Annapolis: various publishers since 1939, now USNI.
106. Farago, Ladislas. *Burn After Reading*. New York: Pinnacle, 1972.
107. Farer, T. J. *The Laws of War 25 Years after Nuremburg*. New York: Carnegie Endowment for International Peace, 1971.
108. Finn, J. (ed.). *Conscience and Command: Justice and Discipline in the Military*. New York: Random House, 1971.
109. Forbes, Harriette M. *New England Diaries, 1602-1800, a Descriptive Catalogue of Diaries, Orderly Books and Sea Journals*. Topsfield, Massachusetts: Privately printed, 1923.
110. Fox, Edward Whiting. *Atlas of American History*. Ithaca: Cornell University Press, 1964.
111. Fox, J. Ronald. *How the U.S. Buys Weapons*. Cambridge: Harvard University Press, 1974.
112. Fox, L. J., and T. O. Sullivan, and M. I. McCubbin. *Literature Review: Research on Military Offenders*. Ft. Riley, Kansas: U.S. Army Correctional Facility, March, 1970.
113. Friedman, Leon. *Law of War*. 2 vols. New York: Random House, 1973.
114. Galloway, Eilene. *History of the United States Military Policy on Reserve Forces, 1775-1957*. Prepared for the House Committee on Armed Services by U.S. Library of Congress, Legislative Reference Service. Washington: G.P.O., 1957.
115. Garraty, John A. (ed.), and Jerome Sternstein (assoc. ed.). *Encyclopedia of American Biography*. New York: Harper & Row, 1974.
116. Gatlin, Jr., Col. Jesse C. *The U.S. Air Force in Fiction: The First Twenty-Five Years*. Research Report 73-3. USAF Academy: 1973.
117. Generous, Jr., William T. *Swords and Scales: The Development of the Uniform Code of Military Justice*. Port Washington: Kennikat, 1973.
118. Glazier, Kenneth M. "Recent Acquisitions of Important Military Papers at the Hoover Institution on War, Revolution and Peace, Stanford University," *Military Affairs*, December 1969.
119. The Goldentree Bibliographies (Northbrook, Illinois: AHM)
    Shy, John. *The American Revolution* (1974)
    Taylor, George Rogers. *American Economic History before 1860* and . . . *since 1860* (1969 & 197-)

Grob, Gerald N. *American Social History before 1860* (1970).
Bremner, Robert H. *American Social History since 1860* (1971).

120. Graber, Doris A. *Crisis Diplomacy: A History of U.S. Intervention Policies and Practices.* Washington: Public Affairs Press, 1959.

121. Great Britain. Ministry of Defence. MOD Library (Central and Army) *Index of Book Lists*, 19 . . . London: MOD Library, annual.

122. Greenfield, Kent Roberts. *The Historian and the Army.* New Brunswick, New Jersey: Rutgers University Press, 1954.

123. Greenwood, John. *American Defense Policy since 1945: A Preliminary Bibliography.* Lawrence: University Press of Kansas, 1973.

124. Greene, Robert E. *Black Defenders of America, 1775-1973: A Reference and Pictorial History.* Chicago: Johnson [*Ebony* magazine], 1973.

125. Grinker, Lt Col. R. R. *Men Under Stress: War Neuroses of our Air Forces Personnel.* Glenview: Anthony Maita, 1945.

126. Groene, Bertram Hawthorne (sic). *Tracing Your Civil War Ancestor.* Winston-Salem, North Carolina: Blair, 1973.

127. Gurney, Gene. *The United States Coast Guard: A Pictorial History.* New York: Crown Pub., 1973.

128. Hale, Jr., Richard W. (ed.). *Guide to Photocopied Historical Materials in the United States and Canada.* Ithaca: Cornell University Press, 1961.

129. Halleck, Maj Gen. H. W. *Elements of Military Art and Science: Or Course of Instruction in Strategy, Fortifications, Tactics of Battles, etc.; Adapted to the Use of Volunteers of Militia.* (Reprint of 1846 ed.) Westport, Connecticut: Greenwood Press, 1971.

130. Hamer, Philip M., ed. *A Guide to Archives and Manuscripts in the United States.* New Haven: Yale University Press, 1961. [NARS revisions in process, 1975]

131. Hamilton, Andrew. *Helpless Giant: The Metaportrait of the Defense Budget.* New York: Schocken, 1972.

132. Hammond, Paul Y. *Organizing for Defense: The American Military Establishment in the Twentieth Century.* Princeton: Princeton University Press, 1961.

133. Harral, Rear Admiral Brooks J. *Service Etiquette.* Annapolis: U.S. Naval Institute, 1969.

134. *Harvard Guide to American History* revised in two volumes; Frank Freidel, edition. Cambridge: Harvard University Press, 1974.

135. Hassler, Warren W., Jr. *The President as Commander in Chief.* Reading, Massachusetts: Addison-Wesley, 1971.

136. Heath, Jim F. "Domestic America during World War II: research opportunities for historians," *Journal of American History*, September 1971, 384-419.

137. Heinl, Col. Robert D., Jr. *Dictionary of Military and Naval Quotations.* Annapolis: U.S. Naval Institute, 1966.

138. Heitman, Francis B. *Historical Register and Dictionary of the United States Army* (2 vols., 1903).

139. Helmer, John. *Bringing the War Home: The American Soldier in Vietnam and After.* Glencoe, Illinois: Free Press, 1974.

140. Helmbold, R. L. *Air Battles and Ground Battles—A Common Pattern?* Santa Monica: Rand Corp, 1971.
141. Henri, Florette. *Bitter Victory: A History of Black Soldiers in World War I.* New York: Doubleday, 1970.
142. Hicken, V. *The American Fighting Man: An Analysis of the Essential Qualities of American Soldiers, Sailors and Marines from the American Revolution to the War in Vietnam.* New York: Macmillan, 1969.
143. Hicks, Maj. J. E. *Notes on U.S. Ordnance (v.2)—1776-1941.* Reprint of 1941 ed. Greens Farms, Connecticut: Modern Books and Crafts, Inc., 1971.
144. Higham, Robin. *Air Power: A Concise History.* New York: St. Martin's, 1973.
145. Higham, Robin, and Abigail T. Siddall. *Flying Combat Aircraft of the USAAF-USAF.* Ames: Iowa State University Press, 1975.
146. Higham, Robin, ed. *A Guide to the Sources of British Military History.* Berkeley: University of California Press, 1971.
147. Higham, Robin, ed. *Intervention or Abstention: The Dilemma of American Foreign Policy.* Lexington: University of Kentucky Press, 1975.
148. Higham, Robin. *Official Histories: Essays and Bibliographies from Around the World.* Manhattan: Kansas States University Libr., 1970.
149. Higham, Robin. "The Russians on the Eastern Seaboard: a maritime Chronology, 1863-64." *The American Neptune,* January, 1960, 49-61.
150. Hill, Jim Dan. *The Minute Man in Peace and War: A History of the National Guard.* Harrisburg: Stackpole, 1964.
151. Hilliard, Jack B. *An Annotated Reading List of United States Marine Corps History.* Washington: Historical Division, HQ, USMC, 1971.
152. Historical Abstracts. Santa Barbara, Calif.: ABC-Clio, 1955-   .
153. Hittle, Gen. James D. *The Military Staff: Its History and Development.* Harrisburg: Stackpole, 1961.
154. Hogg, Ian, and John Batchelor. *Artillery.* London: MacDonald & Co., Ltd., 1972.
155. Hogg, Ian V. *Barrage: The Guns in Action.* Weapons Book No. 18 in Ballantine's Illustrated History of World War II. New York: Ballantine, 1970.
156. Hogg, Ian V. *The Guns, 1939-45.* Weapons Book No. 11 in Ballantine's Illustrated History of World War II. New York: Ballantine, 1970.
157. Hollingsworth, T. H. *Historical Demography.* Ithaca: Cornell University Press, 1969.
158. Holt, W. Stull. *The Office of the Chief of Enginerrs of the Army* (1923).
159. Howe, George Frederick, *et al. The American Historical Association's Guide to Historical Literature.* New York: Macmillan, 1961.
160. Huntington, Samuel P., ed. *Changing Patterns of Military Politics. (International Yearbook of Political Behavior Research,* Vol. 3). New York: Free Press of Glencoe, 1962.

161. Huntington, Samuel P. "Recent Writing in Military Politics—Foci and Corpora," *Changing Patterns of Military Politics*. Edited by Samuel P. Huntington. New York: Free Press of Glencoe, 1962.

162. Huntington, Samuel P. *The Soldier and the State: The Theory and Politics of Civil-Military Relations*. Cambridge: Harvard University Press, 1956.

163. Huston, James A. *The Sinews of War: Army Logistics, 1775-1953*. United States Army Historical Series. Washington: Office of the Chief of Military History, 1966.

164. Huzar, Elias. *The Purse and the Sword: Control of the Army by Congress through Military Appropriations, 1933-1950*. Ithaca: Cornell University Press, 1950.

165. Icks, Robert J. *Famous Tank Battles*. New York: Doubleday, 1972.

166. Israel, Fred L., ed. *Major Peace Treaties of Modern History, 1648-1967*. New York: Chelsea House, 1967. 4 vols.

167. James, Edwart T., ed. *Notable American Women, 1607-1950*. Cambridge: Harvard University Press, 1971-1974.

168. James, D. Clayton. *The Years of MacArthur, I, 1880-1941*. Boston: Houghton Mifflin, 1970.

169. *Jane's Fighting Ships*. London: Sampson, Low Marston, 1898- .

170. Janowitz, Morris. *The Professional Soldier: A Social and Political Portrait*. Glencoe, Illinois: Free Press, 1960, 1973.

171. Janowitz, Morris. *The New Military*. New York: Russell Sage Foundation., 1964.

172. Janowitz, M., and J. Van Doorn, (eds.). *Contributions to Military Sociology*. Rotterdam: University Press, 1971- . (See #74)

173. Javits, Jacob K., *et al*. *The Defense Sector and the American Economy*. New York: University Press, 1973.

174. Jehens, Lt Col. F. *Not in the Book: A Guide for the Junior Officer*. A. A. Johnston, 1951.

175. Johnson, Lt Col. Ann R. "The WASP of World War II," *Aerospace Historian*, XVII, Nos 2 & 3, Summer-Fall 1970, 76-82.

176. Johnson, Thomas H. *The Oxford Companion to American History*. New York: Oxford University Press, 1966.

177. Just, Ward. *Military Men*. New York: Knopf, 1970.

178. Kahn, David. *The Code Breakers: History of Secret Communications*. New York: Macmillan, 1967.

179. Keehan, R. J., I. D. Goldberg, and G. W. Beebe. *Twenty-four Year Mortality Follow-up of Army Veterans with Disability Separations for Psycho-Neurosis in 1944, Psychomatic Medicine*, Jan-Feb 1974.

180. Kelleher, Catherine M. (ed.). *Political Military Systems: A Comparative Analysis*. Beverly Hills: Sage Publications, Inc., Summer 1974.

181. Kemble, Robert C. *The Image of the Army Officer in America: Background for Current Views*. Westport, Connecticut: Greenwood, 1973.

182. Kennedy, Don H. *Ship Names: Origins and Usages During Forty-Five Centuries*. Charlottesville: University Press of Virginia for The Mariners Museum, 1974.

183. Kirkendall, Richard S. (ed.). *The Truman Period as a Research*

Field. Columbia: University of Missouri Press, 1967.

184. Knight, Rear Admiral Austin M., USN. *Modern Seamanship.* Tenth edition rewritten and revised by the officers of the Department of Seamanship and Navigation, United States Naval Academy, Annapolis, Maryland. New York: Van Nostrand 1937, revised January 1943.

185. Knox, Commodore Dudley W. *A History of the United States Navy.* Revised and enlarged edition. New York: Putnam's, 1948.

186. Kuehl, Warren F. (comp.). *Dissertations in History: An Index to Dissertations Completed in History Departments of United States and Canadian universities, 1873-1960.* Lexington: University of Kentucky Press, 1965. Vol. II (*1961-June 1970*). Lexington: University Press of Kentucky, 1972.

187. Kyre, Martin and Joan Kyre. *Military Occupation and National Security.* Washington: Public Affairs Press, 1968.

188. Lang, Kurt. *Military Institutions and the Sociology of War: A Review of the Literature with an Annotated Bibliography.* Beverly Hills: Sage, 1972.

189. Langer, William L. *An Encyclopedia of World History.* Boston: Houghton, Mifflin, revised 1972.

190. Langley, Harold D. *Social Reform in the United States Navy, 1798-1862.* Urbana: University of Illinois Press, 1967.

191. Larrabee, Eric. "Books on Guerrilla Warfare—Fifteen Years Overdue." *Harper's,* May 1964.

192. Larson, Arthur D. *Civil-Military Relations and Militarism: A Classified Bibliography Covering the United States and Other Nations of the World with Introductory Notes.* Manhattan: Kansas State University Library Bibliographical Series, No. 9, 1971.

193. Larson, Arthur D., editor-in-chief. *Information Sources in American Government and History.* Detroit: Gale Research, 1975- , 17 vols.

194. Larson, Arthur D. *Research Note: A Guide to Bibliographies* [on national security, civil military relations, military history, military sociology, war, peace, arms control, and disarmament]. Parkside, Wis.: the author, University of Wisconsin-Parkside, 1972.

195. Leckie, Robert. *The Wars of America.* New York: Harper & Row, 1968.

196. Lee, Ulysses. *The Employment of Negro Troops.* Washington: OCMH, USA, 1966.

197. Leopold, Richard W. "The 'Foreign Relations' Series Revisited: One Hundred Plus Ten." *Journal of American History,* March 1973.

198. Lewis, Berkeley R. *Small Arms and Ammunition in the United States Service 1776-1865.* Newton Abbot, England: David & Charles, 1972.

199. Lewis, Emanuel R. *Seacoast Fortifications of the United States: An Introductory History.* Newton Abbot, England: David & Charles, 1972.

200. Licklider, Roy E. *The Private Nuclear Strategists.* Columbus: Ohio State University Press, 1971.

201. Little, Roger W. *Handbook of Military Institutions.* Beverly Hills: Sage, 1971.

202. Love, Edmund. *War is a Private Affair*. New York: Harcourt, Brace, 1951.
203. Luttwak, Edward. *A Dictionary of Modern War*. New York: Harper & Row, 1971.
204. Lyons, George M. and Louis Morton. *Schools for Strategy: Education and Research in National Security Affairs*. New York: F. A. Praeger, 1965.
205. MacDonald, Capt. E. A. *Polar Operations*. New York: Arco Books, 1971.
206. MacDonald, Scot. *Evolution of Aircraft Carriers*. Washington: Navy Department, Office of the Chief of Naval Operatiɔns, 1964.
207. Mack-Forlist, D. M., and A. Newman. *The Conversion of Shipbuilding from Military to Civilian Markets*. Praeger Special Studies In U.S. Economic and Social Development. New York: Praeger, 1970.
208. Macksey, Kenneth, and John H. Batchelor. *Tank: A History of the Armoured Fighting Vehicle*. New York: Ballantine, 1971.
209. The Macmillan Wars of the United States, Louis Morton, (ed.).
    Clendennen, Clarence C. *Blood on the Border: the United States Army and the Mexican Irregulars* (1969).
    Higginbotham, Don. *The War of American Independence: Military Attitudes, Policies and Practice, 1763-1789* (1971).
    Leach, Douglas. *Arms for Empire: A Military History of the British Colonies in North America, 1607-1763* (1973).
    DeWeerd, Harvey A. *President Wilson Fights His War: World War I and the American Intervention* (1968).
    Prucha, Father Paul. *The Sword of the Republic: The United States Army on the Frontier, 1783-1846* (1969).
    Utley, Robert M. *Frontiersmen in Blue: The United States Army and the Indian, 1846-1865* (1967).
    Utley, Robert M. *Frontier Regulars: The United States Army and the Indian, 1866-1891* (1973).
    Weigley, Russell F. *History of the United States Army* (1967).
    Weigley, Russell F. *The American Way of War: A History of United States Military Strategy and Policy* (1973).
    Bauer, K. Jack. *The Mexican War* (1974).
    Hurley, Alfred F. *History of the United States Air Force* (197).
    Connelly, Thomas L. *The Civil War* (197).
    Preston, R. A., and S. F. Wise. *The War of* 1812 (197).
    Morton, Louis, *World War II* (*Pacific*) (197).
    Fox, Annette Baker. *American Military Intervention in Latin America* (197).
    O'Connor, Raymond G. *History of the United States Navy* (197).
    Grenville, J. A. S., and David Trask. *The Spanish-American War* (197).
    Cole, Hugh M. *World War II (Europe and Africa)* (197).
    Blumenson, Martin. *The Korean War* (197).
    Millett, Allan R. *The History of the Marine Corps* (197).

210. Marshall, Brig. Gen. S. L. A. "Slam". *The Officer as Leader*. Harrisburg: Stackpole, 1966.

211. Maslowski, Pete. "A Study of Morale in Civil War Soldiers," *Military Affairs*, December 1970, 122-126.

212. Mason, Elizabeth B., and Louis M. Starr. *The Oral History Collection of Columbia University*. 3rd ed. New York: Microfilm Corporation of America, 1973.

213. "An Interview with John T. Mason, Jr., Director of Oral History at the U.S. Naval Institute," *United States Naval Institute Proceedings*, July 1973.

214. Matloff, Maurice. *American Military History*. Washington: G.P.O., 1969.

215. Matthews, William, comp. *American Diaries: An Annotated Bibliography of American Diaries Written Prior to the Year 1861*. Berkeley and Los Angeles: University of California Press, 1945.

216. Matthews, William. *American Diaries in Manuscript, 1580-1954*. Athens: University of Georgia Press, 1973.

217. May, Ernest R. "The Development of Political-Military Consultation in the United States." *Political Science Quarterly*, June 1955.

218. May, Ernest R., (ed.). *The Ultimate Decision: The President as Commander in Chief*. New York: George Braziller, 1960.

219. Melhorn, Charles M. (USN Ret.). *Two-Block Fox: The Rise of the Aircraft Carrier, 1911-1929*. Annapolis: U.S. Naval Institute Press, 1974 (Sept).

220. Melman, S. (ed.). *The Defense Economy; Conversion of Industries and Occupations to Civilian Needs*. Praeger Special Studies in U.S. Economic and Social Development, 1970.

221. Melman, Seymour (ed.). *The War Economy of the United States: Readings in Military Industry and Economy*. New York: St. Martin's, 1971.

222. Merillat, Lt. Col. Louis A., and Lt. Col. Delwin M. Campbell. *Veterinary Military History of the United States with a Brief Record of the Development of Education, Practice, Organization and Legislation*. The Haven-Glover Laboratories, Kansas City, Mo., 1935. 2 vols.

223. Military Affairs. *Cumulative Indices to Military Affairs, 1937-1969: Indices to Volumes I-XXXII by Author, Title and Subject, Plus an Index to the Reviews. Compiled by Norma K. Lambert*. Manhattan: Kansas State University Library Bibliographical Series No. 6, 1969.

224. *Military Review Consolidated Index, 1922-1965*. Ft. Leavenworth, Kansas: *Military Review*, 1967.

225. Miller, Everett B. *United States Army Veterinary Service in World War II*. Washington: Office of the Surgeon-General, Dept. of the Army, 1961.

226. Miller, Wayne C. *An Armed America: Its Face in Fiction—History of the American Military Novel*. New York: New York University Press, 1970.

227. Millett, Allan R. "American Military History: Over the Top," *The*

State of American History. Edited by Herbert J. Bass. Chicago: Quadrangle, 1970.

228. Millett, Allan R., and B. Franklin Cooling, III. *Doctoral Dissertations in Military Affairs: A Bibliography.* Manhattan: Kansas State University Library Bibliography Series No. 10, 1972.

229. Millis, Walter. *American Military Thought.* New York: Bobbs-Merrill, 1966.

230. Millis, Walter. *Arms and Men: A Study in American Military History.* New York: Putnam's, 1956.

231. Moran, Capt. John B. (USMC, Ret.). *Creating the Legend: A Descriptive Catalogue of Writing about the U.S. Marine Corps.* Chicago: Publishing Division, Moran/Andrews, 1973.

232. Morison, Samuel Eliot, Frederick Merck, and Frank Freidel. *Dissent in Three American Wars.* Cambridge: Harvard University Press, 1970.

233. Morris, Dan and Inez. *Who was Who in American Politics.* New York: Hawthorne, 1974.

234. Morris, Richard B., (ed.). *Encyclopedia of American History.* Updated and rev. ed. New York: Harper & Row, 1965.

235. Moskos, Charles C., Jr. *The American Enlisted Man: The Rank and File in Today's Military.* New York: The Russell Sage Foundation, 1970.

236. Moskos, Charles C., Jr., (ed.). *Public Opinion and the Military Establishment.* Beverly Hills: Sage, 1971.

237. Mugridge, Donald H., and Helen F. Conover. *An Album of American Battle Art 1755-1918.* New York: DaCapo Press, Inc., 1972.

238. Murray, Robert A. *Brief Guide to Research on Army Posts.* Quantico, Virginia: Council on Abandoned Military Posts, 1969.

239. Mylander, Maureen. *The Generals: Making It, Military Style.* New York: Dial Press, 1974.

240. Nalty, B. C., and R. F. Moody. *A Brief History of U.S. Marine Corps Officer Procurement, 1775-1969.* (Revised edition) U.S. Marine Corps Hist. Branch, 1970.

241. National Academy of Sciences. National Research Council. Advisory Board on Quartermaster Research and Development. *Man Living in the Arctic.* Washington: NAS, 1961.

242. *The National Union Catalog of Manuscript Collections.* Ann Arbor, Michigan: J. W. Edwards, 1962-   . Annual.

243. *The National Union Catalog of Manuscript Collections: Index: 1959-1962.* Hamden, Connecticut: Shoe String Press, 1964.

244. NATO. Information Service. *NATO Handbook.* Brussels: annual.

245. *A Naval Encyclopaedia: Comprising a Dictionary of Nautical Words and Phrases; Biographical Notices, and Records of Naval Officers; Special Articles on Naval Art and Science, Written Expressly for This Work by Officers and Others of Recognized Authority in the Branches Treated by Them. Together with Descriptions of the Principal Naval Stations and Seaports of the World.* Philadelphia: L. R. Hamersly & Co., 1884. Republished by Gale Research Co., Detroit, 1971.

246. Naval Historical Foundation. *The Navy Department: A Brief History until 1945.* Washington: NHF, 1970.

247. Nexus, PO Box 1517, Costa Mesa, Calif., 92626, or phone 800-854-3379.

248. Ney, Col. Virgil. "Military Sociology—A Select Bibliography," *Military Affairs*, Winter 1966.

249. Noel, Capt J. V. (USN), and Capt E. L. Beach (USN). *Naval Terms Dictionary*. 3rd edition. Annapolis: U.S. Naval Institute, 1971.

250. *Notable American Women, 1607-1950: A Biographical Dictionary* edited by Janet Wilson, Edward T. James and Paul S. Boyer. Cambridge: Harvard University Press, 1971-1974.

251. O'Connor, Raymond G. *American Defense Policy in Perspective: From Colonial Times to the Present*. New York: John Wiley, 1965.

252. Organization of American Historians. *The Fifty Year Index to the Mississippi Valley Historical Review (1914-1964)*. Bloomington, Indiana: OAH, 1974.

253. Padfield, Peter. *Guns at Sea*. New York: St. Martin's, 1974.

254. Paine, T. O. *Submarining: Three Thousand Books and Articles*. Santa Barbara, California: General Electric Co., TEMPO Center for Advanced Studies, 1971.

255. Pappas, Col. George S. *Prudens Futuri: The U.S. Army War College, 1901-1967*. Carlisle, Pennsylvania: Alumni Association of the U.S. Army War College, 1967.

256. Parker, W. D. *A Concise History of the United States Marine Corps, 1775-1969*. Washington: G.P.O., 1970.

257. Paullin, Charles O., (ed.). *Atlas of the Historical Geography of the United States*. Washington and New York: Carnegie Institution and American Geographical Society, 1932.

258. Peterson, Clarence S. *Consolidated Bibliography of County Histories in Fifty States*. 2d ed. Baltimore, Maryland: Genealogical Publishing Co., 1963.

259. Peterson, H. L. *Round Shot and Rammers*. Harrisburg: Stackpole, 1969.

260. Peterson, Harold L. *The Treasury of the Gun*. New York: Golden Press, 1962.

261. Platt, Brig. Gen. George Washington, USAR (Ret.). *National Character in Action: Intelligence Factors in Foreign Relations*. New Brunswick, New Jersey: Rutgers University Press, 1961.

262. Ponko, Vincent. *Public Opinion and American Naval Policy*. Chicago: Nelson-Hall, 1975.

263. Polmar, Norman. *Aircraft Carriers*. London: Macdonalds, 1969.

264. Potter, E. B. *The Naval Academy Illustrated History of the United States Navy*. New York: Thomas Y. Crowell, 1971.

265. Potter, E. B., and Fleet Admiral Chester W. Nimitz. *Sea Power*. Englewood Cliffs, New Jersey: Prentice-Hall, various editions.

266. Profile Publications. *Armoured Fighting Vehicles in Profile*. 4 vols. New York: Doubleday, 1972- .

267. Prucha, Francis Paul. *A Guide to the Military Posts of the United States, 1789-1895*. Madison: State Historical Society of Wisconsin, 1964 and 1966.

268. Pruitt, Dean G., and Richard C. Snyder. *Theory and Research on the Causes of War*. Englewood Cliffs, New Jersey: Prentice-Hall, 1969.

269. Pursell, Carroll W., Jr. *"Bibliographic Notes*: Some Recent Government Publications Concerning Technology," *Technology and Culture*, January 1968, 90-93.
270. Quick, John. *Dictionary of Weapons and Military Terms*. New York: McGraw-Hill, 1973.
271. RAND Corporation. *Index of Selected Publications of the RAND Corporation, 1946-1962*. Santa Monica, California: 1962.
272. Rankin, Col. R. H. (USMC). *Uniforms of the Sea Services*. Arco Books, 1971.
273. Republique française. Comité d' histoire de la 2ᵉ. Guerre mondiale. *Publications*.
274. Rickey, Don, Jr. *Forty Miles a Day on Beans and Hay*. Norman: University of Oklahoma Press, 1963.
275. Riker, William H. *Soldiers of the States: The Role of the National Guard in American Democracy*. Washington: Public Affairs Press, 1958.
276. Rivkin, Robert. *Rights of Servicemen*. New York: Avon, 1972.
277. Robinson, Douglas H. *The Dangerous Sky: A History of Aviation Medicine*. Seattle: University of Washington Press, November 1973.
278. Robinson, Fayette. *An Account of the Organization of the Army of the United States*. 1848. 2 vols.
279. Rodberg, Leonard, and Derek Shearer. *Pentagon Watchers: Students Report on the National Security State*. Garden City: Doubleday, 1970.
280. Robles, P. K. *United States Military Medals and Ribbons*. Rutland, Vermont: C. E. Tuttle, 1971.
281. Ropp, Theodore. *War in the Modern World*. Durham, North Carolina: Duke University Press, 1959.
282. Russell, Carl P. *Guns on the Early Frontiers*. Berkeley: University of California Press, 1957.
283. Sabin, Joseph et al. *A Dictionary of Books Relating to America from Its Discovery to the Present Time*. New York: 1868-1936. 29 vols.
284. Sarkesian, Sam C. (ed.). *The Military-Industrial Complex: A Reassessment*. Vol. 2. Chicago: Univ. of Chicago, 1972.
285. Sarkesian, Sam C. *The World of the Professional Military Officer*. Chicago: Nelson-Hall, 1974.
286. Schlesinger, Arthur M., Jr., and Roger Bruns (eds.). *The History of U.S. Congressional Investigations (1792-1974)*. 5 vols. Ann Arbor, Michigan: R. R. Bowker, 1975.
287. Schmeckebier, Laurence F., and Roy B. Eastin. *Government Publications and Their Use*. 2nd revised ed. Washington: Brookings Institution, 1969.
288. Sellers, Robert C. (ed.). *Armed Forces of the World: A Reference Handbook*. 3rd ed. New York: Praeger, 1971.
289. SHAPE. *SHAPE and Allied Command Europe, 1951-1971: Twenty Years in the Service of Peace and Security*. SHAPE, Belgium: 1971.
290. Shelburne, James C., and Kenneth H. Groves. *Education in the*

Armed Forces. New York: Center for Applied Research in Education, 1965.

291. Silverstone, P. H. *U.S. Warships of World War I.* London: Ian Allan, 1970.

292. Silverstone, Paul H. *U.S. Warships of World War II.* New York: Doubleday, n.d., (1966).

293. Skallerup, Harry R. *Books Afloat and Ashore: A History of Books, Libraries, and Reading among Seamen during the Age of Sail.* Hamden, Connecticut: Archon Books, 1974.

294. Smith, Myron J. *American Naval Bibliography.* 4 vols. Metuchen, New Jersey: Scarecrow Press, 1973-   .

295. Smith, W. H. B., and Joseph E. Smith. *Small Arms of the World: The Basic Manual of Military Small Arms. . . .* Harrisburg: Stackpole, 1943-   , many editions.

296. Smithsonian Institution. Smithsonian Miscellaneous Collections Vol. 129 (whole volume). *Small Arms and Ammunition in the United States Service,* by Berkeley R. Lewis. Washington: Smithsonian Institution, August 14, 1956.

297. Social Science Research Council, Committee on Civil-Military Relations Research. *Civil-Military Relations: An Annotated Bibliography,* 1940-1952. New York: Columbia University Press, 1954.

298. Sprout, Harold and Margaret. *The Rise of American Naval Power, 1776-1918.* Princeton: Princeton University Press, 1942.

299. *The Standard Periodical Directory: 1970.* 3rd ed. New York: Oxbridge Publishing, 1969.

300. *The Statesman's Yearbook, 1974/75.* 111th edition. New York: St. Martin's, 1974.

301. Steele, Matthew Forney. *American Campaigns.* 2 vols. Washington: War Department. Office of the Chief of Staff, Second Section, General Staff, No. 13, Washington: Byron S. Adams, 1909.

302. Steffen, Randy. *United States Military Saddles, 1812-1943.* Norman, Oklahoma: University of Oklahoma Press, 1973.

303. Steiner, Paul E. *Medical-Military Portraits of Union and Confederate Generals.* Philadelphia, Pennsylvania: Whitmore, 1968.

304. Steiner, Paul R. *Disease in the Civil War: Natural Biological Warfare, 1861-1865.* Springfield, Illinois: Charles C Thomas, 1968.

305. Stevens, Lt. Col. Phillip H. *Search Out the Land: A History of American Military Scouts.* Chicago: Rand, McNally, 1969.

306. Stillman, Richard J., II. *Integration of the Negro in the U.S. Armed Forces.* New York: Praeger, 1968.

307. Stoflet, Ada M. and Earl M. Rogers (comp.). "A Bibliography of Civil War Articles, 1972," *Civil War History* XIX, 1973.

308. Stone, Richard. *The Kentucky Militia.* Lexington: University Press of Kentucky, 1976.

309. Stouffer, S. A., *et al. The American Soldier in Combat and After.* 2 vols. New York: Wiley, 1965 (originally Princeton University Press, 1949).

310. Strecker, Ed. A., MD. *Psychiatry in Modern Warfare: A Compara-*

tive Study of the Neuropsychiatry of the Two World Wars. Glenview: Anthony Maita, 1945.

311. Stubs, Mary Lee, and Stanley Russell Connor. *Armor—Cavalry, Part 1: Regular Army and Army Reserve.* Washington: G.P.O., 1969.

312. Swanborough, Gordon, and Peter M. Bowers. *United States Military Aircraft Since 1908.* London: Putnam, 1963, revised 1971.

313. Swanborough, Gordon, and Peter M. Bowers. *United States Navy Aircraft Since 1911.* London: Putnam, 1971.

314. Treadwell, Mattie E. *The Women's Army Corps.* Washington: Department of the Army, Office of the Chief of Military History, 1954.

315. Ulmer, S. S. *Military Justice and the Right to Counsel.* Lexington: Kentucky University Press, 1970.

316. *Ulrich's International Periodicals Directory.* 14th ed. New York: R. R. Bowker, 1971. Supplement published in 1972.

317. USAF Air University Library. *Abstracts of Student Research Reports.* Maxwell AFB: Air University Library, annual.

318. USAF Academy Library: Special Bibliographical Series. No. 49. *The Military History of the American Revolution.* USAF Academy Library: 1974.

319. USAF Historical Division, Study No. 55. *Women Pilots in the AAF, 1941-1944* by J. M. England and J. Reither. Maxwell AFB: 1946.

320. USAF. Office of Air Force History. *United States Air Force: an annotated bibliography.* Washington: AFCHO and G.P.O., 1971.

321. USAF. Office of Air Force History. *United States Air Force History: a guide to documentary sources* compiled by Lawrence J. Paszek. Washington: AFCHO and G.P.O., 1973.

322. USAF Office of Scientific Research. *Prisoners of War and Political Hostages: a select bibliography.* Report A10-1. Springfield, Virginia: The Monroe Corporation, 1973.

323. USAF. Office of the Secretary of the Air Force. Office of Information (SAFOI). *Military Forces Handbook: military forces of the USSR and Peoples Republic of China.* Washington: SAFOI, 1974.

324. USAF. 1361st Photo Squadron, (AAVS) (MAC), 221 South Fern St., Alexandria, Virginia, 22202.

325. U.S. Air Force Systems Command. Aerospace Medical Division. Arctic Aeromedical Laboratory. *Review of Research on Military Problems in Cold Regions.* Technical Documentary Report AAL-TDR-64-28. December 1964.

326. United States Armed Forces Institute. *The Military Novel.* Prepared by Russell S. Spindler. (No. A 1001.1). Madison: USAFI, 1964.

327. U.S. Army. Combat Developments Command. *Directory of Vietnam Combat Operational Data (VCOD).* Alexandria, Virginia: Defense Documentation Center, June 1973.

328. U.S. Department of the Army. Center for Military History. *Army Museum Newsletter*, No. 11, October 1974, "Tape Transcripts from the Museum Conference."

329. U.S. Army. Headquarters, Department of the Army. The Adjutant General's Office. Administrative Services Directorate. The Army

Library. Catalog Section. *Checklist of Periodicals Currently Received in the Army Library.* Revised edition, September 1964. Washington: DA, 1964.

330. U.S. Army. Historical Office of the Chief of the Chemical Corps. *History of German Chemical Warfare in World War II* by Generaleutenant Herman Ochsner. 2 vols., n.d., but copy in Air University Library, Maxwell AFB.

331. U.S. Department of the Army. Army Medical Department. *The Medical Department of the United States Army in the World War,* XIII, Part II, *The Army Nurse Corps* by Julia C. Stimson. Washington: Department of the Army. Army Medical Department, 1927.

332. U.S. Department of the Army. *Civilian in Peace, Soldiers in War . . . , A bibliographic Survey of the Army and National Guard.* Washington: G.P.O., 1967.

333. U.S. Department of the Army. Army Library. *Strength in Reserve: a bibliographic survey of the United States Army Reserve.* Washington: G.P.O., 1968.

334. U.S. Department of the Army. *Medical Department of the United States Army in World War II, The Army Nurse Corps* by Pauline E. Maxwell. Washington: Department of the Army. U.S. Army Medical Department (19).

335. U.S. Army Medical Research Laboratory, Ft. Knox, Ky., The Blood Bank Center. *Military Blood Banking, 1941-1973: lessons learned applicable to civil disasters and other considerations* by Col. Frank R. Camp, Sr., MSC, Col. Nicholas F. Conte, MC (MD), and Lt Col. Jerry R. Brewer, MSC. Ft. Knox, Kentucky: USAMRL, The Blood Bank Center, 1973.

336. U.S. Army. Military History Research Collection Special Bibliographic Series:
   a. *The US Army and Domestic Disturbances* (1970)
   b. *The US Army and the Negro with supplement* (1971)
   c. *Language Dictionaries with an emphasis on military dictionaries* (1971)
   d. *United States Army Unit Histories* (1971)
   e. *The Volunteer Army* (1972)
   f. *Manuscript Holdings of the Military History Research Collection* (1972)
   g. *The Mexican War* (1973)
   h. *A Suggested Guide to the Curricular Archives of the U.S. Army War College, 1907-1940* (1973)
   i. *The U.S. Army and the Spanish-American War Era, 1895-1910* (two parts, 1974)
   j. *Pennsylvania Military History* (1974).

337. U.S. Army Still Photo Library. US Army Audio-Visual Agency (ATTN: CEPA-POS-R), Pentagon Rm 5A518, Washington, D.C., 20310.

338. U.S. Army Audio-Visual Agency. Washington, D.C. 20310.

339. U.S. Bureau of the Census. *Methods and Materials of Demography* by Henry S. Shyrock *et al.* Washington: G.P.O., 1971.

340. United States, Bureau of the Census. *The statistical history of the*

United States from colonial times to the present. Stamford, Connecticut: Fairfield Publishers, 1965.

341. U.S. Department of Transportation, U.S. Coast Guard. *United States Coast Guard Annotated Bibliography, 1972.* (CG-230) (available upon request to USCG, GAPI/83), 400 Seventh St., SW, Washington, D.C. 20509.

342. U.S. General Services Administration. National Archives and Records Service. Dwight D. Eisenhower Library. *Historical Materials in the Dwight D. Eisenhower Library.* Abilene, Kansas: DDEL, 1974.

343. U.S. Joint Chiefs of Staff. *A Dictionary of United States Military Terms.* Washington: Public Affairs, 1963.

344. U.S. Joint Chiefs of Staff. *Department of Defense Dictionary of Military and Associated Terms.* Washington, 1972.

345. U.S. Library of Congress. *National Union Catalog of Manuscript Collections, 1966 with Index 1963-1966.* Washington; DC, 1967.

346. U.S. Marine Corps. Headquarters. History and Museums Division. *The Marines in Vietnam, 1954-1973: an anthology and annotated bibliography.* Washington: USMC, 1974.

347. U.S. Military Academy. *The Centennial of the United States Military Academy.* 20 vols., 1904.

348. United States Military Academy. HI 401-402. *History of the Military Art.* West Point: USMA Department of History, 1973.

349. United States Military Academy. *The Library Map Collection: Period of the American Revolution, 1753-1800.* West Point: USMA Library, 1971.

350. United States Military Academy. *Official Records of the American Civil War: a researcher's guide* by Conrad Alan Aimone. West Point, New York: USMA Library Bulletin No. 11.

351. U.S. Military Academy. *The West Point Atlas of American Wars, 1689-1953.* 2 vols., edited by Col. Vincent J. Esposito. New York: Praeger, 1959.

352. U.S. Military Academy, West Point Library. *Subject Catalogue of the Military Art and Science Collection. . . .* Westport, Connecticut: Greenwood, 1969.

353. U.S. Navy Department, Office of Information, Still Photo Branch, Washington, D.C., 20360.

354. U.S. Dept. of the Navy. Naval History Division. *The Battleship in the United States Navy.* Washington: G.P.O., 1970.

355. U.S. Naval History Division. *Dictionary of American Naval Fighting Ships.* 5 vols. Washington: USNHD, 1959-   .

356. U.S. Department of the Navy. Naval History Division. *United States Naval History: a bibliography.* 6th edition. Washington: Naval History Division, 1972.

357. U.S. Naval History Division. *U.S. Naval History Sources in the Washington Area and Suggested Research Subjects.* 3rd revised and enlarged edition compiled by D. C. Allard and Betty Bern. Washington: USNHD, 1971.

358. U.S. *Strategic Bombing Survey.* Washington: 1947.

359. U.S. War Department. *America's Munitions . . .* by Benedict Crowell. Washington: G.P.O., 1919.

360. U.S. War Industries Board. *American Industry in the War: a report of the War Industries Board* by Bernard M. Baruch, Chairman. Washington: G.P.O., 1921.

361. U.S. Naval Academy Museum. *Catalogue of the Henry Huddleston Rogers Collection of Ship Models, United States Naval Academy Museum.* Annapolis: USNI, 1954.

362. *United States Naval Institute Proceedings. Index to the Proceedings Vols. 1-66 and Vols. 67-83* on microfilm with *supplement, Vols. 81-93* (1874-1973). Newport News, Virginia: Mariner's. Museum, 1957-1974.

363. Vagts, Alfred. *The Military Attaché.* Princeton: Princeton University Press, 1967.

364. Vail, R. W. G., (ed.). *The voice of the old frontier.* Philadelphia: University of Pennsylvania Press, 1949.

365. Van Der Veer, Lt. Norman R. *The Bluejacket's Manual, United States Navy.* Sixth edition 1918. New York: Military Publishing Co., 1918.

366. Van Fleet, Gen. James A. *Rail Transport and the Winning of Wars.* Washington: AAR, 1956.

367. Van Gils, M. R. (ed.). *Contributions to Military Sociology—The Perceived Role of the Military.* Rotterdam: University Press, 1971.

368. Van Riper, Paul P. "A Survey of Materials for the Study of Military Management," *American Political Science Review,* September 1955.

369. Van Riper, Paul P., and Darab B. Unwalla. "Voting Patterns among High-Ranking Military Officers," *Political Science Quarterly,* March, 1965.

370. Wagner, Ray. *American Combat Planes: a history of military aircraft in the USA.* London: Macdonald's, 1960 and later editions.

371. Walch, J. Weston. *Complete Handbook on Weapons Control.* 2 vols. Portland, Maine: Published by author, 1964. Supplement published in 1965.

372. Watrous, Livingston. *A Brief History of the Adjutant General's Department* (1927).

373. Warner, W. Lloyd, *et al. The American Federal Executive: A Study of the Social and Personal Characteristics of the Civilian and Military Leaders of the United States Federal Government.* New Haven: Yale University Press, 1963.

374. Warner, W. Lloyd. *Social Class in America: the evaluation of status.* New York: Harper & Row, 1960.

375. Weber, Richard H. *Monitors of the U.S. Navy, 1861-1937.* Washington: G.P.O., 1969.

376. *Webster's American Biographies.* Edited by Charles Van Doren and Robert McHenry. Springfield, Massachusetts: G. & C. Merriam, 1974.

377. Weeks, John. *Infantry Weapons.* Weapons Book No. 25 in Ballantine's Illustrated History of the Violent Century. New York: Ballantine, 1971.

378. Westmoreland, Guy T. *An Annotated Guide to Basic Reference Books on the Black American Experience.* Wilmington, Delaware: Scholarly Resources, 1974.

379. Whittingham, Richard. *Martial Justice: The Last Mass Execution in the United States*. Chicago: Cowles Book Co., 1971.
380. *Who's Who in.* . . . London: Publishing and Distributing Company, annual.
381. Wiener, Frederick Bernays. *Civilians under Military Justice: the British practice since 1689, especially in North America*. Chicago: University of Chicago Press, 1967.
382. Wiley, Bell I. *The Kentuckian as Fighting Man*. Lexington: University Press of Kentucky, 1976.
383. Williams, T. Harry. *Americans at War: The Development of the American Military System*. Baton Rouge: Louisiana State University Press, 1960.
384. Winchell, Constance M. *Guide to Reference Books*. 8th ed. Chicago: American Library Association, 1967. Supplements issued every other year.
385. Windrow, Martin and Gerry Embleton. *Military Dress of North America 1665-1970*. New York: Scribners, 1973.
386. Wisdom, Don, and William P. Kilroy (compilers). *Popular Names of U.S. Government Reports: a catalog*. Washington, D.C.; 1966.
387. Wohlstetter, Roberta. "Cuba and Pearl Harbor: Hindsight and Foresight," *Foreign Affairs*, July 1965.
388. Wolter, John. "Some Materials for the History of American Cartography," *American Studies*, Spring 1974, 12-27.
389. Wool, Harold. *The Military Specialist: Skilled Manpower for the Armed Forces*. Baltimore: Johns Hopkins Press, 1968.
390. Xerox University Microfilms. Comprehensive Dissertation Index. 37 vols. Ann Arbor, Michigan: Xerox, 1973-   .
391. Yarmolinsky, Adam. *The Military Establishment: Its Impact on American Society*. Twentieth Century Fund Study. New York: Harper & Row, 1971.
392. *Yearbook of the United Nations*. New York: United Nations, 1947-   .
393. Ziegler, Janet. *World War II: books in English, 1945-1965*. Stanford: Hoover Institution Press, 1971. (Supplement expected 1975).
394. Ziel, R. *Steel Rails to Victory: a photographic history of Railway Operations during World War II*. New York: Hawthorn, 1970.

PRESIDENTIAL LIBRARIES
395. Herbert Hoover Library, West Branch, Ia. 52358
      Franklin D. Roosevelt Library, Hyde Park, NY 12538
      Harry S. Truman Library, Independence, Missouri 64050
      Dwight D. Eisenhower Library, Abilene, Kansas 67410
      John F. Kennedy Library, 380 Trapelo Rd. Waltham, Massachusetts 02154
      Lyndon B. Johnson Library, Austin, Texas 78712

NEWSPAPERS
396. *Chicago Tribune*
      Christian Science Monitor
      Los Angeles Times

New York Herald Tribune. Ceased publication 1967.
New York Times
The Times (London)
Wall Street Journal
Washington Post

JOURNALS

397. *Aerospace Historian* (formerly *Airpower Historian*). Washington, D.C., 1954. Manhattan, Kans.: 1970-   . Index 1954-1973.
398. *Air Force Magazine* (formerly *Air Force and Space Digest*). Washington, D.C.: 1946-   . Indexed: Air Univ. Lib. Ind.
399. *Air University Review*. Maxwell Field, Ala.: 1947-   . Indexed: Air Univ. Lib. Ind.; Eng. Ind.; P.A.I.S.
400. *American Historical Review*. Washington, D.C.: 1895-   . Index. Cum. index every 10 yrs. Indexed: R.G.
401. *American Political Science Review*. Washington, D.C.: 1906-   . Index. Cum. Index, Indexed: Int. Polit. Sci. Abstr.; Soc. Sci. & Hum. Ind.; P.A.I.S.
402. *Annals of Iowa*—Des Moines: 1863-   . Cum index every 2 years; indexed—American Hist & Life. R.G.
403. *Annals of the American Academy of Political and Social Science*. Philadelphia: 1891-   . Cum. index. Indexed: Bk. Rev. Ind.; Curr. Cont.; P.A.I.S.; R.G.
404. *Arctic Bulletin*. Washington: National Science Foundation for the Interagency Arctic Research Coordinating Committee, 1973-   .
405. *Arkansas Historical Quarterly*. Fayetteville, Ark.: 1942-   . Cum index: V 1-25 under consideration.
406. *Armed Forces and Society: an interdisciplinary journal*. Chicago: Inter-University Seminar on Armed Forces and Society, 1974-   .
407. *Armed Forces Journal* (formerly *Journal of the Armed Forces*). Washington, D.C.: 1863-   . Indexed: Air Univ. Lib. Ind.
408. *Armor*. Washington, D.C.: 1888-   . Index. Indexed: Air Univ. Lib. Ind. (formerly *Cavalry Journal*. Cum. Index *1888-1968,* Manhattan, KS.: Kansas State University Library, 1974.)
409. *Army*. Washington, D.C.: 1950-   . Index. Indexed: Air Univ. Lib. Ind.
410. *Army Aviation*. 1953-   . Westport, Conn.: and as *Army Aviation Digest*. Washington: 1955-   . Index: indexed. Air Univ. Lib. Ind.
411. *Army Finance Journal*. Alexandria, Virginia: 1953-   .
412. *Army in Europe*. Issued as a USAREUR PAM. 1962-   .
413. *Army Logistician*. Washington: 1969-   .
414. *Army National Guard Strength*, 1968-   .
415. *Army Personnel Letter*. Washington: 1971-   .
416. *Army Research and Development Magazine*. Washington: 1960-   .
417. *Army Reserve Magazine*. Washington, 1954-   . Index.
418. *Army Times*. Washington, 1940-   .
419. *Assembly (West Point) 1970-*   .
420. *Atlantic Monthly*. Boston: 1857-   . Indexed: R.G.
421. *Aviation Week & Space Technology*. New York: 1916-   . Indexed: R.G.; B.P.I.

422. *Barron's: National Business and Financial Weekly.* New York: 1921- . Indexed: B.P.I.
423. *Bulletin of the Atomic Scientists* (formerly *Science and Public Affairs*). Chicago: 1945- . Index: Indexed: Biol. Abstr.; P.A.I.S.; Psychol. Abstr., R.G.
424. *Business Week.* New York: 1929- . Indexed: R.G.; B.P.I.; P.A.I.S.
425. *By Valor and By Arms; the journal of American military history.* Ft. Collins, Colorado: Valor and Arms Press, 1974- .
426. *Chaplain.* Washington, D.C.: 1944- .
427. *Chronicles of Oklahoma.* Oklahoma City: 1921- . Cum. index.
428. *Civil War History.* Kent, Ohio: 1955- . Index.
429. *Civil War Times Illustrated.* Harrisburg, Pennsylvania: 1959- . Index.
430. *Collier's.* Springfield, Ohio: 1888-1957. Indexed: R.G.
431. *Command Comment* 1961- .
432. *Command Communication* 1967- .
433. *Commanders Digest* (formerly: *For the Commanders—This Changing World*) (Armed Forces News Bureau). Washington: n.d.
434. *Confederate Veteran,* 1866- .
435. *Congressional Digest.* Washington, D.C.: 1921- . Index. Indexed: P.A.I.S.; R.G.
436. *Congressional Record.* Washington: n.d.
437. *Current History.* Philadelphia: 1914- . Index. Indexed: R.G.; P.A.I.S.
438. *Defense Documentation Center Digest.* Alexandria, Virginia: 1966-
439. *Defense Indicators.* Washington, 1968- .
440. *Defense Management Journal.* Washington, 1945- . n.d.
441. DOD—*War Department Telephone Directory.*
442. *Dissertation Abstracts International* (Section A: Humanities & Social Sciences; Section B: Physical Sciences & Technology) (Formerly *Dissertation Abstracts)* Ann Arbor, Michigan: 1938; Index: Indexed. Biol. Abstr, Chem. Abstr., Music, Psychol. Abstr.
443. *Federal Library Center Newsletter.* Washington, 1965- .
444. *Federal Times.* Washington, 1965- .
445. *Field Artilleryman* 1957- .
446. *Flight International.* London: 1909- . Index. Indexed: Air Uni. Lib. Ind.; Br. Tech. Ind.; Eng. Ind.
447. *Florida Historical Quarterly.* Gainesville, Florida: 1908- . Index.
448. *Foreign Affairs.* New York: 1922- . Index 1922-1972. Indexed P.A.I.S.; R.G.; Soc. Soc. Sci. & Hum. Ind.
449. *Foreign Service Journal.* Washington, D.C.: 1924- . Index. Indexed: P.A.I.S.
450. *Fortitudine.* Quantico, Virginia: Marine Corps Museum, 1973- . 2 vols, 1973.
451. *Fortune.* New York: 1930- . Indexed: B.P.I.; P.A.I.S.; R.G.
452. *Georgia Historical Quarterly.* Savannah, Georgia: 1917- . Index.
453. *Harper's.* New York: 1850- . Index. Indexed: R.G.
454. *Headline Series.* New York: 1935- . Indexed: P.A.I.S.; Soc. Sci. & Hum. Ind.

455. *Health of the Army.* 1972-   .
456. *Historian.* Allentown, Pennsylvania: 1938-   . Index. Indexed: Soc. Sci. & Hum. Ind.
457. *History: reviews of new books.* Washington: Heldref, 1972-   .
458. *Infantry.* Ft. Benning, Georgia: 1921-   . Indexed: Air Un. Lib. Ind.
459. *International Affairs.* London: 1922-   . Index. Indexed: Br. Hum. Ind.; P.A.I.S.; Soc. Sci. & Hum. Ind.
460. *JAG Journal.* Washington: 1947-   . Index. Indexed:
461. *Journal of American History* (formerly *Mississippi Valley Historical Review*). Bloomington, Indiana: 1914-   . Index. Indexed: Soc. Sci. & Hum. Ind.
462. *Journal of Defense Research.*
463. *Illinois State Historical Society Journal.* Springfield, Illinois: 1908-   . Index.
464. *Journal of Mississippi History.* Jackson, Mississippi: 1939-   . Index.
465. *Journal of Politics.* Gainesville, Fla.: 1939-   . Index. Indexed: Curr. Cont.; Hist. Abstr.; Int. Ind.; Int. Polit. Sci.; P.A.I.S.; Soc. Sci. & Hum. Ind.
466. *Journal of Southern History.* New Orleans, La.: 1935-   . Index: Indexed: Soc. Sci. & Hum. Ind.
467. *Kansas Historical Quarterly.* Topeka, Kans.: 1931-   . Index.
468. *Leatherneck.* Washington, D.C.: 1917-   . Index.
469. *Life.* Chicago: 1936-1972. Indexed: R.G.
470. *Look.* Des Moines, Iowa: 1937-1971. Indexed: R.G.
471. *Louisiana History.* Baton Rouge: 1960-   . Index.
472. *Marine Corps Gazette.* Quantico, Va.: 1916-   . Index. Indexed: Air Un. Lib. Ind.
473. *Maryland Historical Magazine.* Baltimore, Md.: 1906-   . Index.
474. *Military Affairs.* Washington, D.C.: 1937-1968. Manhattan, Kans.: 1968-   . Index 1937-1968. Indexed: Air Un. Lib. Ind.; Hist. Abstr.
475. *Military Chaplains Review.* Ft. Meade, Md.: 1972-   . (There is also a *Military Chaplain,* Washington, 1931-   . Indexed: Air Univ. Lib. Ind.)
476. *Military Engineer.* Washington, D.C. 1920-   . Indexed: Air Un. Lib. Ind.; Chem. Abstr.; Eng. Ind.
477. *Military Medicine.* Chevy Chase, Md.: 1891-   . Index. Cum. Index. Indexed: Biol. Abstr.; Chem. Abstr.; Ind. Med.; Psychol. Abstr.
478. *Military Police Journal.* Ft. Benning, Ga.: 1952-   . Index.
479. *Military Policy Journal.* 1959-   .
480. *Military Review.* Ft. Leavenworth, Kans.: 1922-   . Index *1922-1965.* Indexed: Air Un. Lib. Ind.; P.A.I.S.
481. *Mississippi Valley Historical Review* (See Journal of American History).
482. *Nation.* New York: 1865-   . Index. Indexed: R.G.
483. *National Guardsman.* Washington, D.C.: 1947-   . Indexed: Air Un. Lib. Ind.
484. *National War College Forum* 1965.

485. NATO *Review (Belgium)* (Originally of *NATO Letter*) Brussels, Belgium: 1953- .
486. *NATO's Fifteen Nations.* Amsterdam, Netherlands: 1956- Indexed: Air Un. Lib. Ind.
487. *Naval Engineers Journal.* Washington, D.C.: 1889- . Indexed: Chem. Abstr.; Eng. Ind.; Met. Abst.
488. *New Mexico Historical Review.* Albuquerque, NM.: 1926- . Index: Cum. Index every 15 years; Indexed: Curr. Cont.; Hist. Abstr.
489. *New Republic.* Washington, D.C.: 1914- . Indexed: R.G.
490. *Newsweek.* New York: 1933- . Indexed: R.G.
491. *North Carolina Historical Review.* Raleigh, N.C.: 1924- . Index: Cum Index *1924-63.*
492. *Officer.* Washington, D.C.: 1924- . Ineexed: Air Univ. Lib. Ind.
493. *Ordnance.* Washington, D.C.: 1920- . Index. Indexed: Air Un. Lib. Ind.; Chem. Abstr.; Eng. Ind.
494. *Outlook (Army Retirement Services)* 1972- .
495. *Overseas Weekly.* Frankfort, W. Germany: 1950- . (Tabloid format)
496. *Papers of the Military Historical Society of Massachusetts.*
497. *Parameters—The Journal of the Army War College.* Carlisle Barracks, Pa.: 1971- .
498. *Pennsylvania Magazine of History and Biography.* Philadelphia, Pa.: 1877- . Index: Cum. index published irregularly.
499. *Political Science Quarterly.* New York: 1886- . Index. Indexed: A.B.C. Pol. Sci.; Int. Pol. Sci. Abstr.; P.A.I.S.; Soc. Sci. & Hum. Ind.
500. *Quartermaster.* 19- .
501. *Quartermaster Review* (now *American Logistics Association Review).* Washington, D.C.: 1921- . Index. Indexed: Air Un. Lib. Ind.
502. *Register of the Kentucky Historical Society.*
503. *Review (DSA).* Now *Defense Supply Agency News.*
504. *Reviews in American History.* Westport, Conn.: Redgrave Information Services, 1973- . Index.
505. *Royal United Service Institution Journal.* London: 1857- . Index. Indexed: Air Un. Lib. Ind.; Br. Hum. Ind.; P.A.I.S.
506. *Saturday Evening Post.* Philadelphia, Pa.: 1821-1969. Indexed: R.G.
507. *Soldiers* (Old *Army Information Digest).* Washington: 1946- . Index. Indexed: Air Un. Lib. Ind.; P.A.I.S.
508. *The Soldier Shop Quarterly.* New York: The Soldier Shop, 1972- .
509. *South Carolina Historical Magazine.* Charleston, S.C.: 1900- Index: subject. Index vol. 1-61 (1900-1960).
510. *Southern Historical Society Papers.*
511. *Southwestern Historical Quarterly.* Austin, Tex.: 1897- . Index: Cum index.
512. *Strength of the Army* (annual).

513. *Tennessee Historical Quarterly.* Nashville, Tenn.: 1942-   . Index: Cum. index first 25 vols.
514. *Time.* Chicago: 1923-   . Indexed: R.G.
515. *Tips; The Army Personnel Magazine.* Washington: 1971-   .
516. *Today in France.* New York: 1961.
517. *Tyler's Quarterly. A journal of American History, Biography, and Geneology* (originally *Tyler's Quarterly: an Historical and Geneological Magazine*). Nashville, Tenn.: 1952.
518. *U. S. Department of State. Bulletin.* Washington, D.C.: 1939-   . Index. Indexed: P.A.I.S.; R.G.
519. *United States Naval Institute Proceedings.* Annapolis, Md.: 1873-   . Index *1874-1956.* Indexed: Air Un. Lib. Ind.; Chem. Abstr.; P.A.I.S.
520. *U.S. News and World Report.* Washington, D.C.: 1933-   . Title was *U.S. News,* 1933-1948. Indexed: R.G.
521. *Vietnam Bulletin* (RVN). Washington, 1967-1972.
522. *Vietnam Courier* (Hanoi). 1964.
523. *Vital Speeches of the Day.* Southold, Long Island, N.Y.: 1934-   . Index *1934-1959.* Indexed: R.G.
524. *Western Historical Quarterly.* Logan, Utah: 1970-   . Index. Indexed: Air Un. Lib. Ind.; Amer. Hist. & Life.
525. *Yale Review.* New Haven, Conn.: 1911-   . Index. Indexed: P.A.I.S.; R.G.

INDICES
526. *ABC Pol Sci.* Santa Barbara, Calif.: 1969-   .
527. *Air University Library Index to Military Periodicals.* Maxwell Field, Ala.: 1949-   .
528. *America, History and Life: A Guide to Periodical Literature.* Santa Barbara, Calif.: 1964-   .
529. *Dissertation Abstracts International.* Two sections: Section A: *Humanities & Social Sciences;* Section B: *Physical Sciences & Technology.* Ann Arbor, Mich.: 1938-   .
530. *Historical Abstracts: Bibliography of the World's Periodical Literature.* Part A: *Modern History Abstracts, 1450-1914;* Part B: *Twentieth Century Abstracts, 1914 to Present.* Santa Barbara. Calif.: 1955-   .
531. *Index to The Times* (London). London: 1907-   .
532. *International Political Science Abstracts.* Oxford, England: 1951-   .
533. *Masters Abstracts.* Ann Arbor, Mich.: 1962-   .
534. *Monthly Catalog of United States Government Publications.* Washington, D.C.: 1895-   .
535. *The New York Times Index.* 1851-   .
536. *Public Affairs Information Service Bulletin.* New York: 1915-   .
537. *Reader's Guide to Periodical Literature.* New York: 1900-   .
538. *Social Science and Humanities Index.* New York: 1907-   . Titles have changed: *International Index to Periodicals,* 1907-1955; *International Index,* 1955-1965.

FEDERAL RECORDS CENTERS—NATIONAL

539. Washington National Records Center, GSA
Washington, D.C. 20409
Tel. (301) 763-7000
Area served: District of Columbia, Maryland, Virginia, West Virginia

540. National Personnel Records Center, GSA
(Civilian Personnel Records)
111 Winnebago Street
St. Louis, Missouri 63118
Tel: (314) 622-5722
Area served: Entire Federal Government (for personnel and pay records of separated civilian employees; other designated records)

541. National Personnel Records Center, GSA
(Military Personnel Records)
9700 Page Boulevard
St. Louis, Missouri 63132
Tel: (314) 268-7247
Area served: Designated records of the Military Departments and the U.S. Coast Guard

FEDERAL RECORDS CENTERS—REGIONAL

542. Federal Records Center, GSA (Archives Branch)
380 Trapelo Road
Waltham, Massachusetts 02154
Tel: (617) 223-2657
Area served: Maine, Vermont, New Hampshire, Massachusetts, Connecticut, Rhode Island

543. Federal Records Center, GSA (Archives Branch)
641 Washington Street
New York, New York 10014
Tel. (212) 620-5757
Area served: New York, New Jersey, Puerto Rico, Virgin Islands

544. Federal Records Center, GSA (Archives Branch)
5000 Wissahickon Avenue
Philadelphia, Pennsylvania 19144
Tel: (215) 438-5200 Ext. 591
Area served: Delaware and Pennsylvania east of Lancaster

545. Federal Records Center, GSA
Naval Supply Depot, Building 308
Mechanicsburg, Pennsylvania 17055
Tel: (717) 766-8511 Ext. 3477
Area served: Pennsylvania except areas east of Lancaster

546. Federal Records Center, GSA (Archives Branch)
1557 St. Joseph Avenue
East Point, Georgia 30344
Tel: (404) 526-7475
Area served: Kentucky, North Carolina, South Carolina, Tennessee, Mississippi, Alabama, Georgia, Florida

547. Federal Records Center, GSA (Archives Branch)
7201 South Leamington Avenue
Chicago, Illinois 60638
Tel: (312) 353-5720
Area served: Illinois, Wisconsin, Minnesota

548. Federal Records Center, GSA
2400 West Dorothy Lane
Dayton, Ohio 45439
Tel: (513) 461-5597
Area served: Indiana, Michigan, Ohio

549. Federal Records Center, GSA (Archives Branch)
2306 East Bannister Road
Kansas City, Missouri 64131
Tel: (816) 361-0860 Ext. 7271
Area served: Kansas, Iowa, Nebraska, Missouri except greater St. Louis area (St. Louis area see National Personnel Records Center, Civilian Records) (540).

550. Federal Records Center, GSA (Archives Branch)
4900 Hemphill Street
P. O. Box 6216
Fort Worth, Texas 76115
Tel: (817) 334-5515
Area served: Texas, Oklahoma, Arkansas, Louisiana, New Mexico

551. Federal Records Center, GSA (Archives Branch)
Denver Federal Center, Building 48
Denver, Colorado 80225
Tel: (303) 234-3185
Area served: North Dakota, South Dakota, Colorado, Wyoming, Utah, Montana

552. Federal Records Center, GSA (Archives Branch)
100 Harrison Street, Building 1
San Francisco, California 94105
Tel: (415) 556-3484
Area served: Nevada (except Clark County, California (except southern California), Hawaii, Pacific Ocean area

553. Federal Records Center, GSA (Archives Branch)
4747 Eastern Avenue
Bell, California 90201
Tel: (213) 268-2548
Area served: Clark County (Nevada), Southern California (counties of San Luis Obispo, Kern, San Bernardino, Santa Barbara, Ventura, Los Angeles, Riverdale, Orange, Imperial, Inyo, and San Diego), Arizona

554. Federal Records Center, GSA (Archives Branch)
6125 Sand Point Way
Seattle, Washington 98115
Tel: (206) 442-4502
Area served: Washington, Oregon, Idaho, Alaska

II

EUROPEAN BACKGROUND OF AMERICAN
MILITARY AFFAIRS

Russell F. Weigley

In his famous address delivered at the West Point commencement of 1963, General Maxwell D. Taylor pointed out that by mid-twentieth century the arrival of the United States at the pinnacle of world military power was affirmed by the emulation of American military methods and the adoption of American military thought all around the globe. As the kepi of the Civil War American infantryman had symbolized the post-Napoleonic predominance of France in all things military, including military fashion, and the sprouting of spiked helmets from military heads throughout the world soon thereafter signified the eclipse of France by Prussia-Germany, so American military styles permeate the military world today, at least outside the Iron Curtain and often across it. But for generations before this Americanization of the military world, and through most of the time span of American military history (even though Taylor rightly saw the Civil War as a turning point), the United States remained militarily a colony of Europe, in tutelage to the military powers and military thinkers of the mother continent of its civilization. It could afford to be in tutelage because the oceans rendered it militarily secure, the United States Army serving mainly as a constabulary for the pacification of the Indian frontier, the United States Navy a collection of cruisers and lesser ships showing the flag in foreign ports to influence minor commercial disputes. Military thought, institutions, tactics, and weapons were largely borrowed from Europe, European innovations often arriving several years belatedly, and the borrowings often occurring with insufficient regard for their appropriateness to the American scene, as with the application of European infantry tactics to the Second Seminole War.

Thus a guide to the sources of American military history has to devote at least a chapter to the European background of that history. The books listed in the chapter fall into two principal categories. A lesser number of them are secondary historical works describing the institutions, methods, and ideas of military Europe that were to cross the Atlantic, as they had evolved to the time of their crossing. A larger number are a selection of books published by European military writers during the years when

American soldiers and sailors remained in their period of tutelage, with these books being carried to America to tutor them.

Because the circumstances attending their historical evolution often conditioned the manner in which European military exports would be applied in America, even the circumstances of their development in times long before they reached the New World have to be considered thus a number of the historical works selected for inclusion here reach far back into European military history, to help the student understand why the deepest roots of American military institutions displayed the particular shape they did. Among them are major works surveying British military history, which most especially determined much of the initial form that American military history was to take: Sir John Fortescue's monumental *History of the British Army* (98), Charles M. Clode's old but richly detailed *Military Forces of the Crown* (57), and Corelli Barnett's recent, critcal history of the British army in its social context, *Britain and Her Army* (16). The Royal Navy, not only an initial source of American naval institutions but long an object of continuing emulation for the American Navy as the British army, after independence, no longer was for the American Army), lacks an all-inclusive modern survey history; there is Wm. Laird Clowes's older *The Royal Navy: A History: From the Earliest Times to the Present* (58); and among more recent works, G. J. Marcus's two books, *A Naval History of England: The Formative Centuries* (185) and *The Age of Nelson: The Royal Navy, 1793-1815* (184); Michael Lewis's short *History of the British Navy* (166) and his pioneering work of military social history, *England's Sea-Officers: The Story of the Naval Profession* (165); Christopher Lloyd's *The Nation and the Navy: A History of Naval Life and Policy* (167); and Leslie Gardiner's *The British Admiralty* (107). E. H. H. Archibald's *The Wooden Fighting Ship in the Royal Navy, A.D. 897-1860* (8) surveys the instruments of British sea power when the American Navy branched away.

Some American military institutions, most notably the militia system, can trace their descent to the earliest formal military organizations of Anglo-Saxon and Norman England. John Beeler has explored these remote roots in his article "The Composition of Anglo-Norman Armies" (20) and his book *Warfare in England, 1066-1189* (21). C. Warren Hollister carries the study from *Anglo-Saxon Military Institutions on the Eve of the Norman Conquest* (132) to the later Middle Ages with "The Annual Term of Military Service in Medieval England" (133) and *The Military Organization of Medieval England* (134). John Schlight—in *Monarchs and Mercenaries* (261)—argues cogently for the rejection of certain of Sir Charles Oman's (216) theories about the medieval predominance of cavalry and, more pertinently for the relevant institutional history, about feudalism—Schlight contending that mercenary soldiers became much more important to the military service of the English kings much earlier than has recently been acknowledged by most historians. More conventional views than Schlight's are ably presented in Iver John Sanders's *Feudal Military Service in England: A Study of the Constitutional and Military Powers of the Barons in Medieval England* (254).

In the transition from the medieval to the modern period in England, out of militia and mercenaries there gradually evolved two divergent military institutional traditions, from which the United States in turn was to draw a dual military history running along two separate main lines—that of the citizen-soldier and that of the regular, standing forces. The English militia can be followed to the opening of American military history in Michael Powicke's *Military Obligation in Medieval England: A Study in Liberty and Duty* (232), Richard Ager Newhall's *Muster and Review: A Problem of English Military Administration, 1420-1440* (210), and John R. Western's *The English Militia in the Eighteenth Century* (314). The background of the standing army lies in Charles Cruickshank's *Elizabeth's Army* (71), Sir Charles Firth's *Cromwell's Army* (265), Leo F. Solt's *Saints in Arms: Puritanism and Democracy in Cromwell's Army* (265), Michael Roberts's *The Military Revolution, 1560-1660* (244), Clifford Walton's older but still valuable *History of the British Standing Army, AD 1660-1700* (311), R. E. Scouller's *The Armies of Queen Anne* (263), Charles Dalton's *George the First's Army, 1714-1727* (75), and Lieutenant General Sir Reginald Savory's *His Britannic Majesty's Army in Germany during the Seven Years War* (256). H. G. De Watteville deals with a less formal part of the background of the formative experiences of the American Army in *The British Soldier: His Daily Life from Tudor to Modern Times* (83).

Though from time to time the United States was to direct efforts toward a naval version of the citizen-soldier in a naval militia, once warships had definitely evolved into a separate type from merchant ships such efforts could promise only slight success, and British sea power had shifted its foundations from citizen-seamen to professionals before the American Navy began to fashion itself upon the British naval model. There are roots of the naval-militia idea, as well as of American privateering, to be found in Kenneth R. Andrews's *Elizabethan Privateering* (7) and Michael Oppenheim's *A History of the Administration of the Royal Navy and of Merchant Shipping in Relation to the Navy, from MDIX to MDCLX with an Introduction Treating of the Preceding Period* (219). The transition to a regular naval service develops through Sir Herbert Richmond's *The Navy as an Instrument of Policy, 1558-1727* (243), Sir Julian Corbett's *Drake and the Tudor Navy, with a History of the Rise of England as a Maritime Power* (66), Walter Oakeshott's *Founded upon the Seas: A Narrative of Some English Maritime and Overseas Enterprises during the Period 1550 to 1616* (215), Arthur W. Tedder's *The Navy of the Restoration* (273), and Reginald Dundas Merriman's *Queen Anne's Navy: Documents Concerning the Administration of the Navy of Queen Anne, 1702-1714* (189). Naval history meets military history at large in Sir Julian Corbett's *England in the Seven Years War: A Study in Combined Strategy* (68).

Because France, too, contributed to the shaping of American military institutions, through conflict during the colonial wars, alliance with the rebels in the American Revolution, and military prestige in the age of Napoleon and after, basic surveys of French military history are also listed, including the offical *Historiques des corps de troupe de l'armée française (1569-1900)* (100), and, more directly bearing on the immediate background of American military history, Lee Kennett's *The French Armies in the Seven Years' War: A Study in Military Organization and Administration* (151) and Émile G. Léonard's *L'Armée et ses problemes au XVIIIᵉ siècle* (163). For France and the continent in an earlier period there is Ferdinand Lot's *L'Art militaire et les armées au moyen age* (172).

Some of these roots of American military history can be seen as the founders of American military institutions saw them, in contemporary accounts and analyses that reached America. John Trenchard's *History of Standing Armies in England* (278) interpreted the rise of the standing army as a threat to English liberties and a betrayal of the Glorious Revolution of 1688, with an eloquence that made the book a major source of the American Revolutionaries' eventual determination to eject the British from their shores and to countenance no home-grown equivalent of the redcoats. The militia who if properly organized might obviate the need for an American standing army could be nourished from an English officer's *Essay on Defensive War and a Constitutional Militia; with an Account of Queen Elizabeth's Arrangement for Resisting the Projected Invasion of the Year 1588* (94), Colonel Martin's *Plan for Establishing and Disciplining a National Militia in Great Britain, Ireland, and in All the British Dominions of America* (187), and William Windham's *Plan of Discipline, Composed for the Use of the Militia of the County of Norfolk* (318). Whether championing a citizens' militia as the proper reliance of free men for defense, and believing like Thomas Jefferson that it would be best for both citizen and soldier that the distinction between them should be erased, or believing like George Washington that standing armed forces of at least modest proportions were essential to the national safety and dignity, Americans of the generation that fought the Revolution and founded the Republic all believed they required books to guide them to a knowledge of European tactics to turn upon the British. Colonel Washington of the Virginia militia first studied war from the leading British military manual of his day, Humphrey Bland's *Treatise of Military Discipline* (28), first published in 1727.

Later tactical manuals exported to America from Europe can be found listed here in profusion, along with A. F. Becke's European-oriented survey of the principles found in them, his *Introduction to the History of Tactics* (19), because American tactics continued to be borrowed from those of Europe—as Winfield Scott trained the regiments of Chippewa and Lundy's Lane from the European manuals, mainly French, that he carried in his baggage, and then based his own tactical manuals on the same sources. American tactics were essentially European borrowings at least until the innovations of Emory Upton after the Civil War. Even later, Americans continued to draw from the tactical sources of Europe; Walter Krueger, the future commander of the Sixth Army in World War II, translated Balck's *Tactics* from the German and the U.S. Cavalry Association published the manual at Fort Leavenworth in 1911-1914 (11), and so nationalist a soldier as General John J. Pershing was to feel obliged to subject his American Expeditionary Force to the tactical instruction of the French and the British before committing it to battle in 1917-1918.

Though Jefferson, who wanted to eliminate the distinction between the civilian and the military, signed the legislation establishing the Military Academy at West Point in hopes that the school would become a center whence military knowledge would eventually be disseminated among the citizens' militia, with a scattering of academy graduates throughout the country and into militia commissions, complex circumstances decreed that an American standing army should become a permanent institution and West Point the nursery of the military profession in the United States. Many of the books listed here are the European volumes collected at West Point by the first great professionalizing superintendent of the Military Academy, Sylvanus Thayer (2, 3, 12, 17, 18, 23, 24, 31, 33, 34, 35, 36, 39, 40, 41, 43, 53, 60, 79, 80, 82, 90, 91, 95, 102, 103, 104, 105, 108, 110, 111, 121, 122, 123, 135, 144, 145, 155, 156, 157, 158, 160, 164, 168, 170, 171, 174, 175, 178, 179, 180, 182, 183, 188, 190, 191, 194, 198, 199, 200, 201, 202, 203, 214, 226, 228, 229, 230, 231, 237, 240, 247, 249, 251, 253, 258, 264, 266, 276, 277, 281, 282, 312, 317). Upon these volumes and upon the military teachings of Thayer's faculty, which on the level of military theory meant mainly those of Dennis Hart Mahan, teachings also initially borrowed directly from Europe and overwhelmingly from France, the Military Academy built a foundation of military knowledge upon which in turn could be erected within about half a century an American professional military literature—in the reports of European observations by Richard Delafield, Alfred Mordecai, and George B. McClellan and in the military writings of Henry Wager Halleck and of D. H. Mahan himself—of remarkable maturity especially in proportion to the still diminutive size of the American standing army, and attesting to the precociously rapid rise of the military profession in the New World.

For a military profession to be born, military literature had to reach beyond tactical manuals to a historical and philosophical approach to the study of war, seeking to draw from the history of warfare general principles underlying the art and science of war. Where hitherto military books imported from Europe were merely manuals of tactics and discipline, and occasionally guides to forms of organization, the word strategy entered the military lexicon in the early nineteenth century, and the literature became strategic as well as tactical. The impetus for developing a historical and theoretical military literature and thence a military career as a profession rather than simply a craft came of course from the cataclysmic changes in war during the French Revolutionary era and especially those in strategy introduced by Napoleon. The work of the first European military theorists began with the effort to express the genius of Napoleon in principles comprehensible to ordinary mortals. In the long run, the most influential of these interpreters of Napoleon in America as well as elsewhere were to be Jomini (138-143) and Clausewitz (55, 56); but the latter's influence in the United States came only in the very long run, for while the mid-nineteenth-century French translation of *Vom Kriege* was available in the War Department Library and the West Point Library, it was not until after an English translation was published in 1873 and, more importantly, until after the Franco-Prussian War turned American soldiers from French to German military preceptors, that Clausewitz became a familiar name to Americans.

Meanwhile the foundation of West Point and of its library coincided in time with the transformation of military officership from a craft into a profession, and consistent with the subsequent rapid growth of American professionalism with West Point as its fountainhead, an important part of the military library collected by Sylvanus Thayer at the Military Academy introduced into America the new intellectualizing of the study of war. In the War Department Library, too, appeared such Napoleonic-era and immediately pre-Napoleonic historical and theoretical works on war as those of Jomini and Clausewitz, the eccentric Freiherr von Bülow's *Spirit of the Modern System of War* (39), the Archduke Charles's *Principes de la stratégie* (52), and the Comte de Guibert's *Essai général de tactique* (119) and *Oeuvres militaires* (120). Many of the books listed here are from the bibliographical citations of H. W. Halleck's *Elements of Military Art and Science* (Third Edition, New York: Appleton, 1862) (1, 3, 4, 18, 22, 24, 29, 34, 40, 44, 45, 52, 54, 56, 60, 69, 70, 78, 95, 108, 113, 119, 140, 144, 154, 155, 157, 169, 171, 177, 178, 181, 201, 203, 204, 206, 221, 241, 250, 260, 264, 279, 305, 306, 312).

The graduates of West Point rapidly approached military professionalism, but that aspect of West Point and early American military development which Samuel P. Huntington has described as "technicism" has also been rightly emphasized by military historians, albeit Huntington in his own stress upon the technicism of early American soldiers may unduly minimize the professionalizing developments of the period before the Civil War. Jefferson in sponsoring the Military Academy envisioned it as a school for engineers both civil and military as well as a source of militia officers; the former part of his design proved to be fulfilled, because the engineering emphasis not only accorded with Jefferson's plans for the academy's civic utility, but engineering had long been the one branch of military officer-ship that demanded efforts approaching professional study and long continued to support a voluminous part of the imported literature of military affairs (*e.g.*, 3, 12, 13, 22, 23, 24, 29, 31, 34, 44, 45, 54, 60, 65, 69, 70, 73, 90, 91, 93, 95, 99, 108, 111, 126, 153, 154, 161, 177, 182, 183, 199, 201, 203, 218, 229, 247, 248, 249, 251, 264, 277, 279, 280, 297, 305, 306).

This chapter on the sources for examining the European background of American military history might have confined itself to works describing or embodying the European influence up to the founding of the military institutions of the United States during the American Revolution. But the founding of American military institutions was hardly synonymous with the attainment of their mature form, and throughout their formative years, and well beyond the emergence of a vigorous American military profession and professional literature, the tutelage to Europe persisted. Thus the listing includes the largely nineteenth-century European works that Sylvanus Thayer assembled, and it encompasses such modern historical studies of the nature of European military thought and practice in the French Revolutionary and Napoleonic eras as David Chandler's *The Campaigns of Napoleon* (51), the best historical study of Napoleon's way of war, and Peter Paret's *Yorck and the Era of Prussian Reform* (222), the best study of the rise of light-infantry tactics; Jean Colin's and Count Yorck von Wartenburg's classic studies of *The Transformations of War* (63) and *Napoleon as a General* (319), respectively; and, more recently, David B. Ralston's *The Army of the Republic* (239) and Colonel R. W. Phipps's *The Armies of the First French Republic and the Rise of the Marshals of Napoleon I* (227). Necessarily the list includes the first textbook on the art of war to become standard at West Point, Captain J. M. O'Connor's translation of S. M. Gay de Vernon's *Treatise on the Science of War and Fortification* (118).

The list also extends to evidences of the persisting American dependence on European military models throughout the nineteenth century and into the early twentieth. Thus there are the reports of the principal American military observers of European institutions: Delafield, Mordecai, and McClellan (303); J. A. Dahlgren (74); Emory Upton (304); French Ensor Chadwick (50); Caspar F. Goodrich (112); and Nelson A. Miles (192, 291), along with Henry Barnard (14), W. D. Connor (65), W. B. Hazen (127), and Charles P. Echols (87) on European military schools. There are representative publications of the Military Information Divisions first of the Adjutant General's Office and then of the General Staff on foreign armies (283-295, 298-301). There are American studies of European campaigns, Colonel Arthur L. Wagner's of *Koniggratz* (310), Captain John Bigelow's of *Mars-la-Tour and Gravelotte* (27), and R. M. Johnston's—one of the first professional historians to turn to war studies—on *The French Revolution: A Short History* (136) and *Napoleon: A Short Biography* (137). European military studies in American editions or translations and thus manifestly used in America are included, such as an early translation of Freiherr von Swieten on *The Diseases Incident to Armies* (270); a translation of M. P. E. Berthelet and Karl Braun on explosives (26) the latter two being among the relatively few European works on the specialized auxiliary services or on logistics that could be found definitely to have reached America;(see also 38, 101, 106, 123, 155, 156, 160, 171, 174, 176, 198, 223, 225, 226, 245, 266); Lieutenant Colonel William Gerlach's translation of Volume I of Verdy du Vernois's *Studies in the Leading of Troops* (308), and Harry Bell's translation of *Extracts from Moltke's Correspondence Pertaining to the War, 1870-71* (196), to say nothing of Halleck's translation of Jomini's *Life of Napoleon* (139) and the much used though flawed translation of the *Précis de l'art de la guerre* by Major C. F. Winship and Lieutenant E. E. McLean (140). The reach of American interests in European military affairs by the late nineteenth and early twentieth centuries, after the Franco-Prussian War had ended the almost monopolistic influence of France, is suggested by two translations from the Russian, one by Captain Tasker H. Bliss, later Chief of Staff of the Army, of Pashkievitsch's *Exterior Ballistics* (223), the other by Lieutenant Commander John B. Bernadou of A. Brynk's *Properties of Powders* (38).

The widening of American military horizons after 1870 brought the military studies undertaken by the Prussian Great General Staff into American military libraries (*e.g.*, 235, 236), and two books describing the Prussian-German General Staff reached the attention of Secretary of War Elihu Root through Colonel William Harding Carter to shape Root's creation of the American General Staff: Spenser Wilkinson's *The Brain of an Army* (316) and Paul Bronsart von Schellendorf's *The Duties of the General Staff* (37). A modern military writer traces the history of such staffs in J. D. Hittle's *The Military Staff: Its History and Development* (130). By the time Root borrowed from Germany some of the basic elements of his reforms of the American Army, however, the period of European military tutelage of America was approaching its end. Despite Root's reading of Wilkinson and Bronsart von Schellendorf, the American General Staff was far from a carbon copy of the German; in more important ways it was a response to American constitutional and political pressures, and indeed American dilutions of the German model helped make Root's

General Staff relatively ineffective until World War I, when again the improvements that rendered it functional were pragmatic and American.

The beginning of World War I in Europe in fact has been chosen as the point at which to terminate the study of the European background of American military history for the purposes of this chapter and listing. By the eve of World War I, Lord Haldane's conscious and acknowledged borrowing from the American Root reforms for his reforms of the British army marks the beginning of a major, and not merely occasional, flow of military influences eastward across the Atlantic, reversing the previously predominant direction. In 1917-1918, to be sure, Pershing continued to borrow tactical training from the Europeans, but by the Armistice of 1918 the United States Army had surely come of age as one of the major armies of the European military world, and the mainstreams of European and American military history had merged. Thereafter, it becomes no longer possible to speak of transatlantic interchanges of military influence in terms of a European background for American developments.

For the United States Navy, this condition of liberation from European tutelage and achievement of maturity among the major navies of the world probably arrived earlier than for the Army. The ship designs for the new Navy of the 1880s and 1890s had to be bought at first from European naval architects, but that and other forms of technical dependence were brief, and with Alfred Thayer Mahan the United States Navy clearly occupied the forefront of the development of naval strategic thought. Because American naval strategists in turn were influenced by the Britons P. H. Colomb (64), Sir Julian Corbett (67, 68), and Sir Herbert Richmond (242, 243) and by the Frenchman Gabriel Darrieus (76), their representative works are listed here, as are Stephen W. Roskill's and Donald M. Schurman's studies of the evolution of naval strategic thought; some of this work, Corbett's in particular, demands inclusion also because of its contribution to our knowledge of the roots of earlier American naval history. But the modern European naval strategists were themselves so much influenced by A. T. Mahan that their inclusion strains the concept of a European background to American military and naval history, and certainly it brings us to the limits of a study of that background.

The United States Military Academy's *Earliest Printed Catalogue of Books in the United States Military Academy Library* (302); the *Subject Catalog of the Military Art and Science Collection in the Library of the United States Military Academy* (269), in which the volumes of Thayer's original collection are indicated by the designation "WPT" above the call number; and Thomas H. Spaulding and Louis C. Karpinski, *Early Military Books in the University of Michigan Libraries* (267) give invaluable indications which European military literature reached the United States. Along with the libraries of the Military Academy and the Naval Academy, the principal depository in which the books forming at least the literary embodiment of the European background of American military history can be found and examined is the United States Army Military History Research Collection at Carlisle Barracks, Pennsylvania, the official Army depository for books of historical value. Included in the collection is the former War Department Library, which began to be assembled almost at the beginning of that Department's existence.

H. W. Halleck's bibliography in his *Elements of Military Art and Science*, mentioned earlier, is a practically unique source of information about what a scholarly American officer knew of the European military literature of his day—or at least of what Halleck was aware of, since while he lists Clausewitz, for example, there is little in the text to indicate that Halleck had read much of or digested the Prussian military philosopher. (Not all the works listed by Halleck seemed of sufficient importance or relevance to be listed here.) American soldiers generally tell us little of the forces that have shaped their military thought and practice, American or foreign; here Ulysses S. Grant is almost unique, for his acknowledgment in his memoirs of the influence of Winfield Scott upon his generalship. Nevertheless, further study especially in private papers aimed at discovering more fully the extent of awareness of European military thought and developments among American officers may yet reveal more to us of what we now understand only vaguely, the transit of military culture from Europe to America. The development of the West Point curriculum is reasonably well understood, but further studies of the curricula of other, including the higher, military schools, on which little work has yet been done, may also add to our knowledge of the specific processes by which Americans became aware of the military inheritance on which they surely drew. And the work of studying the content of American military thought itself is just beginning, while an examination of the European thought that laid the foundations is a necessary part of such study.

BIBLIOGRAPHY

1. Adys, Ralph Willett. *The Bombardier, and Pocket Gunner.* First American, from the Second London Edition. Printed for E. Larkin, no. 47, Cornhill, Boston, by William Greenough, Charleston, 1804.
2. Adys, S[tephen] Payne. *A Treatise on Courts Martial; Also an Essay on Military Punishments and Rewards.* 7th Edition. London: Vernor, Hood, and Sharpe, 1805.
3. Allent, Pierre Alexandre Joseph. *Historie du Corps impériale du génie; des siéges et des travaux qu'il a dirigés, et des changements que l'attaque, la défense, la construction el l'administration des fortresses ont reçus, en France. . . . 1. ptie., depuis l'origine de la fortification moderne jusqu'à la fin de règne de Louis XIV.* Paris: Magimel, 1805. (No more published.)
4. Allix, Jacques Alexandre François. *Système d'artillerie de campagne, comparé avec les systèmes du Comité d'artillerie de France, de Gribeauval, et de l'an XI.* Paris: Anselin, 1827.
5. Almon, John. *A New Military Dictionary: or, The Field of War. Containing a Particular . . . Account of the Most Remarkable Battles, Sieges, Bombardments, and Expeditions, Whether by Sea or Land. Such as Relate to Great Britain and Her Dependencies, Deduced from the Descent of Julius Caesar to the Present Time. . . . Added, An Essay on Fortificaton; and a Table, Explaining the Military and Naval Terms of Art.* Comp. . . . by a Military Gentleman. London: J. Cooke, 1760.

6. Alombert, P.-C., and J. Colin. *La campagne de 1805 en Allemagne. Publié sous la direction de la Section Historique de l'État-Major de l'Armée.* Paris: Librairie militaire R. Chapelot, 1902-1908. 4 vols. in 6.

7. Andrews, Kenneth R. *Elizabethan Privateering: English Privateering during the Spanish War, 1585-1603.* Cambridge, England: The University Press, 1964.

8. Archibald, E. H. H. *The Wooden Fighting Ship in the Royal Navy, A.D. 897-1860.* London: Blandford Press, 1968.

9. Ardant du Picq, Charles Jean Jacques-Joseph. *Études sur le combat, combat antique et combat moderne.* Paris: Chapelot, 1904.

10. *The Art of War, Containing:* I. *The Duties of All Military Officers in Actual Service* . . . by Monsieur de Lamont . . . II. *The Duties of Soldiers in General* . . . [By a French Officer] III. *The Rules and Practice of the Greatest Generals* . . . By the Chevalier de la Valiere. Philadelphia: Printed and sold by Robert Bell, in Third Street, 1776.

11. Balck, William. *Tactics,* by Balck. . . . Tr. by Walter Kreuger. . . . 4th completely rev. ed. . . . Fort Leavenworth, Kansas: U.S. Cavalry Association, 1911-1914.

12. Bardet de Villeneuve, P. P. A. *Traité de l'attaque* [*et la défense*] *des places; ou l'on enseigne d'une manière courte et facile la methode la plus avantageuse* . . . *avec les remarques necessaires sur les methodes de M. de Vauban et autres habiles maitres.* . . . La Haye: Jean van Duren, 1742. 2 vols. in 1. (*Cours de la science militaire* . . . , t. 9-10.)

13. Baker, John. *Treasury of Fortification.* . . . London: Boscile, 1707.

14. Barnard, Henry. *Military Schools and Courses of Instruction in the Science and Art of War, in France, Prussia, Austria, Russia, Sweden, Switzerland, Sardinia, England, and the United States.* Revised Edition. New York: Steiger, 1872.

15. Barnes, Alfred H., and Peter Young. *The Great Civil War: A Military History of the First Civil War, 1642-1646.* London: Eyre & Spottiswoode, 1959.

16. Barnett, Correlli. *Britain and Her Army, 1509-1970.* New York: William Morrow, 1970.

17. Beauchamp, Alphonse de. *Historie des campagnes de 1814 et de 1815, comprenant l'histoire politique et militaire des deux invasions de la France, de l'enterprise de Buonaparte au mois de mars, de la chute totale de sa puissance, de la double restoration du trone, et de tous les événemens dont la France à éte la théâtre, jusqu'à la seconde paix de Paris, inclusivement. Redigée sur des matériaux authentiques ou inédits.* . . . Paris: Le Normant, 1816-1817. 4 vols.

18. Beauvais de Preau, Charles Theodore, ed. *Victoires, conquêtes, désastres, revers et guerres civiles des Francais, de 1792 a 1815, par une societé de militaires et de gens de lettres.* . . . Paris: C. L. F. Panckouke, 1821-1834. 35 vols. in 34.

19. Becke, A. F. *An Introduction to the History of Tactics.* London: Rees, 1909.

20. Beeler, John. "The Composition of Anglo-Norman Armies." *Speculum*, XL (1965), 398-414.
21. Beeler, John. *Warfare in England 1066-1189*. Ithaca: Cornell University Press, 1966.
22. Belair, Alexandre Pierre Julienne de. *Elemens de fortification.* . . . 2. ed. Paris: Magimel, 1793.
23. Belidor, Bernard Forest de. *Oeuvres diverses . . . concernant l'artillerie et la génie*. Amsterdam: Arkstee, 1764.
24. Bélidor, Bernard Forest de. *La science des ingenieurs dans la conduite des travaux de fortification et d'architecture civile.* . . . Paris: Jombert, 1739. 5 vols. in 1.
25. Bernhardi, Friedrich Adam Julius von. *Cavalry in War and Peace*. Tr. from the German by Major G. T. M. Bridges . . . with a Preface by General Sir J. D. P. French. . . . Fort Leavenworth, Kansas: U.S. Cavalry Association, 1910.
26. Berthelet, Marcellin Pierre Eugène. *Explosive Materials. A Series of Lectures Delivered before the College de France at Paris*. Tr. by Marcus Benjamin. . . . *To Which Is Added a Short Historical Sketch of Gunpowder*. Tr. from the German of Karl Braun, by John P. Wisser, U.S.A. *And a Bibliography of Works on Explosives. Reprinted from Van Nostrand's Magazine*. New York: Van Nostrand, 1883.
27. Bigelow, John. *Mars-la-Tour and Gravelotte*. Washington: G. P. O. 1884.
28. Bland, Humphrey. *A Treatise of Military Discipline in Which Is Laid Down and Explained the Duty of the Officer and Soldier, Thro' the Several Branches of the Service*. 5th Edition. Dublin: P. Crampton, 1743.
29. Blondel, A. *Nouvelle manière de fortifier les places*. Paris: Langlois, 1683.
30. Boguslawski, Albrecht von. *Tactical Deductions from the War of 1870-1871.* . . Tr. from the German by Col. Lumley Graham. . . . . Leavenworth, Kansas: Spooner, 1891.
31. Boistard, Louis Charles. *Experiences sur la main-d'oeuvre de differens trauvaux dependans du service des ingenieurs des ponts et chausses.* . . . Paris: Merlin, 1804.
32. Boitet, Maurice. *Monographies de l'arme blanche (1789-1870) et de l'arme à feu porative (1718-1900) des armées francaise de terre et de mer*. Paris: Editions Haussmann, 1959. Originally published as two separate works in 1905 and 1906.
33. Bourcet, Pierre Joseph. *Mémoires historiques, sur la guerre que les françois ont soutenue en Allemagne depuis 1757 jusqu' en 1762. . . . Auxquels on a joint divers supplémens, & notamment une relation impartiale des campagnes de M. le maréchal de Broglie, rédigée d'après ses propres papiers, & les pièces originales existantes dans les archives du Département de la guerre.* . . . Paris: Maraden, 1792. 3 vols.
34. Bousmard, Henri Jean de. *Essai general de fortification et d'attaque et défense des places.* . . . Berlin: Decker, 1797-1799. 3 vols. and

atlas. New edition, revised, Paris: Magimel, 1814. 4 vols. in 2 and atlas.

35. Briquet, de. *Code militaire: ou, Compilation des ordonnances des rois de France, concernant les gens de guerre.* Nouvelle édition, augmentée des derniers ordannances. Paris: Prault, 1761. 8 vols.

36. Breze, Marquis de. *Réflexions sur les préjuges militaires. . . .* Turin: Freyres Reycends, 1779.

37. Bronsart von Schellendorf, Paul Leopold Eduard Heinrich Anton. *The Duties of the General Staff.* 4th Edition, 1905. Tr. for the General Staff, War Office, 1905. London: H. M. S. O., 1907.

38. Brynk, A. *Properties of Powders and Their Action in Closed Chambers and in Cannon,* tr. fr. the Russian by Lieut. Com. John B. Bernadou, U.S. Navy. Washington: G. P. O., 1904.

39. Bülow, Adam Heinrich Dietrich, Freiherr von. *The Spirit of the Modern System of War.* By a Prussian General Officer. With a Commentary, by C. Malorti de Martemont. London: Sold by T. Egerton, 1806.

40. Bynkershoek, Cornelis van. *A Treatise on the Law of War. Translated from the Original Latin of Cornelis van Bynkershoek. Being the First Book of His Quaestiones juris publici.* With Notes, by Stephen Du Ponceau. . . . Philadelphia: Pub. by Farrand & Nicholas; Fry and Kammerer, printers, 1810.

41. Caesar, C. Julius. *The Commentaries of Caesar, Translated into English: To Which Is Prefixed, A Discourse Concerning the Roman Art of War.* By William Duncan. London: J. Cuthell, 1819. 2 vols.

42. Calef, John Haskell. Part I. *Military Policy and Institutions.* Part II. *Ancient and Modern Armies.* Fort Monroe, Va.: U.S. Artillery School, 1896.

43. Carel, Auguste. *Précis historique de la guerre d'Espagne et de Portugal, de 1808 à 1814; contenant la réfutation des ouvrages de MM. Sarrazin et Alphonse de Beauchamps, avec des détails sur la bataille de Toulouse.* Paris: Jeunehomme, 1815.

44. Carnot, Lazare Nicolas Marguerite, comte. *De la défense des places fortes, ouvrage composé par ordre de Sa Majesté imperiale et royale pour l'instruction des élèves du Corps du génie. . . .* 3e edition. Paris: Courcier, 1812.

45. Carnot, Lazare Nicolas Marguerite, comte. *Mémoire sur la fortification primitive, pour servir de suite au traité de la défense des places fortes. . . .* Paris: Bachelier, 1823.

46. Cary, R. Milton, comp. and tr. *Skirmishers' Drill and Bayonet Exercise (As Now used in the French Army) with Suggestions for the Soldier in Actual Conflict.* Comp. and Tr. for the Use of the Volunteers of the State of Virginia and the South. Richmond: West & Johnston, 1861.

47. *The Cavalry Journal.* London: G. Gilbert Wood. 1904-

48. *Cavalry Studies from Two Great Wars, Comprising the French Cavalry in 1870,* by Lieutenant [Jean Jacques Theophile] Bonie. *The German Cavalry in the Battle of Vionville-Mars-la-Tour,* by Major Kaehler. *The Operation of the Cavalry in the Gettysburg*

Campaign by Lieutenant Colonel George B. Davis. Kansas City, Missouri: Hudson-Kimberly Publishing Co., 1896.

49. [Cavan, Richard Lambert, 6th Earl of]. *A New System of Military Discipline, Founded upon Principle.* By a General Officer. Philadelphia: Printed and sold by R. Aitken, 1776.

50. Chadwick, F[rench] E. . . . *Report on the Training Systems for the Navy and Mercantile Marine of England, and on the Naval Training System of France, Made to the Bureau of Equipment and Recruiting, U.S. Navy Department, September, 1879.* Washington: G.P.O., 1880.

51. Chandler, David. *The Campaigns of Napoleon: The Mind and Method of History's Greatest Soldier.* New York: Macmillan, 1966.

52. Charles, Archduke. *Principès de la stratégie, développés par la relation de la campagne de 1796 en Allemagne, par S. A. I. et R. l'Archduce Charles. Traduit de l'allemand par le General en Chef Jomini . . . avec cartes et plans.* Nouvelle édition, revue et corrigée par l'auteur. . . . Brussels: Librairie militaire de J. B. Petil, 1840.

61. Cole, Major D[avid] H[enry], and Major E. C. Priestley. *An Outline of British Military History, 1660-1936.* London: Sifton Praed, 1936.

62. Colin, J[ean Lambert Alphonse]. *L'Éducation militaire de Napoléon.* Paris: Libraire militaire R. Chapelot, 1901. (Typescript translation by Richard U. Nicholas, Lieut. Col., Corps of Engineers, in U.S. Army Military History Research Collection from Army War College Library, May 25, 1938.)

63. Colin, J[ean Lambert Alphonse]. *The Transformations of War.* . . . Tr. by Brevet-Major L. H. R. Pope-Hennessy. London: H. Rees, 1912.

64. Colomb, P. H. *Naval Warfare, Its Ruling Principles and Practice Historically Treated.* London: W. H. Allen, 1891.

65. Connor W[illiam] D. . . . *(I) The School of Military Engineering, Royal Engineers, British Army (Chatham, England); (II) Civil Engineering Schools Annexed to the University of Ghent (Brussels, Belgium); (III) Comparison of the United States Engineer School, Washington Barracks, D.C., with the Above-Named Schools and the National School of Bridges and Highways, Paris, France.* . . . Washington Barracks, D.C.: Press of the Engineer School, 1913.

66. Corbett, Sir Julian S. *Drake and the Tudor Navy, with a History of the Rise of England as a Maritime Power.* New ed. New York: Longmans, Green, 1899.

67. Corbett, Sir Julian S. *England in the Seven Years' War: A Study in Combined Strategy.* London: Longmans, Green, 1907. 2 vols.

68. Corbett, Sir Julian S. *Some Principles of Maritime Strategy.* New York: Longmans, Green, 1911.

69. Cormontaigne, Louis de. *Mémorial pour l'attaque des places. Ouvrage posthume de Cormontaigne.* Paris: Anselin, 1815.

70. Cormontaigne, Louis de. *Memorial pour la défénse des places. Faisant suite au Mémorial pour l'attaque; ouvrage posthume de Cormontaigne.* Paris: Barrois, 1806.

71. Cruickshank, C[harles] G. *Elizabeth's Army.* 2d ed. Oxford: Clarendon Press, 1966.

72. Cugnac, Captain de. *Campagne de l'Armée de Réserve en 1800. Publié sous la direction de la Section Historique de l'État-Major de*

l'Armée. Paris: Libraire militaire R. Chapelot, 1900. 2 vols. (Extracts translated in typescript from Command and General Staff School Library, 1931, now in U.S. Army Military History Research Collection.

73. Cullum, George Washington. *Systems of Military Bridges in Use by the United States Army, Those Adopted by the Great European Powers, and Such as Are Employed in British India—With Directions for the Preservation, Destruction, and Re-establishment of Bridges*. New York: Van Nostrand, 1863.

74. Dahlgren, J[ohn] A[dolphus]. *Shells and Shell Guns*. Philadelphia: King & Baird, 1856.

75. Dalton, Charles. *George the First's Army, 1714-1727*. . . . London: Eyre and Spottiswoode, 1910-1912. 2 vols.

76. Darrieus, [Pierre Joseph] Gabriel [Georges]. *War on the Sea, Strategy and Tactics*. . . . Translated by Philip R. Alger. Annapolis: United States Naval Institute, 1908.

77. Decker, C[arl]. *La petite guerre, ou Traité des opérations secondaires de la guerre*. Traduit de l'allemard, avec des notes, par M. Ravichio Peretsdorf . . . suivie de l'instruction de Frédéric II. Brussels: Société de libraire belge, 1838.

78. Decker, E. *Traité élémentaire d'artillerie, à l'usage des militaires de toutes les armes* . . . *tr. de l'allemand, avec des notes et des additions relatives a l'artillerie française*. . . . Paris: Levrault, 1825.

79. Dedon, [Francois Louis]. *Précis historique des campagnes du l'armeé de Rhin et Moselle, pendant l'an IV et l'an V; contenant le recit des toutes les operations de cette armée, sous* . . . *Général Moreau, depuis la rupture de l'armistice conclu à la fin de l'an III, jusqu'à la signature des preliminaires de paix a Léoben*. . . . Paris: Magimel, [180?].

80. [Delbare, F. Théodore]. *Relation circumstanciée de la derniere campagne de Buonaparte, terminée par la bataille de Mont-Saint-Jean, dite de Waterloo ou de la Belle-Alliance*; 4. ed., rev., cor., augm. et ornée . . . Par un témpin oculaire. Paris: Dentu, 1816.

81. Derrécagaix, V[ictor Bernard]. *Modern War* . . . Tr. by C. W. Foster. . . . Washington: J. J. Chapman, 1888-1890. 2 vols. and atlas. *(La Guerre moderne*. Paris: L. Baudoin, 1885. 2 vols. and atlas.)

82. Desjardins, O. *Campagnes des français en Italie; ou, Historie militaire, politique et philosophique de la révolution*. . . . Paris: Ponthieu, 1799. 6 vols.

83. De Watteville, Herman Gaston. *The British Soldier: His Daily Life from Tudor to Modern Times*. With a foreword by Sir John Harding. Second Edition. New York: Putnam, 1956.

84. Du Coudray, Charles Tronson. *L'artillerie nouvelle; ou, Examen des changements faits dans l'artillerie française depuis 1765, par* . . . *ci-devant Lieutenant au Corps Royal d'artillerie*. Amsterdam, 1772.

85. Du Coudray, Charles Tronson. *L'ordre profond et l'ordre mince, considerès par rapport aux effets de l'artilleire*. . . . Metz: Ruault, 1776.

86. Dufour, G[uillaume] H[enri]. *Strategy and Tactics*. Tr. from the Latest French Edition by Wm. P. Craighill. New York: Van Nostrand, 1864.

87. Echols, Charles P. *Report upon Foreign Schools*. West Point: United States Military Academy Press, 1907.

88. Eckardt, Werner, and Otto Morawietz. *Die Handwaffen des branden-*

burgischpreussischdeutschen Heeres 1640-1945. Hamburg: G. H. Schulz, 1957.

89. Edelsheim, Franz, Freiherr von. *Operations upon the Sea: A Study, by Freiherr von Edelsheim, in the Service of the German General Staff in 1901; tr. from the German.* New York: Outdoor Press, 1914.

90. [Eggers.] *Journal du siège de Bergopsoom, en MDCCXLVII.* Redigée par un lieutenant-colonel ingenieur volontaire de l'armée des assiégeans. . . . Amsterdam: Arkstee, 1750.

91. *The Elements of Fortification.* Tr. from the French. 2d ed. [Philadelphia:] Printed for the War Office, by C. P. Wayne, 1801. "Translator's note" signed Jonathan Williams.

92. Entick, John. *A New Naval History; or, Compleat View of the British Marine. In Which the Royal Navy and the Merchant's Service are Traced through All Their Periods and Different Branches: With the Lives of the Admirals and Navigators, Who Have Honour'd this Nation.* . . . London: R. Manby, 1757.

93. *An Epitome of the Whole Art of War, In Two Parts. The First of Military Discipline. . . . The Second of Fortification and Gunnery.* London: J. Moxon, 1692.

94. *Essay on Defensive War and a Constitutional Militia; with an Account of Queen Elizabeth's Arrangement for Resisting the Projected Invasion of the year 1588 . . . by an Officer.* London: Evans, 1782.

95. Fallois, Joseph de. *L'École de la fortification; ou, Les Élemens de la fortification permanente, régulière et irrégulière.* . . . Dresden: Walther, 1768.

96. ffoulkes, Charles. *Arms and Armament: A Historical Survey of the Weapons of the British Army.* London: Harrap, 1945.

97. Firth, Sir Charles Harding. *Cromwell's Army: A History of the English Soldier during the Civil Wars, the Commonwealth and the Protectorate.* With a new introd. by P. H. Hardacre. New York: Barnes and Noble, 1962.

98. Fortescue, Sir John. *A History of the British Army.* London: Macmillan, 1910-1935. 13 vols.

99. *Fortification and Military Discipline, in two parts. The First shows the principles and practice of all manner of fortifications, regular or irregular, as now used by the Dutch, English, Italian, German and French ingeniers. . . . The second part treats of the rules for the exercise of horse and foot, with all sorts of instructions and other observations belonging to the whole art of war, as now practised. . . .* Improved and designed by Capt. J. S. London: R. Morden, 1688-1689. 2 vols. in 1.

100. France. Ministère de la guerre. *Historiques des corps de troupe de l'armée française (1569-1900).* . . . Paris: Berger-Levrault, 1900.

101. France. Ministère de la guerre. *Mémorial du dépôt général de la guerre, imprimé par ordre du ministre.* Paris: Picquet, 1829-1832. 6 vols.

102. France. Ministère de la guerre. *Ordonnance pour regler le service dans les places et dans les quartiers, du 1.e mars 1768.* . . . .Paris: Magimel, XVI (1795).

103. France. Ministère de la guerre. *Reglement concernant le service interieur, la police et la discipline des troupes à cheval.* Du 24 juin 1792. Paris: Magimel, 1818.

104. France. Ministère de la guerre. *Reglement provisoire sur le service interieur des troupes à cheval, dont l'execution est ordonée par S. Ex. M. le Duc de Feltre, Ministère secretaire d'état au departement de la guerre.* 2. ed. Paris: Magimel, 1816.

105. Frederick II, the Great, King of Prussia. *Military Instruction from the Late King of Prussia to His Generals . . . to Which Is Added, (By the Same Author) Particular Instruction to the Officers of His Army, and Especially those of the Cavalry.* Translated from the French, by Lieut. Foster. . . . 2d edition. Sherborne: Cruttwell, 1797.

106. Furse, George Armand. *Provisioning Armies in the Field.* London: W. Clowes & Sons, 1899.

107. Gardiner, Leslie. *The British Admiralty.* London: Blackwood, 1968.

108. Gay de Vernon, Simon François, baron. *Traité elementaire d'art militaire et de fortification, à l'usage des élèves de l'École polytechnique, et des élèves des écoles militairs.* . . . Paris: Allais, XIII (1805). 2 vols. and atlas. (Translated as : *A Treatise on the Science of War and Fortification; composed for the use of the Imperial polytechnick school, and military schools; and translated for the War department, for the use of the Military academy of the United States; to which is added a summary of the principles and maxims of grand tactics and operations.* By John Michael O'Connor. . . . New York: J. Seymour, 1817. 2 vols. and atlas.

109. George II, King of Great Britain. *New Exercise, To Be Observed by His Majesty's Troops on the Establishment of Great Britain and Ireland.* . . . New York: Re-printed . . . by J. Parker, 1757.

110. Geuss, J. M. *Théorie de l'art du mineur, trad. de l'allemand.* Maestricht: Dufour, 1778.

111. Gillot, O. *Traité de fortification souteraine; ou, Des mines offensives et defensives.* . . . Paris: Magimel, 1805.

112. Goodrich, Caspar F. . . . *Report of the British Naval and Military Operations in Egypt, 1882.* Washington: G. P. O., 1885.

113. Gouvion Saint-Cyr, [Laurent] marquis de. *Mémoires pour servir à l'histoire militaire sous le directoire, le consulat et l'empire.* . . . Paris: Anselin, 1831. 4 vols. and atlas.

114. Grandmaison. *A Treatise on the Military Service, of Light Horse, and Light Infantry, in the Field, and in Fortified Places.* By Major General de Grandmaison. . . . Tr. from the French, by Major Lewis Nicola. Philadelphia: Robert Bell, 1777.

115. Great Britain. Adjutant General's Office. *The Manual Exercise as Ordered by His Majesty, in 1764. Together with Plans and Explanations of the Method Generally Practised at Reviews and Field Days.* . . . . Lancaster, Pa.: Printed by Francis Bailey in King's Street, 1775. (Also New York: Printed by R. Gaine, 1775.)

116. Great Britain. Adjutant General's Office. *A Plan of Exercise for the Militia of the Province of the Massachusetts-Bay; Extracted from the Plan of Discipline, for the Norfolk Militia.* Boston: Printed by Richard Draper, 1768.

117. Greene, Francis Vinton. *Report on the Russian Army and Its Campaigns in Turkey in 1877-1878.* . . . Published by Order of the Honorable Secretary of War, on the Recommendation of the General of the Army. New York: Appleton, 1879.

118. Grosse, Francis. *Military Antiquities Respecting a History of the English Army from the Conquest to the Present Time.* A New Edition with Material Additions and Improvements. London: I. Stockdale, 1812. 2 vols.

119. Guibert, Jacques Antoine Hippolyte, comte de. *Essai général de tactique; précéde d'un discours sur l'état actuel de la politique & de la science militaire en Europe; avec le plan d'un ouvrage intitulé: La France politique et militaire.* . . . London: Librairies associés, 1772. 2 vols. (*A General Essay on Tactics, with an Introductory Discourse, upon the Present State of Politics, and the Military Science of Europe.* . . . Translated from the French of M. Guibert, by an Officer. London: Printed for J. Millan, 1781, 2 vols.)

120. Guibert, Jacques Antoine Hippolyte, comte de. *Oeuvres militaires de Guibert, publiées par sa veuve, sur les manuscrits et d'après les corrections de l'auteur.* Paris: Magimel, XII (1803). 5 vols.

121. Guischardt, Karl Gottlieb, called Quintus Tellius. *Mémoires critiques et historiques sur plusieurs points d'antiquités militaires.* . . . Berlin: Haude et Spener, 1773-1774. 4 vols.

122. Guischardt, Karl Gottlieb, called Quintus Iellius. *Mémoires militaires sur les Grecs et les Romains, pour servir de suite & d'éclairissement à l'histoire de Polybe commentée par le chevalier Folard, avec une dissertation sur l'attaque & la défense des places des anciens; la traduction d'Onosander & de la tactique d'Arrien, et l'analyse de la campagne de Jules César en Afrique.* Lyon: J. M. Bruyset, 1760.

123. Gumpertz, H. *Traité pratique et théorique des mines, par MM. H. Gumpertz et Lebrun.* Paris: Levrault, 1805.

124. Hall, Alfred Rupert. *Ballistics in the Seventeenth Century: A Study in the Relations of Science and War with Reference Principally to England.* Cambridge, England: Cambridge University Press, 1959.

125. Hanson, Thomas. *The Prussian Evolutions in Actual Engagements; Both in Platoons, Sub, and Grand-Divisions; Explaining, All the Different Evolutions and Manoeuvres, in Firing, Standing, Advancing and Retreating, Which Were Exhibited before His Present Majesty, May 8, 1769; and before John Duke of Argyle on the Links of Leith, near Edinburgh, in 1771.* . . . *To Which Is Added, the Prussian Manual Exercise: Also the Theory and Some Practices of Gunnery.* . . . . Philadelphia: Printed for the author, by J. M. M'Dougall, 1775.

126. Hauser, George, Freiherr von. *Abhandlung über die Befestigungskunst, zum gebrauche der k. k. Ingeniersakademie.* . . . Vienna: Aus der k. k. hof-und staats-aerarial druckery, 1826. 2 vols.

127. Hazen, W[illiam] B. *The School and the Army in Germany and France, with a Diary of Siege Life at Versailles.* New York: Harper, 1872.

128. Hewes, Robert, ed. *Rules and Regulations for the Sword Exercises of the Cavalry* . . . *Added, the Review Exercise.* 1st American from the London Edition. Boston: Norman, 1802.

129. Hicks, James Ernest, assisted by Andre Jandot. *French Military Weapons, 1717 to 1938.* New Milford, Connecticut: N. Flayderman, 1964.

130. Hittle, J[ames] D. *The Military Staff: Its History and Development.* 3d ed. Harrisburg: Military Service Publishing Co., 1961. [First edition 1944.]

131. Hohenloke-Ingelfingen, Kraft Karl August Eduard Friedrich, Prins zu. *Letters on Cavalry.* Tr. by Lieut.-Col. N. L. Walford, R.A. Leavenworth, Kansas: George A. Spooner, 1892.

132. Hollister, C. Warren. *Anglo-Saxon Military Institutions on the Eve of the Norman Conquest.* Oxford: Clarendon Press, 1962.

133. Hollister, C. Warren. "The Annual Term of Military Service in Medieval England." *Mediaevalia et Humanistica.* XIII, 40-47.

134. Hollister, C. Warren. *The Military Organization of Medieval England.* Oxford: Clarendon Press, 1965.

135. *Instructions for the Conduct of [French] Infantry on Actual Service.* . . . . Tr. from the French by John Macdonald. London: Egerton. 1807. 2 vols.

136. Johnston, R. M. *The French Revolution: A Short History.* New York: Henry Holt, 1909.

137. Johnston, R. M. *Napoleon: A Short Biography.* New York: Henry Holt, 1904.

138. Jomini, Antoine Henri, baron de. *Histoire critique et militaire des guerres de la révolution.* Nouv. éd., redigée sur des nouveaux documens, et augmentee d'un grand nombre de cartes et de plans. . . . Paris: Anselin et Pochard, 1820-1824. 15 vols. and atlas.

139. Jomini, Antoine Henri, baron de. *Life of Napoleon.* Tr. from the French, with Notes, by H. W. Halleck. . . . New York: Van Nostrand, 1864. 4 vols. plus atlas. (Also published in 2 vols. plus atlas, Kansas City, Mo.: Hudson-Kimberly, 1897.)

140. Jomini, Antoine Henri, baron de. *Precis de l'art de la guerre.* Paris: Librarie militaire de L. Baudoin, 1894. 2 vols. (*Summary of the Art of War; or, A New Analytical Compend of the Principal Combinations of Strategy, of Grand Tactics, and of Military Policy.* Tr. from the French by Maj. C. F. Winship and Lieut. E. E. McLean. New York: Putnam, 1854.)

141. Jomini, Antoine Henri, baron de. *Précis politique et militaire de la campagne de 1815, pour servir de supplément et de rectification à la Vie politique et militaire de Napoléon, recontée par lui-même.* Par le général J. . . . Paris: Anselin et Laguyonie, 1839. (*The Political and Military History of the Campaign of Waterloo.* Translated from the French of General Baron de Jomini by Capt. S. V. Benet. 2d edition. New York: Van Nostrand, 1862.)

142. Jomini, Antoine Henri, baron de. *Traité des grandes opérations militaires, contenant L'Histoire critique des campagnes de Frédéric II, comparées à celles de l'empereur Napoléon.* . . . Paris: Magimel, 1811. 4 vols.

143. Jomini, Antoine Henri, baron de. *Traité des grandes opérations militaires; ou, Histoire critique des guerres de Frédéric le Grand . . . avec un recueil des principes les plus importants de l'art de la guerre* . . . . 4. édition. Paris: Dumaine, 1851. 3 vols. (*Treatise on Grand Military Operations; or, A Critical and Military History of the Wars of Frederick the Great, as Contrasted with the Modern System. To-*

gether with a few of the Most Important Principles of the Art of War. Translated from the French by Col. S. B. Holabird. New York: Van Nostrand, 1865. 2 vols.)

144. Jones, Sir John T[homas]. *Account of the War in Spain, Portugal, and the South of France, from 1808 to 1814 Inclusive.* . . . 2d edition. London: Egerton, 1821.

145. Jourdan, [Jean Baptiste]. *Mémoires pour servir à l'histoire de la campagne de 1796, contenant les opérations de l'armée de Sambre et Meuse, sous les ordres du général en chef Jourdan.* Paris: Magimel, 1818.

146. *Journal des armes spéciales et de l'état-major, publié sur les documents fournis par les officiers des armées françaises et étrangeres.* . . . Paris: J. Correard, 1834-1869. 72 vols.

147. *Journal des sciences militaires.* Sixteen series, 1825-1914. United with *Revue militaire des armées étrangères* (Vols. 1-83, 1872-1914) and *Revue d'histoire, redigée a l'état-major de l'armée* (Vols. 1-54, 1899-1914) in 1921 to form *Revue militaire française.*

148. *The Journal of the Royal Artillery,* 1858-   [Title varies; 1858-March 1905, *Minutes of Proceedings of the Royal Artillery Institution.*]

149. *The Journal of the Royal United Service Institution.* London: Royal United Service Institution, 1858-   .

150. Kane, Richard. *Campaigns of King William and Queen Anne; from 1689 to 1712. Also, a New System of Military Discipline, for a Battalion of Foot on Action; with the Most Essential Exercise of the Cavalry.* London: Millan, 1745.

151. Kennett, Lee. *The French Armies in the Seven Years' War: A Study in Military Organization and Administration.* Durham: Duke University Press, 1967.

152. Kosciuszko, Tadeues Andrsez Bonawentura. *Manoeuvres of Horse Artillery; Written at Paris in the Year 1800, at the Request of General Wm. R. Davie, then Envoy from the United States to France.* Translated, with Notes and Descriptive Plates, by Jonathan Williams. Published by Direction of the [U.S. Military Philosophical] Society. New York: Sold by Campbell & Mitchell, 1809.

153. Lallemand, Henri Dominique. *Complete Treatise upon Artillery* . . . added, *Summaries of Field Fortification, of the Attack and Defense of Places, of Castramentation, and of Military Reconnoitrings.* Tr. from the French. New York: Van Winkle, 1819-1820. 2 vols.

154. Lallemand, Henri Dominique. *A Treatise on Artillery: To Which is Added a Summary of Military Reconnoitring, of Fortification, of the Attack and Defence of Places, and of Castramentation.* Tr. from the Manuscript of the Author by James Renwick. New York, 1820. 2 vols.

155. La Martillière, Jean Fabre, comte de. *Reflexions sur la Fabrication en général des bouches à feu, et observations sur les épreuves extraordinaires et comparatives de differentes especes de bouches à feu qui ont en lieu à Douai, en 1786, par ordre du ministère de la guerre.* . . . . 2. éd. augm. de quelques notes. Paris: Magimel, 1796.

156. Landmann, Isaac. *Treatise on Mines, for the Use of the Royal Military Academy at Woolwich.* London: Egerton, 1815.

157. La Roche-Aymon, Charles-Étienne Paul, comte de. *Introduction à l'étude de l'art de la guerre.* . . . Weimar: Bureau d'industrie, 1802-1804. 5 vols. and atlas.
158. Latrille, G. *Considérations sur la guerre, et particulierment sur la dernière guerre.* . . . Paris: Magimel, 1804.
159. Lavisse, Emile Charles. . . . *Comparative Studies of the Field Equipment of the French and Foreign Armies.* Translated for the General Staff, U.S. Army, by Capt. Edward F. Lawton. . . . Washington: G. P. O., 1906.
160. Leblond, Guillaume. *L'Artillerie raisonnée, contenant le description & l'usage des différentes bouches à feu* . . . *la théorie & la practique des mines, & du jet des bombes.* . . . Paris: Jombert, 1781.
161. Leblond, Guillaume. *The Military Engineer; or, A Treatise on the Attack and Defence of All Kinds of Fortified Places* . . . *to Which Is Added, a Succinct Account of Three Remarkable Sieges at Different Periods, by Which the Progress of the Art is Pointed Out.* . . . London: J. Nourse, 1759.
162. Lemly, Henry Rowan. . . . *Changes Wrought in Artillery in the 19th Century, and Their Effect upon the Attack and Defense of Fortified Places.* Fort Monroe: U.S. Artillery School, 1886.
163. Leonard, Emile G. *L'Armée et ses problemes au XVIII siecle.* Paris: Plon, 1958.
164. Lespinasse, L. N. *Traité de lavis des plans, appliqué principalmente aux reconnaissances militaires. Ouvrage fondé sur les principes de l'art qui a pour objet l'imitation de la nature, et ou l'on enseigne à rendre, avec toute l'exactitude possible, sur de grandes échelles un terrain quelconque.* . . . Paris: Magimel, IX (1801).
165. Lewis, Michael. *England's Sea-Officers: The Story of the Naval Profession.* London: G. Allen & Unwin, 1939.
166. Lewis, Michael. *The History of the British Navy.* Baltimore: Penguin Books, 1957.
167. Lloyd, Christopher. *The Nation and the Navy: A History of Naval Life and Policy.* London: Cresset Press, 1965.
168. Lloyd, Henry. *History of the Late War in Germany, between the King of Prussia and the Empress of Germany and Her Allies.* . . . By a General Officer Who Served Several Campaigns in the Austrian Army. . . . London: Printed for the author, 1766-1781. 3 vols.
169. Lloyd, Henry, and Tempelhoff, [Colonel]. *History of the Seven Years War in Germany, with Observations and Maxims Extracted from the Treatise of General Jomini.* . . . Translated from the German and French by Captain C. H. Smith. London: Clarke, n.d.
170. Lo-Looz, Robert de. *Recherches d'antiquites militaires, avec la défense du Chevalier Follard, contre les allegations inferés dans les Mémoires militaires sur les Grecs & sur les Romains.* Paris: Jombert, 1770.
171. Lombard, Jean Louis. *Traité du mouvement des projectiles, appliqué au tir des bouches a feu.* . . . Dijon: Frantin, 1797.
172. Lot, Ferdinand. *L'Art Militaire et les armees au moyen age.* Paris: Payot, 1946. 2 vols.

173. Luvaas, Jay. *The Education of an Army: British Military Thought, 1815-1940*. Chicago: University of Chicago Press, 1964.
174. Macdonald, John. *A Treatise on Telegraphic Communication, Naval, Military, and Political*. . . . London: T. Egerton, 1808.
175. Machiavelli, Niccolo. *The Art of War*. In Seven Books. Written by Nicholas Machiavel. . . . To Which Is Added, *Hints Relative to Warfare*, by a Gentleman of the State of New York. Albany: Printed by H. C. Southwick, 1815.
176. Macleod, [Sir] George H. B. *Notes on the Surgery of the War in the Crimea*. Richmond, Va.: J. W. Randolph, 1862.
177. Maigret. *Traite de la sureté et conservation des états, par le moyen des fortresses*. Paris: E. Billiot, 1725. (Translated as: *A Treatise on the Safety and Maintenance of States by the Means of Fortresses*. . . . London: Davis, 1747.)
178. Maizeroy, [Paul Gedeon] Joly de. *Mémoire sur les opinions qui partagent les militaires; suivi, Du traité des armes défénsives*. . . . Paris Jombert, 1773.
179. Maizeroy, [Paul Gedeon] Joly de. *La Tactique discutée, et réduite à ses veritables loix*. . . . Paris: Jombert, 1773.
180. Maizeroy, [Paul Gedeon] Joly de. *Théorie de la guerre*. . . . Paris: Jombert, 1777.
181. Maizeroy, [Paul Gedeon] Joly de. *Traité sur l'art des sièges et les machines des anciens*. . . . Paris: Jombert, 1778.
182. Malortie de Martemont, Charles Stanislas de. *Practical Field-Fortification, Being intended as a supplement to the Theory of Field-Fortification*. London: Egerton, 1813.
183. Malortie de Martemont, Charles Stanislas de. *The Theory of Field-Fortification*. . . . 3d ed. London: W. J. & J. Maynard, 1834.
184. Marcus, G[eoffrey]. J. *The Age of Nelson: The Royal Navy 1793-1815*. New York: Viking, 1971.
185. Marcus, Geoffrey. *A Naval History of England: The Formative Centuries*. Boston: Little, Brown, 1962.
186. Margerand, J. *Armement et équipement de l'infanterie francaise du XVI au XX siècle*. Paris: Editions militaires illustrées, 1945.
187. [Martin, Colonel.] *A Plan for Establishing and Disciplining a National Militia in Great Britain, Ireland, and in All the British Dominions of America. A New Edition, with a Preface Suited to the Present State of Affairs*. London: A. Millas, 1745. Reprinted Chicago (?), 1936.
188. Martin, P. *Histoire de l'expédition française en Égypte*. . . . Paris: Eberhart, 1815. 2 vols.
189. Merriman, Reginald Dundas, ed. *Queen Anne's Navy: Documents concerning the Administration of the Navy of Queen Anne, 1702-1714*. London: Printed for the Navy Records Society, 1961.
190. Mésnil-Durand, François Jean de Graindorge d'Orgeville, baron de. *Fragments de tactique; ou, Seis mémoires*. . . . Paris: C. A. Jombert pere, 1774.
191. Meunier, Claude Marie, baron. *Évolutions par brigades; ou, Instruction servant de developpement aux manoeuvres de ligne, indiquées dans les reglemens*. . . . Paris: Magimel, 1814.

192. Miles, Nelson A. *Military Europe: A Narrative of Personal Observation and Personal Experience.* New York: Doubleday & McClure, 1898.
193. *The Military Mentor. Being a Series of Letters Recently Written by a General Officer to His Son, on His Entering the Army; Comprising a Course of Elegant Instruction, Calculated to Unite the Characters and Accomplishments of the Gentleman and the Soldier.* 1st American from the 2d London ed. . . . Salem: Cushing & Appleton, 1808.
194. Mirabeau, [Honore Gabriel Requetti] Comte de. *Système militaire de la Prusse et principes de la tactique actuelle des troupes les plus perfectionnées. Extract de la monarchie prussienne.* London: n.p., 1788.
195. Moltke, Helmuth Karl Bernhard, Graf von. *Essays, Speeches, and Memoirs of Field-Marshal Count Helmuth von Moltke.* The essays tr. by Charles Flint McClumpha, Ph.D.; the speeches, by Major C. Barter, D.A.A.C.; and the memoirs, by Mary Herms. . . . New York: Harper, 1893.
196. Moltke, Helmuth Karl Bernhard, Graf von. *Extracts from Moltke's Correspondence Pertaining to the War, 1870-71.* Tr. by Harry Bell. Fort Leavenworth, Kansas: Army Service Schools Press, 1911.
197. Moltke, Helmuth Karl Bernhard, Graf von. *The Franco-German War of 1870-71.* Tr. by Clara Bell and Henry W. Fischer. New York: Harper, 1892.
198. Monge, Gaspard, comte de Peluse. *Description de l'art de fabriquer les canons, faits en exécution de l'arrêté du Comité de salut public, du 18 pluviôse de l'an 2 de la République française, une et indivisible.* . . . Paris: Impr. du Comite de Salut Public, II (1794).
199. Montalembert, Marc René, marquis de. *La fortification perpendiculaire; ou, Essai sur plusieurs manières de fortifier la ligne droit, le triangle, le quarré, et tous les polygônes, de quelqu' êtendue qu'en socient les côtés, en donnant à leur défense une direction perpendiculaire.* . . . Paris: Impr. de P.D. Pierres, 1776-1793. 10 vols.
200. Montecuccoli, Raimondo, Conte, Duca di Melfi. *Mémoires de Montecuculi, generalissime des troupes de l'empereur.* Divisés en trois livres, I. *De l'art militaire en général.* II. *De la guerre contre le Turc.* III. *Relation de la campagne de 1664.* Nouv. ed., rev., cor. en plusieurs endroits par l'auteur, & augm. de notes historique & geographiques. . . . . Strasbourg: Doulssecker, 1735.
201. Mouze. *Traité de fortification souterraine, suivi de quatre mémoires sur les mines; par le chef de bataillon du génie Mouze.* . . . Paris: Levrault, Schoell et C. , XII (1804).
202. Mudford, William. *An Historical Account of the Campaign in the Netherlands, in 1815, under His Grace the Duke of Wellington, and Marshal Prince Blücher, Comprising the Battles of Ligny, Quatre Bras, and Waterloo; with a Detailed Narrative of the Political Events Connected with those Memorable Conflicts, down to the Surrender of Paris, and the Departure of Bonaparte for St. Helena.* . . . London: H. Colburn, 1817.
203. Musset, V[ictor] D[onatien de, called Musset-Pathey]. *Relations des principaux sièges faits ou soutenus en Europe par les armées françaises depuis 1792; redigées par MM. les officiers-généraux et*

supérieurs du Corps impérial du génie qui en ont conduit l'attaque ou la défénse; précédees d'un précis historique et chronologique des guerres de la France depuis 1792 jusqu' au traité de Presbourg en 1806. . . . Paris: Magimel, 1806.

204. Napier, Sir W[illiam] F[rancis] P[atrick]. *History of the War in the Peninsula and in the South of France from the Year 1807 to the Year 1814.* London: Boone, 1835-1840. 6 vols. (3-vol. edition, Kansas City: Hudson-Kimberly, 1904.)

205. Napoleon I. *Correspondance de Napoleon I publiee par ordre de l'Empereur Napoleon III.* Paris: Henri Plon and J. Dumain, 1859-1870. 32 vols.

206. Napoleon I. *Mémoires pour servir à l'histoire de France, sous Napoléon, écrits à Sainte-Hélène, par les généraux qui ont partagé sa captivité et publiés sur les manuscrits entièrement corrigés de la main de Napoléon. . . .* Paris: F. Didot, 1823-1825. 8 vols. (Translated as *Memoirs of the History of France during the Reign of Napoleon, Dictated by the Emperor at Saint Helena to the Generals Who Shared His Captivity; and Published from the Original Manuscripts Corrected by Himself. . . .* London: H. Colburn, 1823-1824. 7 vols.)

207. Napoleon I. *Napoleon and Modern War: His Military Maxims, Revised and Annotated by Conrad H. Lanza . . .* Harrisburg: Military Service Publishing Co., 1943.

208. Napoleon I. *A Selection from the Letters and Dispatches of the First Napoleon.* Ed., with explanatory notes, by Captain D. A. Bingham. London: Chapman and Hall, 1884. 3 vols.

209. Napoleon I. *Unpublished Correspondence of Napoleon I Preserved in the War Libraries.* Pub. by Ernest Picard and Louis Tuetey. Tr. by Louise Seymour Harrington. New York: Duffield, 1913. 3 vols. (*Correspondance inédite de Napoléon I conservée aux Archives de la Guerre. Publiée sous la direction de la Section Historique de l'État Major de l'Armée.* Paris: Henri Charles-Lavauzelle, 1912. 3 vols.

210. Newhall, Richard Ager. *Muster and Review: A Problem of English Military Administration, 1420-1440.* Cambridge: Harvard University Press, 1940.

211. Nicolas, Sir Nicholas Harris. *A History of the Royal Navy, From the Earliest Times to the Wars of the French Revolution.* London: Richard Bentley, 1847. 2 vols.

212. Nolan, Lewis Edward. *Cavalry: Its History and Tactics.* 1st American, from the 2d London, ed. Columbia, S.C.: Evans and Cogswell, 1864.

213. Norton, C. B., and W. J. Valentine. *Report to the Government of the U.S. on the Munitions of War Exhibited at the Paris Universal Exposition, 1867.* New York: Army and Navy Journal, 1868.

214. *Nouveau dictionnaire historique des sièges et batailles mémorables, et des combats maritimes les plus fameux, de tous les peuples du monde, anciens et modernes, jusqu' à nos jours. . . .* Par P. M. M. . . . . Paris: Gilbert, 1808. 6 vols.

215. Oakeshott, Walter. *Founded upon the Seas: A Narrative of Some English Maritime and Overseas Enterprises during the Period 1550 to 1616.* Cambridge, England: The University Press, 1942.

216. Oman, C. W. C. *The Art of War in the Middle Ages, A.D. 378-1515.* Ed. John Beeler. New York: Great Seal, 1953.

217. Oman, Sir Charles. *A History of the Art of War in the Sixteenth Century.* New York: Dutton, 1937.

218. O'Neil, Bryan Hugh St. John. *Castles and Cannon: A Study of Early Artillery Fortifications in England.* Oxford: Clarendon Press, 1960.

219. Oppenheim, Michael. *A History of the Administration of the Royal Navy and of Merchant Shipping in Relation to the Navy, from MDIX to MDCLX with an Introduction Treating of the Preceding Period.* Hamden, Connecticut: Shoe String Press, 1961.

220. Paixhans, Henri Joseph. *Expériences faites par la marine française, sur une arme novelle. Changements qui paraissent devoir en résulter dans le système naval, et examen de quelques questions relatives à la marine, à l'artillerie, à l'attaque et à la défense des côtes et des places.* . . . . Paris: Bachelier, 1825.

221. Paixhans, Henri Joseph. *Nouvelle force maritime, et application de cette force à quelques parties du service de l'armée de terre.* . . . Paris: Bachelier, 1822.

222. Paret, Peter. *Yorck and the Era of Prussian Reform, 1800-1815.* Princeton: Princeton University Press, 1966.

223. Pashkievitsch. *Interior Ballistics.* Tr. from the Russian by Tasker H. Bliss. Washington: G. P. O., 1892.

224. Pargiter, Major R[obert] B[everley], and Major H. G. Eady. *The Army and Sea Power: A Historical Outline.* London: Ernest Benn, 1927.

225. Persy, N. *Elementary Treatise on the Forms of Cannon and the Various Military Academy from the French of Professor N. Persy of Metz.* West Point: Lithographed by Geo. Aspinwall, 1832.

226. Peyre. *Le mouvement igne considere principalement, dans la charge d'une pièce d'artillerie, precede Des reflexions phisiques sur les calculs de Mr. Robins, concernant le fluide elastique de la poudre.* Toulon: Peyre, 1809.

227. Phipps, Colonel Ramsay Weston. *The Armies of the First French Republic and the Rise of the Marshals of Napoleon I.* Oxford University Press. London: Humphrey Milford, 1926-1939. 5 vols.

228. *Pièces diverses relatives aux operations militaires et politiques au Général Bonaparte.* Paris: Didot, [1800-1801]. 2 vols.

229. Poissac, de. *Traité théorie-pratique et élémentaire de la guerre des retranchmens. Precédé des notions de géométrie dont la connaissance est nécessaire à tous les militaires, et d'un discours sur l'art de la guerre.* . . . Strasbourg: Levrault, 1769. 2 vols. in 1.

230. Polard, [Jean Charles de]. *Abregé des commentaires de M. de Polard, sur l'histoire de Polybe, Par* . . . *mestre de camp de cavalerie.* Paris: Gandouin, 1754. 3 vols.

231. Poumet. *Essai sur l'art de pointer, toute especè d'arme à feu, et particulièrement les pièces de campagne.* . . . Paris: Magimel, 1816.

232. Powicke, Michael. *Military Obligation in Medieval England: A Study in Liberty and Duty.* Oxford: Clarendon Press, 1962.

233. Pringle, Sir John. *Observations on the Diseases of the Army.* New Edition. London: J. J. Stockdale, 1810.

234. Prower. *The Militiaman at Home and Abroad; Being the History of a Militia Regiment from Its First Training to Its Disembodiment; with Sketches of the Ionian Islands, Malta and Gibraltar.* London: Smith-Elder, 1857.
235. Prussia. Grosser Generalstab. *Kriegsgechichtliche Einzelschriften.* Herausgegeben von Grosser Generalstabe, Abteiluing fur Kriegsgechichte. Berlin: Ernst Siegfried Mitter und Sohn, 1885-1914, 10 Banden, 50 Hefte.
236. Prussia. Grosser Generalstab. *Studien zur Kriegsgeschichte und Taktic.* Herausgegeben vom Grosser Generalstabe, Kriegsgeschichtliche Abteilung I. Berlin: Ernst Siegfried Mittler und Sohn, 1901-1913. 6 vols.
237. Puységur, [J. F. de C. de,] marquis. *Art de la guerre, par principes et par regles. . . .* Paris: Jombert, 1749. 2 vols.
238. Quimby, Robert S. *The Background of Napoleonic Warfare: The Theory of Military Tactics in Eighteenth-Century France.* New York: Columbia University Press, 1957.
239. Ralston, David B. *The Army of the Republic: The Place of the Military in the Political Revolution of France, 1871-1914.* Cambridge: M.I.T. Press, 1967.
240. Retzow, [F. A.] von. *Nouveaux mémoires historiques sur la guerre de sept ans. . . .* Tr. de l'allemand. Paris: Treuttel, 1803. 2 vols.
241. Révéroni Saint-Cyr, Jacques Antoine, baron de. *Statique de la guerre, ou principes de stratégie et de tactique, domonstrés par la statique . . . ou nouv. éd. du Mécanisme de la guerre, considerable augm. . . .* Paris: Anselin et Pochard, 1826.
242. Richmond, Sir Herbert. *British Strategy, Military and Economic: A Historical Review and Its Comtemporary Lessons.* Cambridge, England: The University Press, 1941.
243. Richmond, Sir Herbert. *The Navy as an Instrument of Policy, 1558-1727.* Edited by E. A. Hughes. Cambridge, England: The University Press, 1953.
244. Roberts, Michael. *The Military Revolution, 1560-1660: An Inaugural Lecture Delivered before the Queen's University of Belfast.* Belfast: M. Boyd, 1956.
245. Roguet, Christoph Marie Michel, comte. *De l'approvisionement des armées au XIXme siècle.* Paris: Dumaine, 1848.
246. Roskill, Stephen W. *The Strategy of Sea Power: Its Development and Application.* Based on the Lees-Knowles Lectures Delivered in the University of Cambridge, 1961. London: Collins, 1962.
247. Rotberg, baron de. *L'ingenieur moderne; ou, Essai de fortification. . . .* Nouvelle ed. La Haye: Scheurleer, 1756.
248. *The Royal Engineers Journal.* Chatham: Royal Engineers Institute, 1905-
249. Rozard. *Nouvelle fortification française; où il est traité de la construction des places, ensemble l'explicacion des trois systèmes du maréchal de Vauban. . . .* Nuremberg: Lochner, 1731.
250. Saint-Auban. *Ouvrages sur l'artillerie.* Paris: Neumann, 1775. 2 vols.
251. Saint Julien, chevalier de. *Architecture militaire; ou, L'art de fortifier les villes . . . suivi d'un abregé de geometrie.* La Haye: von Millinge, 1750.

252. *St. Privat. German sources.* Translations by Harry Bell, . . . U.S. Army. Fort Leavenworth, Kansas: Staff College Press, 1914.

253. Samuel, E. *An Historical Account of the British Army, and of the Law Military, as Declared by the Ancient and Modern Statutes and Articles of War for Its Government; with a Free Commentary on the Mutiny Act, and the Rules and Articles of War; Illustrated by Various Decisions of Courts Martial.* London: W. Clowes, 1816.

254. Sanders, Iver John. *Feudal Military Service in England: A Study of the Constitutional and Military Powers of the Barons in Medieval England.* London: Oxford University Press, 1956.

255. Sarrazin, Jean. *Historie de la guerre de Russie et d'Allemagne, depuis le passage du Niémen, juin 1812, jusqu' au passage du Rhin, novembre 1813.* . . . Paris: Rosa, 1815.

256. Savory, Lieut.-General Sir Reginald. *His Britannic Majesty's Army in Germany during the Seven Years War.* Oxford: Clarendon Press, 1966.

257. Saxe, [Maurice], comte de. *Lettres et mémoires choisis parmi les papiers originaux du Maréchal de Saxe, et relatifs aux evenemens auxquels il a en part, ou qui se sont passes depuis 1733 jusqu' en 1750, notamment aux campagnes de Flandre de 1744 à 1748.* Paris: Smets, 1794. 5 vols.

258. Saxe, [Maurice], comte de. *Esprit des loix de la tactique et de différentes institutions militaires.* . . . *avec un mémoire militaire sur les Tartares et les Chinois.* . . . La Haye: Gosse je., 1762. 2 vols.

259. Saxe, [Maurice], comte de. *Mes reveries. Ouvrage posthume . . . augm d'une histoire abregie de sa vie.* . . . Amsterdam: Arkstee et Merkus, 1757. (*Reveries on the Art of War.* Translated and Edited by Brig. General Thomas R. Phillips. Harrisburg: Military Service Publishing Co., 1944.)

260. Scheel, Henri Othon de. *A Treatise of Artillery; Containing a New System, on the Alterations Made in the French Artillery, since 1765.* Tr. from the French of M. de Scheel [by J. Williams]. Philadelphia: Printed for the War Office by John W. Fenno, 1800.

261. Schlight, John. *Monarchs and Mercenaries: A Reappraisal of the Importance of Knight Service in Norman and Early Angevin England.* Studies in British History and Culture, Volume I. Bridgeport, Connecticut. Conference on British Studies at the University of Bridgeport, 1968. Produced and distributed by New York University Press.

262. Schurman, Donald M. *The Education of a Navy: The Development of British Naval Strategic Thought, 1867-1914.* Chicago: University of Chicago Press, 1965.

263. Scouller, R. E. *The Armies of Queen Anne.* Oxford: Clarendon Press, 1966.

264. Sea. *Mémoire sur la fortification permanente, pour servir à la construction d'un front de fortification sur le terrain.* St. Petersburg: Impr. de Pluchart, 1811.

265. Solt, Leo F. *Saints in Arms: Puritanism and Democracy in Cromwell's Army.* Stanford: Stanford University Press, 1959.

266. Somerville, Robert. *Memoir of the Medical Arrangements Necessary to Be Observed in Camps; the Means of Rendering the Clothing of Soldiers Proof against Moisture; of Promoting Cleanliness and*

Regularity; and of Preventing the Introduction or Spreading of Infectious Diseases. . . . London: Egerton, 1796.

267. Spaulding, Thomas M., and Louis C. Karpinski. *Early Military Books in the University of Michigan Libraries.* Ann Arbor: University of Michigan Press, 1941.

268. Stocqueler, J. H. [Joachim Heyward Siddons]. *A Familiar History of the British Army, from the Restoration in 1660 to the Present Time, Including a Description of the Volunteer Movement, and the Progress of the Volunteer Organization.* London: Edward Stanford, 1871.

269. *Subject Catalog of the Military Art and Science Collection in the Library of the United States Military Academy with Selected Author and Added Entries including a Preliminary Guide to the Manuscript Collection.* Westport, Connecticut: Greenwood, 1969. 4 vols.

270. Swieten, Gerard, Freiherr von. *The Diseases Incident to Armies. With the Method of Cure. Translated from the Original of Baron von Swieten. . . . To Which are Added: The Nature and Treatment of Gunshot Wounds.* By John Ranby. *. . . Likewise, Some Brief Directions, To Be Observed by Sea Surgeons in Engagements. Also, Preventatives of the Scurvy at Sea.* By William Northcote. *. . .* Published for the Use of Military and Naval Surgeons in America. . . . Boston: Reprinted for E. Draper, by J. D. M'Dougall, 1777.

271. *A System of Camp Discipline, Military Honours, Garrison Duty, and Other Regulations for the Land Forces. Collected by a Gentleman of the Army. In Which Are Included, Kane's Discipline for a Battalion in Action. . . . To Which is Added General Kane's Campaigns of King William and the Duke of Marlborough . . . with His Remarks on the Several Stratagems by Which Every Battle Was Won or Lost, from 1689-1712.* 2nd Ed. London: J. Millan, 1757.

272. Taylor, Franck. *Rifled Field Pieces: A Short Compilation of What Is Known of the New Field Artillery of Europe, with Some Account of Our Own.* Washington, D.C. The author, 1862.

273. Tedder, Arthur W. *The Navy of the Restoration, from the Death of Cromwell to the Treaty of Breda: Its Work, Growth and Influence.* Cambridge, England: The University Press, 1916.

274. *Theory and Practice of Gunnery.* Tr. from the *Cours de balistique* of Prof. Persy of Metz, for the use of the Department of Artillery, U.S. Military Academy. West Point: Geo. Aspinwall, 1833.

275. Thomas Lynall. *Rifled Ordnance . . . The Application of the Principle of the Rifle to Guns and Mortars of Every Calibre . . . Added, a New Theory of the Initial Action and Force of Fired Gunpowder. . . .* 1st American from 5th English Edition, Revised. New York: Van Nostrand, 1864.

276. Tielcke, J[ohann Theodor]. *Account of Some of the Most Remarkable Events of the War between the Prussians, Austrians, and Russians, from 1756 to 1763; and a Treatise on Several Branches of the Military Art. . . .* Translated from the 2d Ed. of the German Original by Captain C. Craufurd and Captain R. Craufurd. London: Printed for the Translators, 1787. 2 vols. (Also: *Beytrage zur Kriegs-kunst und Geschichte des Krieges von 1756, bis 1763. . . .* Freyberg: Barthelischen, 1775-1786. 6 vols.)

277. Touzac, de. *Traité de la défense interieure et exterieure des redoutes..* . . . Paris: Jombert jeune, 1785.
278. Trenchard, John. *A Short History of Standing Armies in England.* London: Printed in the year 1698, and now reprinted and sold by W. France, 1731.
279. Trincano, Didier Gregoire. *Élemens de fortification, de l'attaque et de la défense des places.* . . . Toul: Carez, 1786. 2 vols.
280. Turner, Hilary L. *Town Defences in England and Wales: An Architectural and Documentary Study, A.D. 900-1500.* Hamden, Connecticut: Archon Books, 1971.
281. Turpin de Crissé, [Lancelot,] comte. *Commentaries sur les mémoires de Montecuculi.* . . . Paris: Lacombe. 1769. 3 vols.
282. Turpin de Crissé, [Lancelot,] comte. *Essai sur l'art de la guerre.* . . . Paris: Prault, 1754. 2 vols.
283. U.S. Adjutant General's Office. Military Information Division. . . . *The Autumn Maneuvers of 1894. Austria-Hungary, France and Germany.* . . . Washington: G.P.O., 1895.
284. U.S. Adjutant General's Office. Military Information Division. *The Autumn Maneuvers of 1896 in Europe.* Washington: G. P. O., 1897.
285. U.S. Adjutant General's Office. Military Information Division. . . . *The Autumn Maneuvers of 1898. Austria-Hungary, France, Germany, Great Britain, Russia, and Switzerland.* Washington: G.P.O., 1899.
286. U.S. Adjutant General's Office. Military Information Division. . . . *The Autumn Maneuvers of 1899. Austria-Hungary, Germany, Great Britain, Italy, and Norway.* Washington: G.P.O., 1900.
287. U.S. Adjutant General's Office. Military Information Division. *The Military Schools of Europe, and Other Papers Selected for Publication.* Washington: G.P.O., 1896.
288. U.S. Adjutant General's Office. Military Information Division. *The Military System of Sweden* [by H. T. Allen] *and Other Papers Prepared for Publication.* Washington: G.P.O., 1896.
289. U.S. Adjutant General's Office. Military Information Division. . . . *Notes and Statistics of Organization, Armament, and Military Progress in American and European Armies.* . . . Washington: G.P.O., 1894. (Also 1896.)
290. U.S. Adjutant General's Office. Military Information Division. . . . *Notes of Military Interest for 1900.* Washington: G.P.O., 1901. (Similar volumes for 1901 and 1902.)
291. U.S. Adjutant General's Office. Military Information Division. . . . *Report of Major General Nelson A. Miles, Commanding U.S. Army, of His Tour of Observation in Europe.* May 5 to October 10, 1897. Washington: G.P.O., 1899.
292. U.S. Adjutant General's Office. Military Information Division. . . . *Reports on Military Operations in South Africa and China.* July, 1901. Washington: G.P.O., 1901.
293. U.S. Adjutant General's Office. Military Information Division. *Report on the Organization of the German Army.* By Major Theodore Schwan, Assistant Adjutant General, U.S. Army. Washington: G.P.O., 1894.
294. U.S. Adjutant General's Office. Military Information Division. *Select-*

ed Professional Papers Translated from European Military Publications. Washington: G.P.O., 1898.

295. U.S. Adjutant General's Office. Miliatry Information Division. *Subsistence and Messing in European Armies*. Washington: G.P.O., 1897.

296. U.S. Board of Engineers for Fortifications. . . . *Report upon the Practice in Europe with the Heavy Armstrong, Woolwich, and Krupp Rifled Guns, Submitted by the Board of Engineers for Fortifications*. Colonel Z. B. Tower, Corps of Engineers . . . President of the Board. Washington: G.P.O., 1883.

297. U.S. Engineer School. . . . *Russian Provisional Fortifications . . . A Series of Studies . . . by Russian Officers* . . . translated by 1st Lieutenant Elliott J. Dent . . . and 1st Lieutenant George R. Spalding. . . . Washington: Press of the Engineer School, 1905.

298. U.S. General Staff. 2d (Military Information) Division. . . . *Bulletin of Military Notes*. Washington: G.P.O., 1904-1905. 3 vols.

299. U.S. General Staff. 2d (Military Information) Division. . . . *Epitome of the Russo-Japanese War*. . . . Washington: G.P.O., 1907.

300. U.S. General Staff. 2d (Military Information) Division. *Reports of Military Observers Attached to the Armies in Manchuria during the Russo-Japanese War*. . . . Washington: G.P.O., 1906-1907. 5 vols.

301. U.S. General Staff 2d (Military Information) Division. . . . *Selected Translations Pertaining to the Boer War*. April 1, 1905. Washington: G. P. O., 1905.

302. U.S. Military Academy. *The Earliest Printed Catalogue of Books in the United States Military Academy Library*. Foreword by Sidney Forman. West Point, 1962 (?).

303. U.S. Military Commission in Europe, 1855-1856. *The Armies of Europe: Compromising Descriptions in Detail of the Military Systems of England, France, Russia, Prussia, and Sardinia, Adapting Their Advantages to All Arms of the United States Service; and Embodying the Report of Observations in Europe during the Crimean War*. . . . Philadelphia: Lippincott, 1861.

304. Upton, Emory. *The Armies of Asia and Europe, Embracing Official Reports on the Armies of Japan, China, India, Persia, Italy, Russia, Austria, Germany, France, and England*. . . . New York: Appleton, 1878.

305. Vauban, Sebastian Le Prestre, marquis de. *De l'attaque de la défense des places*. La Haye: Pierre de Hondt. 2 vols.

306. Vauban, Sebastian Le Prestre, marquis de. *Oeuvres militaires*. Nouvelle édition, rev . . . Par P. P. Foissac. Paris: Magimel, 1796. 3 vols.

307. Verdy du Vernois, [Julius Adrian Friedrich Wilhelm von]. *A Simplified War Game*. Tr. from the French and Arranged for American Students be Captain Eben Swift, Kansas City: Hudson-Kimberly, 1897. (Essai du simplification du jeu de guerre; *exemple d'opération des trois armes sans l'aide de tables ni de des.* . . . Tr. avec autorisation de l'auteur par Morhange. . . . Brussels: C. Muquardt, 1877.

308. Verdy du Vernois, J[ulius Adrian Friedrich Wilhelm von]. *Studies in the Leading of Troops*. . . . Volume I. *The Infantry Division as Part of an Army Corps*. Revised by Colonel von Gossler. . . .

Translated from the German by Lieutenant Colonel William Gerlach. Kansas City: Hudson Press, 1906.

309. Very, Edward Wilson. *Navies of the World; Giving Concise Descriptions of the Plans, Armament and Armor of the Naval Vessels of Twenty of the Principal Nations. Together with the Latest Developments in Ordnance, Torpedoes, and Naval Architecture, and a Concise Summary of the Principal Naval Battles of the Last Twenty Years, 1860-1880.* By Lieut. Edward W. Very, U.S.N. New York: Wiley, 1880.

310. Wagner, Arthur Lockwood. *The Campaign of Königgratz, A Study of the Austro-Prussian Conflict in the Light of the American Civil War.* Fort Leavenworth, Kansas, 1889.

311. Walton, Clifford. *History of the British Standing Army, AD 1660-1700.* London: Harrison & Sons, 1894.

312. Warnery, Charles Emmanuel de. *Melange de remarques, sur-tout sur César et auteurs militaires, anciens et modernes, pour servir de continuation aux commentaries des Commentaries de Turpin sur Montecucoli, et sur le tactique de Guibert.* Warsaw, 1782.

313. Webb, Henry J. *Elizabethan Military Science: The Books and the Practice.* Madison: University of Wisconsin Press, 1965.

314. Western, John R. *The English Militia in the Eighteenth Century: The Story of a Political Issue, 1660-1802.* London: Routledge & K. Paul, 1965.

315. Wilcox, Cadmus M., tr. *Evolutions of the Line, As Practiced by the Austrian Infantry and Adopted in 1853.* New York: Van Nostrand, 1860.

316. Wilkinson, [Henry] Spencer. *The Brain of an Army: A Popular Account of the German General Staff.* New Edition, with Letters from Count Moltke and Lord Roberts. London: Constable, 1895.

317. Wimpffen, Christian Peter von. *Commentaires des Mémoires de Monsieur le comte de Saint-Germain. . . .* London, 1780.

318. Windham, William. *A Plan of Discipline, Composed for the Use of the Militia of the County of Norfolk.* London: Printed for J. Shuckburgh, at the Sun, next Richard's Coffee-House, Fleet street, 1760.

319. Yorck von Wartenburg, Count. *Napoleon as a General.* London: Kegan Paul, Trench, Trubner, 1902. 2 vols.

320. Zepelin, Constantin von. *Die Heere and Flotten der Gegenwort.* Berlin: Schall, 1896.

III

COLONIAL FORCES
1607-1766

Douglas Edward Leach

There has never been any dearth of published material dealing with the colonial military history of British North America, but much of this has been tainted by racial or religious bias, ethnocentrism, romantic filiopietism, patriotic mythology, and the glorification of combat. Modern scholars now are working to reconstruct the military history of those times by careful study of all surviving evidence, within the overall framework of the entire colonial experience. This chapter confines itself to the sources for the period from the founding of the first British colony in 1607 to the conclusion of Pontiac's Indian uprising in 1766, with emphasis on published material of British and American origin. Although other powers, notably the Netherlands, Sweden, Spain, and France, were involved in colonial American warfare, the focus here is primarily upon that portion of North America that was to be included within the United States east of the Mississippi River, from New England and New York south to Florida. Students wishing to explore beyond these confines will find helpful bibliographies in such works as Bannon, *The Spanish Borderlands Frontier, 1513-1821* (9), Beers, *The French & British in the Old Northwest* (13), Beers, *The French in North America* (14), Eccles, *The Canadian Frontier, 1534-1760* (64), Gipson, *The British Empire Before the American Revolution,* vols. 14-15 (76), and Lanctot, *A History of Canada,* vols. 1-3 (150).

The military endeavors of Britain's colonies were basically an extension of earlier and contemporary British experience. Moreover, during the first half of the eighteenth century British regular forces came to play an increasing role in American colonial warfare, and therefore exerted an increasing influence upon the conduct of affairs. For this reason the student should not fail to consult Robin Higham's *Guide to the Sources of British Military History* (129). Fortescue (74) remains the standard history of the British Army, supplemented by Cannon's *Historical Records* (48) which provides the history of every regular regiment.

As in all military history, a good knowledge of geography is essential for an understanding of warfare in the American wilderness. Especially useful are the accurate topographical maps published (now by the U.S.

Coast and Geodetic Survey), but because both time and man may effect changes in terrain these maps should be compared with others closer in time to the events being studied. Archival collections include many old maps and plans, some of which have been reproduced in Fite and Freeman (71), Gipson (76), and Winsor (361).

GENERAL SURVEYS. *France and England in North America*, the 9-volume masterpiece of Francis Parkman (200), although permeated with cultural bias still stands as the most vivid and comprehensive narrative of the Anglo-French imperial struggle. Osgood's classic surveys (191) (192), primarily institutional in emphasis, contain informative chapters on colonial systems of defense as well as the various wars. The international dimensions of imperial rivalry are explored with great competence by Max Savelle (323), while Graham (114) provides a scholarly survey of the maritime aspects, and Bannon (9), Eccles (64), and Leach (159) focus on the frontier experience, including border warfare. Following Parkman there have been several attempts to construct overall surveys of the colonial wars. Hamilton's *French and Indian Wars* (123), though tending to reflect Parkman's own perception, adds much useful information on weapons, tactics, and the soldier's life. Peckham's *Colonial Wars, 1689-1762* (206) is rather severely condensed but serves well as a general introduction to the subject, while his "Speculations on the Colonial Wars" (208) provides a penetrating analysis of long-range implications. The latest and most detailed modern account, covering the entire period from 1607 to 1763, is Leach's *Arms for Empire* (155).

GENERAL DOCUMENTARY SOURCES. Collections of documents pertaining to colonial military history, located throughout the United States and elsewhere, are too numerous and varied to be described here. Spain's Archivo General de Indias, France's Archives Nationales, and England's Public Record Office, all have extensive collections. Fortunately, some of this material has been copied for deposit in American archives and libraries. Other important collections are in the Canadian Archives, the Library of Congress, and the various provincial and state archives. In addition, the Massachusetts Historical Society, the American Antiquarian Society, the New York Historical Society, the William L. Clements Library, the Henry E. Huntington Library, and many other state and local historical societies, have rich collections. The nature of these may be ascertained by consulting Hamer's *Guide to Archives and Manuscripts in the United States* (121), *The National Union Catalog of Manuscript Collections* (184), or the guide published by the repositories themselves. In most cases a serious researcher with a definite project in hand will have no difficulty gaining access to the materials he needs.

GENERAL PUBLISHED SOURCES. Kavanagh's *Foundations of Colonial America: A Documentary History* (144) is a good basic collection including many different types of documents. Because the events of colonial military history were intertwined with other important aspects of colonial life, much of the information needed must be gleaned from a variety of records covering a wide range of topics. Certainly this is true of the extensive published records of the various colonial governments, where items of military import are scattered throughout. To a greater or lesser extent the official records and other public documents of every British colony in North America have been published, usually with indexes. The most important sets will be found listed in the Bibliography below under the heading "Governmental Records and Public Documents". In addition, the published papers of various individuals active in colonial affairs may provide further useful information. Prominent among the persons or families whose papers have been published are Cadwallader Colden (230), Benjamin Franklin (240), Sir William Johnson (251), Henry Laurens (254), the Saltonstalls (280), and William Shirley (282). Nor should one neglect to comb the many colonial newspapers, beginning in 1704, for items of military interest. The standard guide to these is Brigham's *History and Bibliography of American Newspapers, 1690-1820* (43). Many libraries have extensive collections of colonial newspapers in photocopy, but the greatest collection of originals is in the library of the American Antiquarian Society.

ORGANIZATION AND WEAPONRY. Each of the colonies, sooner or (as in the case of Quaker Pennsylvania) later, found it necessary to organize a citizens' militia for defense against pirates, Indians, and potential European foes. Such organizations provided basic military training on a fairly regular basis for a large proportion of the white male colonists. Actually, the significance of the militia system transcends strictly military history, for the militia served also as an arm of established authority against internal dissension, and the commissioned officers of the militia commonly held important civil posts as well, being closely identified in most colonies with the upper class. Morton's "Origins of American Military Policy" (183) and the first chapters of both Leach's *Arms for Empire* (155) and Weigley's *History of the United States Army* (357) provide brief introductions to the colonial militia. *Backgrounds of Selective Service* (112) reviews the early history of compulsory military training in America, and presents a convenient compilation of pertinent legislation, colony by colony. A major study of the beginnings is Darrett B. Rutman's dissertation on "A Militant New World, 1607-1640" (318), while Shy's article "A New Look at Colonial Militia" (330) opens up the ongoing issues. The private notebook of Captain Henry True (289) gives fascinating glimpses of the actual administration of a New England militia company during the early years of the eighteenth century.

There are numerous studies of the militia in particular regions or colonies. For New England we have Sharp's article in the *American Historical Review* (236), as well as his dissertation on "The New England Trainbands in the Seventeenth Century" (327). The same topic has been pursued into the eighteenth century by Archibald Hanna, Jr. (125). Leach's article on Plymouth Colony (158), Radabaugh's article (310) and dissertation (309) on Massachusetts Bay, Kenny's article (145) on Rhode Island, and Marcus' dissertation (172) on Connecticut help fill in the picture for New England. Indian as well as English military systems in that region are considered in Patrick M. Malone's dissertation (169). Informative works dealing with the militia in colonies to the south include De Valinger's *Colonial Military Organization in Delaware, 1638-1776* (59), Scisco's

"Evolution of Colonial Militia in Maryland" (325), Aldridge's "Organization and Administration of the Militia System of Colonial Virginia" (1), Wheeler's "Development and Organization of the North Carolina Militia" (360), Cole's "Organization and Administration of the South Carolina Militia System, 1670-1783" (55), and Jabb's "South Carolina Militia, 1663-1733" (138). An article by Benjamin Quarles (308) ably describes the role of Blacks in the colonial militia.

Weapons and other equipment employed by colonial forces have been described and depicted in a number of publications, among which are Blackmore's *British Military Firearms, 1650-1850* (41), Brown's *American Polearms, 1526-1865* (44), and Sawyer's *Firearms in American History* (324). Also authoritative on this topic are Peterson's three works: *Arms and Armor in Colonial America, 1526-1783* (302), *Round Shot and Rammers* (304), and "The Military Equipment of the Plymouth and Bay Colonies, 1620-1690" (303). The colonial militiaman generally owned and maintained his personal equipment, including his musket. This meant that in a typical company of militia the advantage of complete standardization was seldom enjoyed. Only on the occasional major expedition, when arms and other equipment might be supplied by the British government out of its own stocks, could standardization be achieved.

CONFLICTS WITH INDIANS. Indians were involved in virtually all the colonial wars, usually as allies of one or another of the contending European colonies, and from them, whether as friends or foes, colonial commanders learned some important lessons in the techniques of wilderness fighting. Studying the Indians in colonial times presents special problems in the selection and use of sources. For one thing, the Indians themselves left no written records of their own; all primary sources, even the recorded speeches of Indian leaders, have been filtered through the white man's inkpot. Beyond this, the prolonged conflict between the two peoples, red and white, has been so pervasive and so destructive in the American experience that few if any historians, from colonial times to the present, have been able to break completely free of cultural bias. This bias runs to opposite extremes. Some writers have portrayed the Indian as a bloody-handed savage, reveling in slaughter. In this version he is always seen as an obstacle in the path of civilization. Other writers have portrayed the Indian as Nature's innocent child whose beautiful, harmonious world was befouled by the greedy, polluting Europeans. In this version he is always seen as the blameless victim. The careful student will be alert for traces of either kind of bias in any source consulted.

A good place to begin is with Sheehan's thoughtful article "Indian-White Relations in Early America: A Review Essay" (328), which argues that cultural incompatibility rather than territorial displacement was the fundamental cause of Indian-White conflict. Wilbur R. Jacobs, a scholar who displays much empathy for the Indians, presents some important and provocative insights in *Dispossessing the American Indian* (140), a collection of essays. A book which ably defends the Indian policy pursued by the New England colonies during the seventeenth century is Alden T. Vaughan's *New England Frontier* (347); included is a good account of the Pequot War of 1637. Charles Orr (190) has conveniently assembled the contemporary narratives of the Pequot War written by John Mason, John Underhill, Philip Vincent, and Lion Gardiner. For King Philip's War, which ravaged New England in 1675-76, there is a rich supply of primary sources, nearly all heavily biased against the Indians. Major narratives have been left by Benjamin Church (53), William Hubbard (131), and Increase Mather (175), the first of whom was an outstanding commander in the war. Half a dozen briefer accounts have been gathered and edited by Charles H. Lincoln in his *Narratives of the Indian Wars, 1675-1699* (161). A modern analysis that attempts to explore the causes of the conflict and its impact upon colonial society is Leach's dissertation on "The Causes and Effects of King Philip's War" (156), while the same author's *Flintlock and Tomahawk* (157) provides a comprehensive narrative. The warfare between Indians and colonists in Virginia preceding and accompanying Bacon's Rebellion, roughly concurrent with King Philip's War in New England, also produced some contemporary accounts, three of which have been published in Charles M. Andrews' *Narratives of the Insurrections, 1675-1690* (4). Wilcomb E. Washburn's dissertation on "Bacon's Rebellion" (353) is supplemented by the same author's provocative book *The Governor and the Rebel* (354), which sharply challenges the interpretation offered by Wertenbaker in his *Torchbearer of the Revolution* (359). The flaring of Indian warfare in northern New England during the 1720s may be viewed through the contemporary accounts provided by Symmes (339) and Penhallow (209), and the letters published by William B. Trask (288). Pontiac's Uprising, which swept through much of the Old West in 1763 with devastating effect, was the last serious outbreak of Indian warfare prior to the American Revolution. William Smith's *Historical Account* (331) and Alexander Henry's *Travels and Adventures* (249) provide contemporary insights, as does the journal of Thomas Morris published by Thwaites (286). The best comprehensive modern study is Howard H. Peckham's *Pontiac and the Indian Uprising* (207). This interesting book challenges the view presented in Parkman's older *Conspiracy of Pontiac* (203) that the Ottawa chief instigated a widespread conspiracy against the British colonies. All students of Indian relations should be cognizant of DePuy's *Bibliography of the English Colonial Treaties with the American Indians, Including a Synopsis of Each Treaty* (58), covering the period 1677-1768.

EVOLUTION OF TACTICS. Anyone who studies with some care the military history of the British colonies prior to 1763 will become aware that the wilderness environment, as well as the peculiar skills and methods of the Indians, revealed grave inadequacies in the ordinary tactics which the colonists had brought with them from Europe. Indeed, even some familiar and trusted weapons such as the pike soon had to be modified or discarded altogether and more suitable weapons acquired. The necessary modifications in tactics were accomplished rather gradually through bitter experience and often with stubborn reluctance on the part of traditional-minded officers. Four studies which provide an introduction to the subject are Hamilton's "Colonial Warfare in North America" (122), Mahon's "Anglo-American Methods of Indian Warfare, 1676-1794" (168), Pares' "American Versus Continental Warfare, 1739-1763" (193), and Parker's dissertation on "Anglo-American Wilderness Campaigning, 1754-1764" (198). By the latter part of the 1750s the essential lessons had been fairly well absorbed, even by the British Army.

PRISONERS. Many Americans—soldiers, seamen, and noncombatants—had the unpleasant and often fatal experience of being captured by the enemy and held as prisoners. Of those who subsequently escaped or were released, a considerable number produced narratives of their adventures. In fact, captivity narratives constitute an entire species of early American literature which, if studied with care and skill, may reveal much about colonial and Indian attitudes and culture. For guidance into this body of material the student may consult R. W. G. Vail's *The Voice of the Old Frontier* (346), a most useful bibliography of frontier sources. A number of the captivity narratives have been gathered and published by Isabel M. Calder (225) and Richard VanDerBeets (290).

KING WILLIAM'S WAR, 1689-1697. In North America hostile activity on land consisted mostly of sporadic but destructive raids against isolated outposts and settlements along the northern frontier, with Indians participating on both sides. A biased but informative account of this warfare has been left by the Massachusetts clergyman Cotton Mather in his "Decennium Luctuosum," republished in Lincoln's *Narratives of the Indian Wars* (161). New France's problems at the same time are analyzed in Hardcastle's dissertation on "The Defense of Canada Under Louis XIV, 1643-1701" (126). The successful English attack upon France's principal settlement in what is now Nova Scotia in the spring of 1690 may be viewed through *A Journal of the Proceedings in the Late Expedition to Port-Royal* (215), an eyewitness account. A New England commander's recollections of his raiding activity against the Indians and the French along the coast of Maine and the Bay of Fundy are set forth in Church's *History of the Eastern Expeditions* (54). John Gyles' *Memoirs of Odd Adventures* (246) is an absorbing narrative by an English colonist who was captured by Indians at Pemaquid, Maine, in 1689. The greatest single military operation of the war took place in 1690, when New England sent an amphibious expedition under the command of Sir William Phips up the St. Lawrence River to seize Quebec, a bold enterprise that ended in failure. Accounts of this somewhat ludicrous affair were written by two leading participants, Thomas Savage (281) and John Walley (291), as well as by Cotton Mather in his biography of Phips (32). The commander of the French forces during King William's War, Count Frontenac, has been ably portrayed in a biography by W. J. Eccles (21) which serves as a corrective for Parkman's earlier appraisal (35). See also Eccles' article "Frontenac's Military Policies, 1689-1698: A Reassessment" (65).

QUEEN ANNE'S WAR, 1702-1713. In the second war, unlike the first, Spain as well as France was an active enemy of the British, which meant that the southern frontier also was involved. The Carolinians organized an expedition to seize St. Augustine, Florida, in 1702, but failed in their attempt to capture the major fortification guarding the town and eventually had to withdraw. That expedition has been well described by Charles W. Arnade (7). On the northern frontier there were numerous actions, with Quebec or Montreal again the ultimate target of British endeavors. The French and Indian raid on Deerfield, Massachusetts, in 1704, and the subsequent experiences of English captives taken in that action, have been vividly narrated by one of the victims, the Reverend John Williams (296). A Connecticut chaplain, Thomas Buckingham, has left personal journals (224) of his experiences in the capture of Port Royal in 1710 and on an expedition into the Champlain Valley the following year. In 1711 the British government provided a large fleet and army, augmented by colonial ships and troops, to seize Quebec, but the venture was abandoned after eight of the ships were wrecked in the trecherous St. Lawrence River. Important documents relating to that ill-fated attempt have been edited and published by Gerald S. Graham (116), providing an interesting insight into problems not only of joint military-naval operations but of Anglo-American relations as well. New York's ambivalent role in Queen Anne's War is discussed in an article by G. M. Waller (351). The same author's *Samuel Vetch* (38) is the best biography of an American colonial leader in that war.

THE WAR OF THE 1740s. After a relatively long period of uneasy peace, a new war between Britain and Spain broke out in 1739, with France joining Spain as an ally in 1744. The Anglo-Spanish conflict is known as the War of Jenkins' Ear, while New Englanders generally referred to their latest conflict with the French as King George's War. A fundamental study of this complex struggle is Devine's dissertation on "The British North American Colonies in the War of 1739-1748" (60). The existence of a new British colony, Georgia, at the southern end of the British bloc was a serious challenge to Spain's hold on the Florida peninsula; inevitably, the southern frontier again became the scene of major military activity. Three important studies are Lanning's *Diplomatic History of Georgia* (153), Wright's *Anglo-Spanish Rivalry in North America* (363), and Ivers' *British Drums on the Southern Frontier* (137). General James Oglethorpe's unsuccessful campaign against St. Augustine in 1740, an effort that spawned a legacy of ill-will between Georgians and Carolinians, is described in several contemporary sources, notably *The St. Augustine Expedition of 1740* (107) and *An Impartial Account of the Late Expedition* (5). Important correspondence from Don Manuel de Montiano, who commanded in the defense of St. Augustine, has been published in the *Collections of the Georgia Historical Society,* Volume 7 (267). Part 3 of the same volume (334) includes other Spanish documents relating to the unsuccessful Spanish invasion of Georgia in 1742. Torres-Reyes has provided a brief, modern account of the 1740 siege of St. Augustine (343).

In 1744 the northern frontier again became a zone of hostilities. Benjamin Doolittle's *Short Narrative* (62) is a contemporary account of frontier warfare in western Massachusetts, emphasizing the hardships endured by the pioneers in that area and pointing out the inadequacies of New England's defensive response. The skill and daring of French and Indian raiders from Canada are demonstrated in the Frenchman Marin's journal (264) of his expedition against Saratoga, New York, in 1745. Captivity narratives by Nehemiah How (250), William Pote, Jr. (277), and John Norton (271) tell of prison life in Quebec. Ziebarth's dissertation on "The Role of New York in King George's War, 1739-1748" (365) deals with a key colony.

From New England's point of view, the most notable event of the entire war was the astonishing capture of the great French fortress of Louisbourg on Cape Breton Island by colonial militiamen, aided by a squadron of the Royal Navy, in 1745. Many documents concerning this operation are to be found in the library of the Massachusetts Historical Society, especially among the papers of William Pepperrell the American commander (272), the Louisbourg Papers (164), and the Parkman Papers (199). The American Antiquarian Society published Pepperrell's official journal in 1910 (273). A collection of personal journals kept by participants in the operation has been edited by De Forest (234). Separate journals and private accounts include those by an anonymous French inhabitant of Louisbourg (216), the Reverend Adonijah Bidwell (218), Benjamin Cleaves (228), Benjamin Craft (231), James Gibson (242), Daniel Giddings (243), Seth Pomeroy (276), and Roger Wolcott (299). The Louisbourg operation has been described and analyzed by historians such as McLennan (167) and Rawlyk (312) (313).

THE GREAT WAR FOR THE EMPIRE, 1755-1763. The most thoroughly documented, researched, and narrated of all the colonial wars prior to the American Revolution is the climatic struggle of 1755-63 which resulted in the expulsion of Spain from Florida and of France from the mainland of North America. Space permits mention only of the most important documentary collections, dissertations, books, and articles. Pease (204) and Grenier (118) have published significant collections of documents relating to British and French rivalry in the West, while Pargellis (197) has made available an excellent selection of military documents from the Cumberland Papers in Windsor Castle.

Leaders on both sides deserve careful study. In the Bibliography below are listed many of the important availble sources under the headings "Biography" and "Personal Papers, Journals, and Accounts," as appropriate. Prominent among the leaders included are General James Abercromby (33) (211), Lord Jeffery Amherst (18) (30) (212) (213) (214), Colonel Henry Bouquet (220), Governor Robert Dinwiddie of Virginia (235), General John Forbes (239), General Thomas Gage (241), Sir William Johnson (24) (27) (36) (251), the Marquis de Montcalm (259) (260) (266), Governor William Shirley of Massachusetts (37) (282), George Washington (17) (23) (25) (28) (292) (293) (294), and General James Wolfe (26) (39) (300) (301).

Many orderly books and personal journals kept by relatively obscure individuals who served in or observed the war have survived. For the French one may consult *Relations et journaux de differentes expeditions faites durant les années 1755-56-57-58-59-60* (262), and for Massachusetts soldiers Clark's "Journals and Orderly Books" (227). John Knox's *Historical Journal* (252) is an account by a well-informed participant, covering the major campaigns during the period 1757-60. Thwaites' *Early Western Journals* (286) contains accounts by Conrad Weiser, George Croghan, and Christian Frederick Post. John Bremner, an inquisitive and perceptive Scot who served with the 55th Regiment, kept a journal covering the period 1756-64 which now is in the library of the New York Historical Society (223). Published journals include those of Stephen Cross (232), Moses Dorr (236), John Thomas (285), and John Winslow (298). The latter two relate specifically to the action against Fort Beauséjour and the expulsion of the Acadians in 1755. Much attention has been focused upon the stunning defeat of Braddock's army near the Forks of the Ohio that same year. We have approximately a dozen eyewitness accounts of the fateful encounter, most of which are referred to in Pargellis' article (195). See also the reports edited by Charles Hamilton (247), and the dissertation by Franklin T. Nichols (185).

The capture of Quebec by Wolfe's army in 1759 and the subsequent British effort to hold that key center were crucial to the outcome of the war. Much source material is included in Doughty's six volumes (63) and in Samuel's *Seven Years War in Canada* (320). Governor James Murray's *Journal* (269) describes the activities at Quebec from 18 September 1759 to 25 May 1760. Three modern accounts are those by C. P. Stacey (335), Christopher Lloyd (163), and Gordon Donaldson (61).

More attention should be given to the impact of this long and difficult war upon the civilian population of the colonies, and the concomitant tensions that arose between the colonists on the one hand and imperial authorities on the other. In this connection a few helpful works should be noted: McCormac's *Colonial Opposition to Imperial Authority during the French and Indian War* (165), Rogers' *Empire and Liberty: American Resistance to British Authority, 1755-1763* (317), and Young's dissertation on "The Effects of the French and Indian War on Civilian Life in the Frontier Counties of Virginia" (364).

Only two years after the outbreak of this last great colonial war there appeared the first significant attempt to trace its advent. This was in the form of a small book attributed to William Livingston (162). Covering the period 1753-56, it was strongly biased in favor of Governor Shirley and against his rival, William Johnson. Less partisan and far more comprehensive is the 5-volume work by the Reverend John Entick (69) which began emerging from the press soon after the war's end. Another early survey, this one covering the entire war in Noth America, was produced by Thomas Mante (170), who had served with Colonel John Bradstreet. Since Mante's time a great many historians have written about this war. Of the more recent works, two deserve special mention for their scope and scholarship. Guy Frégault, in his *Canada: The War of the Conquest* (75), describes the tragic demise of a vital culture under the relentless hammer blows of expansive British imperialism. Lawrence H. Gipson has devoted volumes 4-8 of his masterful survey of the British Empire before the American Revolution (76) to explaining in terms of British imperial interests the origins, the course, and the outcome of the Great War for the Empire. No better account is available anywhere.

SUGGESTIONS FOR FURTHER RESEARCH. In addition to fresh, intensive studies of particular campaigns and battles, there is a continuing need for carefully researched biographies of military and civilian leaders whose decisions and actions had important consequences in the colonial wars. This is especially true for certain 17th-century pattern-setters such

COLONIAL FORCES 1607-1766 • 79

as Benjamin Church and Sir William Phips, or less-well-known figures of the eighteenth century such as John Barnwell and Israel Williams. Even more urgent are other great problems and questions still largely neglected. What actual effects did colonial warfare have upon the complex and closely interwoven strands of colonial society? To what degree were the fisheries and maritime commerce helped or hindered by war? What other forms of economic activity were stimulated or stagnated? Did some colonies benefit from the disproportionately heavy sacrifices of other colonies, as was frequently suspected and sometimes loudly asserted? If so, what effects did this have on civilian morale and intercolonial relations? Is it really true that the economic burden of the colonial wars, especially the last, rested heavily and painfully on the shoulders of the British government while the colonies grew and flourished? Certainly we need additional intensive studies of particular colonies and communities in order to be able to assess more accurately the full impact of war in colonial America. Much raw data is available in the sources, and if modern techniques of research and analysis are intelligently applied to these kinds of problems and questions, some new and hopefully enlightening answers may be obtained.

BIBLIOGRAPHY

1. Aldridge, Frederick S. "Organization and Administration of the Militia System of Colonial Virginia." Doctoral dissertation, American University, 1964.
2. Anderson, Niles. "Bushy Run: Decisive Battle in the Wilderness: Pennsylvania and the Indian Rebellion of 1763." *Western Pennsylvania Historical Magazine*, 1963, 46, 211-45.
3. Anderson, Niles. "The General Chooses a Road : The Forbes Campaign of 1758 to Capture Fort Duquesne." *Western Pennsylvania Historical Magazine*, 1959, 42, 109-38, 241-58, 383-401.
4. Andrews, Charles M., ed. *Narratives of the Insurrections, 1675-1690.* New York: Scribner's, 1915.
5. Anonymous. *An Impartial Account of the Late Expedition against St. Augustine under General Oglethorpe.* London: J. Huggonson, 1742.
6. Arnade, Charles W. "The English Invasion of Spanish Florida, 1700-1706." *Florida Historical Quarterly*, 1962, 41, 29-37.
7. Arnade, Charles W. *The Siege of St. Augustine in 1702.* Gainesville: University of Florida Press, 1959.
8. Baker-Crothers, Hayes, *Virginia and the French and Indian War.* Chicago: University of Chicago Press, 1928.
9. Bannon, John Francis. *The Spanish Borderlands Frontier, 1513-1821.* New York: Holt, Rinehart and Winston, 1970.
10. Bean, Walton E. "War and the British Colonial Farmer: A Reevaluation in the Light of New Statistical Records." *Pacific Historical Review*, 1942, 11, 439-47.

11. Beatson, Robert. *Naval and Military Memoirs of Great Britain, from 1727 to 1783*. With a new introd. and pref. by George Athan Billias. Boston: Gregg Press, 1972. 6 vols.
12. Becker, Donald Eugene. "North Carolina, 1754-1763: An Economic, Political, and Military History of North Carolina during the Great War for Empire." Doctoral dissertation, University of North Carolina, 1971.
13. Beers, Henry Putney. *The French & British in the Old Northwest: A Bibliographical Guide to Archive and Manuscript Sources*. Detroit: Wayne State University Press, 1964.
14. Beers, Henry Putney. *The French in North America: A Bibliographical Guide to French Archives, Reproductions, and Research Missions*. Baton Rouge: Louisiana State University Press, 1957.

BIOGRAPHY
15. Alberts, Robert C. *The Most Extraordinary Adventures of Major Robert Stobo*. Boston: Houghton Mifflin, 1965.
16. Alden, John Richard. *John Stuart and the Southern Colonial Frontier: A Study of Indian Relations, War, Trade, and Land Problems in the Southern Wilderness, 1754-1775*. Ann Arbor: University of Michigan Press, 1944.
17. Cleland, Hugh. *George Washington in the Ohio Valley*. Pittsburgh: University of Pittsburgh Press, 1955.
18. Cognets, Louis des, Jr. *Amherst and Canada*. Princeton: The author, 1962.
19. Crouse, Nellis M. *Lemoyne d'Iberville: Soldier of New France*. Ithaca: Cornell University Press, 1954.
20. Cuneo, John R. *Robert Rogers of the Rangers*. New York: Oxford University Press, 1959.
21. Eccles, W. J. *Frontenac: The Courtier Governor*. Toronto: McClelland and Stewart, 1959.
22. Ettinger, Amos A. *James Edward Oglethorpe, Imperial Idealist*. Oxford and New York: Clarendon Press, 1936.
23. Flexner, James Thomas. *George Washington: The Forge of Experience, 1732-1775*. Boston: Little, Brown, 1965.
24. Flexner, James Thomas. *Mohawk Baronet: Sir William Johnson of New York*. New York: Harper, 1959.
25. Freeman, Douglas Southall. *George Washington, A Biography*. New York: Scribner's, 1948-57. 7 vols.
26. Hibbert, Christopher. *Wolfe at Quebec*. Cleveland: World Publishing Co., 1959.
27. Inouye, Frank T. "Sir William Johnson and the Administration of the Northern Indian Department." Doctoral dissertation, University of Southern California, 1951.
28. Knollenberg, Bernhard. *George Washington: the Virginia Period, 1732-1775*. Durham: Duke University Press, 1964.
29. Labaree, Leonard W. "Benjamin Franklin and the Defense of Pennsylvania, 1754-1757." *Pennsylvania History*, 1962, 29, 7-23.
30. Long, John Cuthbert. *Lord Jeffery Amherst, A Soldier of the King*. New York: Macmillan, 1933.

31. McCardell, Lee. *Ill-starred General: Braddock of the Coldstream Guards.* Pittsburgh: University of Pittsburgh Press, 1958.
32. Mather, Cotton. *The Life of Sir William Phips.* Mark Van Doren, ed. New York: Covici-Friede, 1929.
33. Mullett, Charles F. "James Abercromby and French Encroachments in America." *Canadian Historical Review*, 1945, 26, 48-59.
34. Pargellis, Stanley McCrory. *Lord Loudoun in North America, 1756-1758.* New Haven: Yale University Press, 1933. Reprinted, Hamden, Connecticut: Archon Books, 1968.
35. Parkman, Francis. *Count Frontenac and New France under Louis XIV.* Boston: Little, Brown, 1877.
36. Pound, Arthur (in collaboration with R. E. Day). *Johnson of the Mohawks: A Biography of Sir William Johnson, Irish Immigrant, Mohawk War Chief, American Soldier, Empire Builder.* New York: Macmillan, 1930.
37. Schutz, John A. *William Shirley: King's Governor of Massachusetts.* Chapel Hill: University of North Carolina Press, 1961.
38. Waller, G. M. *Samuel Vetch: Colonial Enterpriser.* Chapel Hill: University of North Carolina Press, 1960.
39. Whitton, F. E. *Wolfe and North America.* Boston: Little, Brown, 1929.
40. Wright, Wyllis E. *Colonel Ephraim Williams: A Documentary Life.* Pittsfield, Massachusetts: Berkshire County Historical Society, 1970.
41. Blackmore, Howard L. *British Military Firearms, 1650-1850.* London: Herbert Jenkins, 1961.
42. Bodge, George M. *Soldiers in King Philip's War: Being a Critical Account of That War, with a Concise History of the Indian Wars of New England from 1620-1677.* 3rd ed. Boston: The author, 1906.
43. Brigham, Clarence S. *History and Bibliography of American Newspapers, 1690-1820.* Worcester: American Antiquarian Society, 1947. 2 vols.
44. Brown, Rodney Hilton. *American Polearms, 1526-1865: The Lance, Halberd, Spontoon, Pike, and Naval Boarding Weapons.* New Milford, Connecticut: N. Flayderman, 1967.
45. Buffinton, Arthur H. "The Policy of the Northern English Colonies towards the French to the Peace of Utrecht." Doctoral dissertation, Harvard University, 1925.
46. Buffinton, Arthur H. "The Puritan View of War." *Publications of the Colonial Society of Massachusetts*, 1935, 28, 67-86.
47. Caldwell, Norman W. "The Southern Frontier during King George's War." *Journal of Southern History*, 1941, 7, 37-54.
48. Cannon, Richard, ed. *Historical Records of the British Army, Comprising the History of Every Regiment in His Majesty's Service.* London: Parker, Furnivall, and Parker, 1835-53. 70 vols.
49. Casgrain, Henri Raymond. *Guerre du Canada, 1756-60; Montcalm et Levis.* Quebec: L. J. Demers & frere, 1891. 2 vols.
50. Chapin, Howard Millar. *Privateer Ships and Sailors: The First Century of American Colonial Privateering, 1625-1725.* Toulon: G. Mouton, 1926.

51. Chapin, Howard Millar. *Privateering in King George's War, 1739-1748*. Providence: E. A. Johnson, 1928.

52. Chatelain, Verne E. *The Defenses of Spanish Florida, 1565 to 1763*. Washington: Carnegie Institution, 1941.

53. Church, Thomas. *Entertaining Passages Relating to Philip's War Which Began in the Month of June, 1675*. Boston, 1716. Republished by Henry Martyn Dexter, ed. as *The History of King Philip's War*. Boston, 1865.

54. Church, Thomas. *The History of the Eastern Expeditions of 1689, 1690, 1692, 1696, and 1704 against the Indians and French*. Henry Martyn Dexter, ed. Boston: J. K. Wiggin and W. P. Lunt, 1867.

55. Cole, David William. "The Organization and Administration of the South Carolina Militia System, 1670-1783." Doctoral dissertation, University of South Carolina, 1953.

56. Cooper, Johnson G. "Oswego in the French-English Struggle in North America, 1720-1760." Doctoral dissertation, Syracuse University, 1961.

57. Crane, Verner W. *The Southern Frontier, 1670-1732*. Durham: Duke University Press, 1932.

58. DePuy, Henry F., comp. *A Bibliography of the English Colonial Treaties with the American Indians, Including a Synopsis of Each Treaty*. New York: Lenox Club, 1917.

59. De Valinger, Leon. *Colonial Military Organization in Delaware, 1638-1776*. Wilmington: Delaware Tercentenary Commission, 1938.

60. Devine, Joseph A., Jr. "The British North American Colonies in the War of 1739-1748." Doctoral dissertation, University of Virginia, 1968.

61. Donaldson, Gordon. *Battle for a Continent: Quebec 1759*. Garden City: Doubleday, 1974.

62. Doolittle, Benjamin. *A Short Narrative of Mischief Done by the French and Indian Enemy, on the Western Frontiers of the Province of the Massachusetts-Bay*. Boston: S. Kneeland, 1750.

63. Doughty, Arthur G. *The Siege of Quebec and the Battle of the Plains of Abraham*. Quebec: Dussault & Proulx, 6 vols., 1901.

64. Eccles, W. J. *The Canadian Frontier, 1534-1760*. New York: Holt, Rinehart and Winston, 1969.

65. Eccles, W. J. "Frontenac's Military Policies, 1689-1698: a reassessment." *Canadian Historical Review*, 1956, 37, 201-24.

66. Eccles, W. J. "The Social, Economic, and Political Significance of the Military Establishment in New France." *Canadian Historical Review*, 1971, 52, 1-22.

67. Eckstorm, Fannie H. "The Attack on Norridgewock: 1724." *New England Quarterly*, 1934, 7, 541-78.

68. Edmonds, Walter D. *The Musket and the Cross: The Struggle of France and England for North America*. Boston: Little, Brown, 1968.

69. Entick, John. *The General History of the Late War: Containing It's Rise, Progress, and Event, in Europe, Asia, Africa, and America*. London: E. and C. Dilly, 1763-64. 5 vols.

70. Fisher, John S. "Colonel Armstrong's Expedition against Kittanning." *Pennsylvania Magazine of History and Biography*, 1927, 51, 1-14.
71. Fite, Emerson D. and Archibald Freeman, eds. *A Book of Old Maps Delineating American History from the Earliest Days down to the Close of the Revolutionary War*. Cambridge: Harvard University Press, 1926.
72. Folmer, Henry. "Franco-Spanish Rivalry in North America, 1524-1763." Doctoral dissertation, University of Chicago, 1948.
73. Foote, William A. "The American Independent Companies of the British Army, 1664-1765." Doctoral dissertation, University of California (Los Angeles), 1966.
74. Fortescue, John W. *A History of the British Army*. London: Macmillian. 1910-35. 13 vols. plus atlases.
75. Frégault, Guy. *Canada: the War of the Conquest*. Margaret M. Cameron, trans. Toronto: Oxford University Press, 1969.
76. Gipson, Lawrence H. *The British Empire before the American Revolution*. Caldwell and New York: Alfred A. Knopf, 1936-70. 15 vols.
77. Gipson, Laurence H. "A French Project for Victory Short of a Declaration of War, 1755." *Canadian Historical Review*, 1945, 26, 361-71.
78. Giraud, Marcel. *Histoire de la Louisiane française*. Paris: Presses universitaires de France, 2 vols., 1953-58. *Vol. one: The reign of Louis XIV, 1698-1715* was published in English by the Louisiana State University Press in 1974.
79. Gold, Robert L. *Borderland Empires in Transition: The Triple-Nation Transfer of Florida*. Carbondale: Southern Illinois University Press, 1969.
80. Goldstein, Robert A. *French-Iroquois Diplomatic and Military Relations, 1609-1701*. The Hague: Mouton, 1969.

GOVERNMENTAL RECORDS AND PUBLIC DOCUMENTS

GREAT BRITAIN
81. *Acts of the Privy Council of England, colonial series*. W. L. Grant and James Munro, eds. Hereford and London: H. M. S. O., 1908-1912. 6 vols.
82. *British Royal Proclamations Relating to America, 1603-1783*. Clarence S. Brigham, ed. Worcester: American Antiquarian Society, 1911.
83. *Calendar of State Papers, Colonial Series, America and the West Indies*. W. N. Sainsbury *et. al.*, eds. London: H. M. S. O., 1860-1953. 42 vols. to date.
84. *Journal of the Commissioners for Trade and Plantations* (1704-82). London: H. M. S. O., 1920-38. 14 vols.
85. *Proceedings and Debates of the British Parliaments Respecting North America*. Leo F. Stock, ed. Washington: Carnegie Institution, 1924-41. 5 vols.

86. *Royal Instructions to British Colonial Governors, 1670-1776.* Leonard W. Labaree, ed. New York: D. Appleton-Century, 1935. 2 vols.

CONNECTICUT

87. *The Public Records of the Colony of Connecticut.* J. H. Trumbull and C. J. Hoadly, eds. Hartford, 1850-90. 15 vols.

GEORGIA

88. *The Colonial Records of the State of Georgia.* A. D. Candler, ed. Atlanta, 1904-16. 26 vols. Reprinted, New York: AMS Press, 1970.

MAINE

89. *Province and Court Records of Maine.* C. T. Libby *et. al.*, eds. Portland: Maine Historical Society, 1928-64. 5 vols.

MARYLAND

90. *Archives of Maryland.* Baltimore: Maryland Historical Society, 1883-1972. 72 vols.

MASSACHUSETTS

91. *The Acts and Resolves, Public and Private, of the Province of the Massachusetts Bay* (1692-1786). Boston: Wright & Potter, 1869-1922. 21 vols.

92. *Journals of the House of Representatives of Massachusetts.* Boston: Massachusetts Historical Society, 1919-73. 43 vols. to date.

93. *Records of the Court of Assistants of the Colony of the Massachusetts Bay, 1630-1692.* Boston, 1901-28. 3 vols.

94. *Records of the Governor and Company of the Massachusetts Bay in New England* (1628-1686). Nathaniel B. Shurtleff, ed. Boston: W. White, 1853-54. 5 vols.

NEW HAMPSHIRE

95. *New Hampshire Provincial, Town, and State Papers.* N. Bouton *et. al.*, eds. Concord [etc.], 1867-1943. 40 vols.

NEW JERSEY

96. *Archives of the State of New Jersey.* Newark [etc.], 1880-1931. 34 vols.

NEW YORK

97. *Journal of the Legislative Council of the Colony of New-York* (1691-1775). Albany: Weed, Parsons, 1861. 2 vols.

98. *Journal of the Votes and Proceedings of the General Assembly of the Colony of New-York.* New York: Hugh Gaine, 1764-66. 2 vols.

NORTH CAROLINA

99. *The Colonial Records of North Carolina.* William L. Saunders, ed. Raleigh: Josephus Daniels, 1886-90. 10 vols.

PENNSYLVANIA

100. *Colonial Records of Pennsylvania.* Philadelphia and Harrisburg, 1852-53. 16 vols.

101. *Pennsylvania Archives.* Samuel Hazard *et. al.*, eds. Philadelphia and Harrisburg, 1852-1935. 138 vols.

PLYMOUTH

102. *Records of the Colony of New Plymouth in New England.* Nathaniel B. Shurtleff and David Pulsifer, eds. Boston: William White, 1855-61. 12 vols. Reprinted, New York: AMS Press, 1968.

RHODE ISLAND

103. *The Correspondence of the Colonial Governors of Rhode Island, 1723-1775.* Gertrude S. Kimball, ed. Boston and New York: Houghton Mifflin, 1902-3. 2 vols.

104. *Records of the Colony of Rhode Island, and Providence Plantations, in New England.* John R. Bartlett, ed. Providence, 1856-65. 10 vols.

SOUTH CAROLINA

105. *The Journal of the Commons House of Assembly of South Carolina* (1692-1727). A. S. Salley, Jr., ed. Columbia: Historical Commission of South Carolina, 1907-46. 19 vols.

106. *The Journal of the Commons House of Assembly* (1736-1750). J. H. Easterby and Ruth S. Green, eds. Columbia, 1951-62. 9 vols.

107. *The St. Augustine Expedition of 1740: A Report to the South Carolina General Assembly Reprinted from the Colonial Records of South Carolina with an Introduction by John Tate Lanning.* Columbia: South Carolina Archives, 1954.

VIRGINIA

108. *Executive Journals of the Council of Colonial Virginia (1680-1775).* H. R. McIlwaine et. al., eds. Richmond: Virginia State Library, 1925-66. 6 vols.

109. *Journals of the House of Burgesses of Virginia (1619-1776).* H. R. McIlwaine and J. P. Kennedy, eds. Richmond: Virginia State Library, 1905-15. 13 vols.

110. *Legislative Journals of the Council of Colonial Virginia* (1680-1776). H. R. McIlwaine, ed. Richmond: Virginia State Library, 1918-19. 3 vols.

111. *Minutes of the Council and General Court of Colonial Virginia, 1622-1632, 1670-1676.* H. R. McIlwaine, ed. Richmond: Virginia

UNITED STATES

112. Selective Service System. *Backgrounds of Selective Service.* Washington: G. P. O., 1947. 2 vols.

113. Graham, Dominick. "The Planning of the Beausejour Operation and the Approaches to War in 1755." *New England Quarterly*, 1968, 41, 551-66.

114. Graham, Gerald S. *Empire of the North Atlantic: The Maritime Struggle for North America.* Toronto: University of Toronto Press, 1950.

115. Graham, Gerald S. "The Naval Defence of British North America, 1739, 1763." *Transactions of the Royal Historical Society*, 1948, 4th ser., 30, 95-110.

116. Graham, Gerald S., ed. *The Walker Expedition to Quebec, 1711* (Publications of the Champlain Society, Vol. 32). Toronto, Champlain Society, 1953.

117. Grant, Charles S. "Pontiac's Rebellion and the British Troop Moves of 1763." *Mississippi Valley Historical Review*, 1953, 40, 75-88.

118. Grenier, Fernand, ed. *Papiers Contrecoeur et autres documents concernant le conflit Anglo-Français sur l'Ohio de 1745 a 1756.* Quebec: Presses universitaires Laval, 1952.

119. Hamer, P. M. "Anglo-French Rivalry in the Cherokee Country,

1754-1757." *North Carolina Historical Review*, 1925, 2, 303-22.

120. Hamer, P. M. "Fort Loudoun in the Cherokee War, 1758-1761." *North Carolina Historical Review*, 1925, 2, 442-58.

121. Hamer, P. M., ed. *A Guide to Archives and Manuscripts in the United States*. New Haven: Yale University Press, 1961.

122. Hamilton, Edward P. "Colonial Warfare in North America." *Proceedings of the Massachusetts Historical Society*, 1969, 80, 3-15.

123. Hamilton, Edward P. *The French and Indian Wars: The Story of Battles and Forts in the Wilderness*. Garden City: Doubleday, 1962.

124. Hammelef, John Christensen. "British and American Attempts to Coordinate the Defenses of the Continental Colonies to Meet French and Northern Indian Attacks, 1643-1754." Doctoral dissertation, University of Michigan, 1955.

125. Hanna, Archibald, Jr. "New England Military Institutions, 1693-1750." Doctoral dissertation, Yale University, 1951.

126. Hardcastle, David P. "The Defense of Canada under Louis XIV, 1643-1701." Doctoral dissertation, Ohio State University, 1970.

127. Hargreaves, Reginald. *The Bloodybacks: The British Serviceman in North America and the Caribbean, 1655-1783*. New York: Walker, 1968.

128. Harman, Joyce Elizabeth. *Trade and Privateering in Spanish Florida, 1732-1763*. St. Augustine: St. Augustine Historical Society, 1969.

129. Higham, Robin, ed. *A Guide to the Sources of British Military History*. Berkeley and Los Angeles: University of California Press, 1971.

130. Hitsman, J. MacKay (in collaboration with C. C. J. Bond). "The Assault Landing at Louisbourg, 1758." *Canadian Historical Review*, 1954, 35, 314-30.

131. Hubbard, William. *A Narrative of the Troubles with the Indians in New-England*. Boston, 1677. Republished by Samuel G. Drake, ed. as *The History of the Indian Wars in New England from the First Settlement to the Termination of the War with King Philip, in 1677*. Roxbury, Massachusetts, 1865.

12. Hulbert, Archer B. *Historic Highways of America*. Cleveland: A. H. Clark, 1902-5. 16 vols. Note especially Vol. 2 (Indian thoroughfares), Vol. 3 (Washington's road), Vol. 4 (Braddock's road), and Vol. 5 (Forbes' road).

133. Hunter, William A. *Forts on the Pennsylvania Frontier, 1753-1758*. Harrisburg: Pennsylvania Historical and Museum Commission, 1960.

134. Hunter, William. "Thomas Barton and the Forbes Expedition." *Pennsylvania Magazine of History and Biography*, 1971, 95, 431-83.

135. Irvine, Dallas. "The First British Regulars in North America." *Military Affairs*, 1945, 9, 337-54.

136. Israel, Fred L., ed. *Major Peace Treaties of Modern History, 1648-1967*. New York: Chelsea House, 1967. 4 vols.

137. Ivers, Larry E. *British Drums on the Southern Frontier: The Military Colonization of Georgia, 1733-1749*. Chapel Hill: University of North Carolina Press, 1973.

138. Jabbs, Theodore H. "The South Carolina Militia, 1663-1733." Doctoral dissertation, University of North Carolina, 1973.

139. Jacobs, Wilbur R. *Diplomacy and Indian Gifts: Anglo-French Rivalry Along the Ohio and Northwest Frontiers, 1748-1763.* Stanford: Stanford University Press, 1950.
140. Jacobs, Wilbur R. *Dispossessing the American Indian: Indians and Whites on the Colonial Frontier.* New York: Scribner's, 1972.
141. James, Alfred P. and Charles M. Stotz. "Drums in the Forest." *Western Pennsylvania Historical Magazine,* 1958, 41, 3-56, 59-227.
142. Jameson, John Franklin, ed. *Privateering and Piracy in the Colonial Period: Illustrative Documents.* New York: Macmillan, 1923.
143. Johnson, James G. "The Colonial Southeast, 1732-1763: An International Contest for Territorial and Economic Control." *University of Colorado Studies,* 1932, 19, 163-225.
144. Kavanagh, W. Keith, ed. *Foundations of Colonial America: A Documentary History.* New York: Chelsea House, 1973. 3 vols.
145. Kenny, Robert W. "The Beginnings of the Rhode Island Train Bands." *Collections of the Rhode Island Historical Society,* 1940, 33, 25-38.
146. Kent, Donald H. "The French Advance into the Ohio country." *Western Pennsylvania Historical Magazine,* 1954-55, 37, 135-51.
147. Kent, Donald H. "The French Occupy the Ohio country." *Pennsylvania History,* 1954 21, 301-15.
148. Ketcham, Ralph L. "Conscience, War, and Politics in Pennsylvania, 1755-1757." *William and Mary Quarterly,* 1963, 20, 416-39.
149. Koontz, Louis K. *The Virginia Frontier, 1754-1763* (Johns Hopkins University studies in historical and political science, Vol. 43). Baltimore: Johns Hopkins Press, 1925.
150. Lanctot, Gustave. *A History of Canada* (to 1763). Cambridge: Harvard University Press, 1963-65. 3 vols.
151. Lanning, John Tate. "The American Colonies in the Preliminaries of the War of Jenkins' Ear." *Georgia Historical Quarterly,* 1927, 11, 129-55.
152. Lanning, John Tate. "American Participation in the War of Jenkins' Ear." *Georgia Historical Quarterly,* 1927, 11, 191-215.
153. Lanning, John Tate. *The Diplomatic History of Georgia: A Study of the Epoch of Jenkins' Ear.* Chapel Hill: University of North Carolina Press, 1936.
154. Larrabee, Edward Conyers McMillan. "New Jersey and the Fortified Frontier System of the 1750's." Doctoral dissertation, Columbia University, 1970.
155. Leach, Douglas Edward. *Arms for Empire: A Military History of the British Colonies in North America, 1607-1763.* New York: Macmillan, 1973.
156. Leach, Douglas Edward. "The Causes and Effects of King Philip's War." Doctoral dissertation, Harvard University, 1950.
157. Leach, Douglas Edward. *Flintlock and Tomahawk: New England in King Philip's War.* New York: Macmillan, 1958. Reprinted, New York: W. W. Norton, 1966.
158. Leach, Douglas Edward. "The Military System of Plymouth Colony." *New England Quarterly,* 1951, 24, 342-64.

159. Leach, Douglas Edward. *The Northern Colonial Frontier, 1607-1763.* New York: Holt, Rinehart and Winston, 1966.
160. Lee, E. Lawrence. *Indian Wars in North Carolina, 1663-1763.* Raleigh: Carolina Charter Tercentenary Commission, 1963.
161. Lincoln, Charles H., ed. *Narratives of the Indian Wars, 1675-1699.* New York: Scribner's, 1913.
162. [Livingston, William]. *A Review of the Military Operations in North America* (1753-1756). Dublin: P. Wilson and J. Exshaw, 1757.
163. Lloyd, Christopher. *The Capture of Quebec.* New York: Macmillan, 1959.
164. Louisbourg Papers, Massachusetts Historical Society.
165. McCormac, Eugene I. *Colonial Opposition to Imperial Authority during the French and Indian War* (University of California Publications in History, Vol. 1). Berkeley: The University Press, 1911.
166. McCully, Bruce T. "Catastrophe in the Wilderness: New Light on the Canada Expedition of 1709." *William and Mary Quarterly.* 1954, 11, 440-56.
167. McLennan, John S. *Louisbourg, from Its Foundation to Its Fall, 1713-1758.* London: Macmillan, 1918.
168. Mahon, John K. "Anglo-American Methods of Indian Warfare, 1676-1794." *Mississippi Valley Historical Review*, 1958, 45, 254-75.
169. Malone, Patrick Mitchell. "Indian and English Military Systems in New England in the Seventeenth Century." Doctoral dissertation, Brown University, 1971.
170. Mante, Thomas. *The History of the Late War in North-America, and the Islands of the West-Indies, Including the Campaigns of MDCCLXIII and MDCCLXIV against His Majesty's Indian Enemies.* London: W. Strahan and T. Cadell, 1772.
171. Marcus, Richard H. "The Connecticut Valley: A Problem in Inter-Colonial Defense." *Military Affairs*, 1969, 33, 230-42.
172. Marcus, Richard H. "The Militia of Colonial Connecticut, 1639-1775: An Institutional Study." Doctoral dissertation, University of Colorado, 1965.
173. Marietta, Jack D. "Conscience, the Quaker community, and the French and Indian War." *Pennsylvania Magazine of History and Biography*, 1971, 95, 3-27.
174. Mather, Cotton. *Decennium Luctuosum. An History of Remarkable Occurrences, in the Long War, Which New-England Hath Had with the Indian Salvages, from the Year 1688, to the Year 1698.* Boston: B. Green & J. Allen, 1699. Reprinted in C. H. Lincoln, ed. *Narratives of the Indian Wars, 1675-1699.* New York: Scribner's, 1913.
175. Mather, Increase. *A Brief History of the War with the Indians in New-England.* Boston and London, 1676. Republished by Samuel G. Drake, ed. as *The History of King Philip's War, by the Rev. Increase Mather, D.D.* Boston, 1862.
176. Millar, David R. "The Militia, the Army, and the Independency in Colonial Massachusetts." Doctoral dissertation, Cornell University, 1967.

177. Milot, Victor. "Le Richelieu, route militaire de la Nouvelle-France." Doctoral dissertation, Laval University, 1949.

178. [Mitchell, John]. *The Contest in America between Great Britain and France, with Its Consequences and Importance.* London: A. Millar, 1757.

179. Morgan, Gwenda. "Virginia and the French and Indian War: A Case Study of the War's Effects on Imperial Relations." *Virginia Magazine of History and Biography*, 1973, 81, 23-48.

180. Morgan, William Thomas. "English Fear of "Encirclement' in the Seventeenth Century." *Canadian Historical Review*, 1929, 10, 4-22.

181. Morgan, William Thomas. "The South Sea Company and the Canadian Expedition in the Reign of Queen Anne." *Hispanic American Historical Review*, 1928, 8, 143-66.

182. Morris, John L. "The French Regime in Illinois, 1689-1763." Doctoral dissertation, University of Illinois, 1926.

183. Morton, Louis. "The Origins of American Military Policy." *Military Affairs*, 1958, 22, 75-82.

184. *The National Union Catalog of Manuscript Collections.* Compiled by the Library of Congress. Ann Arbor, Washington, [etc.], 1962—.

185. Nichols, Franklin T. "The Braddock Expedition." Doctoral dissertation, Harvard University, 1947.

186. Nichols, Franklin T. "The Organization of Braddock's Army." *William and Mary Quarterly*, 1947, 4, 125-47.

187. Norkus, Nellie. "Virginia's Role in the Capture of Fort Duquesne, 1758." *Western Pennsylvania Historical Magazine*, 1962, 45, 291-308.

188. O'Meara, Walter. *Guns at the Forks.* Englewood Cliffs, New Jersey: Prentice-Hall, 1965.

189. O'Neil, Emmett Francis. "English Fear of French Encirclement in North America, 1680-1763." Doctoral dissertation, University of Michigan, 1941.

190. Orr, Charles, ed. *History of the Pequot War: The Contemporary Accounts of Mason, Underhill, Vincent and Gardener.* Cleveland: Helman-Taylor, 1897.

191. Osgood, Herbert L. *The American Colonies in the Seventeenth Century.* New York: Macmillan, 1904-7. 3 vols.

192. Osgood, Herbert L. *The American Colonies in the Eighteenth Century.* New York: Columbia University Press, 1924-25. 4 vols.

193. Pares, Richard. "American versus Continental Warfare, 1739-1763." *English Historical Review*, 1936, 51, 429-65. Republished in Pares, *The Historian's Business and Other Essays.* Oxford: Clarendon Press, 1961.

194. Pares, Richard. *Colonial Blockade and Neutral Rights, 1739-1763.* Oxford: Clarendon Press, 1938.

195. Pargellis, Stanley. "Braddock's Defeat." *American Historical Review*, 1936, 41, 253-69.

196. Pargellis, Stanley. "The Four Independent Companies of New York." In *Essays in Colonial History Presented to Charles McLean*

Andrews by his Students. New Haven: Yale University Press, 1931.

197. Pargellis, Stanley, ed. *Military Affairs in North America, 1748-1765: Selected Documents from the Cumberland Papers in Windsor Castle.* New York and London: D. Appleton-Century, 1936. Reprinted, Hamden, Connecticut: Archon Books, 1969.

198. Parker, King Lawrence. "Anglo-American Wilderness Campaigning, 1754-1764: Logistical and Tactical Developments." Doctoral dissertation, Columbia University, 1970.

199. Parkman Papers, Massachusetts Historical Society.

200. Parkman, Francis. *France and England in North America.* Boston: Little, Brown, 1865-92. 9 vols. Important for the colonial wars are:
    Count Frontenac and New France under Louis XIV (cited above under Biography)

201. *A Half-Century of Conflict.* Boston, 1892. 2 vols.

202. *Montcalm and Wolfe.* Boston, 1884. 2 vols.

203. *The Conspiracy of Pontiac and the Indian War after the Conquest of Canada.* 10th ed. Boston, 1893. 2 vols.

204. Pease, Theodore Calvin, ed. *Anglo-French Boundary Disputes in the West, 1749-1763* (Collections of the Illinois State Historical Library, Vol. 27). Springfield: Trustees of the Illinois State Historical Library, 1936.

205. Pease, Theodore Calvin and Ernestine Jenison, eds. *Illinois on the Eve of the Seven Years' War, 1747-1755* (Collections of the Illinois State Historical Library, Vol. 29). Springfield: Trustees of the Illinois State Historical Library, 1940.

206. Peckham, Howard H. *The Colonial Wars, 1689-1762.* Chicago: University of Chicago Press, 1964.

207. Peckham, Howard H. *Pontiac and the Indian Uprising.* Princeton: Princeton University Press, 1947.

208. Peckham, Howard H. "Speculations on the Colonial Wars." *William and Mary Quarterly*, 1960, 17, 463-72.

209. Penhallow, Samuel. *The History of the Wars of New-England with the Eastern Indians* (1703-1725). Boston: T. Fleet, 1726. Facsimile reprint by Corner House, Williamstown, Massachusetts, 1973.

210. Pennington, Edgar L. "The South Carolina Indian War of 1715, as seen by the clergymen." *South Carolina Historical and Genalogical Magazine*, 1931, 32, 251-67.

PERSONAL PAPERS, JOURNALS, AND ACCOUNTS

211. Abercomby, Gen. James. Papers. Henry E. Huntington Library.

212. Amherst, Gen. Jeffery. Papers. William L. Clements Library. 8 vols.

213. Amherst, Gen. Jeffery. Papers (transcripts). Public Archives of Canada ("British Officers").

214. *The Journal of Jeffery Amherst, Recording the Military Career of General Amherst in America from 1758 to 1763.* J. Clarence Webster, ed. Chicago: University of Chicago Press, 1931.

215. Anonymous. *A Journal of the Proceedings in the Late Expedition to Port-Royal.* Boston: Benjamin Harris, 1690.

216. Anonymous. *The anonymous lettre d'un habitant de Louisbourg*

(University of Toronto Studies. History; Second Series, Vol. 1). George M. Wrong, ed. Toronto: The University, 1897.

217. Barnwell, John. "The Tuscarora Expedition: letters of Colonel John Barnwell." *South Carolina Historical and Genealogical Magazine*, 1908, 9, 28-54 (Reprinted from *The Virginia Magazine of History and Biography*, 1898, 5 and 6, 391-402, 42-55).

218. Bidwell, Adonijah. Journal. Massachusetts Historical Society. Published in *The New England Historical and Genealogical Register*, 1873, 27, 153-60.

219. Bougainville, Col. Louis Antoine de. *Adventure in the Wilderness: The American Journals of Louis Antoine de Bougainville, 1756-1760*. Edward P. Hamilton, trans. and ed. Norman: University of Oklahoma Press, 1964.

220. Bouquet, Col. Henry. *The Papers of Henry Bouquet (1755-1758)*. S. K. Stevens *et. al.*, eds. Harrisburg: Pennsylvania Historical and Museum Commission, 1951-72. 2 vols.

221. Bowen, Ashley. "Journal Kept on the Quebec Expedition, 1759, by Ashley Bowen of Marblehead." *Essex Institute Historical Collections*, 1934, 70, 227-66.

222. Bradstreet, Col. John. Papers. American Antiquarian Society. 5 vols.

223. Bremner, John. Journal (1756-64). New York Historical Society.

224. Buckingham, Thomas. *The Private Journals Kept by Rev. John [i.e., Thomas] Buckingham, of the Expedition against Canada, in the Years 1710 & 1711*. New York: Wilder & Campbell, 1825.

225. Calder, Isabel M., ed. *Colonial Captivities, Marches, and Journeys*. New York: Macmillan, 1935.

226. [Carver, Jonathan]. *A Short History and Description of Fort Niagara, with an Account of Its Importance to Great Britain, Written by an English Prisoner, 1758*. Paul Leicester Ford, ed. New York: B. Franklin, 1971 (reprint of the 1890 edition).

227. Clark, David S., comp. "Journals and Orderly Books Kept by Massachusetts Soldiers during the French and Indian War." *New England Historical and Genealogical Register*, 1941, 95, 118-21.

228. Cleaves, Benjamin. "Benjamin Cleaves's Journal." *New England Historical and Genealogical Register*, 1912, 66, 113-24.

229. Cohen, Sheldon S. "Triumph on the St. Lawrence: A New Historical Account." *Mid-America*, 1971, 53, 245-63.

230. Colden, Cadwallader. *The Letters and Papers of Cadwallader Colden (1711-1775)* (Collections of the New York Historical Society, Vols. 50-56, 67-68). New York: New York Historical Society, 1918-37. 9 vols.

231. Craft, Benjamin. "Craft's Journal of the Siege of Louisbourg." W. P. Upham, ed. *Essex Institute Historical Collections*, 1864, 6, 181-94.

232. Cross, Stephen. "Journal of Stephen Cross of Newburyport" (1956-57). *Essex Institute Historical Collections*, 1940, 76, 14-42.

233. Davis, Sylvanus. "The Declaration of Sylvanus Davis" (1690). *Collections of the Massachusetts Historical Society*, Third Series, Vol. 1, 101-12.

234. De Forest, Louis Effingham, ed. *Louisbourg Journals, 1745*. New

York: Society of Colonial Wars in the State of New York, 1932.
Includes ten journals.

235. Dinwiddie, Robert. *The Official Records of Robert Dinwiddie, Lieutenant-Governor of the Colony of Virginia, 1751-1758, Now First Printed from the Manuscript in the Collections of the Virginia Historical Society, With an Introduction and Notes by R. A. Brock* (Collections of the Virginia Historical Society, Vols. 3-4). Richmond, 1883-84. 2 vols.

236. Dorr, Moses. "A Journel of an Expedition against Canaday" (1758). *New York History*, 1935, 16, 452-64.

237. Eastburn, Robert. *A Faithful Narrative of the Many Dangers and Sufferings, as Well as Wonderful and Surprizing Deliverances of Robert Eastburn, during his Late Captivity among the Indians* (1756). Philadelphia: William Dunlap, 1758.

238. Forbes, Harriette Merrifield, comp. *New England Diaries, 1602-1800, a Descriptive Catalogue of Diaries, Orderly Books and Sea Journals.* Topsfield, Massachusetts: Privately printed, 1923.

239. Forbes, Gen. John. *Writings of General John Forbes Relating to His Service in North America.* Alfred P. James, ed. Menasha, Wisconsin: Collegiate Press, 1938.

240. Franklin, Benjamin. *The Papers of Benjamin Franklin.* Leonard W. Labaree *et. al.*, eds. New Haven: Yale University Press, 1959—. 17 vols. to date.

241. Gage, Gen. Thomas. Papers. William L. Clements Library. 180 vols.

242. Gibson, James. *A Journal of the Late Siege by the Troops from North America against the French at Cape Breton, the City of Louisbourg, and the Territories thereunto Belonging.* London: J. Newbery, 1745.

243. Giddings, Daniel. "Journal kept by Lieut. Daniel Giddings of Ipswich during the Expedition against Cape Breton in 1744-5." *Essex Institute Historical Collections*, 1912, 48, 293-304.

244. Gist, Thomas. "Thomas Gist's Indian Captivity, 1758-1759." Howard H. Peckham, ed. *Pennsylvania Magazine of History and Biography*, 1956, 80, 285-311.

245. Green, Samuel A., ed. *Three Military Diaries Kept by Groton Soldiers in Different Wars.* Groton, Massachusetts: J. Wilson and Son, 1901. Includes the 1745 Louisbourg diary of Lieut. Dudley Bradstreet and the 1760 diary of Sgt. David Holden.

246. Gyles, John. *Memoirs of Odd Adventures, Strange Deliverances, &c. in the Captivity of John Gyles, Esq; Commander of the Garrison on St. George's River* (1689-98). Boston: S. Kneeland and T. Green, 1736. Reprinted, Cincinnati: Spiller & Gates, 1869.

247. Hamilton, Charles, ed. *Braddock's Defeat: The Journal of Captain Robert Cholmley's Batman, the Journal of a British Officer, Hal-Kett's Orderly Book.* Norman: University of Oklahoma Press, 1959.

248. Harris, William. *A Rhode Islander Reports on King Philip's War: The Second William Harris Letter of August, 1676.* Douglas Edward Leach, ed. Providence: Rhode Island Historical Society, 1963.

249. Henry, Alexander. *Travels and Adventures in Canada and the Indian Territories between the Years 1760 and 1776.* New York: I. Riley, 1809. Republished by David A. Armour, ed. as *Massacre at Mackinac.* Mackinac Island, Michigan: Mackinac Island State Park Commission, 1966.

250. How, Nehemiah. *A Narrative of the Captivity of Nehemiah How, Who Was Taken by the Indians at the Great-Meadow Fort above Fort-Dummer, Where he was an Inhabitant, October 11th 1745.* Boston, 1748.

251. Johnson, William. *The Papers of Sir William Johnson.* Richard E. Day *et. al.*, eds. Albany: The University of the State of New York, 1921-62. 13 vols.

252. Knox, John. *An Historical Journal of the Campaigns in North-America, for the Years 1757, 1758, 1759, and 1760.* London, 1769. 2 vols. Republished by Arthur G. Doughty, ed. as Vols. 8-10 of the *Publications of the Champlain Society.* Toronto, 1914-16. 3 vols.

253. Kregier, Martin. "Journal of the Esopus War" (1663-64). In B. Fernow, ed., *Documents Relating to the Colonial History of the State of New York,* Vol. 13, 323-54. Albany: Weed, Parsons, 1881.

254. Laurens, Henry. *The Papers of Henry Laurens* (1746—). Philip M. Hamer and George C. Rogers, Jr., eds. Columbia: University of South Carolina Press, 1968—. 3 vols. to date.

255. Lévis, François Gaston de. *Collection des manuscrits du Maréchal de Lévis.* H. R. Casgrain, ed. Montreal and Quebec: L. J. Demers & frère, 1889-95. 12 vols. Among these volumes are the following:

256. *Journal des campagnes du chevalier de Lévis en Canada de 1756 à 1760.*

257. *Lettres du chevalier de Levis concernant la guerre du Canada (1756-1760).*

258. *Lettres et pièces militaires, instructions, ordres, mémoires, plans de campagne et de défense 1756-1760.*

259. *Lettres du marquis de Montcalm au chevalier de Lévis.*

260. *Journal du marquis de Montcalm durant ses campagnes au Canada de 1756 à 1760.*

261. *Lettres du marquis de Vaudreuil au chevalier de Lévis.*

262. *Relations et journaux de différentes expéditions faites durant les annees 1755-56-57-58-59-60.*

263. Loudoun, Earl of. Papers. Henry E. Huntington Library.

264. Marin Journal of the campaign of Saratoga, 1745. New York Public Library (Schuyler Papers, "Indians").

265. Monckton, Gen. Robert. Papers. Public Archives of Canada. 90 vols.

266. Montcalm, Marquis de. "Montcalm's Correspondence." In the *Report of the Public Archives of Canada for the Year 1929,* 31-108. Ottawa: F. A. Acland, 1930.

267. Montiano, Gov. Manuel de. *Letters of Montiano, Siege of St. Augustine* (Collections of the Georgia Historical Society, Vol. 7, Part 1). Savannah, 1909.

268. Murray, Gen. James. Papers. Public Archives of Canada ("Quebec and Lower Canada: Political Figures"). 5 vols., transcripts.

269. Murray, Gen. James. *Governor Murray's Journal of the Siege of Quebec, from 18th September, 1759, to 25th May, 1760.* Toronto: Rous & Mann, 1939.

270. Nicholson, Col. Francis. "Journal at the Capture of Annapolis, 1710" (Collections of the Nova Scotia Historical Society, Vol. 1). Halifax, 1878.

271. Norton, John. *The Redeemed Captive, Being a Narrative of the Taking and Carrying into Captivity the Reverend Mr. John Norton, When Fort-Massachusetts Surrendered to a Large Body of French and Indians, August 20th 1746.* Boston, 1748.

272. Pepperrell, William. Papers. Massachusetts Historical Society. 2 vols. A portion of this collection has been published in the *Collections of the Massachusetts Historical Society*, First Series, Vol. 1 (Boston, 1792), and Sixth Series, Vol. 10 (Boston, 1899).

273. *The Journal of Sir William Pepperrell Kept during the Expedition against Louisbourg, March 24-August 22, 1745.* C. H. Lincoln, ed. Worcester, Massachusetts: American Antiquarian Society, 1910.

274. Perry, David. *Recollections of an Old Soldier.* Cottonport, Louisiana: Polyanthos Press, 1971.

275. Pitt, William. *Correspondence of William Pitt, When Secretary of State, with Colonial Governors and Military and Naval Commissioners in America.* G. S. Kimball, ed. New York: Macmillan, 1906. 2 vols.

276. Pomeroy, Seth. *The Journals and Papers of Seth Pomeroy, Sometime General in the Colonial Service.* L. E. De Forest, ed. New York: Society of Colonial Wars in the State of New York, 1926.

277. Pote, William, Jr. *The Journal of Captain William Pote, Jr. during His Captivity in the French and Indian War from May, 1745, to August, 1747.* New York: Dodd, Mead, 1896.

278. Procter, Jonathan. "Diary Kept at Louisburg, 1759-1760, by Jonathan Procter of Danvers." *Essex Institute Historical Collections*, 1934, 70, 31-57.

279. Rogers, Robert. *Journals* (1755-61). Howard H. Peckham, ed. New York: Corinth Books, 1961.

280. *The Saltonstall Papers, 1607-1815*, Vol. 1 (Collections of the Massachusetts Historical Society, Vol. 80). Robert E. Moody, ed. Boston, 1972.

281. Savage, Maj. Thomas. *An Account of the Late Action of the New-Englanders, under the Command of Sir William Phips, against the French at Canada.* London: Thomas Jones, 1691.

282. Shirley, William. *Correspondence of William Shirley, Governor of Massachusetts and Military Commander in America, 1731-1760.* C. H. Lincoln, ed. New York: Macmillan, 1912, 2 vols. Reprinted, New York: AMS Press, 1973.

283. Shirley, William. *A letter . . . to . . . the Duke of Newcastle: With A Journal of the Siege of Louisbourg, and Other Operations of the Forces, during the Expedition against the French Settlements on Cape Breton.* London: E. Owen, 1746.

284. Smith, Col. James. *An Account of the Remarkable Occurrences in*

the Life and Travels of Col. James Smith. Lexington, Kentucky: John Bradford, 1799.

285. Thomas, John. "Diary" (1755). *Collections of the Nova Scotia Historical Society,* 1878, 1, 119-40.

286. Thwaites, Reuben Gold, ed. *Early Western Journals, 1748-1765, by Conrad Weiser, 1748; George Croghan, 1750-1765; Frederick Post, 1758; and Thomas Morris, 1764.* Cleveland: Arthur H. Clark, 1904.

287. Townshend, Gen. George. Papers. Public Archives of Canada. 15 vols.

288. Trask, William B., ed. *Letters of Colonel Thomas Westbrook and Others Relative to Indian Affairs in Maine, 1722-1726.* Boston: G. E. Littlefield, 1901.

289. True, Capt. Henry. Memorandum and account book, 1696-1719. Manuscript Room, New York Public Library.

290. VanDerBeets, Richard, ed. *Held Captive by Indians: Selected Narratives, 1642-1836.* Knoxville: University of Tennessee Press, 1973.

291. Walley, John. "Major Walley's Journal in the Expedition against Canada in 1690." In Thomas Hutchinson, *The History of the Colony and Province of Massachusetts-Bay,* Vol. 1, 459-67. Lawrence Shaw Mayo, ed. Cambridge: Harvard University Press, 1936.

Washington, George.

292. *The Diaries of George Washington, 1748-1799.* John C. Fitzpatrick, ed. Boston and New York: Houghton Mifflin, 1925. 4 vols.

293. *The Journal of Major George Washington: An Account of His First Official Mission, Made as Emissary from the Governor of Virginia to the Commandant of the French Forces on the Ohio, October 1753-January 1754.* Williamsburg: William Hunter, 1754. Facsimile edition. Charlottesville. Virginia: University Press of Virginia, 1959.

294. *The Writings of George Washington, from the Original Manuscript Sources, 1745-1799.* Washington, D.C.: G. P. O., 1931-44. 39 vols.

295. Williams, Col. Israel. Papers. Massachusetts Historical Society. 2 vols.

296. Williams, John. *The Redeemed Captive Returning to Zion.* Boston: B. Green, 1707. Republished Springfield, Massachusetts: H. R. Huntting, 1908.

297. Williamson, Peter. *French and Indian Cruelty; Exemplified in the Life and Various Vicissitudes of Fortune, of Peter Williamson.* York: The author, 1757.

298. Winslow, Gen. John. "Journal" (1755-56). *Collections of the Nova Scotia Historical Society,* 1882-83, 3, 71-196, 1884, 4, 113-246.

299. Wolcott, Gen. Roger. "Journal of Roger Wolcott at the Siege of Louisbourg." *Collections of the Connecticut Historical Society,* 1860, 1, 131-62.

300. Wolfe, Gen. James. Papers. Public Archives of Canada ("British Officers"). 10 vols.

301. Wolfe, Gen. James. *The Life and Letters of James Wolfe.* Beckles Wilson, ed. London: W. Heinemann, 1909.

302. Peterson, Harold L. *Arms and Armor in Colonial America, 1526-1783*. Harrisburg, Pennsylvania: Stackpole, 1956.
303. Peterson, Harold L. "The Military Equipment of the Plymouth and Bay Colonies, 1620-1690." *New England Quarterly*, 1947, 20, 197-208.
304. Peterson, Harold L. *Round Shot and Rammers*. Harrisburg, Pennsylvania: Stackpole, 1969.
305. Powell, William S. "Aftermath of the Massacre: The First Indian War, 1622-1632." *Virginia Magazine of History and Biography*, 1958, 66, 44-75.
306. Pownall, Thomas. *Considerations Towards a General Plan of Measures for the English Provinces*. New York: J. Parker and W. Weyman, 1756.
307. Preston, Richard A. and Leopold Lamontagne, eds. *Royal Fort Frontenac* (Publications of the Champlain Society, Vol. 42). Toronto: Champlain Society, 1958.
308. Quarles, Benjamin. "The Colonial Militia and Negro Manpower." *Mississippi Valley Historical Review*, 1959, 45, 643-52.
309. Radabaugh, Jack S. "The Military System of Colonial Massachusetts, 1690-1740." Doctoral dissertation, University of Southern California, 1965.
310. Radabaugh, Jack S. "The Militia of Colonial Massachusetts." *Military Affairs*, 1954, 18, 1-18.
311. Rashed, Zenab Esmat. *The Peace of Paris, 1763*. Liverpool: University Press, 1951.
312. Rawlyk, G. A. "New England and Louisbourg, 1744-1745." Doctoral dissertation, University of Rochester, 1966.
313. Rawlyk, G. A. *Yankees at Louisbourg* (University of Maine Studies, Second Series, No. 85). Orono: University of Maine Press, 1967.
314. Reese, Trevor R. "Britain's Military Support of Georgia in the War of 1739-1748." *Georgia Historical Quarterly*, 1959, 43, 1-10.
315. Rice, Otis K. "The French and Indian War in West Virginia." *West Virginia History*, 1963, 24, 134-46.
316. Rice, Otis K. "The Sandy Creek Expedition of 1756." *West Virginia History*, 1951, 13, 5-19.
317. Rogers, J. Alan. *Empire and Liberty: American Resistance to British Authority, 1755-1763*. Berkeley: University of California Press, 1974.
318. Rutman, Darrett B. "A Militant New World, 1607-1640: America's First Generation, Its Martial Spirit, Its Tradition of Arms, Its Militia Organization, Its Wars." Doctoral dissertation, University of Virginia, 1959.
319. Rutman, Darrett B. "The Virginia Company and Its Military Regime." In D. B. Rutman, ed., *The Old Dominion: Essays for Thomas Perkins Abernethy*. Charlottesville: University Press of Virginia, 1964.
320. Samuel, Sigmund, comp. *The Seven Years War in Canada, 1756-1763*. Toronto: Ryerson Press, 1934.
321. Savelle, Max. "The Appearance of an American Attitude toward External Affairs, 1750-1775." *American Historical Review*, 1947, 52, 655-66.

322. Savelle, Max. *The Diplomatic History of the Canadian Boundary, 1749-1763*. New Haven: Yale University Press, 1940.

323. Savelle, Max. *The Origins of American Diplomacy: The International History of Anglo-America, 1492-1763*. New York: Macmillan, 1967.

324. Sawyer, Charles W. *Firearms in American History*. Boston: The author, 1910-20. 3 vols.

325. Scisco, Louis Dow. "Evolution of Colonial Militia in Maryland." *Maryland Historical Magazine*, 1940, 35, 166-77.

326. Sharp, Morrison. "Leadership and Democracy in the Early New England System of Defense." *American Historical Review*, 1945, 50, 244-60.

327. Sharp, Morrison. "The New England Trainbands in the Seventeenth Century." Doctoral dissertation, Harvard University, 1938.

328. Sheehan, Bernard W. "Indian-White Relations in Early America: A Review Essay." *William and Mary Quarterly*, 1969, 26, 267-86.

329. [Shirley, William]. *Memoirs of the Principal Transactions of the Last War between the English and French in North America (1744-1748)*. London: R. & J. Dodsley, 1757.

330. Shy, John W. "A New Look at Colonial Militia." *William and Mary Quarterly*, 1963, 20, 175-85.

331. Smith, William. *An Historical Account of the Expedition against the Ohio Indians, in the year 1764*. Philadelphia: William Bradford, 1765. Also published in London, 1766. Reprinted, Cincinnati: Ohio Valley Historical Society, 1868.

332. Smoyer, Stanley C. "Indians as Allies in the Intercolonial Wars." *New York History*, 1936, 17, 411-22.

333. Sosin, Jack M. "Louisburg and the Peace of Aix-la-Chapelle." *William and Mary Quarterly*. 1957, 14, 516-35.

334. *The Spanish Official Account of the Attack on the Colony of Georgia, in America, and of Its Defeat on St. Simons Island by General James Oglethorpe* (Collections of the Georgia Historical Society, Vol. 7, Part 3). Savannah, 1913.

335. Stacey, C. P. *Quebec, 1759: The Siege and the Battle*. New York: St. Martin's Press, 1959.

336. Stacey, C. P. "Quebec, 1759: Some New Documents." *Canadian Historical Review*, 1966, 47, 344-55.

337. Stanley, John Henry. "Preliminary Investigation of Military Manuals of American Imprint Prior to 1800." Master's thesis, Brown University, 1964.

338. Sylvester, Herbert M. *Indian Wars of New England*. Boston: W. B. Clarke, 1910. 3 vols.

339. Symmes, Thomas. *Historical Memoirs of the Late Fight at Piggwacket, with a Sermon Occasion'd by the Fall of the Brave Capt. John Lovewell and Several of His Valiant Company, in the Late Heroic Action There*. 2nd ed. Boston: B. Green, Jr., 1725.

340. TePaske, John Jay. *The Governorship of Spanish Florida, 1700-1763*. Durham: Duke University Press, 1964.

341. Thayer, Theodore. "The Army Contractors for the Niagara Campaign, 1755-1756." *William and Mary Quarterly*, 1957, 14, 31-46.

342. Tottle, James Roger. "Anglo-Indian Relations in the Northern

Theatre of the French and Indian War, 1748-1761." Ph.D. dissertation, Ohio State University, 1972.

343. Torres-Reyes, Ricardo. *The British Siege of St. Augustine in 1740.* Denver Service Center (National Park Service), 1972.

344. Trask, Kerry Arnold. "In the Pursuit of Shadows: A Study of Collective Hope and Despair in Provincial Massachusetts during the Era of the Seven Years War, 1748 to 1764." Doctoral dissertation, University of Minnesota, 1971.

345. Trudel, Marcel. "The Jumonville Affair" (Translated and abridged by Donald H. Kent). *Pennsylvania History*, 1954, 21, 351-81.

346. Vail, R. W. G., comp. *The Voice of the Old Frontier.* Philadelphia: University of Pennsylvania Press, 1949.

347. Vaughan, Alden T. *New England Frontier: Puritans and Indians, 1620-1675.* Boston: Little, Brown, 1965.

348. Vaughan, Alden T. "Pequots and Puritans: The Causes of the War of 1637." *William and Mary Quarterly*, 1964, 21, 256-69.

349. Waitley, Douglas. *Roads of Destiny: The Trails That Shaped a Nation.* Washington: Robert B. Luce (distributed by David McKay Company, New York), 1970.

350. Wall, Robert Emmet, Jr. "Louisbourg, 1745." *New England Quarterly*, 1964, 37, 64-83.

351. Waller, G. M. "New York's Role in Queen Anne's War, 1702-1713." *New York History*, 1952, 33, 40-53.

352. Ward, Harry M. *"Unite or Die": intercolony relations, 1690-1763.* Port Washington: Kennikat Press, 1971.

353. Washburn, Wilcomb E. "Bacon's Rebellion." Ph.D. dissertation, Harvard University, 1955.

354. Washburn, Wilcomb E. *The Governor and the Rebel: A History of Bacon's Rebellion in Virginia.* Chapel Hill: University of North Carolina Press, 1957.

355. Webb, Stephen S. "Officers and Governors: The Role of the British Army in Imperial Politics and the Administration of the American colonies, 1689-1722." Doctoral dissertation, University of Wisconsin, 1965.

356. Webster, J. Clarence. *The Forts of Chignecto: A Study of the Eighteenth Century Conflict between France and Great Britain in Acadia.* Shediac, New Brunswick: The author, 1930.

357. Weigley, Russell F. *History of the United States Army.* New York: Macmillan, 1967.

358. Wellenreuther, Hermann. *Glaube und politik in Pennsylvania 1681-1776: die wandlungen der obrigkeitsdoktrin und des* peace testimony *der Quaker.* Cologne: Bohlau Verlag, 1972.

359. Wertenbaker, Thomas J. *Torchbearer of the Revolution: The Story of Bacon's Rebellion and Its Leader.* Princeton: Princeton University Press, 1940.

360. Wheeler, E. Milton. "Development and Organization of the North Carolina Militia." *North Carolina Historical Review*, 1964, 41, 307-23.

361. Winsor, Justin. *Narrative and Critical History of America.* Boston and New York: Houghton Mifflin, 1884-89. 8 vols.

362. Wood, William, ed. *The Logs of the Conquest of Canada* (Publications of the Champlain Society, Vol. 4). Toronto: Champlain Society, 1909.
363. Wright, J. Leitch, Jr. *Anglo-Spanish Rivalry in North America.* Athens: University of Georgia Press, 1971.
364. Young, Chester Raymond. "The Effects of the French and Indian War on Civilian Life in the Frontier Counties of Virginia, 1754-1763." Doctoral dissertation, Vanderbilt University, 1969.
365. Ziebarth, Robert E. "The Role of New York in King George's War, 1739-1748." Doctoral dissertation, New York University, 1972.
366. Zoltvany, Yves F. "New France and the West, 1701-1713." *Canadian Historical Review*, 1965, 46, 301-22.

IV

THE AMERICAN REVOLUTION

Hugh F. Rankin

The American Revolution was America's first great military emotional experience, a conflict that involved all segments of the colonial population. The military phase of that rebellion has undergone just about every pattern of historical exposure, ranging from tomes ringing in patriotism and nationalism to debunking that sometimes borders on the vicious. In a like manner, military history has ofttimes been utilized as a vehicle for national aggrandizement.

EARLY AMERICAN ACCOUNTS. In a young nation, desperate for heroes upon which to hang their stars, there were few bad soldiers or lost battles, merely unfortunate leaders and temporary setbacks. The American Revolution provided a strong impetus to historical writing in the young United States for military exploits furnished an initial foundation for national braggadocio.

Among the first to thrust themselves into this national exuberance were Doctor David Ramsay (234) and the Reverend William Gordon (119), although Orin Libby has indicted both for copying at great length from the *Annual Register*. Yet perhaps too much as been made of these charges of plagiarism in the writings of early American historians. For one thing, plagiarism was not so heinous an intellectual crime in the late eighteenth century as it became in later years. And it should be noted that these people considered the *Annual Register* to be a prime source of information. It seems a shame that Gordon did not follow through with his original concept, for he did correspond with the military leaders of the Revolution to gain their views in those engagements in which they participated. Unfortunately he carried his plagiarism beyond the periodical in that he lifted much of his material from David Ramsay's *History of the Revolution in South Carolina* (235) which he borrowed in manuscript and never acknowledged as a source. The good preacher seems to have altered his manuscript because of the spirit of the times; neither England nor the United States was in a mood for an impartial account of the Revolution. After Gordon's book was published, John Adams wryly commented, "His Object was profit. He was told that his book would not sell if printed according to his manuscript . . . Had the original manuscript been printed, the work would have appeared very differently."

100

Ramsay, who might have added much from his own experiences, followed the same approach as Gordon, while Mercy Otis Warren's (296) account of the struggle is steeped in bias and patriotic overtones, necessary ingredients for a young country with ambitions. This early romantic surge reached its climax in the writings of Mason Locke "Parson" Weems, whose enthusiastic (and often fictional) biographies of George Washington and Francis Marion were so encased in romantic froth that they suggested the author relied more heavily on his vivid imagination than the sources. Peter Horry, who rode with Marion, did an account of the life of the partisan leader which Weems reworked with ruffles and flourishes. Perhaps Horry expressed a critique of most of the historical writings of that early period when he reviewed Weem's revision and sadly noted, "Most certainly, 'tis not my history but your romance."

Not until the latter half of the nineteenth century did American writers attempt to push aside the veil of national pride and seek a true picture. But even then such writers as George Bancroft structured their accounts on a nationalistic base, seemingly finding it difficult to remove the romantic and patriotic varnish from their subjects. But again, it should be noted that the country, flushed with growing pains, needed heroes in its past and a heroic tradition on which to base its future.

MODERN SCHOLARSHIP. Modern works tend to be either analytical or narrative with a greater examination of the documents reflecting both views of military actions. In modern general histories of the American Revolution there has been a tendency to meld political, social, and economic factors into the web of the military story. Yet some modern studies, because of the tyranny of word limitation imposed by the rising cost of printing, have often confined themselves to straight narratives of military actions with little emphasis on their impact in other areas. But military history can never entirely be divorced from political, economic, and social aspects, especially in those nations whose lands have become battlefields. The best general works are Alden (5), Miller (198), and Higginbotham (141).

GENERAL BIBLIOGRAPHICAL MATERIALS. There are no bibliographies devoted exclusively to the military history of the American Revolution, although all modern studies contain extensive listings of the sources examined or bibliographical essays.

In any undertaking of a military history of the Revolution, a good initial point of departure is Grace Gardner Griffin et al., *Writings in American History* (130). Chapter VII of Henry P. Beers, *Bibliographies in American History* (26) confines itself to military and naval history. Although not designed as a primary bibliograpical guide, volume VI of Justin Winsor's *Narrative and Critical History* (307) should not be by-passed just because of its age. The notes and bibliographical essays can prove to be a gold mine in recalling often overlooked items, including long forgotten pamphlets. Among the several older bibliographical works that may be checked at the beginning of a project are Conrad H. Lanza, *List of Books on Military History and Related Subjects* (169), and Joseph H. Sabin and others, *A Dictionary of Books Relating to America* (247). Nor should *American Diaries: An Annotated Bibliography of American Diaries Prior to the Year 1861* (192) be overlooked. Newspapers are often a source for battlefield accounts, albeit exaggerated, for their only reporters were officers who wrote back from the army. For guidance in this area check Clarence S. Brigham, *History and Bibliography of American Newspapers, 1690-1800* (48).

British military accounts are well covered in William A. Foote, "The British Army in the Eighteenth Century," in *A Guide to the Sources of British Military History* (142). In a like manner, should there be a need to consult British manuscript sources, there is B. R. Crick and Miriam Alman, *A Guide to Manuscripts Relating to America in Great Britain and Ireland* (75). There is no comparable volume for the United States, although such manuscript depositories as the Library of Congress, the National Archives, the William L. Clements, the Huntington, and the New York Public Libraries, along with a number of other libraries and state archival departments have partial or complete guides to their collections. A number of these, however, are out of date.

JOURNALS. There are no periodicals devoted exclusively to the military history of the American Revolution, although both *Military Affairs* (196) and *The Military Collector and Historian* (197) often contain articles of interest, although in the latter most discussions are slanted more toward the uniforms, equipment, and weapons of the period. The *Guide* of the American Historical Association (9) to dissertations in progress and completed is more than valuable. As a suggestion to the serious researcher or the buff, early volumes of the state and regional historical societies should not be overlooked, for they contain much on the Revolution both in primary and secondary materials, with perhaps the *Pennsylvania Magazine of History and Biography* (225) being the most fruitful. Particularly significant are some of those magazines that have since ceased publication, the old *Journal of American History* (157), the *Magazine of American History* (184), and the *Historical Magazine* (143). And among the unlikely periodicals no longer publishing are such magazines as the *Orion* (215), the *Magnolia* (185), and the *Southern Literary Messenger* (261) which sometimes have useful material tucked away within their pages. Several contemporary English periodicals and publications should be kept in mind: the *Annual Register* (13), the *Gentleman's Magazine* (115), the *Remembrancer* (240), the *London Magazine* (174), and the *Political Magazine* (231).

REPRINTS. There has been a rash of reprints of earlier publications on the Revolution, the most extensive project so far is that by the Arno Press of the New York *Times*. Howard K. Rice, Jr., in his revised translation and edition of Chastellux's *Travels* (56), provides an excellent model for those inclined to travel the same path.

GENERAL WORKS. Among those older works that should be looked into when studying battlefield actions are those of Dawson (84) and Carrington (54), although some of their interpretations have been revised by later studies. And although published just before the outbreak of the Civil War, *Lossing's Pictorial Field Book* (175) still contains interesting material, especially those sketches he made of revolutionary relics that were still extant when he made his swing around the country. Fisher's two-volume *Struggle for American Independence* (98), although published in 1908, still makes for good reading, for it contains more detail than many later volumes on the war. Modern studies include those by Belcher (27), Ward (294), Alden (5), Mackesy (182), Miller (198), Lancaster (168), Peckham (223), Rankin (236), Wallace (292), and Higginbotham (141). But not all limit themselves to military actions, but weave social, political, and economic factors into the whole fabric. The encyclopedic volume by Boatner (42) is a valuable quick reference work and will save many a trip to the library.

For those who enjoy reading military history as told by the participants there are several choices: Commager and Morris (74), Scheer and Rankin (250), Dorson (89), and Rankin (236). Cast in a similar mold is Moore (203), who made his selections from contemporary newspapers.

MILITARY BIOGRAPHY. As might be expected, George Washington has long been a favorite subject for biographers. Some have been laudatory, others cast in a debunking vein. Those by Douglas Southall Freeman (108) and James Flexner (102) are multivolumed and the most complete, covering all facets of the general's life, although Freeman's style akes it appear that the author is standing at attention and saluting. Two short interpretations by Cunliffe (77) and Wright (309) are well worth reading. Other generals have been studied, some more than one time. It should be pointed out that a few of the older works are more valuable for the researcher than modern studies in that they often carry letters and documents in full, some of which are no longer extant. For Charles Lee there are Alden (6) and Patterson (218); Greene (128) and Thayer (279) on Nathanael Greene; Patterson (219) on Gates; Lossing (176) and Gerlach (116) on Philip Schuyler; Stille (265), Preston (232), Wildes (304), and Tucker (283) on Anthony Wayne; Martyn (191) on Artemus Ward; Arnold (14), Wallace (293), Boylan (46), and Flexner (103) on Benedict Arnold; Drake (90) and Callahan (51) on Henry Knox; Graham (124) and Higginbotham (140) on Daniel Morgan; Kapp (159) and Palmer (217) on Steuben; Valentine (287) on Stirling; and Amory (10) and Whittemore (301) on John Sullivan. Shortly after the Revolution and through the first half of the nineteenth century there were a number of biographies of Israel Putnam, but there are no modern studies, apparently because of the realization that "Old Put" was more of a folk hero than a battlefield general of any real significance.

A number of biographies on lesser military figures have been done. These include Broadus Mitchell's (200) comprehensive study of Alexander Hamilton; Esther Forbes (105) and Goss (120) on Paul Revere; Pell (224), Holbrook (144), and Jellison (151) on Ethan Allan; James (148), Pease (221), and Bakeless (18) on George Rogers Clark; Jacobs (147) on James Wilkinson; Billias (33) on John Glover; Lovell (177) on Israel Angell; and Rossman (246) on Thomas Mifflin.

For foreign military men who fought with the Americans during this war there are Kapp (160) on Kalb, Haiman (135) on Kosciuszko, Manning (188) on Pulaski, and Kite (164) on Duportail.

Partisan leaders have been done by Gregorie (129) and Bass (22) on Thomas Sumter; Bass (24) and Rankin (237) on Francis Marion; Davidson (81) on William Lee Davidson; and Robinson (244) on William R. Davie.

George Billias (34, 35) has edited volumes of short interpretive essays on American and British generals, each by a different author.

Modern studies of British generals include Alden (7) on Thomas Gage;

Troyer Anderson (11) and Ira Gruber (131) on the Howes; Willcox (306) on Clinton; the Wickwires (302) on Cornwallis; Gerson (118) and Huddleston (146) on Burgoyne; and Bradley (47) on Guy Carleton. Other than the work on Banastre Tarleton by Bass (23) there has been little done on the lesser figures.

Although not biographies, there are two listings for officers that are valuable, Ford (106) for the British, and Heitmann (139) for the Continental Army, although both are not complete and should be brought up to date.

BATTLES AND CAMPAIGNS. In general there have been but few studies of campaigns, as most studies have concentrated on specific battles. Again, Dawson (84) and Carrington (54) may be used as a point of departure. For the early stages of the war there are works by French (109, 110), Murdock (207), Tourtellot (280), and Coburn (68), although the latter's study of Lexington has good information buried under a layer of patriotism. For the activity around Boston there are Frothingham (113), Murdock (206), and Ketchum (163); while French (112) has a slim volume on the taking of Ticonderoga.

For the fighting around New York there are Bliven (39, 40), Johnston (153, 154), and Sklarsky (255). Trenton and Princeton have attracted the attention of a number of writers, including Stryker (272), Bill (30), Smith (259), and Collins (73). Stryker (271) and Smith (258) have studied the battle of Monmouth. Stryker (273) has also done the fall of the forts on the Delaware River. Valley Forge has been studied by Bill (32), Reed (239), and Stoudt (269).

The Canadian campaigns have received their share of attention with the different facets of those invasions worked over by Smith (256), Codman (69), Bird (36), Dabney (79), Bennett (28), and Nickerson (212).

Treacy (281) is the only work on the southern campaign, although Davis (83) has published the Cowpens to Guilford campaign. The old standby, Draper (91), is still the best thing on King's Mountain. Yorktown has come in for its share of attention, with Arthur (15), Chidsey (60), Davis (82), Fleming (99), and Johnston (155) all making contributions.

For casualty figures there is a compilation by Peckham (222) which lists the losses in 1331 military and 215 naval engagements. So far nothing has surpassed volume III of Fortescue's *History of the British Army* (107) for an overall view of British actions. And British accounts should be supplemented with the study of the organization of the British army by Curtis (78).

UNIT HISTORIES AND PERIPHERAL STUDIES. There are no unit histories of any significance as such, that is of a particular battalion or regiment (the designations were used interchangeably among contemporaries). The nearest thing is the study by Billias (33) of Glover and his Marblehead group. Works that fall into the broad meaning of this category are those of the Delaware and North Carolina Continentals by Ward (295) and Rankin (238). Berg (29) has a compilation of the various state regiments and other units, but it is incomplete, although providing a point of departure for more intense studies. Montross (202) uses the Continental Army as a core around which to construct his military history of the Revolution, while Mitchell (201) has an overall study.

Peripheral works involving the whole or part of the Continentals include such things as Hatch (137) on the organization, Johnson (152) on the Commissariat, and Bowman (45) on morale. As for weapons and accoutrements, a number of significant articles may be found in the *Military Collector and Historian* (197), although there are volumes on the subject authored by Peterson (228) and Neumann (209).

Another area in which the army was concerned was mutiny, with Van Doren (288) reporting the mutinies of the Pennsylvania and New Jersey Lines. And although Benedict Arnold and John André are the super spies of the Revolution, others have studied lesser figures, including French (111), Van Doren (289), and Pennypacker (226).

And there have been no studies on the private soldier of the revolutionary army since Bolton (43), now badly out of date. Quarles (233), Neel (208), White (298), and Kaplan (158) have all worked on the question of black participation on the Revolution. Dandridge (80) and Metzger (195) have studied prisoners of war. Other than histories of British Regiments, Katcher (161) has an encyclopedic volume of the British, Provincial, and Hessian units; while Shy (253) discusses the British Army prior to the Revolution.

REGIONAL AND STATE HISTORIES. Alden's (4) account of the Revolution in the south covers more than just military affairs. Other works on the Southern Campaign are Treacy (281), Agniel (3), and Arthur (15). There are few state histories of the area's military participation in the Revolution larger than pamphlet size. New Jersey has attracted the efforts of Lundin (179), Bill (31), and Fleming (100); while Taylor (277) and New comer (211) studied Massachusetts. Coleman (71) did a history of Georgia in the Revolution.

Stone's (267) earlier work on the frontier has been updated by Sosin (260) and Van Every (290). Related studies are Graymont (125) on the Iroquois and O'Donnell (214) on the southern Indians.

TACTICS AND TRAINING. The primary military knowledge utilized in the training of troops on both sides customarily was gleaned from European military manuals. Many Americans who fancied themselves possessed of a military mind often studied the writings of Frederick the Great and in the manuscript letters of the age there are frequent references to the "King of Prussia." One would guess that James Wolfe's *Instructions for Young Officers* (308) was used rather extensively prior to the war, but this is a guess in that few military leaders made reference to the manuals in which they sought their information. With the onset of the fighting Timothy Pickering (230) composed *An Easy Plan of Discipline for a Militia* in 1775 which was adopted by Massachusetts in 1776, and was widely used throughout the American army until replaced by Steuben's famous "blue book" (263) in 1779. One primary text used rather extensively throughout the war was *Bland's Treatise of Military Discipline* (38), published in many English editions and reprinted by the Americans during the war, with the plates for the edition published in New York in 1775 engraved by Paul Revere. *A New System of Military Discipline* by Richard, Earl of Cavan (242), published in Philadelphia in 1776, was used by Nathanael Greene.

Most biographies are concerned with the strategy and tactics of their subjects. Palmer (216) in his study of Washington's strategy gives the general high marks.

FRENCH PARTICIPATION. General works covering French participation include volumes by Bonsal (44), Stone (266), Perkins (227), Merlant (193), and Balch (19), although several contain material other than military. Much of the interest in French participation is centered on the activities of the youthful and colorful Lafayette. Brand Whitlock's (299) old biography still has merit, but it has been surpassed in every way by the masterful and multivolumed work by Gottschalk (121, 122, 123). Doniol (88), Noailles (213), and Merlant (194) have volumes on the soldiers and sailors of France who fought in the American Revolution. Whitridge (300) has a biography of Rochambeau, and there are the memoirs of Deux-Ponts (87) and Dumas (92).

Two contemporary accounts that make for good reading have recently been published. One is that of the Baron Ludwig von Closen, a German who served as an aide to Rochambeau, whose journal was translated and annotated by Acomb (1). A beautiful printing job is that edited by Rice and Brown (241) on the campaigns of the French army, the first volume made up of itineraries and maps, and the second composed of the journals of three French officers.

THE HESSIANS. The two standard works on the Hessians for many years have been the volumes by Lowell (178) and von Eelking (93), the latter a translation by J. G. Rosengarten of the two-volume German work published in Hanover in 1863. There have been translations of the German documents that Lowell used in writing his *Hessians*. In 1891 William Lee Stone (268) published *Letters of Brunswick and Hessian Officers During the American Revolution* in Munsell's Historical Series. Because several of the letters had been but briefly paraphrased, some had been overlooked, and there were errors in translation Ray W. Pettingill (229) translated them anew in 1924 and republished them under the title, *Letters from America, 1776-1779*. In 1876 George Washington Greene (127) published *The German Element in the War of American Independence*, containing three essays on Steuben, Johann Kalb, and German mercenaries.

In recent years there have been several more excellent volumes of letters and journals. Two of the best of these have been translated and edited by Uhlendorf from the Von Jungkenn Papers in the William L. Clements Library at the University of Michigan. The first of these, the *Siege of Charleston* (285), contains three diaries by officers and five letters to Jungkenn describing the progress of the siege. Even more interesting is the collection of confidential journals and letters of Adjutant General Major Baurmeister, *Revolution in America* (284). And one should not overlook Uhlendorf's brilliant introductory essay, "The Hessians in America," in the latter. And reading Brown's (49) translation and editing of the Baroness von Riedesel's journals is like finding a lace valentine in an old cartridge box.

THE LOYALISTS. The loyalists have attracted the attention of many historians, but more have been interested in the philosophical and political activities than the military. Callahan (52) and Chidsey (57) have works on the military activities of loyalists, while Smith's (257) *Loyalists and Redcoats* is excellent for the role that they were to play in British strategy. Sabine's (248) *American Loyalists*, published in 1847, contains a number of biographical sketches, but a number of military leaders, especially those active in the south, are missing. Swiggett (274) covers much of the frontier activities of loyalists, while the *Collections* of the New York Historical Society for 1884-1885 contain the journals of Stephen Kemble (162), a loyalist officer.

NAVAL AFFAIRS. Older histories of the Continental Navy were done by Paullin (220), Allen (8), and Mahan (186). More recent works have been done by Miller (199), while the study by Coggins (70) covers ships, seamen, weapons, and tactics. Mahan (187) has a work on the Royal Navy during this period and there are later volumes by James (149), Stout (270), and Marcus (189). Detailed accounts of a number of naval engagements are given in Dawson (84) and Lewis (173), while Mackesy (182) ties in the operations of the navy with land forces. Specific engagements are by Jones (156) on the activities of the French fleet during the siege of Savannah, while Larrabee (170) tells the story of the battle off the Capes of the Chesapeake during the Yorktown campaign.

Much naval history can be gleaned from the biographies and documents now in print. Barrow's (21) life of Richard, Lord Howe, and Anderson (11) on the command of the Howe brothers have been relegated to second best by a similar study by Gruber (131). Among the printed sources useful for a study of the British Navy are the papers of Graves (55), Rodney (205), and Sandwich (20). Although Beatson's *Naval and Military Memoirs* (25) is old, it is still useful for amphibious operations. The journal of Ambrose Serle (251) has much to offer as a civilian view of naval operations by Lord Howe's secretary.

For the Americans, Clark has done biographies of Nicholas Biddle (63) and John Barry (64), Gurn (132) has also written on Barry, Ferguson (96) on Truxton, Howard (145) on Seth Harding, while Wagner (291) has covered David Bushnell and his submarine. Samuel Eliot Morison's (204) biography of John Paul Jones has replaced the older studies of that colorful figure.

For peripheral activities there are the studies of privateers by Clark (62) and Maclay (183). Harrison Bird (37) has studied the naval engagement on Lake Champlain, while Clark (65) and Knox (165) have written on the naval operations under the command of George Washington. The collection of Documents (64) now being published by the Department of the Navy and originally edited by Clark promises to offer much in the way of source materials for work on the Continental Navy.

CARTOGRAPHY. Carrington's little *Battle Maps and Charts of the American Revolution* (53) designed to accompany his *Battles* (54) is still useful. A number of contemporary publications were used by the military, among them Jeffrey's *American Atlas* (150) of several editions, and the Sayer *American Military Pocket Atlas* (249), the latter often referred to as the "Holster Atlas" inasmuch as it was designed to be carried by mounted officers. The above aids were based on information collected before 1775. In

1777 William Faden (95) brought out his *North American Pocket Atlas*, encompassing fairly accurate military surveys. A number of these maps provided the basis for Faden's later work in 1793, *Atlas of the Battles of the American Revolution* (94).

Periodicals of the day, the *Annual Register* (13), *Gentleman's Magazine* (115), *Political Magazine* (231), and the *Universal Magazine* (286) published a number of battle maps, while the *Atlantic Neptune* (15) carried a number of coastal charts.

Equally important are the maps of contemporary origin in the memoirs and accounts of Stedman (262), Tarleton (276), and Simcoe (254). Among modern works is *The Fate of a Nation* by Cumming and Rankin (76) which contains a number of contemporary maps and illustrations. *The American Campaigns of Rochambeau's Army*, edited by Rice and Brown (241), has a number of excellent line maps of march routes.

Randolph Adams (2) describes the maps used by Sir Henry Clinton, while Guthorn (133) has *British Maps of the American Revolution* as well as a study of *American Maps and Map Makers of the Revolution* (134). Although not strictly a cartographic volume, Boatner's (41) *Landmarks of the American Revolution* has its uses.

CONTEMPORARY ACCOUNTS. Many of the British accounts published following the war were written in a defensive vein, yet despite their justification of mistakes they are still useful. These include narratives by Stedman (262), Tarleton (276), Simcoe (254), and Clinton (67), although the account by Clinton was not published until the twentieth century. Tarleton's (276) *Campaigns* should be used in conjunction with the *Strictures* of Roderick Mackenzie (181) who was angry with and who disagreed with many of the Green Dragoon's claims. The pamphlet war between Clinton and Cornwallis attempting to place responsibility for the Yorktown disaster has been collected in a two-volume edition by Benjamin Franklin Stevens (264). Then there are the diaries of John André (12), Frederick Mackenzie (180), and Archibald Robertson (243) for the day-to-day experiences of British officers. The *Journal* (167) and *Memoir* (166) of Roger Lamb are valuable for the observations of a noncommissioned officer, although it should be kept in mind that Sergeant Lamb was better educated than the average British soldier of his day.

There are a whole spate of personal accounts written by American participants. William Heath, who refers to himself as "our General" throughout his *Memoirs* (138), has been reprinted several times. There have been interesting accounts left by Samuel B. Webb (297), John Trumbull (282), and James Wilkinson (305). For the later stages of the war there are Henry "Lighthorse Harry" Lee's *Memoirs of the War in the Southern Department*, the best version that edited by his son, Robert E. Lee (172), while Gerson (117) has the best biography of the dashing cavalry leader.

For two delightful reminiscences by men of the ranks, one is urged to read the *Narrative* of Joseph Plumb Martin as edited by George F. Scheer (190) as well as the memories of James Collins (72), although the latter is difficult to come by. Equally interesting is the *Journal* of Surgeon James Thacher (278).

It should be noted that as the war moved south in 1780, personal accounts are not so numerous, perhaps because of a lack of education in the region, or possibly because the war was no longer the great adventure it had been during its earlier stages. Some of the older magazines such as the *Historical Magazine* (143) and the *Magazine of American History* (184), as well as the early issues of the *Pennsylvania Magazine of History and Biography* (225) contain shorter diaries, journals, and reminiscences. The *Journal* of Lieutenant William Seymour (252) of the Delaware Continentals is useful, but his battle accounts are sketchy and he seemed more interested in the number of miles he marched each day than other events.

SUGGESTIONS FOR FURTHER INVESTIGATION. Biographies are needed for many of the lesser military figures of the war, along with studies of the common soldier on both sides. In fact, some of the older biographies of major figures could be reworked in the light of new materials that have been uncovered or the later publications that could add perspectives to the situations in which these individuals found themselves. There is a need to look at the workings of the state governments behind the military with regard to their logistical and general support, perhaps even of in-depth studies of such special organizations as the Boards of War established in several states. The same might be attempted for those special wartime agencies created by the Continental Congress. There is a real need to study the Continental units of each state as well as for a work on the Continental Army. And because of the great faith in the citizen soldier held by the American public there should be investigations as to how the militia were organized, trained, and supplied, and how they behaved on the battlefield to clear up many misconceptions as to the value of this group. There is more than enough material to make such studies.

There is a need for a detailed study of logistics and the problems concerned therewith both on the Contenental and State levels. And there should be investigations of strategy and tactics and the changes dictated by the American terrain.

Although the loyalists have been investigated many times, there should be more on the military activities of these people. This becomes particularly important in the light of the intensity of the vicious little civil wars that raged in New York, the Carolinas, and Georgia. And there are no modern studies of such loyalists as Tarleton's British Legion (Bass [23] worked on Tarleton), Simcoe's Queen's Rangers, or the Volunteers of Ireland.

BIBLIOGRAPHY

1. Acomb, Evelyn M., trans. and ed. *The Revolutionary Journal of Baron Ludwig Von Closen, 1780-1783*. Chapel Hill: University of North Carolina Press, 1958.
2. Adams, Randolph G. *British Headquarters Maps and Sketches Used by Sir Henry Clinton*. Ann Arbor: William L. Clements, 1928.

3. Agniel, Lucien. *The Late Affair Has Almost Broke My Heart; the American Revolution in the South, 1780-1781.* Riverside, Connecticut: Chatham Press, 1972.

4. Alden, John R. *The South in the Revolution, 1763-1789.* Baton Rouge: Louisiana State University Press, 1957.

5. Alden, John Richard. *The American Revolution, 1775-1783.* New York: Harper, 1954.

6. Alden, John Richard. *General Charles Lee: Traitor or Patriot?* Baton Rouge: Louisiana State University Press, 1951.

7. Alden, John Richard. *General Gage in America: Being Principally His Role in the American Revolution.* Baton Rouge: Louisiana State University Press, 1948.

8. Allen, Gardner W. *A Naval History of the American Revolution.* Williamstown, Mass.: Corner House, 1970 (1913). 2 vols.

9. American Historical Association. *List of Doctoral Dissertations in History now in Progress at Universities in the United States.* Washington: American Historial Association, 1902- .

10. Amory, Thomas Coffin. *The Military Services and Public Life of Major-General John Sullivan of the American Revolutionary Army.* Port Washington, New York: Kennikat Press, 1968 (1868).

11. Anderson, Troyer Steele. *The Command of the Howe Brothers during the American Revolution.* New York: Oxford University Press, 1936.

12. André, John. *André's Journal: An Authentic Record of the Movements and Engagements of the British Army in America from June 1777 to November 1778 as Recorded from Day to Day by Major John André.* Edited by Henry Cabot Lodge. Boston: Bibliophile Society, 1903.

13. *Annual Register.* London, 1758-

14. Arnold, Isaac Newton. *The Life of Benedict Arnold: His Patriotism and His Treason.* Chicago: Jansen, McClung & Co., 1880.

15. Arthur, Robert. *The End of a Revolution.* New York: Vantage Press, 1966.

16. *Atlantic Neptune.* London, 1774-1781.

17. Bakeless, John E. *Turncoats, Traitors, and Heroes.* Philadelphia: Lippincott, 1960.

18. Bakeless, John Edwin. *Background to Glory: The Life of George Rogers Clark.* Philadelphia: Lippincott, 1957.

19. Balch, Thomas. *The French in America during the War of Independence of the United States, 1777-1783.* Philadelphia: Porter & Coates, 1891-95. 2 vols.

20. Barnes, R. G. and J. H. Owen, eds. *The Sandwich Papers.* London: Navy Records Society, 1932-38. 4 vols.

21. Barrow, Sir John. *Life of Richard, Earl Howe.* London: Murray, 1838.

22. Bass, Robert Duncan. *Gamecock: The Life and Campaigns of General Thomas Sumter.* New York: Holt, Rinehart and Winston, 1961.

23. Bass, Robert Duncan. *The Green Dragoon: The Lives of Banastre Tarleton and Mary Robinson.* New York: Holt, 1957.

24. Bass, Robert Duncan. *Swamp Fox: The Life and Campaigns of General Francis Marion.* New York: Holt, 1959.

25. Beatson, Robert. *Naval and Military Memoirs of Great Britain from 1727 to 1783*. London: Longman, Hurst, Rees and Orme, 1804. 6 vols.
26. Beers, Henry P., ed. *Bibliographies in American History: Guide to Materials for Research*. New York: H. W. Wilson, 1942.
27. Belcher, Henry. *The First American Civil War; First Period 1775-1778*. London: Macmillan, 1911. 2 vols.
28. Bennett, Clarence E. *Advance and Retreat to Saratoga in the American Revolution*. Boston: Gregg, 1972 (1927).
29. Berg, Fred Anderson. *Encyclopedia of Continental Army Units: Battalions, Regiments and Independent Corps*. Harrisburg: Stackpole, 1972.
30. Bill, Alfred Hoyt. *The Campaign of Princeton, 1776-1777*. Princeton: Princeton University Press, 1948.
31. Bill, Alfred Hoyt. *New Jersey and the Revolutionary War*. Princeton: van Nostrand, 1964.
32. Bill, Alfred Hoyt. *Valley Forge: The Making of an Army*. New York: Harper, 1952.
33. Billias, George Athan. *General John Glover and His Marblehead Mariners*. New York: Holt, 1960.
34. Billias, George Athan, ed. *George Washington's Generals*. New York: Morrow, 1964.
35. Billias, George Athan. *George Washington's Opponents: British Generals and Admirals in the American Revolution*. New York: Morrow, 1969.
36. Bird, Harrison. *March to Saratoga: General Burgoyne and the American Campaign, 1777*. New York: Oxford University Press, 1963.
37. Bird, Harrison. *Navies in the Mountains: The Battles on the Waters of Lake Champlain and Lake George, 1609-1814*. New York: Oxford University Press, 1962.
38. Bland, Major-General Humphrey. *A Treatise of Military Discipline, in which Is Laid Down and Explained the Duty of the Officer and Soldier thro' the Several Branches of the Service*. London: S. Buckley, 1727.
39. Bliven, Bruce. *Battle for Manhattan*. New York: Holt, 1956.
40. Bliven, Bruce. *Under the Guns: New York, 1775-1776*. New York: Harper, 1972.
41. Boatner, Mark M. *Landmarks of the American Revolution: A Guide to Locating and Knowing What Happened at the Sites of Independence*. Harrisburg: Stackpole, 1973.
42. Boatner, Mark Mayo. *Encyclopedia of the American Revolution*. New York: McKay, 1966.
43. Bolton, Charles Knowles. *The Private Soldier under Washington*. London: George Newnes, 1902.
44. Bonsal, Stephen. *When the French Were Here: A Narrative of the Sojourn of the French Forces in America, and Their Contribution to the Yorktown Campaign*. Garden City: Doubleday, Doran and Company, 1945.
45. Bowman, Allen. *The Morale of the American Revolutionary Army*. Washington: American Council on Public Affairs, 1943.

46. Boylan, Brian Richard. *Benedict Arnold, the Dark Eagle.* New York: Norton, 1973.
47. Bradley, Arthur Granville. *Sir Guy Carleton (Lord Dorchester).* Toronto: Toronto University Press, 1966.
48. Brigham, Clarence S. *History and Bibliography of American Newspapers.* Worcester, Mass.: American Antiquarian Society, 1947. 2 vols.
49. Brown, Marvin L., trans. and ed. *Baroness von Riedesel and the American Revolution: Journal and Correspondence of a Tour of Duty, 1776-1783.* Chapel Hill: University of North Carolina Press, 1965.
50. Brown, Wallace. *The Good Americans: The Loyalists in the American Revolution.* New York: Morrow, 1969.
51. Callahan, North. *Henry Knox: George Washington's General.* New York: Rinehart, 1958.
52. Callahan, North. *Royal Raiders: The Tories of the American Revolution.* Indianapolis: Bobbs-Merrill, 1963.
53. Carrington, Henry B. *Battle Maps and Charts of the American Revolution.* New York: A. S. Barnes, 1881.
54. Carrington, Henry B. *Battles of the American Revolution, 1775-1781.* New York: A. S. Barnes, 1876.
55. Chadwick, French E., ed. *The Graves Papers Relating to the Naval Operations of the Yorktown Campaign, July to October, 1781.* New York: Devinne Press, 1916.
56. Chastellux, Marquis De. *Travels in North America in the Years 1780, 1781 and 1782.* Translated and edited by Howard C. Rice, Jr. Chapel Hill: University of North Carolina Press, 1963. 2 vols.
57. Chidsey, Donald Barr. *The Loyalists: The Story of those Americans Who Fought against Independence.* New York: Crown, 1973.
58. Chidsey, Donald Barr. *The Siege of Boston: An On-the-Scene Account of the Beginnings of the American Revolution.* New York: Crown, 1966.
59. Chidsey, Donald Barr. *The Tide Turns: An Informal History of the Campaign of 1776 in the American Revolution.* New York: Crown, 1966.
60. Chidsey, Donald Barr. *Victory at Yorktown.* New York: Crown, 1962.
61. Chidsey, Donald Barr. *The War in the North: An Informal History of the American Revolution in and near Canada.* New York: Crown, 1967.
62. Clark, William Bell. *Ben Franklin's Privateers: A Naval Epic of the American Revolution.* Baton Rouge: Louisiana State University Press, 1956.
63. Clark, William Bell. *Captain Dauntless, the Story of Nicholas Biddle of the Continental Navy.* Baton Rouge: Louisiana State University Press, 1949.
64. Clark, William Bell. *Gallant John Barry, 1745-1803.* New York: Macmillan, 1938.
65. Clark, William Bell. *George Washington's Navy: Being an Account*

of His Excellency's Fleet in New England Waters. Baton Rouge: Louisiana State University Press, 1960.

66. Clark, William Bell, et al., eds. *Naval Documents of the American Revolution.* Washington: Government Printing Office, 1964- .

67. Clinton, Sir Henry. *The American Rebellion.* Edited by William B. Willcox. Hamden: Archon Books, 1971 (1954).

68. Coburn, Frank W. *The Battle of April 19, 1775.* Lexington, Mass.: Lexington Historical Society, 1912.

69. Codman, John. *Arnold's Expedition to Quebec.* New York: Macmillan 1902.

70. Coggins, Jack. *Ships and Seamen of the American Revolution: Vessels, Crews, Weapons, Gear, Naval Tactics, and Actions of the War for Independence.* Harrisburg: Stackpole, 1969.

71. Coleman, Kenneth. *The American Revolution in Georgia.* Athens: University of Georgia Press, 1958.

72. Collins, James P. *Autobiography of a Revolutionary Soldier.* Edited by John M. Roberts. Clinton, La.: Feliciana Democrat, 1859.

73. Collins, Varnum Lansing, ed. *A Brief Narrative of the Ravages of the British and Hessians at Princeton in 1776-1777.* New York: New York Times, 1968 (1906).

74. Commager, Henry Steele, and Richard B. Morris, eds. *The Spirit of Seventy-Six.* Indianapolis: Bobbs-Merrill, 1958.

75. Crick, B. R., and Miriam Alman. *A Guide to Manuscripts Relating to America in Great Britain and Ireland.* London: Oxford University Press, 1961.

76. Cumming, William P., and Hugh F. Rankin. *Fate of a Nation.* London: Phaidon, 1975.

77. Cunliffe, Marcus. *George Washington: Man and Monument.* Boston: Little, Brown, 1958.

78. Curtis, Edward Ely. *The Organization of the British Army in the American Revolution.* St. Clair Shores, Mich.: Scholarly Press, 1972 (1926).

79. Dabney, William M. *After Saratoga: The Story of the Convention Army.* Albuquerque: University of New Mexico Press, 1954.

80. Dandridge, Danske. *American Prisoners of the Revolution.* Charlottesville, Va.: The Michie Company, 1911.

81. Davidson, Chalmers. *Piedmont Partisan: The Life and Times of Brigadier-General William Lee Davidson.* 2d ed. Davidson, N.C.: Davidson College, 1968.

82. Davis, Burke. *The Campaign that Won America: The Story of Yorktown.* New York: Dial, 1970.

83. Davis, Burke. *The Cowpens-Guilford Courthouse Campaign.* Philadelphia: Lippincott, 1962.

84. Dawson, Henry B. *Battles of the United States by Sea and Land.* New York: Johnson, Fry, 1858.

85. Decker, Malcolm. *Benedict Arnold, Son of the Havens.* New York: Antiquarian Press, 1961 (1932).

86. De Peyster, John Watts. *The Burgoyne Campaign of July-October, 1777.* Philadelphia: L. R. Hammersley, 1883.

87. Deux-Ponts, William D. *My Campaign in America.* Translated by Samuel A. Greene. Boston: J. K. Wiggin and W. P. Lunt, 1868.
88. Doniol, Henri. *Historie de la Participation de la France à l'établissement des Etats-Unis d'Amerique.* Paris: Imprimerie Nationale, 1884-92. 6 vols.
89. Dorson, Richard M., ed. *American Rebels.* New York: Pantheon, 1953.
90. Drake, Francis S. *The Life and Correspondence of Major-General Henry Knox.* Boston: John Wilson and Son, 1873.
91. Draper, Lyman C. *King's Mountain and Its Heroes: History of the Battle of King's Mountain, October 7th, 1780, and the Events which Led to it.* Cincinnati: Peter G. Thompson, 1881.
92. Dumas, Mathieu. *Memoirs of His Own Time.* Philadelphia: Lea & Blanchard, 1839. 2 vols.
93. Eelking, Max von. *The German Allied Troops in the North American War of Independence, 1776-1783.* Translated and abridged by Joseph G. Rosengarten. Albany: Munsell, 1893.
94. Faden, William. *Atlas of the Battles of the American Revolution.* Reprint of 1793 edition. New York: Bartlett and Welford, 1845.
95. Faden, William. *The North American Atlas.* London, 1777.
96. Ferguson, Eugene S. *Truxton of the Constellation: The Life of Commodore Thomas Truxton, U.S. Navy, 1755-1822.* Baltimore: Johns Hopkins Press, 1956.
97. Field, I. W. "Battle of Long Island," *Memoirs of the Long Island Historical Society,* III. Brooklyn: Long Island Historical Society, 1869.
98. Fisher, Sydney George. *The Struggle for American Independence.* Philadelphia: Lippincott, 1908. 2 vols.
99. Fleming, Thomas J. *Beat the Last Drum: The Siege of Yorktown, 1781.* New York: St. Martin's, 1963.
100. Fleming, Thomas J. *The Forgotten Victory: The Battle for New Jersey, 1780.* New York: Reader's Digest Press, 1973.
101. Fleming, Thomas J. *Now We Are Enemies.* New York: St. Martin's, 1960.
102. Flexner, James Thomas. *George Washington in the American Revolution (1775-1783).* Boston: Little, Brown, 1968.
103. Fleming, Thomas J. *The Traitor and the Spy: Benedict Arnold and John André.* New York: Harcourt, Brace, 1953.
104. Footner, Hulbert. *Sailor of Fortune: The Life and Adventures of Commodore Barney, U.S.N.* New York: Harper, 1940.
105. Forbes, Esther. *Paul Revere and the World He Lived in.* Boston: Houghton Mifflin, 1942.
106. Ford, Worthington Chauncey. *British Officers Serving in the American Revolution, 1774-1783.* Brooklyn: Historical Printing Club, 1897.
107. Fortescue, Sir John. *History of the British Army.* London: Macmillan, 1910-35. 13 vols.
108. Freeman, Douglas Southall. *George Washington: A Biography.* New York: Scribner, 1948-57. 7 vols.
109. French, Allen. *The Day of Lexington and Concord.* Boston: Houghton Mifflin, 1925.

110. French, Allen. *The First Year of the American Revolution.* Boston: Houghton Mifflin, 1934.
111. French, Allen. *General Gage's Informers: New Materials upon Lexington and Concord.* New York: Greenwood Press, 1968 (1932).
112. French, Allen. *The Taking of Ticonderoga in 1775: The British Story: A Study of Captors and Captives.* Cambridge: Harvard University Press, 1928.
113. Frothingham, Richard. *History of the Siege of Boston, and of the Battles of Lexington, Concord and Bunker Hill.* Boston: Little, Brown, 1872.
114. Frothingham, Thomas G. *Washington, Commander in Chief.* Boston: Houghton Mifflin, 1930.
115. *Gentleman's Magazine.* London: 1730- .
116. Gerlach, Don R. *Philip Schuyler and the American Revolution, 1733-1777.* Lincoln: University of Nebraska Press, 1964.
117. Gerson, Noel Bertram. *Light-Horse Harry: A Biography of Washington's Great Cavalryman, General Henry Lee.* Garden City, N.Y.: Doubleday, 1966.
118. Gerson, Noel Bertram. *The Man Who Lost America: A Biography of Gentleman Johnny Burgoyne.* New York: Dial Press, 1973.
119. Gordon, William. *The History of the Rise, Progress, and Establishment of the Independence of the United States of America: Including an Account of the Late War and of the Thirteen Colonies, from Their Origin to that Period.* London, 1788. 4 vols.
120. Goss, Elbridge Henry. *The Life of Colonel Paul Revere.* Boston: Joseph George Cupples, 1891. 2 vols.
121. Gottschalk, Louis R. *Lafayette and the Close of the American Revolution.* Chicago: University of Chicago Press, 1942.
122. Gottschalk, Louis R. *Lafayette Comes to America.* Chicago: University of Chicago Press, 1935.
123. Gottschalk, Louis R. *Lafayette Joins the American Army.* Chicago: University of Chicago Press, 1937.
124. Graham, James. *The Life of General Daniel Morgan, of the Virginia Line of the Army of the United States, with Portions of His Correspondence: Compiled from Authentic Sources.* New York: Derby and Jackson, 1858.
125. Graymont, Barbara. *The Iroquois in the American Revolution.* Syracuse: Syracuse University Press, 1972.
126. Greene, Francis Vinton. *The Revolutionary War and the Military Policy of the United States.* New York: Scribners, 1911.
127. Greene, George Washington. *The German Element in the War of American Independence.* New York: Hurd & Houghton, 1876.
128. Greene, George Washington. *The Life of Nathanael Greene, Major-General in the Army of the Revolution.* New York: Putnam, 1867-71. 3 vols.
129. Gregorie, Anne King. *Thomas Sumter.* Columbia, S.C.: R. L. Bryan, 1931.
130. Griffin, Grace Garner, *et. al.*, eds. *Writings on American History.* Washington: G.P.O., 1902- .
131. Gruber, Ira D. *The Howe Brothers and the American Revolution.* New York: Atheneum, 1972.

132. Gurn, Joseph. *Commodore John Barry, Father of the American Navy.* New York: P. J. Kennedy & Sons, 1933.
133. Guthorn, Peter J. *British Maps of the American Revolution.* Monmouth, N.J.: Philip Freneau Press, 1972.
134. Guthorn, Peter J. *American Maps and Map Makers of the Revolution.* Monmouth Beach, N.J.: Philip Freneau Press, 1966.
135. Haiman, Miecislaus. *Kosciuzko in the American Revolution.* New York: Polish Institute of Arts and Sciences in America, 1943.
136. Hamilton, Edward Pierce. *Fort Ticonderoga, Key to a Continent.* Boston: Little, Brown, 1964.
137. Hatch, Louis Clinton. *The Administration of the American Revolutionary Army.* New York: Longmans, Green, 1904.
138. Heath, William. *Memoirs of Major-General William Heath, by Himself, to Which Is Added the Accounts of Bunker Hill by Generals Dearborn, Lee and Wilkinson.* Edited by William Abbatt. New York: William Abbatt, 1901.
139. Heitman, Francis B. *Historical Register of Officers of the Continental Army.* Washington: Rare Book Shop Publishing Co., 1914.
140. Higginbotham, Don. *Daniel Morgan, Revolutionary Rifleman.* Chapel Hill: University of North Carolina Press, 1961.
141. Higginbotham, Don. *The War of American Independence: Military Attitudes, Policies, and Practice, 1763-1789.* New York: Macmillan, 1971.
142. Higham, Robin. *A Guide to the Sources of British Military History.* Berkeley: University of California Press, 1971.
143. *Historical Magazine.* 3d series. Boston, Jan. 1872-April 1875.
144. Holbrook, Stewart Hall. *Ethan Allen.* New York: Macmillan, 1940.
145. Howard, James Leland. *Seth Harding, Mariner: A Naval Picture of the Revolution.* New Haven: Yale University Press, 1930.
146. Huddleston, Francis Joseph. *Gentleman Johnny Burgoyne: Misadventures of an English General in the Revolution.* Indianapolis: Bobbs-Merrill, 1927.
147. Jacobs, James R. *Tarnished Warrior: Major-General James Wilkinson.* New York: Macmillan, 1938.
148. James, James Alton. *The Life of George Rogers Clark.* New York: AMS Press, 1970 (1928).
149. James, Sir William Milburne. *The British Navy in Adversity: A Study of the War for Independence.* New York: Russell and Russell, 1970 (1926).
150. Jeffreys, Thomas. *The American Atlas.* London, 1775.
151. Jellison, Charles A. *Ethan Allen: Frontier Rebel.* Syracuse: Syracuse University Press, 1969.
152. Johnson, Victor Leroy. *The Administration of the American Commissariat During the Revolutionary War.* Philadelphia: University of Pennsylvania Press, 1941.
153. Johnston, Henry P. *The Battle of Harlem Heights.* New York: Columbia University Press, 1897.
154. Johnston, Henry P. "The Campaign of 1776 Around New York and Brooklyn," *Memoirs of the Long Island Historical Society,* Vol. III. Brooklyn: Long Island Historical Society, 1878.

155. Johnston, Henry Phelps. *The Yorktown Campaign and the Surrender of Cornwallis*, 1781. New York: Harper, 1881.
156. Jones, Charles Colcock. *The Siege of Savannah by the Fleet of Count d'Estaing in 1779*. New York: New York Times, 1968 (1874).
157. *Journal of American History*. New Haven, 1907- .
158. Kaplan, Sydney. *The Black Presence in the Era of the American Revolution, 1770-1800*. New York: New York Graphic Society, 1973.
159. Kapp, Friederich. *The Life of Frederick William von Steuben, Major General in the Revolutionary Army*. New York: Mason Brothers, 1859.
160. Kapp, Friederich. *The Life of John Kalb, Major-General in the Revolutionary Army*. New York: privately printed, 1884.
161. Katcher, Philip R. N. *Encyclopedia of British, Provincial and German Army Units, 1775-1783*. Harrisburg: Stackpole, 1973.
162. Kemble, Stephen. *The Kemble Papers* (New-York Historical Society *Collections*, XVI-XVII). New York: New-York Historical Society, 1884-85. 2 vols.
163. Ketchum, Richard M. *The Battle for Bunker Hill*. Garden City: Doubleday, 1962.
164. Kite, Elizabeth Sarah. *Brigadier-General Louis Lebeque Duportail, Commandant of Engineers in the Continental Army, 1777-1783*. Baltimore: Johns Hopkins Press, 1933.
165. Knox, Dudley Wright. *The Naval Genius of George Washington*. Boston: Houghton Mifflin, 1932.
166. Lamb, R[oger]. *Memoir of His Own Life; Formerly a Sergeant in the Royal Welch Fuzileers*. Dublin: J. Jones, 1811.
167. Lamb, R[oger]. *An Original and Authentic Journal of Occurrences During the Late American War from its Commencement to the Year 1783*. Dublin: Wilkinson and Courtney, 1803.
168. Lancaster, Bruce. *From Lexington to Liberty*. Garden City, N.Y.: Doubleday, 1955.
169. Lanza, Conrad Hammond. *List of Books on Military History and Related Subjects*. Fort Leavenworth: General Service Schools Press, 1923.
170. Larrabee, Harold Atkins. *Decision at the Chesapeake*. New York: C. N. Potter, 1964.
171. Lawrence, Alexander A. *Storm over Savannah: The Story of Count d'Estaing and the Siege of the Town in 1779*. Athens: University of Georgia Press, 1951.
172. Lee, Henry. *Memoirs of the War in the Southern Department of the United States*. Edited by Robert E. Lee. New York: University Publishing Co., 1870.
173. Lewis, Charles Lee. *Admiral de Grasse and American Independence*. Annapolis: United States Naval Institute, 1945.
174. *London Magazine; or, Gentleman's Monthly Intelligencer*. London, 1732-1785.
175. Lossing, Benson J. *The Pictorial Field-Book of the Revolution*. New York: Harper, 1860. 2 vols.
176. Lossing, Benson John. *The Life and Times of Philip Schuyler*. New York: Da Capo Press, 1973 (1872).

177. Lovell, Louise Lewis. *Israel Angell, Colonel of the 2nd Rhode Island Regiment*. New York: Putnam, 1921.
178. Lowell, Edward J. *The Hessians and the Other German Auxiliaries of Great Britain in the Revolutionary War*. New York: Harper and Brothers, 1884.
179. Lundin, Leonard. *Cockpit of the Revolution: The War for Independence in New Jersey*. Princeton: Princeton University Press, 1940.
180. Mackenzie, Frederick. *Diary of Frederick Mackenzie, Giving a Daily Narrative of His Military Service as an Officer of the Regiment of Royal Welsh Fusiliers During the Years 1775-1781 in Massachusetts, Rhode Island and New York*. Cambridge: Harvard University Press, 1930. 2 vols.
181. Mackenzie, Roderick. *Strictures on Lt. Col. Tarleton's History "Of the Campaigns of 1780 and 1781, in the Southern Provinces of North America." Wherein Military Characters and Corps Are Vindicated from Injurious Aspersions, and Several Important Transactions Placed in Their Proper Point of View. In a Series of Letters to a Friend. To Which Is Added, a Detail of the Siege of Ninety Six, and the Recapture of the Island of New-Providence*. London, 1787.
182. Mackesy, Piers. *The War for America, 1775-1783*. Cambridge: Harvard University Press, 1964.
183. Maclay, Edgar Stanton. *A History of American Privateers*. London: Sampson, Low, Marston & Co., 1899.
184. *Magazine of American History*. New York, 1877-93.
185. *Magnolia; or, Southern Appalachian*. Charleston, S.C., 1840-1843.
186. Mahan, Alfred Thayer. *The Major Operations of the Navies in the War of American Independence*. London: Sampson, Low, Marston & Co., 1899.
187. Mahan, Alfred Thayer. *Major Operations of the Royal Navy, 1762-1783*. Boston: Little, Brown, 1913.
188. Manning, Clarence Augustus. *Soldier of Liberty, Casimir Pulaski*. New York: Philosophical Library, 1945.
189. Marcus, G. J. *A Naval History of England: The Formative Centuries*. London: Longmans, 1961.
190. Martin, Joseph Plumb. *Private Yankee Doodle: Being a Narrative of Some of the Adventures, Dangers and Sufferings of a Revolutionary Soldier*. Edited by George F. Scheer. Boston: Little, Brown, 1962.
191. Martyn, Charles. *The Life of Artemus Ward, the First Commander-in-Chief of the American Revolution*. New York: A. Ward, 1921.
192. Mathews, William. *American Diaries: An Annotated Bibliography of American Diaries Prior to the Year 1861*. Berkeley: University of California Press, 1945.
193. Merlant, Joachim. *La France et la guerre de l'Independence Americaine*. Paris: Bibliotheque France-Amerique, 1918.
194. Merlant, Joachim. *Soldiers and Sailors in the American War of Independence*. Translated by Mary B. Coleman. New York: Scribner, 1920.

195. Metzger, Charles Henry. *The Prisoner in the American Revolution.* Chicago: Loyola University Press, 1971.

196. *Military Affairs.* Washington, D.C., 1937-1968; Manhattan, Kansas, 1968-   .

197. *Military Collector and Historian.* Washington, D.C.; 1949-   .

198. Miller, John C. *The Triumph of Freedom, 1775-83.* Boston: Little, Brown, 1948.

199. Miller, Nathan. *Sea of Glory: The Continental Navy Fights for Independence, 1775-1783.* New York: David McKay, 1974.

200. Mitchell, Broadus. *Alexander Hamilton, Youth to Maturity, 1755-1788.* New York: Macmillan, 1957.

201. Mitchell, Joseph Brady. *Discipline and Bayonets: The Armies and Leaders in the War of the American Revolution.* New York: Putnam, 1967.

202. Montross, Lynn. *Rag, Tag, and Bobtail, the Story of the Continental Army.* New York: Harper, 1952.

203. Moore, Frank, ed. *Diary of the American Revolution. From Newspapers and Original Documents.* New York: Scribner, 1860. 2 vols.

204. Morison, Samuel Eliot. *John Paul Jones, a Sailor's Biography.* Boston: Little, Brown, 1959.

205. Mundy, G. B. *Life and Correspondence of Lord Rodney.* London: Murray, 1830.

206. Murdock, Harold. *Bunker Hill: Notes and Queries on a Famous Battle.* Boston: Houghton Mifflin, 1927.

207. Murdock, Harold. *The Nineteenth of April 1775.* Boston: Houghton Mifflin, 1923.

208. Neel, William Cooper. *The Colored Patriots of the American Revolution.* New York: Arno Press, 1968 (1855).

209. Neumann, George 'C. *The History of Weapons of the American Revolution.* New York: Harper & Row, 1967.

210. Neumann, George C. *Swords & Blades of the American Revolution.* Harrisburg: Stackpole, 1973.

211. Newcomer, Lee Nathaniel. *The Embattled Farmers: A Massachusetts Countryside in the American Revolution.* New York: Russell and Russell, 1971 (1953).

212. Nickerson, Hoffman. *The Turning Point of the Revolution; or, Burgoyne in America.* Boston: Houghton Mifflin, 1928.

213. Noailles, Louise Marie, vicomte de. *Marins et Soldats Français en Amerique pendant la Guerre de l'Independence des États-Unis, 1778-1783.* Paris: Perrin et Cie., 1917.

214. O'Donnell, James H. *The Southern Indians in the American Revolution.* Knoxville: University of Tennessee Press, 1973.

215. *Orion, The.* Penfield, Ga., 1942-44.

216. Palmer, Dave R. *The Way of the Fox.* Westport, Connecticut: Greenwood, 1975.

217. Palmer, John M. *General Von Steuben.* New Haven: Yale University Press, 1937.

218. Patterson, Samuel White. *Knight Errant of Liberty: The Triumph and Tragedy of General Charles Lee.* New York: Lantern Press, 1958.

219. Patterson, Samuel White. *Horatio Gates, Defender of American Liberties.* New York: Columbia University Press, 1941.
220. Paullin, Charles Oscar. *The Navy of the American Revolution: Its Administration, Its Policy, and Its Achievements.* New York: Haskell House, 1971 (1906).
221. Pease, Theodore Calvin. *George Rogers Clark and the Revolution in Illinois, 1763-1787.* Springfield: Illinois State Historical Library, 1929.
222. Peckham, Howard H., ed. *The Toll of Independence: Engagements & Battle Casualties of the American Revolution.* Chicago: University of Chicago Press, 1974.
223. Peckham, Howard H. *The War for Independence, a Military History.* Chicago: University of Chicago Press, 1958.
224. Pell, John. *Ethan Allen.* Boston: Houghton Mifflin, 1929.
225. *Pennsylvania Magazine of History and Biography.* Philadelphia, 1877- .
226. Pennypacker, Morton. *General Washington's Spies on Long Island and in New York.* Brooklyn: Long Island Historical Society, 1931.
227. Perkins, James Breck. *France in the American Revolution.* Williamstown, Massachusetts: Corner House, 1970 (1911).
228. Peterson, Harold L. *Arms and Armor in Colonial America, 1526-1783.* Harrsiburg: Stackpole, 1956.
229. Pettingill, Ray W., trans. *Letters from America, 1776-1779.* Boston: Houghton Mifflin, 1924.
230. Pickering, Timothy. *An Easy Plan of Discipline for a Militia.* Boston, 1775.
231. *Political Magazine and Parliamentary, Naval, Military, and Literary Journal.* London, 1780-1790.
232. Preston, John Hyde. *A Gentleman Rebel, Mad Anthony Wayne.* Garden City, Carden City Publishing Co., 1930.
233. Quarles, Benjamin A. *The Negro in the American Revolution.* Chapel Hill: University of North Carolina Press, 1961.
234. Ramsay, David. *The History of the American Revolution.* London: John Stockdale, 1793. 2 vols.
235. Ramsay, David. *The History of the Revolution in South Carolina. From a British Province to an Independent State.* Trenton: Isaac Collins, 1785.
236. Rankin, Hugh F. *The American Revolution.* New York: Putnam, 1964.
237. Rankin, Hugh F. *Francis Marion: The Swamp Fox.* New York: Crowell, 1973.
238. Rankin, Hugh F. *The North Carolina Continentals.* Chapel Hill: University of North Carolina Press, 1971.
239. Reed, John Frederick. *Campaign to Valley Forge, July 1, 1772-December 19, 1777.* Philadelphia: University of Pennsylvania Press, 1965.
240. *Remembrancer, The.* London, 1775-84.
241. Rice, Howard C., Jr., and Anne S. K. Brown, trans. and eds. *The American Campaigns of Rochambeau's Army 1780, 1781, 1782, 1783.* Princeton, N.J. and Providence, R.I.: Princeton and Brown University Presses, 1972. 2 vols.

242. Richard, Earl of Cavan. *A New System of Military Discipline, Founded upon Principle.* Philadelphia, 1776.

243. Robertson, Archibald. *His Diaries and Sketches in America, 1762-1780.* Edited by Harry Miller Lydenberg. New York: New York Public Library, 1930.

244. Robinson, Blackwell P. *William R. David.* Chapel Hill: University of North Carolina Press, 1957.

245. Robson, Erie. *The American Revolution in Its Political and Military Aspects, 1763-1783.* London: Batchworth Press, 1955.

246. Rossman, Kenneth. *Thomas Mifflin and the Politics of the American Revolution.* Chapel Hill: University of North Carolina Press, 1952.

247. Sabin, Joseph. *Bibliotheca Americana. A Dictionary of Books Relating to America, from Its Discovery to the Present Time.* New York: various publishers, 1868-1936. 29 vols.

248. Sabine, Lorenzo. *The American Loyalists, or Biographical Sketches of Adherents to the British Crown in the War of the Revolution.* Boston: Little, Brown, 1847.

249. Sayer, R., and J. Bennett. *American Military Pocket Atlas.* London, 1776.

250. Scheer, George F., and Hugh F. Rankin. *Rebels and Redcoats.* Cleveland: World Publishing Co., 1957.

251. Serle, Ambrose. *The American Journal of Ambrose Serle, Secretary to Lord Howe, 1776-1778.* Edited by Edward H. Tatum, Jr. San Marino: Huntington Library, 1940.

252. Seymour, William. *A Journal of the Southern Expedition, 1780-1783.* Wilmington: Historical Society of Delaware, 1896.

253. Shy, John W. *Toward Lexington; the Role of the British Army in the Coming of the American Revolution.* Princeton: Princeton University Press, 1965.

254. Simcoe, J. G. *A Journal of the Operations of the Queen's Rangers, from the End of the Year 1777, to the Conclusion of the Late American War.* New York: Bartlett & Welford, 1844.

255. Sklarsky, I. W. *The Revolution's Boldest Venture: The Story of General "Mad Anthony" Wayne's Assault on Stony Point.* Fort Washington, New York: Kennikat Press, 1965.

256. Smith, Justin H. *Our Struggle for the Fourteenth Colony: Canada and the American Revolution.* New York: Putnam, 1907.

257. Smith, Paul H. *Loyalists and Redcoats: A Study in British Revolutionary Policy.* Chapel Hill: University of North Carolina Press, 1964.

258. Smith, Samuel Stelle. *The Battle of Monmouth.* Monmouth Beach, N.J.: Philip Freneau Press, 1964.

259. Smith, Samuel Stelle. *The Battle of Trenton.* Monmouth Beach, N.J.: Philip Freneau Press, 1965.

260. Sosin, Jack M. *The Revolutionary Frontier, 1763-1785.* New York: Rinehart and Winston, 1967.

261. *Southern Literary Messenger.* Richmond, Va., 1834-1864.

262. Stedman, Charles. *The History of the Origin, Progress, and Termination of the American War.* London, 1794. 2 vols.

263. Steuben, Baron Friedrich Wilhelm Ludolf Gerhard Augustin Von. *Regulations for the Order and Discipline of the Troops of the United*

States. Columbus, Ohio: Ohio State Museum, 1956 (1778-1779).

264. Stevens, Benjamin Franklin, ed. *Clinton-Cornwallis Controversy Growing out of the Campaign in Virginia, 1781.* London, 1888. 2 vols.

265. Stille, Charles Janeway. *Major-General Anthony Wayne and the Pennsylvania Line in the Continental Army.* Philadelphia: Lippincott, 1893.

266. Stone, Edwin Martin. *Our French Allies, Rochambeau and His Army, Lafayette and His Devotion, D'Estaing, Deternay, Barras, De Grasse, and Their Fleets, in the Great War of the American Revolution, from 1778 to 1782. . . .* Providence: Providence Press Co., 1884.

267. Stone, William L. *Border Wars of the American Revolution.* New York: A. Fowle, 1900.

268. Stone, William L., trans. *Letters of Brunswick and Hessian Officers during the American Revolution.* Albany: Joel Munsell's Sons, 1891.

269. Stoudt, John Joseph. *Ordeal at Valley Forge: A Day-by-Day Chronicle from December 17, 1777 to June 18, 1778.* Philadelphia: University of Pennsylvania Press, 1963.

270. Stout, Neil, R. *The Royal Navy in America, 1760-1775: A Study of British Colonial Policy in the Era of the American Revolution.* Annapolis: Naval Institute Press, 1973.

271. Stryker, William S. *The Battle of Monmouth.* Edited by William Starr Myers. Princeton: Princeton University Press, 1927.

272. Stryker, William Scudder. *The Battles of Trenton and Princeton.* Boston: Houghton Mifflin, 1898.

273. Stryker, William Scudder. *The Forts on the Delaware in the Revolutionary War.* Trenton, N.J.: J. L. Murphy, 1901.

274. Swiggett, Howard. *War out of Niagara: Walter Butler and the Tory Rangers.* New York: Columbia University Press, 1933.

275. Tallmadge, Benjamin. *Memoir of Colonel Benjamin Tallmadge.* Edited by Henry Phelps Johnston. New York: New York Society of Sons of the Revolution, 1914.

276. Tarleton, Lt. Col. Banastre. *A History of the Campaigns of 1780 and 1781, in the Southern Provinces of North America.* London: T. Cadell, 1787.

277. Taylor, Robert J. *Western Massachusetts in the Revolution.* Providence: Brown University Press, 1954.

278. Thacher, James, M.D. *A Military Journal during the American Revolutionary War, from 1775-1783; Describing Interesting Events and Transactions of this Period; with Numerous Historical Facts and Anecdotes, from the Original Manuscript. To Which Is Added, an Appendix, Containing Biographical Sketches of Several General Officers.* Hartford: Hurlburt, Williams, 1862.

279. Thayer, Theodore. *Nathanael Greene: Strategist of the American Revolution.* New York: Twayne, 1960.

280. Tourtellot, Arthur B. *William Diamond's Drum: The Beginning of the War of the American Revolution.* Garden City: Doubleday, 1959.

281. Treacy, M. F. *Prelude to Yorktown: The Southern Campaign of Nathanael Greene, 1780-1781.* Chapel Hill: University of North Carolina Press, 1963.

282. Trumbull, John. *Autobiography, Reminiscences and Letters of John Trumbull, from 1756 to 1841.* New York: Wiley and Putnam, 1841.
283. Tucker, Glenn. *Mad Anthony Wayne and the New Nation: The Story of Washington's Front Line General.* Harrisburg: Stackpole, 1973.
284. Uhlendorf, Bernhard A., trans. and ed. *Revolution in America: Confidential Letters and Journals, 1776-1784, of Adjutant General Major Baurmeister of the Hessian Forces.* New Brunswick: Rutgers University Press, 1957.
285. Uhlendorf, Bernhard A. trans. and ed. *The Siege of Charleston, with an Account of the Province of South Carolina: Diaries and Letters of Hessian Officers from the von Jungkenn Papers in the William L. Clements Library.* Ann Arbor: University of Michigan Press, 1938.
286. *Universal Magazine of Knowledge and Pleasure.* London, 1747-1815.
287. Valentine, Alan. *Lord Stirling.* New York: Oxford University Press, 1969.
288. Van Doren, Carl. *Mutiny in January: The Story of a Crisis in the Continental Army Now for the First Time Fully Told from Many Hitherto Unknown or Neglected Sources, both American and British.* New York: Viking, 1943.
289. Van Doren, Carl. *The Secret History of the American Revolution.* New York: Viking Press, 1941.
290. Van Every, Dale. *A Company of Heroes, the American Frontier, 1775-1783.* New York: Morrow, 1962.
291. Wagner, Frederick. *Submarine Fighter of the American Revolution, the Story of David Bushnell.* New York: Dodd, Mead, 1963.
292. Wallace, Willard. *Appeal to Arms: A Military History of the Revolution.* New York: Harper, 1951.
293. Wallace, Willard M. *Traitorous Hero: The Life and Fortunes of Benedict Arnold.* New York: Harper, 1954.
294. Ward, Christopher. *The War of the Revolution.* Edited by John R. Alden. New York: Macmillan, 1952. 2 vols.
295. Ward, Christopher L. *The Delaware Continentals, 1776-1783.* Wilmington: Historical Society of Delaware, 1941.
296. Warren, Mercy Otis. *History of the Rise, Progress and Termination of the American Revolution.* Boston: Manning and Loring, 1805.
297. Webb, Samuel B. *Correspondence and Journals of Samuel Blachley Webb.* Edited by Worthington C. Ford. New York, 1894. 3 vols.
298. White, David Oliver. *Connecticut's Black Soldiers, 1775-1783.* Chester, Connecticut: Pequot Press, 1973.
299. Whitlock, Brand. *Lafayette.* New York, London: Appleton, 1929. 2 vols.
300. Whitridge, Arnold. *Rochambeau.* New York: Macmillan, 1965.
301. Whittemore, Charles Park. *A General of the Revolution; John Sullivan of New Hampshire.* New York:Columbia University Press, 1961.
302. Wickwire, Franklin and Mary. *Cornwallis: The American Adventure.* Boston: Houghton Mifflin, 1970.
303. Wilbur, C. Keith. *Picture Book of the Continental Soldier.* Harrisburg: Stackpole, 1969.
304. Wildes, Harry Emerson. *Anthony Wayne: Trouble Shooter of the*

Revolution. Westport, Connecticut: Greenwood Press, 1970 (1941).
305. Wilkinson, James. *Memoirs of My Own Times.* Philadelphia: A Small, 1816. 3 vols.
306. Willcox, William B. *Portrait of a General: Sir Henry Clinton in the War of Independence.* New York: Knopf, 1964.
307. Winsor, Justin, ed. *Narrative and Critical History of America.* Boston: Houghton Mifflin, 1889. 8 vols.
308. Wolfe, General James. *Instructions to Young Officers; also His Orders for a Battalion and an Army. Together with the Orders and Signals Used in Embarking and Debarking an Army by Flat Bottomed Boats, etc. . . .* London: J. Milan, 1768, 1780. Reprinted Ottawa, Ontario: Museum Restoration Service, 1967.
309. Wright, Esmond. *Washington and the American Revolution.* New York: Macmillan, n. d.

V

FROM THE REVOLUTION TO THE
MEXICAN WAR

Roger L. Nichols

Before World War II most American historians considered military history a necessary evil, more evil than necessary much of the time. Those who practiced the craft tended to concentrate on technical studies of battles, campaigns, and strategy. As a result, they paid little attention to the era between Independence and the Mexican War because for most of those sixty years the nation remained at peace—with the exception of the War of 1812 and a few minor Indian campaigns—and the army did little beyond routine, peacetime chores.

During the past three decades, however, people in all walks of life have recognized the increasing impact the military has on American life. As a result a host of books and articles now focus on military subjects. This recent upsurge of attention has aided those interested in the army during the first sixty years of national independence. At first glance, few subjects seem worth considering. For most of the period national preoccupation with territorial expansion and internal economic developments precluded much support for the army. It remained tiny, or only modest-sized at best. As a fighting force the soldiers deserve little further consideration. Nevertheless, recent studies continue, usually examining the army as a social, economic, and political institution within the country instead of merely looking at its combat efforts. This approach has provided significant findings and continues to raise new questions.

GENERAL REFERENCES. Several standard references provide biographical information about army leaders prior to the Mexican War. Only a small portion of officers received formal training at West Point, but George W. Cullum, *Biographical Register of the Officers and Graduates of the United States Military Academy* (54), discusses the careers of those who did. Two other compilations list briefly the unit assignments of all regular army officers who served at the time. These are Thomas Hamersly, *Complete Regular Army Register of the United States* (103), and Francis Heitman, *Historical Register and Dictionary of the United States Army* (109). Both of these gathered their material from the annual *Army Register* and in the process included some errors. In most cases Heitman is more accurate.

Most soldiers lived in small, scattered forts throughout the country. In his *Guide to the Military Posts of the United States* (192), Father Francis P. Prucha locates the forts and camps on detailed maps. In addition, he gives the dates of founding and closure as well as the location and other pertinent information for each installation. Although forts offer one view of army operations, the geographic divisions and shifting organization of the service provides a second. Raphael Thian, *Notes Illustrating the Military Geography of the United States, 1813-1880* (225), traces the territorial changes in command during the nineteenth century. At the same time he considers congressional legislation related to army size and command structure, thereby offering an excellent vantage point from which operations may be considered.

Civilian control of the army brought a continuing flood of legislation and regulation for the military, as for example, in Raphael Thian, *Legislative History of the General Staff of the United States Army* (224). Congress kept a tight rein on the purse strings for military spending, limited army size sharply, and made promotion for officers and enlisted men slow. As a result, brevet ranks came to assume an important place in command relationships. James Fry, *The History and Legal Effect of Brevets in the Armies of Great Britain and the United States . . .* (80), traces this confusing matter with some degree of clarity.

Several studies concentrate on branches or departments of the army. Among these, William Birkhimer, *Historical Sketch of the Organization, Administration, Materiel, and Tactics of the Artillery of the United States Army* (26), deals with that important group. W. Stull Holt, *The Office of the Chief of Engineers of the Army; Its Non-Military History, Activities and Organization* (118), is a limited administrative study and, as such, offers little for most military historians. In *A History of the Medical Department of the United States Army* (12), Percy Ashburn examines the medical and administrative problems which limited army effectiveness. Erna Risch, *Quartermaster Support of the Army: A History of the Corps, 1775-1939* (199), considers the difficulties of transporting and supplying soldiers in the pre-railroad decades.

GENERAL HISTORIES. The trend of including the army within the broader context of American social and economic history has opened new vistas for military historians and at the same time seems to have reduced the suspicion with which many American academicians view military history. One outstanding example of this is the Macmillan series, *Wars of the United States*, edited by Louis Morton. This ambitious, twenty-volume effort now has nine books in print. Of those, Russell F. Weigley, *History of the United States Army* (244), offers a general overview based on the most recent findings and ideas of American military historians. Any consideration of the army must include this volume.

Three older general histories also deserve consideration. William A. Ganoe, *The History of the United States Army* (84), stands as an early attempt to chronicle American military history. Ganoe strove to consider army activity during both peace and war, and brought his story through the demobilization following World War I. He gave a balanced account and devoted one-third of the study to the era preceding the Mexican War

—something unusual when he wrote. Despite the title, *The United States Army in War and Peace* (216), Oliver L. Spaulding takes a more traditional view. He focuses on actual campaigns with only a few scattered chapters devoted to other topics. A more recent and rather breezy account is found in R. Ernest Dupuy, *The Compact History of the United States Army* (63). Dupuy brings the story of the army up beyond the Korean War but presents only three chapters in the entire book on the period under consideration here. When reading his book one needs large doses of solid material to fill the gaps and correct the oversimplifications.

In addition to the narrative histories of the army, two other types of studies deserve mention here. C. Joseph Bernardo and Eugene H. Bacon, *American Military Policy: Its Development Since 1775* (24), offer some good ideas on military thought for the period. An early student of this subject, Emory Upton, provides one of the best discussions for the War of 1812 era in *The Military Policy of the United States* (237). Russell F. Weigley offers more recent ideas on the topic in two books, *The American Way of War* (243), and *Towards an American Army: Military Thought from Washington to Marshall* (245). In the latter book, Weigley concentrates on policy controversies affecting army development and utilization. Two books related to army thought discuss officer training at West Point. Sidney Forman, *West Point: A History of the United States Military Academy* (73), was the best discussion of the topic but left much undone. A more recent study, Stephen Ambrose, *Duty, Honor, Country: A History of West Point* (5), has filled earlier gaps in the story.

JOURNALS. Few contemporary journals dealing with military activity appeared in the pre-Mexican War years. Nevertheless, those which did contained printed correspondence between army leaders and copies of legislation and other official material. In 1811 Hezikiah Niles began publishing *Niles Weekly Register* (173), a small news magazine which includes much of value and interest. Strongly anti-British and pro-expansionist, he filled his journal with army and western news until the late 1840s. During the War of 1812, *The War* (240) appeared several times a week in New York. This included many of the same kinds of items that *Niles Register* did and is the only source for some valuable correspondence on military matters of the day. During the 1830s two distinctly military journals appeared. The *Military and Naval Magazine* (163) was published from 1833 until 1836. It discusses legislation dealing with both branches of service, as well as publishing correspondence from widely scattered officers. In 1835, the Washington-based *Army and Navy Chronicle* (11) began its eight-year life. Its editors aimed the magazine at military officers and provided an outlet for writers as well as a place to express opinions about existing practices within the military. As such, they offer researchers a wealth of material on widely related topics for the pre-1840 era.

OFFICIAL PAPERS. The publications of the various agencies and branches of the United States Government constitute a treasure house of primary information about all phases of early army activity. For the period 1783 to 1824 the *Annals of Congress* (9) include some of the recorded debates there. In 1824 the name of the publication changed to *Register of Debates* (197), and this gave way during the mid-1830s to the *Congressional Globe* (48). In addition to congressional debates, these publications record motions, speeches, and some vote tallies.

Even more important are the actual congressional documents, reports, and investigations which consider all questions related to the army. The vast serial set of congressional documents fills many hundred volumes and no serious student of army affairs during the 1783-1845 period can avoid it. The *American State Papers* : *Military Affairs* (7) and *Indian Affairs* (6) add material to that found in the serial set. Three guides are available in most research libraries. Benjamin P. Poore, *A Descriptive Catalogue of the Government Publications of the United States 1774-1881* (187), is the first place to look. The superintendent of documents prepared two other useful guides. These are the *Checklist of United States Public Documents 1789-1909* (235) and *Tables of and Annotated Index to the Congressional Series of United States Public Documents* (236). When used with a documents librarian's help, these volumes make it relatively easy to find pertinent material.

In addition to this published material, a vast bulk of official correspondence, reports, and routine paperwork may be found in the holdings of the National Archives and Records Service. Along with the published federal material, these archival holdings include the most complete records available for studying early army activity. Some of the more important and most-often used documents have been microfilmed as part of an ambitious project to make the records more accessible to scholars. The most recent catalog, published in 1968, is the *List of National Archives Microfilm Publications* (234). Unfortunately, this includes only those items filmed since the preceding list had been published, and therefore it is best to correspond directly with the National Archives to learn just what is available on film.

Most of the material has not been filmed yet, but the archives staff has prepared some finding aids of which the most ambitious is the *Preliminary Inventory of the Records of United States Army Continental Commands, 1821-1920* (264). This multiple-volume guide has an introduction which describes the army in 1821, traces the development of regional commands and staff departments, while it also gives a brief comment on the responsibilities of the various parts of the army. Then it lists each collection of records, gives the dates for the material, and explains its arrangement. Several other guides are of more modest proportions. For example, Marie Bouknight, et al., *Guide to Records in the Military Archives Division Pertaining to Indian-White Relations* (263), concentrates on that one issue. It lists the archival record groups which include pertinent material and describes holdings within each group. Despite existing guides and inventories, most scholars still have to burrow into the archival record groups in order to benefit from the material.

Although the National Archives holdings offer the best single collection of material, they are weak for the pre-1800 years. In that year a fire destroyed most War Department records. Some other records were lost when the British burned part of Washington in 1814, but that loss proved slight compared to the almost total destruction of the earlier material.

Despite such losses, at least four records groups are major sources for army materials for the 1800-1840 era. Of these the Records of the Office of the Adjutant General, Record Group 94, are the most voluminous and probably give the best indication of what soldiers were doing at the time. Operating under the secretary of war, the adjutant general's office served as the clerk for the entire army. From 1812 on, clerks in this office abstracted and recorded each letter. This information is in the Registers of Letters Received, and using the Registers to locate correspondence can save hours or even days of time.

The Records of United States Army Continental Commands, Record Group 393, are a second major source for the old army. This record group includes not only much that is merely routine, but also numerous special orders, correspondence about personnel and supply problems, and letter books keeping senders' copies of correspondence offer much that is valuable. Correspondence which came directly to the secretary of war is located in the Records of the Office of the secretary of war, Record Group 107. This collection has some material dated as early as 1789 as well as letter book copies of outgoing correspondence beginning in 1800. Separate files exist for material related to military affairs, Indian affairs, and messages to and from the President.

A last archival collection of major significance is the Records of the Office of Indian Affairs (later the Bureau of Indian Affairs, or BIA), Record Group 75. This material relates the story of American-Indian relations from 1824 when the Indian Office began as a new agency. The records consist of directives to Indian agents and their correspondence and reports sent to their superiors. Organized by tribal agencies and regional superintendencies, this material provides a valuable addition to the purely military documents already discussed because it shows what civilian officials were doing about Indian problems at the time.

In addition to these large record groups, several others have equally significant material that is usually more limited in scope. These include the Records of the Chief of Engineers, Record Group 77; Records of the Headquarters of the Army, Record Group 108; Records of the Office of the Quartermaster General, Record Group 92; Records of the Office of the Inspector General, Record Group 159; Records of the Office of the Commissary General of Subsistence, Record Group 192; Records of the Office of the Surgeon General, Record Group 112; Records of the Office of the Judge Advocate General, Record Group 153; the Records of United States Regular Army Mobile Units, Record Group 391; and the Records of United States Army Commands, Record Group 98.

The National Archives staff make all of these early records available to scholars with a minimum of fuss or paperwork. No special permission is needed to use any of the material dealing with the army during the first half of the nineteenth century. In addition to the main archives collections in Washington, D.C., there are two personnel records centers, and thirteen regional records centers. These latter now include items which used to be in Washington but which are of most significance to the region. Therefore they have been made available to scholars at the regional centers in an effort to help people avoid costly research trips to Washington whenever possible.

PRIVATE PAPERS. This category of material is less rewarding for general studies of military history because most manuscript collections are small and items pertaining to a single topic or person may well be scattered all over the country. Nevertheless, for some topics personal papers add the needed ingredients for success. The best guide to manuscripts is Philip Hamer, ed., *A Guide to Archives and Manuscripts in the United States* (102). Some individual research libraries also have published guides to their holdings, but Hamer is certainly the place to start. Major university libraries, state historical societies, and private research institutions such as the Newberry Library and the Huntington Library and Art Gallery all have extensive manuscript collections. The Manuscript Division of the Library of Congress also houses the papers of many national leaders—including leading political and military figures.

ESTABLISHING A PEACETIME ARMY, 1783-1812. During the years immediately following Independence the army fared badly. Lacking funds to pay or equip it, and fearing military interference with the civil government, Congress allowed the army to disintegrate. The most detailed coverage of the era is in James R. Jacobs, *The Beginning of the U.S. Army, 1783-1812* (128). He considers the difficulties political and military leaders had in getting support and show how ineffectively soldiers performed many of their tasks. A more recent article by Louis Morton, "The Origins of American Military Policy" (165), adds a theoretical approach. Randolph G. Adams and Howard H. Peckham in *Lexington to Fallen Timbers, 1775-1794* (3) offers a series of essays which discuss early army problems, too. In *The Sword of the Republic* (193), Francis P. Prucha studies army development for the entire 1783-1846 period. He focuses on the pioneering efforts of soldiers and the army role in Indian affairs, describing the army as an "agent of empire" and claiming that it played a major role in American territorial expansion.

Certainly army activities remained tied closely to expansion and defending the frontiersmen and Indians from each other. Two general studies of the problem are Randolph C. Downes, *Council Fires on the Upper Ohio* (60), and Reginald Horsman, *The Frontier in the Formative Years, 1783-1815* (121). The latter considers all aspects of frontier develpment and thus helps put army efforts into the broadest perspective for the era. In a related article, "American Indian Policy in the Old Northwest" (119), Horsman depicts the army as the agency through which the government acquired land from the Indians. Dwight L. Smith, "Provocation and Occurrence of Indian-White Warfare in the Early American Period in the Old Northwest" (211), sees provocations by whites and Indians alike as making warfare inevitable and almost continuous.

Because much early army effort dealt with the Indians, articles on the topic abound. In particular, Josiah Harmar's expedition against the Ohio tribes which ended in his rout has received much attention. Two of the better discussions of that episode are Randolph G. Adams, "The Harmar Expedition of 1790" (2), and Howard H. Peckham, "Josiah Harmar and His Indian Expedition" (181). Harmar's crushing defeat and that of St. Clair several years later brought reorganization of the army and the appointment of Anthony Wayne as commander of the new force sent west. Two biographies of Wayne offer competent analysis of his frontier campaign. Thomas A. Boyd, *Mad Anthony Wayne* (30), is colorful and anecdotal but also competent. Harry E. Wildes, *Anthony Wayne, Trouble Shooter of the American Revolution* (250), concentrates on Wayne's earlier experience but does also consider his Ohio activities.

The federal government used the army for frontier exploration often during the first decade of the nineteenth century. Meriwether Lewis and William Clark provide the most obvious example of this. As yet there is no study of Clark's life, so scholars must depend on limited articles and on John Bakeless, *Lewis and Clark: Partners in Discovery* (16), a sort of joint biography which concentrates on their famous expedition. For Lewis, Richard Dillon, *Meriwether Lewis, A Biography* (57), completes the story. Numerous edited journals from the expedition are available, including William Clark, *The Field Notes of Captain William Clark, 1803-1805* (44), and Meriwether Lewis and William Clark, *Original Journals of the Lewis and Clark Expedition* (146). Among other early explorers, Zebulon Pike deserves brief mention. There are several editions of his journals but the best is Donald Jackson, *The Journals of Zebulon Montgomery Pike with Letters and Related Documents* (186). This has excellent annotations and maps to help the reader. W. Eugene Hollon studied Pike's army career in *The Lost Pathfinder* (117).

Clearly the most controversial figure in the pre-War-of-1812 era, General James Wilkinson has attracted much attention. Frontier speculator, Spanish agent, and regular army officer—sometimes all at the same time —his career provides an understanding of army duties and problems. His *Memoirs of My Own Times* (251) is a three-volume compilation of documents with which Wilkinson attempted to depict his army career in heroic terms. He also used the documents to rebut, usually unsuccessfully, charges of incompetence and cowardice made against him. Among the studies of his career, R. O. Schreve, *The Finished Scoundrel* (204), is the most negative. In *Tarnished Warrior* (129), James R. Jacobs comes to similar negative conclusions about Wilkinson.

THE WAR OF 1812. Among the general histories of this conflict, the most recent and comprehensive is John K. Mahon, *The War of 1812* (265). This is an exhaustive study of all military aspects of the war which provides a detailed but understandable discussion of the campaigns. It includes extensive notes and an excellent bibliography from which scholars can move in many directions. Harry Coles, *The War of 1812* (47), and Francis F. Beirne, *The War of 1812* (22), offer older and briefer studies. An interesting description of the war taken largely from contemporary newspapers is Glen Tucker, *Poltroons and Patriots* (229). Benson Lossing provides a monumental compilation of contemporary items and sketches in his *Pictorial Field Book of the War of 1812* (148).

Several books discuss the Canadian-British side of the war. William James, *Full and Correct Account of the Military Occurrences of the Late War Between Great Britain and the United States of America* (132), appeared in 1818 and is obviously anti-American throughout. Nevertheless, it provides the contemporary British view and includes many documents. A recent study from the Canadian viewpoint is J. Mackay Hitsman, *The*

Incredible War of 1812 (115), which also quotes much primary material. Mahon, *The War of 1812* (265), has combed British and Canadian archival holdings and, more than any other American, includes this material in his recent study.

Monographs and articles on limited aspects of the war abound. The best contemporary discussion of the 1812-13 campaigns in the west is Robert B. McAfee, *History of the Late War in the Western Country* (150), which appeared in 1816. Louis L. Babcock, *The War of 1812 on the Niagara Frontier* (15), is a good secondary account of regional campaigning in the northeast. The best modern regional study is Alec R. Gilpin, *The War of 1812 in the Old Northwest* (85). The campaign around New Orleans was first discussed by Alexander Walker in his *Jackson and New Orleans* (239), written in the mid-nineteenth century. The more recent Charles B. Brooks, *The Siege of New Orleans* (33) has revised and updated the Walker study. For an analysis of British tactics at New Orleans see John K. Mahon, "British Command Decisions Relative to the Battle of New Orleans" (155). In a related article, "The British at New Orleans: Strategy or Blunder?" (195), Hugh Rankin claims that the American forces took advantage of British mistakes to win.

As they had in previous American wars, the Indians played a major role in all three theaters. The only general article on the subject is George F. G. Stanley, "The Indians in the War of 1812" (218), and even this concentrates on U.S.–Canadian border areas. John K. Mahon, "British Strategy and Southern Indians: War of 1812" (156), demonstrates how the Indians aided British regulars in the New Orleans campaign. According to Frank L. Owsley, Jr., the Creek War in Alabama began with "The Fort Mims Massacre" (176) in 1813. Much has appeared about this conflict in biographies of the major participants. A solid, though old study of the war is Henry S. Halbert and T. H. Ball, *The Creek War of 1813 and 1814* (99). Arthur H. Hall, "The Red Stick War: Creek Indian Affairs During the War of 1812" (101), is a briefer and more recent study, but adds little.

In the Old Northwest the Indian confederacy under the Shawnee leader Tecumseh caused much difficulty for American forces. One of the few efforts at writing a book-length biography of an Indian leader is Glenn Tucker, *Tecumseh: Vision of Glory* (230). He depicts the Indians as fighting a brave but futile delaying action against the advancing frontiersmen. In his "Tecumseh, Harrison and the War of 1812" (209), Marshall Smelser considers the competition between these leaders as a significant factor in leading the west to war. William Henry Harrison, Tecumseh's protagonist, has received much favorable study. Typical of these is Freeman Cleaves, *Old Tippecanoe* (45). To get an accurate balance it is necessary to consider Logan Esarey, ed., *The Messages and Letters of William Henry Harrison* (106).

General Hull's 1812 surrender of Detroit to the Canadian Isaac Brock raised the loudest outcry of any campaign during the entire war. According to Harry Coles (47), Brock frightened Hull into "mental and moral paralysis" which in turn produced the surrender—"one of the most disgraceful episodes in the military history of the United States." Certainly contemporaries would have accepted this judgment wholeheartedly. In fact, within two years Hull had been convicted by court-martial and sentenced to be hanged for his cowardly behavior. The general tried to defend himself years later when he published his *Memoirs* (124). History has been hard on Hull, and a more balanced discussion of his leadership may be found in Milo M. Quaife, "General William Hull and His Critics" (194). Quaife recognizes Hull's ineptitude but reminds the reader that most of his fellow officers were as mediocre or semicompetent as was Hull.

The interested researcher will find many collections of published documents from the War of 1812. Hull's campaign may be seen through two such compilations. The first, "Documents Relating to Detroit and Vicinity, 1805-1813" (58), includes correspondence from Hull, Dearborn, and Eustis. Two larger compilations describing the northern campaigns are Ernest A. Cruikshank, *Documents Relating to the Invasion of Canada and the Surrender of Detroit, 1812* (53) and *The Documentary History of the Campaign upon the Niagara Frontier, 1812-14* (52). Unfortunately, Cruikshank's work includes numerous errors and so must be used with caution. Probably the best set of documents covering the entire war is John Brannan, *Official Letters of the Military and Naval Officers of the United States During the War with Great Britain. . . .* (32). This includes excellent coverage for all phases of wartime operations and should be used with John Armstrong, *Notices of the War of 1812* (10). Armstrong served as secretary of war for much of the conflict and published the documents to settle long-standing disputes begun during the war.

The two most useful collections of British documents are Ferdinand B. Tupper, *The Life and Correspondence of Major-General Sir Isaac Brock* (231), which is indispensable for any study of his career, and William C. H. Wood, *Select British Documents of the Canadian War of 1812* (253). Added to the American documents already discussed, these help provide balance and understanding of things which otherwise remain unclear.

Only a few relatively technical studies of the war have appeared. Brereton Greenhous, "A Note on Western Logistics in the War of 1812" (92), notes that problems related to logistics not only included the usual poor communication and transportation facilities, but also financial, bureaucratic, and political weaknesses as well. Jeffrey Kimball offers one of the few tactical studies in "The Battle of Chippawa: Infantry Tactics in the War of 1812" (140). Louise Phelps Kellogg presents a more narrative approach in "The Capture of Mackinac in 1812" (138) but still gives some sense of campaign activity. In a broader study, *Medical Sketches of the Campaigns of 1812, 1813, 1814* (159), James Mann offers contemporary accounts of medical problems, treatment, and personnel.

THE POSTWAR ARMY. Once the War of 1812 ended, Congress cut the size of the army and the War Department hurried soldiers west to strengthen American control over areas recently cleared of British forces. Edgar B. Wesley, *Guarding the Frontier: A Study of Frontier Defense from 1815 to 1825* (246), provides a detailed, yet lucid account of both these topics. Francis P. Prucha's *Broadax and Bayonet* (190) shows the army role in the "attack on the wilderness." In his more recent *Sword of the Republic* (193) he develops the theme that the soldiers served as "agents of empire" for an expanding nation. Certainly this was the case at times, but enough examples of army incompetence and bureaucratic mismanagement exist to raise doubts too. In "The Army and the Indians 1800-1830—A Reappraisal: The Missouri Valley Example" (169), Roger L. Nichols disputes claims for army accomplishments during the early decades of the century. He demonstrates that soldiers rarely accomplished any of their major assignments in the Missouri Valley prior to 1830. In fact, by 1827 the army had retreated back down the valley to Fort Leavenworth and control of the region reverted to the Indians.

From 1817 on, John C. Calhoun served as secretary of war and he pushed army movement into frontier areas aggressively. His edited correspondence (38, 39) gives a good picture of cabinet-level decision making and shows how haphazard and personal such planning was. Between 1815 and 1821 two reorganizations and reductions of the army occurred. The first came immediately after the war ended and the second resulted from the depression following the Panic of 1819. Raphael P. Thian (225) describes the new organization and how the remaining units were deployed. One part of the 1821 reorganization created the office of Commanding General of the Army. William B. Skelton, "The Commanding General and the Problem of Command in the United States Army, 1821-1841" (207), is an excellent study of the numerous problems which resulted from the creation of this office. While bureaucrats argued, political leaders continued to debate the need for an army. Richard L. Watson, Jr., "Congressional Attitudes Toward Military Preparedness, 1829-1835" (241), discusses the issue and claims that the small army resulted from a compromise between the militia supporters and those who wanted to keep a regular army.

Throughout the period 1815-1845 soldiers carried out many of the same tasks which they had done earlier—but now they worked farther to the west. Soldiers continued to explore, map, and survey portions of the frontier. Stephen H. Long was one important explorer. No good study of his explorations exists, although Richard G. Wood discusses them in *Stephen Harriman Long, 1784-1864* (252). Published journals by John R. Bell (23) and Edwin James (130) provide the story of Long's 1819-20 expeditions up the Missouri and onto the plains, while William H. Keating (137) reported the 1823 expedition north up the Mississippi and Red rivers into Canada.

Nearly two decades later John C. Fremont's expeditions captured the imagination of thousands. Allan Nevins, *Fremont: Pathmarker of the West* (168), is an excellent discussion. Fremont's own account of his 1842-44 expeditions (79) appeared the next year, and his *Memoirs of My Life* (78) round out the story. William H. Goetzmann has written two studies, *Army Exploration in the American West, 1803-1863* (87) which traces the use the federal government made of the corps of topographical engineers as explorers, and *Exploration and Empire* (88), which considers this work within the broader context of exploration in general.

Soldiers did more than explore, however. The vast scope of army efforts may be seen in Francis P. Prucha's two studies (190, 193) as well as in Henry P. Beers, *The Western Military Frontier, 1815-1846* (21). In "Military Escorts on the Santa Fe Trail" (185), Fred S. Perrine analyzes this work which began in 1829. Leo E. Oliva, *Soldiers on the Santa Fe Trail* (174), shows what other activities military units carried out on the southern plains. Along the Mississippi Valley mounted troops were first used during the mid-1830s. Louis Pelzer, *Marches of the Dragoons in the Mississippi Valley* (183), chronicles their work. Two items which consider military transportation projects are William T. Jackson, *Wagon Roads West* (127), and Roger L. Nichols, "Army Contributions to River Transportation, 1818-1825" (170).

Most of the time soldiers had to build their own forts, and numerous books and articles relate these efforts. Several of the most competent studies include: Edwin C. Bearss and Arrell M. Gibson, *Fort Smith: Little Gibraltar on the Arkansas* (20), Marcus Hansen, *Old Fort Snelling, 1819-1858* (105), Elvid Hunt, *History of Fort Leavenworth, 1827-1927* (125), and Bruce E. Mahan, *Old Fort Crawford and the Frontier* (154).

Biographies and career studies of army leaders provide ideas about army activities and problems too. Andrew Jackson, the most famous general of the era, has several biographies, but Marquis James, *Andrew Jackson, The Border Captain* (131), gives the best account of his military career. From 1821 until the early 1840s, Generals Winfield Scott and Edmund P. Gaines bickered continuously while each commanded one of the two army departments. Their rivalry and careers are best discussed in James W. Silver, *Edmund Pendleton Gaines: Frontier General* (206), and Charles W. Elliott, *Winfield Scott: The Soldier and the Man* (67). General Henry Atkinson remained the officer most closely supervising army activity beyond the Mississippi during the 1819-42 era. Roger L. Nichols, *General Henry Atkinson* (172), considers his contributions there. Many of Atkinson's subordinates later rose to positions of significance within the western army. Among these were Henry Dodge (182), William S. Harney (196), Stephen Watts Kearny (43), Stephen H. Long (252), and Zachary Taylor (104, 64).

In addition to these biographies, numerous eyewitness accounts, diaries, and reminiscences survive. As an inspector-general, George Croghan traveled throughout the Mississippi and Missouri valleys for several decades. Parts of his edited reports are available as *Army Life on the Western Frontier* (50). John Gale, *The Missouri Expedition, 1818-1820* (82), details the incredible mismanagement and hardships involved in that movement. For those interested in the health and diet of the regulars, Samuel Forry, *Statistical Report on the Sickness and Mortality of the Army of the United States* (76), includes reports from garrison commanders, as well as statistics compiled by regimental surgeons prior to 1840. Numerous officers left diaries or letters which have been published. Among these the following seem the most informative: Philip St. George Cooke (49), James Hildreth (110), Ethan Allan Hitchcock (113), Erasmus Darwin Keyes (139), George A. McCall (151), and Winfield Scott (205).

THE ARMY AND THE INDIANS. As one of the branches of the federal government on the frontier, the army often had to enforce laws and treaties related to the Indians. This assignment was clearly the most important and difficult one soldiers received during the three decades after 1815. Francis P. Prucha (193) gives a thorough discussion of this matter. Once the Indian Removal policy went into effect, troops had to locate and escort Indians west. At other times the government used the army to separate warring bands of Indians from each other as well as to keep whites and

Indians apart. The biographies of Henry Atkinson (172), Edmund P. Gaines (206), and Stephen W. Kearny (43) provide examples of these tasks. Grant Foreman, *Indian Removal: The Emigration of the Five Civilized Tribes of Indians* (72), gives the traditional view of removal by the army as brutal and degrading. In a bold challenge to this thesis, Francis P. Prucha's article, "Andrew Jackson's Indian Policy: A Reassessment" (189), claims that Jackson was no Indian hater and worked for their best interests.

Whichever view one accepts, removal proved a hateful experience for the Indians and some resisted bitterly. The first case of this occurred in Illinois and Wisconsin when a portion of the Sac and Fox tribes refused to stay west of the Mississippi River. In early 1832 a band of one thousand Indians followed Black Hawk, an aging Sac warrior, east across the Mississippi into Illinois. Panic swept the frontier and the resulting campaign came to be known as the Black Hawk War. Black Hawk's personal account is in *Ma-Ka-Tai-Me-She-Kia-Kiak—Black Hawk, an Autobiography* (27). He claims that his people wanted only to return to their corn fields and that the unrestrained Illinois militiamen caused the war. William T. Hagan, "General Henry Atkinson and the Militia" (97), and Roger L. Nichols, *General Henry Atkinson* (172), agree. For years Frank Stevens, *The Black Hawk War* (220), provided the only book-length study. It includes a narrative with numerous contemporary documents and, except for its anti-Indian bias, is a good account. A recent book by Cecil Eby, "*That Disgraceful Affair," the Black Hawk War* (65), includes the latest ideas on the topic. Unfortunately, the author annotates only direct quotations.

Only three years later, in late 1835, the Seminole Indians in Florida rose up in one of the longest and most expensive Indian conflicts in American history—the Second Seminole War. Shortly after the war ended in the mid-1840s, John T. Sprague published *The Origin, Progress, and Conclusion of the Florida War* (217). This contained a narrative, contemporary documents, and an excellent analysis of the war. In the mid-1960s John K. Mahon wrote the *History of the Second Seminole War, 1835-1842* (158). This is the definitive work on all phases of the conflict, and it seems unlikely that more need be done unless some new body of material should become available. For the Indians' side of this conflict see Edwin C. McReynolds, *The Seminoles* (153).

SUGGESTIONS FOR FURTHER RESEARCH. Although the period from 1783 until 1845 has enjoyed considerable attention from military historians in the past several decades, there are still topics untouched and others which need further study. Except for a minor article on establishing the first infantry school by Nichols (171), little has been done with training, particularly of the enlisted men. For later periods scholars have considered the army as a social institution, but this has not been done for the decades under consideration here. Therefore, studies of the enlistment process, the sources of regular army soldiers, the problems of diet, malnutrition and desertion, and the life of enlisted men within the army are yet to be done.

Most scholars recognize that the use of Indian warriors as scouts, messengers, spies, and allies was widespread. In fact, Indians served both for and against the army in practically every campaign west of Pennsylvania from 1783 until 1845. Despite this, almost no studies of Indian participation in army campaigns exist for the period. An examination of Indian recruitment and pay, of the duties assigned warriors, of their degree of success and failure, and of their contributions to American military history remain unwritten.

Military historians tend to shy away from legal studies, yet frequently in the nineteenth century soldiers served as local posses and officers received directives to enforce the laws regulating trade with the Indians. Such orders brought soldiers into conflict with the civilian population and caused much difficulty. The legal basis for such army activity, the frequency of soldiers being called upon as law enforcers, and the degree of success and failure of these efforts provide fruitful avenues for research.

Finally, the debate over army competence and the degree of positive contributions soldiers made to solving early national problems is by no means concluded. How often did army units succeed in carrying out their orders as understood by the War Department? When they failed, who was to blame? These and related questions need more study.

BIBLIOGRAPHY

1. Adams, George R. "Caloosahatche Massacre: Its Significance in the Second Seminole War." *Florida Historical Quarterly*, XLVIII (April, 1970), 368-380.
2. Adams, Randolph G. "The Harmar Expedition of 1790." *Ohio State Archaeological and Historical Quarterly*, (January-March, 1941), 60-62.
3. Adams, Randolph G. and Howard H. Peckham. *Lexington to Fallen Timbers, 1775-1794*. Ann Arbor: University of Michigan Press, 1942.
4. "Captain James Allen's Dragoon Expedition from Fort Des Moines, Territory of Iowa in 1844." Ed., Jacob Van der Zee. *Iowa Journal of History and Politics*, XI (January, 1913), 68-108.
5. Ambrose, Stephen. *Duty, Honor, Country: A History of West Point*. Baltimore: Johns Hopkins Press, 1966.
6. *American State Papers: Indian Affairs*. Washington: Gales and Seaton, 1832-1834. 2 vols.
7. *American State Papers: Military Affairs*. Washington: Gales and Seaton, 1832-1861. 7 vols.
8. Anderson, Robert. "Reminiscences of the Black Hawk War." *Wisconsin Historical Collections*, X (1888), 167-176.
9. *Annals of Congress, 1789-1824*. Washington: Gales and Seaton, 1834-1856.
10. Armstrong, John. *Notices of the War of 1812*. New York: Wiley and Putnam, 1840. 2 vols.
11. *Army and Navy Chronicle*. Washington; 1835-1842.
12. Ashburn, Percy M. *A History of the Medical Department of the United States Army*. Boston: Houghton Mifflin, 1929.

13. "Journal of the Atkinson-O'Fallon Expedition, 1825." Ed., Russell Reid and Clell G. Gannon. *North Dakota Historical Quarterly*, IV (October, 1929), 4-56.
14. Babcock, Elkhanah. *A War History of the Sixth United States Infantry, From 1798 to 1903.* Kansas City, Missouri: Hudson-Kimberly Publishing Co., 1903.
15. Babcock, Louis L. *The War of 1812 on the Niagara Frontier.* Buffalo, New York: Buffalo Historical Society, 1927.
16. Bakeless, John. *Lewis and Clark, Partners in Discovery.* New York: W. Morrow, 1947.
17. Barr, James. *A Correct and Authentic Narrative of the Indian War in Florida.* New York: J. Narine, printer, 1836.
18. Barron, Alice E. "In Defense of the Frontier: The Work of General Henry Atkinson, 1819-1842." Master's thesis, (Chicago) Loyola University, 1937.
19. Barry, Louise. "The Fort Leavenworth-Fort Gibson Military Road and the Founding of Fort Scott." *Kansas Historical Quarterly*, XI (May, 1942), 115-129.
20. Bearss, Edwin C. and Arrell M. Gibson. *Fort Smith: Little Gibraltar on the Arkansas.* Norman: University of Oklahoma Press, 1969.
21. Beers, Henry P. *The Western Military Frontier, 1815-1846.* Philadelphia: University of Pennsylvania Press, 1935.
22. Beirne, Francis F. *The War of 1812.* New York: E. P. Dutton & Co., Inc., 1949.
23. *The Journal of Captain John R. Bell, Official Journalist for the Stephen H. Long Expedition to the Rocky Mountains, 1820.* Ed., Harlin M. Fuller and LeRoy R. Hafen. Glendale, Calif.: Arthur H. Clark, 1957.
24. Bernardo, C. Joseph and Eugene H. Bacon. *American Military Policy: Its Development Since 1775.* Harrisburg: Military Service Publishing Co., 1955.
25. Bittle, George C. "First Campaign of the Second Seminole War." *Florida Historical Quarterly*, XLVI (July, 1967), 39-45.
26. Birkhimer, William E. *Historical Sketch of the Organization, Administration, Materiel, and Tactics of the Artillery of the United States Army.* Washington : J. J. Chapman, 1884.
27. *Ma-Ka-Tai-Me-She-Kai-Kaik—Black Hawk, an Autobiography.* Ed., Donald Jackson. Urbana: University of Illinois Press, 1955.
28. Bond, Beverley W., Jr. "William Henry Harrison in the War of 1812." *Mississippi Valley Historical Review*, XIII (March, 1927), 499-516.
29. Boyd, Mark F. "Florida Aflame: Background and Onset of the Seminole War, 1835." *Florida Historical Quarterly*, XXX (July, 1951), 3-115.
30. Boyd, Thomas A. *Mad Anthony Wayne.* New York: Charles Scribner's Sons, 1929.
31. Brackett, Albert G. *History of the United States Cavalry, from the Formation of the Federal Government to the 1st of June, 1863.* New York: Harper & Brothers, 1865.
32. Brannan, John. Compiler. *Official Letters of the Military and Naval Officers of the United States During the War with Great Britain*

in the Years 1812, 13, 14, & 15. Washington: Printed by Way & Gideon, for the editor, 1823.

33. Brooks, Charles B. *The Siege of New Orleans*. Seattle: University of Washington Press, 1961.

34. Brooks, Noah. *Henry Knox: A Soldier of the Revolution*. New York: G. P. Putnam's Sons, 1900.

35. Burt, A. L. *The United States, Great Britain and British North America, from the Revolution to the Establishment of Peace after the War of 1812*. Toronto: The Ryerson Press, 1940.

36. Caldwell, Norman W. "The Enlisted Soldier at the Frontier Post, 1790-1814." *Mid-America*, XXXVII (October, 1955), 195-204.

37. Caldwell, Norman W. "The Frontier Army Officer, 1794-1814." *Mid-America*, XXXVII (April, 1955), 101-128.

38. *Correspondence of John C. Calhoun*. Ed., J. Franklin Jameson. *American Historical Association Annual Report, 1899*. Washington: Historical Association, 1900.

39. *The Papers of John C. Calhoun*. Ed. Robert L. Meriwether and W. Edwin Hemphill. 7 vols. Columbia: University of South Carolina Press, 1959—.

40. Callan, John F. *The Military Laws of the United States.* . . . Philadelphia: G. W. Childs, 1863.

41. Carleton, James Henry. *The Prairie Logbooks: Dragoon Campaigns to the Pawnee Village in 1844, and to the Rocky Mountains in 1845*. Ed. Louis Pelzer. Chicago: The Caxton Club, 1943.

42. Cassell, Frank A. "Baltimore in 1813: A Study of Urban Defense in the War of 1812." *Military Affairs*, XXXIII (December, 1969), 349-361.

43. Clark, Dwight L. *Stephen Watts Kearny: Soldier of the West*. Norman: University of Oklahoma Press, 1961.

44. *The Field Notes of Captain William Clark, 1803-1805*. Ed. Ernest S. Osgood. New Haven: Yale University Press, 1964.

45. Cleaves, Freeman. *Old Tippecanoe: William Henry Harrison and His Time*. New York: Charles Scribner's Sons, 1939.

46. Coe, Charles H. *Red Patriots: The Story of the Seminoles*. Cincinnati: Editor Publishing Co., 1898.

47. Coles, Harry L. *The War of 1812*. Chicago: University of Chicago Press, 1965.

48. *Congressional Globe, 1834-1845*. Washington: Globe Office, 1834-1845.

49. Cooke, Philip St. George. *Scenes and Adventures in the Army: or Romance of Military Life*. Philadelphia: Lindsay & Blakiston, 1857.

50. Croghan, George. *Army Life on the Western Frontier: Selections from the Official Reports Made Between 1826 and 1845*. Ed. Francis P. Prucha. Norman: University of Oklahoma Press, 1958.

51. Crowe, Fletcher S. "National Policy of Frontier Defense, 1815-1825." Master's thesis. St. Louis: Washington University, 1922.

52. Cruikshank, Ernest A., ed. *The Documentary History of the Campaign upon the Niagara Frontier, 1812-14*. Welland, Ontario: Printed at the Tribune, 1896-1908. 9 vols.

53. Cruikshank, Ernest A., ed. *Documents Relating to the Invasion of*

Canada and the Surrender of Detroit, 1812. Ottawa: Government Printing Bureau, 1912.

54. Cullum, George W., compiler. *Biographical Register of the Officers and Graduates of the United States Military Academy.* New York: P. Van Nostrand, 1868-1879. 2 vols.

55. Cunliffe, Marcus. "The American Military Tradition." In H. C. Allen and C. P. Hill, eds., *British Essays in American History.* New York: St. Martin's Press, 1957.

56. Cutright, Paul C. *Lewis and Clark: Pioneering Naturalists.* Urbana: University of Illinois Press, 1969.

57. Dillon, Richard. *Meriwether Lewis, A Biography.* New York: Coward-McCann, 1965.

58. "Documents Relating to Detroit and Vicinity, 1805-1813." *Michigan Historical Collections,* XL (1929).

59. Dodge, Henry. "Journal of the March of a Detachment of Dragoons Under the Command of Colonel Dodge during the Summer of 1835." *American State Papers: Military Affairs,* VI, 133-138.

60. Downes, Randolph C. *Council Fires on the Upper Ohio.* Pittsburgh: University of Pittsburgh Press, 1940.

61. Downes, Randolph C. *Frontier Ohio, 1788-1803. Ohio Historical Collections,* III (1935).

62. Downey, Fairfax. *Indian Wars of the United States Army, 1776-1865.* Garden City: Doubleday, 1963.

63. Dupuy, R. Ernest. *The Compact History of the United States Army.* New York: Hawthorn Books, Inc., 1956.

64. Dyer, Brainerd. *Zachary Taylor.* Baton Rouge: Louisiana State University Press, 1946.

65. Eby, Cecil. *"That Disgraceful Affair," the Black Hawk War.* New York: W. W. Norton & Company, Inc., 1973.

66. Eller, William B. "The Arickara Conquest of 1823." *Transactions and Reports of the Nebraska Historical Society,* V (1893), 35-42.

67. Elliott, Charles W. *Winfield Scott: The Soldier and the Man.* New York: The Macmillan Company, 1937.

68. "Employment of Indians Against the Seminoles." *American State Papers: Military Affairs,* VII, 518-525.

69. Fisher, Robert L. "The Western Prologue to the War of 1812." *Missouri Historical Review,* XXX (April, 1936), 267-281.

70. Fisher, Vincent J. "Mr. Calhoun's Army." *Military Review,* XXXVII (September, 1957), 52-58.

71. Foreman, Grant. *Advancing the Frontier, 1830-1860.* Norman: University of Oklahoma Press, 1933.

72. Foreman, Grant. *Indian Removal: The Emigration of the Five Civilized Tribes of Indians.* Norman: University of Oklahoma Press, 1932.

73. Forman, Sidney. *West Point: A History of the United States Military Academy.* New York: Columbia University Press, 1950.

74. Forman, Sidney. "Why the United States Military Academy was Established in 1802." *Military Affairs,* XXIX (Spring, 1965), 16-28.

75. "Letters of Samuel Forry, Surgeon, U.S. Army, 1837, '38." *Florida Historical Quarterly,* VI (January, 1928), 133-148; (April, 1928), 206-219; VII (July, 1928), 88-105.

76. Forry, Samuel, compiler. *Statistical Report on the Sickness and Mortality of the Army of the United States.* Washington: Printed by J. Gideon, Jr., 1840.

77. Forsyth, Thomas. "Fort Snelling. Colonel Leavenworth's Expedition to Establish it in 1819." *Minnesota Historical Collections,* III (1880), 139-167.

78. Fremont, John C. *Memoirs of My Life.* Chicago: Belford, Clarke & Company, 1887.

79. Fremont, John C. *Report of the Exploring Expedition to the Rocky Mountains in the Year 1842, and to Oregon and North California in the Years 1843-'44.* Washington: Gales and Seaton Printers, 1845.

80. Fry, James B. *The History and Legal Effect of Brevets in the Armies of Great Britain and the United States From Their Origin in 1692 to the Present Time.* New York: D. Van Nostrand, 1877.

81. Gaines, William H., Jr. "The Forgotten Army: Recruiting for a National Emergency (1799-1800)." *Virginia Magazine of History and Biography,* LVI (July, 1948), 267-279.

82. Gale, John. *The Missouri Expedition, 1818-1820: the Journal of Surgeon John Gale with Related Documents.* Ed. Roger L. Nichols. Norman: University of Oklahoma Press, 1969.

83. Gallaher, Ruth A. "The Military-Indian Frontier 1830-1835." *Iowa Journal of History and Politics,* XV (July, 1917), 393-428.

84. Ganoe, William Addleman. *The History of the United States Army.* New York: D. Appleton-Century-Co., Inc., 1936. Reprinted, Augusta, West Virginia: Lundberg, 1964.

85. Gilpin, Alec R. *The War of 1812 in the Old Northwest.* East Lansing: Michigan State University Press, 1958.

86. Godfrey, Carlos E. "Organization of the Provisional Army of the United States in the Anticipated War with France, 1798-1800." *Pennsylvania Magazine of History and Biography,* XXXVIII (April, 1941), 129-182.

87. Goetzmann, William H. *Army Exploration in the American West, 1803-1863.* New Haven: Yale University Press, 1959.

88. Goetzmann, William H. *Exploration and Empire, the Explorer and Scientist in the Winning of the American West.* New York: Alfred A. Knopf, 1966.

89. Goodman, Warren H. "The Origins of the War of 1812: A Survey of Changing Interpretations." *Mississippi Valley Historical Review,* XXVIII (September, 1941), 171-186.

90. Goodpasture, Albert V. "Indian Wars and Warriors of the Old Southwest, 1730-1807." *Tennessee Historical Magazine,* Second Series, IV (March, 1918), 3-49; (June, 1918), 106-145; (September, 1918), 161-210; (December, 1918), 252-289.

91. Goodwin, Cardinal L. "A Larger View of the Yellowstone Expedition, 1819-1820." *Mississippi Valley Historical Review,* IX (December, 1917), 299-313.

92. Greenhous, Bereton. "A Note on Western Logistics in the War of 1812." *Military Affairs,* XXXIV (April, 1970), 41-44.

93. Gregg, Kate L. "Building the First American Fort West of the

Mississippi." *Missouri Historical Review*, XXX (July, 1936), 345-364.
94. Gregg, Kate L. "The History of Fort Osage, 1815-1827." *Missouri Historical Review*, XXXIV (July, 1940), 439-488.
95. Grey, Charles. *Crisis in the Canadas, 1838-39; The Grey Journals and Letters.* Ed. William Ormsby. Toronto: Macmillan of Canada, 1964.
96. Hagan, William T. "The Black Hawk War." Doctoral dissertation, University of Wisconsin, 1950.
97. Hagan, William T. "General Henry Atkinson and the Militia," *Military Affairs*, XXII (Winter, 1959-60), 194-197.
98. Hagan, William T. *The Sac and Fox Indians.* Norman: University of Oklahoma Press, 1958.
99. Halbert, Henry S. and T. H. Ball. *The Creek War of 1813 and 1814.* Chicago: Donohue & Henneberry, 1895.
100. Hale, Henry. "The Soldier, the Advance Guard of Civilization." *Proceedings of the Mississippi Valley Historical Association, 1913-14.* VII (1914), 93-98.
101. Hall, Arthur H. "The Red Stick War: Creek Indian Affairs During the War of 1812." *Chronicles of Oklahoma*, XII (September, 1934), 264-293.
102. Hamer, Philip, ed. *A Guide to Archives and Manuscripts in the United States.* New Haven: Yale University Press, 1961.
103. Hamersly, Thomas H. S., compiler. *Complete Regular Army Register of the United States: For One Hundred Years (1779-1878).* Baltimore: William K. Boyle, Printer, 1880.
104. Hamilton, Holman. *Zachary Taylor, Soldier of the Republic.* Indianapolis: Bobbs-Merrill Co., 1941.
105. Hansen, Marcus L. *Old Fort Snelling, 1819-1858.* Iowa City: State Historical Society of Iowa, 1918.
106. *Governors Messages and Letters, Messages and Letters of William Henry Harrison.* 2 vols. Ed. Logan Esarey. *Indiana Historical Collections*, vols. VII and IX. Indianapolis: Indiana Historical Commission, 1922.
107. Hay, Thomas R. and M. R. Werner. *The Admirable Trumpeter: A Biography of General James Wilkinson.* Garden City: Doubleday, Doran & Company, Inc., 1941.
108. Haynes, Robert V. "The Southwest and the War of 1812." *Louisiana History*, V (Winter, 1964), 41-51.
109. Heitman, Francis B., compiler. *Historical Register and Dictionary of the United States Army.* 2 vols. Washington: G.P.O., 1903.
110. Hildreth, James. *Dragoon Campaigns to the Rocky Mountains* . . . . New York: Wiley & Long, 1836.
111. Hill, Forest G. *Roads, Rails & Waterways: The Army Engineers and Early Transportation.* Norman: University of Oklahoma Press, 1957.
112. Hinton, Harwood P. "The Military Career of John Ellis Wool, 1812-1863." Doctoral dissertation, University of Wisconsin, 1960.
113. Hitchcock, Ethan Allen. *Fifty Years in Camp and Field: Diary of Major*

General Ethan Allen Hitchcock, U.S.A. Ed. E. A. Croffut. New York: G. P. Putnam's Sons, 1900.

114. Hitsman, J. Mackay. "Alarum on Lake Ontario, Winter 1812-1813." *Military Affairs*, XXIII (Fall, 1959), 129-138.

115. Hitsman, J. Mackay. *The Incredible War of 1812*. Toronto: University of Toronto Press, 1965.

116. Holland, James W. "Andrew Jackson and the Creek War: Victory at the Horseshoe." *Alabama Review*, XXI (October, 1968), 243-275.

117. Hollon, W. Eugene. *The Lost Pathfinder: Zebulon Montgomery Pike*. Norman: University of Oklahoma Press, 1949.

118. Holt, W. Stull. *The Office of the Chief of Engineers of the Army; Its Non-Military History, Activities and Organization*. Baltimore: The Johns Hopkins Press, 1923.

119. Horsman, Reginald. "American Indian Policy in the Old Northwest, 1783-1812." *William and Mary Quarterly*, XVIII (January, 1961), 35-53.

120. Horsman, Reginald. *The Causes of the War of 1812*. Philadelphia: University of Pennsylvania Press, 1962.

121. Horsman, Reginald. *The Frontier in the Formative Years, 1783-1815*. New York: Holt, Rinehart and Winston, 1970.

122. Hughes, Willis B. "The Army and Stephen Watts Kearny in the West." Doctoral dissertation, University of Minnesota, 1955.

123. Huidekoper, Frederick L. *The Military Unpreparedness of the United States: A History of the American Land Forces from Colonial Times until June 1, 1915*. New York: The Macmillan Company, 1916.

124. Hull, William. *Memoirs of the Canpaign of the North Western Army of the United States, A.D. 1812*. Boston: True and Green, 1824.

125. Hunt, Elvid. *History of Fort Leavenworth, 1827-1927*. Fort Leavenworth, Kansas: The General Service Schools Press, 1926.

126. *Correspondence of Andrew Jackson*. Ed. John Bassett. Washington: Carnegie Institution, 1926-1935. 7 vols.

127. Jackson, William T. *Wagon Roads West*. Berkeley: Universty of California Press, 1952.

128. Jacobs, James R. *The Beginning of the U.S. Army, 1783-1812*. Princeton: Princeton University Press, 1947.

129. Jacobs, James R. *Tarnished Warrior: Major General James Wilkinson*. New York: The Macmillan Company, 1938.

130. James, Edwin, compiler. *Account of an Expedition from Pittsburgh to the Rocky Mountains performed in the years 1819-1820 . . . Under the command of Major S. H. Long*. 4 vols. Ed. Reuben G. Thwaites, in *Early Western Travels*. Cleveland: Arthur C. Clark, 1905.

131. James, Marquis. *Andrew Jackson, The Border Captain*. Indianapolis: Bobbs-Merrill Co., 1933.

132. James, William. *Full and Correct Account of the Military Occurrences of the Late War between Great Britain and the United States of America*. London: Printed for the author, 1818. 2 vols.

133. Johnson, Sally A. "Cantonment Missouri, 1819-1820." *Nebraska History*, XXXVII (June, 1956), 121-133.
134. Johnson, Sally A. "The Sixth's Elysian Fields: Fort Atkinson on the Council Bluffs." *Nebraska History*, XL (March, 1959), 1-38.
135. Jones, Roger. "General Brown's Inspection Tour up the Lakes in 1819." *Publications of the Buffalo Historical Society*, XXIV (1920), 295-323.
136. Kaufman, Martin. "War Sentiment in Western Pennsylvania: 1812." *Pennsylvania History*, XXXI (October, 1964), 436-448.
137. Keating, William H. *Narrative of an Expedition to the Source of St. Peter's River, Lake Winnepeek, Lake of the Woods, &c. Performed in the Year 1823 . . . Under the Command of Stephen H. Long, U.S.T.E.* Philadelphia: Carey & Lea, 1824. 2 vols.
138. Kellogg, Louise Phelps. "The Capture of Mackinac in 1812." *Proceedings of the State Historical Society of Wisconsin*, (1912), 124-145.
139. Keyes, Erasmus Darwin. *Fifty Years' Observation of Men and Events, Civil and Military.* New York: C. Scribner's Sons, 1884.
140. Kimball, Jeffrey. "The Battle of Chippawa: Infantry Tactics in the War of 1812." *Military Affairs*, XXXI (Winter, 1967-1968), 169-186.
141. Knopf, Richard C. *Anthony Wayne, A Name in Arms . . . The Wayne-Knox-Pickering-McHenry Correspondence.* Pittsburgh: University of Pittsburgh Press, 1960.
142. Knopf, Richard C. "Crime and Punishment in the Legion, 1792-1793." *Bulletin of the Historical and Philosophical Society of Ohio*, XIV (July, 1956), 232-238.
143. Kreidberg, Marvin A. and Merton G. Henry. *History of Military Mobilization in the United States Army, 1775-1945.* Washington: Department of the Army, 1955.
144. Lambert, Joseph I. "The Black Hawk War: A Military Analysis." *Journal of the Illinois State Historical Society*, XXXII (December, 1939), 442-473.
145. *Letters of the Lewis and Clark Expedition, With Related Documents, 1783-1854.* Ed. Donald Jackson. Urbana: University of Illinois Press, 1962.
146. *Original Journals of the Lewis and Clark Expedition.* Ed. Reuben G. Thwaites. New York: Dodd, Mead & Company, 1904-1905. 8 vols.
147. *The Journals of Captain Meriwether Lewis and Sergeant John Ordway.* . . . Ed. Milo M. Quaife. Madison: State Historical Society of Wisconsin, 1916.
148. Lossing, Benson J. *Pictorial Field Book of the War of 1812.* . . . New York: Harper & Brothers, 1868.
149. Lowe, Richard G. "American Seizure of Amelia Island." *Florida Historical Quarterly*, XLV (July, 1966), 18-30.
150. McAfee, Robert B. *History of the Late War in the Western Country.* Lexington, Kentucky: Worsley & Smith, 1816.
151. McCall, George A. *Letters from the Frontiers.* Philadelphia: J. B. Lippincott & Co., 1868.

152. McKenny, Thomas L. "The Winnebago War of 1827." *Wisconsin Historical Collections*, V (1868), 178-204.
153. McReynolds, Edwin C. *The Seminoles*. Norman: University of Oklahoma Press, 1957.
154. Mahan, Bruce E. *Old Fort Crawford and the Frontier*. Iowa City: State Historical Society of Iowa, 1926.
155. Mahon, John K. "British Command Decisons Relative to the Battle of New Orleans," *Louisiana History*, VI (Winter, 1965), 53-76.
156. Mahon, John K. "British Strategy and Southern Indians: War of 1812." *Florida Historical Quarterly*, XLIV (April, 1966), 285-302.
157. Mahon, John K. "History of the Organization of the United States Infantry." *The Army Lineage Book*, Washington: Defense Department, 1953, 1-61.
158. Mahon, John K. *History of the Second Seminole War, 1835-1842*. Gainesville: University of Florida Press, 1967.
159. Mann, James. *Medical Sketches of the Campaigns of 1812, 1813, 1814. . .* Dedham, Massachussetts: H. Mann and Co., 1816.
160. Mason, Philip P., ed. *After Tippecanoe: Some Aspects of the War of 1812*. East Lansing: Michigan State University Press, 1963.
161. Mattison, Ray H. "The Military Frontier on the Upper Missouri." *Nebraska History*, XXXVII (September, 1956), 159-182.
162. Meek, Basil. "General Harmar's Expedition." *Ohio State Archaeological and Historical Quarterly*, XX (January, 1911), 74-108.
163. *Military and Naval Magazine*. 6 vols. 1833-1836.
164. Miller, John. "The Military Occupation of Green Bay." *Mississippi Valley Historical Review*, XIII (March, 1927), 549-553.
165. Morton, Louis. "The Origins of American Military Policy." *Military Affairs*, XXII (Summer, 1958), 75-82.
166. Motte, Jacob Rhett. *Journey into Wilderness: An Army Surgeon's Account of Life in Camp and Field During the Creek and Seminole Wars, 1836-1838*. Ed. James Sunderman. Gainesville: University of Florida Press, 1953.
167. Neal, Annie. "Policing the Frontier, 1816-1827." Master's thesis, University of Wisconsin, 1923.
168. Nevins, Allan. *Fremont: Pathmarker of the West*. New York: Longmans, Green and Co., Inc., 1939.
169. Nichols, Roger L. "The Army and the Indians 1800-1830--A Reappraisal: The Missouri Valley Example." *Pacific Historical Review*, XLI (May, 1972), 151-168.
170. Nichols, Roger L. "Army Contributions to River Transportation, 1818-1825," *Military Affairs*, XXXIII (April, 1969), 242-249.
171. Nichols, Roger L. "General Henry Atkinson and the Building of Jefferson Barracks." *Bulletin of the Missouri Historical Society*, XXII (April, 1966), 321-326.
172. Nichols, Roger L. *General Henry Atkinson: A Western Military Career*. Norman: University of Oklahoma Press, 1965.
173. *Niles Weekly Register*. 1811-1849.
174. Oliva, Leo E. *Soldiers on the Santa Fe Trail*. Norman: University of Oklahoma Press, 1967.
175. Owsley, Frank L., Jr. "British and Indian Activities in Spanish West

Florida During the War of 1812." *Florida Historical Quarterly*, XLVI (October, 1967), 111-123.

176. Owsley, Frank L., Jr. "The Fort Mims Massacre." *Alabama Review*, XXIV (July, 1971), 192-204.

177. Owsley, Frank L., Jr. "Jackson's Capture of Pensacola." *Alabama Review*, XIX (July, 1966), 175-185.

178. Paine, Charles R. "The Seminole War of 1817-1818." Master's thesis, University of Oklahoma, 1938.

179. Patrick, Rembert W. *Aristocrat in Uniform: General Duncan L. Clinch*. Gainesville: University of Florida Press, 1963.

180. Patrick, Rembert W. *Florida Fiasco: Rampant Rebels on the Georgia-Florida Border, 1810-1815*. Athens: University of Georgia Press, 1954.

181. Peckham, Howard H. "Josiah Harmar and His Indian Expedition." *Ohio State Archaeological and Historical Quarterly*, LV (July-September, 1946), 227-241.

182. Pelzer, Louis. *Henry Dodge*. Iowa City: State Historical Society of Iowa, 1911.

183. Pelzer, Louis. *Marches of the Dragoons in the Mississippi Valley: an account of marches and activities of the First regiment United States dragoons . . . between the years 1833 and 1850*. Iowa City: State Historical Society of Iowa, 1917.

184. Perkins, Bradford. *Prologue to War: England and the United States, 1805-1812*. Berkeley: University of California Press, 1962.

185. Perrine, Fred S. "Military Escorts on the Santa Fe Trail." *New Mexico Historical Review*, II (April, 1927), 175-193; (July, 1927), 269-304; III (July, 1928), 265-300.

186. *The Journals of Zebulon Montgomery Pike With Letters and Related Documents*. Ed. Donald Jackson. Norman: University of Oklahoma Press, 1966. 2 vols.

187. Poore, Benjamin P. *A Descriptive Catalogue of the Government Publications of the United States 1774-1881*. Washington: G.P.O., 1895. 2 vols.

188. Potter, Woodburne. *The War in Florida: Being an Exposition of Its Causes, and an Accurate History of the Campaigns of Generals Clinch, Gaines and Scott. . . .* Baltimore: Lewis and Coleman, 1836.

189. Prucha, Francis P. "Andrew Jackson's Indian Policy: A Reassessment." *Journal of American History*, LVI (1969), 527-541.

190. Prucha, Francis P. *Broadax and Bayonet, the Role of the United States Army in the Development of the Northwest, 1815-1860*. Madison: State Historical Society of Wisconsin, 1953.

191. Prucha, Francis P. "Distribution of Regular Army Troops Before the Civil War." *Military Affairs*, XVI (Winter, 1952), 169-173.

192. Prucha, Francis P. *Guide to the Military Posts of the United States, 1789-1895*. Madison: State Historical Society of Wisconsin, 1964.

193. Prucha, Francis P. *The Sword of the Republic, The United States Army on the Frontier, 1783-1846*. Toronto: The Macmillan Company, 1969.

194. Quaife, Milo M. "General Hull and His Critics." *Ohio State Archaeo-*

logical and Historical Quarterly, XLVII (April, 1938), 168-182.
195. Rankin, Hugh F. "The British at New Orleans: Strategy or Blunder?" *Louisiana Studies,* IV (Fall, 1965), 179-186.
196. Reavis, Logan U. *Life and Military Services of General William Selby Harney.* St. Louis: Bryan, Brand & Co., 1878.
197. *Register of Debates, 1824-1837.* Washington: Gales and Seaton, 1826-1838. 29 vols.
198. *The First Military Escort on the Santa Fe Trail, 1829: From the Journal and Reports of Major Bennet Riley and Lieutenant Philip St. George Cooke.* Ed. Otis E. Young. Glendale, California: Arthur H. Clark, 1952.
199. Risch, Erna. *Quartermaster Support of the Army: A History of the Corps, 1775-1939.* Washington: Office of the Quartermaster General, 1962.
200. Robbins, Roy M. "The Defense of the Western Frontier, 1825-1840." Unpublished Master's thesis, Madison: University of Wisconsin, 1926.
201. Robinson, Doane. Ed. "Official Correspondence of the Leavenworth Expedition of 1823 into South Dakota for the Conquest of the Ree Indians." *South Dakota Historical Society Collections,* I (August, 1902), 179-256.
202. Rodenbough, Theophilus F. *The Army of the United States: Historical Sketches of Staff and Line with Portraits of Generals-in-Chief.* New York: Maynard, Merrill, & Co., 1896.
203. St. Clair, Arthur. *A Narrative of the Manner in Which the Campaign Against the Indians, in the Year One Thousand Seven Hundred and Ninety-one, Was Conducted Under the Command of Major General St. Clair. . . .* Philadelphia: Printed by Jane Aitken, 1812.
204. Schreve, R. O. *The Finished Scoundrel: General James Wilkinson.* Indianapolis: Bobbs-Merrill Co., 1933.
205. Scott, Winfield. *Memoirs of Lieut. General Scott.* New York: Sheldon & Company, 1864. 2 vols.
206. Silver, James W. *Edmund Pendleton Gaines: Frontier General.* Baton Rouge: Louisiana State University Press, 1949.
207. Skelton, William B. "The Commanding General and the Problem of Command in the United States Army, 1821-1841." *Military Affairs,* XXXIV (December, 1970), 117-122.
208. Slocum, Charles Elihu. *The Ohio Country Between the Years 1783 and 1815. . . .* New York: G. P. Putnam's Sons, 1910.
209. Smelser, Marshall. "Tecumseh, Harrison and the War of 1812." *Indiana Magazine of History,* LXV (March, 1969), 25-44.
210. Smith, Alice. *The History of Wisconsin: From Exploration to Statehood.* Madison: State Historical Society of Wisconsin, 1973.
211. Smith, Dwight L. "Provocation and Occurrence of Indian-White Warfare in the Early American Period in the Old Northwest." *Northwest Ohio Quarterly,* XXXIII (Summer, 1961), 132-146.
212. Smith, Dwight L. "Wayne's Peace with the Indians of the Old Northwest." *Ohio State Archaeological and Historical Quarterly,* LIX (July, 1950), 239-255.
213. Smith, Eudora. "Stephen Watts Kearny as a Factor in the Westward

Movement, 1812-1834." Master's thesis, (St. Louis) Washington University, 1925.

214. Smith, William Henry. *The St. Clair Papers: The Life and Public Services of Arthur St. Clair.* Cincinnati: R. Clarke & Co., 1882. 2 vols.

215. Snelling, William J. "Early Days at Prairie du Chien and Winnebago Outbreak of 1827." *Wisconsin Historical Collections,* V (1868), 123-153.

216. Spaulding, Oliver Lyman. *The United States Army in War and Peace.* New York: G. P. Putnam's Sons, 1937.

217. Sprague, John T. *The Origin, Progress, and Conclusion of the Florida War.* . . . New York: D. Appleton & Company, 1848.

218. Stanley, George F. G. "The Indians in the War of 1812." *Canadian Historical Review,* XXXI (June, 1950), 145-165.

219. Stephen, Walter W. "Andrew Jackson's Forgotten Army." *Alabama Review,* XII (April, 1959), 126-131.

220. Stevens, Frank E. *The Black Hawk War, Including a Review of Black Hawk's Life.* . . . Chicago: F. E. Stevens, 1903.

221. Swift, Joseph Gardner. *The Memoirs of Joseph Gardner Swift . . . Chief Engineer, U.S.A. From 1812 to 1818. 1800-1865.* Ed. Ellery Harrison. Worcester, Mass.: Private printing press of F. S. Blanchard & Co., 1890.

222. Symons, T. W. "The Army and the Exploration of the West." *Journal of the Military Service Institution of the United States,* IV (1883), 205-249.

223. Taylor, Mendell L. "The Western Services of Stephen Watts Kearny, 1815-1848." *New Mexico Historical Review,* XXI (July, 1946), 171-184.

224. Thian, Raphael P., compiler. *Legislative History of the General Staff of the United States Army.* Washington: Adjutant General's Dept., 1901.

225. Thian, Raphael P. *Notes Illustrating the Military Geography of the United States, 1813-1880.* Washington: Adjutant General's Office, 1881.

226. Thoburn, Joseph B. "The Dragoon Campaigns to the Rocky Mountains." *Chronicles of Oklahoma,* VII (March, 1930), 35-41.

227. Thwaites, Reuben G. "The Black Hawk War." *Wisconsin Historical Collections,* XII (1892), 217-265.

228. *Public Papers of Daniel D. Tompkins, Governor of New York, 1807-1817, Military.* Ed. Hugh Hastings. Albany: Wynhoop, Hallenbeck, Crawford Co., State Printers, 1898-1902. 3 vols.

229. Tucker, Glenn. *Poltroons and Patriots, a Popular Account of the War of 1812.* Indianapolis: Bobbs-Merrill Co., Inc., 1954. 2 vols.

230. Tucker, Glenn. *Tecumseh: Vision of Glory.* Indianapolis: Bobbs-Merrill Co., Inc., 1956.

231. Tupper, Ferdinand B. *The Life and Correspondence of Major-General Sir Isaac Brock.* London: Simpkin, Marshall & Co., 1847.

232. Turner, Andrew J. "The History of Fort Winnebago." *Wisconsin Historical Collections,* XIV (1898), 65-103.

233. United States, Department of the Army. *American Military History, 1607-1953* (ROTC Manual 145-20). Washington: G.P.O., 1956.

234. United States, National Archives and Record Service. *List of National Archives Microfilm Publications—1968.* Washington: G.P.O., 1968.

235. United States, Superintendent of Documents. *Checklist of United States Public Documents 1789-1909.* Washington: G.P.O., 1911.

236. United States, Superintendent of Documents. *Tables of and Annotated Index to the Congressional Series of the United States Public Documents.* Washington: G.P.O., 1902.

237. Upton, Emory. *The Military Policy of the United States.* Washington: G.P.O., 1904.

238. Wakefield, John A. *History of the War between the United States and the Sac and Fox Nations of Indians . . . in the Years Eighteen Hundred and Twenty-seven, Thirty-one, and Thirty-two.* Jacksonville, Ill.: Printed by C. Goudy, 1834.

239. Walker, Alexander. *Jackson and New Orleans. . . .* New York: J. C. Derby, 1856.

240. *The War.* New York, 1812-1815.

241. Watson, Richard L., Jr. "Congressional Attitudes Toward Military Preparedness, 1829-1835." *Mississippi Valley Historical Review,* XXXIV (March, 1948), 185-208.

242. Webb, Henry B. "Sketch of Jefferson Barracks." *New Mexico Historical Review,* XXI (July, 1946), 185-208.

243. Weigley, Russell F. *The American Way of War, A History of United States Military Strategy and Policy.* New York: Macmillan Publishing Co., Inc., 1973.

244. Weigley, Russell F. *History of the United States Army.* New York: Macmillan Publishing Co., Inc., 1967.

245. Weigley, Russell F. *Towards an American Army, Military Thought from Washington to Marshall.* New York: Columbia University Press, 1962.

246. Wesley, Edgar Bruce. *Guarding the Frontier: A Study of Frontier Defense from 1815 to 1825.* Minneapolis: University of Minnesota Press, 1935.

247. Wesley, Edgar Bruce. "Life at Fort Atkinson." *Nebraska History,* XXX (December, 1949), 348-358.

248. Wesley, Edgar Bruce "A Still Larger View of the So-Called Yellowstone Expedition." *North Dakota Historical Quarterly,* V (July, 1931), 219-226.

249. Wheelock, Thompson B. "Journal of Colonel Dodge's Expedition from Fort Gibson to the Pawnee Pict Village, August, 1834." *American State Papers: Military Affairs,* V, 373-374.

250. Wildes, Harry Emerson. *Anthony Wayne, Trouble Shooter of the American Revolution.* New York: Harcourt, Brace and Company, 1941.

251. Wilkinson, James. *Memoirs of My Own Times.* Philadelphia: Printed by Abraham Small, 1816. 3 vols.

252. Wood, Richard G. *Stephen Harriman Long, 1784-1864: Army*

Engineer, Explorer, Inventor. Glendale, California: Arthur H. Clark, 1966.

253. Wood, William C. H., ed. *Select British Documents of the Canadian War of 1812.* Toronto: Champlain Society, 1920-1928. 4 vols.

254. Wright, J. Leitch, Jr. "A Note on the First Seminole War as Seen by the Indians, Negroes, and Their British Advisers." *Journal of Southern History,* XXXIV (November, 1968), 565-575.

255. Wright, J. Leitch, Jr. "British Designs on the Old Southwest: Foreign Intrigue on the Florida Frontier, 1783-1803." *Florida Historical Quarterly,* XLIV (April, 1966), 265-284.

256. Young, Hugh. "A Topographical Memoir on East and West Florida. . . ." Ed. Mark F. Boyd. *Florida Historical Quarterly,* XIII (July, 1934), 16-50; (October, 1934), 82-104; (January, 1935), 129-164.

257. Zaslow, Morris and Wesley B. Turner. Editors. *The Defended Border: Upper Canada and the War of 1812.* Toronto: Macmillan Co. of Canada, 1964.

PRIVATE PAPERS

Many collections of manuscripts may be found in university and historical society libraries. Some of the more useful follow.

258. Illinois State Historical Library, Centennial Building, Springfield, 62706.
Robert Anderson Papers
Henry Atkinson Letterbooks and Orderbooks
Albert S. Johnston Journals

259. Library of Congress, Manuscript Division, Washington, D.C., 20400.
Jacob Brown Letterbooks
Andrew Jackson Papers
Thomas S. Jessup Papers
Zachary Taylor Papers

260. Missouri Historical Society, Jefferson Memorial Building, St. Louis, 63112.
Army Papers
William Beaumont Papers
Forts Papers
Stephen W. Kearny Papers

261. Historical Society of Pennsylvania, 1300 Locust Street, Philadelphia 19107.
Dreer collection includes Letters of Officers of the War of 1812
Joel R. Poinsett Papers

262. State Historical Society of Wisconsin, 816 State Street, Madison, 53706.
Fort Crawford Papers
William Henry Papers
Joseph M. Street Papers
Fort Winnebago Papers

SUPPLEMENTARY ITEMS

263. Bouknight, Marie *et. al.* Compilers. *Guide to Records in the Military Archives Division Pertaining to Indian-White Relations.* Washington: General Services Administration, 1972.

264. Everly, Elaine *et al.* Compilers. *Preliminary Inventory of the Records of United States Army Continental Commands, 1821-1920.* Washington: General Services Administration, 1973. 6 vols.

265. Mahon, John K. *The War of 1812.* Gainesville: University of Florida Press, 1972.

266. Mahon, John K. *The American Militia, Decade of Decision, 1789-1800.* Gainesville: University of Florida Press, 1960.

267. Skelton, William B. "The United States Army, 1821-1837: An Institutional History." Master's thesis, Northwestern University, 1968.

VI

THE NAVY IN THE
NINETEENTH CENTURY
1789-1889

Kenneth J. Hagan

GENERAL HISTORIES. The classic study of American naval history in the nineteenth century is still Harold and Margaret Sprout's *The Rise of American Naval Power, 1776-1918* (231). The Sprouts place the Navy in a chronological and institutional context, emphasizing the fundamental fiscal relationship between Congress and the Navy. A companion volume with emphasis on the Navy's internal history is *Paullin's History of Naval Administration, 1775-1911* (181). Dudley W. Knox's *History of the United States Navy* (121) is nicely balanced, although occasionally inaccurate. Knox fully appreciates the varied peacetime roles of the Navy, and he is temperate in assessing the strategic decisiveness of naval battles.

Several general histories of the United States Navy were written by members of the faculty of the Naval Academy. Carroll S. Alden and Allan Westcott's *The United States Navy* (5) strikes a balance between battle history and important peacetime naval activities, as does Elmer B. Potter's *The Naval Academy Illustrated History of the United States Navy* (189). William O. Stevens set himself the same goal, but he was less successful with *The Story of Our Navy* (234) because he fell too much under the influence of Alfred Thayer Mahan, the apostle of sea power.

Authors who put American naval history into the context of world naval history frequently arrange their narratives around the Mahanian hypothesis of the importance of sea power to national development. This viewpoint is evident in William O. Stevens and Allan Westcott, *A History of Sea Power* (235), E. B. Potter and Chester W. Nimitz, eds., *Sea Power: A Naval History* (190), and Clark G. Reynolds, *Command of the Sea: The History and Strategy of Maritime Empires* (198). Bernard Brodie is less deterministic. In *Sea Power in the Machine Age* (38) he simply contends that the technological revolutions beginning in the nineteenth century have completely transformed the maritime affairs of nations.

Two general histories reveal more about the mental set of late nineteenth-century naval leaders than about American naval history. John D. Long, McKinley's Secretary of the Navy, paid homage to the "old Navy" in the first four chapters of his two-volume study, *The New American Navy* (132). A few years earlier Lieutenant James D. J. Kelley perfectly reflected the mood of naval officers advocating a "new Navy" in the 1880s with *Our Navy: Its Growth and Achievements* (117). Kelley's premise was that commercial supremacy and naval greatness are handmaidens.

Finally, two volumes graphically illustrate the Navy under sail: Theodore Roscoe and Fred Freeman, *Picture History of the U.S. Navy* (204), and an earlier survey, Francis J. Reynolds, *The United States Navy from the Revolution to Date* (199).

HISTORIES OF PERIODS OF PEACE. The many peaceful decades of nineteenth-century American naval history have not been systematically analyzed, although there have been some attempts to fill the gaps. Marshall Smelser has followed in the Sprouts' footsteps with *The Congress Founds the Navy, 1787-1798* (222). He makes the simple but elusive point that naval policy is a facet of national politics and must be studied from that perspective.

Well over a century ago James Fenimore Cooper wrote his *History of the Navy of the United States of America* (55). It remains the most detailed analysis of the Navy through the War of 1812. After Cooper there is a hiatus until the birth of the "new Navy" of steam and steel in the 1880s. Donald W. Mitchell devotes four solid chapters to the period 1865-1890 in his *History of the Modern American Navy from 1883 through Pearl Harbor* (162). His bibliography, notes and chronology are as valuable as his text.

Mitchell, however, is an exception and treatment of the post-Civil War years remains uneven. Daniel J. Carrison's *The Navy from Wood to Steel, 1860-1890* (44) is misleadingly titled as it has only one chapter on the post-Civil War period. Walter R. Herrick, Jr., also allots only a single chapter to the years before 1889 in *The American Naval Revolution* (99). George T. Davis, in his standard work, *A Navy Second to None* (65), likewise limits discussion of the period before 1890 to about forty pages. Such brief treatment of the 1870s and 1880s, however competent, distorts and magnifies the significance of the naval events of the 1890s.

NAVIES AT WAR. The United States Navy played a prominent role in at least four wars before 1890. First came the Quasi War. Gardner W. Allen's *Our Naval War with France* (9) is a highly nationalistic account, but it does unite the twin themes of naval and diplomatic history which are generally treated separately. Howard P. Nash, Jr., blends American politics and the fighting at sea in *The Forgotten Wars: The Role of the U.S. Navy in the Quasi War with France and the Barbary Wars, 1798-1805* (167). Those two struggles are usually treated distinctly, but in terms of underscoring the importance of free trade to the young American republic they ought properly to be treated as one.

Three authors trace the origins of a coherent American naval policy to the Barbary Wars. Gardner W. Allen used the records of the Navy Department before they were published. In *Our Navy and the Barbary Corsairs* (10) he stresses the romantic nature of the conflict and the growth of American nationalism as revealed by the gradual realization that paying tribute was a demeaning policy. Glen Tucker is sympathetic to the North Africans in *Dawn Like Thunder: The Barbary Wars and the Birth of the U.S. Navy* (246). Popular in style, and critical in approach is Donald B. Chidsey's *The Wars in Barbary: Arab Piracy and the Birth of the United States Navy* (47).

For many years, books by two ardent Anglophiles were the standard accounts of the Navy in the War of 1812. Theodore Roosevelt's *The Naval War of 1812* (203) concedes that the Navy did little materially to affect the outcome of the war, but the victories at sea sustained the morale of a people whose Army was suffering defeat. Alfred Thayer Mahan was an Anglophile as well as a navalist. In *Sea Power in Its Relations to the War of 1812* (146) he sympathizes with Britain's fight for its life against Napoleon. Mahan's conclusion about the importance of concentrating force at sea is typical of all his histories.

Recently, John K. Mahon published *The War of 1812* (147). This highly detailed study gives ample attention to the Navy and to the social and cultural backdrop behind battles. Mahon isolates romanticism as the leitmotiv of the war and the age.

Andrew Jackson's victory at New Orleans has attracted many commentators. Wilbur S. Brown interprets the campaign as a classic amphibious operation in which the attackers had overwhelming local naval superiority. His book is *The Amphibious Campaign for West Florida and Louisiana, 1814-1815: A Critical Review of Strategy and Tactics at New Orleans* (39). David Porter was as daring as Jackson, but less successful. His *Journal of a Cruise Made to the Pacific Ocean* (187) recounts his attempt to drive the British from that ocean with the lone frigate *Essex.*

Surfboats and Horse Marines: U.S. Naval Operations in the Mexican War, 1846-48 (21) is K. Jack Bauer's readable and probably definitive study of a war which saw extensive amphibious operations.

A great deal has been written about the naval history of the Civil War, and yet there are relatively few comprehensive studies. One fully documented, three-volume survey is *The Civil War at Sea* (114) by Virgil C. Jones. Still useful is an earlier triad, *The Navy in the Civil War*, written by a naval historian and two officers almost a century ago. James R. Soley analyzed *The Blockade and the Cruisers* (227) and concluded that victory would have come to the North much earlier if there had been a sufficient force-in-being when the war began. Daniel Ammen discussed other operations along *The Atlantic Coast* (13), and Alfred Thayer Mahan covered the western theater of operations, *The Gulf and Inland Waters* (144). Less scholarly and highly personalized is *The Naval History of the Civil War* (188), published in 1886 by the senior admiral of the service, David Dixon Porter.

Scholars have analyzed the Union Navy from several perspectives. John Niven and Richard S. West, Jr., have written biographies of Lincoln's Secretary of the Navy, Gideon Welles (170, 275). West has also carried the story from the office of the secretary to the bureaus and commanders at sea in *Mr. Lincoln's Navy* (276). James M. Merrill critically dissected northern naval strategy in his fast-paced narrative, *The Rebel Shore: The Story of Union Sea Power in the Civil War* (158). The same author also wrote a scholarly account of the topic, first treated by Mahan, in *Battle*

Flags South: The Story of the Civil War Navies on Western Waters (156). The strategic importance of northern amphibious operations and the irreparable damage done to the Confederacy by the fall of Vicksburg are the subjects of John D. Milligan's *Gunboats Down the Mississippi* (161).

The Confederate Navy's struggle against insurmountable odds has received more attention than the less romantic northern effort. Joseph T. Durkin used an abundance of printed and unpublished sources for the first biography of *Stephen R. Mallory: Confederate Navy Chief* (69). An affectionate account of that Navy by a former officer is J. Thomas Scharf's *History of the Confederate States Navy from Its Organization to the Surrender of Its Last Vessel* (209). A critical analysis of psychological, material, and administrative problems is Tom H. Wells, *The Confederate Navy: A Study in Organization* (274). William N. Still, Jr., believes that the Confederate Navy's structural weaknesses were but a mirror of the flaws of the Confederacy itself. He examines two aspects of this thesis in *Confederate Shipbuilding* (237) and *Iron Afloat: The Story of the Confederate Armorclads* (238).

The most famous Confederate ship was the C.S.S. *Virginia*, whose strategic significance lay in denying the James River to Union forces. The importance of this accomplishment is the subject of Harrison A. Trexler's *The Confederate Ironclad "Virginia" ("Merrimac")* (245) and R. W. Daly's more recent *How the Merrimac Won: The Story of the C.S.S. Virginia* (60).

The most crippling blow dealt the North by the Confederate Navy was to its merchant marine, according to George W. Dalzell, author of *The Flight from the Flag: The Continuing Effect of the Civil War upon the American Carrying Trade* (61). The same thesis undergirds Frank L. Owsley, Jr.'s *The C.S.S. Florida: Her Building and Operations* (174). The first-hand narrative of the acquisition of the *Florida* and the other raiders is James D. Bulloch's *The Secret Service of the Confederate States in Europe, or How the Confederate Cruisers Were Equipped* (41).

The commander of the most illustrious raider, Raphael Semmes of the *Alabama*, wrote the lucid and comprehensive *Memoirs of Service Afloat, During the War Between the States* (217), now available in condensed form as Philip Van Dorn Stern, ed., *The Confederate Raider Alabama* (233). A well-edited description of what it was like to sail with Semmes is Charles G. Summersell, ed., *The Journal of George Townley Fullum, Boarding Officer of the Confederate Sea Raider Alabama* (239). Equally vivid is a biography based largely on the papers of its subject, William S. Hoole's *Four Years in the Confederate Navy: The Career of Captain John Low on the C.S.S. Fingal, Florida, Alabama, Tuscaloosa, and Ajax* (104). Somewhat less engaging are the reminiscences of the commander of the raider *Shenandoah*, as edited by James D. Horan (106).

Running the blockade was another primary Confederate naval mission, but surprisingly little has been written on the subject. The best study is a half-century old, Francis B. C. Bradlee's *Blockade Running During the Civil War* (35). James D. Hill's *Sea Dogs of the Sixties* (100) studies eight naval leaders who faced problems that typify different aspects of the Civil War at sea, from maintaining a blockade to running past one. Clarence E. Macartney focused on the blockade and perhaps overemphasized its influence on the outcome of the war in *Mr. Lincoln's Admirals* (138), a study of eleven Union naval leaders.

Miscellaneous aspects of Civil War naval operations are covered in three books: *Civil War Naval Chronology, 1861-1865* (259), *Civil War Ironclads: The Dawn of Naval Armor* (139), and *The Confederate Navy: A Pictorial History* (232).

Apart from administration, operations, and technology, the focus of naval historians of the Civil War has been upon diplomacy. In *Squall Across the Atlantic: American Civil War Prize Cases and Diplomacy* (30), Stuart L. Bernath explains that Washington and London reversed their traditional interpretations of neutral rights during the war. The magisterial analysis of the Confederacy's attempts to win European intervention in a diplomatically unprecedented environment is Frank L. Owsley, *King Cotton Diplomacy* (173). Frank J. Merli has a narrower focus, but his study of *Great Britain and the Confederate Navy, 1861-1865* (155) is valuable for its precision. A twentieth century complement has yet to be written, and until it is John Bigelow's *France and the Confederate Navy* (32) will remain useful.

Of all the diplomatic problems generated by the Civil War, none was as vexatious as the dispute over damages between the United States and Great Britain, a running debate commonly referred to as the *Alabama* claims. Caleb Cushing wrote the first comprehensive analysis of the dangerous debate and its settlement over a century ago. His *Treaty of Washington* (58) has been reprinted recently.

BIOGRAPHIES. Officers have received far more attention from biographers than their civilian superiors. Most biographies of secretaries of the Navy devote relatively little space to the politicians' years as secretaries. An exception is Claude H. Hall's *Abel Parker Upshur: Conservative Virginian, 1790-1844* (92), which concludes that Upshur set the stage for a powerful modern navy. Although John Niven has written the definitive biography of *Gideon Welles, Lincoln's Secretary of the Navy* (170), Richard S. West, Jr.'s *Gideon Welles: Lincoln's Navy Department* (275) is still useful. The Democrat who ruined a Republican shipbuilder and simultaneously continued building the "new Navy" was *William C. Whitney: Modern Warwick* (101).

Collective biographies of naval officers are numerous. *Makers of Naval Tradition* (4), by Carroll S. Alden and Ralph Earle, sketches several officers from John Paul Jones through George Dewey with the premise that naval tradition is the common heritage of the American people. Equally didactic is Charles L. Lewis's *Famous American Naval Officers* (128). James Fenimore Cooper had a fascination with the Navy, and he extolled heroism in his *Lives of Distinguished American Naval Officers* (56). Charles B. Davenport absorbed Mahan's assumptions of racially determined aptitudes for the sea before writing *Naval Officers: Their Heredity and Development* (62). Leonard Guttridge and Jay D. Smith have recently traced the early history of the Navy through the lives of its most senior officers, *The Commodores: The U.S. Navy in the Age of Sail* (90). However, Fletcher Pratt's earlier study, *Preble's Boys: Commodore Preble and the Birth of American Sea Power* (192), is still essential because it underscores the attitudinal differences between Americans of the age of Jefferson and those of today.

Biographies of individual officers concentrate heavily on battles and leaders. *Gallant John Barry* (51) was one who fought in the American Revolution and the Quasi War. Probably the most professional officer of his generation, Barry would have modeled American naval policy after Britain's. *Truxton of the Constellation* (77) was intellectually gifted and personally vain, in the view of his biographer, Eugene S. Ferguson. The leader who inspired more junior officers than any other at the end of the eighteenth century is the subject of Christopher McKee's *Edward Preble: A Naval Biography, 1761-1807* (194). Stephen Decatur was the most dashing of "Preble's boys," and Charles L. Lewis accurately emphasizes the concept of honor as the central interpretive theme of *The Romantic Decatur* (129). *Oliver Hazard Perry* (70), who defended Lake Erie during the War of 1812, was almost as popular as Decatur. Less fortunate in every respect was the officer who lost his life and ship in that war, *James Lawrence, Captain, United States Navy: Commander of the "Chesapeake"* (83).

Naval officers of the early nineteenth century spent much of their time on distant station. Charles O. Paullin wrote a careful biography of one of them, *Commodore John Rodgers: Captain, Commodore, and Senior Officer of the American Navy, 1773-1838* (179). A companion volume by Robert E. Johnson tells a balanced story of the son, *Rear Admiral John Rodgers, 1812-1882* (112). A bold and frustrated officer, David Porter, tried to lead America into the Pacific during the War of 1812, adopted young David Farragut, and sired a son who would follow Farragut as the second full admiral in American naval history. David F. Long's biography of the elder Porter, *Nothing Too Daring* (131), is well researched, thorough, and fair. Three older, less scholarly biographies by members of their families throw some light on the activities of American naval officers far from home between 1815 and 1861. Rebecca P. Meade, *Life of Hiram Paulding, Rear-Admiral, U.S.N.* (150), Sophie Radford de Meissner, *Old Naval Days: Sketches from the Life of Rear Admiral William Radford, U.S.N.* (151), and Charles H. Davis, *Life of Charles Henry Davis, Rear Admiral, 1807-1877* (64).

The essence of nineteenth-century naval diplomacy was that a small amount of force was more than sufficient in the "semi-civilized" world. Carroll S. Alden shows that this fact was perfectly understood by the officer who commanded the American East India Squadron during the Opium War, *Lawrence Kearny: Sailor Diplomat* (3). The master of the art was Matthew C. Perry, whose definitive biography is Samuel Eliot Morison's *Old Bruin* (164). An earlier work, *The Great Commodore* (19), by Edward M. Barrows, judges Perry's attitudes towards flogging and grog judiciously and praises him as a visionary who foresaw American greatness on the seas. Late nineteenth-century respect for dedication to duty, humanitarianism, and faith in a Christian God are mirrored in William E. Griffis's *Matthew Calbraith Perry: A Typical American Officer* (88).

David Porter's adopted son won several crucial victories in the Civil War and became the first American four-star admiral. One of the best biographies of Farragut was written by his own son, Loyall Farragut (76).

Alfred T. Mahan drew heavily on that study for his biography (142), which is concerned largely with the character of great leaders. At the turn of the present century a journalist, John R. Spears, eulogized *David G. Farragut* (230) as a typical, hardworking, aggressive American sprung from the frontier. Similar admiration for the admiral's bravery, patriotism, and determination shape Charles L. Lewis's biography, *David Glasgow Farragut* (126).

Porter's other son had fewer biographers. James R. Soley wrote an early eulogy, *Admiral Porter* (226), at the admiral's request. Much more judicious is Richard S. West, Jr.'s *The Second Admiral: A Life of David Dixon Porter, 1813-1891* (277).

There are relatively few biographies of other northern naval officers. John M. Ellicott's *The Life of John Ancrum Winslow* (71), recounts the life of the skipper of the *Kearsarge*. William B. Cushing survived some extremely dangerous small-boat raids to become the Navy's youngest commander. He is the subject of a well-written biography, *Lincoln's Commando* (205), by Ralph J. Roske and Charles Van Doren. A century ago James M. Hoppin of Yale eulogized one of the commanders on the western rivers in his *Life of Andrew Hull Foote* (105). Henry A. DuPont is thoroughly partisan in defense of the kinsman who failed to capture Charleston, *Rear-Admiral Samuel Francis DuPont* (68).

The most important naval officer on the Confederate side was Raphael Semmes (154), whose *Alabama* helped drive northern commerce from the high seas. Emma M. Maffitt, the widow of the commanding officer of another commerce-raider, the C.S.S. *Florida*, used his correspondence to depict *The Life and Services of John Newland Maffitt* (141). Perhaps the most readable biography of any Confederate naval officer is Charles L. Lewis's study of the first superintendent of the U.S. Naval Academy who later opted for the South and defended Mobile Bay against Farragut, *Admiral Franklin Buchanan: Fearless Man of Action* (125).

Two post-Civil War officers merit special attention. Rear Admiral Stephen B. Luce reformed the Navy's enlisted training system and conceived the Naval War College. His biographies are by fellow naval officers, Caspar F. Goodrich, *In Memoriam, Stephen Bleecker Luce* (86), and Albert Gleaves, *Life and Letters of Rear Admiral Stephen B. Luce* (84). Mahan's writing belongs to the 1890s and beyond, but his ideas were formed earlier. The best biography is W. D. Puleston, *Mahan* (195). Charles C. Taylor wrote a British appreciation in 1920, when the American Navy first approached parity with the Royal Navy, *The Life of Admiral Mahan, Naval Philosopher, Rear Admiral, United States Navy* (242). The most trenchant criticism of Mahan's naval theories is in William E. Livezey, *Mahan on Sea Power* (130).

Naval scientists and technicians have received some biographical attention. Matthew Fontaine Maury is the subject of several biographies, the most exhaustively researched being *Matthew Fontaine Maury: Scientist of the Sea* (281). The naval officer who won a Nobel Prize is the topic of Bernard Jaffe's *Michelson and the Speed of Light* (109). Michelson's painful inability to win support for his studies from the Navy and understanding from a wife descended from naval officers is explained by John H. Wilson, Jr., in *Albert A. Michelson: America's First Nobel Prize Physicist* (282).

The most accomplished uniformed naval engineer of the nineteenth century now has a fine, judicious biography, Edward W. Sloan, III's *Benjamin Franklin Isherwood, Naval Engineer: The Years as Engineer in Chief, 1861-1869* (220). Isherwood's implacable civilian rival was the designer of the *Monitor*, whose triumphs were long ago charted by William C. Church in *The Life of John Ericsson* (49). Church was a contemporary as well as a partisan of Ericsson, as is made clear in Donald N. Bigelow's important study, *William Conant Church and The Army and Navy Journal* (31).

Others contributed to modernization of the nineteenth-century Navy. John Stevens was well ahead of his time with a dream of an armored and mobile fleet bearing heavy guns for use against enemy fleets. His biography is Archibald D. Turnbull, *John Stevens: An American Record* (247). The man who built the first ships of the "new Navy" of steam and steel was later ruined by his Democratic critics, and Leonard A. Swann, Jr., has accurately measured his subject's contributions in *John Roach, Maritime Entrepreneur: The Years as Naval Contractor, 1862-1886* (240). The submarine had an uncertain future during the first years of that "new Navy," as Richard K. Morris reveals in *John P. Holland, 1841-1914: Inventor of the Modern Submarine* (165).

Despite the importance of exploration, there have been few biographies of naval explorers. Among the best are George W. Corner's *Doctor Kane of the Arctic Seas* (57), Chauncey C. Loomis's biography of Charles F. Hall, *Weird and Tragic Shores* (133), and William H. Hobbs's *Peary* (102). Too partisan to its subject is Daniel Henderson's *The Hidden Coasts: A Biography of Admiral Charles Wilkes* (97).

One officer is studied because of his uniqueness. He regarded himself as "an American, a sailor and a Jew," and he was the only member of his ethnic group to reach the rank of captain when it was the highest grade in the Navy. Donovan Fitzpatrick and Saul Saphire have written the biography of a *Navy Maverick: Uriah Phillips Levy* (80).

Students seeking a brief summary of an officer's life may find it in one of three places: Lewis R. Hamersly, *The Records of Living Officers of the U.S. Navy and Marine Corps* (93), published intermittently between 1870 and 1902, Allen Johnson and Dumas Malone, eds., *Dictionary of American Biography* (111), or Karl Schuon, *U.S. Navy Biographical Dictionary* (214).

CORRESPONDENCE AND MEMOIRS. The nature of the profession demanded that nineteenth-century naval officers write a great deal. Incessant travel and frequent movement of families also meant that much correspondence was lost to posterity. What remains is therefore fragmentary but nonetheless illuminating. Gardner W. Allen has edited one valuable collection, *Commodore Hull: Papers of Isaac Hull* (8), which provides a rare glimpse of life on American warships in the Mediterranean during the 1830s and 1840s. *Reminiscences of the Old Navy* (140), the correspondence and journals of Edward Trenchard and his son, Stephen Decatur Trenchard, illustrate the nature of naval diplomacy before the Civil War as well as operations during that conflict. Another source for naval life abroad during the thirty years preceding 1861 is the memoir of Benjamin F. Sands, who rose *From Reefer to Rear-Admiral* (208). Rear Admiral

Daniel Ammen's *The Old Navy and the New* (14) is also valuable for the period before 1870.

Some memoirs cast light on isolated cruises or episodes. Hiram Paulding recounted the first visit to Hawaii by an American warship and described the commonplace naval function of chasing mutinous civilian sailors in *Journal of a Cruise of the United States Schooner Dolphin Among the Islands of the Pacific Ocean and a Visit to the Mulgrave Islands, In Pursuit of the Mutineers of the Whale Ship Globe* (177). Raphael Semmes served as an aide to an admiral and a general, as he recalls in *Service Afloat and Ashore During the Mexican War* (218). Commodore Perry wrote his version of the opening of Japan. It is printed as a *Narrative of the Expedition of an American Squadron to the China Seas and Japan* (184) and as *The Japan Expedition, 1852-1854* (185). *With Perry in Japan* (52) was the young Edward Y. McCauley, who would later become a rear admiral. Also valuable for perspective and balance is Lieutenant George H. Preble's *The Opening of Japan* (241). Naval officers who tested Perry's success in Tokyo Bay by visiting other Japanese ports quickly learned that the United States was now caught between the rivalries of Japan, China and Russia. The first-hand accounts of their awakening appears under the somewhat misleading title, *Yankee Surveyors in the Shogun's Seas* (53).

The Civil War did not produce as many naval memoirs as one might have anticipated. His widow edited and published a *Memoir of John A. Dahlgren* (59), composed of selections from the letters and journals of the Union Navy's top ordnance specialist. The most carefully edited collection of letters in print illustrates the daily life of a commander of a blockading squadron, *Samuel Francis DuPont* (95). A South Carolinian who chose the northern side commented incisively on battles, strategy and the course of the war generally in *Naval Letters from Captain Percival Drayton, 1861-1865* (67). James I. Waddell fought for the Confederacy and recorded the day-to-day life of the South's second most important commerce-raider, *C.S.S. Shenandoah* (106). Hundreds of merchant marine officers who volunteered for the northern Navy were mustered out as junior officers at the end of the war. Edward Shippen spoke for the silent majority in his *Thirty Years at Sea: The Story of a Sailor's Life* (219).

Two works are essential for understanding policy making during the Civil War. Secretary of the Navy Gideon Welles altered some entries after the fact, but Howard K. Beale's edition identifies these and reestablishes the *Diary of Gideon Welles* (23) as the most important unofficial primary source for the Union Navy. The complement to Welles's diary is the *Confidential Correspondence of Gustavus Vasa Fox* (244), Assistant Secretary of the Navy during the war.

The post-Civil War generation of naval officers was especially prolific. Each of the following volumes is very useful for understanding the last decades of the "old Navy" and the first years of the new one: Albert S. Barker, *Everyday Life in the Navy* (16); Robley D. Evans, *A Sailor's Log* (72); Bradley A. Fiske, *From Midshipman to Rear-Admiral* (79); Caspar F. Goodrich, *Rope Yarns from the Old Navy* (87); Winfield S. Schley, *Forty-Five Years Under the Flag* (210); Seaton Schroeder, *A Half Century of Naval Service* (212); and Thomas O. Selfridge, Jr., *Memoirs* (216). Alfred Thayer Mahan, the most influential officer of the late nineteenth century, wrote *From Sail to Steam: Recollections of a Naval Life* (143), twelve chapters of which deal with the period before 1890. Much earlier, Mahan had described his experiences as a midshipman at the Naval Academy to his closest friend of adolescence in *Letters of Alfred Thayer Mahan to Samuel A'Court Ashe, 1858-59* (48).

Enlisted men have left very few records of their difficult existence. To generalize the reader must extrapolate from Henry J. Mercier's description of a cruise in 1839 entitled, *Life in a Man-of-War: Or, Scenes in "Old Ironsides" During Her Cruise in the Pacific, By a Fore-Top-Man* (153). William Lloyd Garrison's brother was an alcoholic who served on several naval vessels. His memoir, *Behold Me Once More* (82), demonstrates how extensively corporal punishment was used to maintain discipline. Joseph G. Clark criticized drunkenness, physical punishment, and the severity of Charles Wilkes in his sailor's-eye account of the famous Pacific exploring expedition, *Lights and Shadows of a Sailor's Life* (50).

In the nineteenth century men occasionally shipped aboard naval vessels for the sake of adventure and observation. Herman Melville was on the frigate *United States* from 1843 to 1844. His experiences formed the basis for *White-Jacket, or The World in a Man-of-War* (152). Charles Nordhoff served aboard warships, whalers, and merchantmen and took three volumes to describe *Life on the Ocean* (171). Nathaniel Hawthorne avoided the sea as too dangerous, but his lifelong friend Horatio Bridge went on the first slavery patrol following the Webster-Ashburton Treaty of 1842. Hawthorne edited Bridge's *Journal of an African Cruiser* (37). Enoch C. Wines did not achieve literary fame, but he wrote a fresh description of life on the *Constellation* during a cruise in the Mediterranean between 1829 and 1831 entitled, *Two Years and a Half in the American Navy* (283).

A unique perspective was gained by Samuel P. Boyer, who was a medical officer in the Navy during the 1860s. At the end of the decade he sailed to the Far East. His diary, *Naval Surgeon* (17), contains keen descriptions of naval life, nineteenth century medicine, and the Orient.

Two collections of miscellaneous first-hand accounts of experiences in the Navy contribute colorful and often typical examples of naval life. The better of the two is James M. Merrill, ed., *Quarter-Deck and Fo'c'sle* (157); the other volume is W. Adolphe Roberts and Lowell Brentano, eds., *The Book of the Navy* (201).

NAVAL DIPLOMACY. American warships frequently showed the flag and occasionally used force to stimulate overseas economic activity, protect lives, and accomplish miscellaneous national goals. Two recent studies which trace portions of American naval diplomacy over long periods of time are James A. Field, Jr., *America and the Mediterranean World, 1776-1882* (78) and Robert E. Johnson, *Thence Round Cape Horn: The Story of United States Naval Forces on Pacific Station, 1818-1923* (113).

Episodic illustrations of the geographic breadth of interest is provided by Clayton R. Barrow, Jr., ed., *America Spreads Her Sails* (18). Barrow should be read alongside the pioneering work of Charles O. Paullin, *Diplomatic Negotiations of American Naval Officers, 1778-1883* (180). Paullin also examined merchant and naval activities in China, Japan and some Pacific islands in *American Voyages to the Orient, 1690-1865* (178).

The global reach of naval protection of lives and property after the Civil War is described in Kenneth J. Hagan, *American Gunboat Diplomacy and the Old Navy, 1877-1889* (91). The Incidents where force was actually employed during the nineteenth century are listed in Milton Offutt, *The Protection of Citizens Abroad by the Armed Forces of the United States* (172) and David M. Cooney, *A Chronology of the U.S. Navy, 1775-1965* (54).

Before the Civil War the Navy was involved in Latin America in a variety of ways. The difficulty of maintaining strict neutrality while protecting commerce is competently examined in Edward B. Billingsley's *In Defense of Neutral Rights: The United States Navy and the Wars of Independence in Chile and Peru* (33). The dissolution of the Spanish empire after 1819 created a vacuum in the Caribbean. Two books describe how the U.S. Navy was drawn in as a police force: Gardner W. Allen, *Our Navy and the West Indian Pirates* (11) and Richard Wheeler, *In Pirate Waters* (279). By the 1850s American attention had shifted to the Central American isthmus, where the Navy was used to exert influence. *In Filibusters and Financiers: The Story of William Walker and His Associates* (215), William O. Scroggs analyzes a celebrated soldier of fortune and the Navy's attempt to check him.

The most vexatious maritime problem in the Atlantic was suppression of the slave trade, which the United States attempted only halfheartedly. Henry Wheaton examined it legally in *Enquiry into the Validity of the British Claim to a Right of Visitation and Search* (278) and Hugh G. Soulsby historically in *The Right of Search and the Slave Trade in Anglo-American Relations, 1814-1862* (229). Further east, the Navy at least once intervened in continental politics. Andor Klay has described Commander Duncan Ingraham's demand for release of Hungarian revolutionary Martin Kosta from an Austrian warship in *Daring Diplomacy* (120).

Matthew C. Perry's mission to Japan is the quintessential example of naval diplomacy. It is set into political and naval context in William L. Nuemann, *America Encounters Japan* (169) and Edwin A. Falk, *From Perry to Pearl Harbor* (74).

The global atmosphere of naval diplomacy is perhaps best conveyed by first-hand accounts. William H. Beehler's *The Cruise of the Brooklyn* (24) portrays Africa and the Indian Ocean from the viewpoint of a naval officer of the early 1880s. Francis B. C. Bradlee has collected vivid descriptions of the naval operations of the 1820s in *Piracy in the West Indies and Its Suppression* (36). The commercial aspect, as distinct from the naval facet of maritime activity, is described in Edmund Fanning, *Voyages Round the World* (75). Andrew H. Foote was in the African Squadron in 1850-51, and he explains its dual role in *Africa and the American Flag* (81). The distinctive perspectives of chaplain and officer on a cruise through the Indian Ocean are revealed in Fitch W. Taylor, *The Flagship* (243) and Joshua S. Henshaw, *Around the World* (98).

Joseph F. Loubat kept a journal of a unique naval mission. It is printed as *Narrative of the Mission to Russia, in 1866, of the Hon. Gustavus Vasa Fox, Assistant-Secretary of the Navy* (136). Perry told his own story about his voyage to Japan (184, 185). Edmund Roberts, who conceived the idea of commercial treaties with eastern nations, recorded his diplomatic trip aboard the sloop-of-war *Peacock* in *Embassy to the Eastern Courts of Cochin-China, Siam, and Muscat* (200). Accompanying Roberts was a surgeon, William S. W. Ruschenberger, whose account describes the people and lands visited as well as the process of diplomacy. It is entitled *A Voyage Round the World* (207). Two other cruises of the early nineteenth century are recounted in Charles S. Stewart, *A Visit to the South Seas* (236) and Francis Warriner, *Cruise of the United States Frigate Potomac Round the World* (270).

NAVAL EXPLORATIONS. The Navy helped push the frontiers of knowledge further north, west and south during the nineteenth century, as Vincent Ponko, Jr., recently explained in *Ships, Seas, and Scientists* (186). The first major voyage was to the Pacific. Its leader, Lieutenant Charles Wilkes, described his experiences and findings in the massive *Narrative of the United States Exploring Expedition During the Years 1838, 1839, 1840, 1841, 1842* (280). Wilkes's British rival, James C. Ross, contested some of the American's claims in *A Voyage of Discovery and Research in the Southern and Antarctic Regions, During the Years 1839-43* (206). A scholarly description of the background of the Wilkes expedition and an appraisal of its results is contained in Philip I. Mitterling, *America in the Antarctic to 1840* (163).

Matthew F. Maury, a cartographer and naval contemporary of Wilkes, attempted to systematize all of the information then available regarding *The Physical Geography of the Sea* (148). In the introduction to the 1963 edition, John Leighly contrasts Maury's valuable contributions to oceanic navigation with his naive scientific syntheses.

Beginning with the 1850s, the attention of naval explorers was drawn increasingly to the Arctic. John E. Caswell sensibly interprets the expeditions made between 1850 and 1909 as comprising a movement of intellectual and scientific significance rather than as isolated adventures along *Arctic Frontiers* (45). George W. Corner is equally judicious in his biography of the naval surgeon who went further north than any predecessor, *Doctor Kane of the Arctic Seas* (57). Kane himself recalled his experiences for the general reader in *Arctic Explorations: The Second Grinnell Expedition in Search of Sir John Franklin, 1853, '54, '55* (115). Kane's competence as a scientist and fairness as a leader were questioned by at least one member of his crew, and the challenge has been printed as *Dr. Kane's Voyage to the Polar Lands* (269). This intense American naval interest in the Arctic was not duplicated in any other geographical region, but one expedition of the 1850s shows that no area was too remote to claim some attention. William F. Lynch, the commanding officer, wrote a *Narrative of the United States' Expedition to the River Jordan and the Dead Sea* (137).

After the Civil War the Navy again sponsored Arctic explorations. Charles Francis Hall led one of them, and in *Weird and Tragic Shores* (133) Chauncey C. Loomis shrewdly interprets him as one of a breed of fierce individualists reacting against the homogenizing process of industrialization. Hall's was not the only expedition to be overwhelmed by the ice of the north, and Lieutenant Commander George W. DeLong described the nightmare of clinging to life after an Arctic shipwreck ended

The Voyage of the Jeannette (66). The great naturalist, John Muir, was among those who searched for DeLong. He made careful observations about the north during *The Cruise of the Corwin* in 1881 (166). In the same year an Army officer led an expedition which became trapped in the ice. He was finally saved by Commander Winfield S. Schley, who dramatically described *The Recue of Greely* (211), a story retold seventy-five years later in a conversational style without citations by Theodore Powell, *The Long Rescue* (191). By the mid-1880s the worst was over. Robert E. Peary began his epochal discoveries with an expedition to Greenland in 1886. It constitutes the first part of his *Northward Over the "Great Ice"* (182). The decade ended as had the 1850s, with the Navy occasionally looking elsewhere than just to the Arctic. In 1889, for example, scientist Eben J. Loomis boarded the U.S.S. *Pensacola* for *An Eclipse Party in Africa* (134).

SPECIAL STUDIES. The most provocative book on American naval history ever to appear is Peter Karsten's *The Naval Aristocracy: The Golden Age of Annapolis and the Emergence of Modern American Navalism* (116). Karsten contends that naval officers constitute an élite group seeking primarily the enhancement of their own power and prestige. A less hostile but nonetheless pathbreaking study of the society of naval officers and men is Harold D. Langley, *Social Reform in the United States Navy, 1798-1862* (123).

Ships are as essential to a navy as men, and as a result many ships' histories have been written. John Jenning's *Tattered Ensign* (110) is a popular history of the *Constitution* based on a wide variety of sources. Polly Burroughs has written the latest biography of a ship whose extended record of polar service with the Navy and Coast Guard is unequalled, *The Great Ice Ship Bear: Eighty-Nine Years in Polar Seas* (42).

The standard by which to judge all other collective histories is Howard I. Chapelle's classic design study, *The History of the American Sailing Navy: The Ships and Their Development* (46). More recently, Alexander Laing carefully traced the evolution of naval and merchant vessels in *American Ships* (122). Warships and the battles they fought are arranged chronologically in Joseph Leeming, *The Book of American Fighting Ships* (124), while K. Jack Bauer has arranged combatants by class in *Ships of the Navy* (20). When completed, the definitive list will be the Navy Department's multi-volume *Dictionary of American Naval Fighting Ships* (260).

Several less sweeping histories of naval architecture exist. John D. Alden's *The American Steel Navy* (6) contains some good photographs of the "new Navy" of the 1880s. Two officers provided incentive for building that fleet by carefully studying and describing other nations' navies. Lieutenant Edward W. Very produced *Navies of the World* (268) in 1880 and a year later Chief Engineer James W. King published his equally comprehensive survey, *The War-Ships and Navies of the World* (119). Very, King, and others sold their case to Congress, and by 1896 Passed Assistant Engineer Frank M. Bennett could write a history of *The Steam Navy of the United States* (28). Four years later he published *The Monitor and the Navy under Steam* (27).

J. D. Jerrold Kelley was another articulate naval officer of the 1880s. In

The Question of Ships (118), which was published the same year that Mahan was called to the Naval War College, Kelley made a vigorous argument for reviving the American merchant marine as well as the Navy. The relationship between navy and merchant marine was systematically explained in 1947 by Samuel W. Bryant in *The Sea and the States* (40). John G. B. Hutchins had demonstrated earlier that the United States is a hesitant seapower in his *American Maritime Industries and Public Policy, 1789-1914* (108).

The technological revolution culminating in the "new Navy" began well before the Civil War. The crucial factor determining the transition from wood to steel was the invention of the shell gun, according to James P. Baxter, III, author of the classic *Introduction of the Ironclad Warship* (22). Like Baxter, Peter Padfield neatly sets American contributions against the European context in *The Battleship Era* (175) and *Guns at Sea* (176). The same global perspective shapes William Hovgaard's *Modern History of Warships* (107).

This nineteenth century revolution in naval technology made the old tactics obsolete and spurred a search for new ones, a topic comprising part of Samuel S. and Mary L. Robison's *A History of Naval Tactics from 1530 to 1930* (202). One outdated tactic was boarding, and Robert H. Rankin's *Small Arms of the Sea Services* (197) contains many illustrations of the hand weapons that had been used by boarding parties of the sailing Navy.

The Navy is more than men, ships, weapons and tactics. It is a composite of several administrative entities. Of these, perhaps the most important is the Naval Academy, where officers are educated and trained. At the direction of the academy's superintendent, James R. Soley wrote an encyclopedic *Historical Sketch of the United States Naval Academy* (228). A quarter of a century later Park Benjamin contrasted the differences between an officer's education before and after establishment of *The United States Naval Academy* (26). On the eve of World War II, Captain William D. Puleston praised the institution in *Annapolis: Gangway to the Quarterdeck* (194).

There are surprisingly few histories of Navy yards. At the end of the nineteenth century, Rear Admiral George H. Preble wrote an official *History of the United States Navy-Yard, Portsmouth, N.H.* (193). Not until 1949 was the nineteenth-century Navy's ordnance center adequately described by Taylor Peck, *Round-Shot to Rockets: A History of the Washington Navy Yard and U.S. Naval Gun Factory* (183). For most of the century only one yard existed on the west coast. Arnold S. Lott chronicles Mare Island's history as shipyard and operational base in *A Long Line of Ships* (135).

Even fewer histories have been written of the other varied shore establishments of the Navy. Richmond C. Holcomb set an example of how to combine technical and administrative history in *A Century with Norfolk Naval Hospital, 1830-1930* (103). Gustavus A. Weber claimed a whole field to himself with three tightly written, concise analyses of scientific agencies connected with the Navy: *The Coast and Geodetic Survey* (271), *The Hydrographic Office* (272), and *The Naval Observatory* (273).

The Marine Corps and Coast Guard are somewhat autonomous, but they are also operationally subordinate to the Navy. Robert D. Heinl, Jr.'s *Soldiers of the Sea* (96) is the best history of the Marines. Other studies are Clyde H. Metcalf, *A History of the United States Marine Corps* (159), and Willis J. Abbot, *Soldiers of the Sea* (1). Charles L. Lewis compiled biographies of *Famous American Marines* (127), as did Karl Schuon (213).

The most carefully documented study of nineteenth century antecedents of the Coast Guard is Stephen H. Evans, *The United States Coast Guard, 1790-1915* (73). Popular histories are Howard V. L. Bloomfield, *The Compact History of the United States Coast Guard* (34), and Kensil Bell, *"Always Ready!": The Story of the United States Coast Guard* (25). Gene Gurney collected some rare photographs of the ships and men of the nineteenth century Revenue Cutter Service for *The United States Coast Guard: A Pictorial History* (89).

Of the several technical corps of the Navy itself, only one has been the subject of a history. The Bureau of Naval Personnel commissioned *The History of the Chaplain Corps, United States Navy, 1778-1957* (257).

BIBLIOGRAPHIES. Myron J. Smith, Jr.'s stunningly comprehensive *American Naval Bibliography Series* (233, 224, 225) embraces the century between 1789 and 1889. Included without annotation are books, articles, dissertations, and many government documents. For the few documents that Smith missed, two older bibliographies remain essential: Robert W. Neeser, *Statistical and Chronological History of the United States Navy, 1775-1909* (168), and Charles T. Harbeck, *A Contribution to the Bibliography of the History of the United States Navy* (94). The standard annotated bibliography is Robert G. Albion, *Naval and Maritime History* (2), now in its fourth edition. The Naval History Division of the Navy Department regularly revises two brief and suggestive guides, *United States Naval History: A Bibliography* (261), and *U.S. Naval History Sources in the Washington Area and Suggested Research Subjects* (7).

Two specialized compilations deserve mention. Edward W. Sloan, III's *Maritime History: A Basic Bibliography* (221) explicitly excludes naval history but is nonetheless useful for closely related topics such as the law of the seas, protection of overseas commerce, and the relationship between the Navy and merchant marine. In 1888 the Navy Department issued a *Catalogue of Works by American Naval Authors* (258) which remains a valuable index to the writings of naval officers published prior to that date.

PERIODICALS. Three periodicals were regularly used as forums for debating American naval policy in the middle and late nineteenth century: the *Army and Navy Journal* (15), *The United Service* (248), and the *United States Naval Institute Proceedings* (267). The latter is also extremely valuable for historical essays on the nineteenth century Navy, as are *The American Neptune* (12) and *Military Affairs* (160).

Myron Smith's bibliography (223, 224, 225) is an excellent guide to articles in the periodicals listed and in a wide variety of other journals and magazines. He catalogues most articles by author and subject.

PUBLISHED DOCUMENTS. The relatively few sets of published documents dealing exclusively with the Navy leave many chronological gaps, as is evident from the following list. The most important of these is the *Annual Report of the Secretary of the Navy* (254), beginning about 1798, although it often does not include the valuable reports of his subordinates. These may be available only in manuscript at the National Archives. In 1824, Charles W. Goldsborough collected some rare documents for *The United States Naval Chronicle* (85). Reports submitted by the Navy to Congress between 1794 and 1836 are contained in the *American State Papers* (249).

Congressional control of the purse strings has always resulted in debates on naval policy. These can be traced in the *Annals of the Congress, 1789-1824* (250), *American State Papers* (249), *Abridgement of the Debates of Congress, From 1789 to 1856* (29), *The Congressional Globe* (251), covering 1833 to 1873, and the *Congressional Record* (252), for the Forty-Third Congress of 1873 and beyond. The committee investigations forming the basis for debate are contained in a bewildering variety of incompletely indexed House and Senate reports. Harbeck (94), Neeser (168), and Smith (223, 224, 225) have listed the great majority of these invaluable sources. Finally, a handy compilation of naval appropriations beginning with the "new Navy" of the 1880s is the *Navy Yearbook* (196).

The stand reference work for diplomatic matters related to the Navy is the State Department's *Papers Relating to the Foreign Relations of the United States* (266), first published in 1861. Two other collections contain portions of the diplomatic record: *State Papers and Publick Documents of the United States* (253), for the period to 1819, and *American State Papers* (249), for the years 1794-1836. Jules Davids has edited an extremely valuable specialized collection containing a great deal of correspondence by naval officers in the Far East: *American Diplomatic and State Papers: The United States and China* (63), of which the series covering 1842-1860 is now in print. The basic source for the dangerous diplomatic aftermath of Confederate commerce-raiding is the *Correspondence Concerning the Claims Against Great Britain* (265).

Substantially more material related to the Navy in war has been printed, beginning with the *Naval Documents Related to the Quasi-War between the United States and France* (262). The extended record of American naval involvement with North Africa is contained in the *Naval Documents Related to the United States War with the Barbary Powers* (263), and in the supplementary *Register of Officer Personnel, United States Navy and Marine Corps, and Ships' Data, 1801-1807* (264). The Navy Department collected and published the *Official Records of the Union and Confederate Navies in the War of the Rebellion* (255), which has a separately issued general index (256). Prize-taking was a major function of nineteenth century navies, and the American experience can be reconstructed from *Prize Cases Decided in the United States Supreme Court, 1789-1918* (43).

DEPOSITORIES. Research into manuscript sources for nineteenth century American naval history must begin in the Washington area, and frequently it will end there as well because the collections are so remarkably concentrated. The naval section of the Old Military Records Division of the National Archives (285) is an inestimably rich trove. Record Group 45 contains the bulk of the material. There are fully indexed finding guides for that record group and the others that may be pertinent to a particular topic.

The second richest source in Washington is the Manuscript Division of the Library of Congress (284). Personal papers are catalogued under the individual's name. The quality of indexes varies, but those papers belonging to the Naval History Foundation are usually well indexed.

The Naval History Division of the Department of the Navy, located in the Navy Yard (286), holds rather little material from the period before 1890. However, the archivists there are most knowledgeable and helpful, and they maintain a card index to manuscript sources across the United States. In addition, they know most of the scholars working in the field and can identify those who share mutual interests.

At Annapolis, the Naval Academy's newly completed Nimitz Library (287) houses the nation's finest collection of printed secondary and primary material on nineteenth century American naval history. The rare books collection is especially valuable, and scholars are very welcome.

After exhausting Annapolis and Washington, the researcher may be drawn to isolated collections in other parts of the country. However, these are so specialized that it would not be feasible or meaningful to describe them in this guide.

RESEARCH NEEDED. With the publication of Peter Karsten's *Naval Aristocracy* (116) a field of history long given over largely to antiquarians and students of strategy and tactics has come alive. The controversy surrounding Karsten's book insures a ready audience for naval histories. Some scholar now ought to apply Karsten's methodology to the period before 1845 and sociologically analyze the messmates of Stephen Decatur and David Porter. Decatur is especially intriguing in that he was killed duelling with a fellow naval officer. His biographers either simply neglect to observe the instrument of his demise or lament the waste of a man cut down in his full maturity. What they should examine is the effect of the duelling code upon the style of early American naval leadership. Did it and surrounding social mores insure a characteristic of recklessness that was lauded as patriotic heroism when exhibited by naval officers? If so, did the priates of the Mediterranean and Caribbean whom those naval officers chased operate under a social imperative very similar to that working upon their conquerors?

Using Karsten and Harold Langley (123) as points of departure, one may hope for extensive studies of the enlisted men of the Navy. There is at least one dissertation on the subject, and there are rumors of such studies being in progress; but little has yet emerged. The subject would be more difficult than Karsten's, but careful analysis would fill in what is a nearly blank page of American social history.

When building the "new Navy" of the late nineteenth century American naval officers frequently called for commensurately "new" sailors who would be well equipped with brains rather than brawn. The officers wanted crewmen who could regulate steam boiler pressure and not simply hoist and douse sails by brute force. Parallels with the needs of the technologically revolutionary post-World War II American Navy are obvious, and that alone would justify close analysis of the social and intellectual composition of the nineteenth century enlisted corps of the Navy. But purely historical questions could also be raised and answered. For example, was discipline maintained through vicious corporal punishment in part because of the immense social gap separating officers and men? The relative weight of the following factors in the gradual amelioration of harsh physical punishment should be determined: humanitarian reform, increasing social similarity between officers and enlisted men, impossibility of recruiting technologically competent crewmen who would tolerate physical abuse.

It is also possible that the attitude of officers towards a host of matters was substantially different at the end of the century from what it had been at the beginning. The existing body of biographies is of little help in making distinctions between David Dixon Porter and Stephen B. Luce on the one hand, and "Preble's boys" on the other. As noted above, with the exception of a few recent studies, biographies of naval officers uniformly eulogize bravery in battle, devotion to country, and unfaltering worship of a Christian God. Needed today is a series of biographies that asks individually the sort of question Karsten asks collectively, thereby testing his thesis in depth as well as providing the reading audience with sophisticated studies of men who were important to American national development.

If the course of American history was determined to some extent by the Navy, there ought to be careful analyses of that institution's political and administrative history. The Sprouts (231), Smelser (222), and Paullin (181) have pointed the way. But each of those works has limitations. As several scholars have recently pointed out—and as the Sprouts themselves apparently later realized—*The Rise of American Naval Power* (231) overrates the importance of Mahan and too easily accepts his ideas as valid. Thus what went before is slighted. Paullin's reprinted collection of articles is not indexed, a substantial obstacle to the serious scholar. Smelser is limited to a short period of time. Thus the field is open for studies of the political and administrative history of the Navy from 1799 through 1889. Neeser (168), Harbeck (94), and Smith (223, 224, 225) identify very many of the relevant documentary sources.

In the realm of ideas and strategy, a lacuna exists. Because of the preeminence of Mahan, it is generally assumed that the United States Navy had no real theoretical framework before publication of *The Influence of Sea Power upon History* (145) in 1890. Yet doubts are being expressed. As noted above, James A. Field, Jr. (78) and Kenneth Hagan (91) have suggested that the pre-Mahanian Navy had a mature concept of its role in national and international affairs. But there has been no comprehensive examination of the Navy's concept of its function and strategy between about 1803 and 1877. The National Archives and the Manuscript Division of the Library of Congress hold a vast array of materials that should be scrutinized in order to determine just what were the strategic postulates and assumptions of the nineteenth century American Navy.

Those depositories also hold records relevant to a host of more conventional topics. Heading that list is Alfred Thayer Mahan himself. With the publication by the U.S. Naval Institute *Proceedings* of Soviet Admiral Gorshkov's articles on naval history and strategy a staggering question arises: how good a historian and strategist was Mahan? The U.S. naval establishment remains committed to Mahan as scholar and theorist. But there is an element of determinism in Mahan that is eerily reflected in Gorshkov. Late nineteenth century Social Darwinism and mid-twentieth century Soviet Marxism seem to have led to similar conclusions. A careful examination of Mahan's historical viewpoints, stressing the intellectual milieu of the Navy of the 1870s and 1880s as well as the derivative nature of many of his conclusions, might at least put him in perspective. If so, the floodgates might be opened to reconsideration of contemporary American strategic principles, such as the immutable desirability and feasibility of commanding all the seas all the time.

More broadly, as suggested in the body of the present essay, there exists no current survey of American naval history. Dudley Knox's is the best, but it was last printed in 1948. In addition to absence of material on the twenty-five years since World War II, Knox's *History of the United States Navy* (121) neglects several important nineteenth century topics, notably, the pre-Civil War beginnings of the technological modernization of the Navy. Nor does Knox write much about the period 1865-1890 and the building of the "new Navy."

Several more restricted but conventional topics also need treatment. There exists no modern history of medicine in the Navy. The only treatment of the chaplain's corps is a quasi-official six-volume compendium. A study of the office of the Secretary of the Navy over several decades would reveal much about the power of cabinet officials in the nineteenth century as well as something about the style of presidential leadership. Analysis of the impact of the bureaus upon naval administration from their inception until creation of the office of the Chief of Naval Operations would document a decentralized Navy strikingly in contrast with its twentieth century successor.

There is no recent history of the U.S. Naval Academy, the latest being by Captain William D. Puleston (194), whose work is more propaganda than scholarship. The Naval Academy should be compared with other institutions of higher learning in terms of perceived needs of society at any given time, curricula, faculties, social origins of students, and impact of graduates upon American life. Likewise, there is no published study of the Naval War College, a prime element in the professionalization of the American Navy in the late nineteenth century.

Miscellaneous topics abound. Histories of individual squadrons can prove fruitful, as Robert E. Johnson (113) has shown. Barrow (18), Billingsly (33), Field (78), Hagan (91), Paullin (180), and Ponko (186), have made beginnings in the study of naval diplomacy, but as a whole the story between 1803 and 1877 is untold. The collective attitude of naval officers and leaders toward Great Britain ought to be examined. To what extent, if any, did navalists realize that the British navy was a shield of their republic? Conversely, to what extent did they perceive the Royal Navy as a persistent threat? In a related vein, did the American Navy have a consistent position on freedom of the seas, of what did it consist, and under what circumstances was it substantially modified? Finally, with a hint of presentism, some scholar might examine the means by which contracts were let and purchases made in the navy yards and bureaus. Was there already a suggestion of the "military-industrial complex" in the nineteenth-century American naval establishment? If so, was its beginning coexistent with the very founding of the Navy, or was it yet one more ramification of post-Civil War industrialization of the United States?

It should be emphasized in closing that this list of topics by no means exhausts a field that should enjoy a scholarly renaissance in the next decade or so.

BIBLIOGRAPHY

1. Abbot, Willis J. *Soldiers of the Sea: The Story of the United States Marine Corps.* New York: Dodd, Mead, 1919.
2. Albion, Robert G. *Naval and Maritime History: An Annotated Bibliography.* 4th ed. rev. Mystic, Connecticut: Marine Historical Association, 1972.
3. Alden, Carroll Storrs. *Lawrence Kearny: Sailor Diplomat.* Princeton: Princeton University Press, 1936.
4. Alden, Carroll S., and Ralph Earle, *Makers of Naval Tradition.* Boston: Ginn, 1925. Rev. ed., 1942.
5. Alden, Carroll S., and Allan Westcott. *The United States Navy: A History.* Chicago: J. B. Lippincott, 1943. Rev. ed., 1945.
6. Alden, John D. *The American Steel Navy.* Annapolis: U.S. Naval Institute, 1972.
7. Allard, Dean C., and Betty Bern, comps. *U.S. Naval History Sources in the Washington Area and Suggested Research Subjects.* 3rd ed. rev. Washington: G.P.O., 1970.
8. Allen, Gardner W., ed. *Commodore Hull: Papers of Isaac Hull, Commodore, United States Navy.* Boston: Boston Athenaeum, 1929. Reprinted, 1970.
9. Allen, Gardner W. *Our Naval War with France.* Boston: Houghton Mifflin, 1909. Reprinted, Hamden, Connecticut: Archon Books, 1967.
10. Allen, Gardner W. *Our Navy and the Barbary Corsairs.* Boston: Houghton, Mifflin, 1905. Reprinted, Hamden, Connecticut: Archon Books, 1965.
11. Allen, Gardner W. *Our Navy and the West Indian Pirates.* Salem, Massachusetts: Essex Institute, 1929.
12. *The American Neptune.* 1941- .
13. Ammen, Daniel. *The Atlantic Coast.* Vol. II of *The Navy in the Civil War.* New York: Scribner's, 1883.
14. Ammen, Daniel. *The Old Navy and the New: Memoirs of Rear-Admiral Daniel Ammen.* Philadelphia: J. B. Lippincott, 1891. 2nd ed., 1898.
14a. Anderson, RADM Bern. *By Sea and By River: The Naval History of the Civil War.* New York: Knopf, 1962.

15. *Army and Navy Journal.* 1863-1950.
16. Barker, Albert S. *Everyday Life in the Navy: Autobiography of Rear Admiral Albert S. Barker.* Boston: Richard G. Badger, 1928.
17. Barnes, Elinor, and James A. Barnes. *Naval Surgeon: The Diary of Dr. Samuel Pellman Boyer.* Bloomington: Indiana University Press, 1963. 2 vols.
18. Barrow, Clayton R., Jr., ed. *America Spreads Her Sails: U.S. Seapower in the 19th Century.* Annapolis: U.S. Naval Institute, 1973.
19. Barrows, Edward M. *The Great Commodore: The Exploits of Matthew Calbraith Perry.* Indianapolis: Bobbs-Merrill, 1935.
20. Bauer, K. Jack. *Ships of the Navy.* Vol. I, *Combat Vessels.* Troy, New York: Rensselaer Polytechnic Institute, 1970.
21. Bauer, K. Jack. *Surfboats and Horse Marines: U.S. Naval Operations in the Mexican War, 1846-48.* Annapolis: U.S. Naval Institute, 1969.
22. Baxter, James P., III. *The Introduction of the Ironclad Warship.* Cambridge: Harvard University Press, 1933. Reprinted, Hamden, Connecticut: Archon Books, 1968.
23. Beale, Howard K., ed. *Diary of Gideon Welles.* New York: Norton, 1960. 3 vols.
24. Beehler, William H. *The Cruise of the Brooklyn.* Philadelphia: Lippincott, 1885.
25. Bell, Kensil. *"Always Ready!": The Story of the United States Coast Guard.* New York: Dodd, Mead, 1943.
26. Benjamin, Park. *The United States Naval Academy.* New York: Putnam's, 1900.
27. Bennett, Frank M. *The Monitor and the Navy under Steam.* Boston: Houghton, Mifflin and Company, 1900.
28. Bennett, Frank M. *The Steam Navy of the United States: A History of the Growth of the Steam Vessel of War in the U.S. Navy, and of the Naval Engineer Corps.* Pittsburgh: Warren, 1896. Reprinted, 1972.
29. Benton, Thomas Hart. *Abridgement of the Debates of Congress from 1789 to 1856.* New York: D. Appleton & Company, 1857-1863. 16 vols.
30. Bernath, Stuart L. *Squall Across the Atlantic: American Civil War Prize Cases and Diplomacy.* Berkeley and Los Angeles: University of California Press, 1970.
31. Bigelow, Donald N. *William Conant Church and The Army and Navy Journal.* Columbia University Studies in History, Economics and Public Law, No. 576. New York: Columbia University Press, 1952. Reprinted, 1968.
32. Bigelow, John. *France and the Confederate Navy.* New York: Bergman Publishers, 1968.
33. Billingsley, Edward B. *In Defense of Neutral Rights: The United States Navy and the Wars of Independence in Chile and Peru.* Chapel Hill: University of North Carolina Press, 1967.
34. Bloomfield, Howard V. L. *The Compact History of the United States Coast Guard.* New York: Hawthorn, 1966.

35. Bradlee, Francis B. C. *Blockade Running During the Civil War.* Salem, Massachusetts: The Essex Institute, 1925.
36. Bradlee, Francis B. C. *Piracy in the West Indies and Its Suppression.* Salem, Massachusetts: The Essex Institute, 1923.
37. Bridge, Horatio. *Journal of an African Cruiser.* London: Dawsons of Pall Mall, 1968.
38. Brodie, Bernard. *Sea Power in the Machine Age.* Princeton: Princeton University Press, 1941. 2nd ed., 1943.
39. Brown, Wilburt S. *The Amphibious Campaign for West Florida and Louisiana, 1814-1815: A Critical Review of Strategy and Tactics at New Orleans.* University, Alabama: University of Alabama Press, 1969.
40. Bryant, Samuel W. *The Sea and the States: A Maritime History of the American People.* New York: Crowell, 1947.
41. Bulloch, James D. *The Secret Service of the Confederate States in Europe, or How the Confederate Cruisers Were Equipped.* New York: Thomas Yoseloff, 1959. 2 vols.
42. Burroughs, Polly. *The Great Ice Ship Bear: Eighty-Nine Years in Polar Seas.* New York: Van Nostrand Reinhold, 1970.
43. Carnegie Endowment for International Peace. *Prize Cases Decided in the United States Supreme Court, 1789-1918.* Oxford: Clarendon Press, 1923. 3 vols.
44. Carrison, Daniel J. *The Navy from Wood to Steel, 1860-1890.* New York: Franklin Watts, 1965.
45. Caswell, John E. *Arctic Frontiers: United States Explorations in the Far North.* Norman: University of Oklahoma Press, 1956.
46. Chapelle, Howard I. *The History of the American Sailing Navy: The Ships and Their Development.* New York: Norton, 1949.
47. Chidsey, Donald B. *The Wars in Barbary: Arab Piracy and the Birth of the United States Navy.* New York: Crown Publishers, Inc., 1971.
48. Chiles, Rosa P., ed. *Letters of Alfred Thayer Mahan to Samuel A'Court Ashe, 1858-59.* Duke University Library Bulletin, No. 4. Durham: n.p., 1931.
49. Church, William C. *The Life of John Ericsson.* New York: Scribner's, 1891. 2 vols.
50. Clark, Joseph G. *Lights and Shadows of Sailor Life.* Boston: Benjamin B. Mussey, 1848.
51. Clark, William B. *Gallant John Barry, 1745-1803: The Story of a Naval Hero of Two Wars.* New York: Macmillan, 1938.
51a. Cochran, Hamilton, *Blockade Runners of the Confederacy.* New York: Bobbs Merrill, 1958.
52. Cole, Allan B., ed. *With Perry in Japan: The Diary of Edward Yorke McCauley.* Princeton: Princeton University Press, 1942.
53. Cole, Allan B., ed. *Yankee Surveyors in the Shogun's Seas: Records of the United States Surveying Expedition to the North Pacific Ocean, 1853-1856.* Princeton: Princeton University Press, 1947.
54. Cooney, David M. *A Chronology of the U.S. Navy, 1775-1965.* New York: Watts, 1965.

55. Cooper, James Fenimore. *History of the Navy of the United States of America.* New York: G. P. Putnam & Co., 1854. Reprinted, 1970.

56. Cooper, James Fenimore. *Lives of Distinguished American Naval Officers.* Philadelphia: Carey and Hart, 1846. 2 vols.

57. Corner, George W. *Doctor Kane of the Arctic Seas.* Philadelphia: Temple University Press, 1972.

58. Cushing, Caleb. *The Treaty of Washington.* New York: Harper & Brothers, 1873. Reprinted, 1970.

59. Dahlgren, Madeleine V. *Memoir of John A. Dahlgren.* Boston: James R. Osgood, 1882.

60. Daly, R. W. *How the Merrimac Won: The Story of the C.S.S. Virginia.* New York: Thomas Y. Crowell Company, 1957.

61. Dalzell, George W. *The Flight from the Flag: The Continuing Effect of the Civil War upon the American Carrying Trade.* Chapel Hill: University of North Carolina Press, 1940.

62. Davenport, Charles B. *Naval Officers: Their Heredity and Development.* Washington: Carnegie Institution, 1919.

63. Davids, Jules, ed. *American Diplomatic and State Papers: The United States and China.* Series I: *The Treaty System and the Taiping Rebellion, 1842-1860.* Wilmington: Scholarly Resources, 1973. 21 vols.

64. Davis, Charles H. *Life of Charles Henry Davis, Rear Admiral, 1807-1877.* Boston: Houghton, Mifflin, 1899.

65. Davis, George T. *A Navy Second to None.* New York: Harcourt, Brace, 1940. Reprinted, 1971.

66. DeLong, Emma, ed. *The Voyage of the Jeanette.* Boston: Houghton, Mifflin, 1883-84. 2 vols.

67. Drayton, Percival. *Naval Letters from Captain Percival Drayton, 1861-1865.* New York: [n.p.], 1906.

68. DuPont, Henry A. *Rear-Admiral Samuel Francis DuPont.* New York: National Americana Society, 1926.

69. Durkin, Joseph T. *Stephen R. Mallory: Confederate Navy Chief.* Chapel Hill: University of North Carolina Press, 1954.

70. Dutton, Charles J. *Oliver Hazard Perry.* New York: Longmans, Green and Co., 1935.

71. Ellicott, John M. *The Life of John Ancrum Winslow, Rear Admiral, United States Navy.* New York: G. P. Putnam's Sons, 1902.

72. Evans, Robley D. *A Sailor's Log: Recollections of Forty Years of Naval Life.* New York: Appleton, 1901.

73. Evans, Stephen H. *The United States Coast Guard, 1790-1915: A Definitive History.* Annapolis: U.S. Naval Institute, 1949.

74. Falk, Edwin A. *From Perry to Pearl Harbor: The Struggle for Supremacy in the Pacific.* New York: Doubleday, Doran, 1943.

75. Fanning, Edmund. *Voyages Round the World.* New York: Collins & Hanney, 1833. Reprinted, 1970.

76. Farragut, Loyall. *The Life and Letters of Admiral Farragut, First Admiral of the United States Navy.* New York: D. Appleton, 1879.

77. Ferguson, Eugene S. *Truxtun of the Constellation: The Life of Commodore Thomas Truxtun, U.S. Navy, 1755-1822.* Baltimore: Johns Hopkins Press, 1956.

78. Field, James A., Jr. *America and the Mediterranean World, 1776-1882.* Princeton: Princeton University Press, 1969.
79. Fiske, Bradley A. *From Midshipman to Rear-Admiral.* New York: Century, 1919.
80. Fitzpatrick, Donovan, and Saul Saphire. *Navy Maverick: Uriah Phillips Levy.* Garden City, New York: Doubleday, 1963.
81. Foote, Andrew H. *Africa and the American Flag.* New York: D. Appleton, 1854. Reprinted, 1970.
82. Garrison, James H. *Behold Me Once More: The Confessions of James Holley Garrison, Brother of William Lloyd Garrison.* Boston: Houghton Mifflin, 1954.
83. Gleaves, Albert. *James Lawrence, Captain, United States Navy: Commander of the "Chesapeake".* New York: G. P. Putnam's Sons, 1904.
84. Gleaves, Albert. *Life and Letters of Rear Admiral Stephen B. Luce.* New York: Putnam's, 1925.
85. Goldsborough, Charles W. *The United States Naval Chronicle.* Washington: Wilson, 1824.
86. Goodrich, Caspar F. *In Memoriam, Stephen Bleecker Luce.* New York: Naval History Society, 1919.
87. Goodrich, Caspar F. *Rope Yarns from the Old Navy.* New York: Naval History Society, 1931.
88. Griffis, William E. *Matthew Calbraith Perry: A Typical American Naval Officer.* Boston: Cupples and Hurd, 1887.
89. Gurney, Gene. *The United States Coast Guard: A Pictorial History.* New York: Crown, 1973.
90. Guttridge, Leonard and Jay D. Smith. *The Commodores: The U.S. Navy in the Age of Sail.* New York: Harper & Row, 1969.
91. Hagan, Kenneth J. *American Gunboat Diplomacy and the Old Navy, 1877-1889.* Westport, Connecticut: Greenwood, 1973.
92. Hall, Claude H. *Abel Parker Upshur: Conservative Virginian, 1790-1844.* Madison: State Historical Society of Wisconsin, 1964.
93. Hamersly, Lewis R. *The Records of Living Officers of the U.S. Navy and Marine Corps.* Philadelphia: L. R. Hamersly, 1870. Rev. ed., 1870, 1878, 1890, 1894, 1898, 1902.
94. Harbeck, Charles T., comp. *A Contribution to the Bibliography of the History of the United States Navy.* Cambridge: Riverside Press, 1906. Reprinted, 1970.
95. Hayes, John D., ed. *Samuel Francis Du Pont: A Selection from His Civil War Letters.* Ithaca: Cornell University Press, 1969. 3 vols.
96. Heinl, Robert D., Jr. *Soldiers of the Sea: The United States Marine Corps, 1775-1962.* Annapolis: U.S. Naval Institute, 1962.
97. Henderson, Daniel. *The Hidden Coasts: A Biography of Admiral Charles Wilkes.* New York: William Sloane, 1953. Reprinted, 1969.
98. Henshaw, Joshua S. *Around the World: A Narrative of a Voyage in the East India Squadron.* New York: Charles S. Francis, 1840. 2 vols.
99. Herrick, Walter R., Jr. *The American Naval Revolution.* Baton Rouge: Louisiana State University Press, 1966.
100. Hill, Jim D. *Sea Dogs of the Sixties: Farragut and Seven Con-*

temporaries. Minneapolis: University of Minnesota Press, 1935.

101. Hirsch, Mark D. *William C. Whitney: Modern Warwick.* New York: Dodd, Mead, 1949. Reprinted, Hamden, Connecticut: Archon Books, 1969.

102. Hobbs, William H. *Peary.* New York: Macmillan, 1937.

103. Holcomb, Richmond C. *A Century with Norfolk Naval Hospital, 1830-1930.* Portsmouth, Virginia: Printcraft, 1930.

104. Hoole, William S. *Four Years in the Confederate Navy: The Career of Captain John Low on the C.S.S. Fingal, Florida, Alabama, Tuscaloosa, and Ajax.* Athens: University of Georgia Press, 1964.

105. Hoppin, James M. *Life of Andrew Hull Foote, Rear Admiral United States Navy.* New York: Harper, 1874.

106. Horan, James D., ed. *C.S.S. Shenandoah: The Memoirs of Lieutenant Commanding James I. Waddell.* New York: Crown Publishers, Inc., 1960.

107. Hovgaard, William. *Modern History of Warships.* London: E. & F. Spon, Ltd., 1920. Reprinted, 1971.

108. Hutchins, John G. B. *The American Maritime Industries and Public Policy, 1789-1914.* Harvard Economic Studies, No. 71. Cambridge: Harvard University Press, 1941.

109. Jaffe, Bernard. *Michelson and the Speed of Light.* Garden City, New York: Doubleday, 1960.

110. Jennings, John. *Tattered Ensign.* New York: Crowell, 1966.

111. Johnson, Allen, and Dumas Malone, eds. *Dictionary of American Biography.* New York: Scribner's, 1930.

112. Johnson, Robert E. *Rear Admiral John Rodgers, 1812-1882.* Annapolis: U.S. Naval Institute, 1967.

113. Johnson, Robert E. *Thence Round Cape Horn: The Story of United States Naval Forces on Pacific Station, 1818-1923.* Annapolis: U.S. Naval Institute, 1963.

114. Jones, Virgil C. *The Civil War at Sea.* New York: Holt, Rinehart, Winston, 1960-1962. 3 vols.

115. Kane, Elisha K. *Arctic Explorations: The Second Grinnell Expedition in Search of Sir John Franklin, 1853, '54, '55.* Philadelphia: Childs & Peterson, 1856. 2 vols. Reprinted, 1971.

116. Karsten, Peter. *The Naval Aristocracy: The Golden Age of Annapolis and the Emergence of Modern American Navalism.* New York: Free Press, 1972.

117. Kelley, J. D. Jerrold. *Our Navy: Its Growth and Achievements.* Hartford, Connecticut: American Publishing Co., 1892.

118. Kelley, J. D. Jerrold. *The Question of Ships.* New York: Scribner's, 1884.

119. King, James W. *The War-Ships and Navies of the World.* Boston: A. Williams and Company, 1881.

120. Klay, Andor. *Daring Diplomacy: The Case of the First American Ultimatum.* Minneapolis: University of Minnesota Press, 1957.

121. Knox, Dudley W. *A History of the United States Navy.* New York: Putnam's, 1936. Rev. ed., 1948.

122. Laing, Alexander. *American Ships.* New York: American Heritage, 1971.

123. Langley, Harold D. *Social Reform in the United States Navy, 1798-1862.* Urbana: University of Illinois Press, 1967.
124. Leeming, Joseph. *The Book of American Fighting Ships.* New York: Harper, 1939.
125. Lewis, Charles L. *Admiral Franklin Buchanan: Fearless Man of Action.* Baltimore: Norman, Remington Company, 1929.
126. Lewis, Charles L. *David Glasgow Farragut.* Annapolis: U.S. Naval Institute, 1941-1943. 2 vols.
127. Lewis, Charles L. *Famous American Marines.* Boston: L. C. Page & Company, 1950.
128. Lewis, Charles L. *Famous American Naval Officers.* Boston: L. C. Page, 1924. Rev. ed., 1948.
129. Lewis, Charles L. *The Romantic Decatur.* Philadelphia: University of Pennsylvania Press, 1937.
130. Livezey, William E. *Mahan on Sea Power.* Norman: University of Oklahoma Press, 1947.
131. Long, David F. *Nothing Too Daring: A Biography of Commodore David Porter, 1780-1843.* Annapolis: U.S. Naval Institute, 1970.
132. Long, John D. *The New American Navy.* New York: Outlook, 1903. 2 vols.
133. Loomis, Chauncey C. *Weird and Tragic Shores: The Story of Charles Francis Hall, Explorer.* New York: Knopf, 1971.
134. Loomis, Eben J. *An Eclipse Party in Africa.* Boston: Roberts Brothers, 1896.
135. Lott, Arnold S. *A Long Line of Ships: Mare Island's Century of Naval Activity in California.* Annapolis: U.S. Naval Institute, 1954.
136. Loubat, Joseph F. *Narrative of the Mission to Russia, in 1866, of the Hon. Gustavus Vasa Fox, Assistant-Secretary of the Navy.* New York: D. Appleton, 1873. Reprinted, 1970.
137. Lynch, William F. *Narrative of the United States' Expedition to the River Jordan and the Dead Sea.* Philadelphia: Blanchard and Lee, 1854.
138. Macartney, Clarence E. *Mr. Lincoln's Admirals.* New York: Funk & Wagnalls, 1956.
139. MacBride, Robert. *Civil War Ironclads: The Dawn of Naval Armor.* Philadelphia: Chilton Company, 1962.
140. Maclay, Edgar S., ed. *Reminiscences of the Old Navy.* New York: G. P. Putnam's Sons, 1898.
141. Maffitt, Emma M. *The Life and Services of John Newland Maffitt.* New York: Neale Publishing Company, 1906.
142. Mahan, Alfred T. *Admiral Farragut.* New York: D. Appleton, 1892. Reprinted, 1970.
143. Mahan, Alfred T. *From Sail to Steam: Recollections of Naval Life.* New York: Harper, 1907. Reprinted, 1968.
144. Mahan, Alfred T. *The Gulf and Inland Waters.* Vol. III of *The Navy in the Civil War.* New York: Scribner's, 1883.
145. Mahan, Alfred T. *The Influence of Sea Power upon History, 1660-1783.* Boston: Little, Brown and Company, 1890. Reprinted, 1957.
146. Mahan, Alfred T. *Sea Power in Its Relations to the War of 1812.* Boston: Little, Brown, 1905. 2 vols.

147. Mahon, John K. *The War of 1812.* Gainesville: University of Florida Press, 1972.
148. Maury, Matthew F. *The Physical Geography of the Sea.* Cambridge: Belknap Press, 1963.
149. McKee, Christopher. *Edward Preble: A Naval Biography, 1761-1807.* Annapolis: U.S. Naval Institute Press, 1972.
150. Meade, Rebecca P. *Life of Hiram Paulding, Rear-Admiral, U.S.N.* New York: Baker & Taylor, 1910.
151. Meissner, Sophie Radford de. *Old Naval Days: Sketches from the Life of Rear Admiral William Radford, U.S.N.* New York: Henry Holt, 1920.
152. Melville, Herman. *White-Jacket, or The World in a Man-of-War.* Evanston and Chicago: Northwestern University Press and The Newberry Library, 1970.
153. Mercier, Henry J. *Life in a Man-of-War: Or, Scenes in "Old Ironsides" during Her Cruise in the Pacific, by a Fore-Top-Man.* Boston: Houghton Mifflin, 1927.
154. Meriwether, Colyer. *Raphael Semmes.* Philadelphia: George W. Jacobs & Company, 1913.
155. Merli, Frank J. *Great Britain and the Confederate Navy, 1861-1865.* Bloomington: Indiana University Press, 1970.
156. Merrill, James M. *Battle Flags South: The Story of the Civil War Navies on Western Waters.* Cranbury, New Jersey: Associated University Presses, Inc., 1970.
157. Merrill, James M., ed. *Quarter-Deck and Fo'c'sle: The Exciting Story of the Navy.* Chicago: Rand McNally, 1963.
158. Merrill, James M. *The Rebel Shore: The Story of Union Sea Power in the Civil War.* Boston: Little, Brown, 1957.
159. Metcalf, Clyde H. *A History of the United States Marine Corps.* New York: G. P. Putnam's Sons, 1939.
160. *Military Affairs.* 1937- .
161. Milligan, John D. *Gunboats Down the Mississippi.* Annapolis: U.S. Naval Institute, 1965.
162. Mitchell, Donald W. *History of the Modern American Navy from 1883 through Pearl Harbor.* New York: Knopf, 1946.
163. Mitterling, Philip I. *America in the Antarctic to 1840.* Urbana: University of Illinois Press, 1959.
164. Morison, Samuel E. *Old Bruin: Commodore Matthew C. Perry, 1794-1858.* Boston: Little, Brown, 1967.
165. Morris, Richard K. *John P. Holland, 1841-1914: Inventor of the Modern Submarine.* Annapolis: U.S. Naval Institute, 1966.
166. Muir, John. *The Cruise of the Corwin: Journal of the Arctic Expedition of 1881 in Search of DeLong and the Jeanette.* Boston: Houghton Mifflin, 1917.
167. Nash, Howard P., Jr. *The Forgotten Wars: The Role of the U.S. Navy in the Quasi War with France and the Barbary Wars, 1798-1805.* New York: A. S. Barnes, 1968.
168. Neeser, Robert W. *Statistical and Chronological History of the United States Navy, 1775-1909.* New York: Macmillan, 1909. Reprinted, 1970. 2 vols.

169. Neumann, William L. *America Encounters Japan: From Perry to MacArthur*. Baltimore: Johns Hopkins Press, 1963.
170. Niven, John. *Gideon Welles, Lincoln's Secretary of the Navy*. New York: Oxford University Press, 1973.
171. Nordhoff, Charles. *Life on the Ocean*. Cincinnati: Wilstach Baldwin, 1874. 3 vols. Reprinted, 1970.
172. Offutt, Milton. *The Protection of Citizens Abroad by the Armed Forces of the United States*. Johns Hopkins University Studies in Historical and Political Science, Vol. 46, No. 4. Baltimore: Johns Hopkins Press, 1928. Reprinted, 1974.
173. Owsley, Frank L. *King Cotton Diplomacy: Foreign Relations of the Confederate States of America*. Chicago: University of Chicago Press, 1931. 2nd ed. rev., 1959.
174. Owsley, Frank L., Jr. *The C.S.S. Florida: Her Building and Operations*. Philadelphia: University of Pennsylvania Press, 1965.
175. Padfield, Peter. *The Battleship Era*. New York: David McKay Company, Inc., 1972.
176. Padfield, Peter, *Guns at Sea*. London: Hugh Evelyn, 1973.
177. Paulding, Hiram. *Journal of a Cruise of the United States Schooner Dolphin Among the Islands of the Pacific Ocean and a Visit to the Mulgrave Islands, in Pursuit of the Mutineers of the Whale Ship Globe*. New York: Carvill, 1831. Reprinted, 1970.
178. Paullin, Charles O. *American Voyages to the Orient, 1690-1865*. Annapolis: U.S. Naval Institute, 1971.
179. Paullin, Charles O. *Commodore John Rodgers: Captain, Commodore, and Senior Officer of the American Navy, 1773-1838*. Cleveland: Arthur H. Clark, 1910. Reprinted, 1967.
180. Paullin, Charles O. *Diplomatic Negotiations of American Naval Officers, 1778-1883*. Baltimore: Johns Hopkins Press, 1912.
181. Paullin, Charles O. *Paullin's History of Naval Administration, 1775-1911*. Annapolis: U.S. Naval Institute, 1968.
182. Peary, Robert E. *Northward Over the "Great Ice"*. New York: Frederick A. Stokes, 1898.
183. Peck, Taylor. *Round-Shot to Rockets: A History of the Washington Navy Yard and U.S. Naval Gun Factory*. Annapolis: U.S. Naval Institute, 1949.
184. Perry, Matthew C. *Narrative of the Expedition of an American Squadron to the China Seas and Japan*. New York: AMS Press, 1967. 3 vols.
185. Pineau, Roger, ed. *The Japan Expedition, 1852-1854: The Personal Journal of Commodore Matthew C. Perry*. Washington: Smithsonian Institution, 1968.
186. Ponko, Vincent, Jr. *Ships, Seas, and Scientists: U.S. Naval Exploration and Discovery in the Nineteenth Century*. Annapolis: U.S. Naval Institute, 1974.
187. Porter, David. *Journal of a Cruise Made to the Pacific Ocean*. Philadelphia: Bradford and Inskeep, 1815. 2 vols. Reprinted, 1970.
188. Porter, David D. *The Naval History of the Civil War*. New York: The Sherman Publishing Company, 1886.
189. Potter, Elmer B. *The Naval Academy Illustrated History of the United States Navy*. New York: Crowell, 1971.

190. Potter, E. B., and Chester W. Nimitz, eds. *Sea Power: A Naval History*. Englewood Cliffs, New Jersey: Prentice-Hall, 1960.
191. Powell, Theodore. *The Long Rescue*. Garden City, New York: Doubleday, 1960.
192. Pratt, Fletcher. *Preble's Boys: Commodore Preble and the Birth of American Sea Power*. New York: Sloane, 1950.
193. Preble, George H. *History of the United States Navy-Yard, Portsmouth, N.H.* Washington: G.P.O., 1892.
194. Puleston, W. D. *Annapolis: Gangway to the Quarterdeck*. New York: D. Appleton, 1942.
195. Puleston, W. D. *Mahan: The Life and Work of Captain Alfred Thayer Mahan, U.S.N.* New Haven: Yale University Press, 1939.
196. Pulsifer, Pitman, comp. *Navy Yearbook: A Compilation of Annual Naval Appropriations Including Provisions for the Construction of All Vessels of the "New Navy," with Tables Showing Present Naval Strength*. Washington: G.P.O., 1904-1922.
197. Rankin, Robert H. *Small Arms of the Sea Services*. New Milford, Connecticut: N. Flayderman, 1972.
198. Reynolds, Clark G. *Command of the Sea: The History and Strategy of Maritime Empires*. New York: Morrow, 1974.
199. Reynolds, Francis J. *The United States Navy from the Revolution to Date*. New York: F. P. Collier & Son, 1916.
200. Roberts, Edmund. *Embassy to the Eastern Courts of Cochin-China, Siam, and Muscat*. New York: Harper & Brothers, 1837.
201. Roberts, W. Adolphe, and Lowell Brentano, eds. *The Book of the Navy*. Garden City, New York: Doubleday, Doran, 1944.
202. Robison, Samuel S., and Mary L. Robison. *A History of Naval Tactics from 1530 to 1930*. Annapolis: U.S. Naval Institute, 1942.
203. Roosevelt, Theodore. *The Naval War of 1812*. New York: Putnam's, 1882.
204. Roscoe, Theodore, and Fred Freeman. *Picture History of the U.S. Navy*. New York: Scribner's, 1956.
205. Roske, Ralph J., and Charles Van Doren. *Lincoln's Commando: The Biography of Commander W. B. Cushing, U.S.N.* New York: Harper & Brothers, 1957.
206. Ross, James C. *A Voyage of Discovery and Research in the Southern and Antarctic Regions, During the Years 1839-43*. London: John Murray, 1847. 2 vols. Reprinted, 1971.
207. Ruschenberger, William S. W. *A Voyage Round the World: Including an Embassy to Muscat and Siam, in 1835, 1836, and 1837*. Philadelphia: Carey, Lea & Blanchard, 1838.
208. Sands, Benjamin F. *From Reefer to Rear-Admiral*. New York: Frederick A. Stokes, 1899.
209. Scharf, J. Thomas. *History of the Confederate States Navy from Its Organization to the Surrender of Its Last Vessel*. Atlanta, Georgia: W. H. Shepard & Co., 1887.
210. Schley, Winfield S. *Forty-Five Years Under the Flag*. New York: D. Appleton and Company, 1904.
211. Schley, W. S., and J. R. Soley. *The Rescue of Greely*. New York: Scribner's, 1885.

212. Schroeder, Seaton. *A Half Century of Naval Service.* New York: D. Appleton, 1922.
213. Schuon, Karl, ed. *U.S. Marine Corps Biographical Dictionary.* New York: Watts, 1963.
214. Schuon, Karl. *U.S. Navy Biographical Dictionary.* New York: Watts, 1964.
215. Scroggs, William O. *Filibusters and Financiers: The Story of William Walker and His Associates.* New York: Macmillan, 1916. Reprinted, 1969.
216. Selfridge, Thomas O., Jr. *Memoirs of Thomas O. Selfridge, Jr.* New York: Putnam's, 1924.
217. Semmes, Raphael. *Memoirs of Service Afloat, During the War Between the States.* Baltimore: Kelly, Piet & Co., 1869.
218. Semmes, Raphael. *Service Afloat and Ashore During the Mexican War.* Cincinnati: William H. Moore, 1851.
219. Shippen, Edward. *Thirty Years at Sea: The Story of a Sailor's Life.* Philadelphia: Lippincott, 1879.
220. Sloan, Edward W., III. *Benjamin Franklin Isherwood, Naval Engineer: The Years as Engineer in Chief, 1861-1869.* Annapolis: U.S. Naval Institute, 1965.
221. Sloan, Edward W., III. *Maritime History: A Basic Bibliography.* Choice Bibliographical Essay Series, No. 1. [Chicago]: Association of College and Research Libraries, 1972.
222. Smelser, Marshall. *The Congress Founds the Navy, 1787-1798.* South Bend: University of Notre Dame Press, 1959.
223. Smith, Myron J., Jr. *American Civil War Navies: A Bibliography. American Naval Bibliography Series, Vol. III.* Metuchen, New Jersey: Scarecrow, 1972.
224. Smith, Myron J., Jr. *The American Navy, 1789-1860: A Bibliography. American Naval Bibliography Series, Vol. II.* Metuchen, New Jersey: Scarecrow, 1974.
225. Smith, Myron J., Jr. *The American Navy, 1865-1918: A Bibliography. American Naval Bibliography Series, Vol. IV.* Metuchen, New Jersey: Scarecrow, 1974.
226. Soley, James R. *Admiral Porter.* New York: D. Appleton, 1903.
227. Soley, James R. *The Blockade and the Cruisers.* Vol. II of *The Navy in the Civil War.* New York: Scribner's, 1883.
228. Soley, James R. *Historical Sketch of the United States Naval Academy.* Washington: G.P.O., 1876.
229. Soulsby, Hugh G. *The Right of Search and the Slave Trade in Anglo-American Relations, 1814-1862.* Johns Hopkins University Studies in Historical and Political Science, Ser. 51, No. 2. Baltimore: Johns Hopkins Press, 1933.
230. Spears, John R. *David G. Farragut.* Philadelphia: George W. Jacobs, 1905.
231. Sprout, Harold and Margaret. *The Rise of American Naval Power, 1776-1918.* Princeton: Princeton University Press, 1939. Rev. ed., 1942.
232. Stern, Philip Van Dorn. *The Confederate Navy: A Pictorial History.* Garden City, New York: Doubleday & Company, Inc., 1962.

233. Stern, Philip Van Dorn, ed. *The Confederate Raider Alabama.* Gloucester, Massachusetts: Peter Smith, 1969.
234. Stevens, William O. *The Story of Our Navy.* New York: Harper & Brothers, 1914.
235. Stevens, William O., and Allan Westcott. *A History of Sea Power.* New York: George H. Doran, 1920. Rev. eds., 1937, 1942.
236. Stewart, Charles S. *A Visit to the South Seas, in the U.S. Ship Vincennes, During the Years 1829 and 1830.* New York: John P. Haven, 1831. 2 vols.
237. Still, William N., Jr. *Confederate Shipbuilding.* Athens: University of Georgia Press, 1969.
238. Still, William N., Jr. *Iron Afloat: The Story of the Confederate Armorclads.* Nashville, Tennessee: Vanderbilt University Press, 1971.
239. Summersell, Charles G., ed. *The Journal of George Townley Fullam, Boarding Officer of the Confederate Sea Raider Alabama.* University, Alabama: University of Alabama Press, 1973.
240. Swann, Leonard A., Jr. *John Roach, Maritime Entrepreneur: The Years as a Naval Contractor, 1862-1886.* Annapolis: U.S. Naval Institute, 1965.
241. Szczesniak, Boleslaw, ed. *The Opening of Japan: A Diary of Discovery in the Far East, 1853-1856.* Norman: University of Oklahoma Press, 1962.
242. Taylor, Charles C. *The Life of Admiral Mahan, Naval Philosopher, Rear Admiral, United States Navy.* New York: George H. Doran, 1920.
243. Taylor, Fitch W. *The Flagship: Or a Voyage Around the World, in the United States Frigate Columbia.* New York: D. Appleton, 1840. 2 vols.
244. Thompson, Robert M., and Richard Wainwright, eds. *Confidential Correspondence of Gustavus Vasa Fox.* New York: Naval History Society, 1920. 2 vols.
245. Trexler, Harrison A. *The Confederate Ironclad "Virginia" ("Merrimac").* Chicago: University of Chicago Press, 1938.
246. Tucker, Glenn. *Dawn Like Thunder: The Barbary Wars and the Birth of the U.S. Navy.* Indianapolis: Bobbs-Merrill, 1963.
247. Turnbull, Archibald D. *John Stevens: An American Record.* New York: Century, 1928.
248. *The United Service.* 1879-1905.
249. U.S., Congress. *American State Papers: Documents, Legislative and Executive, of the Congress of the United States.* Washington: Gales and Seaton, 1832-1861. 38 vols.
250. U.S., Congress. *Annals of the Congress, 1789-1824.* Washington: Gales and Seaton, 1789-1842. 42 vols.
251. U.S. Congress. *The Congressional Globe.* Washington: The Globe Office, 1834-1873. 46 vols.
252. U.S., Congress. *Congressional Record.* Washington: G.P.O., 1873- .
253. U.S., Congress. *State Papers and Publick Documents of the United States.* Boston: Thomas B. Wait, 1819. 12 vols.

254. U.S., Navy Department. *Annual Report of the Secretary of the Navy.* Washington: G.P.O., 1798- .

255. U.S., Navy Department. *Official Records of the Union and Confederate Navies in the War of the Rebellion.* Washington: G.P.O., 1894-1922. Series I: 27 vols. Series II: 3 vols.

256. U.S., Navy Department. *Official Records of the Union and Confederate Navies in the War of the Rebellion: General Index.* Washington: G.P.O., 1927.

257. U.S., Navy Department, Bureau of Naval Personnel. *The History of the Chaplain Corps, United States Navy, 1778-1957.* Washington: G.P.O., 1948-1960. 6 vols.

258. U.S., Navy Department, Bureau of Navigation. *Catalogue of Works by American Naval Authors.* Washington: [n.p.], 1888.

259. U.S., Navy Department, Naval History Division. *Civil War Naval Chronology, 1861-1865.* Washington: G.P.O., 1971.

260. U.S., Navy Department, Naval History Division. *Dictionary of American Naval Fighting Ships.* Washington: G.P.O., 1959- . 5 vols.

261. U.S., Navy Department, Naval History Division. *United States Naval History: A Bibliography.* 6th ed. Washington: G.P.O., 1972.

262. U.S., Navy Department, Office of Naval Records and Library. *Naval Documents Related to the Quasi-War between the United States and France.* Washington: G.P.O., 1935-1938. 7 vols.

263. U.S., Navy Department, Office of Naval Records and Library. *Naval Documents Related to the United States Wars with the Barbary Powers.* Washington: G.P.O., 1939-1944. 6 vols.

264. U.S., Navy Department, Office of Naval Records and Library. *Register of Officer Personnel, United States Navy and Marine Corps, and Ships' Data, 1801-1807.* Washington: G.P.O., 1945.

265. U.S., State Department. *Correspondence Concerning the Claims Against Great Britain.* Washington: G.P.O., 1869-1871. 7 vols.

266. U.S., State Department. *Papers Relating to the Foreign Relations of the United States.* Washington: G.P.O., 1861- .

267. *United States Naval Institute Proceedings.* 1873- .

268. Very, Edward W. *Navies of the World.* New York: Wiley, 1880.

269. Villarejo, Oscar M. *Dr. Kane's Voyage to the Polar Lands.* Philadelphia: University of Pennsylvania Press, 1965.

270. Warriner, Francis. *Cruise of the United States Frigate Potomac Round the World, During the Years 1831-34.* New York: Leavitt, Lord, 1835.

271. Weber, Gustavus A. *The Coast and Geodetic Survey: Its History, Activities, and Organization.* Institute for Government Research, Service Monographs of the United States Government, No. 16. Baltimore: Johns Hopkins Press, 1923.

272. Weber, Gustavus A. *The Hydrographic Office: Its History, Activities, and Organization.* Institute for Government Research, Service Monographs of the United States Government, No. 42. Baltimore: Johns Hopkins Press, 1926.

273. Weber, Gustavus A. *The Naval Observatory: Its History, Activities, and Organization.* Institute for Government Research, Service

Monographs of the United States Government, No. 39. Baltimore: Johns Hopkins Press, 1926.

274. Wells, Tom H. *The Confederate Navy: A Study in Organization.* University, Alabama: University of Alabama Press, 1971.

275. West, Richard S., Jr. *Gideon Welles: Lincoln's Navy Department.* Indianapolis: Bobbs-Merrill, 1943.

276. West, Richard S., Jr. *Mr. Lincoln's Navy.* New York: Longman's, Green, 1957.

277. West, Richard S., Jr. *The Second Admiral: A Life of David Dixon Porter, 1813-1891.* New York: Coward-McCann, 1937.

278. Wheaton, Henry. *Enquiry into the Validity of the British Claim to a Right of Visitation and Search of American Vessels Suspected to Be Engaged in the African Slave-Trade.* Philadelphia: Lea and Blanchard, 1842. Reprinted, 1971.

279. Wheeler, Richard. *In Pirate Waters: Captain David Porter, USN, and America's War on Piracy in the West Indies.* New York: Thomas Y. Crowell, 1969.

280. Wilkes, Charles. *Narrative of the United States Exploring Expedition During the Years 1838, 1839, 1840, 1841, 1842.* Philadelphia: C. Sherman, 1844. Reprinted, 1970. 5 vols.

281. Williams, Frances L. *Matthew Fontaine Maury: Scientist of the Sea.* New Brunswick: Rutgers University Press, 1963.

282. Wilson, John H., Jr. *Albert A. Michelson: America's First Nobel Prize Physicist.* New York: Julian Messner, 1958.

283. Wines, Enoch C. *Two Years and a Half in the American Navy.* London: Richard Bentley, 1833. 2 vols.

DEPOSITORIES

284. Library of Congress, Manuscript Division, Washington, D.C.

285. National Archives, Washington, D.C.

286. Navy Department, Naval History Division, Navy Yard, Washington, D.C.

287. U.S. Naval Academy, Nimitz Library, Annapolis, Maryland.

Compilation of this bibliography was made possible by the unstintingly generous help of Ms. Antoinette D. Delisi and her staff in the circulation department of the Nimitz Library.

VII

SCIENCE AND TECHNOLOGY IN THE NINETEENTH CENTURY

Edward C. Ezell

The history of the American armed forces in the nineteenth century is inextricably bound to the increasing momentum of the scientific and technological revolution that began during the previous century in England (25), (96), (202), (313). As the nineteenth century opened, the United States was a net importer of technological concepts and material (350). In the field of military equipment the armed forces were almost totally dependent upon European patterns; e.g., the first musket produced at the National Armory at Springfield in 1795 was simply a copy of the contemporary French weapon (118), (147), (148), (149), (150), (151), (153), (154). By mid-century when the military-technologists of England and the Continent visited the New York Exhibition of 1853, these men came as students not as teachers. Joseph Whitworth and others became enthusiastic proponents of the use of the "labor saving" machinery that characterized the "American System of interchangeable manufacture" (13), (14), (276), (292). A year later, three American officers would visit the Crimean theater of war and tour the arsenals of Europe (89), (194), (223), only to conclude that there were few new ideas to borrow. During the Civil War, the European observers thought differently and assimilated the new ideas and technological elements of that war. These concepts, e.g., the strategic importance of the railroads, would be perfected by the Prussians in their wars of the 1870s (192). Out of the 1861-65 war, which had drawn on the total industrial resources of the divided nation, the United States emerged united and a full-fledged member of the international community. With the naval revolution of the last decades of the century (31), (36), (200), (301), (353), and a growing external expansionism, the United States joined into the community of Imperialism. With the Springfield and the Krag, the United States brought "civilization" to Cuba, the Philippines, and helped to open the Chinese door. Throughout the nineteenth century, science and technology were the conscious handmaidens of the American military. This essay represents an attempt to develop some of the sources for the further exploration of the interrelationships between the world of the military and the worlds of science and technology in the 1800s. The structure that follows, for the sake of convenience, presents a number of topics separately which are obviously part of a larger integrated whole. As in anatomy, where dissection is used as an aid to the understanding of living organisms, the categories developed below are intended to suggest aspects of the history of science and technology that should be studied by the historian of military affairs. This essay is a beginning, not an end. It is intended to be suggestive of the needs for research; not just a catalog of work that has been done.

OVERVIEWS FOR THE HISTORY OF TECHNOLOGY AND SCIENCE. The history of technology and the history of science are broad and relatively new fields of study. Following the practice of Eugene Ferguson (110) technology here is used in the sense of man's activities that result in the creation of artifacts or hardware that extends his physical capabilities. Military technology is often only a slight modification of its civil counterpart, but its use to wage war makes it unique. Civilian and military railroads of the nineteenth century were often identical, but the differing impacts of their respective utilization was dramatic. The Baltimore and Ohio was created to move agricultural and manufactured goods to market, but the same railroad was an important prime mover of strategic military hardware during the Civil War (307). The "American System of interchangeable manufacture," grew out of the need to produce large numbers of military muskets with semiskilled laborers (133), (276), (266), (283), (381). That system would later produce far less militant products such as clocks, McCormick reapers, and ultimately, in one of its most advanced forms, the Ford automobile (156). If technology is neutral and a "double edged sword" that can be used for good and evil, it was an important component in the history of the nineteenth century American Republic. For the military historian who wishes to explore the technological dimension of his field of study there are several general studies in the field. While the five-volume *History of Technology* (296) edited by Charles Singer *et al.* is predominately focused on Europe, it is the primary starting point, especially if used in conjunction with Kranzberg and Pursell, *Technology in Western Civilization* (181). Burlingame, *March of the Iron Men* (56), provides a sense of the unifying effects of technology in the 1800s while it also provides the context in which our military technology developed. John Kouwenhoven's *Made in America* (180) is the single most important essay on the democratizing effects of American technology. This theme of democracy and technology is also developed by Habbakkuk (133) and Mier (214). Oliver, *History of American Technology* (242) is also useful as an introduction to the general subject, but the shortcomings of this volume become abundantly apparent once one gets a better feel for the subject.

The history of American science poses real difficulties for the military historian and his civil counterpart. Unlike the rich tradition of studies in the history of scientific ideas which has prevailed in Europe, American science has received less scholarly attention. It has been argued that this is due to the absence of real science in America of the nineteenth century. As Dupree in *Science in the Federal Government* (98) indicates, science in America took a shape that was unique to the new world. Another view of the subject is to be found in Struik's *Yankee Science in the Making* (306).

For the military historian who is perplexed by the unfamiliar world of technology, Eugene Ferguson's *Bibliography of the History of Technology* (110) is a helpful companion. If at all possible, a newcomer to this field of study should obtain a copy of his essay." The Critical Period of American Technology, 1788-1853," which has been circulated in ditto print only (109). Unfortunately, there is no equivalent bibliography available for the history of American science. The bibliographical essay in Dupree (98) is nevertheless a good starting point.

There are three key contemporary journals for the historian of military technology. The foremost is the old standby *Military Affairs*, as is attested by seventeen citations in the following bibliography. Second in significance is the *U.S. Naval Institute Proceedings* with 7 articles. The third major source is *Technology and Culture* (published by the Society for the History of Technology) which has carried a number of significant articles, but which is in many respects more valuable because of its book reviews and bibliographical materials. Of especial importance are Jack Goodwin's "Current Bibliography in the History of Technology" which has appeared annually since 1964 in *T&C*. Other useful journals include *Civil War History*, the *Journal of the Confederate Historical Society*, and the *Military Collector and Historian*. Occasional articles of real significance to the military historian appear in the *National Defense Review* (formerly *Ordnance*, and before that *Army Ordnance*); e.g., the biographical sketch of the first Chief of Ordnance (263).

For nonmilitary periodicals the general rule is that relevant articles appear in the most unexpected places. The best contemporary description of Springfield Armory appeared in an 1852 issue of *Harpers Weekly* (4). A very comprehensive "Bibliography of the Literature of Submarines, Mines, and Torpedoes," appeared in the 1917 volume of the *General Electric Review* (278). I. Bernard Cohen published an article on Civil War period science in M.I.T.'s *Technology Review* (74), and another on the same subject by Nathan Reingold appeared in *Isis* (75). As a final example, the *American Machinist* carried occasional articles on the actual manufacture of small arms (195), (244).

In addition to the British-oriented bibliography presented by Armytage in Higham's *A Guide to the Sources of British Military History* (24), the following books have particularly useful bibliographies which supplement the citations in this chapter: Baxter, *The Introduction of the Ironclad Warship* (31); Brooks, *Civil War Medicine* (51); Fishlow, *American Railroads and the Transformation of the Antebellum Economy* (111); Hill, *Roads, Rails & Waterways* (156); Hunter, *Steamboats on Western Waters* (165); Huston, *The Sinews of War* (167); Milligan, *Gunboats Down the Mississippi* (216); Ripley, *Artillery and Ammunition of the Civil War* (268); Still, *Iron Afloat* (303); Taylor, *The Transportation Revolution* (309); and Weber, *The Northern Railroads in the Civil War* (343).

MILITARY ENGINEERING AND EDUCATION. At the outset, the Americans followed the lead of the French in military education. The United States Military Academy was established in 1802 to teach potential officers the basics of science and technology as those disciplines were applied to war. Louis Tousard (348) was among the early proponents of a military academy which would stress practical technical education; e.g., see his *American Artillerist's Companion* (88). The basic histories of West Point chronicle the emphasis on engineering education (12), (103), (114), (116), (226), but there was an equally strong stress laid upon ordnance technology. The West Point graduates became the first civil engineers who helped with the exploration of the west (257), (280) and they also assisted the construction of the early railroads and waterways (61), (156), (231), (233). Some of these engineers even served the Confederacy (232) while others sought not to participate in the war and contributed to railroad construction in Mexico and elsewhere (106). Likewise, their fellow academy graduates became "soldier-technologists" (106) and developed a strong scientific movement within the Army Ordnance Department; the important aspects of this latter movement have not yet been presented in published form (106), (104), (105). The careers of Alfred Mordecai— artillery and ballistics (106), (107), (219), (220), (221), (222), (223), Thomas Jackson Rodman—heavy ordnance design and propellant theory (104), (105), (270) are but two of the central ones in the story of the search for a science of ballistics and metallurgy. Their work is paralleled by that of John A. B. Dahlgren of the Navy (80), (81), (317), (318), (319) who came out of the scientific tradition of the Naval Academy to be one of Lincoln's favorite ordnance experts. As central as these figures and their colleagues are to the history of 19th century military technology in the United States very little of their work is known; it is a subject that begs to be explored.

NATIONAL ARMORIES AND ARSENALS. The National Armories, established to produce small arms for the Army, have been central to the development of interchangeable production. Thus it is surprising that so little has been published concerning the Springfield and Harpers Ferry Armories. Following on an earlier doctoral dissertation (345), Constance Green prepared a massive multivolume typescript history of Springfield during her World War II tenure as official historian at the Armory (128), the most accessible copy of which is located in Records Group 336, National Archives. Other material relating to the history of Springfield include (3), (4), (91), (118), (179), (195), (341). Published material concerning Harpers Ferry is equally skimpy (52), (120). The most promising work to date is the unpublished dissertation by M. R. Smith (298) which deals more specifically with the "new technology" of interchangeable manufacture (299). The important work of John H. Hall (299) at Harpers Ferry is just being recognized by the scholarly community, although his weapons have been controversial for years (258), (340), (166). Rock Island Arsenal has fared a better fate (18), (23), (311), (333f). A modest attempt at recording the history of Watervliet Arsenal (19), (20) has been made, but Washington, Frankford, Alleghenny and Benicia Arsenals have been neglected by the historian.

PRIVATE MANUFACTURERS OF SMALL ARMS. There is no dearth of materials on rifles and pistols in the nineteenth century, and the key to this literature is Ray Riling's bibliography (267). A representative sample of the better books on this topic are included in this section; this is only the "tip of the iceberg:" (7), (8), (11), (57), (73), (83), (84), (91), (94),

(102), (119), (120), (121), (122), (124), (137), (144), (166), (185), (188), (199), (244), (248), (264), (292), (300), (339), (354). Histories of specific firearms companies are presented in (121), (137), (142), (152), (199), (248), (300), (314), (339), (354).

THE AMERICAN SYSTEM OF INTERCHANGEABLE MANU-FACTURE. The single most important development in nineteenth century military technology was the evolution of the large scale production of small arms which had interchangeable parts. Again this is a topic, which until comparatively recently, had been talked about without significant research to back up the conclusions. The great myth of Eli Whitney as "father of interchangeability," begun with Olmstead (243) and perpetuated by Green (130) and Mirsky and Nevins (217), first came under attack by Woodbury (358) who also authored monographs on individual machine tools (355), (356), (357). Battison (29) has taken a closer look at the claims that Whitney used a primitive milling machine in the manufacture of his muskets; a study that has been pursued by Smith (298), (299).

Other key sources for the study of interchangeable manufacture include Fitch (112), (113), and (333g) for the production processes and (13), (14), (56), (99), (133), (274), (275), (276), (277), (283), (335), (341), and (360) for the broader implications of this new approach to manufacture. Still, this is a topic that needs much research, especially the question of the transfer of the "American System" to Europe. For example, the American career of James Henry Burton has been touched upon briefly in (336) but his work at Enfield Arsenal, Birmingham Small Arms Company, and Greenwood & Batley of Leeds has thus far been ignored. Greenwood & Batley, a machine tool manufacturer, sold the tooling with which the arsenals of France, Austria, Switzerland, Italy and Russia produced firearms with interchangeable parts. Burton assisted in the installation of the "American System" at the Tula Weapons Factory for the Russian Imperial Government. This one illustration of opportunities in this field could be multiplied. Studies of the manufacturing techniques at the Springfield Armory and Harpers Ferry Armory (298) and (299) and similar studies of the techniques employed at private factories such as Colt, Remington, Pratt & Whitney, and Winchester would be a valuable supplement to the "gun buff literature that predominates the published material currently available.

ORDNANCE DEPARTMENTS: NORTH AND SOUTH. The U.S. Ordnance Department (Army) and the U.S. Ordnance Bureau (Navy) had a major impact upon the shape of American technological development in the nineteenth century. The history of neither has been recorded as fully at that of the Confederate Ordnance Bureau which has been the subject of a major scholarly history (336). With the exception of Green et al. (129), the published materials concerning the Army Ordnance Department concentrate in the Civil War era. Two important doctoral studies are by Mac-Dougall (196) and Davis (84) and (369). The latter presents an alternative thesis to the standard study on small arms procurement by Shannon (293); i.e., the general performance of Army Ordnance was far better than its critics have led later students to believe it was.

The creation of an independent Ordnance Department in 1812, separate from the line services—notably the artillery, was a topic of considerable debate throughout the nineteenth century. This controversy centered on the question of who should control the development and manufacture of military hardware; should it have been the line services or should it have been an independent technical service. The ordnance case for a separate service is made in (35) while the artillery view is presented in (39). The latter favors an integration of hardware into the artillery service.

The sources available for the history of Army Ordnance are plentiful. The *Collection of Annual Reports* (324) is a major source which Holley (158), p. 196) says. "Historians with problems ranging far beyond the confines of ordnance could utilize these documents, which reflect interests in every sphere of public life, social, economic and political." This set has an extremely detailed index, and Vol. III, p. 478ff. provides useful bibliographical data on other Ordnance reports. In the *Annual Reports of the Chief of Ordnance* (335), (326) and *Ordnance Memoranda* (327) a selection of the more significant titles are presented (333c-333g); *Ordnance Notes* (328), (329), and other other ordnance publications (40), (219), (220), (221), (223), (270), (330), (331), (332), (333) begin to indicate the wealth of printed primary sources yet to be tapped. To these published reports must be added the large Record Group 156 of the Office of the Chief of Ordnance in the National Archives. Other printed source materials are presented in (115), (190). Munden and Beers (227) presents a *vade mecum* to the archival materials for the Civil War period.

The basic evolution of naval ordnance must be traced from the fragmentary details presented in books that concentrate on ships and shipbuilding (1), (2), (54), (64), (67), (77), (101), (145), (146), (157), (164), (172), (173), (174), (175), (183), (184), (208), (210), (215), (224), (249), (261), (278), (282), (288), (291), (294), (295), (301), (304), (323), (342), (344). The Ordnance Bureau reports; e.g., (317), (318), (319), provide further background on operations, but the record is not nearly as complete as that for the Army and a Bureau history is badly needed.

The history of Confederate ordnance programs has been given fuller attention by the historian. In addition to popular publications (7), (8), (10), (11), (73), (102), (120), and contemporary accounts (201), (259) there are several basic scholarly studies of ordnance in the South (53), (90), (126), (168), (336). Guides to Confederate ordnance records include (33), (65).

Confederate Naval ordnance and shipbuilding has received considerable scholarly attention (50), (55), (212), (230), (284), (302), (303).

ORDNANCE MATERIEL AND TECHNOLOGY. There is a vast literature on ordnance materiel; a representative sample would include for Artillery and Heavy Ordnance (21), (38), (40), (63), (66), (86), (87), (88), (90), (105), (106), (107), (123), (157), (164), (171), (172), (203), (208), (213), (215), (220), (253), (262), (268), (270), (285), (286), (287), (295), (312), (317), (318), (333b), (338), Rockets (95), (241), (249), for Ammunition (34), (58), (134), (135), (138), (178), (185), (186), (268), (281), (333a), (333c), and for Gunpowder and Explosives (22), (26), (41), (62), (67), (101), (104), (131), (132), (146), (204), (205), (206), (219), (222), (228), (229), (259), (289), (304), (305), (337). In the field of gunpowder and explosives one should not neglect to study the history of that industrial pioneer and giant; E. I.

du Pont de Nemours and Company (16), (17), (67), (100), (176), (337), (347).

The majority of these publications on ordnance materiel were either written as special pleading for a particular type of cannon or piece of equipment, or they were written for the ordnance "buff." Particularly significant as sources for a basic understanding of the technology are Birnie, *Gunmaking in the United States* (40), which deals with artillery manufacture; Tousard, *American Artillerist's Companion* (88); Dew, *Ironmaker to the Confederacy* (90); Ezell, "The Development of Artillery for the United States Land Service" (105); Falk, "Soldier-Technologist" (106); Holley, *A Treatise on Ordnance and Armor* (197); Ripley, *Artillery and Ammunition of the Civil War* (268); and Rodman, *Reports of Experiments on the Properties of Metals for Cannon* (270). See (105) above for more about this particular work and (333b).

NAVAL TECHNOLOGY—NORTH AND SOUTH. There is also a fairly large body of published material relating to the development and utilization of naval technology. Generally, the books in this field are better for the military historians' purposes than those dealing with land service materiel. There are a number of studies that will provide a general overview (30), (31), (46), (48), (49), (69), (155), (200), (282), (301), (316), (322), (342), (344), (353). Then there are a number of specialized books which deal with a particular aspect of naval hardware; such as those studies on Confederate naval hardware (45), (50), (55), (82), (209), (212), (230), (246), (284), (302), (303), Federal naval technology (32), (37), (216), (343), (344), (376), the new steam navy of the post Civil War period (3), (224), (225), (291), (301), (316), (323), the emergence of submarine technology (2), (44), (59), (60), (78), (93), (183), (184), (210), (245), (247), (278), (365), (366), and finally the evolution of torpedoes, mines and related destructive devices (1), (145), (170), (175), (250), (278), (288). An excellent overview of undersea warfare before 1865 is provided in Roland's "A Triumph of Natural Magic" (368).

The more general topic of military supply can be pursued in Huston's *The Sinews of War* (167) and Risch's *Quartermaster Support of the Army* (269). The student interested in the problems of supply and logistics in the Civil War era should look at Weigley's biography of M. C. Meigs for its many insights into the career of Lincoln's Quartermaster General (383). The Meigs biography touches on a number of interesting topics many of which could be studied further; e.g., the shortage of cotton led to the substitution of linen in the manufacture of tents. What similar problems were caused by other shortages of raw materials? How were scarce strategic commodities allocated? In the field of motive power, Weigley touches on the problems of providing horses and fuel for them (i.e., forage); this is a problem that deserves fuller attention as does the whole question of animal power and military vehicles. On the basic topic of wagons and related horse equipments, one should consult Coggin's (73), Scott (379), Shumway, Durell, and Frey (380) and Hutchins's edition of *Ordnance Memoranda no. 29* (382). The atlas volume of the *Official Records* of the War of the Rebellion, discussed in chapter VIII, illustrates many of the contemporary wagons, bridging gear, and related engineer equipments. A handy general reference relating to Civil War accoutrements is Lord's *Civil War Collector's Encyclopedia* which covers 155 major topics in alphabetical order. The actual manufacture of clothing and equipment is another area that needs to be more fully explored, as the fascinating autobiography of General Anson Mills, a pioneer of webbed canvas equipment, attests (377), and (378).

THE TRANSPORTATION AND COMMUNICATION REVOLUTION. While the Army would continue to rely heavily on the horse and the mule as its basic form of motive power until the early decades of the twentieth century, a transportation revolution was influential in changing the pace of warfare. The transportation revolution resulted primarily from the exploitation of the steam engine as a new source of motive power; the extension of that revolution would result in the application of the internal combustion engine to motor trucks and ultimately to armored fighting vehicles. The steam engine was the prologue.

The increased ease and speed of ground and water transportation was one of the major accomplishments of the first half of the nineteenth century. Hill, *Roads, Rails & Waterways* (156), describes the role of the American military in the development of these internal improvements. The first step in the opening of the trans-Appalachian west came with the building of roads for civil and military uses (156), (231), (280). Then came the era of canal building (61) which was followed by the railway boom. The transportation revolution (308) on land was complicated by the bewildering mixture of railway track gauges, but this problem was solved in large part by the Civil War. During that conflict the destructive and reconstructive work of Hermann Haupt (140), (141) and his corps of military railway experts brought standardization in the heat of battle (309), (321).

The rise of railpower as a military asset began most clearly in the American Civil War. The strategic use of the railways to move men and materiel was a major contributory factor in the Union successes on the battlefield (5), (27), (43), (45), (111), (177), (189), (254), (256), (260), (307), (315), (343). In a country in which the prevailing characteristic was the expanse of its territory, rails became the essential route to military victory as is exemplified by Sherman's successful thrust from Chattanooga to Atlanta along a single track railroad. The European observers (192), and more particularly the military planners of the Continent such as the Count von Moltke, were quick to perceive the dynamic force of this element of technology and worked through to the end of the century to integrate it into their strategic plans (256). The Germans were still studying the American Civil War as late as 1875. Their chief borrowing was the incorporation of the American practice of mixing military and railroad administrative staffs into their administration of the railway system (192). Equally significant is the fact that the Germans translated the report (321) of D.C. McCallum, the wartime director of the Federal railroads, for the use of the General Staff.

While less exciting from the European viewpoint, the development of river transportation was very important to the American exploitation of the Mississippi River Valley (165). That same river network was also central to the subsequent plans of the Union forces to divide the Confederacy into two parts. The vessels developed for the western river campaigns, which evolved from the civil craft on the Mississippi, were unique and have been discussed in fairly great detail by naval historians of that era (127), (165), (302).

Coupled with the need for more rapid movement of men and materiel was the movement of information, which was accomplished by the telegraph system which was pressed into military service (28), (240), (255). The use of the telegraph system added a new dimension to battlefield control inasmuch as it gave the commander in the field almost instantaneous contact with the rear. A detailed study of the actual combat utilization of the telegraph by commanders in the field, together with an analysis of the apparent effectiveness of their messages in bringing about the results they desired, would be a significant addition to the anectdotal histories currently available.

A final aspect of the transportation and communication revolution that also deserves fuller attention is the use of observation balloons in the Civil War (79), (139), (362), and (371). There of course is the Block biography of Thaddeus Low (361), and Parkinson's basic study of nineteenth-century aeronautics (367) for this period. For the coming of military aeronautics and air warfare in the twentieth century, the reader should see chapter XV.

THE IMPACT OF WAR UPON THE ECONOMIC GROWTH RATE OF THE CIVILIAN ECONOMY. It is generally agreed among economic historians that the Civil War came at a critical point in the emergence of the industrial economy of the United States. They are quite divided in opinion as to the effect of the war: did it stimulate or did it retard economic growth? The traditional view, as exemplified by Clark's 1918 article, "Manufacturing Development During the Civil War" (70), held that the war greatly stimulated the growth rate of the American economy. Cochran in his thought provoking "Did the Civil War Retard Industrialization?" has argued the contrary (72). Cochran feels that rising growth rate evidenced in the 1850s was in fact slowed by the war. Since 1962, this thesis has been the subject of varying viewpoints which are readily available in Andreano, *The Economic Impact of the Civil War* (15) and Gilchrist and Lewis, *Economic Change in the Civil War Era* (125). A related subject of equal significance which is of growing interest to the scholarly community is the role of the Civil War in modernizing the Southern economy (191). The whole subject of the significance of the 1861-65 conflict on the overall economic history of the United States appears to be a continuing controversy; a technological and economic equivalent of the perennial debate over Turner's "frontier thesis." Whatever the outcome of this debate, the military historian should be aware of the broader implications for military technology and its relationship to the growth patterns of the civilian economy.

ADDITIONAL TOPICS WHICH MERIT FURTHER STUDY AND DEVELOPMENT. In addition to the general paucity of materials in the history of American science, the role of science and scientists within a military context has also generally been neglected. Dupree's *Science in the Federal Government* (98) points the way to the types of studies that can be undertaken. So far the relevant studies in this area are just a handful (74), (75), (143), (169), (187), (265), (320), (351), (370), and (375).

Finally, to close I have selected a topic which should be the central concern of military historians when they address the subject of science and technology. How do military men and their organizations responded to technologically imposed change and to those persons who introduce technological innovations? The officers of the line services often thought that they had a better idea as to the best technology for their troops in the field. The separate technical services, notably the Army Ordnance Department, often expressed the opinion that field personnel did not know how to make the best judgments, since their understanding was based upon intuition rather than upon technical information. Officers, line and technical, often saw new technological concepts as a threat to their established ways of doing things. New weapons often called for new hierarchies, so there was resistance to change. This theme is addressed by Holley, *Ideas and Weapons* (158); indeed, if the compiler were to select one book as essential reading, he would have no hesitancy in recommending this small volume, which while dealing with the acceptance of aircraft by the American military in World War I, sheds light on a host of aspects of the military response to new weaponry. Equally as stimulating on this general topic are Morison, *Admiral Sims, and the Modern American Navy* (224), Morison's essay "Gunfire at Sea" in (225), and Sir Percy Scott's *Fifty Years in the Royal Navy* (290). Two interesting case studies relating to small arms are (47), (83) and the later (84). This concluding category, the military's reception of new techniques and hardware, again only underscores the potential for continued research in the interrelationships between the worlds of science and technology and the world of the military. As much study as has been given the topics in this essay; it can be said with certainty that the real work has yet to be done.

BIBLIOGRAPHY

1. Abbot, Henry L. *Report upon Experiments and Investigations to Develop a System of Submarine Mines for Defending the Harbors of the United States.* Washington: G. P. O., 1881.
2. Abbot, Henry L. "The Beginnings of Modern Submarine Warfare under Captain Lieutenant David Bushnell," *Engineer School of Application.* Willets Point, New York Harbor (1881), 163-198.
3. Abbott, Jacob. *Marco Paul's Adventures in Pursuit of Knowledge.* [Springfield Armory] Boston: T. Harrington Carter & Co., 1843.
4. Abbott, Jacob. "The Springfield Armory," *Harpers Weekly,* V (July, 1852), 143-161.
5. Abdill, George B. *Civil War Railroads.* Seattle: Superior Publishing Co., 1961.
6. Adams, George Worthington. *Doctors in Blue: The Medical History of the Union Army in the Civil War.* New York: H. Schuman, 1952.

7. Albaugh, William A. III. *Tyler, Texas, C.S.A.* Harrisburg: Stackpole, 1958.
8. Albaugh, William A. III. and Steuart, Richard D. *The Original Confederate Colt; the Story of Leech & Rigdon and Rigdon-Ansley Revolvers.* New York: Greenberg, 1953.
9. Albaugh, William A. III. *Confederate Edged Weapons.* New York: Harper, 1960.
10. Albaugh, William A. III. *A Photographic Supplement of Confederate Swords.* [Washington?: The author?,] 1963.
11. Albaugh, William A. III., Benet, Hugh Jr., and Simmons Edward N. *Confederate Handguns: concerning the guns, the men who made them, and the times of their use.* Philadelphia: Riling and Lentz, 1963. Reprinted, York, Pennsylvania: Shumway, 1967.
12. Ambrose, Stephen E. *Duty, Honor, Country: A History of West Point.* Baltimore; Johns Hopkins University Press, 1966.
13. Ames, Edward, and Rosenberg, Nathan. "The Enfield Arsenal in Theory and History," *The Economic Journal*, LXXVII, 312 (December, 1968), 827-842.
14. Anderson, John. *General Statement of the Past & Present Condition of the Several Manufacturing Branches, as Called for by a Letter Dated 8th May, by John Anderson, Inspector of Machinery.* London: George Edward Eyre & William Spottiswoode for H.M.S.O., 1857.
15. Andreano, Ralph., ed. *The Economic Impact of the Civil War.* Cambridge: Mass.: Schenkman, 1962. Second edition, 1967.
16. Anonymous. *The History of The E. I. du Pont de Nemours Powder Company; a century of success.* New York: Business America, 1912.
17. Anonymous. *A History of the Du Pont Company's Relations with the United States Government, 1802-1917.* Wilmington, Delaware: Smokeless Powder Department, E. I. du Pont de Nemours & Co., 1928.
18. Anonymous. *A History of Rock Island and Rock Island Arsenal from Earliest Times to 1954.* 3 vols. and *Synopsis of Events on Rock Island from 1954-1965.* Rock Island, Illinois: U.S. Army Rock Island Arsenal, ca. 1965.
19. Anonymous. *History of Watervliet Arsenal. Sesquicentennial Edition, 1813-1963.* Troy, New York: Watervliet Arsenal, 1963.
20. Anonymous. *A History of Watervliet Arsenal, 1813-1968.* Troy, New York, 1968.
21. Anonymous. *Inefficiency of Heavy Ordnance in this Country and Elsewhere and About Parrott and other Hooped Guns.* Washington: H. Polkinhorn & Son, 1865.
22. Anonymous. "Report of the United States Joint Army and Navy Powder Board in Connection with an Editorial in London *Engineering* on October 6, 1911," *U.S. Naval Institute Proceedings*, XXXVIII, (1911), 133-179).
23. Anonymous. *War's Greatest Workshop; Rock Island Arsenal, historical, topographical and illustrative, its proven usefulness and limitless possibilities in time of peace as well as when put to the test . . .* Rock Island, Illinois: Arsenal Publishing Co. of the Tri-Cities, 1922.

24. Armytage, W. H. G. "Economic, Scientific, and Technological Background for Military Studies, 1815-1914," in Robin Higham, ed. *A Guide to the Sources of British Military History*. London: Routledge & Keagan Paul, 1972, pp. 251-297.
25. Ashton, T. S. *Industrial Revolution, 1760-1830*. London: Oxford University Press, 1948.
26. Barber, F. M. "Gunpowder and its Successors," *Forum*, LX (1890), 579-585.
27. Barriger, John W. "Railroads in the Civil War," *Journal of the Confederate Historical Society*, V, 2 (Summer, 1967), 48-60.
28. Bates, David Homer. *Lincoln in the Telegraph Office; recollections of the United States military telegraph corps during the Civil War*. New York: The Century Co., 1907.
29. Battison, Edwin A. "Eli Whitney and the Milling Machine," *The Smithsonian Journal of History*, I, 2 (Summer, 1966), 9-34.
30. Bauer, K. J. "Naval Shipbuilding Programs, 1794-1860," *Military Affairs*, XXIX, 1 (Spring, 1965), 29-40.
31. Baxter, James P. *The Introduction of the Ironclad Warship*. Cambridge, Massachusetts: Harvard University Press, 1933.
32. Bearss, Edwin C. *Hardluck Ironclad, the Sinking and Salvage of the Cairo*. Baton Rouge: Louisiana State University Press, 1966.
33. Beers, Henry P. ed. *Guide to the Archives of the Government of the Confederate States of America*. Washington: National Archives, 1968.
34. Benet, Stephen Vincent. *Electro-Ballistic Machines; and the Schultz Chronoscope*. New York: D. Van Nostrand, 1866.
35. Benet, Stephen Vincent. *Organization of the Ordnance Department and the Reasons for its Separation from the Line of the Army*. Washington: n.p., 1874.
36. Bennet, Frank M. *The Steam Navy of the United States: A History of the Growth of the Steam Vessel of War in the U.S. Navy and the Naval Engineer Corps*. Pittsburgh: Warren and Co., 1896.
37. Bennet, Frank M. *The Monitor and the Navy under Steam*. Boston: Houghton-Mifflin, 1900.
38. Benton, J. G. *A Course of Instruction in Ordnance and Gunnery compiled for the use of the cadets of the United States Military Academy*. New York: D. Van Nostrand Co., 1861.
39. Birkhimer, William Edward. *Historical Sketch of the Organization, Administration, Materiel and Tactics of the Artillery of the United States Army*. Washington: J. J. Chapman, 1884. Reprinted, Greenwood Press, Inc., ca. 1972.
40. Birnie, Rogers. *Gunmaking in the United States*. New York: Public Service Publishing Co., 1888. Reprinted for the Ordnance Department. Washington: G. P. O., 1914.
41. Bispham, George Tucker. "Smoky Powder and Springfield Rifles," *Journal of the Military Service Institute*, XXVII (1900), 203-218.
42. Black, Robert C. III. "The Railroads of Georgia in the Confederate War Effort," *Journal of Southern History*, XIII (1947), 511-534.
43. Black, Robert C. III. *The Railroads of the Confederacy*. Chapel Hill: The University of North Carolina Press, 1952.

44. Bolander, Louis H. "The *Alligator*, First Federal Submarine of the Civil War," *U.S. Naval Institute Proceedings*, LXIV, 424 (June, 1938), 845-854.

45. Bradlee, Francis Boardman Crowninshield. *Blockade running during the Civil War and the effect of land and water transportation on the Confederacy.* Salem, Massachusetts: The Essex Institute, 1925.

46. Brewington, M. V. "American Naval Guns, 1775-1785," *The American Neptune, III, 1 (January, 1943), 11-18 and III, 2 (April, 1943), 148-158.*

47. Brinckerhoff, Sidney B., and Chamberlain, Peirce. *"The Army's Search for a Repeating Rifle: 1873-1903,"* Military Affairs, XXXII, 1 (April, 1968), 20-30.

48. Brodie, Bernard. "Defense and Technology," *Technology Review*, XLIII, 3 (January, 1941), 107-110.

49. Brodie, Bernard. *Sea Power in the Machine Age*. Princeton: Princeton University Press, 1944.

50. Brooke, John Mercer. "The Virginia or the Merrimac: Her Real Projector," *Southern Historical Society Papers*, XIX (January, 1891), 3-34.

51. Brooks, Stewart. *Civil War Medicine*. Springfield: Charles C Thomas, 1966.

52. Brown, Steuart E. Jr. *The Guns of Harpers Ferry.* Berryville: Virginia Book Co., 1968.

53. Bruce, Kathleen. *Virginia Iron Manufacture in the Slave Era.* New York and London: The Century Co., c 1931. Reprinted, New York: Augustus M. Kelly, 1968.

54. Bruce, Robert V. *Lincoln and the Tools of War.* Indianapolis: Bobbs Merrill, 1956.

55. Bulloch, James D. *The Secret Service of the Confederate States in Europe or How the Confederate Crusiers were equipped.* New York: G. P. Putnam's Sons, 1884. New ed. New York: T. Yoseloff, 1959. 2 vols.

56. Burlingame, Roger. *March of the Iron Men; a social history of union through invention.* New York and London: Charles Scribner's Sons, 1938.

57. Butler, David F. *United States Firearms: the First Century, 1776-1875.* New York: Winchester Press, 1971.

58. Butler, J. S. *Projectiles and Rifled Cannon; a critical discussion of the principal systems of rifling and projectiles, with practical suggestions for their improvement, as embraced in a Report to the Chief of Ordnance, U.S.A.* New York: D. Van Nostrand, 1875.

59. Cable, Frank Taylor. *The Birth and Development of the American Submarine.* New York and London: Harper and Brothers, 1924.

60. Cable, Frank Taylor. "A Submarine Voyage in 1900," *Military Engineer*, XXVI, 147 (1934), 191-192.

61. Calhoun, Daniel Hovey. *The American Civil Engineer; Origins and Conflict.* Cambridge: The M.I.T. Press, 1960.

62. Calvert, Monte Alan. "The Search for a Domestic Source of Saltpeter for Use in Making Gunpowder, 1620-1920." Unpublished

research report Eleutherian Mills Historical Library, Greenville, Delaware, 1961.

63. Canfield, Eugene B. "Civil War Artillery," *Ordnance*, XLI, 219 (November-December, 1956), 436-440.

64. Canfield, Eugene B. *Notes on Naval Ordnance of the American Civil War, 1861-1865.* Washington: American Ordnance Association, 1960.

65. Cappon, Lester J. "A Note on Confederate Ordnance Records," *Military Affairs*, IV, 2 (Summer, 1940), 94-102.

66. Carbutt, Edward Hamer. "Fifty Years of Progress in Gun-Making," *Transactions of the Institute of Mechanical Engineers* (1887).

67. Chandler Alfred D. Jr. "DuPont, Dahlgren, and the Civil War Nitre Shortage," *Military Affairs*, XIII, 3 (Fall, 1949), 142-149.

68. Chandler, Walter. "The Memphis Navy Yard," *West Tennessee Historical Papers*, I (1947), 68-72.

69. Church, William Conant. *The Life of John Ericsson.* New York: Charles Scribner's Sons, 1890. 2 vols.

70. Clark, Victor S. "Manufacturing Development During the Civil War," *The Military Historian and Economist* (April, 1918), 92-100.

71. Clark, Victor S. *History of Manufactures in the United States.* 3 vols. New York: McGraw-Hill, 1929. Reprinted, New York: Peter Smith, 1949.

72. Cochran, Thomas C. "Did the Civil War Retard Industrialization?" *Mississippi Valley Historical Review*, XLVIII (September, 1961), 197-210.

73. Coggins, Jack. *Arms and Equipment of the Civil War.* Garden City: Doubleday, 1962.

74. Cohen, I. Bernard. "Science and the Civil War," *Technology Review*, XLVIII, 3 (1946), 167-170 and 192-193.

75. Cohen, I. Bernard., and Reingold, Nathan. "Science in the Civil War," *Isis*, XLIX (1949), 307-318.

76. Colt, Samuel. *On the Application of Machinery to the Manufacture of Rotating Chambered-Breech Fire-Arms, and their peculiarities,* Ed. by C. Manby. London: W. Clowes & Son, 1853.

77. Cooke, Augustus P. *A Textbook of Naval Ordnance and Gunnery.* New York: Wiley, 1875. 2nd ed., New York, 1880. A revision by the Department of Ordnance and Gunnery, Naval Academy, 1884. Later revised by Meigs and Ingersoll, q.v.

78. Corey, Herbert. ed. *Submarine: Autobiography of Simon Lake.* New York: D. Appleton-Century Co., Inc., 1938.

79. Cornish, Joseph Jenkins. *The Air Arm of the Confederacy; a history of origins and usages of war balloons by the Southern armies during the American Civil War.* Richmond: Richmond Civil War Centennial Committee, 1963.

80. Dahlgren, Madeleine Vinton. *The Petition to the National Government of Madeleine Vinton Dahlgren, Widow of the Later Rear Admiral Dahlgren, Submitting her Claim Asking for Compensation for the Adoption and Use by the United States Navy of Certain Inventions of the Late Rear Admiral Dahlgren Relating to Ordnance.* Washington: Gideon Brothers, 1872.

81. Dahlgren, Madeleine Vinton, *Memoir of John A. Dahlgren, Rear Admiral, U.S.N.* Boston: James R. Osgood & Co., 1882.
82. Daly, Robert W. *How the "Merimac" Won: The Strategic Story of the C.S.S. Virginia.* New York: Crowell, 1957.
83. Davis, Carl L. "Army Ordnance and Inertia Toward a Change in Small Arms through the Civil War," Master's thesis, Oklahoma State University, 1959.
84. Davis, Carl L. "Small Arms in the Union Army, 1861-1865." Doctoral dissertation, Oklahoma State University, 1971. University microfilm no. 72-21853.
85. Davis, Helen E. "A History of the Relations of the Du Pont Company with the United States Government, 1802-1923." Unpublished paper; accession no. 372 Eleutherian Mills Historical Library, Greenville, Delaware.
86. Davis, Madison. "The Old Cannon Foundry above Georgetown, D.C., and its First Owner, Henry Foxall," *Records of the Columbia Historical Society, Washington, D.C.*, 11 (1908), 16-70.
87. Davis, Frederick. "First 'Steam' Gun in Action," *Military Affairs*, II, 3 (Fall, 1938), 172-174.
88. de Tousard, [Anne Marie] Louis. *American Artillerist's Companion, or Elements of Artillery. Treating of all kinds of firearms in detail and of the formation, object and service of the Flying or Horse Artillery, Preceeded by an Introductory Dissertation on Cannon.* 3 vols. Philadelphia: C. and A. Conrad, 1809-1813. Reprinted, ca. 1971 by Greenwood Press, Inc.
89. Delafield, Richard. *Report on the Art of War in Europe in 1854, 1855, 1856.* Washington: George W. Bowman, by government authority, 1861.
90. Dew, Charles B. *Ironmaker to the Confederacy: Joseph R. Anderson and the Tredegar Iron Works.* New Haven: Yale University, Press, 1965.
91. Deyrup, Felicia J. *Arms Makers of the Connecticut Valley: A Regional Study of Economic Development of the Arms Industry, 1798-1870.* Northampton, Massachusetts: Smith College Studies in History XXXIII, 1948. Reprinted, York, Pennsylvania: Shumway, ca 1970.
92. Diamond, William. "Imports of the Confederate Government from Europe and Mexico," *Journal of Southern History*, VI (1940), 470-503.
93. Dickinson, Henry Winram. *Robert Fulton, Engineer and Artist; His Life and Works.* London and New York: John Lane & Co., 1913.
94. Dillin, John Grace Wolf. *The Kentucky Rifle.* 3rd ed. Washington: National Rifle Association, 1946.
95. Donnelly, Ralph W. "Rocket Batteries of the Civil War," *Military Affairs*, XXV, 2 (Summer, 1961), 69-93.
96. Dunham, A. L. *The Industrial Revolution in France, 1815-1848.* New York: Exposition Press, 1955.
97. Du Pont, Bessie G. *E. I. du Pont de Nemours and Company, A History, 1802-1902.* Boston and New York: Houghton-Mifflin, 1920.

98. Dupree, A. Hunter. *Science in the Federal Government: A History of Policies and Activities to 1940.* Cambridge: The Belknap Press of the Harvard University Press, 1957.

99. Durfee, W. F. "The First Systematic Attempt at Interchangeability in Firearms," *Cassier's Magazine* (March, 1894), 469-477.

100. Dutton, William S. *Du Pont, One Hundred and Forty Years.* New York: Charles Scribner's Sons, 1942.

101. Earle, Ralph. "The Development of Our Navy's Smokeless Powder," *U.S. Naval Institute Proceedings,* XL (1914), 1041-1057.

102. Edwards, William B. *Civil War Guns; the complete story of Federal and Confederate small arms: design, manufacture, identification, procurement, issue, effectiveness and postwar disposal.* Harrisburg: The Stackpole Co., 1962.

103. Eliot, George Fielding. *Sylvanus Thayer of West Point.* New York: Messner, 1959.

104. Ezell, Edward C. "Early Propellant Gunpowders; The Development of Mammoth Powder, 1858-1872." Unpublished research report Eleutherian Mills Historical Library; Greenville, Delaware, 1962.

105. Ezell, Edward C. "The Development of Artillery for the United States Land Service before 1861: With Emphasis on the Rodman Gun." Master's thesis, University of Delaware, 1963.

106. Falk, Stanley L. "Soldier-Technologist: Major Alfred Mordecai and the Beginnings of Science in the United States Army." Doctoral dissertation, Georgetown University, 1959. 2 vols.

107. Falk, Stanley L. "Artillery for the Land Service: The Development of a System," *Military Affairs,* XXVIII, 4 (Winter, 1964), 97-110.

108. Farrow, Edward Samuel, ed. *Farrow's Military Encyclopedia.* New York: Published by the editor, 1885. 3 vols.

109. Ferguson, Eugene S. "The Critical Period of American Technology, 1788-1853; A Review Article." Unpublished ditto, print ca., 1962.

110. Ferguson, Eugene S. *Bibliography of the History of Technology.* Cambridge, Massachusetts: Published jointly by the Society for the History of Technology and M.I.T., 1968.

111. Fishlow, Albert. *American Railroads and the Transformation of the Antebellum Economy.* Cambridge: Harvard University Press, 1966.

112. Fitch, Charles H. "Interchangeable Mechanism," in U.S. Census Office, *Report on the Manufacturers of the United States* (Tenth Census, 1880, Vol. 2) Washington: G. P. O., 1883, 613-704.

113. Fitch, Charles E. *The Manufacture of Fire-Arms and Ammunition.* Extra Census Bulletin. Washington: G. P. O., 1882.

114. Flemming, Thomas J. *West Point: The Men and Times of the United States Military Academy.* New York: William Morrow & Co., 1969.

115. Force, Peter. *American Archives; Containing a Collection of Authentick Records, State Papers, Debates and other Notices of Public Affairs.* Washington: Matthew St. Clair Clarke & Peter Force, 1837-1853. 9 Vols.

116. Forman, Sidney, *West Point: A History of the United States Military Academy.* New York: Columbia University Press, 1950.

117. Forman, Sidney. "Early American Military Engineering Books," *Military Engineer*, XLVI (March-April, 1956), 93-95.
118. Fuller, Claud E. Compiler. *Springfield Muzzle-Loading Shoulder Arms; a description of the flintlock muskets, musketoons and carbines and the muskets, musketoons, rifles, carbines and special models from 1795 to 1865 . . . and a sketch of Springfield Armory.* New York: Francis Bannerman Sons, 1930.
119. Fuller, Claud E. *The Breech-Loader in the Service; the developments of one hundred and one years 1816 to 1917.* Topeka, Kansas: The Arms Reference Club of America, 1933. Reprinted, New Milford, Connecticut: N. Flayderman, ca. 1971.
120. Fuller, Claud E. and Steuart, Richard D. *Firearms of the Confederacy; the shoulder arms, pistols and revolvers of the Confederate soldier including the regular United States models, imported arms and those manufactured within the Confederacy.* Huntington, West Virginia: Standard Publications Inc., 1944.
121. Fuller, Claud E. *The Whitney Firearms.* Hunting, West Virginia: Standard Publications Inc., 1946.
122. Fuller, Claud E. *The Rifled Musket.* Harrisburg: The Stackpole Co., 1958.
123. Gaines, William H. Jr. "Guns, Silkworns and Pigs," *Virginia Cavalcade*, III, 2 (Autumn, 1953), 32-37.
124. Gatling, Richard J. *Gatling's System of Firearms, with official reports of recent trials and great success.* New York: n.p., 1870.
125. Gilchrist, David T., and Lewis W. David. *Economic Change in the Civil War Era: Proceedings of a Conference on American Economic Institutional Change, 1850-1873, and the Impact of the Civil War held March 12-14, 1964.* Greenville, Delaware: Eleutherian-Mills Hagley Foundation, 1965.
126. Goff, Richard D. *Confederate Supply.* Durham: Duke University Press, 1969.
127. Gosnell, Harpur Allen. *Guns on the Western Waters: The Story of River Gunboats in the Civil War.* Baton Rouge: Louisiana State University Press, 1949.
128. Green, Constance McLaughlin. "The History of Springfield Armory." Unpublished typescript, Records Group 336, Modern War Records Branch, National Archives.
129. Green, Constance McLaughlin, Thomson, Harry C., and Roots, Peter C. *The Ordnance Department; Planning Munitions for War. United States Army in World War II; Technical Services.* Washington: Office of the Chief of Military History, Department of the Army, 1955.
130. Green, Constance McLaughlin. *Eli Whitney and the Birth of American Technology.* Boston: Little, Brown and Co., 1956.
131. Guttmann, Oscar. *The Manufacture of Explosives: A Theoretical and Practical Treatise on the History, the Physical and Chemical Properties, and the Manufacture of Explosives.* London: n.p., 1895. 2 vols.
132. Guttmann, Oscar. *The Manufacture of Explosives: Twenty Years' Progress.* New York: Whittaker and Co., 1909.
133. Habbakkuk, H. J. *American and British Technology in the 19th*

Century: The Search for Labour-Saving Inventions. Cambridge, England: Cambridge University Press, 1962.

134. Hackley, Frank W. *A Report on Civil War Explosive Ordnance.* Indianhead, Maryland: U.S. Naval Propellant Plant, ca. 1960.

135. Hackley, Frank W., Woodin, William H., and Scranton, E. L. *History of Modern U.S. Small Arms Ammunition.* New York and London: Collier-Macmillan and Macmillan, 1967.

136. Hall, A. R. *The Scientific Revolution, 1500-1800.* Boston: Beacon Paperback, 1956.

137. Hatch, Alden, *Remington Arms in American History.* New York: Reinhart, 1956.

138. Haydon, Frederick Stansbury. "A Proposed Gas Shell, 1862," *Military Affairs,* II, 1 (Spring, 1938), 52-54.

139. Haydon, Frederick Stansbury. *Aeronautics in the Union and Confederate armies, with a Survey of Military aeronautics Prior to 1861.* Baltimore: Johns Hopkins Press, 1941.

140. Haupt, Hermann. *Military bridges; with suggestions of new expedients and constructions for crossing streams and chasms; including also, designs for trestle and truss bridges for military rail roads, adapted especially to the wants of the service in the United States.* New York: D. Van Nostrand, 1864.

141. Haupt, Hermann. *Reminiscences of General Hermann Haupt . . . giving hitherto unpublished official orders, personal narratives of important military operations, and interviews with President Lincoln, Secretary Stanton, General-in-Chief Halleck, and with Generals McDowell, McClellan, Meade, Hancock, Burnside, and others in command of the armies in the field, and his impressions of these men. With notes . . . by Frank Abial Flower.* [Milwaukee: Wright & Joys Co.], 1901.

142. Haven, Charles T., Belden, Frank A. *A History of the Colt Revolver; and Other Arms Made by Colt's Patent Fire Arms Manufacturing Company from 1836 to 1940.* New York: William Morrow & Co., 1940.

143. Hawes, Joseph M. "The Signal Corps and its Weather Service, 1870-1890," *Military Affairs,* XXX, 2 (Summer, 1966), 68-76.

144. Held, R. *The Age of Firearms: a pictorial history.* New York: Harper and Brothers, 1957.

145. Henderson, Robert. "The Naval Torpedo Station," *U.S. Naval Institute Proceedings,* XXIX (1899), 239-249.

146. Henderson, Robert. "The Evolution of Smokeless Powder," *U.S. Naval Institute Proceedings,* XXX (1904), 352-372.

147. Hicks, James E. "United States Military Shoulder Arms, 1795-1935, Part I, The Smoothbore Flintlock as a Military Arm," *Military Affairs,* I, 1 (Spring, 1937), 22-33.

148. Hicks, James E., and Todd F. P. ". . . , Part II, The French Military Musket as an American Weapon," *Military Affairs,* I, 2 (Summer, 1937), 75-79.

149. Hicks, James E. ". . . , Part III, The French Infantry Musket of the Model, 1763 and 1766," *Military Affairs,* II, 1 (Spring, 1938), 36-39.

150. Hicks, James E. ". . . , Part IV, The U.S. Musket Model of 1795," *Military Affairs,* II, 2 (Spring, 1938), 40-42.

151. Hicks, James E. *Notes on French Ordnance, 1717-1936.* Mount Vernon, New York: The author, c. 1938.
152. Hicks, James E. *Nathan Starr; U.S. sword & arms maker.* Mount Vernon, New York: The author, c. 1940.
153. Hicks, James E. *Notes on United States Ordnance.* 2 vols. Mount Vernon, New York: The author, c. 1940.
154. Hicks, James E. *U.S. Firearms, 1776-1957. Notes on U.S. Ordnance,* Vol I. La Canada, California: The author, 1957. Revised edition of vol. I of 153 above.
155. Herrick, Walter R. Jr. *The American Naval Revolution.* Baton Rouge: Louisiana State University Press, 1966.
156. Hill, Forest G. *Roads, Rails & Waterways: The Army Engineers and Early Transportation.* Norman: Oklahoma State University Press, 1957.
157. Holley, Alexander L. *A Treatise on Ordnance and Armor: Embracing Descriptions, Discussions, and Professional Opinions Concerning the Material, Fabrication, Requirements, Capabilities, and Endurance of European and American Guns for Naval, Sea-Coast, and Iron-Clad Warfare, and their Rifling, Projectiles, and Breech-Loading.* New York and London: D. Van Nostrand and Truebner & Company, 1865.
158. Holley, I. B. Jr. *Ideas and Weapons: Exploitation of the Aerial Weapon by the United States during World War I; A Study in the Relationship of Technological Advance, Military Doctrine, and the Development of Weapons.* New Haven: Yale University Press, 1953. Reprinted, Hamden Connecticut: Archon Books, 1971.
159. Hollowell, M. Edgar, Jr. "The Point of Fork Arsenal," *Military Collector and Historian,* XX, 1 (Spring, 1970), 11-13.
160. Holt, William Stull. *The Office of the Chief of Engineers of the Army.* Monograph no. 27. Baltimore: Johns Hopkins University Press, 1923.
161. Hornsby, Thomas. "Oregon and Peacemaker; 12-Inch Wrought-Iron Guns," *The American Neptune,* VI, 3 (July, 1946), 212-222.
162. Hubbard, Guy. "Development of Machine Tools in New England," *American Machinist* LIX-LXI (1923-1924). A 22 part series on this subject.
163. Hughes, J. R. T. *The Vital Few.* Boston: Houghton-Mifflin, 1966.
164. Humphreys, A. A. *Report on Certain Experimental and Theoretical Investigations Relative to the Quality, Form and Combination of Materials for Defensive Armor, together with incidental facts relating to their use for industrial purposes.* Washington: G. P. O., 1870. Professional Papers No. 17, Corps of Engineers, U.S.A.
165. Hunter, Louis C. *Steamboats on Western Rivers.* Cambridge: Harvard University Press, 1949.
166. Huntington, R. T. *Hall's Breechloaders.* York, Pennsylvania: George Shumway Publisher, 1972.
167. Huston, James A. *The Sinews of War: Army Logistics, 1775-1953. U.S. Army Historical Series.* Washington: Office, Chief of Military History, U.S. Army, 1966.
168. Iobst, Richard William. "North Carolina Mobilizes: Nine Crucial Months, December, 1860-August, 1861." Doctoral dissertation,

204 • A GUIDE TO THE SOURCES OF U.S. MILITARY HISTORY

University of North Carolina, 1968. University microfilms no. 69-10171.

169. Jahns, Patricia. *M. F. Maury and Joseph Henry, Scientists of the Civil War*. New York: Hastings, 1961.

170. Jaques, W. H., Barber, F. M., and Very, E. W. "Paper on Naval Torpedo Warfare," Paper prepared for the U.S. Senate Select Committee on Ordnance and Warships. Washington: n.p., 1866.

171. Jaques. W. H. *Heavy Ordnance for National Defence, being a consideration of the present defenceless condition of the coast cities of the United States and of the necessity for immediate production of heavy guns adapted to modern warfare, together with suggestions concerning the best type to accept, and the most advantageous system of construction*. New York and London: G. P. Putnam's Sons, 1884.

172. Jaques, W. H. *The Establishment of Steel Gun Factories in the United States*. Annapolis: United States Naval Institute, 1884.

173. Jaques, W. H. *Ericsson's Destroyer and Submarine Gun*. New York and London: G. P. Putnam's Sons, 1885.

174. Jaques, W. H. *Modern Armor for National Defense; presenting practical information about material, methods of manufacture, cost, development, tests and application, effects of fire, resistance of plates, and a comparison of the results that have been obtained at the most important competitive, together with statistics*. New York and London: G. P. Putnam's Sons, 1886.

175. Jaques, W. H. *Torpedoes for National Defence*. New York and London: G. P. Putnam's Sons, 1886.

176. James, Marquis. *Alfred I. Du Pont, The Family Rebel*. New York: Bobbs-Merrill Co., 1941.

177. Johnston, Angus James. *Virginia Railroads in the Civil War*. Chapel Hill: University of North Carolina Press, 1961.

178. Kerksis, Sydney C., and Dickey, Thomas S. *Heavy Artillery Projectiles of the Civil War, 1861-1865*. Atlanta: Phoenix Press, 1968.

179. King Moses. ed. *King's Handbook of Springfield, Massachusetts*. Springfield: James D. Gill, Publisher, 1884.

180. Kouwenhoven, J. A. *Made in America: The Arts in Modern Civilization*. Garden City: Doubleday, 1962.

181. Kranzberg, Melvin, and Pursell, Carroll W., Jr. *Technology in Western Civilization*. New York: Oxford University Press, 1967. 2 vols.

182. Laidley, T. T. S. *A Course of Instruction in Rifle Firing*. Philadelphia: J. B. Lippincott Co., 1879.

183. Lake, Simon. "Safe Submarine Vessels and the Future of the Art," *Transactions of the Institute of Naval Architects*, XLIX (1907), 37-64.

184. Lake Torpedo Boat Company. *Under-Water Torpedo Boats: The Submarine versus the Submersible*. Bridgeport: n.p., 1906.

185. Lewis, Berkeley R. *Small Arms and Ammunition in the United States Service, 1776-1865*. Washington: Smithsonian Institution, 1956.

186. Lewis, Berkeley R. *Notes on Ammunition of the American Civil*

War, 1861-1865. Washington: American Ordnance Association, 1959.

187. Livingston, Dorothy Michelson. "Michelson in the Navy; the Navy in Michelson," *U.S. Naval Institute Proceedings*, XCV, 796 (June, 1969), 72-79.

188. Lord, Francis A. *Civil War Collector's Encyclopedia; arms, uniforms, and equipment of the Union and Confederacy*. Harrisburg: Stackpole Co., 1963.

189. Lord, Francis A. *Lincoln's Railroad Man; Herman Haupt*. Rutherford, New Jersey: Fairleigh Dickinson University Press, 1969.

190. Lowrie, Walter, and Clarke, Matthew St. Clair. eds. *American State Papers: Documents, Legislative and Executive, of the Congress of the United States* [1st through 25th Congresses, 1789-1838.] Washington: Gales and Seaton, 1832-1861. 32 vols. Class V, Military Affairs in 7 vols.

191. Luraghi, Raemondo. "Civil War and the Modernization of American Society: Social Structure in the Old South before and During the War," *Civil War History*, XVIII, 3 (September, 1972), 230-250.

192. Luvaas, Jay. *The Military Legacy of the Civil War: The European Inheritance*. Chicago: University of Chicago Press, 1959.

193. McCabe, James D. *The Illustrated History of the Centennial Exposition*. Cincinnati: Jones Brothers, 1876.

194. McClellan, George B. *The Armies of Europe comprising descriptions in detail of the military systems of England, France, Russia, Prussia, Austria, and Sardinia adapting their advantages to all arms of the U.S. service*. Philadelphia: J. B. Lippincott, 1861. Also published as a Senate Document, 34th Congress, Special Session, 1857.

195. MacCarty, D. E. "The Krag-Jorgensen Guns Made at the Springfield Armory," *American Machinist*, XXIII (1900), 311-314.

196. MacDougall, Donald A. "The Federal Ordnance Bureau, 1861-1865." Doctoral dissertation, University of California, 1951.

197. McKenzie, Robert Hamlet. "A History of the Shelby Iron Company, 1865-1881." Doctoral dissertation, University of Alabama, 1971. University microfilm no. 71-29218.

198. McLean, James Henry. *Peace-Makers*. New York: Baker & Godwin, 1880.

199. Madis, George. *The Winchester Book*. Lancaster, Texas: Art and Reference House, 1971.

200. Mahan, Alfred Thayer. *From Sail to Steam: Recollections of Naval Life*. New York: Harper's Brothers, 1907.

201. Mallet, John W. "Work of the Confederate Ordnance Bureau," *Southern Historical Society Papers*, XXXVII (1909), 1-20.

202. Mantoux, Paul. *The Industrial Revolution in the Eighteenth Century*. London: Cape, 1961.

203. Manucy, Albert. *Artillery Through the Ages; a short illustrated history of cannon, emphasizing types used in America*. Washington: G. P. O., 1949.

204. Marvin, Joseph Dana. *The Theory and Practice of Granulating Gun Powder*. Annapolis: Naval Experimental Battery, 1875.

205. Maxim, Hiram P. *A Genius in the Family*. New York: Harper, 1936.

206. Maxim, Hudson. "The Story of Smokeless Powder," *Cassier's Magazine Engineering Illustrated*, XIII, (1899), 239-249.
207. Maxim, Hudson. *Reminiscences and Comments as Reported by Clifton Johnson*. Garden City: Doubleday, Page & Co., 1924.
208. Meigs, John Forsyth, and Ingersoll, Royal Rodney. *Text-book of Ordnance and Gunnery, naval b.l.r. guns, prepared and arranged for the use of naval cadets*. Baltimore: Press of Isaac Friedenwald. 1887. Evolves from 77 above, q.v.
209. Melton, Maurice. *The Confederate Ironclads*. New York: Thomas Yoseloff, 1968.
210. Melville, G. W. "The Submarine Boat; Its value as a weapon of naval warfare," *Annual Report of the Smithsonian Institute* (1901), 713-738.
211. Meneely, A. Howard. *The War Department, 1861: A Study of Mobilization and Administration*. New York: Columbia University Press, 1928.
212. Merli, Frank J. *Great Britain and the Confederate Navy, 1861-1865*. Bloomington and London: Indiana University Press, 1971.
213. Metcalfe, Henry. *A Course of Instruction in Ordnance and Gunnery*. 2 vols. 3rd ed. New York: John Wiley & Sons, 1894.
214. Mier, Hugo A. "Technology and Democracy, 1800-1860." *Mississippi Valley Historical Review*, XLII (March, 1957), 618-640.
215. Miles, A. H. "The Princeton' Explosion," *U.S. Naval Institute Proceedings*, LII, 11 (November, 1926), 2225-2245.
216. Milligan, John D. *Gunboats down the Mississippi*. Annapolis: U.S. Naval Institute, 1965.
217. Mirsky, Jeannette, and Nevins, Allan. *The World of Eli Whitney*. New York: Macmillan, 1952.
218. Montross, Lynn. *War through the Ages*. New York and London: Haper & Brothers, 1944.
219. Mordecai, Alfred. *Experiments on Gunpowder Made at Washington Arsenal in 1843 and 1844*. Washington: J. & G. S. Gideon, 1845.
220. Mordecai, Alfred. *Artillery for the United States Land Service; as devised and arranged by the Ordnance board*. Washington: J. & G. S. Gideon, 1849. Available as microfilm print from the National Archives.
221. Mordecai, Alfred. Reviser. *The Ordnance Manual for Use of Officers of the United States Army*. Washington: Gideon & Co., 1850.
222. Mordecai, Alfred. *Second Report of Experiments on Gunpowder Made at Washington Arsenal in 1845-47-48*. Washington: Gideon, 1853.
223. Mordecai, Alfred. *Military Commission to Europe in 1855 and 1856*. Washington: George W. Bowman with Government authority, 1860.
224. Morison, Elting E. *Admiral Sims and the Modern American Navy*. Boston: Houghton-Mifflin, 1942.
225. Morison, Elting E. *Men, Machines and Modern Times*. Cambridge: M.I.T. Press, 1966.
226. Morrison, James Kundsford, Jr. "The United Stats Military

Academy, 1833-1866: Years of Progress and Turmoil." Doctoral dissertation, Columbia University, 1970. University microfilms no. 71-6230.

227. Munden, Kenneth W., and Beers, Henry P. *Guide to Federal Archives Relating to the Civil War.* Washington: National Archives, 1962.

228. Munroe, Charles E. *Index to the Literature of Explosives.* Baltimore: n.p., 1886 and 1893. 2 vols.

229. Munroe, Charles, E. "On the Development of Smokeless Powders," *Journal of the American Chemical Society,* XVIII (1896), 818-846.

230. Neill, John H., Jr. "Shipbuilding in Confederate New Orleans." Master's thesis, Tulane University, 1940.

231. Nelson, Harold L. "Military Road for War and Peace, 1791-1836." *Military Affairs,* XIX, 1 (Spring, 1955), 1-14.

232. Nichols, James Lynn. *Confederate Engineers.* Tuscaloosa: Confederate Publishing Co., 1957.

233. Nichols, Roger L. "Army Contributions to River Transportation, 1818-1825," *Military Affairs,* XXXIII, 1 (April, 1969), 242-249.

234. Nicklason, Fred. "The Civil War Contracts Committee," *Civil War History,* XVII, 3 (September, 1971), 232-244.

235. North, S. N. D., and North, Ralph. *Simeon North; the first official pistol maker of the United States.* Concord: The Rumford Press, 1913. Reprinted, Highland Park, New Jersey: Gun Room, 1972.

236. Norton, Charles B. and Valentine, W. J. *Report to the Government of the United States on the Munitions of War Exhibited at the Paris Universal Exhibition, 1867.* New York: Office of the Army & Navy Journal, 1868.

237. Norton, Charles B. *American Breech-Loading Small Arms: a description of late inventions, including the Gatling gun, and a chapter on cartridges.* New York: F. W. Christern, 1872.

238. Norton, Charles B. *American Inventions and Improvements in Breech-Loading Small Arms, heavy ordnance, machine guns, magazine arms, fixed ammunition, including a chapter on sporting arms.* Springfield: Chapin & Gould, 1880.

239. Norton, Frank, Ed. *Frank Leslie's Historical Register of the United States Centennial Exposition, 1876.* New York: Frank Leslie's Illustrated Weekly, 1876.

240. O'Brien, John Emmet. *Telegraphing in Battle; reminiscences of the Civil War.* Scranton: The Raeder Press, 1910.

241. Olejar, Paul D. "Rockets and Early American Wars," *Military Affairs,* X, 4 (Winter, 1946), 16-34.

242. Oliver, John W. *History of American Technology.* New York: Ronald, 1956.

243. Olmstead, Denison. *Memoir of Eli Whitney.* New Haven: Durrie and Pech, 1846. Reprinted, New York: Arno, 1972.

244. Parkhurst, E. G. "The Manufacture of Military Rifle Barrels," *American Machinist,* XXIII (1900), 387-395.

245. Parks, E. Taylor. "Robert Fulton and Submarine Warfare," *Military Affairs,* XXV, 4 (Winter, 1961), 177-182.

246. Parks, William B. "Building a Warship in the Southern Con-

federacy," *U.S. Naval Institute Proceedings*, LXIX (August, 1923), 1299-1307.

247. Parsons, William Barclay. *Robert Fulton and the Submarine*. New York: Columbia University Press, 1922.

248. Patterson, Robert M. *Samuel Colt vs. the Massachusetts Arms Co.* Boston: Printed for Samuel Colt by White & Potter, 1851.

249. Peck, Taylor. *Round-Shot to Rockets; a history of the Washington Navy Yard and U.S. Naval Gun Factory*. Annapolis: U.S. Naval Institute, 1949.

250. Perry, Milton F. *Infernal Machines; the Story of Confederate submarine and mine warfare*. Baton Rouge: Louisiana State University Press, 1965.

251. Peterson, Harold Leslie. *Encyclopedia of Firearms*. New York: Dutton, c 1964.

252. Peterson, Harold Leslie. *Notes on Ordnance of the American Civil War, 1861-1865*. Washington: American Ordnance Association, 1959.

253. Peterson, Harold Leslie. *Round Shot and Rammers*. Harrisburg: Stackpole Books, 1969.

254. Phillips, Ulrich Bonnell. *A History of Transportation in the Eastern Cotton Belt to 1860*. New York: Columbia University Press, 1908. Reprinted by Octagon Books, 1968.

255. Plum, William Rattle. *The Military Telegraph during the Civil War in the United States, with an Exposition of Ancient and Modern Means of Communication, and of the Federal and Confederate Cipher Systems. . . .* Chicago: Jensen, McClurg & Co., 1882.

256. Pratt, Edwin. *The Rise of Rail-power in War and Conquest, 1833-1914*. London: P. S. Knight and Son, 1915.

257. Prucha, F. Paul. *Broadax and Bayonet: The Role of the United States Army in the Development of the Northwest, 1815-1860*. Madison: University of Wisconsin Press, 1953.

258. Prucha, F. Paul. ed. *Army Life on the Western Frontier*. Norman: University of Oklahoma Press, 1958.

259. Rains, George Washington. *History of the Confederate Powder Works*. Augusta: Chronicle & Constitutionalist Print, 1882.

260. Ramsdell, Charles W. "The Confederate Government and the Railroads," *American Historical Review*, XXII (1916-1917), 794-810.

261. Rankin, Robert H. *Small Arms of the Sea Service: A History of the Firearms and Edged Weapons of the U.S. Navy, Marine Corps and Coast Guard from the Revolution to the Present*. New Milford, Connecticut: N. Flayderman & Co., Inc., 1972.

262. Ranson, Edward. "The Endicott Board of 1885-1886, and the Coast Defenses," *Military Affairs*, XXXI, 2 (Summer, 1967), 74-84.

263. Reed, C. Wingate. "Decius Wadsworth, First Chief of Ordnance, U.S. Army, 1812-1821," *Army Ordnance*, XXIV, 139 (July-August, 1943), 113-116.

264. Reilly, Robert M. *United States Military Small Arms, 1816-1865*. Baton Rouge: The Eagle Press, Inc., 1970.

265. Reingold, Nathan. "Science in the Civil War: The Permanent Commission of the Navy Department," *Isis*, XLIV, 157 (September, 1958), 307-318.

266. Rezneck, Samuel. "The Rise and Early Development of Industrial Consciousness in the United States, 1760-1830," *Journal of Economic and Business History*, IV, 2 (1932), 784-811.

267. Riling, Ray. *Guns and Shooting: A Selected Chronological Bibliography*. New York: Greenberg, 1951.

268. Ripley, Warren. *Artillery and Ammunition of the Civil War*. New York: Van Nostrand Reinhold Company, 1971.

269. Risch, Erna. *Quartermaster Support of the Army: A History of the Corps, 1779-1939*. Washington: Quartermaster Historian's Office, Office of the Quartermaster General, 1962.

270. Rodman, Thomas Jackson. *Reports of Experiments on the Properties of Metals for Cannon; and the qualities of cannon powder, with an account of the fabrication and trial of a 15-inch gun*. Boston: Charles H. Crosby, 1861.

271. Roe, Joseph Wickham. *English and American Tool Builders*. New Haven: Yale University Press, 1916.

272. Roe, Joseph Wickham. "Interchangeable Manufacture," *Transactions of the Newcomen Society*, XVII (1936-37), 165-174.

273. Roe, Joseph Wickham. "Machine Tools in America," *Journal of the Franklin Institute*, CCXXV (1938), 499-511.

274. Rolt, Lionel Thomas Caswell. *A Short History of Machine Tools*. Cambridge: The M.I.T. Press, 1965.

275. Rosenberg, Nathan. "Technological Change in the Machine Tool Industry, 1840-1910." *Journal of Economic History*, XXIII, 4 (December, 1963), 414-446.

276. Rosenberg, Nathan. ed. *The American System of Manufactures: The Report of the Committee on Machinery of the United States 1855, and the Special Reports of George Wallis and Joseph W. Withworth 1854*. Edinburgh: Edinburgh University Press, 1969.

277. Rosenberg, Nathan. *Technology and American Economic Growth*. New York: Harper & Row, Publishers, 1972.

278. Rushmore, D. B., Lanman, W. H., and Lof, E. A. "Bibliography of the Literature of Submarines, Mines, and Torpedoes," *General Electric Review* (Schnectady, New York) XX (1917), 675-685.

279. Russell, Carl Parcher. *Guns on the Early Frontiers: a history of firearms from colonial times through the years of the western fur trade*. Berkeley: University of California Press, 1957.

280. Ryan, Garry David. "War Department Topographical Bureau, 1831-1863; An Administrative History." Doctoral dissertation, The American University, 1968. University microfilm no. 68-14572.

281. Salzer, J. Richard. "Civil War Hand Grenades," *Military Collector and Historian*, XX, 1 (Spring, 1970), 14-18.

282. Sandler, Stanley. "A Navy in Decay: Some Strategic Technological Results of Disarmament, 1865-69 in the U.S. Navy," *Military Affairs*, XXXV, 4 (December, 1971), 138-142.

283. Sawyer, John E. "The Social Basis of the American System of Manufacturing," *Journal of Economic History*, XIV, 4 (Autumn, 1954), 361-379.

284. Scharf, John Thomas. *History of the Confederate States Navy from its Origin to the Surrender of its Last Vessel*. 2nd ed. Albany: Joseph McDonough, 1894.

285. Schreier, Konrad F., Jr. "U.S. Army Field Artillery Weapons, 1866-1918," *Military Collector and Historian*, XX, 2 (Summer, 1968), 40-45.
286. Schreier, Konrad F., Jr. "The Sims-Dudley 2-1/2-inch Dynamite Gun," *Military Collector and Historian*, XXII, 2 (Summer, 1970), 46-50.
287. Schreier, Konrad F., Jr. "The Army 3.2-inch Field Gun," *Military Collector and Historian*, XXIV, 3 (Fall, 1972), 77-84.
288. Schroeder, S. "The Development of Modern Torpedoes," *General Information Series*, VI (Washington: Office of Naval Intelligence, 1887).
289. Schuppaus, Robert. "The Evolution of Smokeless Powder," *Journal of the Military Service Institution*, XVIII (1897), 171-179.
290. Scott, Percy. *Fifty Years in the Royal Navy.* New York: George H. Doran, 1919.
291. Seager, Robert, II. "Ten Years before Mahan: The Unofficial Case for the New Navy," *Mississippi Valley Historical Review*, XL (December, 1953), 491-512.
292. Select Committee on Small Arms. *Report from the Select Committee On Small Arms.* London: Ordered to be printed by the House of Commons, 12 May 1854.
293. Shannon, Fred Albert. *The Organization and Administration of the Union Army, 1861-1865.* Cleveland: The Arthur H. Clark Co., 1928. 2 vols. Reprinted, Peter Smith, 1965.
294. Simpson, Edward. *A Treatise on Ordnance and Naval Gunnery.* Annapolis: Robert F. Bonsall, 1859.
295. Simpson, Edward. *Report on a Naval Mission to Europe; especially devoted to the material and construction of artillery.* Washington: n.p., 1873. 2 vols.
296. Singer, Charles, Holmyard, E. J., Hall, A. R., and Williams, Trevor I., eds. *A History of Technology.* 5 vols. New York and London: Oxford University Press, 1954-1958.
297. Smith, George Winston. *Medicines for the Union Army; the United States Army laboratories during the Civil War.* Madison: American Institute of the History of Pharmacy, 1962.
298. Smith, Merritt Roe. "The Harpers Ferry Armory and the 'New Technology' in America, 1794-1854." Doctoral dissertation, the Pennsylvania State University, 1971. University microfilm no. 72-95531.
299. Smith, Merritt Roe. "John H. Hall, Simeon North, and the Milling Machine: The Nature of Innovation among Antebellum Arms Makers," *Technology and Culture*, XIV, 4 (October, 1973), 573-591.
300. Smith, Winston C. *The Sharps Rifle.* New York: William Morrow, 1943.
301. Sprout, Harold, and Sprout, Margaret. *The Rise of American Naval Power.* Princeton: Princeton University Press, 1939.
302. Still, William N. *Confederate Shipbuilding.* Athens: University of Georgia Press, 1969.
303. Still, William N. *Iron Afloat: The Story of the Confederate Armorclads.* Nashville: Vanderbilt University Press, 1971.

304. Stokesberry, James J. "The Development of Smokeless Gunpowder by the United States Navy, 1889-1900." Master's thesis, University of Delaware, 1965.
305. Strauss, Joseph. "Smokeless Powder," *U.S. Naval Institute Proceedings*, XXVII (1901), 733-738.
306. Struik, Dirk J. *Yankee Science in the Making*. Boston: Little, Brown and Co., 1948.
307. Summers, Festus Paul. *The Baltimore and Ohio in the Civil War*. New York: G. P. Putnam's Sons, 1939.
308. Taylor, George Rogers. *The Transportation Revolution, 1815-1860*. Vol. IV of *The Economic History of the United States*. New York: Reinhart, 1951.
309. Taylor, George Rogers, and Neu, Irene D. *The American Railroad Network, 1861-1890*. Cambridge: Harvard University Press, 1956.
310. Thompson, John T. "The Art of Designing and Constructing Small Arms," *Transactions of the American Society of Civil Engineers. International Engineering Confederence* (1904), 351-387.
311. Tillinghast, B. F. *Rock Island Arsenal: in Peace and in War*. Chicago: Henry O. Shepard Co., 1898.
312. Totten, Robert C. "History of the Fort Pitt Cannon Foundry," *Western Pennsylvania Historical Magazine* (April, 1920), 90-92.
313. Toynbee, Arnold. *The Industrial Revolution*. Boston: Beacon Paperbacks, 1956.
314. Tryon, Charles Z. *The History of a Business Established One Hundred years Ago; 1811-1911*. Philadelphia: Edward K Tryon Co., 1911.
315. Turner, George Edgar. *Victory Rode the Rails; the Strategic Place of the Railroads in the Civil War*. Indianapolis: Bobbs-Merrill, 1953.
316. Tyler, Daniel B. *The American Clyde: A History of Iron and Steel Shipbuilding on the Delaware from 1840 to World War I*. Newark: University of Delaware Press, 1958.
317. U.S. Navy, Bureau of Ordnance. *Naval Percussion Locks and Primers*, by John A. B. Dahlgren. Philadelphia: A. Hart for the Board of Ordnance and Hydrography, 1853.
318. U.S., Bureau of Ordnance. *Shells and Shell Guns*, by John A. B. Dahlgren. Philadelphia: King & Baird, 1856.
319. U.S., Bureau of Ordnance. *Boat Armament of the U.S. Navy*, by John A. B. Dahlgren. Philadelphia: King & Baird, 1856.
320. U.S., Coast and Geodetic Survey. . . . *Military and naval service of the United States Coast Survey, 1861-1865*. Washington: G. P. O., 1916.
321. U.S., Military Railroad Department. *United States Military Railroads*. Report of Bvt. Brig. Gen. D. C. McCallum, director and general manager, from 1861-1866. Washington: n.p., 1866.
322. U.S., Navy Department, Naval History Division. *Riverine Warfare: The U.S. Navy's Operations on Inland Waters*. Washington: G. P. O., 1968.
323. U.S., Office of the Superintendent of Public Documents. *List of United States Public Documents and Reports Relating to Construction of new Navy; also references to debates in Congress on the subject, 1880-1901*. Washington: G. P. O., 1902.

212 • A GUIDE TO THE SOURCES OF U.S. MILITARY HISTORY

324. U.S., Ordnance Department Army. *A Collection of Annual Reports and other Important Papers Relating to the Ordnance Department*, compiled by Brig. Gen. S. V. Benet. (1812-1889) Washington: G. P. O., 1878-1890. 4 vols.

325. U.S., Ordnance Department. *Annual Report of the Chief of Ordnance to the Secretary of War.* Washington: G. P. O., 1873; 1875-1918.

326. U.S., Ordnance Department. *Index to the Reports of the Chief of Ordnance, United States Army, 1867-1887*, by J. C. Ayres. Washington: G. P. O., 1888.

327. U.S., Ordnance Department. *Ordnance Memoranda.* 29 nos. Washington: G. P. O., 1869-1891.

328. U.S., Ordnance Department. *Ordnance Notes.* 351 nos. Washington: G. P. O., 1873-1884. 12 vols.

329. U.S., Ordnance Department. *Index of Ordnance Notes* (Nos. 1 to 357 inclusive). Washington: War Department, 1884.

330. U.S., Board for Testing Iron, Steel, and Other Metals. *Report of the U.S. Board Apppointed to Test Iron, Steel, and Other Metals.* Washington: G. P. O., 1881. 2 vols.

331. U.S., Ordnance Department. *Report of the Tests of Metals and Other Materials for Industrial Purposes . . . at Watertown Arsenal.* Washington: G. P. O., 1882-1919. 38 vols.

332. U.S., Ordnance Department. *Index to the Reports of Tests of Metals . . . from 1881-1912.* Washington: G. P. O., 1913.

333. U.S., Ordnance Department—Important selected publications:
   a. *Reports of Experiments with Small Arms for the Military Service.* Washington: A. O. P. Nicholson, 1856.
   b. *Reports of Experiments on the Strength and Other Properties of Metals for Cannon; with a description of the machines for testing metals, and of the classification of cannons in service.* Philadelphia: Henry Carey Baird, 1856.
   c. *Metallic Ammunition; for the Springfield Breech-Loading Rifle-Musket*, by S. V. Benet. Philadelphia: Frankford Arsenal, 1868. Ordnance Memoranda No. 8. 2nd ed. by T. J. Treadwell. Washington: G. P. O., 1870. No. 9.
   d. *Metallic Cartridges (Regulation and Experimental); as manufactured and tested at Frankford Arsenal, Philadelphia, Pennsylvania.* Washington: G. P. O., 1873. Ordnance Memoranda No. 14.
   e. *Report of the Board of Officers; appointed . . . for the purpose of selecting a breech-system for the muskets and carbines of the military service . . .* Washington: G. P. O., 1873. Ordnance Memoranda 15.
   f. *A History of the Rock Island Arsenal; from its establishment in 1863 to December, 1876, and of the Island of Rock Island, the site of the Arsenal, from 1804 to 1863*, by D. W. Flagler. Washington: G. P. O., 1877. Ordnance Memoranda No. 20.
   g. *The Fabrication of Small Arms for the United States Service*, by James G. Benton. Washington: G. P. O., 1878. Ordnance Memoranda No. 22.

334. U.S., Surgeon-general's Office. *The Medical and Surgical History of the War of the Rebellion, 1861-1865.* Washington: G. P. O., (1970) 1888. 3 vols.

335. U.S., War Department. *The War Department at the Centennial Exposition, Cincinnati, Ohio, 1888.* N.p.: n.p., ca 1888.

336. Vandiver, Frank Emerson. *Ploughshares into Swords: Josiah Gorgas and Confederate Ordnance.* Austin: University of Texas Press, 1952.

337. VanGelder, Arthur P., and Schlatter, Hugo. *History of the Explosive Industry in America.* New York: Columbia University Press, 1927. Reprinted, New York: Arno, 1972.

338. Vreeland, C. E. "The Development of the High-Power Gun," *Naval Mobilization and Improvement in Materiel. General Information Series.* No. VIII. Washington: Office of Naval Intelligence, 1869.

339. Wahl, Paul, and Toppel, Donald R. *The Gatling Gun.* New York: Arco, 1965.

340. Wasson, Robert Gordon. *The Hall Carbine Affair; a study in contemporary folklore.* Rev. ed. New York: Pandick Press, 1948.

341. Waters, Asa H. "Thomas Blanchard, The Inventor," *Harper's New Monthly Magazine,* LXVII (July, 1881), 254-260.

342. Webber, Richard H. *Monitors of the U.S. Navy, 1861-1937.* Washington: Naval History Division, Navy Department, 1969.

343. Weber, Thomas. *The Northern Railroads in the Civil War, 1861-1865.* New York: King's Crown Press, Columbia University, 1952.

344. White, Ruth. *Yankee from Sweden: the Dream and the Reality in the Days of John Ericsson.* New York: Henry Holt and Company, c 1962.

345. Whittlesey, Derwent Stainsthorp. "The Springfield Armory: A Study in Institutional Development." Doctoral dissertation, University of Chicago, 1920.

346. Wiley, Bell, Irvin. *The Life of Johnny Reb; the Common Soldier of the Confederacy.* Indianapolis: Bobbs-Merrill Co., 1943.

347. Wilkinson, Norman B. "The Founding of the DuPont Powder Factory, 1800-1809." Unpublished research report, Eleutherian Mills Historical Library, Greenville, Delaware, 1955.

348. Wilkinson, Norman B. "The Forgotten 'Founder' of West Point," *Military Affairs,* XXIV, 4 (Winter, 1960-61), 177-188.

349. Wilkinson, Norman B. "Brandywine Borrowings from European Technology," *Technology and Culture,* III, 4 (Winter, 1963), 1-13.

350. Wilkinson, Norman B. "In Anticipation of Frederick W. Taylor: a Study of Work by Lammot du Pont, 1872," *Technology and Culture* VI, 2 (Spring, 1966), 208-221.

351. Williams, Francis L. *Matthew Fontaine Maury; Scientist of the Sea.* New Brunswick: Rutgers University Press, 1963.

353. Wilson, Herbert W. *Ironclads in Action, A Sketch of Naval Warfare from 1855 to 1895, with some account of the Development of the Battleship in England.* 2 vols. London: Low Marston & Company, 1896.

354. Williamson, Harold F. *Winchester: The Gun that Won the West.* Washington: Combat Forces Press, 1952.

355. Woodbury, Robert S. *History of the Gear Cutting Machine.* Cambridge: The M.I.T. Press, 1958.
356. Woodbury, Robert S. *History of the Grinding Machine.* Cambridge: The M.I.T. Press, 1959.
357. Woodbury, Robert S. *History of the Milling Machine.* Cambridge: The M.I.T. Press, 1960.
358. Woodbury, Robert S. *History of the Lathe to 1850.* Cleveland: Society for the History of Technology, 1961.
359. Woodbury, Robert S. "The Legend of Eli Whitney and Interchangeable Parts," *Technology and Culture*, I, 3 (Summer, 1963), 235-253.
360. Woodworth, Joseph V. *American Tool Making and Interchangeable Manufacturing.* New York: Norman W. Henley Publishing Company, 1904.
361. Block, Eugene B. *Above the Civil War.* Berkeley: Howell North, 1966.
362. Hennessy, Juliet A. *The United States Army Air Arm. April 1861 to April 1917.* [Montgomery, Alabama] USAF Historical Division, Research Studies Institute, Air University, 1958.
363. Hughes, Thomas Parke. *Elmer Sperry: Inventory & Engineer.* Baltimore: The Johns Hopkins University Press, 1971.
364. Livingston, Dorothy Michelson. *The Master of Light: A Biography of Albert A. Michelson.* New York: Scribner's, 1973.
365. National Research Council—National Academy of Sciences, Committee on Undersea Warfare, *An Annotated Bibliography of Submarine Technical Literature 1557-1953.* Washington, 1954.
366. Paine, T. O. *Submarining: Three Thousand Books and Articles.* Santa Barbara, California: General Electric Company—TEMPO Center for Advanced Studies, 1971.
367. Parkinson, Russell J. "Politics, Patents and Planes: Military Aeronautics in the United States 1863-1907." Doctoral dissertation, Duke University, 1963.
368. Roland, Alex. "A Triumph of Natural Magic: The Development of Undersea Warfare in the Age of Sail, 1578-1865." Doctoral dissertation, Duke University, 1974.
369. Davis, Carl L. *Arming the Union: Small Arms in the Civil War.* Port Washington, New York: Kennikat Press, 1974.
370. Fowler, Don. D. and Fowler, Catherine S. "John Wesley Powell's Journal: Colorado Exploration, 1871-72," *Smithsonian Journal of History*, III, 2 (Summer, 1968), 1-44.
371. Gilman, Roda R. "Count Zeppelin and the American Atmosphere," *Smithsonian Journal of History*, III, 1 (Spring, 1968), 29-40.
372. Hoole, W. Stanley. "The Confederate Armory at Tallassee, Alabama, 1864-65," *Alabama Review*, 25 (January 1972), 3-29.
373. Lewis, Berkley R. *Small Arms Ammunition at the International Exposition*, Philadelphia, 1876. Washington: G. P. O., 1972.
374. Lord, Frank A. *The Civil War Collector's Encyclopedia: Arms, Uniforms, and Equipment of the Union and Confederacy.* Harrisburg: Stackpole, 1963.
375. Manning, Thomas G. *Government in Science; the U.S. Geological Survey, 1867-1894.* Lexington: University of Kentucky Press, 1967.

376. Merrill, James M. "Union Shipbuilding on Western Rivers during the Civil War," *Smithsonian Journal of History*, III, (Winter, 1968-69), 17-44.
377. Mills, Anson. *My Story*. Washington; published by the author, press of Byron S. Adams, 1918.
378. Mills Woven Cartridge Belt Company. *Woven Military Equipment* [Catalogue for Model 1910 Equipment]. Worcester, Massachusetts, ca. 1914.
379. Scott, Michel. "Army Wagons, Westward Ho!" *Translog* (May, 1970), 9-10.
380. Shumway, George, Durell, Edward, and Frey, Howard C. *Conestoga Wagon, 1750-1850; Freight Carrier for 100 Years of America's Westward Expansion*. Williamsburg, Virginia: Early American Industries Association, 1964.
381. Smith, Merritt Roe. "Museum Review: The American Precision Museum (Winsor, Vermont), [Robbins & Lawrence], *Technology and Culture*, XV, 3 (July, 1974), 413-37.
382. U.S., Ordnance Department. *Horse Equipments and Cavalry Accoutrements, as prescribed by G. O. 73, A. G. O.* Washington: G. P. O., 1885. Reprinted with New introduction by James S. Hutchins, Pasadena, California: Sociotechnical, 1970.
383. Weigley, Russell F. *Quartermaster General of the Union Army: a biography of M. C. Meigs*. New York: Columbia University Press, 1959.

VIII

THE MEXICAN WAR AND THE
CIVIL WAR

Grady McWhiney

There are good reasons to consider the sources on the military history of the Mexican War and the Civil War together. In many ways the Mexican War was, as one writer called it, a rehearsal for conflict. It was more than that, of course, and anyone who examines it from such a limited perspective is likely to miss much of importance. On the other hand, it would be equally shortsighted to ignore the relationship between these two wars. There was much continuity despite significant differences. What young Americans saw and did in Mexico in 1846-47 strongly influenced the way they fought each other in 1861-65. Indeed, many of the Union and Confederate officers who led large bodies of men in the Civil War learned much of what they knew about combat in Mexico. This continuity also extends to some of the sources. Many collections of primary material that are useful in studying one war are also valuable in studying the other. This is true not only of certain unpublished papers, but also of some published materials as well—especially biographies, letters, and memoirs.

THE MEXICAN WAR.
General Works. The first military histories of the Mexican War displayed many of the strengths and weaknesses often associated with works authored by participants. A two-volume study by Roswell S. Ripley, an artillery officer, appeared soon after the war (227). It was severely critical of General Zachary Taylor's military ability. Ripley's views were soon attacked by another veteran, Isaac I. Stevens (261). Still another war hero, Cadmus M. Wilcox, praised Taylor's generalship in a lengthy volume (299).

The most thorough study yet produced on the war was written early in the twentieth century by Justin H. Smith (250). The research on which these two volumes were based was so overwhelming that since their appearance historians of the Mexican War have worked in Smith's shadow. Smith intimidated prospective writers so effectively that no general histories of the war appeared for more than two decades, but since 1947 one-volume accounts of the conflict have been written by Alfred H. Bill (20), Robert S. Henry (130), Otis A. Singletary (245), Charles L. Dufour (84), Seymour V. Connor and Odie B. Faulk (56), and K. Jack Bauer (15). Each of these works has some appeal, but only Bauer seems to have used unpublished sources extensively.

Biographies. Some of the best secondary sources on Mexican War military activities are biographies. Two studies of Taylor by Holman Hamilton (115) and by Brainerd Dyer (86) judiciously evaluate the old general and pronounce him a better commander than his critics admitted. General Winfield Scott is also the subject of two adequate if less than definitive biographies by Charles W. Elliott (93) and by A. D. Howden Smith (246).

Among the more useful studies of subordinate officers are Douglas S. Freeman's *R. E. Lee* (97), Charles P. Roland's *Albert Sidney Johnston* (230), Lloyd Lewis's *Captain Sam Grant* (160), T. Harry Williams's *Beauregard* (305), Frank E. Vandiver's *Mighty Stonewall* (284), Lenoir Chambers's *Stonewall Jackson* (43), Grady McWhiney's *Braxton Bragg* (180), Dwight L. Clarke's *Stephen W. Kearny* (47), Allan Nevin's *Fremont* (202), Nathaniel C. Hughes's *William J. Hardee* (140), Freeman Cleaves's *Meade* (48), Edward J. Nichols's *John F. Reynolds* (203), Joseph H. Parks's *Edmund Kirby Smith* (213), Robert G. Hartje's *Earl Van Dorn* (119), Edward S. Wallace's *William J. Worth* (290), Hudson Strode's *Jefferson Davis* (264), and Hazard Stevens's *Isaac Ingalls Stevens* (260), which is valuable because of the extensive number of letters included.

Strategy and Tactics. Good sources on strategy are President James K. Polk's *Diary* (218), Zachary Taylor's Papers (358), William L. Marcy's Papers (342), and Winfield Scott's *Memoirs* (238). "To compel a people, singularly obstinate, *to sue for peace*," Scott stated, "it is absolutely necessary . . . to strike, effectively, at the vitals of the nation." Elliott (93) argued that Scott followed a strategy of annihilation, but one of Scott's officers, Raphael Semmes (240), insisted that the general's objective "was to strike a vital blow at the enemy, by reaching, and possessing himself of his capital." Russell F. Weigley (294) agreed with Semmes. Weigley, who described Scott's strategy as political and based upon a campaign of maneuver, wrote: "Scott did not include as an object of his campaign into Mexico the destruction of the Mexican army."

Both strategy and tactics are explored by Justin H. Smith (250) and by several biographers. Tactics and sometimes other aspects of the art of war are expounded in volumes written by such contemporaries as Winfield Scott (237), Henry W. Halleck (114), and Dennis Hart Mahan (184). Artillery (22) and cavalry (279) tactics are discussed in separate works.

Operations and Logistics. All general military accounts, most biographies, and many primary sources devote varying amounts of space to campaigns, but carefully researched works on specific operations are scarce. Before the war ended or soon afterwards a number of books on campaigns and battles appeared. Some examples are Thomas B. Thorpe's *Our Army on the Rio Grande* (272) and *Our Army at Monterey* (271), Samuel C. Reid's *Scouting Expeditions of McCulloch's Texas Rangers* (225), John Hughes's *Doniphan's Expedition* (139), James H. Carleton's *Buena Vista* (31), H. Judge Moore's *Scott's Campaign* (196), Isaac I. Stevens's *Campaigns of the Rio Grande* (261), Raphael Semmes's *Campaign of General*

Scott (240), and Francis Baylis's *Major General Wool's Campaign* (16). None is a definitive study. But after this prodigious spilling of ink, writers—except for Philip St. George Cooke, who published *The Conquest of New Mexico and California* (57) in 1878—neglected campaign studies for over a hundred years. A few good articles appeared from time to time, but no book length work on Mexican War operations was published until the 1960s. Since then two volumes on operations in northern Mexico have been written: Edward J. Nichols's *Zach Taylor's Little Army* (204) and David Lavender's *Climax at Buena Vista* (157). [Naval operations are covered in chapter VI.]

Primary Sources. Letters, diaries, reports, memoirs—printed and manuscript—are available in abundance on the Mexican War. Justin H. Smith, whose impressive study of that conflict appeared in 1919 (250), listed 379 manuscript collections in his bibliography. More have become accessible since then. But, unfortunately, there is no comprehensive guide to either published or unpublished primary sources on the Mexican War. The ongoing *National Union Catalog of Manuscripts* is helpful; so are Philip M. Hamer's *Guide to Archives and Manuscripts* and William Matthews's *American Diaries in Manuscript* [see chapter I]. Useful for the growing Military History Research Collection at Carlisle Barracks is Richard J. Sommers's *Manuscript Holdings* (251). Kenneth W. Munden and Henry P. Beers's *Guide to Federal Archives* (197) is indispensable to anyone attempting to work through the mountain of manuscripts in the National Archives, especially the important records of the secretary of war (350), the adjutant general (349), the quartermaster general (348), the chief of ordnance (351), and the chief of engineers (347). Benjamin P. Poore's *Descriptive Catalogue of Government Publications* together with other checklists [see chapter XIX] are helpful in locating the many letters, orders, and reports relating to Mexican War military operations that are printed in various House and Senate serial publications of the 29th and 30th Congresses.

Nearly all of the official letters and reports of the principal leaders are in the printed public documents, but the candid views and prejudices of President Polk are best revealed in his diary (218). Those of General Taylor can be examined in his manuscripts at the Library of Congress (358) and the Huntington Library (359), and in his printed letters from the battlefields (268). The views of General Scott can be found in his *Memoirs* (238). Collections of Scott's letters at the Library of Congress, the New York Historical Society, and the University of Arizona are relatively unimportant for the Mexican War. But the papers of Secretary of War Marcy (342) contain important letters from Scott and Taylor.

Other participants in the war left a variety of records; so many, in fact, that it is impossible to do more here than to offer a sampling. These sources range widely in usefulness and readability—from the dullness of a muster roll to the colorful statement by a rustic Virginian that he had joined a volunteer company "thats araising . . . to go and slay them Mexicans."

Some of the best accounts of personalities and operations in Mexico were written by officers who served with both Taylor and Scott. The published diary of Ethan Allen Hitchcock (134) is an excellent source; so are the published letters of John Sedgwick (239), Ulysses S. Grant (110), George

G. Meade (189), Ephraim Kirby Smith (247), and George H. McCall (174). Useful unpublished collections of letters include those by John Porter Hatch, 3rd Infantry (325); John S. Hatheway, 1st Artillery (324); Ethan A. Hitchcock, a staff officer (326); William W. Mackall, 1st Artillery (341); James Duncan, 2nd Artillery (318, 319); John A. Quitman, a volunteer general (345); and Persifor F. Smith, a regular general (356). The best of the published memoirs of officers who served with both Taylor and Scott are by Ulysses S. Grant (111) and Dabney H. Maury (187). But see also the reminiscences of John R. Kenly, a volunteer officer from Maryland who was with Taylor at Monterey but arrived in central Mexico too late to participate in any of Scott's battles (152).

The best accounts of the northern Mexico campaign by officers who served only with Taylor's army are in the published diaries of William S. Henry (131) and Philip N. Barbour (12), and in the published memoirs of Samuel G. French (99) and Luther Giddings (106). Also revealing are the unpublished papers of Benjamin F. Cheatham, a Tennessee volunteer (314); Jefferson Davis, commander of the 1st Mississippi Volunteers (315, 316, 317); Samuel G. French, 3rd Artillery (321); Albert Sidney Johnston, a volunteer (331); and John E. Wool, a regular general (360, 361).

Among the more worthwhile volumes published by officers who served only with Scott are the gossipy and strongly pro-Scott letters of Robert Anderson (8), the diary of George B. McClellan (177), and the reminiscences of P. G. T. Beauregard (18). McClellan and Beauregard were members of Scott's staff. Additional "inside" information can be found in the unpublished papers of McClellan (340) and Beauregard (310, 311), and especially in those of another staff officer, Isaac Ingalls Stevens (357). Valuable material on the campaign in central Mexico is also in the unpublished papers of Robert Anderson, 3rd Artillery (308); John Campbell, an army physician (313); Richard S. Ewell, 1st Dragoons (320); Thomas J. Jackson, 1st Artillery (329); Robert E. Lee, of Scott's staff (335, 336, 337); and George W. Rains, 4th Artillery (346).

Other useful unpublished material relative to various units, individuals, and activities is available. Some of this includes the files of Quartermaster General Thomas S. Jesup (330); thirty-six Mexican War letters from Benjamin Huger, an ordnance officer (344); the William T. Sherman Papers, which include a number of significant letters from his friends who were in Mexico (354); the 1st Infantry Regiment's Papers, that contain letters sent by that unit while it was in Mexico (328); and copies of the orders issued both at Scott's headquarters and at General William J. Worth's division headquarters, July-November 1847 (309).

Perhaps the best published volume by an enlisted man is George Ballentine's *Autobiography* (11). Concerned with Scott's campaign, it was written by a former member of the British army who joined the U.S. army after he had migrated from Scotland but was unable to find work as a weaver in America. Equally enjoyable is Samuel E. Chamberlain's confession (42). It is, the author admits, the recollections of a rogue. Though Chamberlain probably exaggerated his exploits, especially those in the bedroom, his narrative of soldier life is interesting and useful. Accounts by regulars such as Ballentine and Chamberlain are rare; those by volunteers are more numerous, but few are outstanding sources. Some of the better ones have appeared in periodicals. Of those that have been published as books, two of the most frequently cited are by J. Jacob Oswandel (212) and by George C. Furber (103). The letters and dairy of Oswandel, a member of the 1st Pennsylvania Volunteers who served with Scott, appear to have been "revised" for publication. The journal of Furber, a private in a Tennessee cavalry regiment who also was with Scott, is useful on both camp life and military operations.

Edited collections of primary sources include *Chronicles of the Gringos* (248), an elaborate selection of accounts by participants arranged chronologically by George W. Smith and Charles Judah. A less expensive, paperback volume edited by Grady and Sue McWhiney (182) also contains excerpts from contemporary American sources. The views of Mexican participants have been collected by Ramon Alcaraz and others (3).

1848-1861. Between the Mexican War and the Civil War the United States Army was most active in the West. Its military encounters with Indians during this period are described by Robert M. Utley (282). Leonard D. White has analyzed the War Department and the administrative problems of the army (298). The views of Jefferson Davis, who was Secretary of War from 1853 to 1857 and periodically from 1847 until 1861 a member of the Senate's Military Affairs Committee, are revealed in his own writings (67). See also Strode's biography of Davis (264). Winfield Scott's role as commanding general as well as his feud with Secretary Davis is examined by Elliott (93) and by Smith (246). Much useful information on army life can be found in the biographies of Robert E. Lee (97), Albert Sidney Johnston (230), Ulysses S. Grant (160), P. G. T. Beauregard (305), Thomas J. Jackson (284, 43), Braxton Bragg (180), E. Kirby Smith (213), Early Van Dorn (119), William J. Hardee (140), and John F. Reynolds (203). Strategic ideas and influences during this period are discussed in Russell F. Weigley's *American Way of War* (294). Two valuable works are W. Turrentine Jackson's account of the army's role in western road construction (141) and William H. Goetzmann's *Army Exploration in the American West* (107). Various public documents and the unpublished army records in the National Archives (350, 347, 348, 349, 351) contain extensive material on military affairs between 1848 and 1861.

THE CIVIL WAR.

General Works. The most comprehensive and readable military history of the Civil War is Bruce Catton's three-volume *Centennial History* (36), but also worthwhile is the old four-volume study by John C. Ropes and W. R. Livermore (233). The first two volumes, by Ropes, are especially good. The best single volume survey of the whole period is J. G. Randall and David Herbert Donald's *Civil War and Reconstruction* (223); its distinguished bibliography evaluates works on the entire era as well as the wartime milieu. Mark M. Boatner's *Civil War Dictionary* is a handy item (24). Ezra J. Warner's *Generals in Blue* (291) and *Generals in Gray* (292) are excellent biographical dictionaries. E. B. Long's almanac (166) tells briefly and accurately what happened every day of the war. The twelve-volume *Confederate Military History* edited by Clement Evans (94) is still useful. So is Frederick H. Dyer's list of northern units, campaigns, and losses

(87); William F. Amann's two volumes (5) are not as comprehensive, but provide information on both Federal and Confederate units. The basic reference on casualties and battle effectives on both sides is Thomas L. Livermore's *Numbers and Losses* (165). William F. Fox's *Regimental Losses* (95) analyzes only Union casualties. Charles E. Dornbusch's ongoing listing of regimental histories arranged by states (77) is serviceable. A valuable guide to *Civil War Books* has been edited by Allan Nevins, James I. Robertson, Jr., and Bell I. Wiley (201). Old but still the most extensive collection of Civil War pictures is Francis T. Miller's ten-volume *Photographic History* (193); a good one-volume pictorial history of the war is David Herbert Donald's *Divided We Fought* (74). Vincent J. Esposito's *West Point Atlas* (278) provides clear maps for all of the major campaigns; the atlas designed to accompany the *Official Records* (280) is unwieldy in size but quite beneficial. [On naval activities see chapter VI.]

Policy and Strategy. There is no comprehensive treatment of Civil War strategy, but the two chapters devoted to the subject in Russell F. Weigley's *American Way of War* (294) are impressive and suggestive. The strategic views of Lincoln and Davis and their generals are best revealed in their published and unpublished works.

Union strategy and generalship are analyzed in John G. Nicolay and John Hay's ten-volume study (207), J. G. Randall's *Lincoln the President* (224), Colin R. Ballard's *Military Genius of Abraham Lincoln* (10), T. Harry Williams's *Lincoln and His Generals* (303), Kenneth P. Williams's *Lincoln Finds a General* (302), Bruce Catton's *Grant Moves South* (38) and *Grant Takes Command* (39), T. Harry Williams's *McClellan, Sherman and Grant* (304), Warren W. Hassler, Jr.'s *George B. McClellan* (122) and *Commanders of the Army of the Potomac* (120), Adam Badeau's *Military History of U.S. Grant* (9), and Stephen E. Ambrose's *Halleck* (6). Authorities on Union generalship often disagree. One such controversy involves McClellan's ability. He is defended by Hassler and Randall; attacked by T. Harry Williams, Kenneth P. Williams, and Bruce Catton.

The best analysis of Confederate strategy is *The Politics of Command* by Thomas L. Connelly and Archer Jones (55). Other useful works on the subject include Frank E. Vandiver's *Rebel Brass* (286) and *Their Tattered Flags* (287), Archer Jones's *Confederate Strategy* (147), Thomas L. Connelly's *Army of the Heartland* (53) and *Autumn of Glory* (54), Douglas S. Freeman's *R. E. Lee* (97) and *Lee's Lieutenants* (96), Charles P. Roland's *Albert Sidney Johnston* (230), T. Harry Williams's *P. G. T. Beauregard* (305), Gilbert E. Govan and James W. Livingood's *Joseph E. Johnston* (109), Grady McWhiney's *Braxton Bragg* (180), John G. Barrett's *Civil War in North Carolina* (13), David Herbert Donald's *Lincoln Reconsidered* (75), Charles P. Roland's essay on Lee in *Grant, Lee, Lincoln and the Radicals* (181), T. Harry Williams's essay in *Why the North Won the Civil War* (76), and certain essays in Grady McWhiney's *Southerners and Other Americans* (183). There is no satisfactory study of Jefferson Davis either as Confederate commander-in-chief or as strategist. He is treated sympathetically by Vandiver; more critically by Connelly, Jones, and Mc-Whiney. Robert E. Lee's strategic abilities are evaluated favorably by Freeman and Roland; unfavorably by Donald, Williams, Connelly, and Jones.

Several valuable works by foreigners comment on Civil War strategy and generalship. Among the best of these are J. F. C. Fuller's *Grant and Lee* (102) and *The Generalship of Ulysses S. Grant* (101), G. F. R. Henderson's *The Civil War* (127) and *Stonewall Jackson* (128), Frederick Maurice's *Statesmen and Soldiers* (186), B. H. Liddell Hart's *Sherman* (162), A. H. Burne's *Lee, Grant, and Sherman* (30), and Walter B. Wood and James E. Edmonds's *History of the Civil War* (307). These and other foreign observers and their evaluations are analyzed in Jay Luvaas's *Military Legacy of the Civil War* (172) and *Education of an Army* (171).

Several scholars believe that Jomini's strategic and tactical ideas influenced Civil War commanders, but there is disagreement on who was affected and how. See Donald's *Lincoln Reconsidered* (75), T. Harry Williams's essay in *Why the North Won* (76), Roland's essay in *Grant, Lee, Lincoln and the Radicals* (181), Vandiver's *Their Tattered Flags* (287), and Connelly and Jones's *Politics of Command* (55).

Operations in the East. The story of the Army of the Potomac is colorfully told by Bruce Catton in *Mr. Lincoln's Army* (40), *Glory Road* (37), and *A Stillness at Appomattox* (41). Union operations and commanders are evaluated by Warren W. Hassler, Jr. (120), and through the Gettysburg campaign by Kenneth P. Williams (302). Biographies of Civil War military figures range from superb to poor; too many, unfortunately, simply glorify the subject and magnify his accomplishments. Among the most useful studies of Union generals who served in the East are Bruce Catton's excellent *Grant Takes Command* (39), J. F. C. Fuller's analysis of Grant's generalship (101), Warren W. Hassler, Jr.'s carefully researched defense of George B. McClellan (122), Freeman Cleaves's sympathetic study of George G. Meade (48), Walter H. Hebert's evaluation of Joseph Hooker (126), Glenn Tucker's vividly written account of Winfield Scott Hancock (274), Edward J. Nichols's extensively documented biography of John F. Reynolds (203), Richard O'Connor's partial but interesting study of Philip H. Sheridan (211), John A. Carpenter's scholarly treatment of Oliver O. Howard (32), and the early chapters in Stephen E. Ambrose's analysis of Emory Upton (7).

Confederate activities in the East are treated extensively in Douglas S. Freeman's *R. E. Lee* (97) and *Lee's Lieutenants* (96). A four-volume study, *Lee* is a model Civil War biography despite Freeman's sympathy for his hero. The best one-volume study of Lee is by Clifford Dowdey (78). Two men who served briefly as army commanders in the East are the subjects of biographies: P. G. T. Beauregard has been judiciously analyzed by T. Harry Williams (305); Joseph E. Johnston has been sympathetically studied by Gilbert E. Govan and James W. Livingood (109). Lee's principal subordinates have received somewhat uneven evaluation. Frank E. Vandiver's biography of Thomas J. (Stonewall) Jackson is excellent (284). Other worthwhile studies of Jackson include those by Lenoir Chambers (43) and the highly sympathetic account by the British military authority Colonel G. F. R. Henderson (128). The biographies of James Longstreet are less satisfactory; the best is a partisan treatment by Donald B. Sanger and Thomas R. Hay (235). Studies of A. P. Hill by William W. Hassler (123) and Martin Schenck (236) are limited by the failure of many of Hill's own letters to survive. A similar problem plus excessive admiration for his subject hampered Percy G. Hamlin, Richard S. Ewell's biographer (117). More balanced is John P. Dyer's study of John B. Hood (89). Hal Bridges's biography of D. H. Hill (26) is carefully researched but full of the author's strong opinions.

Accounts of battles and campaigns vary considerably in quality. The best study of First Bull Run is by Robert M. Johnston (146). Clifford Dowdey's *The Seven Days* (80) is dramatically written. The most satisfactory account of the Second Bull Run campaign is still John C. Rope's study published in 1881 (232). Antietam is the subject of studies by Edward J. Stackpole (253) and James V. Murfin (199); both are anti-McClellan. The most recent and thorough analysis of Fredericksburg is by Vorin E. Whan (297). John Bigelow's *The Campaign of Chancellorsville* (19) is impressive—one of the best campaign studies ever written. Too much trash has been written about Gettysburg. Some of the better accounts are Edwin B. Coddington's *The Gettysburg Campaign* (50), Warren W. Hassler, Jr.'s *Crisis at the Crossroads* (121), George R. Stewart's *Pickett's Charge* (263), Wilbur S. Nye's *Here Come the Rebels* (209), and Glenn Tucker's *High Tide at Gettysburg* (275) and *Lee and Longstreet at Gettysburg* (276). Edward Steere's *The Wilderness Campaign* (256) is excellent. *Lee's Last Campaign* by Clifford Dowdey (79) is lively. Actions in the Shenandoah Valley in 1864 are covered by Edward J. Stackpole (254) and Frank E. Vandiver (283). Colorful accounts of the Appomattox Campaign have been written by Burleigh C. Rodick (229) and Burke Davis (65). John G. Barrett's *Sherman's March Through the Carolinas* (14) is outstanding.

Artillery in the East is covered in several useful secondary works as well as in some primary sources (4, 228, 175). The story of the Army of the Potomac's artillery is told in L. Van Loan Naisawald's *Grape and Canister* (200). Confederate guns and gunners are described in Jennings C. Wise's *Long Arm of Lee* (306) and in Maury Klein's *Edward Porter Alexander* (155). *The Guns of Gettysburg* are vividly depicted by Fairfax D. Downey (82).

Cavalry operations are less satisfactorily covered. Fairfax D. Downey's *Clash of Cavalry* (81) describes the war's largest cavalry battle at Brandy Station. James H. Wilson, who reorganized the Union Cavalry Bureau, is the subject of a recent biography by Edward G. Longacre (167). Confederate cavalry actions are described sympathetically and at times romantically in biographies of J. E. B. Stuart by Burke Davis (66) and by John W. Thomason (270).

Operations in the West. Until some two decades ago western campaigns had been relatively neglected, but since then a profusion of studies have been produced on the West. Indeed, nearly three-fourths of the significant works on western operations and leaders have appeared since 1954. Many of these volumes reassess military activities outside the East and offer challenging new theses. This reevaluation began with volume three of Kenneth P. Williams's *Lincoln Finds a General* (302), which covered Grant's first year in the West. Before he died in 1958, Williams had added two additional volumes on the western campaigns and had carried his analysis through the Battle of Chickamauga. He concentrated on Union activities, but he also corrected many errors regarding Confederate operations. This analysis of Union commanders and battles begun by Williams continued after his death. In 1960 Bruce Catton published *Grant Moves South* (38), an impressive continuation of the biography begun by Lloyd Lewis (160). A year later important studies of William S. Rosecrans by William M. Lamers (156) and George H. Thomas by Francis F. McKinney (179) appeared. Since then biographies of John A. Logan by James P. Jones (148), John M. Schofield by James L. McDonough (178), and William T. Sherman by James M. Merrill (191) have been published. Before 1954 the only worthwhile accounts of Union commanders who served in the West were two works on Sherman—by Lloyd Lewis (161) and B. H. Liddell Hart (162)—one on Thomas by Freeman Cleaves (49), and one on Nathaniel P. Banks by Fred H. Harrington (118).

Books written since 1954 on Confederate operations in the West are even more abundant. Perhaps the most impressive achievement has been the work of Thomas L. Connelly. His two volumes on the Army of Tennessee (53, 54) not only superseded Stanley F. Horn's book (137); they did for the western Confederacy what Freeman's *Lee's Lieutenants* (96) had done for the East. Whatever one thought of Connelly's conclusions, which were often controversial, they could not be ignored. A number of biographical studies also supplemented and expanded knowledge of Confederate activities in the West. In 1954 only one of the men who commanded the Army of Tennessee had been the subject of a modern biography—John B. Hood (89). A year later T. Harry Williams's scholarly study of Beauregard appeared (305). Next came Gilbert E. Govan and James W. Livingood's biography of Joseph E. Johnston (109), followed by Charles P. Roland's definitive treatment of Albert Sidney Johnston (230), and finally by Grady McWhiney's account of Braxton Bragg (180). Not only had scholarly biographies of the Army of Tennessee's commanders been completed by 1974; so had studies of a number of subordinate generals. Among the best of these are Nathaniel C. Hughes's readable and thorough work on William J. Hardee (140), Joseph H. Parks's sympathetic volumes on E. Kirby Smith (213) and Leonidas Polk (214), Robert G. Hartje's thoughtful analysis of Earl Van Dorn (119), William C. Davis's recent volume on John C. Breckinridge (71), Robert E. Shalhope's evaluation of Sterling Price (241), Albert Castel's careful treatment of that same general's Civil War career (34), Hal Bridges's biography of D. H. Hill (26), and Howell and Elizabeth Purdue's account of Patrick R. Cleburne (222).

The quality of works on special areas of the West and on campaigns are as uneven as those relating to the East. A useful general account of fighting on the western border is by Jay Monaghan (194). Ray C. Colton's study of actions in the western territories is excellent (51). Robert L. Kerby's *Kirby Smith's Confederacy* (153) is important on the Trans-Mississippi; Martin H. Hall provides details on Henry H. Sibley's New Mexico campaign (113). Two old works by James B. Fry (100 and Bromfield L. Ridley (226) concentrate on operations in the central Confederacy. James J. Hamilton has described the Battle of Fort Donelson (116). Otto Eisenschiml's account of Shiloh is valuable but highly opinionated (92). Alexander F. Stevenson's old study is still helpful on Stone's River (262).

Charles L. Dufour has analyzed the fall of New Orleans (85). The Union side of the struggle for Vicksburg is told by Earl Schenck Miers (192); the Confederate side by Peter F. Walker (289). *The Port Hudson Campaign* by Edward C. Cunningham (62) is a thorough study. Ludwell H. Johnson's *Red River Campaign* (142) is excellent. Chickamauga is best covered by Glenn Tucker (273). Fairfax D. Downey's *Storming the Gateway* (83) recounts actions around Chattanooga in 1863. Jacob D. Cox's *Atlanta* (59) is old but still useful; William Key's *Battle of Atlanta and the Georgia Campaign* is too uncritical (154); Samuel C. Carter's *Siege of Atlanta* (33) is new. Still of help are Jacob D. Cox's *The March to the Sea* (61) and *The Battle of Franklin* (60). Thomas R. Hay's account of *Hood's Tennessee Campaign* (124) is thorough. Stanley F. Horn overstated his thesis but his *Decisive Battle of Nashville* (138) is useful.

There are no studies of either Union or Confederate artillery in the West, but cavalry operations and raids are covered in several works. Dee A. Brown's *Grierson's Raid* (27) is a swiftly paced account of an important action. Stephen Z. Starr's *Jennison's Jayhawkers* (255) is a valuable unit history. John W. Powell's *Yankee Cavalrymen* (220) focuses on the Ninth Pennsylvania Regiment. Stephen B. Oates tells the story of Confederate cavalry operations in the Trans-Mississippi (210). Richard S. Brownlee (28) describes western guerrillas. William C. Quantrill is depicted by Albert E. Castell (35). Confederate cavalry leader Nathan Bedford Forrest is the subject of many uncritical works; perhaps the best of these sympathetic studies is by Robert S. Henry (129). John P. Dyer's Joseph Wheeler (88) and Cecil F. Holland's John H. Morgan (135) are biographies of other Confederate cavalrymen.

Special Studies. The problems of raising armies are described by Albert B. Moore (195) and Eugene C. Murdock (198). Alexander H. Meneely (190) and Fred A. Shannon (242) have written on the Union War Department and army administration. See also Stephen E. Ambrose's biography of Henry W. Halleck (6). The best biography of Lincoln's Secretary of War Edwin M. Stanton is by Benjamin P. Thomas and Harold M. Hyman (269).

Bell I. Wiley's *Life of Billy Yank* (300) and *Life of Johnny Reb* (301) are outstanding works on the common soldier. Desertion is discussed by Ella Lonn (169). The best work on Civil War military prisons is by William B. Hesseltine (132), but see also Ovid L. Futch's *Andersonville* (104). Unit histories often leave much to be desired. Four exceptions are the admirable studies by James I. Robertson, Jr. (228), Alan T. Nolan (208), John J. Pullen (221), and Harold B. Simpson (244). The best study of Negro troops in the Union army is by Dudley T. Cornish (58). The story of Negro military laborers in Virginia is told by James H. Brewer (25).

Military railroads are evaluated by Robert C. Black III (23), George E. Turner (277), Angus J. Johnston II (144), and Francis A. Lord (170). Ordnance is the subject of studies by Robert V. Bruce (29), Harold L. Peterson (217), Frank E. Vandiver (285), and Charles B. Dew (72). Richard D. Goff's *Confederate Supply* (108) is a clear analysis of the failure of Confederate logistics. James L. Nichols has written on *Confederate Engineers* (205) and *The Confederate Quartermaster in the Trans-Mississippi*

(206). Russell F. Weigley has done a good biography of the Union's quartermaster general (295). Civil War aeronautics are described by Frederick S. Haydon (125). Military medicine is examined by George W. Adams (1), Paul E. Steiner (257, 258, 259), George W. Smith (249), William Q. Mexwell (188), and Horace H. Cunningham (63, 64). [For more on medicine see chapter XII.]

Primary Sources. Many of the sources as well as the guides to those sources mentioned in the Mexican War section also apply to the Civil War. The best single source for Civil War military history is the 128-volume *War of the Rebellion* (281). Popularly known as the "*Official Records*" or the "*OR*," this enormous compilation includes both Union and Confederate documents—reports, letters, telegrams, etc.—dealing with every campaign of the war. Each volume is indexed, and there is also a general index volume. A researcher's guide to the *OR* appeared recently (2).

Definitive collections of the works of both the Union and Confederate presidents are either available or in preparation. Abraham Lincoln's own writings have been carefully and accurately edited by Roy P. Basler (163, 164). In addition, over 40,000 letters to and from Lincoln are in his papers at the Library of Congress (339).

In 1923 Dunbar Rowland published ten volumes of Jefferson Davis's papers (67), but much new material has been turned up since then. The private letters of Davis, edited by Hudson Strode (68), include documents unavailable to Rowland. Collections of Davis papers at Duke University (316) and at the Library of Congress (317) contain unpublished items. A new and comprehensive collection of Davis's letters is now being prepared. The first volume—edited by Haskell M. Monroe, Jr., and James T. McIntosh—has been published, but only includes material to 1840 (69). Davis's memoirs (70) are highly disputatious, full of errors and distortions, but valuable nevertheless. Editor Bell I. Wiley's foreword to the new edition is a good analysis of Davis.

The personal papers of a few army commanders have been published. Ulysses S. Grant's papers (110) are being meticulously edited by John Y. Simon. When completed, this collection will be *the* comprehensive primary source of Grant's own writing. Unpublished letters to and from Grant in the Library of Congress (322) number more than 47,000. No Civil War student should neglect Grant's *Memoirs* (111), which are clear and direct— some of the best military memoirs ever written—but not without error. There is a useful paperback abridgment with an excellent introduction by E. B. Long (112).

The most complete collection of Robert E. Lee's personal, official, and family letters are his *Wartime Papers*, edited by Clifford Dowdey and Louis H. Manarin (159), but this volume contains only a fraction of the letters Lee wrote during the war. For additional Lee letters see the *OR* (280) and *Lee's Dispatches*, edited by Douglas S. Freeman and Grady McWhiney (158). Unpublished letters to and from Lee are in many archives—two fairly large collections are in the Virginia Historical Society (338) and the Library of Congress (337).

William T. Sherman's *Memoirs* (243B) are among the Civil War's best— admirably clear, temperate, colloquial, and usually trustworthy. There is no comprehensive printed collection of Sherman's papers, but his *Home Letters* (243A) and his correspondence with his brother (243C) contain useful material on the war. The Library of Congress (354) and the Ohio Historical Society (355) house important Sherman manuscripts.

Other significant unpublished collections include information on such high ranking Union and Confederate generals as P. G. T. Beauregard (310, 311), Braxton Bragg (312), Henry W. Halleck (323), Joseph Hooker (327), Albert Sidney Johnston (331), Joseph E. Johnston (332, 333, 334), George B. McClellan (340), William S. Rosecrans (352), George G. Meade (343), and Philip H. Sheridan (353). Unpublished Civil War manuscripts are so multitudinous that it is impossible to list more than a few collections here. E. B. Long, who has examined as many manuscripts as any Civil War scholar, listed nearly a thousand collections in his bibliography (166). Students are advised to check his list as well as the *National Union Catalog of Manuscripts* [see chapter I].

Several published memoirs reveal much about their authors as well as about military affairs. One of the most important of all Confederate memoirs is Joseph E. Johnston's *Narrative* (145). Clearly a defense of its author, it is strongly anti-Davis and anti-Hood, but it is a better book than one might expect. Frank E. Vandiver's introduction to the new edition is a thoughtful evaluation of Johnston. *Advance and Retreat* (136), John B. Hood's recollections of the war, is full of bitterness and errors. Even so, this controversial volume is essential to any understanding of Hood and the army he commanded. Helpful too is Richard Current's introduction to the new edition. Alfred Roman's *Military Operations of General Beauregard* (231) is for all practical purposes Beauregard's personal memoir. By having his former aide's name on the title page, Beauregard could eulogize himself without appearing immodest; he also could mask his attack on Davis and the Johnstons. George B. McClellan wrote his *Own Story* (176) as a defense of his actions after he was relieved of command of the Army of the Potomac. It contains many private letters that are otherwise unavilable; it also inadvertently reveals much about McClellan's personality.

Other important works by high ranking generals include Philip H. Sheridan's *Memoirs* (243), George G. Meade's *Letters* (189), James Longstreet's *From Manassas to Appomattox* (168), Jubal A. Early's *Memoirs* (90), and Richard Taylor's *Destruction and Reconstruction* (266). Sheridan's recollections are balanced and remarkably uncontentious. Meade's letters, edited by his son, are much less than comprehensive. Longstreet's account is somewhat ponderous and biased—a defense of the author's actions, particularly at Gettysburg. The introduction to the new edition by James I. Robertson, Jr., corrects many of Longstreet's errors and gives a balanced evaluation of the senior lieutenant general of the Confederate army. Early's narrative is as blunt and irascible as the general himself, but it is quite judicious. Taylor's reminiscence, which is critical of several Confederate leaders but always temperate, is probably the best-written of the war.

Another significant source is *Battles and Leaders* (143). Issued originally in serial form in the *Century* magazine and reissued in many forms, this four-volume compendium of articles by Union and Confederate officers describing and defending their roles in the various campaigns is uneven and at times inaccurate, but some of the accounts are invaluable.

Among the most useful works by subordinate and staff officers are the eloquent and incisive letters of Colonel Theodore Lyman, a Massachusetts volunteer who served on Meade's staff (173); the papers of Charles Marshall, a member of Lee's staff (185); the diary of Marsena R. Patrick, defender of McClellan and the Army of the Potomac's provost marshal (215); the memoirs of E. Porter Alexander, an excellent critic of operations in the Army of Northern Virginia and one of only three Confederate artillerists to become a general (4); the letters of James A. Garfield, chief of staff in the Army of the Cumberland (105); the candid letters of William Dorsey Pender, who commanded a division in Lee's army and received a mortal wound at Gettysburg (216); the diary of Colonel Charles S. Wainwright, chief of artillery for the Army of the Potomac's I and V Corps (288); the recollections of Samuel G. French, which are particularly helpful on Hood's Tennessee campaign (99); the adventures of Thomas W. Higginson, commander of the first black regiment mustered into the Union service (133); the memoir of Horace Porter, who was Grant's aide from October 1863 until the war's end (219); the recollections of G. Moxley Sorrel, Longstreet's chief of staff (252); and the "inside" account of Walter H. Taylor, of Lee's staff (267).

Four published diaries kept by Union and Confederate government officials are especially important. Gideon Welles's diary (296) is basic for any understanding of the war. This account by Lincoln's Secretary of the Navy is clear, candid, and useful on army as well as naval affairs. Probably the most valuable of all Confederate diaries is John B. Jones's two volumes (149). Jones, a Confederate War Department clerk, recorded military developments clearly, if often impatiently. A condensed, one-volume reissue of the diary, edited by Earl Schenck Miers appeared in 1958 (150). The diary of Robert G. H. Kean (151) is a major account of the Davis government by the Head of the War Bureau. Neither as full nor as gossipy as Jones's journal, Kean's diary is more reliable, more discerning, and better balanced. It is strongly anti-Davis. The diary of Salmon P. Chase, Lincoln's Secretary of the Treasury, covers but sixteen of Lincoln's forty-nine months in office and is often dull reading (44); nevertheless, it is a useful source for military and political information.

Among the better accounts by men in the ranks are John Beatty's journal (17), John Dooley's diary (73), John D. Billings's narrative (21), Carlton McCarthy's memoir (175), and Sam R. Watkins's recollection (293). Beatty's diary is one of the war's best; its author, from Ohio, fought for the Union on the western front. Dooley's little diary gives the best insight into the mind of the average southern soldier. The author's frank account of how a rookie felt when first under fire at Antietam is magnificent. Billings, a Massachusetts artillerist in the Army of the Potomac, penned one of the best descriptions of a soldier's life. McCarthy, a member of the Richmond Howitzer Battalion, wrote one of the most informative and interesting memoirs by a private. Watkins, who was in the Army of Tennessee, is the source for several good anti-Bragg stories. His recollections are lively, frank, full of errors and afterthoughts, but most readable.

Two useful collections of eyewitness accounts are *The Blue and the*

Gray, edited by Henry Steele Commager (52); and *The American Iliad*, edited by Otto Eisenschiml and Ralph G. Newman (91).

Some civilian journals give valuable information on military affairs. Arthur J. L. Fremantle's diary (98) is a charming account by an English officer who managed to meet almost everyone of importance in the Confederacy. Among other adventures, Fremantle was almost shot by Federals in Mississippi, visited Bragg's headquarters in Tennessee, and watched the Battle of Gettysburg from a tree. His account is strongly pro-Confederate. Mary B. Chesnut's diary (45) contains the uninhibited and spicy reflections of a garrulous southern lady whose husband was on Davis's staff. Much space is devoted to military action and commanders. A new and enlarged edition is available (46). The diary of George Templeton Strong (265) is a major source for the entire Civil War era; it reflects not merely the attitudes and ideas of a "proper" New Yorker of the period, but gives significant descriptions, anecdotes, and analyses of local and national events. A surprising amount of space is devoted to military affairs. Volume III covers 1860-1865. Fitzgerald Ross's *Cities and Camps* (234), a complement and a sequel to the Fremantle diary, was also written by a professional soldier with strong southern sympathies.

SUGGESTIONS FOR FURTHER RESEARCH. Despite all that has been written on the military history of the Mexican War and the Civil War, there is still work to be done. A new biography of General Winfield Scott is needed, and several other Mexican War leaders deserve further attention—particularly John A. Quitman and Persifor F. Smith. Civil War General Don Carlos Buell merits a biography; better studies of Generals Philip H. Sheridan and James Longstreet would be welcomed. There is no book length work on tactics for either the Mexican War or the Civil War. Numbers and losses, especially how losses occurred, need additional investigation. More staff studies and analyses of military administration are needed. There are no volumes on Union or Confederate artillery in the West. Nor are there enough good accounts of units and campaigns. Indeed, it is here that some of the most valuable new contributions can be made: the history of many brigades and regiments as well as of many campaigns and battles in both the Mexican War and the Civil War need to be written or rewritten. To be worthwhile, such accounts should combine exhaustive research in the published and unpublished sources with the techniques of quantification and the insights and concerns of the social and military historian.

These suggestions only indicate a few of the possibilities for further research. The topics are almost limitless. The prospects are so exciting, it almost makes one wish that he could start all over again.

BIBLIOGRAPHY

PUBLISHED SOURCES

1. Adams, George Worthington. *Doctors in Blue: The Medical History of the Union Army in the Civil War*. New York: Schuman, 1952.

2. Aimone, Alan Conrad. *The Official Records of the American Civil War: A Researcher's Guide.* West Point: United States Military Academy Library Bulletin No. 11, 1972.

3. Alcaraz, Ramon, and others. *Apuntes Para La Historia de La Guerra entre Mexico y Los Estados Unidos.* Mexico: Payno, 1848, a contemporary translation is Albert C. Ramsey, *The Other Side,* New York: Wiley, 1850.

4. Alexander, Edward Porter. *Military Memoirs of a Confederate.* New ed., Bloomington: Indiana University Press, 1962.

5. Amann, William Frayne, ed. *Personnel of the Civil War.* New York: Yoseloff, 1961. 2 vols.

6. Ambrose, Stephen E. *Halleck: Lincoln's Chief of Staff.* Baton Rouge: Louisiana State University Press, 1962.

7. Ambrose, Stephen E. *Upton and the Army.* Baton Rouge: Louisiana State University Press, 1964.

8. Anderson, Robert. *An Artillery Officer in the Mexican War, 1846-7: Letters of Robert Anderson, Captain, 3rd Artillery, U.S.A.* New York: Putnam's, 1911.

9. Badeau, Adam. *Military History of Ulysses S. Grant, from April, 1861, to April, 1865.* New York: Appleton, 1885. 3 vols.

10. Ballard, Colin Robert. *The Military Genius of Abraham Lincoln.* New ed., Cleveland: World Publishing, 1952.

11. [Ballentine, George]. *Autobiography of an English Soldier in the United States Army. . . .* New York: Stringer and Townsend, 1854.

12. Barbour, Philip Norbourne. *Journals of . . . Brevet Major Philip Norbourne Barbour. . . .* Edited by Rhoda van Bibber Tanner Doubleday. New York: Putnam's, 1936.

13. Barrett, John Gilchrist. *The Civil War in North Carolina.* Chapel Hill: University of North Carolina Press, 1963.

14. Barrett, John Gilchrist. *Sherman's March Through the Carolinas.* Chapel Hill: University of North Carolina Press, 1956.

15. Bauer, K. Jack. *The Mexican War: 1846-1848.* New York: Macmillan, 1974.

16. Baylies, Francis. *A Narrative of Major General Wool's Campaign in Mexico, in the Years 1846, 1847, & 1848.* Albany: Little, 1851.

17. Beatty, John. *The Citizen-Soldier; or, Memoirs of a Volunteer.* Cincinnati: Wilstach, Baldwin, 1879.

18. Beauregard, Pierre Gustave Toutant. *With Beauregard in Mexico: The Mexican War Reminiscences of P. G. T. Beauregard.* Edited by T. Harry Williams. Baton Rouge: Louisiana State University Press, 1956.

19. Bigelow, John. *The Campaign of Chancellorsville: A Strategic and Tactical Study.* New Haven: Yale University Press, 1910.

20. Bill, Alfred Hoyt. *Rehearsal for Conflict: The War with Mexico, 1846-1848.* New York: Knopf, 1947.

21. Billings, John Davis. *Hardtack and Coffee: The Unwritten Story of Army Life.* Edited by Richard Harwell. New ed., Chicago: Donnelley, 1960.

22. Birkhimer, William E. *Historical Sketch of the Organization, Ad-*

ministration, Material and Tactics of the Artillery, United States Army. Washington: Chapman, 1884.
23. Black, Robert C. III. *The Railroads of the Confederacy.* Chapel Hill: University of North Carolina Press, 1952.
24. Boatner, Mark Mayo III. *The Civil War Dictionary.* New York: McKay, 1959.
25. Brewer, James H. *The Confederate Negro: Virginia's Craftsmen and Military Laborers, 1861-1865.* Durham: Duke University Press, 1969.
26. Bridges, Leonard Hal. *Lee's Maverick General, Daniel Harvey Hill.* New York: McGraw-Hill, 1961.
27. Brown, Dee Alexander. *Grierson's Raid.* Urbana: University of Illinois Press, 1954.
28. Brownlee, Richard S. *Gray Ghosts of the Confederacy: Guerrilla Warfare in the West, 1861-1865.* Baton Rouge: Louisiana State University Press, 1958.
29. Bruce, Robert V. *Lincoln and the Tools of War.* Indianapolis: Bobbs-Merrill, 1956.
30. Burne, Alfred H. *Lee, Grant and Sherman: A Study in Leadership in the 1864-65 Campaign.* New York: Scribner's, 1939.
31. Carleton, James Henry. *The Battle of Buena Vista. . . .* New York: Harper, 1848.
32. Carpenter, John Alcott. *Sword and Olive Branch: Oliver Otis Howard.* Pittsburgh: University of Pittsburgh Press, 1964.
33. Carter, Samuel III. *The Siege of Atlanta, 1864.* New York: St. Martin's, 1974.
34. Castel, Albert E. *General Sterling Price and the Civil War in the West.* Baton Rouge: Louisiana State University Press, 1968.
35. Castel, Albert E. *William Clarke Quantrill: His Life and Times.* New York: Fell, 1962.
36. Catton, Bruce. *The Centennial History of the Civil War.* E. B. Long, Director of Research. New York: Doubleday, 1961-1965. 3 vols.
37. Catton, Bruce. *Glory Road: The Bloody Route from Fredericksburg to Gettysburg.* New York: Doubleday, 1952.
38. Catton, Bruce. *Grant Moves South.* Boston: Little, Brown, 1960.
39. Catton, Bruce. *Grant Takes Command.* Boston: Little, Brown, 1969.
40. Catton, Bruce. *Mr. Lincoln's Army.* New York: Doubleday, 1951.
41. Catton, Bruce. *A Stillness at Appomattox.* New York: Doubleday, 1955.
42. Chamberlain, Samuel Emery. *My Confession: The Recollections of a Rogue.* New York: Harper, 1956.
43. Chambers, Lenoir. *Stonewall Jackson.* New York: Morrow, 1959. 2 vols.
44. Chase, Salmon Portland. *Inside Lincoln's Cabinet: The Civil War Diaries of Salmon P. Chase.* Edited by David Herbert Donald. New York: Longmans, Green, 1954.
45. Chesnut, Mary Boykin. *A Diary from Dixie, as Written by Mary Boykin Chesnut. . . .* Edited by Isabella D. Martin and Myrta Lockett Avary. New York: Appleton, 1905.
46. Chesnut, Mary Boykin. *A Diary from Dixie.* Edited by Ben Ames

Williams. Boston: Houghton Mifflin, 1961.
47. Clarke, Dwight L. *Stephen Watts Kearny, Soldier of the West.* Norman: University of Oklahoma Press, 1961.
48. Cleaves, Freeman. *Meade of Gettysburg.* Norman: University of Oklahoma Press, 1960.
49. Cleaves, Freeman. *Rock of Chickamauga: The Life of General George H. Thomas.* Norman: University of Oklahoma Press, 1948.
50. Coddington, Edwin B. *The Gettysburg Campaign: A Study in Command.* New York: Scribner's, 1968.
51. Colton, Ray Charles. *The Civil War in the Western Territories: Arizona, Colorado, New Mexico, and Utah.* Norman: University of Oklahoma Press, 1959.
52. Commager, Henry Steele, ed. *The Blue and the Gray: The Story of the Civil War as Told by Participants.* Indianapolis: Bobbs-Merrill, 1950. 2 vols.
53. Connelly, Thomas Lawrence. *Army of the Heartland: The Army of Tennessee, 1861-1862.* Baton Rouge: Louisiana State University Press, 1967.
54. Connelly, Thomas Lawrence. *Autumn of Glory: The Army of Tennessee, 1862-1865.* Baton Rouge: Louisiana State University Press, 1971.
55. Connelly, Thomas Lawrence, and Archer Jones. *The Politics of Command: Factions and Ideas in Confederate Strategy.* Baton Rouge: Louisiana State University Press, 1973.
56. Connor, Seymour V., and Odie B. Faulk. *North America Divided: The Mexican War, 1846-1848.* New York: Oxford University Press, 1971.
57. Cooke, Philip St. George. *The Conquest of New Mexico and California. . . .* New York: Putnam, 1878.
58. Cornish, Dudley Taylor. *The Sable Arm: Negro Troops in the Union Army, 1861-1865.* New York: Longmans, Green, 1956.
59. Cox, Jacob Dolson. *Atlanta.* New York: Scribner's, 1882.
60. Cox, Jacob Dolson. *The Battle of Franklin, Tennessee, November 30, 1864.* New York: Scribner's, 1897.
61. Cox, Jacob Dolson. *The March to the Sea; Franklin and Nashville.* New York: Scribner's, 1882.
62. Cunningham, Edward. *The Port Hudson Campaign, 1862-1863.* Baton Rouge: Louisiana State University Press, 1963.
63. Cunningham, Horace Herndon. *Doctors in Gray: The Confederate Medical Service.* Baton Rouge: Louisiana State University Press, 1958.
64. Cunningham, Horace Herndon. *Field Medical Service at the Battles of Manassas (Bull Run).* Athens: University of Georgia Press, 1968.
65. Davis, Burke. *To Appomattox: Nine Days, 1865.* New York: Rhinehart, 1959.
66. Davis, Burke. *Jeb Stuart: The Last Cavalier.* New York: Rhinehart, 1957.
67. Davis, Jefferson. *Jefferson Davis, Constitutionalist: His Letters, Papers, and Speeches.* Edited by Dunbar Rowland. Jackson: Mississippi Archives, 1923. 10 vols.

68. Davis, Jefferson. *Jefferson Davis: Private Letters, 1823-1889*. Edited by Hudson Strode. New York: Harcourt, Brace & World, 1956.
69. Davis, Jefferson. *The Papers of Jefferson Davis*. Edited by Haskell M. Monroe, Jr., and James T. McIntosh. Baton Rouge: Louisiana State University Press, 1971- . 1 vol. to date.
70. Davis, Jefferson. *The Rise and Fall of the Confederate Government*. New ed., New York: Yoseloff, 1959. 2 vols.
71. Davis, William C. *Breckinridge: Statesman, Soldier, Symbol*. Baton Rouge: Louisiana State University Press, 1974.
72. Dew, Charles B. *Ironmaker to the Confederacy: Joseph R. Anderson and the Tredegar Iron Works*. New Haven: Yale University Press, 1966.
73. Dooley, John Edward. *John Dooley, Confederate Soldier: His War Journal*. Edited by Joseph T. Durkin. Washington: Georgetown University Press, 1945.
74. Donald, David Herbert, ed. *Divided We Fought: A Pictorial History of the War, 1861-1865*. New York: Macmillan, 1952.
75. Donald, David Herbert. *Lincoln Reconsidered: Essays on the Civil War Era*. New York: Knopf, 1956.
76. Donald, David Herbert, ed. *Why the North Won the Civil War*. Baton Rouge: Louisiana State University Press, 1960.
77. Dornbusch, Charles Emil. *Regimental Publications & Personal Narratives of the Civil War: A Checklist*. New York: New York Public Library, 1961- . 3 vols. to date.
78. Dowdey, Clifford. *Lee*. Boston: Little, Brown, 1965.
79. Dowdey, Clifford. *Lee's Last Campaign: The Story of Lee and His Men Against Grant—1864*. Boston: Little, Brown, 1960.
80. Dowdey, Clifford. *The Seven Days: The Emergence of Lee*. Boston: Little, Brown, 1964.
81. Downey, Fairfax Davis. *Clash of Cavalry: The Battle of Brandy Station, June 9, 1863*. New York: McKay, 1959.
82. Downey, Fairfax Davis. *The Guns of Gettysburg*. New York: McKay, 1958.
83. Downey, Fairfax Davis. *Storming of the Gateway: Chattanooga, 1863*. New York: McKay, 1960.
84. Dufour, Charles L. *The Mexican War: A Compact History*. New York: Hawthorne, 1958.
85. Dufour, Charles L. *The Night the War was Lost*. New York: Doubleday, 1960.
86. Dyer, Brainerd. *Zachary Taylor*. Baton Rouge: Louisiana State University Press, 1946.
87. Dyer, Frederick Henry, ed. *A Compendium of the War of the Rebellion*. New ed., New York: Yoseloff, 1959. 3 vols.
88. Dyer, John Percy. *"Fightin' Joe" Wheeler*. Baton Rouge: Louisiana State University Press, 1941.
89. Dyer, John Percy. *The Gallant Hood*. Indianapolis: Bobbs-Merrill, 1950.
90. Early, Jubal Anderson. *War Memoirs: Autobiographical Sketch and Narrative of the War Between the States*. Edited by Frank E. Vandiver. New ed., Bloomington: Indiana University Press, 1960.

91. Eisenschiml, Otto, and Ralph G. Newman, eds. *The American Iliad: The Epic Story of the Civil War as Narrated by Eyewitnesses and Contemporaries.* Indianapolis: Bobbs-Merrill, 1947.
92. Eisenschiml, Otto. *The Story of Shiloh.* Chicago: Norman Press, 1946.
93. Elliott, Charles Winslow. *Winfield Scott: The Soldier and the Man.* New York: Macmillan, 1937.
94. Evans, Clement Anselm, ed. *Confederate Military History: A Library of Confederate State History . . . Written by Distinguished Men of the South.* Atlanta: Confederate Publishing, 1899. 12 vols.
95. Fox, William Freeman. *Regimental Losses in the American Civil War, 1861-1865.* Albany, New York: Albany Publishing, 1889.
96. Freeman, Douglas Southall. *Lee's Lieutenants: A Study in Command.* New York: Scribner's, 1942-1944. 3 vols.
97. Freeman, Douglas Southall. *R. E. Lee: A Biography.* New York: Scribner's, 1934. 4 vols.
98. Fremantle, Sir Arthur James Lyon. *Three Months in the Southern States: April-June, 1863.* New York: Bradburn, 1864.
99. French, Samuel G. *Two Wars: An Autobiography.* Nashville: Confederate Veteran, 1901.
100. Fry, James Barnet. *Operations of the Army Under Buell from June 10th to October 30th, 1862, and the "Buell Commission."* New York: Van Nostrand, 1884.
101. Fuller, John Frederick Charles. *The Generalship of Ulysses S. Grant.* New York: Dodd, Mead, 1929.
102. Fuller, John Frederick Charles. *Grant & Lee, a Study in Personality and Generalship.* London: Eyre and Spottiswoods, 1933.
103. Furber, George C. *The Twelve Months Volunteer; Or, Journal of a Private in the Tennessee Regiment of Cavalry in the Campaign in Mexico, 1846-7.* Cincinnati: J. A. & U. P. James, 1848.
104. Futch, Ovid L. *History of Andersonville.* Gainesville: University of Florida Press, 1968.
105. Garfield, James Abram. *The Wild Life of the Army: Civil War Letters of James A. Garfield.* Edited by Frederick D. Williams. East Lansing: Michigan State University Press, 1964.
106. [Giddings, Luther]. *Sketches of the Campaign in Northern Mexico . . . By an Officer of the First Ohio Volunteers.* New York: Putnam, 1853.
107. Goetzmann, William H. *Army Exploration in the American West, 1803-1863.* New Haven: Yale University Press, 1959.
108. Goff, Richard D. *Confederate Supply.* Durham: Duke University Press, 1969.
109. Govan, Gilbert E., and James W. Livingood. *A Different Valor: The Story of General Joseph E. Johnston, C.S.A.* Indianapolis: Bobbs-Merrill, 1956.
110. Grant, Ulysses S. *The Papers of Ulysses S. Grant.* Edited by John Y. Simon. Carbondale: Southern Illinois University Press, 1967- . 5 vols to date.
111. Grant, Ulysses S. *Personal Memoirs of U.S. Grant.* New York: Webster, 1885. 2 vols.

112. Grant, Ulysses S. *Personal Memoirs of U.S. Grant.* Edited by E. B. Long. Cleveland: World Publishing, 1952.
113. Hall, Martin Hardwick. *Sibley's New Mexico Campaign.* Austin: University of Texas Press, 1960.
114. Halleck, Henry Wager. *Elements of Military Art and Science; Or, Course of Instruction in Strategy, Fortification, Tactics of Battles, & C., Embracing the Duties of Staff, Infantry, Cavalry, Artillery, and Engineers.* New York: Appleton, 1846.
115. Hamilton, Holman. *Zachary Taylor: Soldier of the Republic.* Indianapolis: Bobbs-Merrill, 1941.
116. Hamilton, James J. *The Battle of Fort Donelson.* New York: Yoseloff, 1968.
117. Hamlin, Percy Gatlin. *"Old Bald Head" (General R. S. Ewell): The Portrait of a Soldier.* Strasburg, Virginia: Shenandoah, 1940.
118. Harrington, Fred Harvey. *Fighting Politician: Major General N. P. Banks.* Philadelphia: University of Pennsylvania Press, 1948.
119. Hartje, Robert G. *Van Dorn: The Life and Times of a Confederate General.* Nashville: Vanderbilt University Press, 1967.
120. Hassler, Warren W., Jr. *Commanders of the Army of the Potomac.* Baton Rouge: Louisiana State University Press, 1962.
121. Hassler, Warren W., Jr. *Crisis at the Crossroads: The First Day at Gettysburg.* University: University of Alabama Press, 1970.
122. Hassler, Warren W., Jr. *General George B. McClellan: Shield of the Union.* Baton Rouge: Louisiana State University Press, 1957.
123. Hassler, William Woods. *A. P. Hill: Lee's Forgotten General.* Richmond: Garrett & Massie, 1957.
124. Hay, Thomas Robson. *Hood's Tennessee Campaign.* New York: Neale, 1929.
125. Haydon, Frederick Stansburg. *Aeronautics in the Union and Confederate Armies, with a Survey of Military Aeronautics Prior to 1861.* Baltimore: Johns Hopkins University Press, 1941.
126. Hebert, Walter H. *Fighting Joe Hooker.* Indianapolis: Bobbs-Merrill, 1944.
127. Henderson, George Francis Robert. *The Civil War: A Soldier's View; a Collection of Civil War Writings.* Edited by Jay Luvaas. Chicago: University of Chicago Press, 1958.
128. Henderson, George Francis Robert. *Stonewall Jackson and the American Civil War.* London: Longmans, Green, 1898. 2 vols.
129. Henry, Robert S. *"First with the Most" Forrest.* Indianapolis: Bobbs-Merrill, 1944.
130. Henry, Robert S. *The Story of the Mexican War.* Indianapolis: Bobbs-Merrill, 1950.
131. Henry, William Seaton. *Campaign Sketches of the War with Mexico.* New York: Harper, 1847.
132. Hesseltine, William Best. *Civil War Prisons: A Study in War Psychology.* Columbus: Ohio State University Press, 1930.
133. Higginson, Thomas Wentworth. *Army Life in a Black Regiment.* New ed., Boston: Houghton, Mifflin, 1900.
134. Hitchcock, Ethan Allen. *Fifty Years in Camp and Field: Diary of . . . Ethan Allen Hitchcock. . . .* Edited by W. A. Croffut. New York: Putnam, 1909.

135. Holland, Cecil Fletcher. *Morgan and His Raiders: A Biography of the Confederate General.* New York: Macmillan, 1942.
136. Hood, John Bell. *Advance and Retreat: Personal Experiences in the United States & Confederate States Armies.* New ed., Bloomington: Indiana University Press, 1959.
137. Horn, Stanley Fitzgerald. *The Army of Tennessee.* Norman: University of Oklahoma Press, 1953.
138. Horn, Stanley Fitzgerald. *The Decisive Battle of Nashville.* Baton Rouge: Louisiana State University Press, 1956.
139. Hughes, John Taylor. *Doniphan's Expedition.* Cincinnati: James, 1848.
140. Hughes, Nathaniel Cheairs, Jr. *General William J. Hardee, Old Reliable.* Baton Rouge: Louisiana State University Press, 1965.
141. Jackson, W. Turrentine. *Wagon Roads West: A Study of Federal Road Surveys and Construction in the Trans-Mississippi West, 1846-1869.* Berkeley: University of California Press, 1952.
142. Johnson, Ludwell H. *Red River Campaign: Politics and Cotton in the Civil War.* Baltimore: Johns Hopkins Press, 1958.
143. Johnson, Robert Underwood, and Clarence Clough Buel, eds. *Battles and Leaders of the Civil War: Being for the Most Part Contributions by Union and Confederate Officers.* New ed., New York: Yoseloff, 1956. 4 vols.
144. Johnston, Angus James II. *Virginia Railroads in the Civil War.* Chapel Hill: University of North Carolina Press, 1961.
145. Johnston, Joseph Eggleston. *Narrative of Military Operations Directed, During the Late War Between the States.* New ed., Bloomington: Indiana University Press, 1959.
146. Johnston, Robert Matteson. *Bull Run: Its Strategy and Tactics.* Boston: Houghton, Mifflin, 1913.
147. Jones, Archer. *Confederate Strategy from Shiloh to Vicksburg.* Baton Rouge: Louisiana State University Press, 1961.
148. Jones, James P. *"Black Jack": John A. Logan and Southern Illinois in the Civil War.* Tallahassee: Florida State University Press, 1967.
149. Jones, John Beauchamp. *A Rebel War Clerk's Diary at the Confederate States Capital.* Philadelphia: Lippincott, 1866. 2 vols.
150. Jones, John Beauchamp. *A Rebel War Clerk's Diary.* Edited by Earl Schenck Miers. New York: Sagamore Press, 1958.
151. Kean, Robert Garlick Hill. *Inside the Confederate Government: The Diary of Robert Garlick Hill Kean, Head of the Bureau of War.* Edited by Edward Younger. New York: Oxford, 1957.
152. Kenly, John Reese. *Memoirs of a Maryland Volunteer.* Philadelphia: Lippincott, 1873.
153. Kerby, Robert L. *Kirby Smith's Confederacy: The Trans-Mississippi South, 1863-1865.* New York: Columbia University Press, 1972.
154. Key, William. *The Battle of Atlanta and the Georgia Campaign.* New York: Twayne, 1958.
155. Klein, Maury, *Edward Porter Alexander.* Athens: University of Georgia Press, 1971.
156. Lamers, William M. *The Edge of Glory: A Biography of General William S. Rosecrans, U.S.A.* New York: Harcourt, Brace, 1961.
157. Lavender, David Sievert. *Climax at Buena Vista: The American*

Campaigns in Northeastern Mexico, 1846-1847. Philadelphia: Lippincott, 1966.

158. Lee, Robert Edward. *Lee's Dispatches: Unpublished Letters of General Robert E. Lee, C.S.A. to Jefferson Davis and the War Department of the Confederate States of America, 1862-65.* Edited by Douglas S. Freeman and Grady McWhiney. New York: Putnam's, 1957.

159. Lee, Robert Edward. *The Wartime Papers of R. E. Lee.* Edited by Clifford Dowdey and Louis H. Manarin. Boston: Little, Brown, 1961.

160. Lewis, Lloyd. *Captain Sam Grant.* Boston: Little, Brown, 1950.

161. Lewis, Lloyd. *Sherman: Fighting Prophet.* New York: Harcourt, Brace, 1932.

162. Liddell Hart, Basil Henry. *Sherman: Soldier, Realist, American.* New York: Dodd, Mead, 1929.

163. Lincoln, Abraham. *The Collected Works of Abraham Lincoln.* Edited by Roy P. Basler. New Brunswick: Rutgers University Press, 1953. 9 vols.

164. Lincoln, Abraham. *The Collected Works of Abraham Lincoln: Supplement, 1832-1865.* Edited by Roy P. Basler. Westport, Connecticut: Greenwood, 1974.

165. Livermore, Thomas Leonard. *Numbers and Losses in the Civil War in America, 1861-65.* New ed., Bloomington: Indiana University Press, 1957.

166. Long, Everette Beach, with Barbara Long. *The Civil War Day by Day: An Almanac, 1861-1865.* New York: Doubleday, 1971.

167. Longacre, Edward G. *From Union Stars to Top Hat: A Biography of the Extraordinary General James Harrison Wilson.* Harrisburg: Stackpole, 1972.

168. Longstreet, James. *From Manassas to Appomattox: Memoirs of the Civil War in America.* Edited by James I. Robertson, Jr. New ed., Bloomington: Indiana University Press, 1960.

169. Lonn, Ella. *Desertion During the Civil War.* New York: Century, 1928.

170. Lord, Francis A. *Lincoln's Railroad Man: Herman Haupt.* Rutherford: Fairleigh Dickinson University Press, 1969.

171. Luvaas, Jay. *The Education of an Army: British Military Thought, 1815-1940.* Chicago: University of Chicago Press, 1964.

172. Luvaas, Jay. *The Military Legacy of the Civil War.* Chicago: University of Chicago Press, 1959.

173. Lyman, Theodore. *Meade's Headquarters, 1863-1865: Letters of Colonel Theodore Lyman from the Wilderness to Appomattox.* Edited by George R. Agassiz. Boston: Atlantic, 1922.

174. McCall, George Archibald. *Letters from the Frontiers. . . .* Philadelphia: Lippincott, 1868.

175. McCarthy, Carlton. *Detailed Minutiae of Soldier Life in the Army of Northern Virginia, 1861-1865.* Richmond: McCarthy, 1882.

176. McClellan, George Brinton. *McClellan's Own Story: The War for the Union, the Soldiers Who Fought It, the Civilians Who Directed It and His Relations to It and to Them.* New York: Webster, 1886.

177. McClellan, George Brinton. *The Mexican War Diary of George B.*

McClellan. Edited by William Starr Myers. Princeton: Princeton University Press, 1917.

178. McDonough, James L. *Schofield: Union General in the Civil War and Reconstruction.* Tallahassee: Florida State University Press, 1972.

179. McKinney, Francis F. *Education in Violence: The Life of George H. Thomas and the History of the Army of the Cumberland.* Detroit: Wayne State University Press, 1961.

180. McWhiney, Grady. *Braxton Bragg and Confederate Defeat: Field Command.* New York: Columbia University Press, 1969.

181. McWhiney, Grady, ed. *Grant, Lee, Lincoln and the Radicals: Essays on Civil War Leadership.* Evanston: Northwestern University Press, 1964.

182. McWhiney, Grady, and Sue McWhiney, eds. *To Mexico with Taylor and Scott, 1845-1847.* Waltham, Mass.: Blaisdell, 1969.

183. McWhiney, Grady. *Southerners and Other Americans.* New York: Basic Books, 1973.

184. Mahan, Dennis Hart. *A Complete Treatise on Field Fortification, with the General Outline of the Principles Regulating the Arrangement, the Attack, and the Defense of Permanent Works.* New York: Wiley & Long, 1836.

185. Marshall, Charles. *An Aide-de-Camp of Lee, being the Papers of Colonel Charles Marshall, Sometime Aide-de-Camp, Military Secretary, and Assistant Adjutant General on the Staff of Robert E. Lee, 1862-1865.* Edited by Sir Frederick Maurice. Boston: Little, Brown, 1927.

186. Maurice, Sir Frederick Barton. *Statesmen and Soldiers of the Civil War: A Study of the Conduct of War.* Boston: Little, Brown, 1926.

187. Maury, Dabney Herndon. *Recollections of a Virginian in the Mexican, Indian, and Civil Wars.* New York: Scribner's, 1894.

188. Maxwell, William Quentin. *Lincoln's Fifth Wheel: The Political History of the United States Sanitary Commission.* New York: Longmans, Green, 1956.

189. Meade, George Gordon. *The Life and Letters of George Gordon Meade. . . .* Edited by George Gordon Meade. New York: Scribner's, 1913. 2 vols.

190. Meneely, Alexander Howard. *The War Department, 1861: A Study in Mobilization and Administration.* New York: Columbia University Press, 1928.

191. Merrill, James M. *William Tecumseh Sherman.* Chicago: Rand McNally, 1971.

192. Miers, Earl Schenck. *The Web of Victory: Grant at Vicksburg.* New York: Knopf, 1955.

193. Miller, Francis Trevelyan, ed. *The Photographic History of the Civil War.* New ed., New York: Yoseloff, 1957. 10 vols.

194. Monaghan, James. *Civil War on the Western Border, 1854-1865.* Boston: Little, Brown, 1955.

195. Moore, Albert Burton. *Conscription and Conflict in the Confederacy.* New York: Macmillan, 1924.

196. Moore, H. Judge. *Scott's Campaign in Mexico. . . .* Charleston: Nixon, 1849.

197. Munden, Kenneth W., and Henry Putney Beers. *Guide to Federal Archives Relating to the Civil War*. Washington: National Archives, 1962.
198. Murdock, Eugene C. *One Million Men: The Civil War Draft in the North*. Madison: State Historical Society of Wisconsin, 1971.
199. Murfin, James V. *The Gleam of Bayonets: The Battle of Antietam and the Maryland Campaign of 1862*. New York: Yoseloff, 1965.
200. Naisawald, L. Van Loan. *Grape and Canister: The Story of the Field Artillery of the Army of the Potomac, 1861-1865*. New York: Oxford University Press, 1960.
201. Nevins, Allan, James I. Robertson, Jr., and Bell I. Wiley, eds. *Civil War Books: A Critical Bibliography*. Baton Rouge: Louisiana State University Press, 1967. 2 vols.
202. Nevins, Allan. *Fremont: Pathmaker of the West*. New York: Longmans, Green, 1939.
203. Nichols, Edward Jay. *Toward Gettysburg: A Biography of General John F. Reynolds*. University Park: Pennsylvania State University Press, 1958.
204. Nichols, Edward Jay. *Zach Taylor's Little Army*. New York: Doubleday, 1963.
205. Nichols, James Lynn. *Confederate Engineers*. Tuscaloosa, Alabama: Confederate Publishing, 1957.
206. Nichols, James Lynn. *The Confederate Quartermaster in the Trans-Mississippi*. Austin: University of Texas Press, 1964.
207. Nicolay, John George, and John Hay. *Abraham Lincoln: A History*. New York: Century, 1890. 10 vols.
208. Nolan, Alan T. *The Iron Brigade: A Military History*. New York: Macmillan, 1961.
209. Nye, Wilbur Sturtevant. *Here Come the Rebels!* Baton Rouge: Louisiana State University Press, 1965.
210. Oates, Stephen E. *Confederate Cavalry West of the River*. Austin: University of Texas Press, 1961.
211. O'Connor, Richard. *Sheridan, the Inevitable*. Indianapolis: Bobbs-Merrill, 1953.
212. Oswandel, J. Jacob. *Notes on the Mexican War, 1846-48*. Philadelphia: The author, 1885.
213. Parks, Joseph Howard. *General Edmund Kirby Smith, C.S.A.* Baton Rouge: Louisiana State University Press, 1954.
214. Parks, Joseph Howard. *General Leonidas Polk, C.S.A.: The Fighting Bishop*. Baton Rouge: Louisiana State University Press, 1962.
215. Patrick, Marsena Rudolph. *Inside Lincoln's Army: The Diary of Marsena Rudolph Patrick, Provost Marshal General, Army of the Potomac*. Edited by David S. Sparks. New York: Yoseloff, 1964.
216. Pender, William Dorsey. *The General to His Lady: The Civil War Letters of William Dorsey Pender to Fanny Pender*. Edited by William W. Hassler. Chapel Hill: University of North Carolina Press, 1965.
217. Peterson, Harold Leslie. *Notes on Ordnance of the American Civil War, 1861-1865*. Washington: American Ordnance Association, 1959.
218. Polk, James K. *The Diary of James K. Polk, During His Presi-*

dency. Edited by Milo M. Quaife. Chicago: McClurg, 1910. 4 vols.
219. Porter, Horace. *Campaigning with Grant.* Edited by Wayne C. Temple. New ed., Bloomington: Indiana University Press, 1961.
220. Powell, John W. *Yankee Cavalrymen: Through the Civil War with the Ninth Pennsylvania Cavalry.* Knoxville: University of Tennessee Press, 1971.
221. Pullen, John J. *The Twentieth Maine: A Volunteer Regiment in the Civil War.* Philadelphia: Lippincott, 1957.
222. Purdue, Howell, and Elizabeth Purdue. *Pat Cleburne, Confederate General: A Definitive Biography.* Hillsboro, Texas: Hill Jr. College Press, 1973.
223. Randall, James Garfield, and David Herbert Donald. *The Civil War and Reconstruction.* Lexington, Massachusetts: Heath, 1969.
224. Randall, James Garfield. *Lincoln the President.* New York: Dodd, Mead, 1945-55. 4 vols.
225. Reid, Samuel Chester. *The Scouting Expeditions of McCulloch's Texas Rangers. . . .* Philadelphia: Zieber, 1848.
226. Ridley, Bromfield Lewis. *Battles and Sketches of the Army of Tennessee.* Mexico, Missouri: Missouri Printing, 1906.
227. Ripley, Roswell Sabine. *War with Mexico.* New York: Harper, 1849. 2 vols.
228. Robertson, James I., Jr. *The Stonewall Brigade.* Baton Rouge: Louisiana State University Press, 1963.
229. Rodick, Burleigh Cushing. *Appomattox: The Last Campaign.* New York: Philosophical Library, 1965.
230. Roland, Charles Pierce. *Albert Sidney Johnston: Soldier of Three Republics.* Austin: University of Texas Press, 1964.
231. Roman, Alfred. *The Military Operations of General Beauregard in the War Between the States, 1861 to 1865; Including a Brief Personal Sketch and a Narrative of His Services in the War with Mexico, 1846-8.* New York: Harper, 1884.
232. Ropes, John Codman. *The Army under Pope.* New York: Scribner's, 1881.
233. Ropes, John Codman, and W. R. Livermore. *The Story of the Civil War: A Concise Account of the War in the United States of America Between 1861 and 1865.* New York: Putnam's, 1894-1913. 4 vols.
234. Ross, Fitzgerald. *Cities and Camps of the Confederate States.* Edited by Richard Barksdale Harwell. New ed., Urbana: University of Illinois Press, 1958.
235. Sanger, Donald Bridgman, and Thomas Robson Hay. *James Longstreet: Soldier, Politician, Officeholder, and Writer.* Baton Rouge: Louisiana State University Press, 1952.
236. Schenck, Martin. *Up Came Hill: The Story of the Light Division and Its Leaders.* Harrisburg, Pennsylvania: Stackpole, 1958.
237. Scott, Winfield. *Infantry Tactics; Or, Rules for the Exercise and Manoeuvers of the United States Infantry.* New York: Harper, 1846. 3 vols.
238. Scott, Winfield. *Memoirs of Lieutenant General Scott. . . .* New York: Sheldon, 1864. 2 vols.

239. Sedgwick, John. *Correspondence of J. Sedgwick.* New York: Battel, 1903. 2 vols.
240. Semmes, Raphael. *The Campaign of General Scott in the Valley of Mexico.* Cincinnati: Moore & Anderson, 1852.
241. Shalhope, Robert E. *Sterling Price: Portrait of a Southerner.* Columbia: University of Missouri Press, 1971.
242. Shannon, Fred Albert. *The Organization and Administration of the Union Army, 1861-1865.* Cleveland: Clark, 1928. 2 vols.
243. Sheridan, Philip Henry. *Personal Memoirs of Philip Henry Sheridan, General, United States Army.* New ed., New York: Appleton, 1902. 2 vols.
243a. Sherman, William Tecumseh. *Home Letters of General Sherman.* Edited by M. A. De Wolfe Howe. New York: Scribner's, 1909.
243b. Sherman, William Tecumseh. *Memoirs of General William T. Sherman.* New York: Appleton, 1875. 2 vols.
243c. Sherman, William Tecumseh. *The Sherman Letters: Correspondence Between General and Senator Sherman from 1837 to 1891.* Edited by Rachel Sherman Thorndike. New York: Scribner's, 1894.
244. Simpson, Harold B. *Hood's Texas Brigade: Lee's Grenadier Guard.* Waco: Texian Press, 1970.
245. Singletary, Otis A. *The Mexican War.* Chicago: University of Chicago Press, 1960.
246. Smith, Arthur D. Howden. *Old Fuss and Feathers: Life and Exploits of Lieutenant General Winfield Scott.* New York: Greystone Press, 1937.
247. Smith, Ephraim Kirby. *To Mexico with Scott: Letters of Captain E. Kirby Smith to His Wife.* Cambridge: Harvard University Press, 1917.
248. Smith, George Winston, and Charles Judah, eds. *Chronicles of the Gringos: The U.S. Army in the Mexican War, 1846-1848.* Albuquerque: University of New Mexico Press, 1968.
249. Smith, George Winston. *Medicines for the Union Army: The United States Army Laboratories During the Civil War.* Madison, Wisconsin: American Institute of the History of Pharmacy, 1962.
250. Smith, Justin H. *The War with Mexico.* New York: Macmillan, 1919. 2 vols.
251. Sommers, Richard J. *Manuscript Holdings of the Military History Research Collection. Special Bibliography No. 6, Part I.* Carlisle Barracks, Pennsylvania: U.S. Army Military History Research Collection, 1972.
252. Sorrel, Gilbert Moxley. *Recollections of a Confederate Staff Officer.* Edited by Bell I. Wiley. New ed., Jackson, Tennessee: McCowat-Mercer, 1958.
253. Stackpole, Edward James. *From Cedar Mountain to Antietam, August-September, 1862: Cedar Mountain, Second Manassas, Chantilly, Harpers Ferry, South Mountain, Antietam.* Harrisburg: Stackpole, 1959.
254. Stackpole, Edward James. *Sheridan in the Shenandoah; Jubal Early's Nemesis.* Harrisburg: Stackpole, 1961.

255. Starr, Stephen Z. *Jennison's Jayhawkers: A Civil War Cavalry Regiment and Its Commander.* Baton Rouge: Louisiana State University Press, 1973.
256. Steere, Edward. *The Wilderness Campaign.* Harrisburg: Stackpole, 1960.
257. Steiner, Paul Eby. *Disease in the Civil War: Natural Biological Warfare in 1861-1865.* Springfield, Illinois: Charles C Thomas, 1968.
258. Steiner, Paul Eby. *Medical-Military Portraits of Union and Confederate Generals.* Philadelphia: Whitmore Publishing, 1968.
259. Steiner, Paul Eby. *Physician-Generals in the Civil War: A Study in Nineteenth Mid-Century American Medicine.* Springfield, Illinois: Charles C Thomas, 1966.
260. Stevens, Hazard. *The Life of Isaac Ingalls Stevens.* Boston: Houghton, Mifflin, 1900. 2 vols.
261. Stevens, Isaac Ingalls. *Campaigns of the Rio Grand and of Mexico, with Notices of the Recent Work of Major Ripley.* New York: Appleton, 1851.
262. Stevenson, Alexander F. *The Battle of Stone's River. . . .* Boston: Osgood, 1884.
263. Stewart, George Rippey. *Pickett's Charge: A Microhistory of the Final Attack at Gettysburg, July 3, 1863.* Boston: Houghton, Mifflin, 1959.
264. Strode, Hudson. *Jefferson Davis.* New York: Harcourt, Brace, 1955-1964. 3 vols.
265. Strong, George Templeton. *The Diary of George Templeton Strong.* Edited by Allan Nevins and Milton Halsey Thomas. New York: Macmillan, 1952. 4 vols.
266. Taylor, Richard. *Destruction and Reconstruction: Personal Experiences of the Late War.* Edited by Charles P. Roland. New ed., Waltham, Massachusetts: Blaisdell, 1968.
267. Taylor, Walter Herron. *Four Years with General Lee.* Edited by James I. Robertson, Jr. New ed., Bloomington: Indiana University Press, 1962.
268. Taylor, Zachary. *Letters of Zachary Taylor, From the Battlefields of the Mexican War. . . .* Edited by William H. Samson. Rochester, New York: Genessee, 1908.
269. Thomas, Benjamin P., and Harold M. Hyman. *Stanton: The Life and Times of Lincoln's Secretary of War.* New York: Knopf, 1962.
270. Thomason, John William. *Jeb Stuart.* New York: Scribner's, 1930.
271. Thorpe, Thomas Bangs. *Our Army at Monterey. . . .* Philadelphia: Carey and Hart, 1847.
272. Thorpe, Thomas Bangs. *Our Army on the Rio Grande.* Philadelphia: Carey and Hart, 1846.
273. Tucker, Glenn. *Chickamauga: Bloody Battle in the West.* Indianapolis: Bobbs-Merrill, 1961.
274. Tucker, Glenn. *Hancock the Superb.* Indianapolis: Bobbs-Merrill, 1960.
275. Tucker, Glenn. *High Tide at Gettysburg: The Campaign in Pennsylvania.* Bobbs-Merrill, 1958.

276. Tucker, Glenn. *Lee and Longstreet at Gettysburg*. Indianapolis: Bobbs-Merrill, 1968.

277. Turner, George Edgar. *Victory Rode the Rails: The Strategic Place of the Railroads in the Civil War*. Indianapolis: Bobbs-Merrill, 1953.

278. U.S. Military Academy, West Point. *The West Point Atlas of the Civil War*. Edited by Vincent J. Esposito. New York: Praeger, 1962.

279. U.S. War Department. *Cavalry Tactics*. Washington: Gideon, 1841. 3 vols.

280. U.S. War Department. *The Official Atlas of the Civil War*. New ed., New York: Yoseloff, 1958.

281. U.S. War Department. *The War of the Rebellion: A Compilation of the Official Records of the Union and Confederate Armies*. Washington: G. P. O., 1880-1901. 128 vols.

282. Utley, Robert M. *Frontiersmen in Blue: The United States Army and the Indian, 1848-1865*. New York: Macmillan, 1967.

283. Vandiver, Frank Everson. *Jubal's Raid: General Early's Famous Attack on Washington in 1864*. New York: McGraw-Hill, 1960.

284. Vandiver, Frank Everson. *Mighty Stonewall*. New York: McGraw-Hill, 1957.

285. Vandiver, Frank Everson. *Ploughshares into Swords: Josiah Gorgas and Confederate Ordnance*. Austin: University of Texas Press, 1952.

286. Vandiver, Frank Everson. *Rebel Brass: The Confederate Command System*. Baton Rouge: Louisiana State University Press, 1956.

287. Vandiver, Frank Everson. *Their Tattered Flags: The Epic of the Confederacy*. New York: Harper's Magazine Press, 1970.

288. Wainwright, Charles Shiels. *A Diary of Battle: The Personal Journals of Colonel Charles S. Wainwright, 1861-1865*. Edited by Allan Nevins. New York: Harcourt, Brace & World, 1962.

289. Walker, Peter Franklin. *Vicksburg: A People at War, 1860-1865*. Chapel Hill: University of North Carolina Press, 1960.

290. Wallace, Edward S. *General William Jenkins Worth: Monterey's Forgotten Hero*. Dallas: Southern Methodist University Press, 1953.

291. Warner, Ezra J. *Generals in Blue: Lives of Union Commanders*. Baton Rouge: Louisiana State University Press, 1964.

292. Warner, Ezra J. *Generals in Gray: Lives of Confederate Commanders*. Baton Rouge: Louisiana State University Press, 1959.

293. Watkins, Samuel R. *"Co. Aytch," Maury Grays, First Tennessee Regiment; Or, A Side Show of the Big Show*. New ed., Jackson, Tennessee: McCowat-Mercer, 1952.

294. Weigley, Russell Frank. *The American Way of War: A History of United States Military Strategy and Policy*. New York: Macmillan, 1973.

295. Weighley, Russell Frank. *Quartermaster General of the Union Army: A Biography of M. C. Meigs*. New York: Columbia University Press, 1959.

296. Welles, Gideon. *Diary*. Edited by Howard K. Beale. New ed., New York: Norton, 1960. 3 vols.

297. Whan, Vorin E. *Fiasco at Fredericksburg.* University Park: Pennsylvania State University Press, 1961.
298. White, Leonard D. *The Jacksonians: A Study in Administrative History. 1829-1861.* New York: Macmillan, 1954.
299. Wilcox, Cadmus Marcellus. *History of the Mexican War.* Edited by Mary Rachel Wilcox. Washington: Church News, 1892.
300. Wiley, Bell Irvin. *The Life of Billy Yank: The Common Soldier of the Union.* Indianapolis: Bobbs-Merrill, 1951.
301. Wiley, Bell Irvin. *The Life of Johnny Reb: The Common Soldier of the Confederacy.* Indianapolis: Bobbs-Merrill, 1943.
302. Williams, Kenneth Powers. *Lincoln Finds a General: A Military Study of the Civil War.* New York: Macmillan, 1949-59. 5 vols.
303. Williams, Thomas Harry. *Lincoln and His Generals.* New York: Knopf, 1952.
304. Williams, Thomas Harry. *McClellan, Sherman, and Grant.* New Brunswick: Rutgers University Press, 1962.
305. Williams, Thomas Harry. *P. G. T. Beauregard: Napoleon in Gray.* Baton Rouge: Louisiana State University Press, 1955.
306. Wise, Jennings C. *The Long Arm of Lee; Or, the History of the Artillery of the Army of Northern Virginia.* Lynchburg: Bell, 1915. 2 vols.
307. Wood, Walter Birkbeck, and James E. Edmonds. *A History of the Civil War in the United States, 1861-5.* New York: Putnam's, 1905.

UNPUBLISHED SOURCES
308. Anderson, Robert, Papers. Library of Congress, Washington, D.C.
309. Army, Army of Mexico, First Division, Second Brigade, Papers. Military History Research Collection, Carlisle Barracks, Pennsylvania.
310. Beauregard, Pierre Gustave Toutant, Papers. Duke University, Durham, North Carolina.
311. Beauregard, Pierre Gustave Toutant, Papers, Library of Congress, Washington, D.C.
312. Bragg, Braxton, Papers. William P. Palmer Collection, Western Reserve Historical Society, Cleveland, Ohio.
313. Campbell, John, Correspondence. University of Virginia, Charlottesville.
314. Cheatham, Benjamin Franklin, Papers. Tennessee State Library, Nashville.
315. Davis, Jefferson, Papers. Chicago Historical Society.
316. Davis, Jefferson, Papers. Duke University, Durham, North Carolina.
317. Davis, Jefferson, Papers. Library of Congress, Washington, D.C.
318. Duncan, James, Papers. Military History Research Collection, Carlisle Barracks, Pennsylvania.
319. Duncan, James, Papers. United States Military Academy, West Point, New York.
320. Ewell, Richard Stoddert, Papers. Library of Congress, Washington, D.C.
321. French, Samuel G., Papers. United States Military Academy, West Point, New York.

322. Grant, Ulysses S., Papers. Library of Congress, Washington, D.C.
323. Halleck, Henry Wager, Papers. Library of Congress, Washington, D.C.
324. Hatheway Family Papers. Cornell University, Ithaca, New York.
325. Hatch, John Porter, Papers. Library of Congress, Washington, D.C.
326. Hitchcock, Ethan Allen, Papers. Library of Congress, Washington, D.C.
327. Hooker, Joseph, Papers. Henry E. Huntington Library, San Marino, California.
328. Infantry, 1st Regiment, Papers. Military History Research Collection, Carlisle Barracks, Pennsylvania.
329. Jackson, Thomas Jonathan, Papers. Library of Congress, Washington, D.C.
330. Jesup, Thomas Sidney, Papers. Library of Congress, Washington, D.C.
331. Johnston, Albert Sidney, and William Preston Johnston, Papers. Mrs. Mason Barret Collection, Tulane University, New Orleans, Louisiana.
332. Johnston, Joseph Eggleston, Papers. Duke University, Durham, North Carolina.
333. Johnston, Joseph Eggleston, Papers. College of William and Mary, Williamsburg, Virginia.
334. Johnston, Joseph Eggleston, Papers. Henry E. Huntington Library, San Marino, California.
335. Lee, Robert and Custis, Papers. Military History Research Collection, Carlisle Barracks, Pennsylvania.
336. Lee, Robert Edward, Letters. University of Virginia, Charlottesville.
337. Lee, Robert E., Family Papers. DeButts-Ely Collection, Library of Congress, Washington, D.C.
338. Lee, Robert Edward, Papers. Virginia Historical Society, Richmond.
339. Lincoln, Abraham, Papers. Library of Congress, Washington, D.C.
340. McClellan, George Brinton, Papers. Library of Congress, Washington, D.C.
341. Mackall, William Whann, Papers. Southern Historical Collection, University of North Carolina, Chapel Hill.
342. Marcy, William L., Papers. Library of Congress, Washington, D.C.
343. Meade, George Gordon, Papers. Historical Society of Pennsylvania, Philadelphia.
344. Pruyn, Olivia S. T., Family Papers. Cornell University, Ithaca, New York.
345. Quitman, John Anthony, Papers. Mississippi Department of Archives and History, Jackson.
346. Rains, George Washington, Papers. Southern Historical Collection, University of North Carolina, Chapel Hill.
347. Record Group 77, Records of the Office of the Chief of Engineers. National Archives, Washington, D.C.
348. Record Group 92, Records of the Office of the Quartermaster General. National Archives, Washington, D.C.

349. Record Group 94, Records of the Adjutant General's Office. National Archives, Washington, D.C.
350. Record Group 107, Records of the Office of the Secretary of War. National Archives, Washington, D.C.
351. Record Group 156, Records of the Office of the Chief of Ordnance. National Archives, Washington, D.C.
352. Rosecrans, William S., Papers. University of California, Los Angeles.
353. Sheridan, Philip Henry, Papers. Library of Congress, Washington, D.C.
354. Sherman, William Tecumseh, Papers. Library of Congress, Washington, D.C.
355. Sherman, William Tecumseh, Papers. Ohio Historical Society, Columbus.
356. Smith, Persifor Frazer, Papers. Historical Society of Pennsylvania, Philadelphia.
357. Stevens, Isaac Ingalls, Papers. University of Washington, Seattle.
358. Taylor, Zachary, Papers. Library of Congress, Washington, D.C.
359. Taylor, Zachary, Papers. Henry E. Huntington Library, San Marino, California.
360. Wool, John Ellis, Papers. Duke University, Durham, North Carolina.
361. Wool, John Ellis, Papers. New York State Library, Albany.
362. U.S. Army Military History Research Collection. *The Era of the Civil War, 1820-1876.* Special Bibliographic Series No. 11, 1975.

IX

CIVIL-MILITARY RELATIONS, OPERATIONS, AND THE ARMY, 1865-1917

Richard N. Ellis

General Works

The starting point for a study of the United States army in this or any other period should be Russell Weigley's *History of the United States Army* (270) which is the best and most recent survey of the place of the army in the nation's history. The major questions raised by Weigley, those of a professional or citizen army and civilian control of the military, are especially clear in this period. While Weigley presents the development of military thought and the history of the army as an institution, *American Military History* (166), a recent survey for the Army Historical Series, is a straightforward account with a greater emphasis upon campaigns and battles. Other older and somewhat dated but still useful studies that evaluate the development of the army as an institution and sketch the army in combat include Ganoe (94), Bernardo and Bacon (14), and Spaulding (240). All three reflect the military point of view and the influence of Emory Upton. Steele's *American Campaigns* (243) is an older history of U.S. military campaigns that also reflects a pro-army bias but which was a standard account for years and is still of use.

Although many recent scholars reflect the civilian point of view, and Weigley in particular has been critical of the Uptonian influence, the major influence on military thinking in the late nineteenth and early twentieth centuries was the writing of Emory Upton who was critical of the nation's military history and contemptuous of the civilian soldier and civilian control of the military. Upton's publications, particularly *The Military Policy of the United States* (259), had an immense impact on the military mind. Junior officers filled the pages of professional journals with Uptonian ideas as Weigley indicates in *Towards an American Army* (271). His career has recently been studied in depth by Ambrose (3) in a balanced work although all scholars dealing with military history and thought in this period have dealt with the Uptonian system.

Civil-military relations provide a major theme in American military history, and if Upton and his followers criticized civilian control, recent scholars tend to favor it. Louis Smith's *American Democracy and Military Power* (237), a comprehensive institutional study of civil-military relations, argues that civilian control has worked. Arthur Ekirch (72) is quite critical of the army and is more vehement in his support of civilian control; Walter Millis presents an important critical analysis of American military policy in *Arms and Men* (179) and an anthology entitled *American Military Thought* (178); Weigley (271) and Williams (279) also evaluate key military thinkers although the latter's work is unfortunately brief. *The Soldier and the State: The Theory and Politics of Civil-Military Relations* by Samuel P. Huntington (131) is an unusually useful and provocative analysis of the intellectual climate and its influence on civil-military relations. Huntington argues that the prevailing climate of liberalism in American thought has been a major factor in shaping military policy, and after the Civil War the mood of "Business pacifism" opposed war and helped isolate the army socially, intellectually, and even physically from the rest of the nation. If these were the "dark ages" of the army as Ganoe (94) and others have stated, they were the dark ages of military political influence, but they were the golden ages of military professionalism, according to Huntington. Two books related to the subject of civil-military relations are Merle Curti's *Peace or War* (55), a general survey of peace movements that devotes considerable attention to the 1865-1917 period, and a more recent study by Marchand (162) which describes the mercurial rise and fall of the American peace movment from 1898 to 1918 and which includes a useful annotated bibliography.

There are several general topical studies that are of considerable importance for this and also for other periods of United States military history. Huston's (132) study of army logistics is unmatched as a survey and deals with ordinance and the medical service as well. Erna Risch provides the same competent scholarship in *Quartermaster Support of the Army* (219) and Honeywell (127) surveys the history of military chaplains. The literature about military medicine is covered in chapter XII. Several general and popular accounts of the cavalry have been written by Whitman (276), Wormser (286), Merrill (171), and Herr and Wallace (118). Thian's *Legislative History of the General Staff . . .* (250) has a misleading title because it covers the period before the creation of the General Staff in 1903, but its description of the various departments and bureaus in the War Department makes it an essential tool for army historians.

During these years West Point saw many changes and was the center of occasional controversy. Dupuy (68), Foreman (87), and Ambrose (2) all have written general histories of the military academy, but the account by Henry Flipper (84), a black cadet, and the story of the controversial court martial of Johnson Whitaker, a black cadet, by Marszalek (164) should also be consulted.

The tasks of raising and demobilizing armies are covered by Kreidberg and Henry (149), who describe the assembling and organizing of troops and equipment, Lerwill (155), and Sparrow (239). All are government publications and are somewhat encyclopedic, but they are essential as sources of information and statistics. During this period the militia, an institution singled out for criticism by Upton but defended by Logan (160), underwent reforms and emerged as the National Guard. Riker (218), Hill (122), and Derthick (61) describe the National Guard and its influence. Riker argues that the guard revived in response to labor troubles in 1877, and Derthick recounts the founding of the National Guard Association.

THE SOLDIER. Two useful studies of the lot of the common soldier are in Foner (85), which is a critical study of the slow process of reform, and Rickey (216), which is a narrative of soldier life in the West. Leckie (151) and Fowler (89) have studies of Black cavalry and infantry regiments, respectively, that deal with conditions in Black regiments and include, in Leckie particularly, descriptions of campaigns in the West. The enlisted man speaks for himself in Merrill (172) and Williams (278). Janowitz (140) describes the evolution of army leadership. Two extremely useful tools are George Cullum's *Biographical Register of the Officers and Graduates of the United States Military Academy* (54) and Francis Heitman's *Historical Register and Dictionary of the United States Army* (117).

PROFESSIONALISM IN THE ARMY. During the post Civil War years, Huntington's (131) golden age of professionalism, William T. Sherman, was the guiding force in the army. His memoirs (232) reveal a perceptive thinker, an assessment confirmed by a number of scholars, including Athearn (7), whose book concentrates on Sherman and the West. It was Sherman who, despite frustration from his relations with the Secretary of War, encouraged professionalism by the development of military schools and encouraged the work of Emory Upton. The results of the professional spirit instilled by Sherman can be seen in the organizations and journals founded during this period.

JOURNALS. Although no journal specializes in the military history of this period, *Military Affairs* carries frequent articles on the subject. Most state, regional, and national historical journals also publish in this area, and a handy guide to appropriate articles for the geographical region of the trans-Mississippi West is Oscar Winther, (282) *A Classified Bibliography of the Periodical Literature of the Trans-Mississippi West* which has been updated several times. A good source is the *Army and Navy Journal* which began publication in 1863. Although not a professional journal, it has carried articles, correspondence, and other items about military topics, and the role of its founder and guiding light, William C. Church, is described by Bigelow (16). A series of professional journals began after the Civil War, which, along with professional associations, symbolized and encouraged professionalism. The *Journal of the Military Service Institution of the United States* began in 1879; the United States Cavalry Association published the *Cavalry Journal* in 1888; the Artillery School at Fort Monroe published *The Journal of the United States Artillery* in 1892; and the United States Infantry Association founded the *Infantry Journal* in 1904. *United Service,* first published in 1879, also included material on naval affairs.

RECONSTRUCTION. Although most of the literature on Reconstruction in the South after the Civil War ignores the role of the army, the military was deeply involved in the administration of federal policy from 1865 to 1877. Harold Hyman (136) has evaluated the role of the army in events leading to the impeachment of President Andrew Johnson, and Hyman and Benjamin Thomas have an excellent biography of Secretary of War Edwin Stanton, (251), but the most recent and complete study is James E. Shefton, *The United States Army and Reconstruction* (230). Shefton argues that the army demonstrated a commendable ability to adjust to frequent changes in federal policy and that military administration was creditable to the army as an institution. He also finds the role of the army to be unique, for there were no precedents for the task, and the experience it gained was largely unneeded in the years that followed. A first hand account by an unusually literate officer can be found in DeForest (59).

One important aspect of military involvement in Reconstruction was the Freedman's Bureau under Oliver O. Howard. There is general agreement that the Bureau was unsuccessful, and McFeely (168) finds that a fair proportion of the blame lies on the shoulders of Howard while Carpenter (32) places more blame on other factors. A study of the Bureau in one state can be found in White (274).

DOMESTIC FUNCTIONS. After the Civil War the army continued to play a role in exploration and scientific work and was involved in a wide range of activity from involvement in labor disputes to medical research and construction projects. Continued exploration in the West is evaluated by Goetzmann (99) and at greater length by Bartlett (10), while the construction of wagon roads is found in Jackson (138). Military exploration in the Arctic, some of which was conducted by the Signal Corps, is described by Caswell (39), while the history of the Signal Corps, which was transferred to civilian administration in 1891, can be found in Whitnah (277). Army administration of Alaska from 1867 to 1877 when Congress provided civil government is credited by Hinckley (123) with beginning the process of Americanization, while army exploration in the territory is adequately described by Sherwood (233). The army was also involved in the administration of national parks from 1886 to 1918, and Hampton (114) argues that the army saved the parks and the national park idea. The involvement of the military in medical work has been described by Ashburn (5), but the life of one pioneer bacteriologist, George Sternberg, who created the Yellow Fever Commission, is available in a laudatory biography by Gibson (97). A recent critical study of civil construction projects by the Corps of Engineers can be found in *Dams and Other Disasters* by Morgan (183), who worked with the Corps for years, and the account of one major project, the Panama Canal, can be found in a biography of Goethals (22) and Padelford's broader study of the canal (196).

The use of troops in labor disputes caused considerable controversy at the time. General surveys can be found in Wilson, *Federal Aid in Domestic Disturbances* (280), a Senate document, and Rich (217), but a thorough study of army activity in the critical year of 1877 is in Bruce (29). A chapter in *Bayonets in the Streets,* edited by Robin Higham, (121) provides a good recent survey.

INDIAN CAMPAIGNS. Although the primary task of the small military establishment between 1865 and 1890 was to control Indian tribes in the trans-Mississippi West, this aspect of military history has not been effectively integrated into general histories of the period. Military historians, too, have often failed to analyze the Indian fighting army and to place it in the broader history of the United States army. The literature about the Indian "wars" is tremendous, but most accounts are relatively narrow and detailed and fail to look at the big picture.

There are only a few general histories of the army in the West. Andrist (4) is uninspired; Downey (63) is popular and selective and lacks analysis; Marshall (163) has considerable experience as a military historian and occasionally adds new insights in his critical evaluations of army officers and Indian leaders, but he lacks a sound knowledge of Indian history and culture, and his book includes numerous errors of fact; Dunn (66) is older and by no means complete, and Brown's (27) recent best seller is an unbalanced attack upon the army and federal policy in general and therefore should be used with care. Robert Utley's *The Frontier Regulars* (261) is unquestionably the finest survey of the topic. It is the best description of the campaigns and provides a thoughtful analysis of the army and its leaders. Utley describes the frontier army as a conventional army fighting unconventional wars and as a force that had more failures than successes.

Because of the limited size of the army, which never totaled thirty thousand after 1870, scholars have concentrated on the careers of individual officers or on individual battles. A dominant force in the early years was William T. Sherman, who, because of the structure of the War Department, operated independently from that institution. His western career is admirably treated by Athearn (7), who concludes that Sherman utilized the army to encourage western settlement. Philip Sheridan, who succeeded Sherman, still awaits an adequate treatment of his post war career although Rister's (220) older work is available. A forthcoming biography of George Crook by James T. King should provide an adequate analysis of the career of the one officer who adjusted to unconventional warfare and developed anti-guerrila tactics by employing Indian soldiers, but until it is published scholars can use Crook's autobiography which was edited by Schmitt (53) and an extremely useful book by one of Crook's aides (24). The use of Indian soldiers is described by Ellis (73) and Downey and Jacobsen (65), but a full scale study is needed. Other sound biographies are Wallace on Ranald Mackenzie (265), King on Eugene Carr (145), Carpenter on O. O. Howard, Heyman on E. R. S. Canby (120), and Ellis on John Pope (74).

George Armstrong Custer deserves special mention because of the controversy surrounding his career and because of the bulk of published material about him. A good starting point is Utley, *Custer and the Great Controversy* (260), which deals with the literature. Balanced accounts are Edgar Stewart, *Custer's Luck* (245), and Monaghan's biography (181). There is an interesting psychological study by Hofling, a professor of psychiatry (126).

There are numerous studies of campaigns against western tribes. Leckie (152) adequately describes activity on the southern plains between 1867 and 1875; Thrapp (255), Faulk (80), and Ogle (193) evaluate the Apache campaigns; Sprague (241) narrates events surrounding the brief conflict with the Utes in 1879; Josephy (145), Beal (11) and others capture the drama of the flight of the Nez Perce in 1877; Utley (262) evaluates the climax of the Indian campaigns at Wounded Knee in 1890 in an exceptional book. A host of books shed light on the history of the Indian fighting army by concentrating on Indian opponents. Examples are Berthrong (15), Grinnell (104), Olson (195), Thrapp (257), and the series of books on the Sioux by George Hyde (133), (134), (135).

One aspect of military involvement in the West can be seen in the history of numerous military posts that were constructed to help control Indians. A popular account of Ft. Leavenworth, departmental headquarters, a major supply point and home of the infantry and cavalry school, is by Walton (266). Emmett's (77) history of Ft. Union demonstrates the importance of that post on the Southwest. Possibly the best study of a military post is Nye's history of Fort Sill (190). Athearn (6) has an excellent history of forts on the Upper Missouri, and Murray has a good account of posts on Powder River. Prucha (211) and Frazer (90) provide brief but useful sketches of military installations in the continental United States.

The army in the West was subject to continual complaints with westerners on one side and defenders of the Indians on the other. Utley (261) believes that stereotypes developed by these groups and by army officers are invalid, and Ellis (75) argues that many officers were sincerely concerned about the welfare of Indians.

The lot of enlisted men in the frontier army was one of hardship and harsh discipline. Rickey describes conditions in *Forty Miles a Day on Beans and Hay* (216); Foner (85) takes a broader look at conditions in the army in general and describes the halting efforts at reform. Both indicate the prevalance of desertion during the late nineteenth century. Until recently historians ignored the role of Black regiments in the West. Leckie (151) and Fowler (89) describe their contributions and the adverse conditions under which they served while Porter has an excellent pioneering article on the Seminole Negro scouts (205).

TACTICS. Emory Upton's own military experience and his inquiring mind led him to develop a new system of infantry tactics after the Civil War. Confident that the breechloading rifle would be the weapon of the future, he recommended abandoning the traditional two or three line formation and urged reliance on groups of four men. Upton's tactics, which continued in use in the twentieth century, were described in his *Infantry Tactics* (258). Another key tactician was Arthur Wagner who helped develop the Command and General Staff College and the Army War College and authored several important studies (264) in the 1890s. Another important text written in the 1890s was John Bigelow's *Principles of Strategy* (17).

WEAPONS. Most general works describe the painfully slow changes in firearms in the late nineteenth century, but Brinckerhoff and Chamberlain (26) in particular recount the delays and conflicts in the army's search for a breechloader. Those interested in small arms can turn to Gluckman (98), who provides a rather thorough identification of U.S. martial weapons. Fuller's (92) study of the breechloader includes both experimental and standard weapons before 1917, and Campbell (30) has a recent work on the 1903 Springfield, the standard shoulder weapon for so many years. Parker (202) provides a first hand account of a Gatling gun detachment in Cuba, and Chinn (43) describes the history of the machine-gun. Although there is no satisfactory history of artillery, Downey (64) and Bishop (20) have popular surveys. Birkhimer's sketch (19), first published in 1884, has recently been reprinted as part of the West Point Military Library. The story of the Endicott Board, created in 1885 to study coastal defenses, can be found in Ranson's (214) article in *Military Affairs*.

SPANISH-AMERICAN WAR. Much of the literature about the Spanish-American War is critical of the army for lack of planning, inefficient administration, and poor leadership. Walter Millis, *The Martial Spirit* (180), has been disparaged by some for being too critical and occasionally satirical, but his is still an excellent history. It should be read, however, in conjunction with *An Army for Empire*, a recent study by Graham Cosmas (49), which is an attempt to reconstruct the War Department's story of the war and to modify the picture of ineptitude. Cosmas defends the War Department and spreads the blame for failures to Congress, the National Guard, and haste. Secretary of War Russell Alger, the target of considerable criticism, defended himself in a book published in 1901 (1).

A brief but useful survey of the period is Morgan's, *America's Road to Empire* (184), but Chadwick's (40) older history is still good. The most detailed account of military operations is Sargent's three volume *The Campaign of Santiago de Cuba* (224) while Freidel's *The Splendid Little War* (91) has superb illustrations. Hill (122) describes the role of the National Guard; Roosevelt (223) praises the Rough Riders; Dyer (71) has a good biography of Fighting Joe Wheeler; Johnson (142) praised the contribution of Black soldiers in a book published in 1899, but it should be supplemented with a recent compilation of material from black soldiers by Gatewood (96).

THE LITTLE WARS. If the Spanish-American War was, as one diplomatic historian has described it, America's "coming out party" into the world arena, the quickening pace of United States involvement in international diplomacy can be seen in part in the "Little Wars" of the United States, to borrow that term from Dupuy and Baumer. Their book of that title (69) is a readable summary of conflict in the Philippines, the China Relief Expedition, and interventions into Mexico and the Caribbean.

American military involvement in the Philippines has not attracted large numbers of scholars, but the most recent, thorough and soundly researched study is John Gate's *Schoolbooks and Krags* (95), a revisionist history. While not denying atrocities by American soldiers, Gates describes them as "Progressives in Uniform" who developed a pacification program that was a mixture of humanitarianism and force. Their's was a well-conceived counter-guerrilla operation stressing political, economic, social, and military activity, he argues. Others, such as Storey and Lichauco (247), have been highly critical of government policy and army conduct. Other useful studies are those by Sexton (229), who is more favorable to the United States, Baclagon (8), LeRoy (154), Grunder & Livezey (106), who evaluate the origins of United States policies in the Philippines, and the autobiography of Frederick Funston (93), who captured Aguinaldo.

One officer who was involved in both the Philippines and the China Relief Expedition during the Boxer Rebellion was Edna R. Chaffee whose biography was written by William Carter (37). The full story of the Boxer Rebellion and the role of American troops has been told by Tan (248), Purcell (212), and Daggett (56).

During the first part of the twentieth century, U.S. troops were also involved in Latin America. Military intervention in Cuba from 1906-1909 has recently been evaluated along lines similar to Gate's work on the Philippines. Allan Millett (177) stresses the role of army officers in policy making and argues that they strongly urged reforms. Lockmiller's older study of Charles Magoon (159) is also useful while Philip Foner (86) offers a richly detailed multivolume study of Cuban-American relations. Robert Quirk (213) praises the work of the military government in the occupation of Vera Cruz, Mexico, while Clarence Clendenen provides a rather full study of Mexican-United States relations along the border in the *United States and Pancho Villa* (45) and the more general *Blood on the Border* (44), which describes army expeditions into Mexico during the Indian campaigns as well as Pershing's invasion in 1916. Tompkins's *Chasing Villa* (254) is a widely used account of the latter event, but must be supplemented with Donald Smythe's (238) excellent and detailed biography of Pershing to 1917. Clendenen and Smythe argue that Pershing accomplished his mission of destroying Villa's principal bands and that he utilized small mobile units rather than ponderous, slow moving forces.

REFORMS. The problems of organization, supply, and planning that became evident during the Spanish-American War resulted in an investigation by the Dodge Commission which delineated weaknesses and recommended reforms. Its report, an important primary source, was printed as a congressional document, and one result was the removal of Secretary of War Russell A. Alger, who subsequently defended himself in print with a history of the war (1).

Elihu Root, Alger's replacement, instituted a series of major reforms of long lasting impact upon the American army that have been evaluated by a variety of scholars. Root lacked a military background, but he utilized capable assistants such as Henry Corbin and William Carter and carefully studied the situation. Root's own account of his efforts can be found in speeches and reports collected by Bacon and Scott (9) and a collection of his annual reports as Secretary of War (222), but one should also see Carter's *Creation of the American General Staff* (35). Root's biographer, Philip Jessup (141), Semsch (228), Ambrose (3), and others describe how Root studied the Dodge Commission Report, read Spenser Wilkinson's *The Brain of an Army*, a British study, and discovered the writings of Emory Upton. It was Root who arranged for publication of Upton's *The Military Policy of the United States.* Weigley (270) argues persuasively that although clearly influenced by Upton, the Secretary drew selectively on the ideas of a variety of military thinkers.

Root's major accomplishment, along with such changes as the creation of the Army War College and the reorganization of the National Guard, was the creation of a general staff. Hittle, *The Military Staff* (125) is a good starting point for an understanding of the staff concept and its implementation in several nations, including the United States. Hammond (113) and Nelson (189) both deal with the broader period of the twentieth century but include useful and favorable analyses of Root's reforms. Both indicate the skill and patience of Root in surmounting hostility to the staff concept in and out of the army, and Nelson, in particular, describes its gradual acceptance. The work of the general staff in subsequent years can best be found in biographies of Secretaries of War William Howard Taft, Henry Stimson, and Newton Baker by Pringle (210), Morison (185), and Palmer (199) respectively and in biographies of Chiefs of Staff Chaffee by Carter (37), Wood by Hagedorn (112), and Bliss by Palmer (198). Also useful is Hugh Scott's autobiography (227). One key controversy mentioned by most of the above is the conflict between Chief of Staff Leonard Wood and Adjutant General Fred Ainsworth which involved the whole staff concept. Most scholars defend Wood, but Deutrich (62) is more generous to Ainsworth and does praise him for inaugurating a system of military record keeping that has aided archivists and scholars alike.

PREPAREDNESS CAMPAIGN. With the outbreak of World War I an increasing number of Americans began to urge military preparedness. The most recent and useful study of Plattsburg Movement with its military training camps is John Clifford's *The Citizen Soldiers* (46), a soundly researched book. Ralph Barton Perry was involved in the movement and left a sympathetic first-hand account (203). Frederic Huidekoper, a friend of Leonard Wood and a leader of the Army League, wrote a history of military unpreparedness in 1915 (129) that was in the Uptonian tradition and served as a major voice for change. Hagedorn's history of the preparedness movement (111) and his biography of Wood (112) are both laudatory, and one sample of Wood's deep involvement in the preparedness movement is his *The Military Obligation of Citizenship* (285). Other useful accounts are Ward (268) on the National Security League, Mooney and Layman (182) on the compulsory military training movement, Herring's article on James Hay, chairman of the House Committee on Military Affairs (119), and Coffman's biography of Peyton March (47). Lockmiller's biography of Enoch Crowder (158) is a good study of his influence on the Selective Service act and on mobilization.

PRIMARY MATERIALS. The largest and most significat body of source material is found in the military records in the National Archives which are divided in a series of record groups based upon the various divisions in the military establishment. A list of record groups is available from the National Archives, and preliminary inventories have been prepared for some record groups. Selections from these documents as well as reports of investigations and collections of testimony on various military topics have been published in the congressional documents, and scholars should not overlook these important sources.

FURTHER RESEARCH. Despite the existence of an impressive body of scholarly material for this period, there are numerous areas that still await research. A variety of officers need modern critical biographies, and a closer look at the Gates-Millett interpretation of army officers as reformers in the Philippines and Cuba would be useful. A new history of the Spanish-American War that utilizes Cuban and Spanish sources is needed, and a variety of topics such as military justice and weaponry need considerable work. A forthcoming study by Emanuel R. Lewis to be entitled, *Seacoast Fortifications of the United States*, should provide a useful description of a hitherto neglected subject, but research is needed on topics such as recruiting and military diets.

BIBLIOGRAPHY

1. Alger, Russell Alexander *The Spanish-American War*. New York: Harper and Bros., 1901.
2. Ambrose, Stephen E. *Duty, Honor, Country: A History of West Point*. Baltimore: John Hopkins University Press, 1966.
3. Ambrose, Stephen. *Upton and the Army*. Baton Rouge: Louisiana State University Press, 1964.
4. Andrist, Ralph K. *The Long Death: The Last Days of the Plains Indian*. New York: Macmillan, 1964.
5. Ashburn, Percy M. *A History of the Medical Department of the United States Army*. Boston: Houghton Mifflin, 1929.
6. Athearn, Robert G. *Forts of the Upper Missouri*. Englewood Cliffs: Prentice-Hall, 1967.
7. Athearn, Robert G. *William Tecumseh Sherman and the Settlement of the West*. Norman: University of Oklahoma Press, 1956.
8. Baclagon, Uldarico S. *Philippine Campaigns*. Manila: Graphic House, 1952.
9. Bacon, Robert and James B. Scott. *The Military and Colonial Policy of the United States: Addresses and Reports by Elihu Root*. Cambridge: Harvard University Press, 1924.
10. Bartlett, Richard A. *Great Surveys of the American West*. Norman: University of Oklahoma Press, 1962.
11. Beal, Merrill D. *I Will Fight No More Forever*. Seattle: University of Washington Press, 1963.
12. Beale, Howard K. *Theodore Roosevelt and the Rise of America to World Power*. Baltimore: Johns Hopkins University Press, 1956.
13. Berdahl, Clarence A. *War Powers of the Executive in the United States*. Urbana: University of Illinois Press, 1921.
14. Bernardo, C. Joseph and Eugene H. Bacon. *American Military Policy: Its Development Since 1775*. Harrisburg: Military Service Publishing Co., 1955.
15. Berthrong, Donald. *The Southern Cheyennes*. Norman: University of Oklahoma Press, 1963.
16. Bigelow, Donald. *William Conant Church and the Army and Navy Journal*. New York: Columbia University Press, 1952.
17. Bigelow, John. *Principles of Strategy*. Philadelphia: J. B. Lippincott, 1894.

18. Bigelow, John. *Reminiscences of the Santiago Campaign.* New York: Harper, 1898.
19. Birkhimer, William E. *Historical Sketch of the Organization, Administration, Material, and Tactics of the Artillery, United States Army.* Washington, D.C. : J. J. Chapman, Agent, 1884.
20. Bishop, Harry G. *Field Artillery, The King of Battles,* Boston: Houghton Mifflin, 1935.
21. Bishop Henry G. *Elements of Modern Field Artillery, U.S. Service.* Menasha, Wisconsin,; G. Banta Publishing Co., 1914.
22. Bishop, Joseph B. and Farnham Bishop. *Goethals: Genius of the Panama Canal.* New York: Harper, 1930.
23. Blount, James H. *The American Occupation of the Philippines, 1898-1912.* New York: Putnam's, 1912.
24. Bourke, John G.; *On the Border With Crook.* New York: Scribner's, 1891.
25. Brimlow, George F. *Cavalryman Out of the West: Life of General William Carey Brown.* Caldwell: Caxton Printers, 1944.
26. Brinckerhoff, Sidney B. and Pierce Chamberlain. "The Army's Search for a Repeating Rifle: 1873-1903." *Military Affairs,* v. 32, p. 20-30, 1968.
27. Dee Brown. *Bury My Heart at Wounded Knee: An Indian History of the American West.* New York: Holt, 1970.
28. Brown, Dee. *Fort Phil Kearny: An American Saga.* New York: Putnam, 1962.
29. Bruce, Robert V. *1877: Year of Violence.* Indianapolis: Bobbs-Merrill, 1959.
30. Campbell, Clark S. *The '90 Springfield.* Beverly Hills, California: Fadco Publishing Co., 1957.
31. Cantor, Louis."Elihu Root and The National Guard: Friend or Foe?" *Military Affairs,* v. 33, p. 361-373, 1969.
32. Carpenter, John. *Sword and Olive Branch.* Pittsburgh: University of Pittsburgh Press, 1964.
33. Carriker, Robert C. *Fort Supply, Indian Territory: Frontier Outpost on the Plains.* Norman: University of Oklahoma Press, 1970.
34. Carter, William Harding. *The American Army.* Indianapolis: Bobbs-Merrill, 1915.
35. Carter, William H. *Creation of the American General Staff.* Washington, G.P.O., 1924.
36. Carter, William H. *From Yorktown to Santiago with the Sixth U.S. Cavalry.* Baltimore: The Friedenwald Co., 1900.
37. Carter, William H. *The Life of Lieutenant General Chaffee.* Chicago: University of Chicago Press, 1917.
38. Castle Henry; *The Army Mule.* Indianapolis: Bobbs-Merrill, 1897.
39. Caswell, John E. *Arctic Frontiers: United States Explorations in the Far North.* Norman: University of Oklahoma Press, 1956.
40. Chadwick, French E. *The Relations of the United States to Spain: The Spanish-American War.* New York: Scribner's, 1911.
41. Challener, Richard D. *Admirals, Generals and American Foreign Policy, 1898-1914.* Princeton: Princeton University Press, 1973.
42. Chew, Abraham. *A Biography of Colonel Charles Young.* Washington, D.C.: Pendleton, 1923.

43. Chinn, George M. *The Machine Gun.* Washington: G.P.O., 1951.
44. Clendenen, Clarence C. *Blood on the Border: The United States Army and the Mexican Irregulars.* New York: Macmillan, 1969.
45. Clendenen, Clarence C. *The United States and Pancho Villa: A Study in Unconventional Diplomacy.* Ithaca: Cornell University Press, 1961.
46. Clifford, John G. *The Citizen Soldiers: The Plattsburg Training Camp Movement, 1913-1920.* Lexington: University Press of Kentucky, 1972.
47. Coffman, Edward M. *The Hilt of the Sword: The Career of Peyton C. March.* Madison: University of Wisconsin Press, 1966.
48. Colby, Elbridge. "Elihu Root and the National Guard," *Military Affairs,* v. 23, p. 28-34, 1959.
49. Cosmas, Graham A. *An Army for Empire: The United States Army in the Spanish-American War.* Columbia: University of Missouri Press, 1971.
50. Cosmas, Graham A. "Military Reform After the Spanish-American War: The Army Reorganization Fight of 1898-1899." *Military Affairs,* v. 35, p. 12-18, 1972.
51. Cox, John and LaWanda Cox. "General O. O. Howard and the Misrepresented Bureau." *Journal of Southern History,* v. 19, p. 427-456, 1972.
52. Cramer, Clarence H. *Newton D. Baker: A Biography.* Cleveland: World, 1961.
53. Crook, George. *General George Crook, His Autobiography.* Norman: University of Oklahoma Press, 1946.
54. Cullum, George W. *Biographical Register of the Officers and Graduates of the U.S. Military Academy at West Point, New York, from its Establishment, in 1802, to 1890.* Boston: Houghton, Mifflin, 1891.
55. Curti, Merle. *Peace or War: The American Stuggle, 1636-1936.* New York: W. W. Norton, 1936.
56. Daggett, Aaron S. *America in the China Relief Expedition.* Kansas City: Hudson-Kimberly, 1903.
57. Davis, Richard H. *The Cuban and Puerto Rican Campaigns.* New York: Scribner's, 1898.
58. Dearing, Mary R. *Veterans in Politics: The Story of the G.A.R.* Baton Rouge: Louisiana State University Press, 1952.
59. DeForest, John W. *A Union Officer in the Reconstruction.* New Haven: Yale University Press, 1948. Reprinted, Hamden, Connecticut: Archon Books, 1968.
60. D'Elia, Donald J. "The Argument over Civilian or Military Indian Control, 1865-1880." *Historian,* v. 24, p. 207-225, 1972.
61. Derthick, Martha. *The National Guard in Politics.* Cambridge: Harvard University Press, 1965.
62. Deutrich, Mabel E. *Struggle for Supremacy: The Career of General Fred C. Ainsworth.* Washington: Public Affairs Press, 1962.
63. Downey, Fairfax. *Indian Fighting Army.* New York: Scribner's 1941.
64. Downey, Fairfax. *Sound of Guns: The Story of American Artillery from Ancient and Honorable Company to the Atom, Canon and Guided Missile.* New York: David McKay Co., 1955.

65. Downey, Fairfax and Jacques N. Jacobsen, Jr. *The Red Bluecoats.* Fort Collins, Colorado: Old Army Press, 1973.

66. Dunn, Jacob P. *Massacres of the Mountains: A History of the Indian Wars of the Far West, 1815-1875.* New York: Harper, 1886.

67. Dupuy, Richard Ernest. *Men of West Point: The First 150 Years of the United States Military Academy.* New York: Sloane, 1951.

68. Dupuy, Richard Ernest. *Where They Have Trod: The West Point Tradition in American Life.* New York: Frederick A. Stokes, 1940.

69. Dupuy, R. Ernest and William H. Baumer. *The Little Wars of the United States.* New York: Hawthorn Books, 1968.

70. Dupuy, R. Ernest and Trevor N. Dupuy; *Military Heritage of America.* New York: McGraw-Hill, 1956.

71. Dyer, John P. *From Shiloh to San Juan: Fighting Joe Wheeler.* Baton Rouge: Louisiana State University Press, 1961.

72. Ekirch, Arthur A., Jr. *The Civilian and the Military.* New York: Oxford University Press, 1956.

73. Ellis, Richard N. "Copper-Skinned Soldiers: The Apache Scouts." *Great Plains Journal,* vol. 5, p. 51-67.

74. Ellis, Richard N. *General Pope and U.S. Indian Policy.* Albuquerque: University of New Mexico Press, 1970.

75. Ellis, Richard N. "The Humanitarian Generals." *The Western Historical Quarterly,* v. 3, p. 169-178.

76. Ellis, Richard N. "Volunteer Soldiers in the West, 1865." *Military Affairs,* v. 34, p. 53-56, 1971.

77. Emmett, Chris. *Fort Union and the Winning of the Southwest.* Norman: University of Oklahoma Press, 1965.

78. Esposito, Vincent J. *The West Point Atlas of American Wars.* New York: Praeger, 1959. 2 vols.

79. Farago, Ladislas. *Patton: Ordeal and Triumph.* Stamford, Connecticut: Astor-Honor, Inc., 1964.

80. Faulk, Odie B. *The Geronimo Campaign.* New York: Oxford University Press, 1969.

81. Fite, Gilbert C. "The United States Army and Relief to Pioneer Settlers, 1874-1875." *Journal of the West,* v. 6, p. 99-107.

82. Fitzgibbon, Russell H. *Cuba and the United States, 1900-1935.* Menasha, Wisconsin: George Banta, 1935.

83. Fleming, Thomas J. *West Point: The Men and Times of the United States Military Academy.* New York: William Morrow, 1969.

84. Flipper, Henry O. *The Colored Cadet at West Point.* New York: Homer Lee, 1878.

85. Foner, Jack D. *The United States Soldier between Two Wars: Army Life and Reforms, 1865-1898.* New York: Humanities Press, 1970.

86. Foner, Philip S. *The Spanish-Cuban-American War and the Birth of American Imperialism, 1895-1902.* New York: Monthly Review Press, 1972.

87. Forman, Sidney. *West Point: A History of the United States Military Academy.* New York: Columbia University Press, 1950.

88. Forsyth, George A. *The Story of the Soldier.* New York: D. Appleton, 1900.

89. Fowler, Arlen L. *The Black Infantry in the West.* Westport, Connecticut: Greenwood, 1971.
90. Frazer, Robert W. *Forts of the West.* Norman: University of Oklahoma Press, 1963.
91. Freidel, Frank B. *The Splendid Little War.* Boston: Little, Brown, 1958.
92. Fuller, Claud E. *The Breech-loader in the Service.* Topeka: American Reference Club of America, 1933.
93. Funston, Frederick. *Memories of Two Wars: Cuban and Philippine Experiences.* New York: Scribner's 1911.
94. Ganoe, William A. *The History of the United States Army.* New York: Appleton, 1924.
95. Gates, John M. *Schoolbooks and Krags: The United States Army in the Philippines, 1898-1902.* Westport, Connecticut: Greenwood Press, Inc., 1973.
96. Gatewood, Willard B. *Smoked Yankees and the Struggle for Empire: Letters from Negro Soldiers, 1898-1902.* Urbana: University of Illinois Press, 1971.
97. Gibson, John M. *Soldier in White: The Life of General George Willis Sternberg.* Durham: Duke University Press, 1958.
98. Gluckman, Arcadi. *United States Muskets, Rifles, and Carbines.* Buffalo: Otto Ulbrich Co., 1948.
99. Goetzmann, William H. *Exploration and Empire.* New York: Knopf, 1966.
100. Gorgas, William C. *Sanitation in Panama.* New York; Appleton, 1915.
101. Graham, W. A. *The Story of the Little Big Horn.* Harrisburg: Military Service Publishing Co., 1941.
102. Greene, Fred. "The Military View of American National Policy, 1904-1940." *American Historical Review,* v. 66, p. 354-377, 1960.
103. Grenville, John and George Young. *Politics, Strategy and American Diplomacy.* New Haven: Yale University Press, 1966.
104. Grinnell, George B. *The Fighting Cheyennes.* New York: Scribner's 1915.
105. Grinnell, George B. *Two Great Scouts and Their Pawnee Battalion.* Cleveland: Arthur H. Clark, 1928.
106. Grunder, Garel A. and William E. Livezey. *The Philippines and the United States.* Norman; University of Oklahoma Press, 1951.
107. Guerney, Gene. *A Pictorial History of the United States Army in War and Peace from Colonial Times to Vietnam.* New York: Crown, 1966.
108. Hacker, Barton. "The United States Army as a National Police Force: The Federal Policing of Labor Disputes, 1877-1898." *Military Affairs,* v. 33, p. 255-264, 1970.
109. Hafen, LeRoy R. and Francis M. Young. *Fort Laramie and the Pageant of the West.* Glendale, California: Arthur H. Clark, 1938.
110. Hafen, LeRoy R. and Ann W. Hafen. *Powder River Campaigns and Sawyer's Expedition of 1865.* Glendale, California: Arthur H. Clark, 1961.
111. Hagedorn, Hermann. *The Bugle that Woke America.* New York: John Day, 1940.

112. Hagedom, Hermann. *Leonard Wood: A Biography.* New York: Harper, 1931.
113. Hammond, Paul Y. *Organizing for Defense: The American Military Establishment in the Twentieth Century.* Princeton: Princeton Univeristy Press, 1961.
114. Hampton, H. D. *How the U.S. Cavalry Saved Our National Parks.* Bloomington: Indiana University Press, 1971.
115. Harbaugh, William H. *Power and Responsibility: The life and Times of Theodore Roosevelt.* New York: Farrar, Straus and Cudahy, 1961.
116. Healy, David F. *The United States in Cuba, 1898-1902: Generals, Politicians, and the Search for Policy.* Madison: University of Wisconsin Press, 1963.
117. Heitman, Francis B. *Historical Register & Dictionary of the United States Army from its Organization Sept. 29, 1789 to March 2, 1903.* Washington: G.P.O., 1903.
118. Herr, John K. and Edward S. Wallace. *The Story of the U.S. Cavalry, 1775-1942.* Boston: Little, Brown, 1953.
119. Herring, George C. "James Hay and the Preparedness Controversy, 1915-1916." *Journal of Southern History,* v. 30, p. 383-404.
120. Heyman, Max, Jr., *Prudent Soldier: A Biography of Major General E. R. S. Canby, 1817-1873.* Glendale, California; Arthur H. Clark, c. 1959.
121. Higham, Robin, ed. *Bayonets in the Streets: The Use of Troops in Civil Disturbances.* Lawrence: University Press of Kansas, 1969.
122. Hill, Jim Dan. *The Minute Men in Peace and War: A History of the National Guard.* Harrisburg: Stackpole, 1964.
123. Hinckley, Ted C. *The Americanization of Alaska, 1867-1897.* Palo Alto: Pacific Books, 1972.
124. Hirshson, Stanley P. *Grenville M. Dodge: Soldier, Politician, Railroad Pioneer.* Bloomington: Indiana University Press, 1967.
125. Hittle, James D. *The Military Staff: Its History and Development.* Harrisburg: Military Service Publishing Co., 1949.
126. Hofling, Charles K. "George Custer: A Psychoanalytic Approach." *Montana, The Magazine of Western History,* v. 21, p. 32-43.
127. Honeywell, Roy J. *Chaplains of the United States Army.* Washington: G.P.O., 1958.
128. Howard, Harry N. *Military Government in the Panama Canal Zone.* Norman: Univeristy of Oklahoma Press, 1931.
129. Huidekoper, Frederic Louis. *The Military Unpreparedness of the United States.* New York: Macmillan, 1915.
130. Hume, Edgar E. *Victories of Army Medicine: Scientific Accomplishments of the Medical Department of the United States Army.* Philadelphia: Lippincott, 1943.
131. Huntington, Samuel P. *The Soldier and the State: The Theory and Politics of Civil-Military Relations.* Cambridge: Harvard University Press, 1957.
132. Huston, James A. *The Sinews of War: Army Logistics, 1775-1953.* Washington: G.P.O., 1966.
133. Hyde, George. *A Sioux Chronicle.* Norman: University of Oklahoma Press, 1956.

134. Hyde, George. *Red Cloud's Folk.* Norman: University of Oklahoma Press, 1937.
135. Hyde, George. *Spotted Tail's Folk: A History of the Brule Sioux.* Norman: University of Oklahoma Press, 1961.
136. Hyman, Harold M. "Johnson, Stanton, and Grant: A Reconsideration of the Army's Role in the Events Leading to Impeachment." *American Historical Review*, v. 66, p. 85-100, 1960.
137. Ingersoll, Lurton D. *A History of the War Department of the United States.* Washington, D. C.: F. B. Mohun, 1879.
138. Jackson, W. Turrentine. *Wagon Roads West: A Study of Federal Road Surveys and Construction in the Trans-Mississippi West, 1846-1869.* Berkeley: University of California Press, 1952.
139. James, Dorris C. *The Years of MacArthur*, Volume I, 1880-1941. Boston: Houghton Mifflin, 1970.
140. Janowitz, Morris. *The Professional Soldier.* Glencoe, Illinois: Free Press, 1960.
141. Jessup, Philip C. *Elihu Root.* New York: Dodd-Mead, 1938.
142. Johnson, Edward A. *History of Negro Soldiers in the Spanish-American War, and other Items of Interest.* Raleigh: Capitol Printing Co., 1899.
143. Johnson, Virginia W. *Unregimented General: A Biography of Nelson A. Miles.* Boston: Houghton Mifflin, 1962.
144. Johnston, Robert M. *Arms and the Race: The Foundations of Army Reform.* New York: Century, 1915.
145. Josephy, Alvin M., Jr. *The Nez Perce Indians and the Opening of the Northwest.* New Haven: Yale University Press, 1965.
146. King, James T. " 'A Better Way': General George Crook and the Ponca Indians." *Nebraska History*, v. 50. p. 239-254.
147. King, James T. *War Eagle: A Life of General Eugene A. Carr.* Lincoln: University of Nebraska Press, 1963.
148. Knight, Oliver. *Following the Indian Wars: The Story of the Newspaper Correspondents Among the Indian Campaigners.* Norman: University of Oklahoma Press, 1960.
149. Kreidberg, Marvin A. and Henry G. Merton; *History of Military Mobilization in the U.S. Army, 1775-1945.* Washington: Department of the Army, 1955.
150. Lane, Ann J. *The Brownsville Affair: National Crisis and Black Reaction.* Port Washington: Kennikat Press, 1971.
151. Leckie, William H. *The Buffalo Soldiers: A Narrative of the Negro Cavalry in the West.* Norman : University of Oklahoma Press, 1967.
152. Leckie, William H. *The Military Conquest of the Southern Plains.* Norman: University of Oklahoma Press, 1963.
153. Leech, Margaret. *In the Days of McKinley.* New York: Harper, 1959.
154. LeRoy, James A. *The Americans in the Philippines: A History of the Conquest and the First Years of Occupation.* Boston: Houghton Mifflin, 1914.
155. Lerwill, Leonard L. *History of the U.S. Replacement System.* Washington: G.P.O., 1954.
156. Lewis, Lloyd. *Sherman; Fighting Prophet.* New York: Harcourt, Brace, 1958.

157. Liddell Hart, B. H. *Sherman: Soldier, Realist, American.* New York: Dodd, Mead, 1929.
158. Lockmiller, David A. *Enoch H. Crowder: Soldier, Lawyer and Statesman.* Columbia: University of Missouri Press, 1955.
159. Lockmiller, David A. *Magoon in Cuba: A History of the Second Intervention, 1906-1909.* Durham: University of North Carolina Press, 1938.
160. Logan, John A. *The Volunteer Soldier in America.* Chicago: R. S. Peale & Co., 1887.
161. Lyons, Gene M. and John W. Masland. *Education and Military Leadership: A Study of the ROTC.* Princeton: Princeton University Press, 1959.
162. Marchand, C. Roland. *The American Peace Movement and Social Reform, 1898-1918.* Princeton: Princeton University Press, 1972.
163. Marshall, S. L. A. *Crimsoned Prairie.* New York: Scribners, 1972.
164. Marszalek, John F. *Court-Martial: A Black Man in America.* New York: Scribner's, 1972.
165. Masland, John W. and Laurence I. Radway. *Soldiers and Scholars: Military Education and National Policy.* Princeton: Princeton University Press, 1957.
166. Matloff, Maurice, ed. *American Military History.* Washington: Office of the Chief of Military History, United States Army, 1969.
167. Mattes, Merril J. *Indians, Infants, and Infantry: Andrew and Elizabeth Burt on the Frontier.* Denver: Old West Publishing Co., 1960.
168. McFeely, William S. *Yankee Stepfather: General O. O. Howard and the Freedmen.* New Haven: Yale University Press, 1968.
169. McIntyre, Benjamin F. *Federals on the Frontier: The Diary of Benjamin F. McIntyre.* Austin: University of Texas Press, 1963.
170. Meredith, Roy. *The American Wars, 1775-1953: A Pictorial History from Quebec to Korea.* Cleveland: World, 1955.
171. Merrill, James M. *Spurs to Glory. The Story of the United States Cavalry.* Chicago, Rand McNally, 1966.
172. Merrill, James M., ed. *Uncommon Valor: The Exciting Story of the Army.* Chicago: Rand McNally, 1964.
173. Michie, Peter S. *Life and Letters of General Emory Upton.* New York: Appleton, 1885.
174. Miles, Nelson A. *Personal Recollections and Observation of General Nelson A. Miles. . . .* Chicago: The Werner Co., 1896.
175. Miles, Nelson A. *Serving the Republic; Memoirs of the Civil and Military Life of Nelson A. Miles.* New York: Harper, 1911.
176. Miley, John D. *In Cuba with Shafter.* New York: Scribner's, 1899.
177. Millett, Allan R. *The Politics of Intervention: The Military Occupation of Cuba, 1906-1909.* Columbus: Ohio State University Press, 1968.
178. Millis, Walter, ed. *American Military Thought.* Indianapolis: Bobbs-Merrill, 1966.
179. Millis, Walter. *Arms and Men: A Study in American Military History.* New York: Putnam, 1956.
180. Millis, Walter. *The Martial Spirit: A Study of our War with Spain.* Boston: Houghton Mifflin Co., 1931.
181. Monaghan, Jay. *Custer.* Boston: Little, Brown, 1959.

182. Mooney, Chase C. & Martha E. Layman. "Some Phases of the Compulsory Military Training Movement, 1914-1920." *Mississippi Valley Historical Review,* v. 38, p. 637-655.
183. Morgan, Arthur E. *Dams and Other Disasters: A Century of the Army Corps of Engineers in Civil Works.* Boston: Porter Sargeant, 1971.
184. Morgan, H. Wayne. *America's Road to Empire: The War with Spain and Overseas Expansionism.* New York: John Wiley, 1965.
185. Morison, Elting E. *Turmoil and Tradition: A Study of the Life and Times of Henry L. Stimson.* Boston: Houghton Mifflin, 1960.
186. Murray, Keith. *The Modocs and their War.* Norman: University of Oklahoma Press, 1959.
187. Murray, Robert A. *Military Posts in the Powder River Country of Wyoming, 1865-1894.* Lincoln: University of Nebraska Press, 1968.
188. Nadeau, Remi. *Fort Laramie and the Sioux Indians.* Englewood Cliffs: Prentice-Hall, 1967.
189. Nelson, Otto L. *National Security and the General Staff.* Washington: Infantry Journal Press, 1946.
190. Nye, Wilbur S. *Carbine and Lance: The Story of Old Fort Sill.* Norman: University of Oklahoma Press, 1943.
191. O'Connor, Richard G. *Black Jack Pershing.* Garden City: Doubleday, 1961.
192. O'Connor, Richard G. *Sheridan, The Inevitable.* Indianapolis: Bobbs-Merrill, 1953.
193. Ogle, Ralph H. *Federal Control of the Western Apaches, 1848-1886.* Albuquerque: University of New Mexico Press, 1970.
194. Oliva, Leo E. *Soldier on the Santa Fe Trail.* Norman: University of Oklahoma Press, 1967.
195. Olson, James C. *Red Cloud and The Sioux Problem.* Lincoln: University of Nebraska Press, 1965.
196. Padelford, Norman. *The Panama Canal in Peace and War.* New York: Macmillan, 1942.
197. Palmer, John McAuley. *America In Arms: The Experience of the United States with Military Organization.* New Haven: Yale University Press, 1941.
198. Palmer, Frederick. *Bliss, Peacemaker: The Life and Letters of General Tasker Howard Bliss.* New York: Dodd, Mead, 1934.
199. Palmer, Frederick. *Newton D. Baker.* New York: Dodd, Mead, 1931.
200. Pappas, George S. *Prudens Futuri! The U.S. Army War College, 1901-1967.* Carlisle: Army War College Alumni Association, 1968.
201. Parker, James. *The Old Army: Memories, 1872-1918.* Philadelphia: Dorrance, 1929.
202. Parker, John H. *History of the Gatling Gun Detachment, Fifth Army Corps, at Santiago.* Kansas City: Franklin Hudson, 1898.
203. Perry, Ralph Barton. *The Plattsburg Movement, a Chapter of America's Participation in the World War.* New York: E. P. Dutton, 1921.
204. Pogue, Forrest C. *George C. Marshall: Education of a General, 1880-1939.* New York: Viking Press, 1963.
205. Porter, Kenneth W. "The Seminole-Negro Indian Scouts, 1870-1881." *Southwestern Historical Quarterly,* v. 55, p. 358-377.

206. Post, Charles J. *The Little War of Private Post*. Boston: Little, Brown, 1960.
207. Pratt, Richard Henry. *Battlefield & Classroom: Four Decades with the American Indian, 1867-1904*. New Haven: Yale University Press, 1964.
208. Price, George F. *Across the Continent with the Fifth Cavalry*. New York: D. Van Nostrand, 1883.
209. Pride, Woodbury F. *The History of Fort Riley*. Fort Riley, Kansas: Cavalry School Book Dept., 1926.
210. Pringle, Henry F. *The Life and Times of William Howard Taft*. New York: Farrar and Rinehart, 1939.
211. Prucha, Francis Paul, S. J. *Guide to Military Posts of the United States*. Madison: State Historical Society of Wisconsin, 1964.
212. Purcell, Victor. *The Boxer Uprising: A Background Study*. Cambridge: University Press, 1963. Reprinted, Hamden, Connecticut: Archon Books, 1974.
213. Quirk, Robert E. *An Affair of Honor: Woodrow Wilson and the Occupation of Vera Cruz*. Lexington: University of Kentucky Press, 1962.
214. Ranson, Edward. "The Endicott Board of 1885-86 and the Coast Defenses." *Military Affairs*, v. 31, p. 74-84.
215. Ranson, Edward. "Nelson A. Miles as Commanding General, 1895-1903." *Military Affairs*, v. 29, p. 179-200.
216. Rickey, Don. *Forty Miles a Day on Beans and Hay: The Enlisted Soldier Fighting the Indian Wars*. Norman: University of Oklahoma Press, 1963.
217. Rich, Bennett M. *The Presidents and Civil Disorder*. Washington: Brookings Institution, 1941.
218. Riker, William H. *Soldiers of the States: The Role of the National Guard in American Democracy*. Washington: Public Affairs Press, 1957.
219. Risch, Erna. *Quartermaster Support of the Army: A History of the Corps, 1775-1939*. Washington: G. P. O., 1962.
220. Rister, Carl C. *Border Command: General Phil Sheridan in the West*. Norman: University of Oklahoma Press, 1944.
221. Rodenbough, Theophilus F. and William L. Haskin, ed.; *The Army of the United States*. New York: Maynard, Merrill & Co., 1896.
222. Root Elihu. *Five Years of the War Department*. Washington: G. P. O., 1904.
223. Roosevelt, Theodore. *The Rough Riders*. New York: Scribner's, 1899.
224. Sargent, Herbert H. *The Campaign of Santiago de Cuba*. Chicago: A. C. McClurg, 1907.
225. Sears, Joseph Hamblen. *The Career of Leonard Wood*. New York: D. Appleton, 1919.
226. Schofield, John M. *Forty Six Years in the Army*. New York: Century, 1897.
227. Scott, Hugh A. *Some Memories of a Soldier*. New York: Appleton Century, 1928.
228. Semsch, Philip L. "Elihu Root and the General Staff." *Military Affairs*, v. 27, p. 16-27.

229. Sexton, William T. *Soldiers in the Sun: An Adventure in Imperialism.* Harrisburg: Military Service Pub. Co., 1939.
230. Shefton, James E. *The United States Army and Reconstruction, 1865-1877.* Baton Rouge: Louisiana State University Press, 1967.
231. Sheridan, Philip H. *Personal Memoirs of P. H. Sheridan, General, United States Army.* New York: C. L. Webster, 1888.
232. Sherman, William T. *Memoirs of William T. Sherman.* Civil War Centennial, ed. Bloomington: Indiana University Press, 1957.
233. Sherwood, Morgan B. *Exploration of Alaska, 1865-1900.* New Haven: Yale University Press, 1965.
234. Shindler, Henry. *History of the United States Military Prison.* Ft. Leavenworth: Army Service Schools Press, 1911.
235. Shindler, Henry and E. E. Booth. *History of the Army Service Schools.* Fort Leavenworth: Staff College Press, 1908.
236. Singletary, Otis A. *Negro Militia and Reconstruction.* Austin: University of Texas Press, 1957.
237. Smith, Louis, *American Democracy and Military Power.* Chicago: University of Chicago Press, 1951.
238. Smythe, Donald. *Guerrilla Warrior: The Early Life of John J. Pershing.* New York: Scribner's, 1973.
239. Sparrow, John C. *History of Personnel Demobilization.* Washington: G. P. O., 1951.
240. Spaulding, Oliver Lyman. *The United States Army in War and Peace.* New York: G. P. Putnam's Sons, 1937.
241. Sprague, Marshall. *Massacre: The Tragedy at White River.* Boston: Little, Brown, 1957.
242. Stanley, David S. *Personal Memoirs of Maj. General D. S. Stanley, U.S.A.* Cambridge, Massachusetts, 1917.
243. Steele, Matthew F. *American Campaigns.* Washington, D.C.: B. S. Adams, 1909.
244. Steward, Theophilus G. *The Colored Regulars in the United States Army, with a Sketch of the History of the Colored American, and an Account of His Services in the Wars of the Country, From the Period of the Revolutionary War to 1899.* Philadelphia: AME Book Concern, 1904.
245. Steward, Edgar I. *Custer's Luck.* Norman: University of Oklahoma Press, 1955.
246. Stimson, Henry L. and McGeorge Bundy. *On Active Service in Peace and War.* New York: Harper, 1947.
247. Storey, Moonfield and Marcial P. Licnauco. *The Conquest of the Philippines by the United States.* New York: G. P. Putnam's Sons, 1926.
248. Tan, Chester C. *The Boxer Catastrophe.* New York: Columbia University Press, 1955.
249. Tanham, George J. "Service Relations Sixty Years Ago." *Military Affairs,* v. 23, p. 139-148.
250. Thian, Raphael P. *Legislative History of the General Staff of the Army of the United States from 1775 to 1901.* Washington, D. C.: Government Printing Office, 1901.
251. Thomas, Benjamin P. and Harold M. Hyman. *Stanton: The Life*

and Times of Lincoln's Secretary of War. New York: Knopf, 1962.
252. Thomas, Robert S. and Inez V. Allen. The Mexican Punitive Expedition Under Brigadier General John J. Pershing, 1916-1917. Washington: U.S. Department of the Army, Office of Military History, 1954.
253. Thompson, Donald A. American Army Chaplaincy: A Brief History. Washington: G. P. O., 1946.
254. Tompkins, Frank. Chasing Villa: The Story Behind the Story of Pershing's Expedition Into Mexico. Harrisburg: The Military Service Pub. Co., 1934.
255. Thrapp, Dan L. The Conquest of Apacheria. Norman: University of Oklahoma Press, 1967.
256. Thrapp, Dan L. General Crook and the Sierra Madre Adventure. Norman: University of Oklahoma Press, 1972.
257. Thrapp, Dan L. Victorio and the Mimbres Apaches. Norman: University of Oklahoma Press, 1973.
258. Upton, Emory. A New System of Infantry Tactics, Double and Single Rank. New York: D. Appleton, 1867.
259. Upton, Emory. The Military Policy of the United States. Washington: G. P. O., 1904.
260. Utley, Robert M. Custer and the Great Controversy: The Origin and Development of a Legend. Los Angles: Westernlore Press, 1962.
261. Utley, Robert M. Frontier Regulars: The United States Army and the Indian, 1866-1890. New York: Macmillan, 1973.
262. Utley, Robert M. The Last Days of the Sioux Nation. New Haven: Yale University Press, 1963.
263. Vaughan, William P. "West Point and the First Negro Cadet." Military Affairs, v. 35, p. 12-18.
264. Wagner, Arthur L. Organization and Tactics. New York: B. Westerman, 1895.
265. Wallace, Ernest. Ranald S. Mackenzie On The Texas Frontier. Lubbock: West Texas Museum Association, 1964.
266. Walton, George. Sentinel of the Plains: Fort Leavenworth and the American West. Englewood Cliffs: Prentice-Hall, 1973.
267. Walton, William. The Army and Navy of the United States. Boston: G. Barrie, 1889-95.
268. Ward, Robert D. "The Origins and Activities of the National Security League." Mississippi Valley Historical Review, v. 47, p. 51-65.
269. Weaver, John D. The Brownsville Raid. New York: W. W. Norton, 1970.
270. Weigley, Russell F. History of the United States Army. New York: Macmillan, 1967.
271. Weigley, Russell F. Towards an American Army: Military Thought from Washington to Marshall. New York: Columbia University Press, 1962.
272. Wheeler, Joseph. The Santiago Campaign. Boston: Lamson, Wolffe and Co., 1898.
273. White, Howard. Executive Influence in Determining Military Policy in the United States. Urbana: University of Illinois Press, 1924.
274. White, Howard A. The Freedman's Bureau in Louisiana. Baton Rouge: Louisiana State University Press, 1970.

275. White, John R. *Bullets and Bolos: Fifteen Years in the Philippine Islands.* New York: Century, 1928.
276. Whitman, Sidney E. *The Troopers: An Informal History of the Plains Cavalry, 1865-1890.* New York: Hastings House, 1962.
277. Whitnah, Donald R. *A History of the United States Weather Bureau.* Urbana: University of Illinois Press, 1961.
278. Williams, Ben A., ed. *Amateurs at War: The American Soldier in Action.* Boston: Houghton-Mifflin, 1943.
279. Williams, T. Harry. *Americans At War: The Development of the American Military System.* Baton Rouge: Louisiana State University Press, 1960.
280. Wilson, Frederick T. *Federal Aid in Domestic Disturbances, 1787-1903.* Washington: G. P. O., 1903.
281. Wilson, James Harrison. *Under the Old Flag: Recollections of Military Operations in the War for the Union, the Boxer Rebellion, etc.* New York: D. Appleton, 1912.
282. Winther, Oscar O. *A Classified Bibliography of the Periodical Literature of the Trans-Mississippi West.* Bloomington: Indiana University Press, 1961.
283. Winther, Oscar O. *Trans-Mississippi West: A Guide to Its Periodical Literature.* Bloomington: University of Indiana Press, 1942.
284. Woff, Leon. *Little Brown Brother.* Garden City: Doubleday, 1961.
285. Wood, Leonard. *The Military Obligation of Citizenship.* Princeton: Princeton University Press, 1915.
286. Wormser, Richard C. *The Yellowlegs: The Story of the United States Cavalry.* Garden City: Doubleday, 1966.

X

SCIENCE AND TECHNOLOGY
IN THE TWENTIETH CENTURY

Carroll W. Pursell, Jr.

Despite the obvious overwhelming importance of war in stimulating and shaping American science and technology, we know remarkably little about the process itself. Only the years during and immediately after World War II have been looked at carefully; for the rest we must make do with detailed "official" administrative histories or equally detailed studies of particular weapons. Any survey of the pre-World War II period should begin with A. Hunter Dupree's *Science in the Federal Government* (62). Eugene Emme, "The Contemporary Spectrum of War" (66) gives textbook coverage to the postwar period, and should be supplemented by *Organization and Administration of the Military Research and Development Programs* (218), issued in 1954 by the House Committee on Government Operations. Clarence G. Lasby, "Science and the Military" (125) surveys the entire period.

What all these surveys show is that the general topic of this chapter, "Science and Technology in the Twentieth Century," deals with two problems which are usually kept separate in both popular and scholarly studies. On the one hand, we have the traditional guns, naval vessels, etc., which are in fact the actual tools of war. On the other hand, there is a growing research and development sector, existing both within and without the military, which not only devises and changes the actual weapons, but which is itself a tool constantly sharpened and applied to new tasks. This bibliography, while biased toward the latter topic, will cover both.

STRATEGY. New tools of war, of course, are frequently used in new ways, and new tactics suggest new strategic thinking as well. I. B. Holley and Theodore Ropp, "Technology and Strategy" (96) is a useful introduction to the interaction between ends and means, while Ralph Sanders and Fred R. Brown, *National Security Management* (172) describe the thinking of the mid-1960s upon the subject. Albert Wohlstetter, "Strategy and the Natural Scientists" (252) and Bernard Brodie, "The Scientific Strategists" (26) both concentrate on that new breed of professional strategist most often found in the universities and "think tanks" of the nation in the post-World War II era.

FACILITIES. Although usually lacking drama, the histories of scientific and technological facilities contributing to the nation's weaponry form an

269

important part of the literature. One of the oldest is covered by Gustavus A. Weber, *The Naval Observatory* (248). An even older facility, the Washington Navy Yard and Naval Gun Factory, is described in Taylor Peck, *Round-Shot to Rockets* (154). The better remembered Naval Research Laboratory is covered in two short pieces by A..Hoyt Taylor, "Thomas A. Edison and the Naval Research Laboratory" (201) and *The First Twenty-Five Years of the Naval Research Laboratory* (200). Studies of more recent facilities include Alfred Rosenthal, *Venture Into Space* (168) which covers the early years of the Goddard Space Flight Center, and the popularly written *Edwards* (15) by John Ball, Jr., a history of the Air Force flight test center in California. Albert B. Christman, *Sailors, Scientists, and Rockets* (44) is the first volume in a projected history of the Naval Ordnance Test Station, Inyokern.

NAVY. Many of the titles listed in this bibliography concern issues which cross service lines, but each has its own literature as well. A good survey, though somewhat dated, of naval affairs is Bernard Brodie, *Sea Power in the Machine Age* (27), which opens with a chapter on "Sea Power and the New Technology" (steam power, iron-clads, etc.) and closes with one on "Naval Invention and National Policy" bringing the story to the eve of World War II. Reminiscences of men deeply involved in the changes in naval technology include William Frederick Durand, *Adventures* (63), Holden A. Evans, *One Man's Fight for a Better Navy* (68), and two by a key figure of World War II, Harold G. Bowen: *Engineering and Research in the U.S. Navy* (22) and the more complete *Ships, Machinery, and Mossbacks* (23). Useful studies of the actual hardware of the Navy include such official reports as *Destroyers of the United States Navy* (240) and *The Submarine in the United States Navy* (242), both by the Naval History Division, and Scot MacDonald, *Evolution of Aircraft Carriers* (128). James C. Fahey, *Ships and Aircraft of the U.S. Fleet* (69) went through eight editions between 1939 and 1965, and contains comprehensive technical data. Peter B. Schroeder, *Contact at Sea* (178), is a good study of maritime radio communications, as is Howeth's official volume (101).

AIRCRAFT. The literature on aircraft, and the flying services, is very large. For the Navy, one can begin with Archibald D. Turnbull and Clifford L. Lord, *History of United States Naval Aviation* (212), Office of Naval Operations, *United States Naval Aviation 1910-1960* (243), and Garland Fulton, "The General Climate for Technological Developments in Naval Aeronautics on the Eve of World War I" (76). M. P. Claussen, *Comparative Histories of Research and Development Policies Affecting Air Material, 1915-1944* (46) is useful, and more particular studies include Philip S. Dickey III, "The Liberty Engine, 1918-1942" (57), Bernard L. Boylan, "The Development of the American Long Range Escort Fighter" (25), and J. DuBuque and R. Gleckner, *The Development of the Heavy Bomber, 1918-1944* (60). A study of a more recent (and more controversial) airplane is Berkeley Rice, *The C-5A Scandal* (165). Lighter-than-air ships are dealt with by Richard K. Smith, *The Airships Akron & Macon* (190).

A valuable congressional study of the subject is *Basic Scientific and Astronautic Research in the Department of Defense* (222), and the Finletter Report, *Survival in the Air Age* (158), issued in 1948, gives considerable insight into the rationale for postwar military aviation. Although technically a civilian organization, the work of the National Advisory Committee for Aeronautics (NACA) was of critical importance for the development of military aircraft. The best introduction to the NACA is George W. Gray, *Frontiers of Flight* (83), which should be supplemented by Jerome C. Hunsaker, *Aeronautics at the Mid-Century* (103).

WORLD WAR I AND AFTER. The record of American science and technology in World War I is varied though far from complete. A brief overview of the war and the decades immediately before is Edward L. Katzenbach, Jr., "The Mechanization of War, 1880-1919" (108). A popular contemporary account of weaponry is Frank Parker Stockbridge, *Yankee Ingenuity in the War* (195), which can be prepared with the heavily illustrated volume edited by Albert A. Hopkins, *The Scientific American War Book* (99). Two articles by Daniel J. Kevles, "Testing the Army's Intelligence: Psychologists and the Military in World War I" (111) and "Flash and Sound in the AEF: The History of a Technical Service" (109) explore interesting aspects of the new way in which both social and natural science were applied to warfare. Thomas Parke Hughes' excellent biography, *Elmer Sperry* (102), treats the close, complicated, and productive relationships between that inventor-engineer and the military services both before and during the war.

Wartime science flourished in several different organizational environments. The activities of the Massachusetts Institute of Technology and its faculty and students are set down in interesting detail in *Technology's War Record* (202). Two official records of old-line military agencies are *Historical Report of the Chief Engineer* (213) and U.S. Navy Department, *Navy Ordnance Activities World War* (237). Some State Councils of Defense set up research agencies, and the record of one has survived: "The Organization and Activities of the Committee on Scientific Research of the State Council of Defense of California" (81).

It was during World War I, for the first time, that civilian scientists succeeded in setting up within the government structure effective agencies for aiding the military. The first of these is officially recorded in the *Naval Consulting Board of the United States* (182), which played a technical role larger than its name implies. The Board was chaired by Thomas Edison, and some insight into his activities can be gotten from Karl T. Compton, "Edison's Laboratory in Wartime" (52). Scientists, as distinct from engineers and inventors, tended to look not to the Board but to the new National Research Council for leadership. A detailed but uncritical history of the first years of the NRC is given in *A History of the National Research Council, 1919-1933* (143). The best study of its origins is Daniel J. Kevles, "George Ellery Hale, the First World War, and the Advancement of Science in America" (110). Hale's efforts are placed in context by Helen Wright, *Explorer of the Universe* (254).

THE WORLD WAR II OFFICE OF SCIENTIFIC RESEARCH AND DEVELOPMENT. The efforts of the Office of Scientific Research and Development (OSRD) form the best documented scientific activities of World War II. Established in 1941 through a metamorphosis of the older Naponal Defense Research Committee (NDRC), set up in 1940, the OSRD was the primary research agency for the entire military (excluding aviation which continued to be the responsibility of the National Advisory Committee for Aeronautics [NACA]). The broadest and most general of the official histories of the OSRD is by James Phinney Baxter 3rd, *Scientists Against Time* (18). The administrative, and to some extent political, history of the group appears in Irvin Stewart, *Organizing Scientific Research for War* (194). In addition, each of the separate sections within OSRD was asked to produce its own history. Among these are John E. Burchard, ed., *Rockets, Guns, and Targets* (32); Joseph C. Boyce, ed., *New Weapons for Air Warfare* (24); C. G. Suits *et al.*, *Applied Physics, Electronics, Optics, Metallurgy* (198); Lincoln R. Thiesmeyer and John E. Burchard, *Combat Scientists* (206), which covers the battlefield aspect of development and testing; and E. C. Andrus *et al.*, *Advances in Military Medicine* (9), covering the work of the Committee on Medical Research (CMR), a coordinate branch, along with the NDRC, of OSRD.

A prominent member of the original NDRC, and after 1941 its chairman, was James B. Conant, whose autobiography, *My Several Lives* (53), sheds some light on his wartime activities. The real leader of the OSRD was the remarkable Vannevar Bush. His autobiography, *Pieces of the Action* (35), is not very detailed about his role in OSRD, but his postwar plan for American research, *Science—the Endless Frontier* (36), and his later collection of essays, *Modern Arms and Free Men* (34), establish his place in the history of military research. A bibliography of his works, published over a decade before his death, is *A Keepsake in Honor of Vannevar Bush* (33).

In addition to the official histories published after the war, the OSRD summarized its activities in a series of seventy-three volumes carrying the overall title "Summary technical report of the National Defense Research Committee." A set of these reports is available for use at the library of the National Science Foundation, Washington, D.C. No independent history of the OSRD yet exists, but a scholarly explanation of its origin and significance will be found in A. Hunter Dupree, "The Great Instauration of 1940: The Organization of Scientific Research for War" (61).

OTHER WORLD WAR II SCIENTIFIC ACTIVITIES. Although the OSRD was the principal American scientific agency during World War II, it did not account for the majority of funds spent on research and development. An overview of the total effort can be gained from the congressional report, *The Government's Wartime Research and Development* (230), part I of which covers the various agencies involved while part II details the committee's findings and recommendations. A congressional inquiry into technical changes in industry forced by the war is found in the detailed but unanalytical *Wartime Technological Developments* (231). Both of these major reports appeared during the first half of 1945 and so do not take into account the latter months of the war. George W. Gray, *Science at War* (84), is a popular report on an activity in progress, and Ralph Sanders, "Three-Dimensional Warfare: World War II" (173), is a scholarly attempt to impose some structure on what was disparate effort.

Other studies of wartime activities range from a very few efforts to trace certain innovations, such as Charles Kittel, "The Nature and Development of Operations Research" (112); a personal account of America's radar research,

Robert Morris Page, *The Origin of Radar* (152); and on through memoirs of wartime reminiscences such as Louis F. Fieser, *The Scientific Method* (71), and Warren Weaver, *Scene of Change* (247). The latter book contains only one chapter on World War II. Julius A. Furer, "Naval Research and Development in World War II" (78), is a short introduction to that service and can be supplemented by his *Administration of the Navy Department in World War II* (77). Particular bureaus and services are being covered by the official history program of the Army (see chapter XIV). Examples include George Raynor Thompson *et al.*, *The Signal Corps: The Test* (208), and Harry C. Thompson and Lida Mayo, *The Ordnance Department: Procurement and Supply* (209). The Navy's ordnance effort is covered in Buford Rowland and William B. Boyd. *U.S. Navy Bureau of Ordnance in World War II* (171), chapter 19 of which deals specifically with research and development. Nonmilitary agencies are not as well researched, but two examples are "A Brief Summary of the Smithsonian Institution's Part in World War II" (1) and the *Administrative History of the National Inventors Council* (142).

MANHATTAN DISTRICT AND POSTWAR NUCLEAR EFFORTS. The literature on the Manhattan District and its consequences is large and growing fast. The starting place for any study must be the excellent and official history of the Atomic Energy Commission (AEC), Richard G. Hewlett and Oscar E. Anderson, Jr., *The New World, 1939-1946* (92), and Richard G. Hewlett and Francis Duncan, *Atomic Shield, 1947-1952* (90). Many of the main themes of the next decade can be picked up from Richard G. Hewlett and Francis Duncan, *Nuclear Navy, 1946-1962* (91), which deals with the professional career of Admiral Rickover. The first official report on the Manhattan District, Henry DeWolf Smyth, *Atomic Energy for Military Purposes* (191), is still useful, as are such personal recollections as those of Leslie Groves, *Now It Can Be Told* (87), by the Corps of Engineers head of the Project; Arthur Holly Compton, *Atomic Quest* (51), by one of the leading physicists; and Samuel A. Goudsmit, *Alsos* (82), the story of the scientific mission which attempted to discover the German atomic bomb project before V-E Day.

Any attempt to understand the Robert Oppenheimer affair, the most celebrated conflict over atomic policy in the early years of the AEC, should begin with the official transcript of his security hearings by the U.S. Atomic Energy Commission, *In the Matter of J. Robert Oppenheimer* (214). Peter Michelmore, *The Swift Years* (136), is a biography of Oppenheimer, and his relations with E. O. Lawrence, the other atomic luminary at the University of California, are described in Nuel Pharr Davis, *Lawrence & Oppenheimer* (54). Thomas Wilson, Jr., *The Great Weapons Heresy* (251) tells the Oppenheimer story in the context of military nuclear policy.

General studies of the early atomic years include Stephane Groueff, *Manhattan Project* (86) and Lansing Lamont, *Day of Trinity* (121). Later developments are covered in Norman Moss, *Men Who Play God* (141), the story of the H-bomb. This should be supplemented with the contemporary essays, pro and con, printed in George Fielding Eliot, ed., *The H-Bomb* (65). More specialized studies include the old but provocative James S. Allen, *Atomic Imperialism* (4), which attempts to link American nuclear and foreign policy to corporate control of the Manhattan Project, as well as the more recent brief critical attack on the University of California's Lawrence Radiation Laboratory, *U.C. Science at War* (182), issued by the SESPA (Scientists and Engineers for Social and Political Action).

POSTWAR ORGANIZATION OF RESEARCH. The organizational history of postwar military research and development is still best gotten at through government documents. The debate over appropriate organizational forms began even before V-E Day and are best seen in the fight over the proposed Research Board for National Security, and may be followed in the variously issued reports and hearings: *Hearings, Surplus Materials . . . Research and Development* (228); *Report, Research and Development* (229); *Permanent Program of Scientific Research in the Interest of National Security* (219); *Hearings, Establishing a Research Board for National Security* (232); and *Report, Establishing a Research Board for National Security* (233). Later attempts by the government to survey the situation are the report of the Steelman committee, *Science and Public Policy* (159), which contains information on military R&D in all five volumes, and two reports of the Hoover Commission (1955): *Research and Development in the Government* (49), in which thirty-two of the fifty pages deal with military matters, and *Subcommittee Report on Research Activities in the Department of Defense and Defense Related Agencies* (50). A brief overview of these activities is given in Donald C. Swain, "Organization of Military Research" (199).

The Navy soon after the war set up its pioneering Office of Naval Research, the origins of which are told in an article by the "Bird Dogs" (the officers who originated the agency), in "The Evolution of the Office of Naval Research" (21). The early days are also described in F. Joachim Weyl, ed., *Research In the Service of National Purpose* (249), especially in articles by Alan T. Waterman on "Pioneering in Federal Support of Basic Research" and William O. Baker in "Science and National Security." A retrospective is offered by Luther J. Carter, "Office of Naval Research: 20 Years Bring Changes" (39). The Air Force in-house activities are covered by Thomas A. Sturm, *The USAF Scientific Advisory Board* (197), and Nick A. Komons, *Science and the Air Force* (119). The spin-off of contract organizations is well covered in Paul Dickson, *Think Tanks* (58), and a history of the most famous is given in Bruce L. R. Smith, *The Rand Corporation* (189). An effort to expand university suppliers of military research is described in the U.S. Department of Defense booklet. *Project Themis* (235). European efforts to support American military research is considered in Scientific Affairs Division, North Atlantic Treaty Organization, *NATO and Science* (148).

MISSILES. The best book for pre-World War II missile efforts in America is Milton Lehman, *This High Man* (126), a biography of Robert H. Goddard. The autobiography of a major wartime figure is Theodore von Karman, *The Wind and Beyond* (245), while the Joint Board on Scientific Information Policy, *U.S. Rocket Ordnance Development and Use in World War II* (236), attempts to cover a broader area of activity. German efforts (carried over to America) are described by a participant in Dieter K. Huzel, *Peenemunde to Canaveral* (105). The bringing to America of German rocket experts is covered in Michel Bar-Zohar, *The Hunt for German Scientists* (17), translated from the French, and more carefully in Clarence G. Lasby, *Project Paperclip* (124).

The Fall 1963 issue of *Technology and Culture* (published also as a separate volume) was devoted to essays on the history of rocketry, notably the Polaris (137), the Atlas, Thor, and Titan (155), and the Redstone, Jupiter, and Juno (244).

The way in which public policy translates into technology is displayed in Michael H. Armacost, *The Politics of Weapons Innovation* (11), which focuses on the Thor-Jupiter controversy. An overall look at Air Force efforts is given by a participant in Ernest G. Schwiebert, *A History of the U.S. Air Force Ballistic Missiles* (179). Histories of particular missiles include John B. Medaris, *Countdown for Decision* (135), by the head of the Redstone Arsenal, John J. Chapman, *Atlas* (42), J. J. DiCerto, *Missile Base Beneath the Sea* (56), concerning Polaris, Constance Green and Milton Lomask, *Vanguard* (85), and Harvey M. Sapolsky, *The Polaris System Development* (174). A study of the still-secret spy satellites is given by Philip J. Klass, *Secret Sentries in Space* (113). The background of the ABM system is contained in Benson D. Adams, *Ballistic Missile Defense* (2), which covers Nike and Zeus as well as Safeguard.

RESEARCH AND DEVELOPMENT. The concept of research and development, of course, is basic to much of what science has contributed to military technology in the twentieth century. Although the process can be studied through histories of research facilities, agencies, and specific projects and devices, the general activity itself has been studied. Edwin Mansfield, *Defense, Science, and Public Policy* (129), is an excellent collection of essays, and Klaus Knorr and Oskar Morgenstern, *Science and Defense* (114), is a brief but searching inquiry into the process. R. A. Solo, "Gearing Military R & D to Economic Growth" (192), R. R. Nelson, "The Impact of Arms Reduction on R & D" (145), and Willis H. Shapely, "Special Problems of Military Research and Development" (185), the last by an important official of the then federal Bureau of the Budget, discusses various economic aspects of the process. A congressional study that is still useful is *Research and Development for Defense* (225) issued in 1961. A controversial study, sponsored by the Pentagon, which seemed to cast doubt on the cost-effectiveness of military support of science is reported in *First Interim Report on Project Hindsight* (234), as well as in Chalmers W. Sherwin and Raymond S. Isenson, "Project Hindsight" (186).

CHEMICAL WARFARE. Chemical warfare was, of course, one of the most dramatic developments of World War I and remains a controversial activity. Leo P. Brophy, "Origins of the Chemical Corps" (30), is a good starting place for its study, and the continuing controversy is covered in Frederick J. Brown, *Chemical Warfare: A Study in Restraints* (31). The situation on the eve of World War II is described in F. A. Hessel *et al.*, *Chemistry in Warfare* (89). The official history of World War II activities is contained in two volumes by Leo P. Brophy *et al.*, *The Chemical Warfare Service: Organizing for War* (29) and *The Chemical Warfare Service: From Laboratory to Field* (28). The chemical work done by civilians in the Office of Scientific Research and Development is described in William Albert Noyes, ed., *Chemistry* (149).

Since World War II research on chemical warfare has continued. Gale E.

Peterson, "The Discovery and Development of 2, 4-D" (156), tells the story of one defoliant developed, in part, with military funds and later used in Vietnam. Nick A. Komons, *A Decade of Chemical Research* (115) describes research carried on by the Air Force in the postwar period. A survey of chemical and biological potentials is presented by J. H. Rothschild, *Tomorrow's Weapons* (170).

RECENT TOPICS AND PROBLEMS. Although we lack the advantages of historical perspective on recent developments in military research and development, they are among the most interesting and important and much more could be done with them than is currently available in the scholarly literature. One such area is that called conversion, that is, the switching of scientific and technical resources from military to civilian projects. The years of the early 1960s, before the increased military activities in Southeast Asia, witnessed a great deal of concern about the problem. Two attempts at an overview are Richard S. Rosenbloom, "The Transfer of Military Technology to Civilian Use" (167), and Steven R. Rivkin, *Technology Unbound* (166). The House Committee on Governmental Operations, *Application of Aerospace and Defense Industry Technology to Environmental Problems* (215) reflects the awareness of pollution problems which surfaced in 1970. Samuel l. Doctors, *The Role of Federal Agencies in Technology Transfer* (59), sets the problem in its bureaucratic context, and Marvin Berkowitz, *The Conversion of Military-oriented Research and Development to Civilian Uses* (19), is a more recent survey of the particular problems involved.

The convergence of interests which President Eisenhower called the Military-Industrial Complex has not received the investigation it deserves. Three detailed surveys, the first two by a physicist and the third by a political scientist, are Ralph E. Lapp, *The Weapons Culture* (122), his more recent *Arms Beyond Doubt* (123), and H. L. Nieburg, *In the Name of Science* (147). Books by participants include *Race to Oblivion* (256) by Herbert F. York, a former research head for the Department of Defense, A. Ernest Fitzgerald, *The High Priests of Waste* (74), which deals with the Lockheed C-5A scandal, and Chalres J. Hitch, *Decision-Making for Defense* (93), by the economist who reformed the management of procurement for Secretary of Defense Robert McNamara. A detailed case study of how well the new plan worked is given in Robert J. Art, *The TFX Decision* (12). Two economic studies on how weapons are developed and purchased are Merton J. Peck and Frederic M. Scherer, *The Weapons Acquisition Process: An Economic Analysis* (153), and F. M. Scherer, *The Weapons Acquisition Process: Economic Incentives* (175).

The literature on military production and use of the social sciences is very small. The most famous case was Project Camelot which involved covert social data gathering in Latin America. A collection of essays dealing with this episode is Irving Louis Horowitz, ed., *The Rise and Fall of Project Camelot* (100), which should be supplemented by the chapter on "Congressional Response to Project Camelot" which appeared in the study *Technical Information for Congress* issued by the House Committee on Science and Astronautics (227). A related and very critical expose is Eric R. Wolf and Joseph G. Jorgensen, "Anthropology on the Warpath in Thailand" (253).

Dissent from postwar American military science and technology have been both scholarly and public, reasoned and violent. Attempts by some of the scientists of the Manhattan District to influence nuclear weapons policy are best covered in Alice Kimball Smith, *A Peril and A Hope* (188), which may be supplemented by Donald A. Strickland, *Scientists in Politics* (196). An international movement of scientists participated in the Pugwash Conferences, the history of which is given in J. Rotblat, *Scientists in the Quest for Peace* (169). An example of their deliberations may be seen in B. T. Feld *et al.*, *Impact of New Technologies on the Arms Race* (70). A particularly important protest against university involvement occurred at the Massachusetts Institute of Technology in 1969. The addresses made on the occasion are collected in Jonathan Allen, ed., *March 4* (5), and the history of the event is covered in Dorothy Nelkin, *The University and Military Research* (145). A critical study of war research at Stanford University is made in *Department of Defense Sponsored Research at Stanford* (80), the first volume of which is entitled "Two Perceptions: The Investigator's and the Sponsor's" and the second, "Its Impact on the University." Two outspoken and activist organizations publish magazines critical of war research: SPARK (193), by the Committee for Social Responsibility in Engineering, and *Science for the People* (180), by Scientists and Engineers for Social and Political Action. The latter group has also issued a pamphlet exposing and criticizing the élite research group known as Jason: *Science Against the People* (181).

When we turn to very recent weapons, of course, the problem of a lack of perspective is reinforced by secrecy. Nevertheless, some of the more important dimensions of modern arms are beginning to appear. John S. Tompkins, *The Weapons of World War III* (210), is an early effort to look at weapons other than nuclear, and the National Security Industrial Association, *Proceedings of the Symposium on Federal Research & Development in the 70's*, (144) is a hopeful attempt to map plans for new weaponry. A less friendly overview is given by Marc Kramer, "Buck Rogers is Alive and Well—And Doing R&D for the Pentagon" (120). Adam Yarmolinsky gave an early description of the use of computers by the military in "The Electronic Revolution at the Pentagon" (255). Vietnam provided a testing ground for several new weapons. One is touched upon in Deborah Shapley, "Weather Warfare: Pentagon Concedes 7-Year Vietnam Effort" (184), and a more detailed study was made by the House Committee on Science and Astronautics, *A Technology Assessment of the Vietnam Defoliant Matter* (221). The Israeli-Arab conflict has been looked at in Edgar O'Ballance, *The Electronic War in the Middle East* (150) and the battles of the Fall of 1973 are covered briefly but perspectively in Robert Gillete, "Military R&D: Hard Lessons of an Electronic War" (79).

SUGGESTIONS FOR FURTHER RESEARCH. Though considerable official work has been done on the histories of wartime scientific and technological work, there is much that remains to be done there and on the peacetime periods. Many of the wartime and immediate postwar assessments were made by participants and some were too close to the events they describe in both time and place. A more objective view from a proper historical perspective would be useful, for instance, in setting World War I developments into the general patterns of scientific and technological work at the time as well as comparing it with historical progress in other similar technologies. Though a great deal has been made of American technological progress, aircraft production in the First World War was a flop with many repercussions. But historians have done little in the way of looking at this compared to the production of artillery, say, and other hardware. Shipbuilding in both World Wars and the work of the U.S. Maritime Commission on the creation of standardized designs as well as of the U.S. Navy's Bureau of Ships still provide much room for a researcher's manouvers. The development of trucks which enabled the armies to do without railroads and the development of railroads themselves are wide open fields. In fact, a history of military railroading is a much needed volume.

Some aspects of military pressure for the development of fuels for ships, vehicles and aircraft and the associated hardware would lend themselves easily to articles. Work on foods and their preservations as well as on the development of special plastics for military uses are also topics which for the period to 1941, at least, leave much to be desired.

From World War II onwards the impact of the Cold War channeled money into research and development, but the combination of World War II, the Cold War, Korea and Vietnam stimulated not only developments in science and technology, but also vastly greater interest on the part of press lords, Congress, and the public, so that there is a plethora of scientific and technological information lying waiting to be exploited in technical journals, Congressional, and other governmental publications (see chapter 1). A researcher does not have to be a trained scientist or engineer to learn to master this and then even more technical material.

Another aspect of this whole field which has been very largely neglected is the economic side of military hardware. Here Brookings Institution studies can provide useful bases (141) and their investigative techniques employed to look into other similar or apparently dissimilar problems.

In other words, the history of science and technology in the twentieth century is largely wide open. At the same time there are some excellent models to follow.

BIBLIOGRAPHY

1. "A Brief Summary of the Smithsonian Institution's Part in World War II," *Annual Report of the Board of Regents of the Smithsonian Institution* . . . 1945 (Washington, 1946), 459-472.
2. Adams, Benson D. *Ballistic Missile Defense*. New York: American Elsevier 1971.
3. Air Ministry. *The Origins and Development of Operational Research in the Royal Air Force*. Air Publication 3368. London: 1963.
4. Allen, James S. *Atomic Imperialism: The State, Monopoly, and the Bomb*. New York: International Publishers 1952.
5. Allen, Jonathan, ed. *March 4: Scientists, Students, and Society*. Cambridge: M.I.T. Press 1970.
6. Anders, Leslie.*The Ledo Road: General Joseph W. Stilwell's Highway to China*. Norman: University of Oklahoma Press, 1965.
7. Anderson, Clinton P. and James T. Ramey."Congress and Research:

Experience in Atomic Research and Development," *Annals of the American Academy of Political and Social Science*, 327 (Jan., 1960), 85-94.

8. Andrade, Ernest, Jr. "The Ship That Never Was: The Flying-Deck Cruiser," *Military Affairs*, 32, no. 3 (Dec., 1968), 132-140.

9. Andrade, Ernest, Jr., "Submarine Policy in the United States Navy 1919-1941", *Military Affairs*, April 1971, 50-56.

10. Andrus, E. C., *et al.* (ed.) *Advances in Military Medicine, made by American Investigators Working under the Sponsorship of the Committee on Medical Research*, Boston, 1948. 2 vols.

11. Armacost, Michael H. *The Politics of Weapons Innovation: The Thor-Jupiter Controversy.* New York, 1969.

12. Art. Robert J. *The TFX Decision: McNamara and the Military.* Boston: Little, Brown 1968.

13. Ashford, Bailey K. *A Soldier in Science.* New York: William Morrow & Co.

14. Baar, James and William E. Howard. *Polaris!* New York: Harcourt Brace 1960.

15. Ball, John, Jr. *Edwards: Flight Test Center of the U.S.A.F.* New York: Duell, Sloan & Pearce 1962.

16. Barnes, Maj. Gen. G. M. X. *Weapons of World War II.* New York, 1947.

17. Bar-Zohar, Michel.*The Hunt for German Scientists.* New York: Hawthorn Books 1967.

18. Baxter, James Phinney 3rd.*Scientists Against Time.* Boston: Little, Brown 1946,

19. Berkowitz, Marvin.*The Conversion of Military-oriented Research and Development to Civilian Uses.* Foreward by Seymour Melman. New York: Praeger 1970.

20. Bibb, Everett I. "The Flying Tank . . . that Didn't," *U.S. Army Combat Forces Jour.*, 1 (Dec., 1950), 25-28.

21. The Bird Dogs. "The Evolution of the Office of Naval Research," *Physics Today*, XIV (Aug. 1961), 30-35.

22. Bowen, Harold G. *Engineering and Research in the U.S. Navy: An Address at New York.* New York: The Newcomen Society 1944.

23. Bowen, Harold G. *Ships, Machinery, and Mossbacks: The Autobiography of a Naval Engineer.* Princeton: Princeton University Press 1954.

24. Boyce, Joseph C. (ed.) *New Weapons for Air Warfare: Fire-Control Equipment, Proximity Fuzes, and Guided Missiles.* Boston: Little, Brown 1947.

25. Boylan, Bernard L. *The Development of the American Long-Range Escort Fighter.* Unpublished doctoral dissertation, University of Missouri, 1955.

26. Brodie, Bernard,"The Scientific Strategists," *Scientists and National Policy-Making*, ed. Robert Gilpin and Christopher Wright, New York: Columbia University Press, 1964, 240-256.

27. Brodie, Bernard.*Sea Power in the Machine Age.* Princeton: Princeton University Press 1941.

28. Brophy, Leo P., Wyndham D. Miles, and Rexmond Cochran *The Chemical Warfare Service: From Laboratory to Field.* Washington: G.P.O., 1959.
29. Brophy, Leo P. and George J. B. Fisher. *The Chemical Warfare Service: Organizing for War.* Washington: G.P.O., 1958.
30. Brophy, Leo P. "Origins of the Chemical Corps," *Military Affairs,* 20 (Winter, 1956), 217-226.
31. Brown, Frederick J. *Chemical Warfare. A Study in Restraints.* Princeton: Princeton University Press 1968.
32. Burchard, John E. (ed.) *Rockets, Guns, and Targets.* Boston: Little, Brown 1949.
33. Bush, Vannevar.*A Keepsake in Honor of Vannevar Bush.* Cambridge, June 15, 1959.
34. Bush, Vannevar.*Modern Arms and Free Men: A Discussion of the Role of Science in Preserving Democracy.* New York: Simon & Schuster 1949.
35. Bush, Vannevar.*Pieces of the Action.* New York: William Morrow & Co., 1970.
36. Bush, Vannevar.*Science—the Endless Frontier.* Washington, 1945. Reprinted by NSF, 1960.
37. Bushnell, David and Nick A. Komons.*History of the Office of Research Analysis.* Washington: Historical Division, Office of Information, Office of Aerospace Research, 1963.
38. Bushnell, David. *The Sacramento Peak Observatory, 1947-1962.* Washington: Historical Division, Office of Information, Office of Aerospace Research, 1962.
39. Carter, Luther J. "Office of Naval Research: 20 Years Bring Changes," *Science,* 153 (22 July 1966), 397-400.
40. Chamberlain, Peter and Chris Ellis.*The Sherman: An Illustrated History of the M4 Medium Tank.* New York: Arco 1969.
41. Chapin, Seymour L. "Patent Interferences and the History of Technology: A High-flying Example," *Technology and Culture,* 12 (July, 1971), 414-446.
42. Chapman, John L. *Atlas: The Story of a Missile.* New York: Harper 1960.
43. Chinn, George N. *The Machine Gun: History, Evolution and Development of Manual, Automatic and Airborne Repeating Weapons.* Washington: G.P.O., 1951-55. 4 vols.
44. Christman, Albert B. *Sailors, Scientists, and Rockets: Origins of the Navy Rocket Program and of The Naval Ordnance Test Station, Inyokern. History of the Naval Weapons Center, China Lake, California, Volume 1.* Washington: Naval History Division, 1971.
45. Clark, Edward B. *William L. Sibert, the Army Engineer.* Philadelphia: Dorrance & Co. 1930.
46. Claussen, M. P. *Comparative Histories of Research and Development Policies Affecting Air Materiel, 1915-1944.* Washington, 1945.
47. Claussen, M. P. *Material Research and Development in the Army Air Arm.* Washington, 1946.
48. Coll, Blanche D., Jean E. Keith, and Herbert H. Rosenthal. *The Corps of Engineers: Troops and Equipment.* Washington: G.P.O., 1958.

49. Commission on Organization of the Executive Branch of the Government. *Research and Development in the Government*. A Report to the Congress by the Commission on Organization of the Executive Branch of the Government. Washington, May 1955.

50. Commission on Organization of the Executive Branch of the Government. *Subcommittee Report on Research Activities in the Department of Defense and Defense Related Agencies*. Prepared for the Commission . . . by the Subcommittee on Research Activities in the Department of Defense and Defense Related Agencies of the Committee on Business Organization of the Department of Defense. Washington, April 1955.

51. Compton, Arthur Holly. *Atomic Quest: A Personal Narrative*. New York: Oxford University Press, 1956.

52. Compton, Karl T. "Edison's Laboratory in Wartime," *Science*, 75 (15 Jan., 1932), 70-71.

53. Conant, James B. *My Several Lives: Memoirs of a Social Inventor*. New York, 1970.

54. Davis, Nuel Pharr. *Lawrence & Oppenheimer*. New York: Simon & Schuster 1968.

55. Davis P. M. and A. C. Fenwick. *Development and Procurement of Gliders in the Army Air Forces, 1941-1944*. Washington, 1946.

56. DiCerto, J. J. *Missile Base Beneath the Sea: The Story of Polaris*. New York: St. Martin's Press 1967.

57. Dickey, Philip S., III. "The Liberty Engine, 1918-1942," *Smithsonian Annals of Flight*, I, no. 3 (1968).

58. Dickson, Paul. *Think Tanks*. New York: Atheneum, 1971.

59. Doctors, Samuel I. *The Role of Federal Agencies in Technology Transfer*. Cambridge: M.I.T. Press, 1969.

60. DuBuque, J. and R. Gleckner. *The Development of the Heavy Bomber, 1918-1944*. Rev. ed., Washington, 1951.

61. Dupree, A. Hunter. "The Great Insaturation of 1940: The Organization of Scientific Research for War," in Gerald Holton (ed.), *The Twentieth Century Science* New York: Norton 1972, 445-454.

62. Dupree, A. Hunter. *Science in the Federal Government: A History of Policies and Activities to 1940*. Cambridge: Harvard University Press 1957.

63. Durand, William Frederick. *Adventures: In the Navy, in Education, Science, Engineering, and in War—A Life Story*. New York: American Society of Mechanical Engineers 1953.

64. Eisenman, Harry J. *History of Mathematical Statistics Research at the Aeronautical Research Laboratories*. Washington: Historical Division, Office of Information, Office of Aerospace Research, 1962.

65. Eliot, George Fielding *et al. The H Bomb*. New York: Didier 1950.

66. Emme, Eugene M. "The Contemporary Spectrum of War," *Technology in Western Civilization, Volume II: Technology in the Twentieth Century*, ed. Melvin Kranzberg and Carroll W. Pursell, Jr. New York, Oxford University Press, 1967, pp. 578-590.

67. Emme, Eugene M. "Technical Change and Western Military Thought, 1914-1945," *Military Affairs*, 24 (Spring, 1960), 6-19.

68. Evans, Holden A. *One Man's Fight for a Better Navy*. New York: Dodd, Mead & Co. 1940.

69. Fahey, James C. *Ships and Aircraft of the U.S. Fleet.* various eds. Annapolis, 1965-

70. Feld, B. T. *et al. Impact of New Technologies on the Arms Race: A Pugwash Monograph.* Cambridge: M.I.T. Press 1971.

71. Fieser, Louis F. *The Scientific Method: A Personal Account of Unusual Projects in War and in Peace.* New York: Reinhold 1964.

72. Fine, Lenore and Jesse A. Remington. *The Technical Services—the Corps of Engineers: Construction in the United States.* Washington: Office of the Chief of Military History, GPO, 1973.

73. Fishbein, Morris (ed.) *Doctors at War* New York: E. P. Dutton 1945.

74. Fitzgerald, A. Ernest *The High Priests of Waste.* New York: Norton 1972.

75. Fuller, J. F. C. *Machine Warfare: An Inquiry into the Influence of Mechanics on the Art of War.* Washington: The Infantry Journal, 1943.

76. Fulton, Garland. "The General Climate for Technological Developments in Naval Aeronautics on the Eve of World War I," *Technology and Culture,* 4 (Spring, 1963), 154-165.

77. Furer, Julius Augustus. *Administration of the Navy Department in World War II.* Washington: G.P.O., 1959.

78. Furer, Julius A. "Naval Research and Development in World War II," *Journal of the American Society of Naval Engineers,* 62 (1950), 21-53.

79. Gillette, Robert. "Military R & D: Hard Lessons of an Electronic War," *Science,* 182 (9 Nov. 1973), 559-561.

80. Glantz, Stanton A. *Department of Defense Sponsored Research at Stanford.* Stanford: Stanford Workshop on Political and Social Issues, 1971. 2 vols.

81. Goodspeed, T.H. "The Organization and Activities of the Committee on Scientific Research of the State Council of Defense of California," *Bulletin of the National Research Council,* 5 part 6, no. 31 (April, 1923), 1-43.

82. Gouldsmit, Samuel A. *Alsos.* New York: Henry Schuman 1947.

83. Gray, George W. *Frontiers of Flight: The Story of NACA Research.* New York, 1948.

84. Gray, George W. *Science at War.* New York: Harper & Bros. 1943.

85. Green, Constance (McLaughlin) and Milton Lomask. *Vanguard: A History.* Washington: G.P.O., 1971.

86. Groueff, Stephane. *Manhatten Project: The Untold Story of the Making of the Atomic Bomb.* Boston: Little, Brown & Co., 1967.

87. Groves, Leslie. *Now It Can Be Told.* New York: Harper, 1962.

88. Helmer, William J. *The Gun That Made the Twenties Roar.* London: Macmillan, 1969.

89. Hessel, F. A., M. S. Hessel, and Wellford Martin *Chemistry in Warfare: Its Strategic Importance.* New York: Hastings House, 1940.

90. Hewlett, Richard G. and Francis Duncan. *Atomic Shield, 1947/1952. A History of the Atomic Energy Commission,* II. University Park: Pennsylvania State University Press 1969.

91. Hewlett, Richard G. and Francis Duncan. *Nuclear Navy, 1946-1962.* Chicago: University of Chicago Press, 1974.

92. Hewlett Richard G. and Oscar E. Anderson, Jr. *The New World, 1939/ 1946. Volume I: A History of the United States Atomic Energy Com-*

mission. University Park: Pennsylvania State University Press, 1962.

93. Hitch, Charles J. *Decision-Making for Defense.* Berkeley: University of California Press, 1966.

94. Holley, I. B. *Development of Aircraft Gun Turrets in the AAF, 1917-1944.* Washington, 1947.

95. Holley, I. B. *Ideas and Weapons.* New Haven: Yale University Press, 1953.

96. Holley, I. B. Jr. and Theodore Ropp· "Technology and Strategy," *Technology in Western Civilization, Volume II: Technology in the Twentieth Century,* ed. Melvin Kranzberg and Carroll W. Pursell, Jr. New York: Oxford, 1967, pp. 590-601.

97. Holmquist, Carl O. and Russell S. Greenbaum. "The Development of Nuclear Propulsion in the Navy," *U.S. Naval Institute Proceedings,* 86 (Sept., 1960), 65-71.

98. Holt, W. Stull. *The Office of the Chief of Engineers of the Army: Its Non-Military History, Activities and Organization.* Baltimore: Johns Hopkins Press 1923.

99. Hopkins, Albert A., ed. *The Scientific American War Book: The Meanism and Technique of Warfare.* New York: Moran & Co., 1916.

100. Horowitz, Irving Louis (ed.). *The Rise and Fall of Project Camelot: Studies in the Relationship Between Social Science and Practical Politics.* Cambridge: MIT Press, 1967.

101. Howeth, Linwood S. *History of Communications-Electronics in the United States Navy.* Washington: G.P.O., 1963.

102. Hughes, Thomas Parke. *Elmer Sperry: Inventor and Engineer.* Baltimore: Johns Hopkins Press, 1971.

103. Hunsaker, Jerome C. *Aeronautics at the Mid-Century.* New Haven: Yale University Press, 1952.

104. Hunsaker, Jerome C. Testimony of Jerome C. Hunsaker, "Research and Development in the Airplane Industry," Feb. 27, 1945, in *Investigation of the National Defense Program,* Hearings before a Special Committee Investigating the National Defense Program, U.S. Senate, Part 33, pp. 16807-16864.

105. Huzel, Dieter K. *Peenemunde to Canaveral.* Englewood Cliffs: Prentice Hall, 1962.

105a. Ickes, Harry E. "The Development of the 60-Inch Anti-aircraft Searchlight by the United States Army." (Unpublished doctoral dissertation), University of Pittsburgh, 1951.

106. Jacobson, H. Karen and E. Stein. *Diplomats, Scientists and Politicians: The U.S. and the Nuclear Test Ban Negotiations.* Ann Arbor: University of Michigan Press, 1966.

107. Johnson, Melvin M. and Charles T. Haven. *Automatic Arms: Their History, Development and Use.* New York: W. Morrow & Co., 1941.

108. Katzenbach, Edward L., Jr. "The Mechanization of War, 1880-1919," *Technology in Western Civilization, Volume II: Technology in the Twentieth Century,* ed. Melvin Kranzberg and Carroll W. Pursell, Jr. New York: Oxford University Press, 1967 pp. 548-561.

109. Kevles, Daniel J. "Flash and Sound in the AEF: The History of a Technical Service," *Military Affairs,* 33, no. 3 (Dec., 1969), 374-384.

110. Kevles, Daniel J. "George Ellery Hale, the First World War, and the

Advancement of Science in America," *Isis*, 59, no. 4 (Winter, 1968), 427-437.

111. Kevles, Daniel J. "Testing the Army's Intelligence: Psychologists and the Military in World War I," *Journal of American History*, 55, no. 3 (Dec., 1968), 565-581.

112. Kittel, Charles."The Nature and Development of Operations Research," *Science*, 105 (Feb. 7, 1947), 150-153.

113. Klass, Philip J. *Secret Sentries in Space*. New York: Random House, 1971.

114. Knorr, Klaus and Oskar Morgenstern.*Science and Defense: Some Critical Thoughts on Military Research and Development*. Policy Memo No. 32, Center of International Studies, Woodrow Wilson School of Public and International Affairs. Princeton, Feb. 18, 1965.

115. Komons, Nick A. *A Decade of Chemical Research: History of the Air Force Office of Scientific Research Chemistry Program*. Washington: Historical Divsion, Office of Information, Office of Aerospace Research, 1962.

116. Komons, Nick A. and David Bushnell. *The Air Force and Nuclear Physics: A History of the Air Force Office of Scientific Research Nuclear Physics Program*. Washington: Historical Division, Office of Information, Office of Aerospace Research, 1963.

117. Komons, Nick A. *Cadmium Sulfide: A History of Semiconductor Research at the Aerospace Research Laboratories*. Washington: Historical Division, Office of Information, Office of Aerospace Research, 1964.

118. Komons, Nick A. *Development of the Air Force Research Grant Program*. Washington: Historical Division, Office of Information, Office of Aerospace Research, 1963.

119. Komons, Nick A. *Science and the Air Force: A History of the Air Force Office of Scientific Research*. Arlington, Virginia: Historical Division, Office of Information, Office of Aerospace Research, 1966.

120. Kramer, Marc."Buck Rogers is Alive and Well—And Doing R&D for the Pentagon," *The Pentagon Watchers: Students Report on the National Security State*, ed. Leonard S. Rodberg and Derek Shearer (Garden City, 1970), pp. 323-334.

121. Lamont, Lansing.*Day of Trinity*. New York: Atheneum, 1965.

122. Lapp, Ralph E. *The Weapons Culture*. New York: Norton, 1968.

123. Lapp, Ralph E. *Arms Beyond Doubt: The Tyranny of Weapons Technology*. New York: Cowels Book Co., 1970.

124. Lasby, Clarence G. *Project Paperclip: German Scientists and the Cold War*. New York: Atheneum, 1971.

125. Lasby, Clarence G. "Science and the Military," *Science and Society in the United States*, ed. David D. Van Tassel and Michael G. Hall. Homewood, Ill.: Dorsey Press, 1966, pp. 251-282.

126. Lehman, Milton.*This High Man: The Life of Robert H. Goddard*. New York: Farrar Straus, 1963.

127. Maass, Arthur.*Muddy Waters: The Army Engineers and the Nation's Rivers*. Cambridge: Harvard University Press, 1951.

128. MacDonald, Scot.*Evolution of Aircraft Carriers*. Washington: Office of the Chief of Naval Operations, 1964.

129. Mansfield, Edwin (ed.) *Defense, Science, and Public Policy.* New York: Norton, 1968.

130. Marshall, Max L. (ed.) *The History of the U.S. Army Signal Corps.* New York: F. Watts, 1965.

131. Matt, Paul R. (comp.) *United States Navy and Marine Corps Fighters, 1918-1962.* Los Angeles, Aero Publishers, 1962.

132. McCarthy, Charles J. "Naval Aircraft Design in the Mid-1930's," *Technology and Culture,* 4 (Spring, 1963), 165-174.

133. McCloskey, Joseph F. "Military Roads in Combat Areas: The Development of Equipment and Techniques by the Corps of Engineers, United States Army, during World War II." (Unpublished doctoral dissertation), University of Pittsburgh, 1948.

134. McGovern, James.*Crossbow and Overcast.* New York: Morrow, 1964.

135. Medaris, John B. *Countdown for Decision.* New York: Putnam, 1960.

136. Michelmore, Peter.*The Swift Years: The Robert Oppenheimer Story.* New York: Dodd, Mead & Co., 1969.

137. Miles, Wyndham D. "The Polaris," *Technology and Culture,* 4 (Fall, 1963), 478-489.

138. Morgan, Arthur E. *Dams and Other Disasters: A Century of the Army Corps of Engineers in Civil Works.* Boston: Porter Sargent, 1971.

139. Morison, Elting E. *Men, Machines, and Modern Times.* Cambridge: MIT Press, 1966.

140. Moss, Norman.*Men Who Play God. The Story of the H-Bomb and How the World Came to Live with It.* New York: Harper & Row, 1969.

141. Mueller, Dennis C., and John E. Tilton. "Research and Development Costs as a Barrier to Entry". Washington: The Brookings Institution, 1970.

142. National Inventors Council.*Administrative History of the National Inventors Council.* Processed, NIC, Department of Commerce, Washington, c. 1946.

143. National Research Council. *A History of the National Research Council, 1919-1933.* Reprint and Circular Series of the National Research Council, No. 106, Washington, 1933.

144. National Security Industrial Association.*Proceedings of the Symposium on Federal Research & Development in the 70's: It's Need and Scope.* Washington: NSIA, 1969.

145. Nelkin, Dorothy.*The University and Military Research: Moral Politics at M.I.T.* Ithaca: Cornell University Press, 1972.

146. Nelson, R. R. "The Impact of Arms Reduction on R & D," *American Economic Review,* (May, 1963).

147. Nieburg, H. L. *In the Name of Science.* Chicago: Quadrangle Books, 1966.

148. North Atlantic Treaty Organization, Scientific Affairs Division.*NATO and Science: Facts about the activities of the Science Committee of the North Atlantic Treaty Organization, 1959-1966.* Paris: NATO, 1967.

149. Noyes, William Albert (ed.) *Chemistry: A History of the Chemistry Components of the National Defense Research Committee, 1940-1946.* Boston: Little, Brown, 1948.

150. O'Ballance, Edgar. *The Electronic War in the Middle East, 1968-70.* Hamden, Connecticut: Archon, 1974.

151. Office of Aerospace Research. *Office of Aerospace Research Chronology.* Washington: Historical Division, Office of Information, Office of Aerospace Research, 1962.

152. Page, Robert Morris. *The Origin of Radar.* New York: Doubleday Anchor, 1962.

153. Peck, Merton J. and Frederic M. Scherer. *The Weapons Acquisition Process: An Economic Analysis.* Boston: Division of Research, Graduate School of Business Administration, Harvard University, 1962.

154. Peck, Taylor. *Round-Shot to Rockets: A History of the Washington Navy Yard and U.S. Naval Gun Factory.* Annapolis: U.S. Naval Institute, 1949.

155. Perry, Robert L. "The Atlas, Thor, and Titan," *Technology and Culture,* 4 (Fall, 1963), 466-477.

156. Peterson, Gale E. "The Discovery and Development of 2, 4-D," *Agricultural History,* 41 (July, 1967), 243-253.

157. Phillips, Robert F. *The Churchill Research Range: A History of Its Acquisition and Management by the Air Force.* Washington: Historical Division, Office of Information, Office of Aerospace Research, 1964.

158. President's Air Policy Commission. *Survival in the Air Age.* A Report of the President's Air Commission. Washington, Jan. 1, 1948. (Finletter Commission).

159. President's Scientific Research Board. *Science and Public Policy: A Report to the President,* by John R. Steelman, Chairman, The President's Scientific Research Board. Washington, 1947. 5 vols.

160. Pupin, Michael. *From Immigrant to Inventor.* New York: Charles Scribner's Sons, 1924.

161. Raborg, Paul C. *Mechanized Might: The Story of Mechanized Warfare.* New York: Whittlesey House, 1942.

162. Reed, John C. and Andreas G. Ronhovde. *Arctic Laboratory: A History (1947-1966) of the Naval Arctic Research Laboratory at Point Barrow, Alaska.* Washington, 1971.

163. Reingold, Nathan (comp.) *Materials Research Chronology, 1917-1957.* Dayton: Directorate of Materials and Process (Materials Control). Wright-Patterson A.F.B. 1962.

164. Reynolds, Carroll F. "The Development of the Military Floating Bridge by the United States Army." (Unpublished doctoral dissertation), University of Pittsburgh, 1950.

165. Rice, Berkeley. *The C-5A Scandal: An Inside Story of the Military-Industrial Complex.* Boston: Houghton Mifflin Co., 1971.

166. Rivkin, Steven R. *Technology Unbound: Transfering Scientific and Engineering Resources from Defense to Civilian Purposes.* New York: Pergamon Press, 1968.

167. Rosenbloom, Richard S. "The Transfer of Military Technology to Civilian Use," *Technology in Western Civilization, Volume II: Technology in the Twentieth Century,* ed. Melvin Kranzberg and Carroll W. Pursell, Jr. New York: Oxford, 1967, pp. 601-612.

168. Rosenthal, Alfred. *Venture Into Space: Early Years of Goddard Space Flight Center.* Washington: NASA, 1968.

169. Rotblat, Joseph. *Scientists in the Quest for Peace: A History of the Pugwash Conferences.* Cambridge: MIT Press, 1972.
170. Rothschild, J. H. *Tomorrow's Weapons: Chemical and Biological.* New York: McGraw-Hill, 1964.
171. Rowland, Buford and William B. Boyd. *U.S. Navy Bureau of Ordnance in World War II.* Washington: G.P.O., 1959.
172. Sanders, Ralph and Fred R. Brown, eds. *National Security Management. Science and Technology: Vital National Assets.* Washington: Industrial Collge of the Armed Forces, 1966.
173. Sanders, Ralph. "Three-Dimensional Warfare: World War II," *Technology in Western Civilization, Volume II: Technology in the Twentieth Century,* ed. Melvin Kranzberg and Carroll Pursell, Jr. New York: Oxford, 1967, pp. 561-578.
174. Sapolsky, Harvey M. *The Polaris System Development: Bureaucratic and Programmatic Success in Government.* Cambridge: Harvard University Press, 1972.
175. Scherer, F.M. *The Weapons Acquisition Process: Economic Incentives.* Cambridge: Harvard University Press, 1964.
176. Schiller, Herbert I. *Mass Communications and American Empire.* New York: A. M. Kelley, 1970.
177. Schofield, William G. *Destroyers—60 Years.* New York: Rand McNally, 1962.
178. Schroeder, Peter B. *Contact at Sea: A History of Maritime Radio Communications.* Ridgewood, New Jersey: Gregg, 1967.
179. Schwiebert, Ernest G. *A History of the U.S. Air Force Ballistic Missiles.* New York: F. A. Praeger, 1965.
180. Scientist and Engineers for Social and Political Action. *Science for the People.* Vol. 1, no. 1 (Feb. 23, 1969), published various places.
181. Scientists and Engineers for Social and Political Action, Berkeley *Science Against the People: The Story of Jason.* Berkeley: SESPA, Dec. 1972. 45 pp.
182. SESPA *U.C. Science at War.* Berkeley: SESPA 1970.
183. Scott, Lloyd N. *Naval Consulting Board of the United States.* Washington: G.P.O., 1920.
184. Shapley, Deborah. "Weather Warfare: Pentagon Concedes 7-Year Vietnam Effort," *Science,* 184 (7 June 1974), 1059-1061.
185. Shapley, Willis H. "Special Problems of Military Research and Development," *Annals of the American Academy of Political and Social Science,* 327 (Jan., 1960), 68-75.
186. Sherwin, Chalmers W. and Raymond S. Isenson. "Project Hindsight," *Science,* 156 (23 June 1967), 1571-1577.
187. Shurcliff, W. A. *Bombs at Bikini: The Official Report of Operation Crossroads.* New York, 1947.
188. Smith, Alice Kimball. *A Peril and A Hope: The Scientists' Movement in America: 1945-47.* Chicago: University of Chicago Press, 1965.
189. Smith, Bruce L. R. *The Rand Corporation: Case Study of a Nonprofit Advisory Corporation.* Cambridge: Harvard University Press, 1966.
190. Smith, Richard K. *The Airships Akron & Macon: Flying Aircraft Carriers of the United States Navy.* Annapolis: U.S. Naval Institute, 1965.

191. Smyth, Henry DeWolf. *Atomic Energy for Military Purposes: The Official Report on the Development of the Atomic Bomb under the Auspices of the United States Government, 1940-45.* Princeton: Princeton University Press, 1945.
192. Solo, R. A. "Gearing Military R&D to Economic Growth," *Harvard Business Review,* (Nov. - Dec., 1962).
193. SPARK Vol 1, no. 1 (March, 1971), published by Committee for Social Responsibility in Engineering.
194. Stewart, Irvin. *Organizing Scientific Research for War: The Administrative History of the Office of Scientific Research and Development.* Boston: Little, Brown, 1948.
195. Stockbridge, Frank Parker. *Yankee Ingenuity in the War.* New York: Harper & Bros. 1920.
196. Strickland, Donald A. *Scientists in Politics: The Atomic Scientists Movement, 1945-46.* Lafayette: Purdue University Studies, 1968.
197. Sturm, Thomas A. *The USAF Scientific Advisory Board: Its First Twenty Years, 1944-1964.* Washington: U.S. Air Force Historical Division Liaison Office, 1967.
198. Suits, C. G., H. Kirk, Edgar Jones, and Louis Jordan. *Applied Physics, Electronics, Optics, Metallurgy.* Boston: Little, Brown, 1948.
199. Swain, Donald C. "Organization of Military Research," *Technology in Western Civilization, Volume II: Technology in the Twentieth Century,* ed. Melvin Kranzberg and Carroll W. Pursell, Jr. New York: Oxford, 1967 pp. 535-548.
200. Taylor, A. Hoyt. *The First Twenty-Five Years of the Naval Research Laboratory.* Washington: Navy Dept., 1948.
201. Taylor, A. Hoyt. "Thomas A. Edison and the Naval Research Laboratory." *Science,* vol. 105 (Feb., 7, 1947), 150.
202. *Technology's War Record: An Interpretation of the Contribution Made by the Massachusetts Institute of Technology . . . in the Great War, 1914-1919.* Cambridge: War Records Committee of the Alumni Assoc. of the M.I.T., 1920.
203. Teller, Edward. *The Legacy of Hiroshima.* Garden City: Doubleday, 1962.
204. Teller, Edward. *The Reluctant Revolutionary.* New York: Columbia University Press, 1964.
205. Thayer, George. *The War Business: The International Trade in Armaments.* New York, 1969.
206. Thiesmeyer, Lincoln R. and John E. Burchard. *Combat Scientists.* Boston: Little, Brown, 1947.
207. Thomas, Morgan. *Atomic Energy and Congress.* Ann Arbor: University of Michigan Press, 1956.
208. Thompson, George Raynor, Dixie R. Harris, Pauline M. Oakes, and Dulany Terrett. *The Signal Corps: The Test.* Washington: G.P.O., 1957.
209. Thompson, Harry C. and Lida Mayo. *The Ordinance Department: Procurement and Supply.* Washington: G.P.O., 1960.
210. Tompkins, John S. *The Weapons of World War III: The Long Road Back from the Bomb.* Garden City: Doubleday, 1966.
211. Toole, V. G. and R. W. Ackerman. *The Modification of Army Aircraft in the United States, 1939-1945.* Washington, 1945.

212. Turnbull, Archibald D. and Clifford L. Lord.*History of United States Naval Aviation*. New Haven: Yale University Press, 1949.

213. U.S. Army. *Historical Report of the Chief Engineer, Including All Operations of the Engineer Department: American Expeditionary Forces, 1917-1919*. Washington: G.P.O., 1919.

214. U.S. Atomic Energy Commission.*In the Matter of J. Robert Oppenheimer, Transcript of Hearing Before Personnel Security Board*. Washington: AEC, 1954.

215. U.S. Cong., H. of R., Committee on Government Operations.*Application of Aerospace and Defense Industry Technology to Environmental Problems*. Hearings before a Subcommittee of the Committee on Government Operations, House of Rep., 91st Cong., 2 sess., Nov. 23 and 24, 1970.

216. U.S. Cong., H. of R., Committee on Government Operations.*Air Force Ballistic Missile Management (Formation of Aerospace Corporation)*. Third Report by the Committee on Government Operations, House of Rep., 87th Cong., 1 sess., 1961.

217. U.S. Cong., H. of R., Select Committee on Government Research *Federal Research and Development Programs*. First Progress Report of the Select Committee on Government Research, House of Rep., 88th Cong., 2 sess., Feb. 17, 1964.

218. U.S. Cong., H. of R., Committee on Government Operations.*Organization and Administration of the Military Research and Development Programs*. 24th intermediate report of the Committee on Government Operations, 83d Cong., 2 sess., 1954.

219. U.S. Congress, H. of R., Committee on Military Affairs. *Permanent Program of Scientific Research in the Interest of National Security*, H.R. 727, 79th Cong., 1 sess., June 11, 1945.

220. U.S. Cong., H. of R., Committee on Military Affairs.*Research and Development*. Hearings before the Committee on Military Affairs, House of Rep., 79th Cong., 1 sess., 1945. On H.R. 2946, an act authorizing appropriations for a permanent program of scientific research in the interest of national security.

221. U.S. Cong., H. of R., Committee on Science and Astronautics, Subcommittee on Science, Research, and Development. *A Technology Assessment of the Vietnam Defoliant Matter: A Case History*. Report to the Subcommittee on Science, Research, and Development of the Committee on Science and Astronautics, House of Rep., 91st Cong., 1 sess., Aug. 8, 1969.

222. U.S. Congress, H. of R., Committee on Science and Astronautics.*Basic Scientific and Astronautic Research in the Department of Defense*. Hearings, 86th Cong., 1 sess. 1959.

223. U.S. Congress, H. of R., Committee on Science and Astronautics "Congressional Response to Project Camelot," *Technical Information for Congress*. Report to the Subcommittee on Science, Research and Development of the Committee on Science and Astronautics, U.S. House of Rep., 92nd Cong., 1 sess., (April 25, 1969, revised April 15, 1971), pp. 126-160.

224. U.S. Cong., H. of R., Committee on Science and Astronautics.*Missile Development and Space Science*. Hearings before Committee on Science and Astronautics, House of Rep., 86th Cong., 1 sess., 1959.

225. U.S. Congress, H. of R., Committee on Science and Astronautics *Research and Development for Defense.* Hearings, 88th Cong., 1 sess., 1961.

226. U.S. Congress, H. of R., Committee on Science and Astronautics "The Supersonic Transport," *Technical Information for Congress.* Report to the Subcommittee on Science, Research, and Development of the Committee on Science and Astronautics, U.S. House of Rep., 92d Cong., 1 sess., (April 25, 1969, revised on April 15, 1971) pp. 685-748.

227. U.S. Congress, H. of R., Committee on Science and Astronautics."The Test Ban Treaty—A Study in Military and Political Cost Effectiveness," *Technical Information for Congress.* Report to the Subcommittee on Science, Research, and Development of the Committee on Science and Astronautics, U.S. House of Rep., 92d Cong., 1 sess. (April 25, 1969, revised April 15, 1971), pp. 193-240.

228. U.S. Congress, H. of R., Select Commitee on Post-War Military Policy.*Hearings, Surplus Materials . . . Research and Development,* 78th Congr., 2 sess., Nov. 1944-Jan. 1945.

229. U.S. Congress, H. of R., Select Committee on Post-War Military Policy.*Report, Research and Development,* HR505, 79th Cong., 1 sess., May 2, 1945.

230. U.S. Congress, Senate, Committe on Military Affairs, Subcommittee on War Mobilization.*The Government's Wartime Research and Development, 1940-44.* Report from the Subcommittee on War Mobilization to the Committe on Military Affairs, U. S. Senate. Subcommittee Report No. 5, 79th Cong., 1 sess., Jan. 23, 1945. *Part I.—Survey of Government Agencies.* Part II.—*Findings and Recommendations* (July, 1945).

231. U.S. Congress, Senate, Committee on Military Affairs, Subcommittee on War Mobilization.*Wartime Technological Developments.* A Study Made for the Subcommittee on War Mobilization of the Committee on Military Affairs, U.S. Senate. Subcommittee Monograph No. 2, 79th Cong., 1 sess., May 1945.

232. U.S. Congress, Senate, Committee on Naval Affairs.*Hearings, Establishing a Research Board for National Security.* 79th Cong., 1 sess., June 20, 1945.

233. U.S. Congress, Senate, Committee on Naval Affairs.*Report, Establishing a Research Board for National Security,* 79th Cong., 1 sess., July 28, 1945.

234. U.S. Dept. of Defense, Office of the Director of Defense Research and Engineering.*First Interim Report on Project Hindsight.* U.S. Dept. of Commerce Clearinghouse for Federal Scientific and Technical Information, 1966.

235. U.S. Dept. of Defense *Project Themis: A Program To Strengthen the Nation's Academic Institutions.* Office of the Director of Defense Research and Engineering, Washington, Jan. 1967.

236. U.S., Joint Board on Scientific Information Policy.*U.S. Rocket Ordnance Development and Use in World War II.* Washington: 1946.

237. U.S. Navy Dept., Bureau of Ordnance. *Navy Ordnance Activities World War, 1917-1918.* Washington: 1920.

238. U.S. Navy Dept., Bureau of Ordnance. *U.S. Navy Bureau of Ordnance in World War II.* By Buford Rowland and William Boyd. Washington: 1953.
239. U.S. Navy, Naval History Division. *Aviation in the United States Navy.* Washington: 1965.
240. U.S. Navy, Naval History Division. *Destroyers in the United States Navy.* Washington: 1962.
241. U.S. Navy Dept., Office of Naval Operations. *The Steam Catapult: Its History and Operation.* Washington: 1957.
242. U.S. Navy, Naval History Division. *The Submarine in the United States Navy.* Washington: 1963.
243. U.S. Navy, Office of Naval Operations. *United States Naval Aviation 1910-1960.* Washington: 1961.
244. von Braun, Wernher. "The Redstone, Jupiter, and Juno," *Technology and Culture*, 4 (Fall, 1963), 452-465.
245. von Karman, Theodore. *The Wind and Beyond: Theodore von Karman, Pioneer in Aviation and Pathfinder in Space.* Boston: Little, Brown, 1967.
246. Watson-Watt, Robert. *The Pulse of Radar: The Autobiography of Sir Robert Watson-Watt.* New York: Dial Press, 1959.
247. Weaver, Warren. *Scene of Change: A Lifetime in American Science.* New York: Charles Scribner's Sons, 1970.
248. Weber, Gustavus A. *The Naval Observatory: Its History, Activities and Organization.* Institute for Government Research, Service Monographs of the United States Government, No. 39. Baltimore, 1926.
249. Weyl, F. Joachim (ed.) *Research In the Service of National Purpose.* Proceedings of the Office of Naval Research Vicennial Convocation. Washington: 1966.
250. Wilson, Andrew. *The Bomb and the Computer: Wargaming from Ancient Chinese Mapboard to Atomic Computer.* London: Barrie & Rockliff, 1968.
251. Wilson, Thomas W., Jr. *The Great Weapons Heresy.* Boston: Houghton Mifflin Co., 1970.
252. Wohlstetter, Albert. "Strategy and the Natural Scientists," *Scientists and National Policy-Making*, ed. Robert Gilpin and Christopher Wright. New York: Columbia University Press, 1964, pp. 174-239.
253. Wolf, Eric R. and Joseph G. Jorgensen. "Anthropology on the Warpath in Thailand," *N.Y. Review of Books*, 15 (Nov. 19, 1970), 26-35.
254. Wright, Helen. *Explorer of the Universe: A Biography of George Ellery Hale.* New York: E. P. Dutton, 1966.
255. Yarmolinsky, Adam. "The Electronic Revolution at the Pentagon," *American Scholar*, 35 (Spring, 1966), 272-274.
256. York, Herbert F. *Race to Oblivion: A Participant's View of the Arms Race.* New York: Simon & Schuster, 1970.

XI

WORLD WAR I AND THE PEACETIME ARMY, 1917-1941

Daniel R. Beaver

In April, 1971, the United States Army was poised for its greatest battle since Appomattox. It was not a new army by any means. Its foundations were set by habitual modes of action and traditional problems and conflicts endemic to the American political, economic, and social life of which it was a part. Less than a year before, the basis of its institutional structure—how and by whom it was commanded, how it regulated its internal administrative apparatus, how and by whom it was supplied—had been debated and reformed to meet new and to an extent unforseeable circumstances. The army was tested and modified during the war, and in 1920 those changes which appeared consistent with American values were incorporated into the system. In 1941,with its historical institutions essentially intact, it faced similar, if more forbidding,challenges. The changes that had occurred were not revolutionary. One student of institutions, C. E. Lindbloom, has labeled the process "incrementalism" of "The Science of Muddling Through." Always in transition, always looking backward toward previous experiences, the United States had succeeded in shaping its military establishment to the requirements of modern war. Although it is not a success story, neither is it a tale of reluctant military neanderthals being pulled kicking and screaming into the twentieth century. This essay is an introduction to the secondary works and research materials for this challenging period.

BIBLIOGRAPHIES. The best general bibliographies for twentieth-century American military history are in the back notes of Russell Weigley, *History of the United States Army* (211), and in the same author's *The Anerican War of War* (210). The best introduction to American sources for the First World War is in Waldo G. Leland and Newton D. Mereness, compilers. *Introduction to American Offical Sources for the Economic and Social History of the World War* (122), and the National Archives, *Handbook of Federal War Agencies and their Records* (148). Good World War I bibliographies are in Daniel R. Beaver, *Newton D. Baker and the American War Effort, 1917-1919* (11), Edward M. Coffman, *The War to End All Wars* (31), and Harvey DeWeerd, *President Wilson Fights His War* (56).

GENERAL WORKS. There is no comprehensive history of the United States Army for this period; nor is there much agreement about what such a history should include if and when it is written. Students have tended to examine episodes, crisis moments, wartime activity, and internal administrative affairs. Even the larger policy studies which have appeared seldom incorporate effectively the broad frames of national and international affairs within which the military acts and upon which it has had such a profound effect. A synthesis of the general works on the American military establishment applicable to this period reveals five dominant themes. The first is concern about military domination of the state. This issue is dealt with in Louis Smith's excellent *American Democracy and Military Power* (185) and C. Joseph Bernardo and Eugene H. Bacon's more pedestrian *American Military Policy: Its Development since 1775* (12). Far more exciting, if at times mildly sinister, is Samuel Huntington's *The Soldier and the State* (99). A second theme is conflict between "Uptonians" who promoted the idea of one professional national army with its own reserves expandable in war, and "citizen soldiers" who supported the traditional tripartite American military establishment. Because of its profound underlying constitutional issues of national and local political power, this theme has intrigued scholars for years. The best statement of the "Uptonian" position is in two older histories of the American Army, William Ganoe, *History of the United States Army* (74), and Oliver Spaulding, *The United States Army in Peace and War* (188). The "citizen soldier" school is best represented by John M. Palmer's *America in Arms* (159), written after the First World War in defense of traditional policy, and Russell Weigley's two recent books, *Towards an American Army* (212) and *History of the United States Army* (211). A third theme focuses on civil-military relations and the accompanying problems of military command in the War Department and in the field. In T. Harry Williams, *Americans at War* (216), and Ernest R. May, *The Ultimate Decision, The President as Commander-in-Chief* (139), the relationships between the President and War Department and the army are explored. Otto Nelson's *National Security and the General Staff* (152) and Paul Y. Hammond's *Organizing for Defense* (86) investigate command and institutional issues inside the War Department and the army. A fourth theme is the organization of the procurement agencies of the army and their connection with the civilian businessmen who supply them in emergencies. Two general histories of supply which devote considerable attention to twentieth-century experiences are by James A. Huston, *The Sinews of War* (102), and Erna Risch, *Quartermaster Support of the Army: A History of the Corps* (173). A last and most fascinating theme involves the institutional relationship of the army to American society as a whole. The pioneer work on this topic is Walter Millis, *Arms and Men* (141). More exciting conceptually and provocative intellectually is Alfred Chandler, *Strategy and Structure* (22). Representative of the most recent work on the topic are Robert Wiebe, *The Search for Order, 1877-1921* (24), James Weinstein, *The Corporate Ideal in the Liberal State* (213), and Robert Cuff, "Business, the State, and World War I: The American Experience," in J. L. Granatstein and R. D. Cuff, eds., *War and Society in North America* (45).

NATIONAL POLICY 1917-1941: THE NATION, THE STATES, AND MANPOWER PROCUREMENT. One important criticism that has been leveled at American military policy makers, especially by those interested in supply and logistics, is the inordinate amount of time and energy given to deliberating manpower procurement and reserve organization. The charge is unfounded. Two great themes, the relationship of the citizen to the nation and that of the state to the federal government, as well as less complex issues of military structure and efficiency are involved. The decision to adopt the "dual oath" in 1916 in order to strengthen the National Guard as a viable reserve force and to strengthen the training of reserve officers through ROTC, and the decision in 1917 to scrap the volunteer system and go to conscription, modified but did not substantially change the traditional tripartite structure of the American military establishment.

PUBLISHED SOURCES. Most valuable for the early period are the War Department *Annual Reports* (239). From 1917 to 1921 they contain, in addition to a general statement by the Secretary of War, the *Annual Report of the Provost Marshal General* who was responsible for administering the draft and the *Annual Report of the Militia Bureau* which handled National Guard matters. The Chief of Staff's *Annual Report* includes important discussions of officer training during the war and reveals the high hopes the army had for the new Reserve Officer Training Program inaugurated by the National Defense Act of 1916. Unfortunately, as an economy measure, the government ceased to publish the reports in full after 1921, and from that date to 1941 we have only the *Annual Reports of the Secretary of War* (248), which are generally too sketchy to be of help except on general policy.

In February, 1917, a statement prepared by the War Department for the United States Senate, *Universal Military Training* (234), was published containing an intimation of what national manpower policy might be in case of war. The *Congressional Record*, 65th Congress, 1st session, has the April-May debates on the Selective Service Act of 1917. The most important congressional hearings on manpower for the entire period, the Senate Hearings, *The Reorganization of the Army* (232), cover the debates on universal military training, the National Guard, and officer training which led to the passage of the National Defense Act of 1920.

SECONDARY WORKS. The representative defense of traditional policy is in Palmer, *America in Arms* (159), and Weigley, *Towards an American Army* (212). A good description of the army's World War expansion is in Marvin A. Kreidberg and Merton G. Henry, *History of Military Mobilization in the United States Army 1775-1945* (116). Edward A. Fitzpatrick's *Conscription and America* (70) is dated. Administering the draft during the First World War is discussed in David A. Lockmiller, *Enoch A. Crowder* (128), and Provost Marshal General Crowder's own *The Spirit of Selective Service* (40). The temporary triumph of the "Uptonians," with the creation of one national army during the First World War, and the return to more traditional policies with the passage of the National Defense Act of 1920 are best analyzed in Edward M. Coffman, *The Hilt of the Sword, The Career of Peyton C. March* (30), and Beaver, *Baker* (11). John Dickinson, *The Building of an Army* (59), although much older, is still very useful as a legislative history. Interwar manpower mobilization planning is described in Mark S. Watson, *Chief of Staff: Pre-War Plans and Preparations* (209). The three best studies of the military role and constitutional status of the National Guard are William H. Riker, *Soldiers of the States: The Role of the National Guard in American Democracy* (171), Martha Derthick, *The National Guard in Politics* (53), and Jim Dan Hill, *The Minute Man in Peace and War: A His-*

tory of the National Guard (90). The most comprehensive book on the ROTC is Gene M. Lyons and John W. Masland, *Education and Military Leadership: A Study of the ROTC* (130). Manpower policy debates in the late thirties are clearly handled in the two volumes by William Langer and Sorell E. Gleason, *The Challenge to Isolation* (119) and *The Undeclared War* (120).

NATIONAL POLICY 1917-1941: THE PROBLEM OF COMMAND. Three significant command relationships—that of the President of the United States with the Secretary of War and the Army Chief of Staff, that of the Chief of Staff with the bureau of chiefs in the War Department, and that of the Chief of Staff with army commanders in the field—established the parameters of debate and shaped the command and administrative structure of the American Army from 1917 to 1941.

PUBLISHED SOURCES. There were no major investigations of the presidential commander-in-chief power during the period, but considerable attention was paid to the War Department chain of command. The most complete discussion of this issue in in *Reorganization of the Army* (232) and in the *Annual Report of the Secretary of War* (248) for 1922 and 1923. For names and date of rank of Regular Army officers, see *The Army Register* (240).

SECONDARY WORKS. The best discussion of the President as commander-in-chief is in Edwin S. Corwin, *The President: Office and Powers* (37). Ernest May's essay on Wilson in *The Ultimate Decision: The President as Commander-in-Chief* (139) insists that Wilson abdicated his role. Beaver's discussion of the President and his Secretary of War in *Baker* (11) comes to an opposite conclusion. For Wilson's difficulties with Pershing, see Beaver, *Baker* (11), and Bullett Lowry, "Pershing and the Armistice" (129). Franklin Roosevelt gloried in the title "Commander-in-Chief." James M. Burns provides a good introduction in *Roosevelt: Soldier of Freedom* (19), but the best insight into the Roosevelt style of leadership is in Maurice Matloff's Harmon Memorial Lecture, *Mr. Roosevelt's Three Wars: F. D. R. as War Leader* (137). For Roosevelt's relations with his Secretary of War, see Elting Morison, *Turmoil and Tradition, A Study of the Life and Times of Henry L. Stimson* (145).

Two important attempts to explain command relationships between the chiefs of staff and the bureaus are Hammond (86) and Nelson (152). The story of the rise of the general staff and the decline of the bureau chiefs during the First World War is in Coffman, *March* (30), Beaver, *Baker* (11) and Beaver, "George W. Goethals and the P. S. and T." (10). Risch (113) gives an excellent account of the virtual disappearance of the Quartermaster Bureau during 1918. The resurgence of bureau power after 1920 and the interwar staff-bureau compromise are handled in Watson (209) and Raymond Cline, *Washington Command Post: The Operations Division* (27). The best discussions of the relationship between Secretary of War Stimson and Chief of Staff Marshall are Morison (145), Forrest Pogue, *George C. Marshall: Education of a General, 1880-1939* (168), and Pogue, *George C. Marshall: Ordeal and Hope, 1939-1942* (169). For a more critical view of Stimson, see Richard N. Current, *Secretary Stimson: A Study in Statecraft* (48).

The struggle for supremacy between the chief of staff and the commander in the field during the First World War is analyzed in Beaver, *Baker* (11) and Coffman, *March* (30). Frank Vandiver discusses Pershing as a military leader in his Harmon Lecture, *John J. Pershing and the Anatomy of Leadership* (204). Pershing wrote of his troubles with Washington in *My Experiences in the War* (166). Chief of Staff Peyton C. March took Pershing to task in *The Nation at War* (133). A fascinating discussion of the actual writing of those volumes is Donald Smythe, "Battle of the Books: Pershing Versus March" (187). Pershing's self-image as "General in Chief" is discussed in Frederick Palmer, *John J. Pershing, General of the Armies* (156), and by Richard O'Connor in his less laudatory *Black Jack Pershing* (153). (New biographies of Pershing by Frank Vandiver and Donald Smythe are in progress.) D. Clayton James, *The Years of MacArthur,* Vol. I, 1889-1941 (104), illumines MacArthur's perception of his role as Chief of Staff and army commander during the thirties. George C. Marshall's reluctant decision to relinquish field command is described in Pogue, *Ordeal and Hope* (169).

The question of command involved more than clashing personalities. The nature of military leadership was changing, and Pershing, March, MacArthur, and, to a lesser extent, Marshall were caught in the midst of the transition. American tradition dictated that the battle leader should be military chief, but the demands of modern war, especially multi-front situations, made some sort of grand coordinator a necessity. As the century moved on, the older view was held tenaciously; but management became more important than old-fashioned leadership, or so it seemed. The way that awareness penetrated military circles can be seen through the study of the curriculum of the army higher education system. The most recent studies of the school systems are Stephen Ambrose, *Duty, Honor, Country: A History of West Point* (1), and John W. Masland and Lawrence I. Radway, *Soldiers and Scholars: Military Education and National Policy* (135). The impact of military higher education before 1920 is described in Edward M. Coffman, "The American Military Generation Gap in World War I: The Leavenworth Clique in the AEF" (29). George S. Pappas has an excellent discussion of the growth of the Army War College curriculum in *Prudens Futuri: The U.S. Army War College 1901-1954* (161).

NATIONAL POLICY 1917-1941: THE PROBLEM OF SUPPLY. Except in special cases, the United States Army historically has supplied itself through its own arsenals and depots in time of peace and relied on the civilian industrial and business community to meet its expanded needs in wartime. On three occasions, 1916, 1920, and again in the 1930s, the country rejected a nationalized munitions industry. From those decisions a cooperative military-industrial system evolved which determined American military supply planning and organization from 1917 to 1941.

PUBLISHED SOURCES. The Senate *Investigation of the War Department* (230) by the Chamberlain Committee reveals the disorganization of the war effort during the winter of 1917-18. The *Report of the Chief of Staff* in the War Department *Annual Reports* (239) for 1919 contains the best account of the work of the Purchase, Storage, and Traffic Division of the General Staff. Benedict Crowell's defense of his work as Assistant Secretary of War and Director of Munitions was published as *America's Munitions 1917-1918*

(238). Bernard Baruch's report, *American Industry in the War* (7), gives the War Industries Board perspective on the story. The *Annual Report of the Council of National Defense* (235) for 1917, 1918, and 1919, is occasionally useful. A vast document reservoir, which has only recently begun to be used creatively, is available in the records of the *Special Committee to Investigate the Munitions Industry* (233), (the Nye Committee). This committee had three important sets of documents published: *The Minutes of the General Munitions Board April 4-August 9, 1917, The Minutes of the War Industries Board*, and *Digest of the Proceedings of the Council of National Defense during the World War*, edited by Franklin H. Martin. The post-Armistice hearings on *Expenditures in the War Department* (228) (the Graham Committee hearings) are a gold mine of information, as are the House and Senate Hearings on the *Reorganization of the Army,* (226,232), which preceded the passage of the National Defense Act of 1920. For the interwar period, the annual Reports of the Secretary of War (248) contain general information. In addition to the Nye Committee Records, the *War Policies Commission Report to the President* (229) reveals the military view of industrial mobilization.

SECONDARY WORKS. The best general introductions to the army and industrial mobilization are Huston (102) and Risch (173). For insight into the relationship between the military and the business community before 1920, see Cuff (45); and for the interwar period, see the excellent selection of articles and commentary in Carroll W. Pursell, Jr., ed., *The Military-Industrial Complex* (170). The traditional view that industrial mobilization during World War I was controlled by the business community is set forth in Grosvenor Clarkson, *Industrial America in the World War* (24), Benedict Crowell and Robert Wilson, *How America Went to War* (41), and Bernard Baruch, *Baruch: The Public Years* (9). Recent discussions of the dispute, which contest the Clarkson-Baruch-Crowell story and give more importance to the War Department's role, include Beaver, *Baker* (11), Robert Cuff's excellent *War Industries Board* (47), and Paul A. C. Koistenen, "The Industrial-Military Complex in Historical Perspective: World War I" (114). Robert Cuff has recently shown how army partisans tried to set the record straight in "Newton D. Baker, Frank A. Scott and 'The American Reinforcement in the World War'" (46).

Articles describing mobilization planning in the Assistant Secretary of War's Office during the interwar period include Albert A. Blum, "Birth and Death of the M Day Plans," in Herbert Stein, ed., *American Civil-Military Relations* (14), his later "Roosevelt, the M Day Plans and the Military-Industrial Complex" (15), Harry B. Yoshpe, "Economic Mobilization between Wars" (223), Gerald D. Nash, "Experiment in Industrial Mobilization: WIB and NRA" (147), and Paul A. C. Koistenen, "The Industrial-Military Complex: The Interwar Years" (115). These studies show the importance of the new Army Industrial College and reveal the growth of industrial-military cooperation before 1941. For the role of Congress in industrial preparedness, see John E. Wiltz, *In Search of Peace: The Senate Munitions Inquiry, 1934-36* (220), Wayne Cole, *Senator Gerald P. Nye and American Foreign Relations* (33), and Edwin H. Rutkowski, *The Politics of Military Aviation Procurement 1926-1934* (176). The most useful studies of the emergency period are Donald Nelson's *Arsenal of Democracy* (149), Eliot Janeway's *The Strug-*

gle for Survival (105), Bruce Catton's *The Warlords of Washington* (20), and R. Elberton Smith's *The Army and Economic Mobilization* (186).

STRATEGY, DOCTRINE AND TECHNOLOGY 1917-1941. Before the First World War, thinking about military strategy—the defining of objectives to be reached in war, military doctrine—the development of methods of organization and application of military power in war, and military technology—the creation of the weapons with which armies are equipped, was isolated and compartmentalized. During the war and after there appeared a growing understanding among soldiers, civilian technologists, scientists, and inventors that the development of new weapons was dependent upon a common understanding of the purpose of those weapons.

SECONDARY WORKS. American strategic thought has only recently begun to attract the attention of scholars. There are no sources printed on the subject and few secondary works. Urs Schwarz, *American Strategy: A New Perspective* (180), is thin and impressionistic, not at all comparable to Russell Weigley's *The American Way of War* (210). Pappas (161 also discusses the early history of American war planning. A pioneer study of army strategic thinking is Fred Green's "The Military View of American National Policy" (80). Ronald Spector's "You're Not Going to Send Soldiers Over There Are You? (189), Beaver, *Baker* (11), and Coffman, *The War to End All Wars* (31), give the background on World War strategic thought and show that American intelligence gathering was not as backward as has been thought. The essence of interwar planning is contained in Watson (209) and Maurice Matloff and Edwin M. Snell, *Strategic Planning for Coalition Warfare* (138). The evolution of war plans against Japan and Germany and the adoption of the Germany-first strategy is explained by Louis Morton in "Germany First," in Kent Roberts Greenfield, ed., *Command Decisions* (81).

The best discussion of American doctrine is in Maurice Matloff, "The American Approach to War 1919-1945" (136). Changes in American infantry doctrine during the twenties and thirties were published as *Infantry in Battle* (244), a study Sir Basil Liddell Hart called at the time the finest infantry text in the world. The relationship of doctrine and technology as it applied to American airpower is analyzed in I. B. Holley's *Ideas and Weapons* (98) and his subsequent, *Buying Aircraft* (97). For the theories and trials of William Mitchell, see Alfred F. Hurley, *Billy Mitchell: Crusader for Air Power* (100), and Wesley F. Craven and James Lee Cate, eds., *The Army Air Forces in World War II*, Vol. I, *Plans and Early Operations* (39). To understand the difficulties of developing effective mechanized warfare doctrine, see Richard Ogorkiewicz, *A History of Mechanized Forces* (154), and George Hoffman, "The Demise of the U.S. Tank Corps and Medium Tank Development Program" (94). Martin Blumenson, ed., *The Patton Papers*, Vol. I, *1880-1940* (16), shows that even the redoubtable George S. Patton, Jr., was slower to give up the horse than the General would later have us believe.

The problems of organizing technology in the interest of the state are discussed in A. Hunter Dupree, *Science in the Federal Government: A History of Policies and Activities to 1940* (62), and David D. Van Tassel and Michael G. Hall, eds., *Science and Society in the United States* (205). James B. Conant shows the possible conflicts that might arise between soldiers, inventors and bureaucrats in *Modern Science and Modern Man* (34). How those difficulties occurred in the tank development program during the 1930s can be seen in Constance M. Green, Harry C. Thomson and Peter C. Roots, *The Ordnance Department: Planning Munitions for War* (79), and George F. Hoffman, "Tactics vs. Technology: The U.S. Cavalry Experience (95). For more detailed materials on air power development and technological change, see chapters X and XV.

THE AMERICAN ARMY AT WAR 1917-1918. During the First World War Americans in large numbers fought in coalition for the first time since the Revolution. The Wilson Administration's determination to play a decisive part in the peace negotiations dictated that an indepenpent American Army under its own command, and of a size and quality to be decisive on the battlefield, appear in France. Three major issues inherent in that decision —diplomacy, military planning and logistics, and battlefield performance —dominate the literature of the First World War.

PUBLISHED SOURCES. The best source for the larger military-strategic problems of the war is *Papers Relating to the Foreign Relations of the United States, 1917, 1918 Supplements I and II, The First World War* (236). Ray Stannard Baker *Woodrow Wilson, Life and Letters* (4), and Charles Seymour, *The Intimate Papers of Colonel House* (183), are essential sources for high administration policy. It was the intention of the War Department to publish a large multivolume history of the war effort, but financial exigencies allowed only the publication of three volumes before World War II. The *Order of Battle of American Land Forces in the World War, AEF Divisions, Order of Battle, AEF-Army Corps, Service of Supply and General Headquarters*, and *The Genesis of the American First Army* (245) make unit identification easy and give a skeleton chronology for American operations in France. After the Second World War two more volumes in the *Order of Battle* series covered the War Department and the Zone of the Interior in the same way. The United States Battle Monuments Commission, *American Armies and Battlefields in Europe* (199), is more than a picture book; it has some of the best summaries of unit actions in American World War I literature. The Commission also published *Summaries of Operations* (201), a set of short World War I divisional histories. In 1948 a seventeen-volume document collection of the greatest significance, *United States Army in the World War 1917-1919* (243), was published which makes it possible to reconstruct the organization and combat history of the AEF with considerable accuracy. The *Final Report* (241) of General Pershing is a good overview; while the *Annual Report* (239) of the Chief of Staff for 1918 and 1919 add the Washington perspective. *The War with Germany: A Statistical Summary* by Leonard P. Ayres (242) should be used with great discretion. Its charts and graphs give the illusion of reliability but within its norms and averages lie many distortions. The *Annual Report* (248) of the Secretary of War for 1926 gives final American casualties for the war.

SECONDARY WORKS. Americans forget that the First World War had been raging for three bloody years when the United States intervened. The most profound, moving and bitter literature on military affairs in European history emerged from those early experiences. Only the outlines of the controversies over strategy and tactics can be mentioned here. A good introduction to the literature is Cyril Falls, *War Books* (69). The most biting attack on the allied western strategy is in Sir Basil Liddell Hart's *The Real War 1914-1918* (124). On the German side Max Hoffman's *The War of Lost Opportunities* (96) is the best of its genre. George S. Viereck, *As They Saw Us* (206), gives a good account of the European view of Americans in battle. A most balanced, compassionate and understanding view of the difficulties of men in battle is found in Cyril Falls, *The Great War* (68), but for grasping the pure pathos and tragic grandeur of the conflict no writer has approached Winston Churchill's *The World Crisis* (23).

The best general history of Americans in the war is Frederic Paxson, *American Democracy and the World War* (162). Mark Sullivan, *Our Times* (193), is impressionistic but helpful. The problems of coalition warfare can be traced in Beaver, *Baker* (11), and David M. Trask, *The United States in the Supreme War Council* (197). The best biography of Tasker Bliss, the American representative at the Supreme War Council, is still Frederick Palmer's *Bliss, Peace Maker* (155). Harry J. Rudin, *Armistice, 1918* (175), gives virtually an hour by hour description of the end of the fighting. The growth of the American Army during the war can be traced in Beaver, *Baker* (11), DeWeerd (51), and Coffman, *The War to End All Wars* (31). The best older study is Thomas G. Frothingham, *The American Reinforcement in the World War* (73). The critical shipping question and the economic issues involved with it have not received the attention they deserve, but see Benedict Crowell and Robert Wilson, *The Road to France* (41), Edward N. Hurley, *The Bridge to France* (101), and Albert Gleaves, *A History of the Transport Service* (76), for a rudimentary introduction to the question. The story of the AEF supply is told in Pershing (166), James G. Harbord, *The American Army in France, 1917-1919* (87), and Johnson Hagood, *The Services of Supply* (84). Charles G. Dawes, *A Journal of the Great War* (52), is the only account of the massive purchasing agency which Pershing established under Dawes' control in Paris to help support the AEF from European sources. The decision to adopt French artillery types and its effect on the American production effort is discussed in Harvey DeWeerd's unique "The American Adoption of French Artillery 1917-1918" (55). The most thoughtful critiques of the AEF in battle are by the Commander of the First Army, Hunter Liggett, in *AEF, Ten Years ago in France* (126) and *Commanding an American Army* (127). Lawrence Stalling's chapter on Belleau Wood in *The Doughboys* (190), which catches the horror of gas warfare and heavy artillery bombardment, is still the best American soldier's narrative of the Great War. Stalling's book also includes an excellent bibliography of divisional and regimental histories. William Langer's memoir, *Gas and Flame in World War I* (118), tells of the effect of the war on a young college man. The biggest "side show" of the war was the Russian intervention. The story is best told by George Kennan in *Soviet American Relations, 1917-1920* (111). The Murmansk and Archangel forces are described in E. M. Halliday, *The Igorant Armies* (85). William Graves, *America's Siberian Adventure* (78), is the best account of that operation from the viewpoint of the soldier who commanded the American contigent. The best war maps are available in Vincent J. Esposito, ed., *The West Point Atlas of American Wars*, Vol. II (67); while the best photography is in Lawrence Stalling, *The First World War: A Photographic History* (191). Beaver, *Baker* (11), and Coffman, *The War to End All Wars* (31), criticize the unnecessary size and poor planning of the American war effort, but the most incisive critique of all levels of activity is in DeWeerd (56).

THE ARMY AND AMERICAN SOCIETY 1917-1941. The most significant questions about the American Army have few satisfactory answers. During the debates over national defense in 1916, 1920, and again in 1940, important questions were raised about the influence of the American military system on the Republic. How should an army be raised, officered, equipped and supported with the least damage to the institutions it was meant to defend? Would the logistical and supply requirements of such an army create a breed of contractors interested in stirring up war for profit? Could and should the army become an instrument for social change? The literature on these topics, much of it highly polemical, reveals the importance of the issues and the difficulties historians have had in developing methodologies to deal with them effectively.

PUBLISHED SOURCES. Every set of published records mentioned in this essay has something to contribute to the study of the army and American society. In addition, the attempts to ameliorate the military life of citizen-soldiers during the First World War are described in Raymond B. Fosdick, *Report of the Chairman on Training Camp Activities to the Secretary of War* (246).

SECONDARY WORKS. One should begin the study of the social impact of the military with Alfred Vagts, *A History of Militarism* (203). A good introduction to the subject for the United States is in Keith L. Nelson. *The Impact of War on American Life: The Twentieth Century Experience* (151). The American soldiers' perceptions of society are best discussed in Morris Janowitz, *The Professional Soldier* (106), but for a more critical view, see C. Wright Mills, *The Power Elite* (142). David F. Trask, ed., *World War I at Home* (198), and Arthur Ekirch, *The Civilian and the Military* (64), cover social aspects of the war and opposition to the military. For the war and civil liberty, see Horace Peterson and Gilbert C. Fite, *Opponents of War 1917-1918* (167), and Donald Johnson, *The Challenge to American Freedoms* (108). The best book on conscientious objection during the First World War is still Norman Thomas, *The Conscientious Objector* (196). Raymond B. Fosdick in his autobiography, *Chronicle of a Generation* (71), tells of the work of the Salvation Army, the YMCA, and the Red Cross at home and with the AEF. For the army's wartime links with the academic community, see Daniel J. Kevles, "Testing the Army's Intelligence: Psychologists and the Military in World War I" (113), and the same author's "George Ellery Hale, the First World War, and the Advancement of Science in America" (112). The best interpretative essay on the First World War and American society is Charles Hirschfeld's "The Transformation of American Life" (92).

The most recent book on interwar pacifism is *The Peace Prophets, American Pacifist Thought, 1919-1941* (150) by John K. Nelson. The literary impact of the war is shown best in Stanley Cooperman, *World War I and the American Novel* (36). For interwar veterans organizations the best study is Roscoe Baker, *The American Legion and American Foreign Policy* (5). The army's role in the Bonus March is shown by Roger Daniels in *The Bonus March* (51). The story of the army and the New Deal is told in John Salmond, *The Civilian Conservation Corps 1933-1942* (177).

During the thirties a whole host of books hostile to the military appeared.

The authors' arguments were usually couched in economic terms, but their overriding fear was loss of liberty and "class control" of American society by a small "war-mongering" elite. Representative of such works are George Seldes, *Iron, Blood, and Profits* (182), and H. C. Englebrecht and F. C. Hanighen, *Merchants of Death* (65). For the alleged discovery of an American conspiracy against peace and democracy, read Seymour Waldman's *Death and Profits, A Study of the War Policies Commission* (207).

The experience of American Black people with the army during the First World War is best chronicled by Emmett J. Scott in *The American Negro in the War* (181). More critical treatments which suggest that the army rejected the role of social catalyst and did little to foster Black upward mobility in American society are Beaver, *Baker* (11), and Coffman, *The War to End All Wars* (31). A recent book on the Black war experience is Florette Henri and Richard Stillman, *Bitter Victory: A History of Black Soldiers in World War I* (89). Charles Johnson's article, "The Army, the Negro and the Civilian Conservation Corps 1933-1942" (107), indicates that army policy changed very little after the war. The background chapters of Richard Dalfiume's *Desegregation of the U.S. Army Forces: Fighting on Two Fronts, 1939-1953* (50), and Ulysses Lee's *The Employment of Negro Troops: The United States Army in World War II* (121) complete the dismal story.

LIBRARIES AND ARCHIVES. The major research sources on American military history from 1917 to 1941 are at the Library of Congress, the National Archives in Washington, D.C., and the Records Center at Suitland, Maryland. Some significant material on interwar industrial mobilization planning is located at the Industrial College of the Armed Forces in Washington, D.C. The Military History Research Collection at Carlisle Barracks, Pennsylvania, contains the records and projects of the Army War College as well as the letters and papers of representative officers and enlisted men. The manuscripts there lend themselves admirably to quantification of army social history, an area sadly neglected by scholars. The reference library in the Office of the Chief of Military History, Washington, D.C., has the contemporary monographs and documents that formed the basis of the U.S. government's massive research effort, *The United States Army in World War II* (202). The Command and General Staff College Library at Fort Leavenworth, Kansas, contains student projects and monographs, many written by officers who later held important command positions, which reveal the direction of army thinking during the twenties and thirties. Many of the manuscript collections in the Library of Congress have restrictions that require prior permission before use. (Write Director of the Manuscript Division of the Library of Congress, Room 3005, Library of Congress Annex, Second and Independence Ave., Washington, D.C., for information and to secure clearances before beginning a research project.) At the National Archives one must secure a user's card to be admitted to the research rooms, and some records are still restricted. (Write Archivist of the United States, U.S. National Archives and Records Service, Washington, D.C., for information on checklist, inventories and particular restrictions on military records.) (For the Records Center, contact Chief, Archives Branch, Washington, D.C.)

MANUSCRIPT SOURCES. The papers of Woodrow Wilson in the Library of Congress show Wilson's concern with military affairs at the highest levels. They are essential for strategic planning and foreign policy studies and contain important exchanges of letters with Secretary Baker on the draft, industrial mobilization and War Department organization. The Newton D. Baker papers, also at the Library of Congress, present certain research difficulties for they contain only sixteen boxes for the war period. Baker wrote his most trenchant comments in the twenties and thirties, and those statements must be checked carefully against the archival records. A selection of the papers of Ralph Hays, Baker's private secretary, are also included at the end of the Baker collection.

The Franklin D. Roosevelt papers at Hyde Park have a remarkable amount of material on military affairs. (Write Director, Roosevelt Library, Hyde Park, New York.) A comparison of the Wilson and Roosevelt papers reveals Wilson's cool, structured approach to problems of military administration and especially his capacity to judge men accurately and delegate authority. Roosevelt's catholic interest and intense curiosity about everything resulted in a disjointed and destructured administrative style which gave an illusion of delegation while retaining the essence of authority in the President's hands. The papers of Roosevelt's Secretary of War, Henry L. Stimson, located in the Yale University Library, include correspondence and diaries that give important insights into the defense period just before World War II.

The papers of Bernard Baruch at Princeton University show his controversial involvement in industrial mobilization during and after the First World War. Of special significance in the Baruch collection are the records and interviews collected by Grosvenor Clarkson for his book, *Industrial America in the World War* (24). The papers of Frank Scott, the first chairman of the War Industries Board, are also at Princeton. The papers of Edward R. Stettinius at the University of Virginia and those of Benedict Crowell at Western Reserve Library in Cleveland, Ohio, are of some interest for World War I industrial mobilization.

The most important set of soldier's papers for the period are those of John J. Pershing. They are in three parts: the organized papers in the Library of Congress which formed the basis for *My Experiences in the World War* (166), the other Pershing papers in the Library of Congress which are relatively unorganized and contain more revealing personal information, and the Pershing papers in Record Group 316 in the National Archives. Pershing knew everybody and his position and influence in the army made his favor important. Every issue of military significance from 1917 to 1941 brought requests for advice and support across his desk. Everyone who was anyone in the army corresponded with Pershing, and his papers are a gold mine. The papers of George C. Marshall at the Marshall Library in Lexington, Virginia, have similar value for the late thirties. They give a remarkable insight into army life and army politics in the interwar years. Neither the papers of Douglas MacArthur at the MacArthur Foundation, Norfolk, Virginia, nor the George S. Patton, Jr., papers at the Library of Congress are at this moment open to the public. The Patton papers become available in 1975.

The papers of Peyton C. March, George W. Goethals, James G. Harbord, Tasker H. Bliss and Leonard Wood at the Library of Congress, and those of Enoch H. Crowder at the Western Historical Collection at the University of

Missouri, Columbia, Missouri, are essential for the First World War. The March papers show the General's view of the importance of the Chief of Staff's office and his conflict with Pershing. Goethals's papers, especially his desk diary, are a day-by-day account of the work of the Purchase, Storage, and Traffic Division of the General Staff. The Harbord papers contain much on AEF supply and interwar problems. The Bliss papers are excellent for grand strategy and interallied relations during and after the war, while the Wood papers give an insight into the thinking of the administration's military and political opponents. The Crowder papers are necessary for the study of conscription.

USING THE ARCHIVES. The main problem in using the National Archives and the Records Center at Suitland is bulk. One never knows for sure what will be uncovered in the strangest places. Where among the hundreds of thousands of feet of records can one find those nuggets of information which bring history alive? In 1917 the War Department introduced the dewey decimal system of classification for correspondence, and a comprehensive guide is available in every search room. All the researcher has to do is outguess the person who assigned the file number. The central depository for army correspondence is the Adjutant General's Office file (RG 94 before 1917 and RG 407 after 1917). The AGO files are so massive that it is better to work toward them from the records of the various other offices and bureaus in the War Department and the Army. *Each division maintained a historical section which compiled documents and monographs on the most important of its activities.* Document numbers and "direction signs" abound there to point the way into the AGO maze.

ARCHIVAL RECORDS. The *Records of the Office of the Secretary of War* (Archives, RG 107) contain not only a significant part of the correspondence of that office but also important records of the Office of Assistant Secretary of War including mobilization planning records, the Army-Navy Munitions Board records, and the records of the interwar War Policies Commissions. The *Records of the AEF* (Archives, RG 120) are deceptive. In addition to the obvious material, they contain the records of the American section of the Supreme War Council and the files and war monographs of the Historical Section of the War Department. The *Records of the Chief of Staff* (Archives and Suitland, RG 165) contain policy documents and the records of the War Plans Division. Those records should be supplemented with records from the Joint Board (Archives, RG 225). The most frustrating records to use in the Chief of Staff record group are the Purchase, Storage, and Traffic records. They are organized under a unique filing system which cannot be broken with the correspondence guide.

The most important other archival records are those of the Quartermaster Corps (Suitland, RG 92), the Ordnance Department (Suitland, RG 156), and the Provost Marshal General's Office (Suitland, RG 163). The records of the Council of National Defense (Suitland, RG 62) and the War Industries Board (Suitland, RG 61), though well organized, have only recently begun to be used systematically by scholars. Four other important collections neglected by scholars which contain information on military affairs are the Archives of the House of Representatives (Archives, RG 233), the Archives of the United States Senate (Archives, RG 46), the records of the General Accounting Office (Suitland, RG 217), and the records of the United States Shipping Board (Archives and Suitland, RG 32).

RESEARCH NEEDED. Much work remains to be done before a solid frame of reference for the study of military affairs in this century can be established. Scholarly work has only really begun on the modern army. There is no history at all of the American Army in the twentieth century. Research on the interwar period is still at the article stage. We need heuristic syntheses and provocative monographs to get our creative and reflective juices flowing. We need more studies on procurement, industrial-military organization, civil-military affairs and war planning. The social role of the army in American society has scarcely been touched. There is not even an adequate recent history of American conscription. The role of army officers in business and of the businessmen in uniform has only been superficially discussed. There is no history of the American enlisted man and only partial and theoretical studies of the officer corps. There is a place almost anywhere in recent American military history for an ambitious young scholar to plunge in and begin creative work.

BIBLIOGRAPHY

1. Ambrose, Stephen E. *Duty, Honor, Country: A History of West Point.* Baltimore: Johns Hopkins Press, 1966.
2. Ambrose, Stephen E. *Upton and the Army.* Baton Rouge: Louisiana State University Press, 1964.
3. Baker, Charles Whiting. *Government Control and Operation of Industry in Great Britain and the United States during the World War.* New York: Oxford University Press, 1921.
4. Baker, Ray Stannard. *Woodrow Wilson, Life and Letters.* Garden City: Doubleday, Page & Co., 1927-1939. 8 vols.
5. Baker, Roscoe. *The American Legion and American Foreign Policy.* New York: Bookman Associates, 1954.
6. Baldwin, Hanson W. *World War I: An Outline History.* New York: Harper & Row, 1962.
7. Baruch, Bernard M. *American Industry in the War.* Washington: G.P.O., 1921.
8. Baruch, Bernard M. *Baruch: My Own Story.* New York: Henry Holt, 1957.
9. Baruch, Bernard M. *Baruch: The Public Years.* New York: Holt, Rinehart and Winston, 1960.
10. Beaver, Daniel R. "George W. Goethals and the P. S. and T.," in Daniel R. Beaver, ed., *Some Pathways in Twentieth Century History.* Detroit: Wayne State University Press, 1969.
11. Beaver, Daniel R. *Newton D. Baker and the American War Effort 1917-1919.* Lincoln: University of Nebraska Press, 1966.

12. Bernardo, C. Joseph, and Eugene H. Bacon. *American Military Policy: Its Development Since 1775*. Harrisburg: Military Publishing Service, 1955.

13. Bliss, Tasker H. "The Evolution of the Unified Command," *Foreign Affairs* (Dec. 15, 1922).

14. Blum, Albert A. "Birth and Death of the M Day Plans," in Harold Stein, ed., *American Civil-Military Decisions*. Montgomery: University of Alabama Press, 1963.

15. Blum, Albert A. "Roosevelt, the M Day Plans and the Military Industrial Complex," *Military Affairs* (April 1972).

16. Blumenson, Martin, ed. *The Patton Papers*. Boston: Houghton Mifflin, 1972-74. 2 vols.

17. Bullard, Robert L. *American Soldiers Also Fought*. Toronto and New York: Longmans Green and Co., Inc., 1936.

18. Bullard, Robert L. *Personalities and Reminiscences of the War*. Garden City: Doubleday, Page & Co., 1925.

19. Burns, James M. *Roosevelt: Soldier of Freedom*. New York: Harcourt, Brace, Jovanovich, 1970.

20. Catton, Bruce. *The Warlords of Washington*. New York: Harcourt, Brace & Co., 1948.

21. Chambers, Frank P. *The War behind the War 1914-1918: A History of the Political and Civilian Fronts*. New York: Harcourt, Brace & Co., 1939.

22. Chandler, Alfred D. *Strategy and Structure: Chapters in the History of the Industrial Enterprise*. Cambridge: MIT Press, 1962.

23. Churchill, Winston S. *The World Crisis, 1916-1918*. New York: Scribner's, 1923-29. 4 vols.

24. Clarkson, Grosvenor B. *Industrial America in the World War: The Strategy behind the Line, 1917-1918*. Boston: Houghton Mifflin, 1923.

25. Clarkson, Jesse, and Thomas Cochran. *War as a Social Institution*. New York: American Historical Association, 1941.

26. Clifford, John Garry. *The Citizen Soldiers, The Plattsburg Training Camp Movement, 1913-1920*. Lexington: University of Kentucky Press, 1972.

27. Cline, Raymond S. *Washington Command Post: The Operations Division*. Washington: Office of the Chief of Military History, Dept. of the Army, 1951.

28. Cochran, Thomas C., and William Miller. *The Age of Enterprise, A Social History of Industrial America*. New York: Macmillan, 1942.

29. Coffman, Edward M. "The American Military Generation Gap in World War I: The Leavenworth Clique in the AEF," in William Geffen, ed., *Command and Commanders in Modern Warfare*. Colorado Springs: U.S. Air Force Academy, 1964.

30. Coffman, Edward M. *The Hilt of the Sword: The Career of Peyton C. March*. Madison: University of Wisconsin Press, 1966.

31. Coffman, Edward M. *The War to End All Wars*. New York: Oxford University Press, 1968.

32. Coit, Margaret. *Mr. Baruch*. Boston: Houghton Mifflin, 1957.

33. Cole, Wayne. *Senator Gerald P. Nye and American Foreign Relations*. Minneapolis: University of Minnesota Press, 1962.

34. Conant, James B. *Modern Science and Modern Man.* New York: Columbia University Press, 1952.
35. Consett, Montagu W. W. P., and Octavius H. Daniel. *The Triumph of Unarmed Forces.* London: Williams and Norgate, 1923.
36. Cooperman, Stanley. *World War I and the American Novel.* Baltimore: Johns Hopkins Press, 1967.
37. Corwin, Edwin S. *The President: Office and Powers, 1781-1957; History and Analysis of Practice and Opinion.* 4th rev. ed. New York: New York University Press, 1957.
38. Cramer, C. H. *Newton D. Baker: A Biography.* Cleveland: World Publishing Co., 1961.
39. Craven, Wesley F., and James L. Cate. *The Army Air Forces in World War II.* Vol. I. *Plans and Early Operations.* Chicago: University of Chicago Press, 1948.
40. Crowder, Enoch H. *The Spirit of Selective Service.* New York: Century, 1920.
41. Crowell, Benedict, and Robert F. Wilson. *How America Went to War, An Account from Official Sources of the Nation's War Activities, 1917-1920.* New Haven, Connecticut: Yale University Press, 1921. 6 vols.
42. Crowell, J. Franklin. *Government War Contracts.* New York: Oxford University Press, 1920.
43. Crozier, Emmet. *American Reporters on the Western Front, 1914-1918.* New York: Oxford University Press, 1959.
44. Crozier, William. *Ordnance and the World War: A Contribution to the History of American Preparedness.* New York: Scribner's, 1920.
45. Cuff, Robert C. "Business, the State, and World War I: The American Experience," in J. L. Granatstein and R. D. Cuff, eds., *War and Society in North America.* Toronto: Thomas Nelson, 1971.
46. Cuff, Robert D. "Newton D. Baker, Frank A. Scott and The American Reinforcement in the World War,'" *Military Affairs* (Feb. 1970).
47. Cuff, Robert D. *War Industries Board, Business-Government Relations during World War I.* Baltimore: Johns Hopkins Press, 1973.
48. Current, Richard N. *Secretary Stimson: A Study in Statecraft.* New Brunswick: Rutgers University Press, 1954. Reprinted, Hamden, Connecticut: Archon Books, 1970.
49. Curti, Merle. *The American Peace Crusade.* Durham: Duke University Press, 1929.
50. Dalfiume, Richard. *Desegregation of the U.S. Army Forces: Fighting on Two Fronts, 1939-1953.* Columbia: University of Missouri Press, 1969.
51. Daniels, Roger. *The Bonus March: An Episode of the Great Depression.* Westport, Connecticut: Greenwood Publishing Co., 1971.
52. Dawes, Charles G. *A Journal of the Great War.* Boston: Houghton Mifflin, 1921. 2 vols.
53. Derthick, Martha. *The National Guard in Politics.* Cambridge: Harvard University Press, 1965.
54. Deutrich, Mabel E. *Struggle for Supremacy: The Career of Fred C. Ainsworth.* Washington: Public Affairs Press, 1962.
55. DeWeerd, Harvey. "The American Adoption of French Artillery, 1917-

1918," *Journal of American Military Institute* [now *Military Affairs*] (Summer, 1939).

56. DeWeerd, Harvey. *President Wilson Fights His War: World War I and the American Intervention.* New York: Macmillan, 1968.
57. DeWitt, Harry M. *The General Staff.* Washington: G.P.O., 1953.
58. Dickinson, John. *The Building of an Army, A Detailed Account of Legislation, Administration and Opinion in the United States, 1915-1920.* New York: Century, 1922.
59. Dickman, Joseph T. *The Great Crusade, A Narrative of the World War.* New York: D. Appleton Co., 1927.
60. Dixon, Frank H. *Railroads and Government: Their Relations in the United States, 1910-1921.* New York: Scribner's, 1922.
61. Dos Passos, John. *Mr. Wilson's War.* Garden City: Doubleday & Co., 1962.
62. Dupree, A. Hunter *Science in the Federal Government: A History of Policies and Activities to 1940.* Cambridge: Harvard University Press, 1957.
63. Earle, Edward Mead, ed. *Makers of Modern Strategy: Military Thought from Machiavelli to Hitler.* Princeton: Princeton University Press, 1941.
64. Ekirch, Arthur A., Jr. *The Civilian and the Military.* New York: Oxford University Press, 1956.
65. Engelbrecht, Helmuth C., and Frank C. Hanighen. *Merchants of Death: A Study of the International Armament Industry.* New York: Dodd, Mead, & Co., 1934.
66. Esposito, Vincent J., ed. *A Concise History of World War I.* New York: Frederick A. Praeger, Inc., 1964.
67. Esposito, Vincent J., ed. *The West Point Atlas of American Wars.* Vol. II, *1900-1953.* New York: Frederick A. Praeger, Inc., 1959.
68. Falls, Cyril. *The Great War.* New York: G. P. Putnam's Sons, 1959.
69. Falls, Cyril. *War Books: A Critical Guide.* London: P. Davies, Ltd., 1930.
70. Fitzpatrick, Edward A. *Conscription and America: A Study of Conscription in a Democracy.* Milwaukee: Richard Publishing Co., 1940.
71. Fosdick, Raymond B. *Chronicle of a Generation.* New York: Harpers, 1959.
72. Fredericks, Pierce G. *The Great Adventure: America in the First World War.* New York: Dutton, 1960.
73. Frothingham, Thomas G. *The American Reinforcement in the World War.* Garden City: Doubleday, Page & Co., 1927.
74. Ganoe, William A. *History of the United States Army.* Rev. ed. New York: D. Appleton and Co., 1943.
75. Gillie, Mildred Hanson. *Forging the Thunderbolt: A History of the Development of the Armored Force.* Harrisburg: Military Service Publishing Co., 1947.
76. Gleaves, Albert. *A History of the Transport Service: Adventures and Experiences of the United States Transports and Cruisers in the World War.* New York: George H. Doran, 1921.
77. Grant, Ulysses S., III. *America's Part in the Supreme War Council during the World War.* New York: Columbia Historical Society Records, 1928.

78. Graves, William S. *America's Siberian Adventure, 1918-1920.* New York: J. Cape and H. Smith, 1931.
79. Green, Constance M., and Harry C. Thomson and Peter C. Roots. *The Ordnance Department: Planning Munitions for War.* Washington: G.P.O., 1955.
80. Green, Fred. "The Military View of American National Policy, 1904-1940," *American Historical Review* (Jan. 1961).
81. Greenfield, Kent Roberts, ed. *Command Decisions.* Washington: G.P.O., 1960.
82. Greer, Thomas H. *The Development of Air Doctrine in the Army Air Force 1917-1941.* Montgomery: Air University Press, 1955.
83. Hagedorn, Hermann. *Leonard Wood, A Biography.* New York and London: Harper & Bros., 1931. 2 vols.
84. Hagood, Johnson. *The Services of Supply: A Memoir of the Great War.* Boston: Houghton Mifflin, 1927.
85. Halliday, E. M. *The Ignorant Armies.* New York: Harper & Bros., 1960.
86. Hammond, Paul Y. *Organizing for Defense: The American Military Establishment in the Twentieth Century.* Princeton: Princeton University Press, 1961.
87. Harbord, James G. *The American Army in France, 1917-1919.* Boston: Little, Brown and Company, 1936.
88. Harbord, James G. *Leaves from a War Diary.* New York: Dodd, Mead & Co., 1925.
89. Henri, Florette, and Richard Stillman. *Bitter Victory: A History of Black Soldiers in World War I.* New York: Doubleday, 1970.
90. Hill, Jim Dan. *The Minuteman in Peace and War: A History of the National Guard.* Harrisburg: Stackpole, 1964.
91. Hines, Walker, D. *War History of American Railroads.* New Haven: Yale University Press, 1928.
92. Hirschfield, Charles. "The Transformation of American Life," in Jack Roth, ed., *World War I: A Turning Point in Modern History.* New York: Alfred A. Knopf, 1967.
93. Hittle, James D. *The Military Staff, Its History and Development.* Harrisburg: Military Service Publishing Co., 1949.
94. Hoffman, George F. "The Demise of the U.S. Tank Corps and Medium Tank Development Program," *Military Affairs* (Feb. 1973).
95. Hoffman, George F. "Tactics vs. Technology: The U.S. Cavalry Experience," *Armour* (Sept.-Oct. 1973).
96. Hoffman, Max. *The War of Lost Opportunities.* New York: International Publishers, 1925.
97. Holley, Irving B., Jr. *Buying Aircraft: Procurement of Air Material in World War II.* Washington: G.P.O., 1964.
98. Holley, Irving B., Jr. *Ideas and Weapons.* New Haven: Yale University Press, 1953. Reprinted, Hamden, Connecticut: Archon Books, 1971.
99. Huntington, Samuel P. *The Soldier and the State.* Cambridge: The Belknap Press, Harvard, 1957.
100. Hurley, Alfred F. *Billy Mitchell: Crusader for Air Power.* New York: Watts, 1964.
101. Hurley, Edward N. *The Bridge to France.* Philadelphia: J. B. Lippincott, 1927.

102. Huston, James A. *The Sinews of War: Army Logistics 1775-1953.* Washington: G.P.O., 1966.
103. Huzar, Elias. *The Purse and the Sword: Control of the Army by Congress through Military Appropriations 1933-1950.* Ithaca: Cornell University Press, 1950.
104. James, D. Clayton. *The Years of MacArthur.* Vol. I, *1880-1941.* Boston: Houghton Mifflin, 1970.
105. Janeway, Eliot. *The Struggle for Survival: A Chronicle of Economic Mobilization in World War II.* New Haven: Yale University Press, 1951.
106. Janowitz, Morris. *The Professional Soldier.* Glencoe: Free Press, 1960.
107. Johnson, Charles. "The Army, the Negro and the Civilian Conservation Corps, 1933-1942," *Military Affairs* (Oct. 1972).
108. Johnson, Donald O. *The Challenge to American Freedoms, World War I and the Rise of the American Civil Liberties Union.* Lexington: University of Kentucky Press, 1963.
109. Johnson, Thomas M. *Our Secret War.* Indianapolis: Bobbs-Merrill, 1929.
110. Johnson, Thomas M. *Without Censor, New Light on Our Greatest World War Battles.* Indianapolis: Bobbs-Merrill, 1928.
111. Kennan, George F. *Soviet American Relations 1917-1920.* Princeton: Princeton University Press, 1956-58. 2 vols.
112. Kevles, Daniel J. "George Ellery Hale, the First World War, and the Advancement of Science in America," *ISIS* (Winter, 1968).
113. Kevles, Daniel J. "Testing the Army's Intelligence: Psychologists and the Military in World War I," *Journal of American History* (Dec. 1968).
114. Koistenen, Paul A. C. "The Industrial-Military Complex in Historical Perspective: World War I," *Business History Review,* (Winter, 1967).
115. Koistenen, Paul A. C. "The Industrial-Military Complex in Historical Perspective: The Interwar Years," *Journal of American History* (Mar. 1970).
116. Kreidberg, Marvin A., and Merton G. Henry. *History of Military Mobilization in the United States Army,1775-1945.* Department of the Army Pamphlet 20-212. Washington, D.C.: GPO, 1955.
117. Kutz, Charles R. *War on Wheels: The Evolution of an Idea.* Harrisburg: Military Service Publishing Co., 1940.
118. Langer, William L. *Gas and Flame in World War I.* Rev. ed. New York: Knopf, 1965.
119. Langer, William L.. and Sorell E. Gleason. *The Challenge to Isolation, 1937-1940.* New York: Harper & Bros., 1952.
120. Langer, William L., and Sorell E. Gleason. *The Undeclared War, 1940-1941.* New York: Harper & Bros., 1952.
121. Lee, Ulysses. *The Employment of Negro Troops: The United States Army in World War II.* Washington: Office of the Chief of Military History, 1966.
122. Leland, Waldo G., and Newton D. Mereness, comps. *Introduction to the American Official Sources for the Economic and Social History of the World War.* New Haven: Yale University Press, 1926.
123. Liddell Hart, Basil. *A History of the World War, 1914-1918.* Boston: Little, Brown and Co., 1935.

124. Liddell Hart, Basil. *The Real War, 1914-1918.* Boston: Little, Brown and Co., 1930.
125. Liddell Hart, Basil. *Reputations Ten Years After.* Boston: Little, Brown and Co., 1928.
126. Liggett, Hunter. *A. E. F. Ten Years Ago in France.* New York: Dodd, Mead & Co., 1928.
127. Liggett, Hunter. *Commanding an American Army.* Boston: Houghton Mifflin, 1925.
128. Lockmiller, David A. *Enoch H. Crowder: Soldier, Lawyer and Statesman.* Columbia: University of Missouri Press, 1955.
129. Lowry, Bullett. "Pershing and the Armistice," *Journal of American History* (Mar. 1968).
130. Lyons, Gene M., and John W. Masland. *Education and Military Leadership: A Study of the ROTC.* Princeton: Princeton University Press, 1959.
131. McClendon, R. Earl. *The Question of Autonomy for the United States Air Arm.* Montgomery Alabama: Air University, 1952.
132. McLean, Rose H. "Troop Movements on the American Railroads during the Great War," *American Historical Review* (Apr. 1921).
133. March, Peyton C. *The Nation at War.* Garden City: Doubleday, Doran & Co., 1932.
134. Marshall, S. L. A. *The American Heritage History of World War I.* New York: American Heritage Publishing Co., 1964.
135. Masland, John W. and Lawrence I. Radway. *Soldiers and Scholars, Military Education and National Policy.* Princeton: Princeton University Press, 1957.
136. Matloff, Maurice. "The American Approach to War, 1919-1945," in Michael Howard, ed., *The Theory and Practice of War: Essays Presented to Capt. Sir Basil Liddell Hart.* London: Cassell, 1965.
137. Matloff, Maurice. *Mr. Roosevelt's Three Wars: F. D. R. As War Leader.* Harmon Lectures #6. Colorado Springs: U.S. Air Force Academy, 1964.
138. Matloff, Maurice, and Edwin M. Snell. *Strategic Planning for Coalition Warfare, 1941-1942.* Washington: G.P.O., 1953.
139. May, Ernest R., ed. *The Ultimate Decision: The President as Commander in Chief.* New York: Braziller, 1960.
140. Millett, John D. *The Organization and Role of the Army Service Forces.* Washington: G.P.O., 1954.
141. Millis, Walter. *Arms and Men, A Study in American Military History.* New York: G. P. Putnam, 1956.
142. Mills, C. Wright. *The Power Elite.* New York: Oxford Univeristy Press, 1956.
143. Mitchell, William. *Memoirs of World War I.* New York: Random House, 1960.
144. Morison, Elting E. *Men, Machines, and Modern Times.* Cambridge: Harvard University Press, 1966.
145. Morison, Elting E. *Turmoil and Tradition, A Study of the Life and Times of Henry L. Stimson.* Boston: Houghton Mifflin, 1960.
146. Morton, Louis. "War Plan ORANGE: Evolution of a Strategy," *World Politics* (Jan. 1959).

147. Nash, Gerald D. "Experiments in Industrial Mobilization: WIB and NRA," *Mid-America* (July, 1963).
148. National Archives. *Handbook of Federal War Agencies and Their Records, 1917-1921.* Washington: G.P.O., 1943.
149. Nelson, Donald M. *Arsenal of Democracy: The Story of American War Production.* New York: Harcourt, Brace, 1946.
150. Nelson, John K. *The Peace Prophets, American Pacifist Thought, 1919-1941.* Chapel Hill: University of North Carolina Press, 1967.
151. Nelson, Keith L., ed., *The Impact of War on American Life: The Twentieth Century Experience.* New York: Holt, Reinhart and Winston, 1971.
152. Nelson, Otto. *National Security and the General Staff.* Washington: Infantry Journal Press, 1946.
153. O'Connor, Richard. *Black Jack Pershing.* Garden City: Doubleday, 1961.
154. Ogorkiewicz, Richard M. *Armour: A History of Mechanized Forces.* Tasker Howard Bliss. New York: Dodd, Mead & Co., 1934.
155. Palmer, Frederick. *Bliss, Peace Maker: The Life and Letters of General Tasker Howard Bliss.* New Yrk: Dodd, Mead & Co., 1934.
156. Palmer, Frederick. *John J. Pershing, General of the Armies: A Biography.* Harrisbrg: Military Service Publishing Co., 1948.
157. Palmer, Frederick. *Newton D. Baker: America at War.* New York: Dodd, Mead & Co., 1931. 2 vols.
158. Palmer, Frederick. *Our Greatest Battle.* New York: Dodd, Mead & Co., 1919.
159. Palmer, John M. *America in Arms: The Experience of the United States with Military Organization.* New Haven: Yale University Press, 1941.
160. Palmer, John M. *Washington, Lincoln, Wilson: Three War Statesmen.* Garden City: Doubleday, Doran & Co., 1930.
161. Pappas, George S. *Prudens Futuri: The U.S. Army War College 1901-1967.* Carlisle Barracks: Alumni Association of U.S. Army War College, 1967.
162. Paxson, Frederic L. *American Democracy and the World War.* Boston: Houghton Mifflin, 1936-48. 3 vols.
163. Paxson, Frederic L. "The American War Government, 1917-1918," *American Historical Review* (Oct. 1920).
164. Paxson, Frederic L. "The Great Demobilization," *American Historical Review* (Jan. 1939).
165. Penick, James L., Jr., et. al., eds. *The Politics of American Science: 1939 to the Present.* Chicago: Rand McNally, 1965.
166. Pershing, John J. *My Experiences in the World War.* New York: Frederick A. Stokes Co., 1931. 2 vols.
167. Petersen, Horace C., and Gilbert C. Fite. *Opponents of War, 1917-1918.* Madison: University of Wisconsin Press, 1957.
168. Pogue, Forrest C. *George C. Marshall: Education of a General, 1880-1939.* New York: The Viking Press, Inc., 1963.
169. Pogue, Forrest C. *George C. Marshall: Ordeal and Hope, 1939-1942.* New York: The Viking Press, Inc., 1966.
170. Pursell, Carroll W., Jr., ed. *The Military-Industrial Complex.* New York: Harper & Row, 1972.

171. Riker, William H. *Soldiers of the States, The Role of the National Guard in American Democracy.* Washington: Public Affairs Press, 1957.

172. Risch, Erna. *The Quartermaster Corps: Organization, Supply and Service.* Washington: G.P.O., 1953. 2 vols.

173. Risch, Erna. *Quartermaster Support of the Army: A History of the Corps, 1775-1939.* Washington: G.P.O., 1962.

174. Roth, Jack J., ed. *World War I: A Turning Point in Modern History.* New York: Alfred A. Knopf, 1967.

175. Rudin, Harry R. *Armistice, 1918.* New Haven: Yale University Press, 1944.

176. Rutkowski, Edwin H. *The Politics of Military Aviation Procurement 1926-1934, A Study in the Political Assertion of Consensual Values.* Columbus: Ohio State University Press, 1967.

177. Salmond, John. *The Civilian Conservation Corps, 1933-1942.* Durham: Duke University Press, 1967.

178. Salter, James A. *Allied Shipping Control, An Experiment in International Administration.* Oxford: Clarendon Press, 1921.

179. Schaffer, Ronald. "General Stanley D. Embick: Military Dissenter," *Military Affairs* (Oct. 1973).

180. Schwarz, Urs. *American Strategy: A New Perspective.* Garden City: Doubleday, 1966.

181. Scott, Emmett J. *The American Negro in the World War.* Chicago: Homewood Press, 1919.

182. Seldes, George. *Iron, Blood and Profits.* New York: Harper & Bros., 1934.

183. Seymour, Charles. *The Intimate Papers of Colonel House Arranged as a Narrative.* Boston: Houghton Mifflin, 1926-28. 4 vols.

184. Sharpe, Henry G. *The Quartermaster Corps in the Year 1917 in the World War.* New York: Century, 1921.

185. Smith, Louis. *American Democracy and Military Power.* Chicago: University of Chicago Press, 1951.

186. Smith, R. Elberton. *The Army and Economic Mobilization.* Washington: G.P.O., 1959.

187. Smythe, Donald. "Battle of the Books: Pershing Versus March," *Army* (Sept. 1972).

188. Spaulding, Oliver. *The United States Army in Peace and War.* New York: G. P. Putnam's Sons, 1937.

189. Spector, Ronald. "You're Not Going to Send Soldiers Over There Are You?: The American Search for an Alternate to the Western Front, 1916-1917," *Military Affairs* (Feb. 1972).

190. Stallings, Lawrence. *The Doughboys: The Story of the AEF, 1917-1918.* New York: Harper & Row, 1963.

191. Stallings, Lawrence. *The First World War: A Photographic History.* New York: Simon and Schuster, 1933.

192. Stimson, Henry L., and McGeorge Bundy. *On Active Service in Peace and War.* New York: Harpers, 1948.

193. Sullivan, Mark. *Our Times.* New York: Charles Scribner's Sons, 1926-35. 6 vols.

194. Swisher, C. B. "Control of War Preparations," *American Political Science Review*, 1940.

195. Thacher, Harold W. *Planning for Industrial Mobilization 1920-1940.* Washington: G.P.O., 1943.

196. Thomas, Norman. *The Conscientious Objector in America.* New York: B. W. Huebsch, Inc., 1923.

197. Trask, David F. *The United States in the Supreme War Council: American War Aims and Inter-Allied Strategy, 1917-1918.* Middletown, Connecticut: Wesleyan University Press, 1961.

198. Trask, David F., ed. *World War I at Home.* New York: John Wiley and Sons, 1970.

199. U.S. American Battle Monuments Commission. *American Armies and Battlefields in Europe.* Washington: G.P.O., 1938.

200. U.S. American Battle Monuments Commission. *First Division, Summary of Operations in the World War.* Washington: G.P.O., 1944. Same for Second, Third, Fourth, Fifth, Seventh, Eighteenth, Twenty-seventh, Twenty-eighth, Thirtieth, Thirty-second, Thirty-third, Thirty-fifth, Thirty-seventh, Forty-second, Seventy-seventh, Seventy-ninth, Eighty-second, Eighty-ninth, Ninetieth, Ninety-first, Ninety-second, and Ninety-third Divisions.

201. U.S. Army War College, Historical Section. *The Genesis of the American First Army.* Washington, D.C.: G.P.O., 1938.

202. *The United States Army in World War II.* Washington, D.C.: G.P.O., 1945 to date. Specific volumes cited in essay. Projected 79 vols.

203. Vagts, Alfred. *A History of Militarism.* Rev. ed. New York: Meridian Books, 1959.

204. Vandiver, Frank. *John J. Pershing and the Anatomy of Leadership.* Harmon Lectures #6. Colorado Springs, Col: U.S. Air Force Academy, 1963.

205. Van Tassel, David D., and Michael G. Hall, eds. *Science and Society in the United States.* Homewood, Illinois: Dorsey Press, 1966.

206. Viereck, George S., ed. *As They Saw Us: Foch, Ludendorff and Other Leaders Write Our War History.* Garden City: Doubleday, Doran & Co., 1929.

207. Waldman, Seymour. *Death and Profits, A Study of the War Policies Commission.* New York: Warren and Putnam, 1932.

208. Ward, Robert D. "Against the Tide: The Preparedness Movement of 1923-1924," *Military Affairs* (Apr. 1974).

209. Watson, Mark S. *Chief-of-Staff: Pre-War Plans and Preparations.* Washington: G.P.O., 1950.

210. Weigley, Russell. *The American Way of War, A History of United States Military Strategy and Policy.* New York: Macmillan, 1973.

211. Weigley, Russell. *History of the United States Army.* New York: Macmillan, 1967.

212. Weigley, Russell. *Towards an American Army: American Military Thought from Washington to Marshall.* New York: Columbia University Press, 1962.

213. Weinstein, James. *The Corporate Ideal in the Liberal State, 1900-1918.* Boston: Beacon Press, 1968.

214. Wiebe, Robert H. *The Search for Order, 1877-1920.* New York: Hill & Wang, 1967.

215. Wilgus, William J. *Transporting the A. E. F. in Western Europe.* New York: Columbia University Press, 1931.

216. Williams, T. Harry. *Americans at War: The Development of the American Military System*. Baton Rouge: Louisiana State University Press, 1960.
217. Willoughby, Charles A. *The Economic and Military Participation of the United States in the World War*. Ft. Leavenworth: Command and General Staff School Press, 1931.
218. Willoughby, Charles A. *Government Organization in Wartime*. New York: Appleton, 1919.
219. Wilson, John R. M. "The Quaker and the Sword: Herbert Hoover's Relations with the Military," *Military Affairs* (Apr. 1974).
220. Wiltz, John E. *In Search of Peace: The Senate Munitions Inquiry, 1934-36*. Baton Rouge: Louisiana State University Press, 1963.
221. Yardley, Herbert O. *The American Black Chamber*. Indianapolis: Bobbs-Merrill, 1931.
222. Yoshpe, Harry B. "Bernard Baruch: Civilian Godfather of the Military M Day Plan," *Military Affairs* (Spring, 1965).
223. Yoshpe, Harry B. "Economic Mobilization between Wars," *Military Affairs* (Winter, 1951, and Summer, 1952).

GOVERNMENT DOCUMENTS
224. U.S. Congress, *Congressional Record*. 1917-1941. Cited by session in essay.
225. U.S. Congress, House, Committee on Military Affairs. *Hearings before the Committee on Military Affairs: A Bill to Increase the Effectiveness of the Military Establishment of the United States*, 64th Cong., 1st sess., 1916. 2 vols.
226. U.S. Congress, House, Committee on Military Affairs. *Hearings before the Committee on Military Affairs: A Bill to Reorganize and Increase the Efficiency of the U.S. Army and Other Purposes*, 66th Cong., 1st sess., 1919-1921. 2 parts.
227. U.S. Congress, House, Committee on Military Affairs. *Hearings, Reorganization of the National Guard*, 65th Cong., 3rd sess., 1919.
228. U.S. Congress, House, Select Committee on Expenditures in the War Department. [Graham Committee]. *Hearings on Expenditures in the War Department*, 66th Cong., 1st-3rd sess., 1919-1921. 15 vols.
229. U.S. Congress, House. *War Policies Commission Report to the President*, 72nd Cong., 1st sess., 1932. House Document no. 163.
230. U.S. Congress, Senate, Committee on Military Affairs. *Hearings, Investigation of the War Department*, 65th Cong., 2nd sess., 1918. 8 parts.
231. U.S. Congress, Senate, Committee on Military Affairs. *Hearings, Reorganization of the Army and Creation of a Reserve Army*, 64th Cong., 1st sess., 1916.
232. U.S. Congress, Senate, Committee on Military Affairs. *Hearings, Reorganization of the Army*, 66th Cong., 1st and 2nd sess., 1919. 2 parts.
233. U.S. Congress, Senate, Special Committee to Investigate the Munitions Industry. [Nye Committee]. *Hearings, Munitions Industry*, 73rd-74th Cong., 1934-1937. 40 parts. Included in the published date are: *Minutes of the General Munitions Board*, Apr. 6 - Aug. 1, 1917; *Minutes of the War Industries Board*, Aug. 1 - Dec. 19, 1918; and

Digest of the Proceedings of the Council of National Defense during the World War. ed. by Franklin H. Martin.

234. U.S. Congress, Senate. *Universal Military Training*, 65th Cong., 1st sess., 1917. Senate Document no. 10.

235. U.S. Council of National Defense. *First Annual Report of the Council of National Defense, 1917.* Washington: G.P.O. Same for *Second Annual Report, 1918*, and *Third Annual Report, 1919.*

236. U.S. Department of State. *Papers Relating to the Foreign Relations of the United States, 1917-1918.* Washington: G.P.O., 1926-1933. 9 vols. with Supplements.

237. U.S. Department of State. *Papers Relating to the Foreign Relations of the United States, 1917-1918: The Lansing Papers.* Washington: G.P.O., 1939-40. 2 vols.

238. U.S. War Department. *America's Munitions, 1917-1918.* The Report of Benedict Crowell, Assistant Secretary of War, Director of Munitions. Washington: G.P.O., 1919.

239. U.S. War Department. *Annual Reports.* Washington: G.P.O., 1917-1921.

240. U.S. War Department. *The Army Register.* Washington: G.P.O., 1917-1941.

241. U.S. War Department. *Final Report of the Commander-in-Chief American Expeditionary Force.* Washington: G.P.O., 1919.

242. U.S. War Department, General Staff. *The War with Germany: A Statistical Summary* by Leonard P. Ayres. Washington: G.P.O., 1919.

243. U.S. War Department, Historical Division, Department of the Army. *The United States Army in the World War.* Washington: G.P.O., 1948, 17 vols.

244. U.S. War Department. *Infantry in Battle.* Washington: Infantry Journal Press, 1934.

245. U.S. War Department. *Order of Battle of the U.S. Land Forces in the World War.* Washington: G.P.O., 1931-1949.

246. U.S. War Department. *Report of the Chairman of the Committee on Training Camp Activities to the Secretary of War.* Washington: G.P.O., 1919.

247. U.S. War Department. *Report of the Military Board of Allied Supply.* Washington: G.P.O., 1924. 3 vols.

248. U.S. War Department, Secretary of War. *Annual Report.* Washington: G.P.O., 1922-1941. Cited by year in essay.

XII

MILITARY AND NAVAL MEDICINE

James O. Breeden

The late Allan Nevins (131) soberly reminded Americans at the beginning of the centennial celebration of their Civil War that all great wars had two sides, "the glorious and the terrible." It is well-known, he contended, that everyone enjoys the former, revelling in accounts of inspired military leadership, decisive campaigns, and battlefield courage; the latter, however, is like a bad dream, and we recoil at reminders of the ravages of battle and the dreadful toll of disease. Yet, it is an incontrovertible fact that injury and disease have been constant companions of the American fighting man and have played a far greater role in deciding engagements than is generally recognized. The fondness of Americans for the "glorious" has produced a marked emphasis on it in the vast literature of our nation's military history. This chapter, then, is something of an anomaly, for it surveys the all too paltry literature devoted to the "terrible."

First-rate historical surveys of military medicine are almost nonexistent. The only one worthy of mention is Fielding H. Garrison's *Notes on the History of Military Medicine* (70). But it is dated and touches only briefly on the American experience. In the absence of a comprehensive study the student of American military medicine is forced to piece together the story himself from available sources. These vary greatly in both quantity and quality, depending upon the period under study.

Among those studies of a general nature, Francis R. Packard's *History of Medicine in the United States* (138) is a good starting point. It has lengthy introductory accounts of Army and Navy medical history, surveying the former through the Spanish-American War and the latter to 1928. More in-depth information can be found in the medical histories of the various branches. The Army has received the lion's share of attention. There have been three noteworthy attempts at recounting its medical history: Harvey E. Brown's *Medical Department of the United States Army from 1775 to 1873* (235); James A. Tobey's *Medical Department of the Army, Its History, Activities and Organization* (193); and Percy M. Ashburn's *History of the Medical Department of the United States Army* (4). These are complemented by William Owen's chronology of Congressional legislation relating to the Medical Department of the Army between 1785 and 1917 (136); James E. Pilcher's *Surgeon Generals of the Army of the United States of America* (149); and James M. Phalen's *Chiefs of the Medical Department, United States Army, 1775-1940* (148). Additional biographical sketches are available in Thacher (190), Williams (249), Gross (85), Hamersly (86), Heitman (91), and Kelly and Burrage (107). Surveys of a special nature but which also help illuminate the Army's medical history are Edgar E. Hume's *Victories of Army Medicine* (97) and Stanhope Bayne-Jones' *Evolution of Preventive Medicine in the United States Army, 1607-1939* (11). A final general source for the Army is the annual reports of the surgeon general to the secretary of war (231). These contain a wealth of valuable primary material and are a must for the serious scholar.

Much less attention, from the earliest days of the nation to the present, has been devoted to the medical history of the Navy. The most significant attempt at presenting an overview is Louis Roddis's *Short History of Nautical Medicine* (163). Roddis supplemented this outline with a series of biographical sketches of the Navy's surgeon generals (164). George P. Bradley's article on the origin and history of the medical corps of the Navy (25) is also worth consulting. The obvious lack of detailed accounts makes the annual reports of the surgeon general of the navy (208) of inestimable value to the student of naval medicine.

The Air Force had its beginning in this century and emerged as a distinct branch only after World War II. It is not surprising, therefore, that there has not been a great deal of activity concerning the history of aviation medicine in America. Green Peyton's *Fifty Years of Aerospace Medicine* (147) and Douglas H. Robinson's *The Dangerous Sky* (162A), although ground breakers at best, are steps in the right direction.

Much material of a general nature relating to each branch of the military establishment can be gleaned from the voluminous periodical literature dealing with military medicine. The chief journals to be consulted are the *Bulletin of the History of Medicine*, the *Journal of the History of Medicine and the Allied Sciences, Military Medicine* (and its predecessors the *Military Surgeon* and the *Journal of the Association of Military Surgeons*), and the *United States Armed Forces Medical Journal* (and its predecessors the *Army Medical Bulletin* and the *U.S. Naval Medical Bulletin*). The leading guides to this plethora of periodical material are the *Bibliography of the History of Medicine* (20), Genevieve Miller's *Bibliography of the History of Medicine of the United States and Canada, 1939-1960* (124), and the *Index-Catalogue of the Library of the Surgeon-General's Office* (218)—especially the reprint of the military section, volume XI, fourth series (219).

THE AMERICAN REVOLUTION. The medical side of the Revolution is the only facet of this heroic struggle for which there is no first-rate study. Attempts have been made, but all have fallen short of the mark: Joseph M. Toner's *Medical Men of the Revolution* (195) has an easily discernible patriotic bias; William O. Owen's administrative history (137), while an excellent compilation of the medical legislation passed by the national and provincial legislatures, lacks interpretation; and Louis C. Duncan's *Medical Men in the American Revolution, 1775-1783* (58) and James E. Gibson's *Dr. Bodo Otto and the Medical Background of the American Revolution* (72) contain a wealth of primary material but are poorly organized to the point of a total loss of cohesion. Although noticeably succinct, one of the best analyses of medicine in the Revolution to appear in recent years is a series of articles by Howard L. Applegate (3).

The student of military medicine in the Revolutionary era is further hampered by a shortage of contemporary material. But that which does exist is quite illuminating. The earliest known medical publication of the Revolution is Dr. John Jones' *Plain Concise Practical Remarks on the Treatment of Wounds and Fractures* (103) which appeared in 1775 shortly after the onset of hostilities. In reality an abstract of the principles of Sir John Pringle, the founder of military medicine, this first medical book published in America proved to be of great value to the Army and Navy surgeons of the Revolution. Within a year it was supplemented by an American edition of Gerard van Swieten's *Diseases Incident to Armies* (187). John Morgan's brief *Recommendation of Innoculation, according to Baron Dimsdale's Method* (126) also appeared in 1776. Two years later William Brown's *Pharmacopoeia* (34) and Benjamin Rush's *Directions for Preserving the Health of Soldiers* (167) were published. The former, often called the *Lititz Pharmacopoeia* because Brown compiled it in his spare time while stationed at an Army hospital in Lititz, Pennsylvania, was the first undertaking of its kind in America. The latter, published by order of the Board of War, briefly, but forcefully, set forth a number of excellent sanitary rules. It has been called the most important work written as a direct result of the Revolution. The winter of 1778-79, of Valley Forge fame, was further marked by the publication of Baron von Steuben's *Regulations for the Order and Discipline of Troops of the United States* (217). Generally regarded as a manual of arms and drill, this book, nevertheless, contains much sound advice on military hygiene. Finally, notice should be made of James Tilton's *Economical Observations on Military Hygiene* (192). This book, based upon the author's extensive experiences in the field and hospital during the Revolution, is a superior study on the preservation of the health of soldiers.

Valuable insights into the history and operations of the Medical Department of the Continental Army can be obtained from an examination of John Morgan's stormy tenure as director general. A recognized leader in the colonial medical profession, Morgan succeeded Dr. Benjamin Church, the medical department's traitorous first head, in November 1775. Church's enigmatic career has been scrutinized by William F. Norwood (132). Morgan worked hard to introduce economy and discipline into the medical service but ended up losing his job in 1777, largely because of the incessant backbiting and insubordination of the regimental surgeons who were jealous of those surgeons assigned to general hospital service. Fiercely proud, he launched a defense of his actions. The result was a published vindication (127). In this lengthy brief, which Packard has called the most interesting literary relic of the Revolution from a medical standpoint, Morgan surveyed his Army career and placed the blame for his misfortune on Dr. William Shippen, Jr., his successor and former friend and colleague in the Medical Department of the University of Pennsylvania. Shippen's career as director general and its equally inglorious ending has been examined by Whitfield J. Bell (19).

A variety of accounts, sampled below, deal with specific aspects of military medicine in the Revolution. James Thacher, best known for his *American Medical Biography* (190), kept a highly informative military journal (189) of his wartime experiences. Thacher's career has, in turn, been studied by Walter Steiner (181). Less extensive but still useful personal accounts are those of Francis Alison (159), Albigence Waldo (191), and Samuel F. Merrick (51). William S. Middleton's "Medicine at Valley Forge" (123) and Phillip Cash's *Medical Men at the Siege of Boston, April, 1775-April, 1776* (37) are noteworthy examinations of particular encampments and engagements. Although old, J. W. Jordan's thoroughly researched and highly informative study of the military hospitals at Bethlehem and Lititz, Pennsylvania (105), is still the best account of American military hospitals. George B. Griffenhagen's *Drug Supplies in the American Revolution* (82) is likewise the best source on that subject. Finally, biographical studies of note exist for John Morgan (18), Benjamin Rush (22 and 76), and Edward Warren (245).

FROM THE REVOLUTION TO THE CIVIL WAR. The end of the Revolution was accompanied by the rapid and almost complete demobilization of the nation's armed forces. By the formal signing of the Treaty of Paris in September 1783, the Medical Department of the Army had been virtually disbanded. Two years later the Navy passed out of existence altogether until 1794. The threat of war with France in 1798 sparked a brief flurry of medical activity, chiefly the appointment of James Craik, a veteran of the Revolution, as physician general. But no hostilities ensued and Craik was mustered out of service in 1800. His brief tour of duty is surveyed in a correspondingly short study by Robert U. Patterson (144).

The outbreak of war with Great Britain in 1812 found no central medical organization in either the Army or the Navy, an almost total ignorance of military medicine on the part of civilian physicians, and an absence of first-hand accounts from the Revolution with which to educate them. In short, a medical organization had to be devised under wartime conditions, a lesson that was painfully repeated with each new war down to World War I. The medical side of this exercise in inefficient mediocrity, as one historian has aptly labeled the War of 1812, is the subject of short studies by James Edgar (61) and Louis C. Duncan (59). No full-scale examination exists.

James Tilton and James Mann were the war's major medical figures. Tilton, of Revolutionary fame, had published his *Economical Observations on Military Hospitals* (192) on the eve of the hostilities. As a result, he was appointed physician general, a post he held until 1815. Tilton tried to institute many of the reforms set forth in his book, but as Mann, in charge of medical affairs for the Northern Army, makes clear in his informative *Medical Sketches of the Campaigns of 1812, 13, 14* (119) such efforts were largely unsuccessful.

Army medicine between the War of 1812 and the Mexican War is in a large measure the story of Joseph Lovell who became the first surgeon general of the Army when the post was created by Congress in 1818. A man of marked ability and foresight, Lovell was ideal for the position, as his accomplishments well illustrate. Chief among them were his meteorological registers, vital statistics of the Army, and Library of the Surgeon General's Office. Shortly after his appointment Lovell ordered Army surgeons to record meteorological observations and to study the relationship between disease and climate. The results, published in four meterological registers encompassing the years 1822-54 (226 and 228-30), provide a wealth of information on epidemiology and preventive medicine. The U.S. Weather Bureau is a direct outgrowth of these investigations. In 1819 Lovell initiated a system of detailed reporting of the Army's vital statistics. The results were collected and published in three volumes covering the years 1819-60 (233). These are a veritable gold mine of primary material for the student of American military history. In 1836 Lovell founded the Library of the Surgeon General's Office, which, after several name changes, became the National Library of Medicine in 1956. The evolution of this truly outstanding facility is thoroughly traced by Edgar E. Hume (96) and Dorothy M. Schullian and Frank B. Rogers (168). Much of its success is the result of the inspired leadership of John Shaw Billings who served as its head from 1865 to 1895. Billings's career has been admirably assessed by Fielding H. Garrison (69) and Frank B. Rogers (21). Lovell is also to be commended for the encouragement and support he offered William Beaumont in his experiments on the physiology of digestion. Accounts of Beaumont's remarkable accomplishments range from his own writings (13-14) to Jesse S. Myer's biography (129).

Naval medicine in the first half of the nineteenth century has attracted little attention from historians of medicine. Several articles, such as Louis H. Roddis's "Naval Medicine in the Early Days of the Republic" (165), are about all that exist. A major reason for lack of reliable in-depth studies is that naval medicine in this era is the story of the activities of a few outstanding individuals acting largely alone. The first of these was Edward Cutbush. Up until Cutbush's time, American naval hygiene was based on the writings of James Lind, Thomas Trotter, and Gilbert Blane, the great medical officers of the British Navy. In 1808 Cutbush published his *Observations on the Means of Preserving the Health of Soldiers and Sailors,* (50), the first American contribution to the literature of naval medicine. Cutbush was also instrumental in the organization of the Medical Department of the Navy and in the professionalization of the medical corps. His activities have earned him the title "Nestor of the medical corps of the Navy." Frank L. Pleadwell (150) is the best authority on Cutbush. Louis Heermann, a contemporary of Cutbush's, waged a lengthy campaign, thoroughly described by W. M. Kerr and Pleadwell (109), for the construction of naval hospitals. His work led to the founding of such outstanding facilities as the Norfolk Naval Hospital, the history of which is recorded by Richmond C. Holcomb (94).

The greatest naval clinician of the first half of the nineteenth century was Usher Parsons, a luminary in both the civilian and the military medical professions. As for the latter, he is best known for his 1820 *Physicians for Ships* (143) which went through five editions by 1867. Accounts of his varied and highly successful life include those of his son Charles (141) and Pleadwell (152). The last of the antebellum giants of naval medicine was William Paul Crillon Barton. Remembered best for his ability as an organizer and administrator, as illustrated by his *Treatise Containing a Plan for the Internal Organization and Government of Marine Hospitals in the United States . . . with a Scheme for Amending and Systematizing the Medical Department of the Navy* (8), he was appointed the first Chief (Surgeon General after 1871) of the Bureau of

Medicine and Surgery when the post was created in 1842. Through the efforts of these farseeing naval surgeons the growth and organization of the medical corps was stimulated and advanced.

The outbreak of war with Mexico in 1846 found the medical departments of the Army and Navy confronted with the same problems which had proved so vexing in 1812. As a result the medical gains of this war did not match those made on the ground. The sole gain of any consequence was the winning of military rank, with commensurate pay and privileges, for medical officers (160). In terms of medical histories, there is a contemporary account by John B. Porter (155) and two vignettes by Louis C. Duncan (56-57) which draw heavily on the former.

THE CIVIL WAR. The literature of the Civil War is overwhelming, easily exceeding that of all other American wars combined. A further indication of the wholesale interest in this struggle is the attention accorded its medical side. For the first time in American military history the historian of medicine has a sufficiency of sources. Valuable guides to this plethora of material have been compiled by Beers (17A), Munden and Beers (128A), and Nevins, Robertson, and Wiley (131A).

The best general studies are George W. Adams' *Doctors in Blue* (1) and Horace H. Cunningham's *Doctors in Gray* (47). Louis C. Duncan's *Medical Department of the United States Army in the Civil War* (60); Stewart M. Brooks' *Civil War Medicine* (31); and Paul E. Steiner's *Physician-Generals in the Civil War* (180) and *Diseases in the Civil War* (179) are also deserving of notice.

This was the first American war for which an official medical history was prepared. *The Medical and Surgical History of the War of the Rebellion* (234), made possible by the renewed emphasis on record keeping growing out of the Crimean War, was designed to preserve every bit of known experience for the use of future Army surgeons. Largely as a result of the loss of the official records of the medical department when the Surgeon General's office burned in the fire which destroyed much of Richmond in the spring of 1865, there is no parallel study for the South. But some Southern sources of an official nature are available, principally the *Regulations for the Medical Department of the C. S. Army* (43), the various compilations of the statutes at large of the Confederacy (41), and the *Confederate States Medical and Surgical Journal* (40). The *Official Records* of the Union and Confederate armies (238) and navies (221) are of importance for both sides.

Contemporary accounts are plentiful. Noteworthy Northern ones are: John Brinton's *Personal Memoirs* (30); Charles B. Johnson's *Muskets and Medicine* (101); John G. Perry's *Letters from a Surgeon of the Civil War* (146); Benjamin F. Stevenson's *Letters from the Army* (184); and Walter D. Briggs' *Civil War Surgeon in a Colored Regiment* (29). The best Northern naval memoir is Samuel P. Boyer's diary (24). Those of John M. Batten (9), Charles S. Foltz (65), and Charles H. Wheelwright (248) have their limitations but are of some value in light of the paucity of material relating to medicine in the Navy. Thomas T. Ellis' *Leaves from the Diary of an Army Surgeon* (62) is an interesting account by a foreign observer. Ellis, an English physician, volunteered his services to the Union Army.

Confederate reminiscences are noticeably less numerous. Those worthy of mention are: John Q. Anderson's *Texas Surgeon in the C. S. A.* (2); Junius N. Bragg's *Letters of a Confederate Surgeon, 1861-65* (26); Joseph Jones' *Medical and Surgical Memoirs* (104); and Spencer G. Welch's *Confederate Surgeon's Letters to His Wife* (246).

Although such important developments for American medicine as the origins of the public health movement and the beginning of the professional nursing service can be traced to the Civil War, it was a medical nightmare for the combatants on each side. It is an incontrovertible fact that little of value for the advancement of American medicine accrued to either side. The medical services provided were adequate at best. That they were as good as they were is the result of the labors of a few farseeing, dedicated individuals. The leading figure in the Southern medical service was Samuel P. Moore. In the North William A. Hammond and Jonathan Letterman should be singled out.

Moore, the southern surgeon general, was directly responsible for any success enjoyed by the Confederate Medical Department. He established it, nurtured it, and kept it functioning throughout the war. This, in itself, is something of a minor miracle. Although highly deserving of a full-scale biography, Moore has received little in-depth attention.

Hammond was appointed Surgeon General of the Union Army in 1862 when only thirty-four. His two-year tenure marked the beginning of a new era in the history of the medical department. Hammond is best known for founding the Army Medical Museum, sponsoring the *Medical and Surgical History of the War of the Rebellion* (234), and proposing the establishment of an Army medical school and an Army general hospital. With the exception of the first-named, these things were accomplished after Hammond had left office. The Army Medical Museum, founded in 1862, was an immediate success, as was the Armed Forces Institute of Pathology to which it was soon to give rise. Their development and contributions are detailed by D. S. Lamb (112), Esmond R. Long (116), Robert S. Henry (92), and Saul Jarcho (100). Hammond was relieved of his post after an 1864 court martial. The reasons, although not the expressed ones, seem to have been a growing antagonism between Hammond and Secretary of War Edwin M. Stanton and the furor resulting from Hammond's removal of calomel from the medical department's supply table. Hammond's published defense (87) sheds much light upon this tragedy.

Letterman was Medical Director of the Army of the Potomac, owing his appointment to Hammond. He is credited with devising the Union Army's system of field hospitals and originating the nation's first ambulance corps. Much needed developments, they attest to Letterman's ingenuity and ability. Their evolution can be traced in Henry I. Bowditch's public plea for an ambulance system (23), Letterman's *Medical Recollections of the Army of Potomac* (114), and Louis C. Duncan's brief historical overview (55). Evacuation of the sick and wounded by sea is discussed in Frederic L. Olmsted's *Hospital Transports* (133).

The origins of the nursing profession and the military nurse are found in the Civil War. Both sides soon came to depend heavily upon women to care for the sick and wounded in their general hospitals. Histories of the Army Nurse Corps, such as those of Julia C. Stimson (185) and Julia

Flikke (63), cite the importance of their work. Studies of a general nature relating directly to the war include Norah Smaridge's *Hands of Mercy* (172); Mary A. Holland's *Our Army Nurses* (95); Marjorie L. Greenbie's *Lincoln's Daughters of Mercy* (81); and Ann D. Wood's recent article dealing with the Union Army (253). Like their physician counterparts, many of these early nurses recorded and later published their memoirs. Representative Northern ones are Mary A. Livermore's *My Story of the War* (115); Adelaide W. Smith's *Reminiscences of an Army Nurse during the Civil War* (173); and Jane S. Woolsey's *Hospital Days* (256). The last-named is the subject of a recent study by Anne L. Austin (5). Walt Whitman's experiences as a male nurse are well described in his *Specimen Days in America* (248A) and *The Wound Dresser* (248B). The Southern side is well represented by Fannie A. Beers' *Memories* (17); Kate Cumming's *Journal of Hospital Life in the Confederate Army of Tennessee* (45-46); and Phoebe Y. Pember's *Southern Woman's Story* (145).

Many, perhaps most, of the advancements made in treating the sick and wounded in the North was the result of the courageous actions of the United States Sanitary Commission, a civilian group modeled after the British Sanitary Commission of the Crimean War and resembling the present day Red Cross. The best biography of this organization has been written by William Q. Maxwell (122). Charles J. Stille's earlier study (239) and Jacob G. Forman's account of its work in the West (66) also add to an understanding of it.

Part of the Sanitary Commission's fight to preserve the health of soldiers was the publication of medical and surgical essays, written by some of the nation's leading physicians, for issuance to medical and line officers. In recognition of the importance of these essays, Surgeon General Hammond, in July 1864, collected and published seventeen of them in a single volume (89). After the cessation of hostilities this organization turned its attention to the medical history of the war and commissoned a two-volume *Surgical Memoirs of the War of the Rebellion* (241) and another two volumes of *Sanitary Memoirs of the War of the Rebellion*, consisting of Austin Flint's *Contributions Relating to· the Causation and Prevention of Disease* (64) and Benjamin A. Gould's *Investigations in the Military and Anthropological Statistics of American Soldiers* (80). The latter's work was greatly extended in 1875 when the Provost Marshal-General's Office published its two large volumes of medical and anthropological statistics (224).

There are many other points of interest that should at least be touched upon in passing. Numerous manuals, texts, and treatises for the use of physicians and surgeons appeared on each side. The most widely used ones in the North were authored by Samuel D. Gross (84), William A. Hammond (88), John H. Packard (139), Stephen Smith (176), John Ordronaux (135), Charles S. Tripler (197), William H. Van Buren (242), and Joseph Woodward (255). The leading Southern ones were prepared by Julian J. Chisolm (38), a committee appointed by Surgeon General Moore (42), Edward Warren (244), and Francis P. Porcher (154). Although the Civil War is not remembered for its research, some important scientific investigations were conducted. In the North, for example, there was the work of S. Weir Mitchell on injuries to the nerves. He has recorded his findings (125) while

Richard D. Walter (243), his most recent biographer, has evaluated their significance. Joseph Jones was the South's leading research scientist. Lacking a biography at this time, the student of medical history is forced to fall back on Jones' lengthy *Medical and Surgical Memoirs* (104) and James O. Breeden's interpretive article (28) for an analysis of his contribution. George W. Smith has written a scholarly study of the Union Army's medicine supply (175). The United States Sanitary Commission sponsored an investigation of the treatment of Union prisoners of war (240). Finally, there are several good medical histories of individual campaigns—Horace H. Cunningham on the battles of Manassas (48), Gordon W. Jones on the Battle of Fredericksburg (102), and James O. Breeden on the Atlanta Campaign (27).

CIVIL WAR TO WORLD WAR I. The size of America's armed forces was severely slashed following the Civil War. The Army was reduced to a series of posts scattered throughout the South and the western plains, and the large naval force which had been assembled to blockade the Southern coast was rapidly dismantled. On the whole it may be safely asserted that for the medical services the period between the end of the Civil War and the turn of the century was largely one of stagnation.

Military action was limited to a number of brief but bloody skirmishes with hostile Indians in the West. Personal reminiscences provide interesting and informative insights into this aspect of military medicine. Noteworthy accounts are Robert H. McKay's *Little Pills* (118), James M. DeWolf's diary (53), William T. Corbusier's *Verde to San Carlos* (44), and Bernard J. Byrne's *Frontier Army Surgeon* (36). State medical histories, such as Frances E. Quebbeman's *Medicine in Territorial Arizona* (158), shed further light. An 1875 report of the surgeon general (225) on the hygiene of the Army, growing out of an increased emphasis on medical reporting, is also useful.

Beginning in the 1870s the bacteriological revolution, which was to usher in modern scientific medicine, began to have an effect on America. Its chief advocate in the armed forces was George M. Sternberg. Already a well-known bacteriologist, Sternberg became Surgeon General in 1893. His decade in office was characterized by extraordinary accomplishment. Chief among the gains made were the establishment of the Army Medical School (54), the Army Nursing Corps (63 and 185), the Dental Corps and the creation of a number of highly effective special scientific boards and commissions. Sternberg's busy life has been recorded and interpreted by his wife (183) and John M. Gibson (74).

Naval medicine between the Civil War and the Spanish-American War continued to be the story of the accomplishments of a handful of dedicated individuals. The major figure in the sixties was Ninian Pinkney, the pioneer of the hospital ship. Frank L. Pleadwell (151) has devoted considerable attention to his career. The seventies opened with the elevation of the Chief of the Bureau of Medicine and Surgery to Surgeon General of the Navy. William Maxwell Wood was the first to hold this post. His long naval career, which did much to enhance the prestige of the medical department, has been studied by W. M. Kerr (108). This decade, however, was dominated by Joseph Wilson, Jr., and Albert L. Gihon. Wilson wrote the first

American book concerned solely with naval hygiene (251), but Gihon's *Practical Suggestions in Naval Hygiene* (75) soon supplanted it and remained the standard work on the subject for years.

Between 1872 and 1883 seven volumes of medical reports (209 and 211-13), selected from reports submitted to the Surgeon General, were published by the Bureau of Medicine and Surgery. These contain many insights into naval medicine in the late nineteenth century. The eighties also witnessed the publication of the first book of instructions for medical officers of the Navy (210). Within a few years it had become the official manual of the medical department. The advancement of naval medicine in the nineties is largely owing to the vision of Surgeon General J. R. Tryon who played important roles in the establishment of a hospital corps in 1898 and the naval medical school in 1902. Unfortunately, no study of his career has been written.

The Spanish-American War lasted less than four months and was an unqualified military success. But the medical picture was quite different. The medical departments of the Army and Navy were unprepared for war, and disease took its usual heavy toll. A short overview of the war's medical side is presented in the article, "Tropical Tryout" (198). The Army's medical problems and gains are examined by Sternberg in his *Sanitary Lessons of the War* (182) and Nicholas Senn in his *Medico-Surgical Aspects of the Spanish-American War* (171). Naval medicine has not received much attention. Louis H. Roddis's brief study of the medical department of Dewey's squadron (166) is the only one deserving of mention. The medical milestone of the Spanish-American War was the appointment of a board composed of Walter Reed, Victor C. Vaughan, and Edward O. Shakespeare to study typhoid fever, one of the contest's biggest health problems. The results of its investigations, in which the role of carriers was clearly noted, was published in 1904 (232).

In 1900 the United States took part in the international expedition which put down the Boxer Rebellion in China. Insights into the medical side of American involvement can be gained from Francis J. Ives' firsthand account (99). This was but an international interlude, however, and the years between the Spanish-American War and the outbreak of World War I found the Army primarily concerned with tropical medicine. Charles M. Wilson survey's its accomplishments in his *Ambassadors in White* (250).

There were others, but the most important gains were made in the Philippines, Cuba, and the Panama Canal Zone. A board of medical officers headed by Richard P. Strong investigated the tropical diseases of America's new insular possessions between 1899 and 1901. Medical conditions in the Philippines are thoroughly described by John M. Banister in his reminiscences as an Army medical officer there (7). Walter Reed headed the Yellow Fever Commission in Cuba between 1900 and 1901 which conclusively proved that yellow fever was caused by a filterable virus and confirmed Carlos Finlay's hypothesis that the disease was transmitted by the *Aedes aegypti* mosquito. Studies of Reed's work include his yellow fever report (257), the detailed examinations of this important period of his life by Albert Truby (199) and Howard A. Kelly (106), Stanhope Bayne-Jones's interpretative article (12), and Laura N. Wood's full-fledged biography (254). William C. Gorgas, who was to serve as Surgeon General during World War I, applied Reed's findings to Havana and soon rid it of yellow fever. Later, as chief sanitary officer of the Panama Canal Zone, he sponsored an extensive program of sanitation and disease control which greatly expedited the construction of the Panama Canal. Gorgas has left accounts of his activities in Cuba (78) and Panama (79). Marie D. Gorgas and Burton J. Hendrick (77) and John M. Gibson (73) are his leading biographers.

Naval medicine in the early twentieth century was dominated by Presley M. Rixey who became Surgeon General in 1902. During his tenure in office the first naval medical school was established, the size of the medical corps was doubled and strengthened by specialization and post-graduate training, a nurse corps was founded, old hospitals were renovated and new ones built, the *United States Naval Medical Bulletin* was launched to stimulate professional interests in the medical department, and the movement which was to culminate in the establishment of the naval dental corps in 1912 was set in motion. The high points of Rixey's outstanding career are explored in his combination autobiography-biography (162). Robert A. Marmion (121) and C. S. Butler and W. M. Kerr (35) have traced the origins of the Naval Medical School. An in-depth chronology of the dental corps (213A) has been compiled by the Bureau of Medicine and Surgery.

WORLD WAR I. When the United States finally entered the war in April 1917, the medical departments of the Army and Navy were in a better position that at the beginning of any previous American war to carry out their missions. This happy circumstance was largely the result of advancements made in both services between the Spanish-American War and World War I, lessons learned by observing the combatants for almost three years, and the mobilization of the nation's scientific resources as part of President Wilson's 1916 preparedness campaign.

With the exception of the Navy, where there was little combat, the medical side of this war has been recorded in the fifteen-volume *Medical Department of the United States Army in the World War* (236), which, like its predecessor for the Civil War, was sponsored by the Surgeon General's office. Even a cursory perusal of this series reveals its thoroughness. Another official study of value, also a product of the Surgeon General's office, is the lengthy *Defects Found in Drafted Men* (227). The only official work on the Navy, and the first of its type published by the Bureau of Medicine and Surgery, is *Medical Department of the United States Navy with the Army and Marine Corps in France in World War I* (210a).

The nonofficial literature on the history of military medicine in World War I contains numerous useful sources. There are several important personal accounts. Harvey Cushing's *From a Surgeon's Journal, 1915-1918* (49) presents the views of this outstanding surgeon as both a member of the Harvard Unit of the American Ambulance and as a senior consultant in neurosurgery in the American Expeditionary Forces. Woods Hutchinson's *Doctor in War* (98) should be consulted because of his extensive travels with the English, French, Italian, and American armies between January and December 1917. Roger I. Lee's letters (113) and Hugh H. Young's autobiography (258) are further useful firsthand accounts.

Frederick A. Pottle's *Stretchers* (156) is an excellent study of a hospital unit on the western front. Histories of hospitals include those for two Base Hospitals in France—no. 10 (201) and no. 53 (202). A useful summary of the vital statistics of the Army has been prepared by Albert G. Love (117). John F. Fulton's biography of Harvey Cushing (68) offers some insight into the war. Carter H. Harrison (90) and Edward D. Toland (194) have produced good accounts of Red Cross participation. Finally, Frederick M. Dearborn's *American Homeopathy in the World War* (52) is of more than passing interest, for it thoroughly explores the activities of the nation's largest irregular sect in this war.

WORLD WAR II. In terms of its medical history, World War II is America's most thoroughly documented war. There are an especially large number of official sources. Of these, the most impressive is the exhaustive *Medical Department of the U.S. Army in World War II* (206). Sponsored again by the Surgeon General's office, it records in extraordinary thoroughness the major activities of the Medical Department of the Army. Forty-three of a projected fifty volumes have now appeared. Two studies of a more general nature are included in the Technical Services sub-series of the multivolume *United States Army in World War II*. These are Clarence M. Smith's examination of hospitalization and evacuation in the zone of the interior (174) and Charles M. Wiltse's survey of the medical service in the Mediterranean and minor theaters (252). The three chemical warfare volumes (32-33 and 110) in this same subseries and Mattie E. Treadwell's *Women's Army Corps* (196) in the Special Studies subseries should also be consulted.

Although still a part of the Army, the Air Force's medical history in World War II has received considerable attention. A large part of the seventh volume of the semi-official *Army Air Forces in World War II* (222) is devoted to it. In addition, Oron P. South (178) and Mae M. Lind and Hubert A. Coleman (200) have produced significant studies on medical support by the Army Air Force.

For the first time there is an official medical history for the Navy during a war. In fact, there are two—the multivolume *U.S. Navy Medical Department Administrative History, 1941-1945* (216) and the shorter *History of the Medical Department of the United Navy in World War II* (215). Samuel Eliot Morison's lengthy *History of the United States Naval Operations in World War II* (128) is also of some value.

These official sources are supplemented by numerous nonofficial ones. Representative personal histories for the Army are Edward D. Churchill's surgical diary (39), Andrew C. Geer's recollections as an ambulance driver with the Eighth Army (71), Gordon S. Seagrave's two volumes of experiences in Burma (169-70), and Edith Aynes' nursing memoirs (6). Robert C. Page has recorded his experiences with the Army Air Force in the Burma theater (140). Naval reminiscences of interest are Charles M. Oman's *Doctors Aweigh* (134) and Herbert L. Pugh's *Navy Surgeon* (157).

Typical hospital histories are those for the Army's 12th (203) and 77th (204) Evacuation Hospitals and Robert P. Parson's (142) account of a naval hospital in a South Seas jungle. Rollin L. Bauchspies' series of articles (10) on the role of the medics in the Anzio campaign is excellent. David Wheeler

(247) has studied comparative physical standards in the allied and enemy armies. Gilbert W. Beebe and Michael De Bakey (16) have produced a solid study of battle casualties. In a later work Beebe teamed with John W. Appel (15) in an examination of the psychological component of ground combat. *Studies in Social Psychology in World War II* (186) is a broader psychological study. The scientific gains accruing from the war have been the subject of several works, ranging from the U.S. Office of Scientific Research and Development's *Advances in Military Medicine* (223) to William H. Taliaferro's *Medicine and the War* (188) to Alexander R. Griffin's *Out of Carnage* (83). George G. Korson has surveyed the activities of the Red Cross (111).

WORLD WAR II TO PRESENT. The history of military and naval medicine in the recent period has received little attention. Two brief general accounts, one dealing with the Army (205) and the other with the Navy (214), have appeared. David E. Goldman has edited a volume on the contributions of the Naval Medical Research Institute (220). As for specific wars, the Army originally planned two volumes on the medicine of the Korean Conflict but neither has been completed. It now looks as if only one might be brought out. Arnold M. Meirowsky's *Neurological Surgery of Trauma* (207) deals with World War II and Korea. Other Korea studies are the Army Medical Service Graduate School's four volumes on surgery (237) and Frank A. Reister's examination (161) of battle casualties and medical statistics. A ten- to twelve-volume *Vietnam Studies* is planned by the Army for the war in Southeast Asia. One volume, Spurgeon Neel's *Medical Support of the U.S. Army in Vietnam, 1965-1970* (130) has already appeared.

SUGGESTIONS FOR FURTHER RESEARCH. The history of military and naval medicine has only had its surfaces scratched—almost to the point of still being virgin territory. A great deal has been written, to be sure, but much of it is now outdated or of dubious quality. Moreover, coverage is noticeably spotty. Some areas, like the Civil War, have received an inordinate amount of attention, while others, like the Navy before World War II, have received far too little. Given this situation, it seems sheer folly to list specific topics that need researching. It is hoped that they are clear from the foregoing. Suffice it to say, then, that the history of military and naval medicine is a most inviting field.

The sources singled out in this chapter, it is further hoped, will serve as a springboard to research. They are not complete but, rather, were selected to depict two things—the cream of the crop and a cross section of the types of material available. There is in addition a great deal of unpublished primarily material in several major repositories. Inquiries as to holdings and availability should be made to the Army Historical Unit, Fort Detrick, Maryland; Chief, Bureau of Medicine and Surgery, Washington, D.C.; the Albert F. Simpson Historical Research Center, Maxwell Air Force Base, Alabama; the National Archives, Washington, D.C.; the National Library of Medicine, Bethesda, Maryland; and the Army Historical Collection, Carlisle Barracks, Pennsylvania.

BIBLIOGRAPHY

1. Adams, George W. *Doctors in Blue: The Medical History of the Union Army in the Civil War.* New York: H. Schuman, 1952.
2. Anderson, John Q. *A Texas Surgeon in the C. S. A.* Tuscaloosa: Confederate Pub. Co., 1957.
3. Applegate, Howard L. "The American Revolutionary Hospital Department," *Milit. Med.,* 1961, *126,* 296-306, 379-82, 450-53, 551-53, 616-18.
4. Ashburn, Percy M. *A History of the Medical Department of the United States Army.* Boston and New York: Houghton Mifflin, 1929.
5. Austin, Anne L. *The Woolsey Sisters of New York: A Family's Involvement in the Civil War and a New Profession (1860-1900).* Philadelphia: American Philosophical Society, 1971.
6. Aynes, Edith A. *From Nightingale to Eagle: An Army Nurse's History.* Englewood Cliffs: Prentice-Hall, 1973.
7. Banister, John M. "Medical and Surgical Observations during a Three Years' Tour of Duty in the Philippines," *J. Assoc. Milit. Surgs.,* 1906, *18,* 149-69, 259-77, 318-34.
8. Barton, William P. C. *A Treatise Containing a Plan for the Internal Organization and Government of Marine Hospitals in the United States: Together with a scheme for amending and systematizing the medical department of the navy.* Philadelphia: Privately printed, 1814.
9. Batten, John M. *Reminiscences of Two Years in the United States Navy.* Lancaster, Pennsylvania: Privately printed, 1881.
10. Bauchspies, Rollin L. "The Courageous Medics of Anzio," *Milit. Med.,* 1958, *122,* 53-65, 119-28, 197-207, 267-72, 338-59, 429-48.
11. Bayne-Jones, Stanhope. *The Evolution of Preventive Medicine in the United States Army, 1607-1939.* Washington: Office of the Surgeon General, 1968.
12. Bayne-Jones, Stanhope. "Walter Reed (1851-1902)," *Milit. Med.,* 1967, *132,* 391-400.
13. Beaumont, William. *Experiments and Observations on the Gastric Juice and the Physiology of Digestion.* Facsim. of the original ed. of 1833 together with a biographical essay, A pioneer American physiologist, by Sir William Osler. New York: Dover, 1959.
14. Beaumont, William. *Wm. Beaumont's Formative Years; Two Early Notebooks, 1811-1821.* With annotations and an introductory essay by Genevieve Miller. New York: Schuman, 1946.
15. Beebe, Gilbert W. and John W. Appel. *Variation in Psychological Tolerance to Ground Combat in World War II.* Washington: National Academy of Sciences, National Research Council, Division of Medical Sciences, Follow-up Agency, 1958.
16. Beebe, Gilbert W. and Michael E. De Bakey. *Battle Casualties: Incidence, Mortality, and Logistic Considerations.* Springfield: Charles C. Thomas, 1952.
17. Beers, Fannie A. *Memories. A Record of Personal Experience and Adventure during Four Years of War.* Philadelphia: J. B. Lippincott, 1888.
17a. Beers, Henry P. *Guide to the Archives of the Government of the*

Confederate States of America. Washington: National Archives, General Services Administration, 1968.
18. Bell, Whitfield J. *John Morgan, Continental Doctor.* Philadelphia: University of Pennsylvania Press, 1965.
19. Bell, Whitfield J. "The Court Martial of Dr. William Shippen, Jr., 1780," *J. Hist. Med. & Allied Sci.,* 1964, *19,* 218-38.
20. *Bibliography of the History of Medicine.* no. 1-, 1965-. Bethesda, Maryland: U.S. Dept. of Health, Education, and Welfare, Public Health Service.
21. Billings, John S. *Selected Papers.* Compiled with a life of Billings, by Frank B. Rogers. Chicago: Medical Library Association, 1965.
22. Binger, Carl A. L., *Revolutionary Doctor: Benjamin Rush, 1746-1813.* New York: Norton, 1966.
23. Bowditch, Henry I. *A Brief Plea for an Ambulance System for the Army of the United States.* Boston: Ticknor and Fields, 1863.
24. Boyer, Samuel P. *Naval Surgeon; The Diary of Dr. Samuel Pellman Boyer.* Edited by Elinor Barnes and James A. Barnes. Bloomington: Indiana University Press, 1963. 2 vols.
25. Bradley, George P. "A Brief Sketch of the Origin and History of the Medical Corps of the United States Navy," *J. Assoc. Milit. Surgs.,* 1901-1902, *10,* 487-514.
26. Bragg, Junius N. *Letters of a Confederate Surgeon.* By Mrs. T. J. Gaughan. Camden? Arkansas, 1960.
27. Breeden, James O. "A Medical History of the Latter Stages of the Atlanta Campaign," *J. Southern Hist.,* 1969, *35,* 31-59.
28. Breeden, James O. "Joseph Jones, a Major Source for Nineteenth-Century Southern Medical History," Tulane University medical faculty, *Bull.,* 1967, *26,* 41-48.
29. Briggs, Walter D. *Civil War Surgeon in a Colored Regiment.* Berkeley, California, 1960.
30. Brinton, John H. *Personal Memoirs of John H. Brinton, Major and Surgeon U. S. V., 1861-1865.* New York: The Neale Publishing Co., 1914.
31. Brooks, Steward M. *Civil War Medicine.* Springfield: Charles C. Thomas, 1966.
32. Brophy, Leo P. and George J. B. Fisher. *The Chemical Warfare Service; Organizing for War.* Washington: Office of the Chief of Military History, Dept. of the Army, 1959.
33. Brophy, Leo P., Wyndham D. Miles, and Rexmond C. Cochrane. *The Chemical Warfare Service: from Laboratory to Field.* Washington: Office of the Chief of Military History, Dept. of the Army, 1959.
34. [Brown, William]. *Pharmacopoeia Simpliciorum et Efficaciorum.* Philadelphia: Styner & Cist, 1778.
35. Butler, C. S. and W. M. Kerr. "The U.S. Naval School, Washington, D.C.," *Milit. Surg.,* 1924, *54,* 641-62.
36. Byrne, Bernard J. *A Frontier Army Surgeon; Life in Colorado in the Eighties.* 2d rev. and enl. ed. New York: Exposition press, 1962.
37. Cash, Philip. *Medical Men at the Siege of Boston, April, 1775-April, 1776.* Philadelphia: American Philosophical Society, 1973.
38. Chisolm, Julian J. *A Manual of Military Surgery, for the Use of*

Surgeons in the Confederate States Army. 2d rev. and improved ed. Richmond: West & Johnson, 1862.

39. Churchill, Edward D. *Surgeon to Soldiers; Diary and Records of the Surgical Consultant, Allied Force Headquarters, World War II.* Philadelphia: J. B. Lippincott, 1972.

40. *Confederate States Medical & Surgical Journal.* Richmond: Ayres & Wade, 1864-65.

41. Confederate States of America. *The Statutes at Large of the Provisional Government of the Confederate States of America, from the Institution of the Government, February 8, 1861, to Its Termination, February 18, 1862.* inclusive. Ed. by James M. Matthews. Richmond: R. M. Smith, 1864.

42. Confederate States of America. Surgeon-General's Office. *A Manual of Military Surgery.* Richmond: Ayres & Wade, 1863.

43. Confederate States of America. War Dept. *Regulations for the Medical Department of the C. S. Army.* Richmond: Ritchie & Dunnavant, 1863.

44. Corbusier, William T. *Verde to San Carlos; Recollections of a Famous Army Surgeon and His Observant Family on the Western Frontier, 1869-1886.* Tucson: D. S. King, 1968.

45. Cumming, Kate. *A Journal of Hospital Life in the Confederate Army of Tennessee, from the Battle of Shiloh to the End of the War.* Louisville: J. P. Morgan & Co., 1866.

46. Cumming, Kate. *Kate: the Journal of a Confederate Nurse.* Ed. by Richard B. Harwell. Baton Rouge: Louisiana State University Press, 1959.

47. Cunningham, Horace H. *Doctors in Gray; the Confederate Medical Service.* Baton Rouge: Louisiana State University Press, 1958.

48. Cunningham, Horace H. *Field Medical Services at the Battles of Manassas (Bull Run).* Athens: University of Georgia Press, 1968.

49. Cushing, Harvey W. *From a Surgeon's Journal, 1915-1918.* Boston: Little, Brown, 1936.

50. Cutbush, Edward. *Observations on the Means of Preserving the Health of Soldiers and Sailors; and on duties of the Medical Department of the Army and Navy: with remarks on hospitals and their internal arrangement.* Philadelphia: Fry & Kammerer, 1808.

51. Davis, David B. "Medicine in the Canadian Campaign of the Revolutionary War: the Journal of Doctor Samuel Fisk Merrick," *Bull. Hist. Med.,* 1970, *44,* 461-73.

52. Dearborn, Frederick M. *American Homeopathy in the World War.* Chicago: Pub. by and under the authority of the Board of Trustees of the American Institute of Homeopathy, 1923.

53. DeWolf, James M. *The Diary and Letters of Dr. James M. DeWolf, Acting Assistant Surgeon, U.S. Army; His Record of the Sioux Expedition of 1876 as Kept until His Death.* Transcribed and editorial notes by Edward S. Luce. Bismarck: State Historical Society, (1958?)

54. Duke, Raymond M. "The Army Medical Service School; Its History and Mission," *U.S. Armed Forces Med. J.,* 1960, *2,* 621-40.

55. Duncan, Louis C. "Evolution of the Ambulance Corps and Field Hospital," *Milit. Surg.,* 1913, *32,* 221-40.

56. Duncan, Louis C. "Medical History of General Scott's Campaign to the City of Mexico," *Milit. Surg.,* 1920, *47,* 436-70.

57. Duncan, Louis C. "Medical History of General Zachary Taylor's Army of Occupation in Texas and Mexico, 1845-1847," *Milit. Surg.,* 1921, *48,* 76-104.

58. Duncan, Louis C. *Medical Men in the American Revolution, 1775-1783.* Carlisle Barracks, Pennsylvania: Medical Field Service School, 1931.

59. Duncan, Louis C. "Sketches of the Medical Service in the War of 1812," *Milit. Surg.,* 1932, *71,* 436-40, 539-42; 1933, *72,* 488-56, 144-50, 241-46, 234-29.

60. Duncan, Louis C. *The Medical Department of the United States Army in the Civil War.* Washington, D.C.?: n. d.

61. Edgar, James E. "The Army Medical Department in the War of 1812," *Milit. Surg.,* 1927, *60,* 301-13.

62. Ellis, Thomas T. *Leaves from the Diary of an Army Surgeon.* New York: J. Bradburn, 1863.

63. Flikke, Julia. *Nurses in Action.* Philadelphia: J. B. Lippincott, 1943.

64. Flint, Austin. *Contributions Relating to the Causation and Prevention of Disease, and to Camp Diseases; Together with a Report of the Diseases, etc., among the Prisoners at Andersonville, Ga.* New York: Pub. for the U.S. Sanitary Commission by Hurd & Houghton, 1867.

65. Foltz, Charles S. *Surgeon of the Seas; the Adventurous Life of Surgeon General Jonathan M. Foltz in the Days of Wooden Ships.* Indianapolis: Bobbs-Merrill, 1931.

66. Forman, Jacob G. *The Western Sanitary Commission.* St. Louis: Pub. for the Mississippi Valley Sanitary Fair by R. P. Studley & Co., 1864.

67. *Friends of France; the Field Service of the American Ambulance Described by Its Members.* Boston and New York: Houghton Mifflin, 1916.

68. Fulton, John F. *Harvey Cushing, a Biography.* Springfield, Ill.: Charles C. Thomas, 1946.

69. Garrison, Fielding H. *John Shaw Billings; a Memoir.* New York: G. P. Putnam's, 1915.

70. Garrison, Fielding H. *Notes on the History of Military Medicine.* Washington: Association of Military Surgeons, 1922.

71. Geer, Andrew C. *Mercy in Hell, an American Ambulance Driver with the Eighth Army.* New York: Whittlesey House, 1943.

72. Gibson, James E. *Dr. Bodo Otto and the Medical Background of the American Revolution.* Springfield, Ill.: Charles C. Thomas, 1937.

73. Gibson, John M. *Physician to the World; the Life of General William C. Gorgas.* Durham: Duke University Press, 1950.

74. Gibson, John M. *Soldier in White; the Life of General George Miller Sternberg.* Durham: Duke University Press, 1958.

75. Gihon, Albert L. *Practical Suggestions in Naval Hygiene.* Washington: G. P. O., 1871.

76. Goodman, Nathan G. *Benjamin Rush, Physician and Citizen, 1746-1813.* Philadelphia: University of Pennsylvania Press, 1934.

334 • A GUIDE TO THE SOURCES OF U.S. MILITARY HISTORY

77. Gorgas, Marie C. and Burton J. Hendrick. *William Crawford Gorgas, His Life and Works.* Garden City: Doubleday, Page, 1924.
78. Gorgas, William C. "A Short Account of the Results of Mosquito Work in Havana, Cuba," *Milit. Surg.,* 1903, *12,* 133-39.
79. Gorgas, William C. *Sanitation in Panama.* New York: D. Appleton, 1915.
80. Gould, Benjamin A. *Investigations in the Military and Anthropological Statistics of American Soldiers.* New York: Pub. for the U.S. Sanitary Commission by Hurd & Houghton, 1869.
81. Greenbie, Marjorie L. *Lincoln's Daughters of Mercy.* New York: G. P. Putnam's, 1944.
82. Griffenhagen, George B. *Drug Supplies in the American Revolution.* Washington: Smithsonian Institution, 1961.
83. Griffin, Alexander R. *Out of Carnage.* New York: Howell, Soskin, 1945.
84. Gross, Samuel D. *A Manual of Military Surgery.* Philadelphia: J. B. Lippincott, 1861.
85. Gross, Samuel D. *Lives of Eminent American Physicians and Surgeons of the Nineteenth Century.* Philadelphia: Lindsay & Blakiston, 1861.
86. Hamersly, Thomas H. S. *Complete Regular Army Register of the United States: for One Hundred Years (1779 to 1879).* Washington: T. H. S. Hamersly, 1880.
87. Hammond, William A. *A Statement of the Causes Which Led to the Dismissal of Surgeon-General William A. Hammond from the Army; with a Review of the Evidence Adduced before the Court.* New York, 1864.
88. Hammond, William H. *A Treatise on Hygiene, with Special Reference to the Military Service.* Philadelphia: J. B. Lippincott, 1863.
89. Hammond, William A. *Military, Medical and Surgical Essays, Prepared for the United States Sanitary Commission.* Philadelphia: J. B. Lippincott, 1864.
90. Harrison, Carter H. *With the American Red Cross in France, 1918-1919.* Chicago: Ralph Fletcher Seymour, 1947.
91. Heitman, Francis B. *Historical Register and Dictionary of the United States Army, from Its Organization, September 29, 1789, to March 2, 1903.* Washington: G. P. O., 1903. 2 vols.
92. Henry Robert S. *The Armed Forces Institute of Pathology, Its First Century, 1862-1962.* Washington: Office of the Surgeon General, Dept. of the Army, 1964.
93. *History of the American Field Service in France, "Friends of France," 1914-1917; Told by Its Members.* Boston: Houghton Mifflin, 1920. 3 vols.
94. Holcomb, Richmond C. *A Century with Norfolk Naval Hospital, 1830-1930.* Portsmouth, Virginia: Printcraft, 1930.
95. Holland, Mary A. *Our Army Nurses.* Boston: B. Wilkins, 1895.
96. Hume, Edgar E. "The Centennial of the World's Largest Military Library: the Army Medical Library in Washington, Founded 1836," *Milit. Surg.,* 1936, *77,* 241-66.
97. Hume, Edgar E. *Victories of Army Medicine; Scientific Accomplish-*

ments of the Medical Department of the United States Army. Philadelphia: J. B. Lippincott, 1943.

98. Hutchinson, Woods. *The Doctor in War.* Boston: Houghton Mifflin, 1918.

99. Ives, Francis J. "The Medical Department in China," *J. Assoc. Milit. Surgs.,* 1903, *13,* 92-111.

100. Jarcho, Saul. "The Influence of the Armed Forces Institute of Pathology on Medicine," *Milit. Med.,* 1963, *128,* 473-82.

101. Johnson, Charles B. *Muskets and Medicine; or, Army Life in the Sixties.* Philadelphia: F. A. Davis, 1917.

102. Jones, Gordon W. "The Medical History of the Fredericksburg Campaign: Course and Significance," *J. Hist. Med. & Allied Sci.,* 1963, *18,* 241-56.

103. Jones, John. *Plain Concise Practical Remarks on the Treatment of Wounds and Fractures.* New York: John Holt, 1775.

104. Jones, Joseph. *Medical and Surgical Memoirs.* New Orleans: Clark Hofeline, 1876-90. 3 vols. in 4.

105. Jordan, J. W. "The Military Hospitals at Bethlehem and Lititz during the Revolution," *Pa. Mag. Hist. & Biog.,* 1896, *20,* 137-57.

106. Kelly, Howard A. *Walter Reed and Yellow Fever.* New York: McClure, Phillips, 1906.

107. Kelly, Howard A. and Walter L. Burrage. *Dictionary of American Medical Biography; Lives of Eminent Physicians of the United States and Canada, from the Earliest Times.* New York: D. Appleton, 1928.

108. Kerr, W. M. "William Maxwell Wood (1809-1880), the First Surgeon-General of the United States Navy," *Ann. Med. Hist.,* 1924, *6,* 387-425.

109. Kerr, W. M. and F. L. Pleadwell. "Louis Heermann, Surgeon in the United States Navy (1779-1833)," *Ann. Med. Hist.,* 1923, *5,* 113-45.

110. Kleber, Brooks E. and Dale Birdsell. *The Chemical Warfare Service; Chemicals in Combat.* Washington: Office of the Chief of Military History, U.S. Army, 1966.

111. Korson, George G. *At His Side; the Story of the American Red Cross Overseas in World War II.* New York: Coward-McCann, 1945.

112. Lamb, D. S. "The Army Medical Museum, Washington, D. C.," *Milit. Surg.,* 1923, *53,* 89-140.

113. Lee, Roger I. *Letters, 1917-1918.* Brookline, Mass., 1962.

114. Letterman, Jonathan. *Medical Recollections of the Army of the Potomac.* New York: D. Appleton, 1866.

115. Livermore, Mary A. *My Story of the War.* Hartford: A. D. Worthington, 1888.

116. Long, Esmond R. "The Army Medical Museum," *Milit. Med.,* 1973, *128,* 367-77.

117. Love, Albert G. "A Brief Summary of the Vital Statistics of the U.S. Army during the World War," *Milit. Surg.,* 1922, *51,* 139-68.

118. McKay, Robert H. *Little Pills; an Army Story.* Pittsburg, Kansas: Pittsburg Headlight, 1918.

119. Mann, James. *Medical Sketches of the Campaigns of 1812, 13, 14.* Dedham, Massachusetts: H. Mann, 1816.

120. Marmion, Robert A. "The Medical Corps of the Navy from the

Outbreak of the War with Spain to the Present Time," J. *Assoc. Milit. Surgs.*, 1901-1902, 10, 515-28.

121. Marmion, Robert A. "The United States Naval Medical School," *J. Assoc. Milit. Surgs.*, 1905, *17*, 23-34.

122. Maxwell, William Q. *Lincoln's Fifth Wheel: the Political History of the United States Sanitary Commission.* New York: Longmans, Green, 1956.

123. Middleton, William S. "Medicine at Valley Forge," *Ann. Med. Hist.*, 1941, 3rd ser., *3*, 461-86.

124. Miller, Genevieve, ed. *Bibliography of the History of Medicine of the United States and Canada, 1939-1960.* Baltimore: Johns Hopkins Press, 1964.

125. Mitchell, Silas W. *Injuries of Nerves and Their Consequences.* Philadelphia: J. B. Lippincott, 1872.

126. Morgan, John. *A Recommendation of Innoculation, According to Baron Dimsdale's Method.* Boston: J. Gill, 1776.

127. Morgan, John. *A Vindication of His Public Character in the Station of Director-General of the Military Hospitals, and Physician in Chief of the American Army.* Boston: Powars and Willis, 1777.

128. Morison, Samuel E. *History of United States Naval Operations in World War II.* Boston: Little, Brown, 1947-62. 15 vols.

128a. Munden, Kenneth W. and Henry P. Beers. *Guide to Federal Archives Relating to the Civil War.* Washington: National Archives, General Services Administration, 1962.

129. Myer, Jesse S. *A New Print of Life and Letters of Dr. William Beaumont.* St. Louis: C. V. Mosby, 1939.

130. Neel, Spurgeon. *Medical Support of the U.S. Army in Vietnam, 1965-1970.* Washington: Dept. of the Army, 1973.

131. Nevins, Allan. "The Glorious and the Terrible," *Sat. Rev.*, Sept. 2, 1961, *44*, 9-11, 46-48.

131a. Nevins, Allan, James I. Robertson, and Bell I. Wiley, eds. *Civil War books; a Critical Bibliography.* Published for the U.S. Civil War Centennial Commission by Louisiana State University Press, 1967-69. 2 vols.

132. Norwood, William F. "The Enigma of Dr. Benjamin Church; High Level Scandal in the American Colonial Army Medical Service," *Med. Arts & Sci.*, 1956, *10*, 71-93.

133. [Olmsted, Frederic L.] *Hospital Transports. A Memoir of the Embarkation of the Sick and Wounded from the Peninsula of Virginia in the Summer of 1862.* Boston: Ticknor & Fields, 1863.

134. Oman, Charles M. *Doctors Aweigh: the Story of the United States Navy Medical Corps in Action.* Garden City: Doubleday, Doran, 1943.

135. Ordronaux, John. *Manual of Instructions for Military Surgeons, on the Examination of Recruits and Discharge of Soldiers.* New York: D. Van Nostrand, 1863.

136. Owen, William O. *A Chronological Arrangement of Congressional Legislation Relating to the Medical Corps of the United States Army from 1785 to 1917.* Chicago: American Medical Association 1918.

137. Owen, William O. *The Medical Department of the United States Army* [*Legislative and Administrative History*] *during the Period of the Revolution* [*1776-1786*]. New York: P. B. Hoeber, 1920.

138. Packard, Francis R. *History of Medicine in the United States.* New York: P. B. Hoeber, 1931. 2 vols.

139. Packard, John H. *A Manual of Minor Surgery.* Philadelphia: J. B. Lippincott, 1863.

140. Page, Robert C. *Air Commando Doc.* New York: B. Ackerman, 1945.

141. Parsons, Charles W. *Memoir of Usher Parsons, M.D., of Providence, R. I.* Providence: Hammond, Angell, 1870.

142. Parsons, Robert P. *Mob 3, a Naval Hospital in a South Sea Jungle.* Indianapolis: Bobbs-Merrill, 1945.

143. Parsons, Usher. *Physician for ships.* 3rd ed. Boston: C. C. Little & J. Brown, 1842.

144. Patterson, Robert U. "James Craik, Physician General," *Milit. Surg.,* 1932, *70*, 152-56.

145. Pember, Phoebe Y. *A Southern Woman's Story; Life in Confederate Richmond.* Edited by Bell I. Wiley. Jackson, Tennessee: McCowat-Mercer, 1959.

146. Perry, John G. *Letters from a Surgeon of the Civil War.* Comp. by Martha D. Perry. Boston: Little, Brown, 1906.

147. Peyton, Green. *Fifty Years of Aerospace Medicine; Its Evolution since the Founding of the United States Air Force School of Aerospace Medicine in January 1918.* Brooks Air Force Base, Texas: Air Force Systems Command, Aerospace Medical Division, 1968.

148. Phalen, James M. *Chiefs of the Medical Department, United States Army, 1775-1940.* Carlisle Barracks: Medical Field Service School, 1940.

149. Pilcher, James E. *The Surgeon Generals of the Army of the United States of America.* Carlisle: The Association of Military Surgeons, 1905.

150. Pleadwell, Frank L. "Edward Cutbush, M.D.; Nestor of the Medical Corps of the Navy," *Ann. Med. Hist.,* 1923, *5*, 113-45.

151. Pleadwell, Frank L. "Ninian Pinkney, M.D., 1811-1877, Surgeon, U.S. Navy," *Ann. Med. Hist.,* 1929, n.s., *1*, 667-97; 1930, n.s., *2*, 89-121.

152. Pleadwell, Frank L. "Usher Parsons (1788-1858), Surgeon, United States Navy," *Milit. Surg.,* 1922, *51*, 351-94.

153. Pleadwell, Frank L. "William Paul Crillon Barton, Surgeon United States Navy, a Pioneer in American Naval Medicine," *Ann. Med. Hist.,* 1919, *2*. 267-301.

154. Porcher, Francis P. *Resources of the Southern Fields and Forests; Medical, Economical and Agricultural.* Richmond: West & Johnston, 1863.

155. Porter, John B. "Medical and Surgical Notes of Campaigns in the War with Mexico, during the Years 1845, 1846, 1847, and 1848," *Am. Jour. Med. Sci.,* 1852, n.s., *23*, 13-37; n.s. *24*, 13-30; 1853, n.s., *25*, 35-42; n.s. 26, 297-333; 1858, n.s. *35*, 347-52.

156. Pôttle, Frederick A. *Stretchers; the Story of a Hospital Unit on the Western Front.* New Haven: Yale University Press, 1929.

157. Pugh, Herbert L. *Navy Surgeon.* Philadelphia: J. B. Lippincott, 1959.

158. Quebbeman, Frances E. *Medicine in Territorial Arizona.* Phoenix: Arizona Historical Foundation, 1966.

159. Radbill, Samuel X. "Francis Alison, Jr.; a Surgeon of the Revolution," *Bull. Hist. Med.*, 1941, *9*, 243-57.

160. Reedy, M. J. "Army Doctors; Long Years Attaining Rank and Command," *Milit. Med.*, 1965, *130*, 813-20.

161. Reister, Frank A. *Battle Casualties and Medical Statistics; U.S. Army experience in the Korean War.* Washington, D.C.: Surgeon General, Dept. of the Army, 1973.

162. Rixey, Presley M. *The Life Story of Presley Marion Rixey.* Strasburg, Virginia: Shenandoah Publishing House, 1930.

162a. Robinson, Douglas H. *The Dangerous Sky.* Seattle: University of Washington Press, 1973.

163. Roddis, Louis H. *A Short History of Nautical Medicine.* New York: P. B. Hoeber, 1941.

164. Roddis, Louis H. "Lives of the Surgeon Generals of the United States Navy," *Milit. Surg.*, 1941, *89*, 811-18; 1942, *90*, 74-75, 196-200, 319-24, 445-49, 580-82, 691-93; *91*, 98-103, 228-32, 353-55, 460-64, 588-91, 696-99; 1943, *92*, 69-73, 209-11, 317-23.

165. Roddis, Louis H. "Naval Medicine in the Early Days of the Republic," *J. Hist. Med. & Allied Sci.*, 1961, *16*, 103-23.

166. Roddis, Louis H. "The Medical Departments of the Ships of Dewey's Squadron in the Battle of Manila Bay," *Milit. Surg.*, 1935, *76*, 141-48.

167. Rush, Benjamin. *Directions for Preserving the Health of Soldiers.* Lancaster, Pennsylvania: John Dunlap, 1778.

168. Schullian, Dorothy M. and Frank B. Rogers, "The National Library of Medicine," *Lib. Quar.*, 1958, *28*, 1-17, 95-121.

169. Seagrave, Gordon S. *Burma Surgeon.* New York: W. W. Norton, 1943.

170. Seagrave, Gordon S. *Burma Surgeon Returns.* New York: W. W. Norton, 1946.

171. Senn, Nicholas. *Medico-Surgical Aspects of the Spanish American War.* Chicago: American Medical Association, 1900.

172. Smaridge, Norah. *Hands of Mercy; the Story of Sister-Nurses in the Civil War.* New York: Benziger Bros., 1900.

173. Smith, Adelaide W. *Reminiscences of an Army Nurse during the Civil War.* New York: Greaves, 1911.

174. Smith, Clarence M. *The Medical Department: Hospitalization and Evacuation, Zone of Interior.* Washington: Office of the Chief of Military History, Dept. of the Army, 1956.

175. Smith, George W. *Medicines for the Union Army; the United States Army Laboratories during the Civil War.* Madison: American Institute of the History of Pharmacy, 1962.

176. Smith, Stephen, *Hand-Book of Surgical Operations.* New York: Bailliere Bros., 1862.

177. Smucker, John R. *USAAS History*. Allentown?: United States Army Ambulance Service Association, 1967.
178. South, Oron P. *Medical Support in a Combat Air Force; a Study of Medical Leadership in World War II*. Maxwell Air Force Base, Alabama: Documentary Research Division, Research Studies Institute, Air University, 1956.
179. Steiner, Paul E. *Diseases in the Civil War; Natural Biological Warfare in 1861-1865*. Springfield: Charles C. Thomas, 1968.
180. Steiner, Paul E. *Physician-Generals in the Civil War; a Study in Nineteenth Mid-century American Medicine*. Springfield: Charles C. Thomas, 1966.
181. Steiner, Walter. "Dr. James Thacher of Plymouth, Massachusetts, an Erudite Physician of Revolutionary and Post-Revolutionary Fame," *Bull. Hist. Med.*, 1933, *1*, 157-73.
182. Sternberg, George M. *Sanitary Lessons of the War, and Other Papers*. Washington: B. S. Adams, 1912.
183. Sternberg, Martha L. *George Miller Sternberg*. Chicago: American Medical Association, 1920.
184. Stevenson, Benjamin F. *Letters from the Army*. Cincinnati: W. E. Dibble, 1884.
185. Stimson, Julia C. *History and Manual of the Army Nurse Corps*. Carlisle Barracks Medical Field Service School, 1937.
186. *Studies in Social Psychology in World War II*. Prepared and edited under the auspices of a special committee of the Social Science Research Council. Princeton: Princeton University Press, 1949-50. 4 vols.
187. Swieten, Gerard *frieherr* van. *The Diseases Incident to Armies*. Philadelphia: R. Bell, 1776.
188. Taliaferro, William H., ed. *Medicine and the War*. Chicago: University of Chicago Press, 1944.
189. Thacher, James. *A Military Journal during the American Revolutionary War, from 1775 to 1783*. Boston: Richardson & Lord, 1823.
190. Thacher, James. *American Medical Biography: or, Memoirs of Eminent Physicians Who Have Flourished in America*. Boston: Richardson & Lord, 1828. 2 v.
191. Thoms, Herbert. "Albigence Waldo, Surgeon; His Diary Written at Valley Forge," *Ann. Med. Hist.*, 1928, *10*, 486-97.
192. Tilton, James. *Economical Observations on Military Hospitals; and the Prevention and Cure of Diseases Incident to an Army*. Wilmington: J. Wilson, 1813.
193. Tobey, James A. *The Medical Department of the Army, Its History, Activities and Organization*. Baltimore: Johns Hopkins University Press, 1927.
194. Toland, Edward D. *The Aftermath of Battle; with the Red Cross in France*. New York: Macmillan, 1916.
195. Toner, Joseph M. *The Medical Men of the Revolution, with a Brief History of the Medical Department of the Continental Army*. Philadelphia: Collins, 1876.
196. Treadwell, Mattie E. *The Women's Army Corps*. Washington: Office of the Chief of Military History, Dept. of the Army, 1954.

197. Tripler, Charles S. *Hand-Book for the Military Surgeon.* Cincinnati: R. Clarke, 1861.
198. "Tropical Tryout," *MD*, 1958, *2*, 154-60.
199. Truby, Albert E. *Memoir of Walter Reed, the Yellow Fever Episode.* New York: P. B. Hoeber, 1943.
200. U.S. Air Force. Medical Service. *Medical Support of the Army Air Forces in World War II.* By Mae M. Link and Hubert A. Coleman. Washington: Office of the Surgeon General, USAF, 1955.
201. U.S. Army. Base Hospital no. 10. *History of the Pennsylvania Hospital Unit (Base Hospital no. 10, U.S.A. in the Great War.* New York: P. B. Hoeber, 1921.
202. U.S. Army. Base Hospital no 53. *Hisotry of Base Hospital Number Fifty-Three, Advance Section, Service of Supply.* Compiled under the direction of Col. W. Lee Hart. Langres: Base Printing Plant, 29th Engineers, U.S. Army, 1919.
203. U.S. Army. Evacuation Hospital no. 12. *History of the 12th Evacuation Hospital, 25 August 1942 to 25 August 1945.* Nurnberg: Sebaldus-Verlag, 1945.
204. U.S. Army. Evacuation Hospital no. 77. *Medicine under Canvas, War Journal of the 77th Evacuation Hospital.* Edited by Max S. Allen. Kansas City, Missouri: Sosland Press, 1949.
205. U.S. Army Medical Dept. Historical Unit. *A Decade of Progress: the United States Army Medical Department, 1959-1969.* Edited by Rose C. Engleman. Washington: Office of the Surgeon General, Dept. of the Army, 1971.
206. U.S. Army Medical Service. *Medical Department U.S. Army in World War II.* Washington: Office of the Surgeon General, Dept. of the Army, 1952- .
207. U.S. Army Medical Service. *Neurological Surgery of Trauma.* Edited by Arnold M. Meirowsky, Washington: Office of the Surgeon General, Dept. of the Army, 1965.
208. U.S. Bureau of Medicine and Surgery. *Annual Report of the Surgeon-General, U.S. Navy.* Washington: G.P.O., 18 -19 .
209. U.S. Bureau of Medicine and Surgery. *Hygienic and Medical Reports by Medical Officers of the U.S. Navy.* Washington: G.P.O., 1879.
210. U.S. Bureau of Medicine and Surgery. *Instructions for Medical Officers of the United States Navy.* Washington:G.P.O., 1873.
210a. U.S. Bureau of Medicine and Surgery. *Medical Department of the United States Navy with the Army and Marine Corps in France in World War I.* Washington: G.P.O., 1947.
211. U.S. Bureau of Medicine and Surgery. *Medical Essays: Compiled from Reports to the Bureau of Medicine and Surgery, by Medical Officers of the U.S. Navy.* Washington: G.P.O., 1872.
212. U.S. Bureau of Medicine and Surgery. *Sanitary and Medical Reports for 1873-74.* Washington: G.P.O., 1875.
213. U.S. Bureau of Medicine and Surgery. *Sanitary and Statistical Report[s] of the Surgeon-General of the Navy for the Year[s] 1879-1881.* Washington: G.P.O., 1881-83.
213a. U.S. Bureau of Medicine and Surgery. *The Dental Corps of the*

United States Navy; a Chronology, 1912-1962. Washington, 1962.

214. U.S. Bureau of Medicine and Surgery. *The History of the Medical Department of the United States Navy, 1945-1955.* Washington: G.P.O., 1958.

215. U.S. Bureau of Medicine and Surgery. *The History of the Medical Department of the United States Navy in World War II.* Rev. ed. Washington: G.P.O., 1953-

216. U.S. Bureau of Medicine and Surgery. *U.S. Navy Medical Department Administrative History, 1941-1945.* Washington, 1946. 2 vols. in 8.

217. U.S. Inspector-General's Office. *Regulations for the Order and Discipline of the Troops of the United States.* Philadelphia: Styner & Cist, 1779.

218. U.S. National Library of Medicine. *Index-Catalogue of the Library of the Surgeon-General's Office, United States Army.* [1st-5th ser.] Washington: G.P.O., 1880-1961.

219. U.S. National Library of Medicine. *Military Medicine.* Washington: G.P.O., 1955.

220. U.S. Naval Medical Research Institute. *The Naval Medical Research Institute, 1942-1962.* Edited by David E. Goldman. Washington: G.P.O., 1966.

221. U.S. Navy Dept. *Official Records of the Union and Confederate Navies in the War of the Rebellion.* Washington:G.P.O., 1894-1922. 30 vols.

222. U.S. Office of Air Force History. *The Army Air Forces in World War II.* Prepared under the editorship of Wesley F. Craven and James L. Cate. Chicago: University of Chicago Press, 1948-58. 7 vols.

223. U.S. Office of Scientific Research and Development. Committee on Medical Research. *Advances in Military Medicine, Made by American Investigators.* Edited by E. C. Andrus and others. Boston: Little, Brown, 1948. 2 vols.

224. U.S. Provost-Marshal-General's Bureau. *Statistics, Medical and Anthropological, of the Provost-Marshal-General's Bureau, Derived from Records of the Examination for Military Service in the Armies of the United States during the Late War of the Rebellion.* Comp. by J. H. Baxter. Washington: G.P.O., 1875. 2 vols.

225. U.S. Surgeon-General's Office. *A Report on the Hygiene of the United States Army, with Descriptions of Military Posts.* Washington: G.P.O., 1875.

226. U.S. Surgeon-General's Office. *Army Meteorological Register, for Twelve Years, from 1843 to 1854.* Washington: A. O. P. Nicholson, 1855.

227. U.S. Surgeon-General's Office. *Defects Found in Drafted Men. Statistical Information Compiled from the Draft Records Showing the Physical Condition of the Men Registered and Examined in Pursuance of the Requirements of the Selective Service Act.* Washington: G.P.O., 1920.

228. U.S. Surgeon-General's Office. *Meteorological Register for the Years 1822, 1823, 1824 & 1825.* E. De Krafft, 1826.

229. U.S. Surgeon-General's Office. *Meteorological Register for the Years 1826, 1827, 1828, 1829, and 1830.* Philadelphia: Haswell, Barrington, & Haswell, 1840.
230. U.S. Surgeon-General's Office. *Meteorological Register for the Years, from 1831 to 1842 Inclusive.* Washington: C. Alexander, 1851.
231. U.S. Surgeon-General's Office. *Report of the Surgeon-General U.S. Army to the Secretary of War.* Washington: G.P.O., 18 -19 .
232. U.S. Surgeon-General's Office. *Report on the Origin and Spread of Typhoid Fever in U.S. Military Camps during the Spanish War of 1898.* By Walter Reed, Victor Vaughan, and Edward O. Shakespeare. Washington: G.P.O., 1904. 2 vols.
233. U.S. Surgeon-General's Office. *Statistical Report on the Sickness and Mortality in the Army of the United States.* Washington: J. Gideon, Jr., 1840-60. 3 vols.
234. U.S. Surgeon-General's Office. *The Medical and Surgical History of the War of the Rebellion.* (1861-65). Washington: G.P.O., 3 vols. in 6.
235. U.S. Surgeon-General's Office. *The Medical Department of the United States Army from 1775 to 1873.* Comp. by Harvey E. Brown. Washington: Surgeon General's Office, 1873.
236. U.S. Surgeon-General's Office. *The Medical Department of the United States Army in the World War.* Washington: G.P.O., 1921-29. 15 vols. in 17.
237. U.S. Walter Reed Army Institute of Research. *Battle Casualties in Korea: Studies of the Surgical Research Team.* Washington, 1955-56. 4 vols.
238. U.S. War Dept. *The War of the Rebellion: a Compilation of the Official Records of the Union and Confederate Armies.* Washington: G.P.O., 1880-1901. 70 vols. in 128.
239. United States Sanitary Commission. *History of the United States Sanitary Commission, Being the General Report of Its Work during the War of the Rebellion.* By Charles J. Stille. New York: Hurd & Houghton, 1868.
240. United States Sanitary Commission. *Narrative of Privations and Sufferings of United States Officers and Soldiers While Prisoners of War in the Hands of the Rebel Authorities.* Philadelphia: King & Baird, 1864.
241. United States Sanitary Commission. *Surgical Memoirs of the War of the Rebellion.* New York: Published for the U.S. Sanitary Commission by Riverside Press, 1870-71. 2 vols.
242. [Van Buren, William H.] *Rules for Preserving the Health of the Soldier.* Washington, 1861.
243. Walter, Richard D. *S. Weir Mitchell, M.D., Neurologist; a Medical Biography.* Springfield: Charles C. Thomas, 1970.
244. Warren, Edward. *An Epitome of Practical Surgery for Field and Hospital.* Richmond: West & Johnston, 1863.
245. Warren, Edward. *The Life of John Warren, M. D.* Boston: Noyes, Holmes, 1874.
246. Welch, Spencer G. *A Confederate Surgeon's Letters to His Wife.* New York & Washington: Neale, 1911.

247. Wheeler, David C. "Physical Standards in Allied and Enemy Armies during World War II," *Milit. Med.*, 1965, *130*, 899-916.
248. Wheelwright, Charles H. *Correspondence of Dr. Charles H. Wheelwright, Surgeon of the United States Navy.* Edited by Hildegarde B. Forbes. Boston? 1958.
248a. Whitman, Walt. *Specimen Days.* Boston: Godine, 1971.
248b. Whitman, Walt. *The Wound Dresser; Letters Written to His Mother from the Hospitals in Washington during the Civil War.* Edited by Richard M. Bucke. New York: Bodley, 1949.
249. Williams, Stephen W. *American Medical Biography; or, Memoirs of Eminent Physicians, Embracing Principally Those Who Have Died since the Publication of Dr. Thacher's Work on the Same Subject.* Greenfield, Massachusetts: L. Merriam, 1845.
250. Wilson, Charles M. *Ambassadors in White, the Story of American Tropical Medicine.* New York: H. Holt, 1942.
251. Wilson, Joseph. *Naval Hygiene.* Washington,: G.P.O., 1870.
252. Wiltse, Charles M. *The Medical Department: Medical Service in the Mediterranean and Minor Theaters.* Washington: Office of the Chief of Military History, Dept. of the Army, 1965.
253. Wood, Ann D., "The war within a War: Women Nurses in the Union Army," *Civil War Hist.*, 1972, *18*, 197-212.
254. Wood, Laura N. *Walter Reed, Doctor in Uniform.* New York: J. Messner, 1943.
255. Woodward, Joseph J. *The Hospital Steward's Manual.* Philadelphia: J. B. Lippincott, 1862.
256. Woolsey, Jane S. *Hospital Days.* New York: D. Van Nostrand, 1868.
257. *Yellow Fever: a Compilation of Various Publications. Results of the Work of Maj. Walter Reed, Medical Corps, United States Army, and the Yellow Fever Commission.* Washington,: G.P.O., 1911.
258. Young, Hugh H. *Hugh Young, a Surgeon's Autobiography.* New York: Harcourt, Brace, 1940.

XIII

THE NAVY IN THE EARLY
TWENTIETH CENTURY, 1890-1941

William R. Braisted

The half century from 1890 to 1941 embraces the golden age of the battleship in the United States and the retreat of that great class before the inexorable rise of air power. Although the Navy distinguished itself in the Spanish-American War as well as in World War I, the period is fully as important for the changes within the service brought about by techno-logical, institutional, and diplomatic developments during peace as for the wars the Navy fought. Limitations of space do not permit a full review of many valuable dissertations listed by Allan R. Millett and B. Franklin Cooling in their *Doctoral Dissertations in Military Affairs* (74).

SURVEY HISTORIES. The survey histories of the Navy are generally deficient either because they do not cover the period or cover it only inade-quately. The two superb volumes by Harold and Margaret Sprout (304, 305) remain the finest, balanced treatment of the growth of American naval power to 1922, notwithstanding the fact that they were completed more than thirty years ago. George T. Davis's *A Navy Second to None* (86) of the same vintage carries the Navy from 1881 almost to World War II but without the assistance of many recent studies based on archival research. Other standard histories such as those by Dudley W. Knox (166), Fletcher Pratt (262). E. B. Potter and Chester W. Nimitz (260), and Brayton Harris (130) tend to stress the Navy's war record to the neglect of crucial activities during the years of peace. Donald W. Mitchell's survey of the Navy from 1883 to Pearl Harbor (223) must be used with caution. Walter Millis's *Arms and Men* (221) and Russell F. Weigley's *The American Way of War* (263) show the Navy's role in the nation's total military effort.

ON THE NEW NAVY TO 1898. Although historians must agree with Robert Seager (294) that the roots of the New Navy of steam and steel should be traced at least a decade before 1890, that year was memorable for the Navy since it saw the famed Policy Board recommend construction of battle fleets for both the Atlantic and the Pacific (338), Congress vote to build the first genuine American battleships, and Alfred Thayer Mahan

344

publish his first and most influential volume on sea power (205). The early years of the New Navy are treated in two recent studies: Walter R. Herrick's *The American Naval Revolution* (139), dealing with the New Navy from about 1880 through the fighting in the Spanish-American War in 1898, and B. Franklin Cooling's biography of Benjamin F. Tracy (74), President Harrison's naval secretary. Hugh B. Hammett's dissertation reviews Hilary A. Herbert's work on behalf of the Navy as congressman as well as his secretaryship in Cleveland's second administration. Except for an article on his political friendships by Walter D. Garrett (112), Secretary of the Navy John D. Long has not been studied. Long's published writings include his journal (197), his letters (195), and his volumes on the New Navy (194).

On the relation of the New Navy to the steel industry, see especially Dean C. Allard's thesis (11) and the history of armor plate manufacturing by the American Iron and Steel Association (14). Frank M. Bennett's volume on the *Steam Navy* (36) is a mine of information on the ships of the New Navy, while *The American Steel Navy* by John D. Alden, Ed Holm, and Arthur D. Baker is a photographic portrait from 1883 to the departure of the Great White Fleet on its world cruise in 1907. Robert W. Neeser's *Statistical and Chronological History of the United States Navy* (240) is both a chronology and detailed bibliography of naval materials to 1907.

At the intellectual heart of the New Navy was the Naval War College together with its founder, Stephen B. Luce, and its most famous professor, Alfred Thayer Mahan. Ronald A. Spector has studied private correspondence to assess the impact of the college on the Navy before World War I (303); and the college itself preserves a useful administrative history prepared in 1916 by its then president, Austin M. Knight, and William D. Puleston (164). Albert L. Gleaves' biography of Luce (117) has been supplemented by John D. Hayes' important articles on Luce's writings (135) and Luce's work in founding the college (134). The standard biographies of Mahan are those by Charles G. Taylor (318) and William D. Puleston (267). William E. Livezey's fine analysis of *Mahan on Sea Power* (192) includes a full bibliography. Also noteworthy is Margaret Sprout's concise article on Mahan in Edward Mead Earle's *Makers of Modern Strategy* (306) as well as B. M. Gilliam's dissertation on Mahan's changing geopolitical views (114). Mahan expressed himself most succinctly on strategy in his first sea power volume (205) and in his book on naval strategy (208).

Among the many books that have assessed the influence of the Navy and Mahan on American foreign relations, especially noteworthy are the studies on imperialism by Walter LaFeber (169) and Julius W. Pratt (264). Arthur J. Marder's classic on *The Anatomy of British Sea Power* (210) is basic for understanding the naval milieu in which the New Navy emerged as well as for Anglo-American naval relations to 1905.

THE SPAINISH-AMERICAN WAR AND AFTER. The Standard account of naval operations during the Spanish American War is that by French E. Chadwick (60), an able officer of the period; Walter Millis's *Martial Spirit* (222) places the naval operations in the total military context; and Frank Freidel (107) and Allen Keller (158) have written of the

"Splendid Little War" in lighter vein. For other perspectives of the war including the Navy, the works of Margaret Leech (178), H. Wayne Morgan (225), Walter LaFeber (169), and Julius Pratt (264) are valuable. William R. Braisted (40) has reviewed the Navy's operations in the Pacific during the war as well as its subsequent involvements in Samoa and the Boxer Uprising. The fate of the battleship *Maine* was recorded by her captain, Charles E. Sigsbee (295); in the report by the American naval court of inquiry into her sinking (339); and in John E. Weems' biography of the ship (361). The best account of the dash by the battleship *Oregon* from the Pacific to the Atlantic is by her skipper Captain, later Rear Admiral, Charles E. Clark (63).

Partly because the reputations of the two senior naval commanders in the Caribbean, William T. Sampson and Winfield S. Schley, were tarnished by a bitter dispute that led to a spectacular naval inquiry (352), George Dewey emerged as the one great naval hero of the war. Richard S. West, Jr., however, has written appreciatively of the war's leading admirals of empire: Dewey, Mahan, Sampson, and Schley (365). Schley presented his case in his autobiography (289); Sampson, in an article in *Century Magazine* (285). Perhaps because Dewey left so little to suggest his real impact on the Navy during the war and after, the Admiral of the Navy waited for fifty years for a serious biographer, Ronald Spector (302). Dewey's autobiography (89) is confined almost entirely to his deeds in Manila Bay and is little more than a revision in the first person of a lauditory account by one of his later aides, Nathan Sargent (286).

Naval actions off Cuba and in Manila Bay are reviewed respectively in popular versions by Anastacio C. M. Azoy (20) and Robert Conroy (73). E. A. M. Laing (170) adds a few details to Thomas A. Bailey's famous article on Dewey and the Germans at Manila (21). The principal sources on gunboat operations against the Philippine Insurgents are the articles by Albert P. Niblack (242) a participant, and the brief studies by David Potter (259) and Frederick L. Sawyer (287).

Much important naval correspondence relating to the war is printed in an appendix to the annual report of the Bureau of Navigation for 1898 (329), but interesting additional material may be found in the volumes on the war and the Boxer Uprising prepared by the Adjutant General's Office of the Army (327). The Office of Naval Intelligence also published a collection of reports on the naval operations by foreign observers (353). Correspondence relating to Rear Admiral Louis Kempff's conduct during the Boxer Uprising is printed in the congressional documents (334). Mahan's volume on the war's lessons (206) is especially noteworthy because the admiral was the most significant member of Secretary Long's strategy board of 1898. His articles reproduced in *The Problem of Asia* (209) are characteristic of American naval opinion, 1899-1900.

FROM THE SPANISH-AMERICAN WAR TO THE NEW FREEDOM. Since Theodore Roosevelt was a potent factor in naval affairs as the Navy's assistant secretary and as president between 1897 and 1909, the studies of him by Henry F. Pringle (266) and Howard K. Beale (26) are important for understanding the man and the Navy. Gordon C. O'Gara's still useful *Theodore Roosevelt and the Rise of the Modern Navy* (246) is based on the printed record. After further research in manuscripts, Albert C. Stillson takes a more disenchanted view of Roosevelt's leadership in his article (310) and his dissertation (309) on the naval establishment, 1901-1909. Roosevelt's letters edited by Elting E. Morison (229) include a very large selection relating to the Navy. The significant naval literature on TR's succession of naval secretaries is limited to the article by Paul T. Heffron on William H. Moody (136). The vigorous record of Secretary of the Navy George von Lengerke Meyer during the Taft administration deserves fuller treatment than that by his biographer, M. A. DeWolfe Howe (145). Naval constructor Holden Evans's memoirs (97) are helpful for the Meyer years.

Pioneer undertakings on naval diplomacy of the period were Seward W. Livermore's dissertation (187) and his articles arising therefrom (188, 189, 190, 191). Outten J. Clinard sought to study Japan's influence on the Navy (67) without consulting the basic naval manuscripts. William R. Braisted's volumes on the Navy in the Pacific (40, 41) are largely concerned with the use of the Navy as a diplomatic instrument in the Far East from 1897 to 1922. John A. S. Grenville has surveyed the Navy's war plans from 1890 to 1940 (121) and collaborated with George B. Young in studying the relation of American naval strategy to diplomacy from 1873 to 1914 (122). More recently, Richard D. Challener has pushed ahead still farther in his *Admirals, Generals, and Foreign Policy, 1898-1914* (61), a magnificently documented treatment of both the Army's and Navy's impact on American foreign policy in the Caribbean and the Pacific. Also noteworthy is the work by Robert E. Johnson on American naval forces on the Pacific Station, 1818-1919 (155), by Richard W. Turk on the Navy's Caribbean policies, 1865-1915 (325), and by Thomas A. Bailey (22) and Charles E. Neu (241) on Roosevelt and Japan. The best accounts of the world cruise by the Atlantic Fleet are those by Robert A. Hart (132), Samuel Carter (58), and the *New York Times* correspondent Franklin Matthews (213, 214). Homer Lea's *The Valor of Ignorance* was a sensational warning of Japanese attack in 1909 that lived again after the outbreak of World War II.

The two most rewarding memoirs of the period are those by Mahan (204) and by Bradley Fiske (104), the brilliant inventor who served as aid for operations from 1913 to 1915. Other flag officers represented by memoirs or biographies of varying significance are Albert S. Barker (23), Robley D. Evans (99, 100, 102), Richard Wainwright (78), Casper F. Goodrich (119), William E. Emory (116), George C. Remey (275), Willard H. Brownson (131), and Seaton Schroeder (292). Drawing chiefly from this type of biographical material and from numerous private manuscript collections, Peter Karsten has written a brilliant interpretation of the manners and mores of what he calls *The Naval Aristocracy* (157), the officer graduates from the Naval Academy at Annapolis from 1842 to about 1930.

THE NEW FREEDOM AND WORLD WAR I. Woodrow Wilson's attitudes towards the Navy remain difficult to determine notwithstanding the mass of Wilson scholarship. Ernest R. May has a suggestive article on Wilson as commander-in-chief in *The Ultimate Decision* (215), and Wilson's naval views will surely become more distinct as Arthur S. Link carries his multivolume biography of the President (185) into World War I. Josephus Daniels's administration of the Navy is treated in Innis L. Jenkins's dissertation (153) as well as by Joseph L. Morrison (233) and the secretary's son Jonathon (80), but Daniels himself is still a prime source for his secretaryship in his volumes on *The Wilson Era* (83, 84) and in his diaries (77), Franklin D. Roosevelt as assistant secretary is best portrayed in the first two volumes of Frank Freidel's biography (106), in an earlier account by the newspaperman Ernest K. Lindley (184), and in Joseph W. Coady's dissertation (69). Daniels's aide for operations, Bradley Fiske, commented tartly on conditions in the service in his autobiography (104) and in *The Navy as a Fighting Machine* (105). In addition to the more general studies by the Sprouts (304), Link (185, 186), and Braisted (41), the dissertation by Edward H. Brooks (45) as well as Armin Rappaport's fine history of the Navy League (271) may be consulted on the preparedness movement that led to the famed 1916 naval bill. The Navy's oil policies during the Wilson administration and later are covered by John L. Bates (25), John A. DeNovo (88), Reginald W. Ragland (270), and Secretary Daniels (81). Jack Sweetman's (316) is the most complete study of the naval landing at Vera Cruze in 1914.

Perhaps because most Americans assumed that World War I was really the war to end all wars until it was overshadowed by World War II, the third volume of Thomas G. Frothingham's history of the war (109) remains the best general survey of the Navy's actions. Moreover, writing about the Navy's role has often been marred by the bitterness that divided the service after William S. Sims' attacks on the Navy Department's administration brought a full Senate investigation into the conduct of the war (340). Much of the best work on the Navy's war effort has centered on Admiral Sims in London: Elting S. Morison's splendid biography of Sims (226), Sims' own account of the *Victory at Sea* (297), and the defense of Sims by his officers, T. B. Kittredge (163) and John L. Leighton (179). Daniels's version may be found in his popular story of the war (82) and in his second volume of *The Wilson Era* (84). Adding significantly to earlier work on naval diplomacy during the war by Warner R. Schilling (288) and William Braisted (41), David F. Trask has searched deeply in British and American archives and private collections to produce the finest study of Anglo-American wartime naval relations (323). The last volume of Arthur J. Marder's *From the Dreadnought to Scapa Flow* (211) views from the British Admiralty the American Navy in the war and at the Paris Peace Conference. American flag officers other than Sims who wrote on the war were Henry B. Wilson, commander of U.S. naval forces in France (374); Hugh Rodman, commander of the American battleships with the Grand Fleet (278); and Albert Gleaves, commander of the naval transport service (115).

In the area of operational history, Reginald R. Belknap (35) wrote on American mining activities in the North Sea that he helped organize; Holloway Frost (108), Peter B. Schroeder (291), and John D. Alden (9), on destroyers; Ray Millholland (220), Harold W. Rose (280), and William W. Nutting (244), on subchasers and other patrols; Lewis P. Clephane (66), on the Naval Overseas Transportation Service [NOTS]; and Henry P.

Beers (34), on the naval port officers at Bordeaux. The important study by Robert G. Albion and Jennie B. Pope on *Sea Lanes in Wartime* (7) includes material on keeping the Atlantic open to Allied shipping. Paul V. Silverstone (296) has prepared the most convenient handbook giving the basic characteristics of American warships in the war. For additional materials, see also the sections on administrative history, naval air, the marines, and submarines which follow below.

Although the Navy never published a documentary collection on the war, the Senate investigation hearings (340), like the Pearl Harbor hearings twenty-five years later, include a large amount of such material. The Office of Naval Records and Library also prepared a monograph series (354) on such topics as mining activities, the Naval Planning Section in London, and the Bureau of Engineering. There are official histories of the war activities of the Bureau of Ordnance (332), the Bureau of Yards and Docks (333), and the Naval Consulting Board (293).

Turning to the several delicate diplomatic episodes in which the Navy was involved at the close of World War I, the fullest study of Admiral Mark L. Bristol as high commissioner in Turkey, 1919-1924, is Peter M. Buzanski's excellent dissertation (49). Anthony C. Davidonis (85) has briefly but factually reviewed the Navy's occupation of Dalmatia, 1918-1921, as have Henry P. Beers and William Braisted its participation in the interventions in North Russia (33) and at Vladivostok (41).

THE ERA OF NAVAL ARMS LIMITATION, 1919-1931. The era from the close of World War I to the Manchurian Incident has been studied in considerable detail from the point of view of naval diplomacy. The Sprouts (305) were the first scholars fully to cover the Navy's readjustment to peace through the Washington Conference, 1921-1922. More recent research by Thomas M. Buckley (46) and William Braisted (41) on the conference has often confirmed what the Sprouts concluded long before the relevant archives and private collections were opened. While the first volume of Stephen W. Roskill's *Naval Policy between the Wars* (284) provides an excellent discussion of the British at the conference as well as a fine overview of the naval situation from 1919 to 1929, Robin Higham (141) is sometimes severely critical of British defense policies between the World Wars (141). Two dissertations add Japanese dimension to the Pacific naval problem: Asada Sadao's survey of Japanese-American relations from 1915 to 1922 (18) and Roger Dingman's comparative history of the politics of national defense in the United States and Japan (90). Raymond Leslie Buell's *Washington Conference* (47) is probably the most intelligent contemporary report, but Yamato Ichihashi's study of the conference (151) deserves attention since Ichihashi served as secretary to Admiral Baron Kato Tomosaburo, the leading Japanese delegate. Merlo J. Pusey's biography of Charles Evans Hughes (268) details the secretary of State's conduct of the conference. John Chalmers Vinson's *The Parchment Peace* (359) assesses the influence of Senator William E. Borah and the Senate in bringing a naval treaty, complementing C. Leonard Hoag's older work on public opinion during the conference (143). Herbert O. Yardley's *The American Black Chamber* (379) tells with numerous quotations from Japanese originals how the United States Navy read the Japanese naval and diplomatic telegrams. The most succinct, American naval critique of the Washington naval agreements is that by Commodore Dudley W. Knox (165).

Gerald E. Wheeler's *Prelude to Pearl Harbor* (368) is the single most useful survey of American naval policy from the Washington Conference to the Manchurian Incident. Wheeler's biography of Admiral William V. Pratt (367) deals with the American naval officer who contributed most to the naval agreements. The later conferences at Geneva (1927) and London (1930) have been studied respectively by Michel J. Brode (42) and Raymond G. O'Connor (245). Revealing for Japanese attitudes toward the latter conference are the Saionji-Harada memoirs translated by Thomas Francis Mayer-Oakes (216). John M. Wilson's studies on Herbert Hoover and the armed forces (375, 376) are illuminating on naval administration and service politics. The surviving memoirs by commanders-in-chief, Admirals Robert E. Coontz (75) and Henry A. Wiley (370), contain little on naval policy. Joseph H. Kitchans's dissertation on William B. Shearer (161) deals with a public relations man charged with working on behalf of arms firms to wreck the Geneva Naval Conference of 1927.

Distinguished among naval writers of the period was Hector C. Bywater, whose *Sea Power in the Pacific* (55) was standard reading and whose vision of *The Great Pacific War* (54) may well have influenced war planning in the United States and Japan. Somewhat later in time, Bernard Brodie's *A Layman's Guide to Naval Strategy* (43) is an excellent introduction to naval strategic thinking before the superiority of air power was fully accepted.

In other areas. *Tragedy at Honda* by Charles A. Lockwood and Hans C. Adamson is the moving tale of seven destroyers that were grounded when they missed the Santa Barbara Channel in 1923 (194). Kemp Tolley's *Yangtze Patrol* (322) is a somewhat nostalgic history of the river gunboats earlier made famous by Richard McKenna's novel *The Sand Pebbles* (203).

FROM THE MANCHURIAN INCIDENT TO PEARL HARBOR.

For too long the principal writing on the Navy and the coming of World War II was limited to the urbane but brief treatment by Samuel Eliot Morison in the first (1947) and third (1948) volumes of his history of the war (230), 231). Thaddeus V. Tuleja later (1961) drew largely on the General Board records to survey the Navy in the Pacific from the Manchurian Incident to Pearl Harbor (324), much as Gerald Wheeler has done for the previous decade. The respective essays by Waldo H. Heinrichs, Jr., (138) and Asada Sadao (19) in *Pearl Harbor as History* are fine reviews of American and Japanese attitudes. In their respective dissertations, Robert H. Levine (182) treats the interaction between the naval construction and New Deal recovery programs while Calvin Enders (96) recounts the development of the Navy under the watchful eye of Carl Vinson, the powerful chairman of the House Naval Affairs Committee. Charles A. Beard's *The Navy: Defense or Portent?* (27) is the most important statement on the Navy by a severe critic, whose debate with "the Big Navy Boys" is covered by Thomas C. Kennedy (159).

In the immense literature on the Far Eastern Crisis, 1931-1933, Christopher Thorne's *Limits of Foreign Policy* (321) is an interpretation from the

Anglo-American viewpoint that includes naval considerations. More specifically directed to the United States Navy is Michael D. Reagen's essay on ". . . Stimson, Hoover, and the Armed Services" (274). Dorothy Borg's study of American Far Eastern Policy during the middle thirties (38) gives attention to the breakdown of the naval treaties and the Navy during the early phases of the China Incident, 1937-1938. The famous sinking of the gunboat *Panay* is covered well from the American side in monographs by Maury T. Koginos (167) and Hamilton D. Perry (256) and the more popular paperback by Joseph B. Icenhower (150).

Since the Navy never undertook comparable official histories of its prewar planning, the relevant volumes of the Army's history of World War II are also important for naval policy, especially those by Mark S. Watson on *Pre-War Plans and Preparations* (360), by Maurice Matloff and Edwin M. Snell on *Strategic Planning for Coalition War* (212), by Louis Morton on *Strategy and Command* (235), by Ray S. Cline on the War Department's Operations Division (68), and by Stetson Conn and Bryan Fairchild on Western Hemisphere defense (71). Morton's article on "War Plan Orange" (236) is a concise review of American planning for war with Japan between the World Wars. The diplomatic histories by William L. Langer and S. Everett Gleason on *The Challenge to Isolation* (174) and *The Undeclared War* (175) are fundamental for understanding the Navy's relation to American foreign policy in both Europe and Asia from 1937 to 1941. Also important is the manuscript on "United States-British Naval Cooperation" from 1939 to 1941 (162) that T. B. Kittredge prepared as part of a projected official history of the Commander U.S. Naval Forces Europe. The opening of the naval records has stimulated a flow of new studies on naval diplomacy on the eve of war. Stephen B. Pelz has read extensively in Japanese and English language materials to examine Japanese and American naval policies during the *Race to Pearl Harbor* (255) from 1936 to 1941; John H. Herzog's *Closing the Open Door* (140) deals chiefly with Admiral Harry E. Yarnell at Shanghai early in the China Incident and with Anglo-American relations in the Pacific, 1940-1941. More directed toward the Atlantic are the well documented dissertations by James R. Leutze on Anglo-American naval relations in 1940 (181) and by Patrick Abbazia on "Mr. Roosevelt's Navy" in the Atlantic from 1939 to 1942 (1). Captain Royal E. Ingersoll's mission to London in 1938 is covered in articles by John McV. Haight (124) from the American point of view and by Lawrence Pratt (264) from the British. For the famed Anglo-American deal on bases and destroyers in 1940, see especially Harold J. Sutphen's dissertation (314) and the semipopular account by Philip Goodhart (118). Robert J. Quinlin (269) details the movements of the Navy's battle forces in 1940-1941 when the United States sought to build up its power in the Atlantic against Germany while preserving a meaningful deterrent in the Pacific against Japan.

The Pearl Harbor disaster is covered most fully by Roberta Wohlstetter's multifaceted inquiry into how the Americans were caught in catastrophe (377). The thirty-nine volumes of hearings by the joint congressional committee to investigate the *Pearl Harbor Attack* (337) is a vast collection of documents and testimony that comprises the single most important printed source on the Navy in the Pacific during the last two years of peace. John B. Potter's biography of Admiral Yamamoto Isoroku (261) includes a full account of the careful Japanese planning before the attack. The role of cryptanalysis in the Pearl Harbor drama is examined in Ladislas Farago's description of "Operation Magic" (103) and in David Kahn's massive study of codebreaking (156). The deeds of Ellis M. Zacharias, the Navy's most famous Japan expert, are celebrated in his autobiography (380) and in the biography by Maria Wilhelm (371). For additional Pearl Harbor materials, see Dean C. Allard's chapter.

Notable among the memoirs of the decade are the frank autobiography by Admiral J. O. Richardson (277), the commander-in-chief of the United States Fleet, 1940-1941; the "Narrative of Events . . ." by Admiral Thomas C. Hart (133), the commander-in-chief of the Asiatic Fleet, 1939-1942; and *Ships, Machinery, and Mossbacks* by Harold G. Bowen (39), chief engineer of the Navy, 1935-1939, and later chief of Naval Research. Other flag officers represented by memoirs are William H. Standley (308), chief of Naval Operations, 1933-1935; Harris Lanning (176), commander-in-chief of the Baltic Fleet, 1935-1937; Emory S. Land (173), chief of the Bureau of Construction and Repair, 1932-1937, and later chairman of the U.S. Maritime Commission; and Yates Stirling, Jr. (311), sometime commander of the Yangtze Patrol. George C. Dyer's biography of Richmond Kelley Turner (94) includes material on Turner's service as War Plans director, 1940-1941, and earlier significant duty.

Contemporary materials on the Navy during the thirties are listed in the bibliographies on naval expansion by Grace Hadley Fuller (110) and on *Sea Power in the Pacific* by Werner B. Ellinger and Herbert Ronsinski (95).

ADMINISTRATIVE, TECHNICAL, AND OTHER SPECIALIZED HISTORIES. Since there is no survey administrative history of the Navy covering the half-century before Pearl Harbor, this important subject must be approached piece by piece through lesser studies. C. O. Paullin's classic articles, now assembled in one volume (250), unfortunately end in 1911. A multivolume administrative history undertaken by Robert G. Albion under the Navy's auspices was cut short after Albion completed only a draft of the first volume on "Makers of Naval Policy, 1798-1947" (4). What historians have missed may be conjectured from Albion's articles (2, 3, 5) and the splendid study by Albion and Robert H. Connery on James H. Forrestal's naval reforms (6). Julius A. Furer's administrative history of World War II (111) includes much detailed information on the pre-war years, as do Connery's monograph on the Navy and industrial mobilization (72) and numerous unpublished official naval administrative histories of the war (351). The first third of Vincent Davis's *The Admiral's Lobby* (87) is devoted to struggles within the Navy Department, the impact of technology on the Navy, and strategic planning before 1941. Paul Y. Hammond (128) and Samuel P. Huntingon (149) have written briefly but perceptively on the clash between the Navy's line and staff officers and its relations with the civil authorities in their more general studies, as has Elting Morison in his biography of Sims (226). Mahan (207) and Bradley Fiske (105) represent moderate and extreme positions taken by line officers in the line-staff controversy. Jarvis Butler's reflections on the General

Board (48) were derived during many years with that august body, whose policies from 1900 to World War I are summarized in Daniel F. Costello's dissertation (76). Henry P. Beers' fine articles on the Office of the Chief of Naval Operations (30) together with his short studies of the Bureau of Equipment (31), the Judge Advocate General (32), and the Bureau of Navigation (29) could form a useful volume on naval administration. Also helpful on the Navy Department and its bureaus are a study by Alfred W. Johnson (154), lively articles by Thomas W. Ray (273) and Elting Morison (227), and a documentary collection assembled by Morison during World War II (228).

Representative studies on individual shore establishments are those by Willis E. Snowbarger on Pearl Harbor (300), James H. West on New York (364), Arnold S. Lott on Mare Island (198), Taylor Peck on the Washington Navy Yard and Gun Factory (254), and Frederick L. Paxson on the Naval Station at Alameda, California (252). William Braisted includes a good deal on shore establishments in his studies of the Navy in the Pacific (40, 41). The reports by two of the three most important boards on the development of yards and bases have been published: the Helm Commission of 1916 and 1918 (336) and the Hepburn Board of 1938 (335). That by the Parks-McKean Board of 1919 is in the National Archives.

Julius W. Pratt (263) deals in rather general terms with the Navy's record in colonial administration. More specific are the studies by Earl S. Pomeroy (258) and Henry P. Beers (28) on Guam, J. A. C. Gray on Samoa (120), and Luther H. Evans on the Virgin Islands (98).

For the impact of technology on naval development, Bernard Brodie's *Sea Power in the Machine Age* (44) remains a classic. Naval engineering of the period is reviewed in Herbert Neuhaus's survey of fifty years (242), Bowen's autobiography (39), and the *Historical Transactions* of the Society of Naval Architects and Marine Engineers (237). Important sources on science and research are Albert H. Taylor's history of the Naval Research Laboratory to 1948 (317), the first volume of Albert B. Christman's account of the rocket program at China Lake, California (62), Robert C. Duncan's brief, authoritative *American Use of Sea Mines* (93), and Thomas P. Hughes' biography of Elmer Sperry (148), the inventor of the gyroscope. Three valuable studies of naval communications are Linwood S. Howeth's history of communications electronics in the Navy (145) and the more comprehensive histories of maritime wireless communications by Harry E. Hancock (129) and Peter B. Schroeder (291). Alan F. Pater's *United States Battleships* (249) includes biographies and pictures of every American battleship.

In the field of polar exploration, Robert E. Peary's quest for the North Pole is recorded in Peary's own account (253) and in biographies of Peary by William H. Hobbs (144) and John E. Weems (362). Dennis Rawlins's article on "the Lingering Doubt" (272) looks again at Frederick A. Cook's claim that he, not Peary, discovered the pole. Richard E. Byrd's Antarctic explorations are covered in his popular volumes (50, 51, 52, 53) and in Edwin P. Hoyt's biography (147).

Frederick S. Harrod deals broadly with enlisted personnel in his important dissertation (394). The Naval Reserves are introduced in William R. Kreh's *Citizen Soldiers* (168) and Harold J. Weiand's dissertation

(369); the chaplains, covered by Clifford M. Drury's five volume history (92). Stephen H. Evans' history of the Coast Guard (101), which ends in 1915, may be supplemented by popular accounts by Henry V. Bloomfield (37) and Walter C. Capron (57). There is also a bibliography on the Coast Guard by Thomas R. Strobridge (312). See chapter XII for naval medicine.

NAVAL AIR. The basic history of naval aviation by Archibald D. Turnbull and Clifford L. Lord (326) has been supplemented but not displaced by Theodore Roscoe's more recent survey (279). George Van Deurs' handsomely illustrated *Wings of the Fleet* (355) and the biographies of the builder-inventor Glenn Curtiss by Clara Studer (313) and Cecil R. Roseberry (281) are important for the early heroic years of naval aviation. The role of naval air during World War I are summarized in the pamphlet by Adrian Van Wyen (357); the war deeds of the famous first naval reserve units from Yale, extolled by Ralph D. Paine (247). The transatlantic flight by the NC-4, first narrated by the effort's participants (366), has been retold in Richard K. Smith's *First Across!* (299). Edward Arpee's biography of Rear Admiral William A. Moffet (16) is really a history of naval aviation from Moffett's appointment as the first chief of the Bureau of Aeronautics in 1921 to his death in the dirigible *Macon* in 1933, including the Navy's defense against General William "Billy" Mitchell. For other materials on the Mitchell controversy see chapter XV. The Navy's lighter-than-air program, whose principal spokesman was Commander Charles E. Rosendahl (282, 283), is reviewed in R. K. Smith's monograph on the *Akron* and the *Macon* (298). The evolution of the Navy's use of carriers before 1941 must be sought in the more general histories of carriers by Scot MacDonald (202), Clark G. Reynolds (276), Garrett L. Pawlowski (251), and Norman Polmar (257). Van Wyen's brief history of the Aeronautical Board, 1916-1947 (356), deals with efforts by the Army and Navy to coordinate their air arms. Van Wyen also collaborated on a useful chronology of naval aviation, 1910-1960 (358). The illustrated data book on *United States Naval Aircraft since 1911* by Gordon Swanborough and Peter M. Powers (315) provides the histories, designs, and types of naval aircraft arranged alphabetically by manufacturer.

Reginald W. Arthur's *Contact!* (17) is a biographical dictionary of the first 2000 naval airmen. Biographies and memoirs of World War II commanders such as Ernest J. King (160), William F. Halsey (125), Marc Mitscher (319), and Joseph J. Clark (64) are also important sources on naval aviation before the war. Eugene E. Wilson's *Slipstream* (373) is the autobiography of a crusading naval officer who became president of the United Aircraft Corporation.

THE MARINE CORPS. The two most important survey histories of the Marine Corps are those by marine historians Clyde Metcalf (218) and Robert D. Heinl (137). Metcalf stops in the 1930s, but Heinl sweeps through the entire period 1890-1941 with characteristic marine élan. The Division of Reserve has prepared its own official history (345). Marine actions in World War I are conveniently surveyed in the early study by the Corps historian Edwin B. McClellan (200). The *Reminiscences* of Major

General John A. Lejeune (180), commander of the 2d Division of the A. E. F., are important for the Marines during the war as well as during the 1920s when Lejeune was thirteenth commandant of the Corps. Major General Albertus W. Catlin's *With the Help of God and a Few Marines* (59) is the record of the commander of the heroic 6th Marine Regiment of Belleau Woods fame. The memoirs of Smedley D. Butler (320), as told to newsman Lowell Thomas, cover that colorful marine's service in the Boxer Uprising, in World War I, and in China and Nicaragua during the 1920s.

Of the marine interventions, those in Nicaragua have received most attention: Bernard C. Nalty's pamphlet in the Marine Corps Historical Reference Series (237), Neill Macaulay's fine account of the *Sandino Affair*, 1927-1933 (199), Lejeune Cummins's older study of the same (79), and Vernon E. Megee's thesis on the military features of Nicaraguan interventions, 1909-1933 (217). James H. McCrocklin's *Garde D'Haiti* (201) is chiefly a reproduction of an official report on the Marines in Haiti, 1915-1934. Outstanding among the marine regimental histories is that by Kenneth W. Condit and Edwin T. Turnblat on the 4th Marines (70), famed for their services at Shanghai before World War II. Louis Morton's "Army and Marines on the China Station" (234) is an analysis of service rivalries in China before 1941. John W. Thomason, the Corps' gifted raconteur, delighted a generation and is himself the stuff of an entertaining biography by Roger Willock (372).

Since space does not permit a really adequate review of the sources of Marine Corps history, the reader is urged to consult further in John Moran's somewhat unorthodox *Creating a Legend* (224), Jack B. Hilliard and Harold A. Bivins' excellent annotated reading list (142), the Corps' history newsletter *Fortitudine*, and the bibliographies brought out by the Marine Corps Historical Division's *Historical Bibliographies* (346) on such topics as the Marines in World War I, the Boxer Uprising, Marine artillery, and marine fiction. The Historical Division has also published a useful chronology in its *Historical Reference Series* (347).

SUBMARINES AND SUBMARINERS. The two best introductions to the Navy's "silent service" are Edward P. Stafford's *The Far and the Deep* (307) and Robert H. Barnes' older *United States Submarines* (24). Submarine pioneers are covered in William K. Morris's brief but well-documented biography of John P. Holland (232); a semi-autobiographic account by one of Holland's associates, Frank T. Cable (56); and the writings of Simon Lake (171, 172), who founded the Lake Torpedo Boat Company that competed with Holland's Electric Boat Company. Carroll S. Alden's articles (8) are the best sources on American submarines in World War I. Also helpful on the war are monographs on keeping the Atlantic sea lanes open by David D. Lewis (183), German submarine operations by Richard H. Gibson and Maurice Prendergast (113), and German submarines off the American Atlantic coast by William B. Clark (65) and Henry J. James (152). Charles A. Lockwood's *Down to the Sea in Subs* (193) is both the story of the admiral's love affair with submarines and a rich source on American submarine history before 1942. Dean C. Allard's essay on "Submarine Qualification" (12) explores efforts to establish standards for officers aspiring to wear the dolphins of the submarine service. The dissertations by Lawrence H. Douglas (91) and D. T. Groeling (123) assess the influence of diplomacy on submarine policy between the World Wars. For more detailed information on submarine literature, there are bibliographies by Frank J. Anderson (15), Thomas O. Paine (248), and the Committee on Undersea Warfare of the National Research Council (238).

JOURNALS. The two most important service news journals throughout the period were the *Army and Navy Journal* and the *Army and Navy Register*. Both provided full coverage, but the *Register* was probably the more widely read in the Navy. The *United States Naval Institute Proceedings* was and remains the most significant journal of professional opinion, containing articles of both contemporary and historical import. Too little used, however, is *United Service*, a magazine to which prominent naval officers contributed until it ceased publication in 1905. Prime sources for naval technology are the *Scientific American*, the *Transactions of the Society of Naval and Marine Engineers*, and the *Journal of the American Society of Naval Engineers*. The best daily news reporting on naval affairs was usually in the *New York Times*. The *Marine Corps Gazette* and *Leatherneck* both contain materials of historical interest. Articles on naval history also appear in *Military Affairs*, the *American Neptune*, the *Pacific Historical Review*, and the *Naval War College Review*. *Sea Power* was the magazine of the Navy League of the United States. See Rappaport (271).

PRINTED GOVERNMENT DOCUMENTS. The most valuable source published by the Navy from 1890 to 1932 was the Navy Department's *Annual Reports* (349) which, in addition to the secretary's report, included those for the bureaus. Only the secretary's *Report* (350) was printed after 1932. Issued separately by the Bureau of Contruction and Repair after 1911 were the *Ships' Data* books (328) that contained concise technical data on all ships. On naval personnel, the monthly *Navy Directory* (330) listed officers according to stations; the annual *Register* (331), according to rank with dates of birth and stations also indicated. Congressional committee hearings, especially those of the House Naval Affairs Committee and of the House Appropriations Committee, contain much factual material together with the testimonies of the naval authorities. There is a convenient list of hearings prepared by the Legislative Reference Section of the Library of Congress (344). Also rich in naval matter are the House and Senate Documents and Reports in the Congressional Serials Set as well as the *Congressional Record*. Issued annually from 1904 to 1921 was the *Navy Yearbook* (342) containing abstracts of the naval appropriations bills from 1883 and current statistical information. The *United States Foreign Relations* (341) includes correspondence relating to matters involving the Navy, usually without the relevant naval letters.

MANUSCRIPT DEPOSITORIES AND LIBRARIES. The richest depositories of naval historical manuscripts are those in the Washington area described in the guide by Dean C. Allard and Betty Bern (13). At the

National Archives (386), the Naval Records Collection of the Office of Naval Records and Library, Record Group 45, embraces a vast amount of material drawn principally from the Navy Department's files. The collection is especially rich for the years through World War I. Also of major importance is Record Group 80, the General Records of the Navy Department, which includes those of the Office of the Secretary and several valuable formerly classified files for 1917-1938. A large number of naval attache reports to 1940 as well as extensive correspondence of the Office of Naval Intelligence are in Record Group 38, misleadingly designated by the National Archives as the Records of the Office of the Chief of Naval Operations since significant Opnav correspondence is located in Record Group 80. O.N.I. Correspondence remains classified as far back as 1913. Since the Navy Department failed to maintain a central file, researchers desiring full naval documentation must consult the records of the various bureaus, offices, and other units concerned, such as those of the Marine Corps (Record Group 127), the Bureau of Navigation (Record Group 24), or the Bureau of Aeronautics (Record Group 72). Several naval record groups have been moved to the Archives Branch of Suitland, Maryland (394). Given the scattered condition of the naval records, those of the State Department (Record Group 59), of the Army (various record groups), of the Joint Army and Navy Boards (Record Group 225), and other agencies assume special significance for naval research. In addition to its *Guide* (348), the National Archives has prepared checklists and inventories for its more important record groups that are also useful sources of information on institutional history.

Apart from the National Archives, the Naval History Division (388) retains several basic files, including the records of the General Board from its establishment in 1900, the War Plans Division from about 1937, and other Operations records from about 1940. It also maintains a card index on the locations of private manuscript collections that supplements the standard national guides (126, 343). Among the private papers held by the Naval History Division are those of Admirals William V. Pratt and Harry E. Yarnell. Access to the Navy's classified records is through the Director of Naval History.

The most important depository of private naval manuscripts is the Manuscript Division at the Library of Congress (384) which, in addition to its own extensive collections, houses most of the papers of the Naval Historical Foundation (387) described in the Foundation's printed catalogue (239). Notable among the latter are the papers of Vice Admiral William S. Sims. The Library of Congress is also the depository for the papers of the Presidents through Woodrow Wilson as well as naval secretaries (especially Josephus Daniels) and others whose lives touched the Navy. The Warren G. Harding Papers are at the Ohio Historical Society (390) while the papers of Presidents Hoover (382) and Franklin D. Roosevelt (381), together with other navy related material, are located at their respective presidential libraries.

The three most important naval libraries are the Navy Department Library (389), the Mahan Library at the Naval War College with its archives (393), and the Naval Academy Library (392). The most useful libraries for Marine history are the Breckinridge Library at Quantico (383) and the Marine Historical Reference Library (385). The latter is shortly to be housed in the Washington Navy Yard with the Corps' extensive private manuscript collections (378). The Submarine Library at Groton, Connecticut (391), holds the papers of the Electric Boat Company and other submarine history materials.

SUGGESTIONS FOR RESEARCH. There are very few areas of American naval history adequate to explain the overall development of the service, the relations between its constituent parts, and their contacts with the outside world. One searches in vain for a first class history of a single bureau, of the Office of Naval Operations, of the General Board, of the Naval War College after 1914, of the Office of Naval Intelligence, or of their relations with each other. Naval shore establishments have been studied in desultory fashion without systematic investigation into the Navy's broad policies on navy yards, the influence of local communities and of patronage, and whether the yards were economically sound. Nor have there been studies of contract and other negotiations between the Navy and private corporations to determine whether there were planted the seeds for the much publicized military-industrial complex. It is ardently to be hoped that Congress may soon make possible full inquiry into naval-congressional relations by opening its records on the same liberal terms that it requires of the Executive. In the area of science and technology, there is need for history by scholars trained in science on the development of new or improved ship types, reflecting advances in ordnance, armor, propulsion, and electronics as well as on the Navy's relations with civilian scientists. Nor have there been adequate studies on the Navy's changing tactics and logistics. Neglected aspects of social history include civilian personnel of the Navy, naval education, the position of women and other minorities, naval law, and recreation. There is no really adequate study of submarines and submariners before 1941 comparable to those for naval air and the Marines. The most promising opportunities in naval air history are probably to be found in the decade before 1941. Although the Navy's relation to foreign policy has attracted many historians, the opening of foreign archives is inducement for a thorough reexamination of American naval diplomacy in terms of the Navy's impact abroad. For the buff on naval operational history, practically all aspects of naval operations during World War I call for serious new study, as do a host of lesser involvements in China, Latin America, and Russia. Still unclaimed by biographers are several significant secretaries and such outstanding officers as Henry C. Taylor, Charles O'Neil, Washington I. Chambers, Richmond P. Hobson, Albert Gleaves, Joseph B. Reeves, Harry E. Yarnell, and Thomas C. Hart. Also rewarding would be shorter studies of less known men chosen for the light they might shed on the Navy, such as a volume on Josephus Daniels's bureau chiefs. Of the tools for further study, perhaps none would be more welcome than a fine biographical dictionary and a factual encyclopedia of American naval history.

I wish to thank the librarians of the Navy Department Library for their generous assistance during the preparation of this chapter and bibliography.

BIBLIOGRAPHY

1. Abbazia, Patrick. "Mr. Roosevelt's Navy: The Little War of the United States Atlantic Fleet, 1939-1942." Doctoral dissertation, Columbia University, 1972.
2. Albion, Robert G. "The Administration of the Navy, 1798-1945," *Public Administration Review* (Chicago), V (Autumn, 1945), 293-302.
3. Albion, Robert G. "Distant Stations." *U.S. Naval Institute Proceedings*, LXXX (March, 1954), 265-273.
4. Albion, Robert G. "Makers of Naval Policy, 1798-1947." Washington: Office of Naval History, 1950. Microfilm copy available from the Widener Library, Harvard University.
5. Albion, Robert G. "The Naval Affairs Committees, 1916-1947." *U.S. Naval Institute Proceedings*, LXXVIII (November 1952), 1227-1239.
6. Albion, Robert G. and Robert H. Connery. *Forrestal and the Navy*. New York: Columbia University Press, 1962.
7. Albion, Robert G. and Jennie B. Pope. *Sea Lanes in Wartime: The American Experience, 1775-1945*. Hamden, Connecticut: Archon Books, 1968.
8. Alden, Caroll S. "American Submarine Operations in the War." *U.S. Naval Institute Proceedings*, XLVI (June 1920), 811-850, (July 1920), 1013-1048.
9. Alden, John D. *Flush Decks and Four Pipes*. Annapolis: U.S. Naval Institute, 1965.
10. Alden, John D., Ed Holm, and Arthur D. Baker. *The American Steel Navy*. Annapolis: U.S. Naval Institute, 1972.
11. Allard, Dean C. "The Influence of the United States Navy Upon the American Steel Industry, 1880-1900." Master's thesis, Georgetown University, 1959.
12. Allard, Dean C. "Submarine Qualification." Typescript in the Navy Department Library.
13. Allard, Dean C., and Betty Bern. *U.S. Naval History Sources in the Washington Area and Suggested Research Subjects*. Washington: Naval History Division, 1970.
14. American Iron and Steel Association. *History of the Manufacture of Armor Plate for the United States Navy*. Philadelphia: The Association, 1899.
15. Anderson, Frank F. *Submarines, Submariners, Submarining: A Checklist of Submarine Books in the English Language, Principally of the Twentieth Century*. Hamden, Connecticut: Shoe String Press, 1963.
15a. Anderson, Frank F. *Submarines, Diving and the Underwater World*. Hamden, Connecticut: Archon Books, 1975.
16. Arpee, Edward. *From Frigates to Flat Tops: The Story of the Life and Achievements of Rear Admiral William Alger Moffett, U.S.N.* Lake Forest, Illinois: The author, 1953.
17. Arthur, Reginald Wright. *Contact! Careers of U.S. Naval Aviators*

Assigned Numbers 1 to 2000. Washington: Naval Aviation Register, 1967.

18. Asada, Sadao, "Japan and the United States, 1915-1925." Doctoral dissertation, Yale University, 1965.
19. Asada, Sadao. "The Japanese Navy and the United States," in Dorothy Borg and Shumpei Okamoto, *Pearl Harbor as History: Japanese-American Relations, 1931-1941*. New York: Columbia University Press, 1974.
20. Azoy, Anastacio. *Signal 250! The Sea Fight Off Santiago*. New York: David McKay, 1964.
21. Bailey, Thomas A. "Dewey and the Germans at Manila Bay," *American Historical Review*, XLV (October, 1939), 59-81.
22. Bailey, Thomas A. *Theodore Roosevelt and the Japanese-American Crises: An Account of the International Complications Arising from the Race Problem on the Pacific Coast*. Stanford: Stanford University Press, 1934.
23. Barker, Albert S. *Everyday Life in the Navy: Autobiography of Rear Admiral Albert S. Barker*. Boston: R. G. Badger, 1928.
24. Barnes, Robert H. *United States Submarines*. New Haven: H. F. Morse, 1944.
25. Bates, James L. *The Origins of Teapot Dome: Progressives, Parties, and Petroleum, 1909-1921*. Urbana: University of Illinois Press, 1973.
26. Beale, Howard K. *Theodore Roosevelt and the Rise of American World Power*. Baltimore: Johns Hopkins Press, 1956.
27. Beard, Charles A. *The Navy: Defense or Portent?* New York: Harper, 1932.
28. Beers, Henry P. *American Naval Occupation and Government of Guam, 1898-1902*. Washington: Navy Department, Administrative Reference Service Report No. 6. 1944.
29. Beers, Henry P. "The Bureau of Navigation, 1862-1942," *American Archivist*, VI (1943), 212-215.
30. Beers, Henry P. "The Development of the Office of the Chief of Naval Operations," *Military Affairs*, X (Spring and Fall, 1947), 40-68, 10-38, XI (Summer and Winter, 1947), 88-99, 229-237.
31. Beers, Henry P. "Historical Sketch of the Bureau of Equipment." Typescript. In Navy Department Library.
32. Beers, Henry P. "Historical Sketch of the Office of the Judge Advocate General, Navy Department," *U.S. Naval Institute Proceedings*, LXVII (May, 1941), 670-674.
33. Beers, Henry P. *U.S. Naval Forces in Northern Russia (Archangel and Murmansk), 1918-1919*. Washington: Navy Department, Administrative Reference Service Report No. 5. 1943.
34. Beers, Henry P. *U.S. Naval Port Officers in the Bordeaux Region, 1917-1919*. Washington: Navy Department, Administrative Reference Service Report No. 3. 1943.
35. Belknap, Reginald R. *The Yankee Mining Squadron*. Annapolis: U.S. Naval Institute, 1920.
36. Bennett, Frank M. *The Steam Navy of the United States*. Pittsburgh: Warren, 1896.

37. Bloomfield, Howard V. L. *The Compact History of the United Coast Guard.* New York: Hawthorn Books, 1966.
38. Borg, Dorothy. *The United States and the Far Eastern Crisis, 1933-1938.* Cambridge: Harvard University Press, 1964.
39. Bowen, Harold G. *Ships, Machinery and Mossbacks: The Autobiography of a Naval Engineer,* Princeton: Princeton University Press, 1954.
40. Braisted, William R. *The United States Navy in the Pacific, 1897-1909.* Austin: University of Texas Press, 1958.
41. Braisted, William R. *The United States Navy in the Pacific, 1909-1922.* Austin: University of Texas Press, 1972.
42. Brode, Michael J. "Anglo-American Relations and the Geneva Disarmament Conference of 1927." Doctoral dissertation, University of Alberta, 1972.
43. Brodie, Bernard. *A Layman's Guide to Naval Strategy.* Princeton: Princeton University Press, 1944.
44. Brodie, Bernard. *Sea Power in the Machine Age.* Princeton: Princeton University Press, 1941.
45. Brooks, Edward H. "The National Defense Policy of the Wilson Administration, 1913-1917." Doctoral dissertation, Stanford University, 1950.
46. Buckley, Thomas H. *The United States and the Washington Conference, 1921-1922.* Knoxville: University of Tennessee, 1970.
47. Buell, Raymond Leslie. *The Washington Conference.* New York: D. Appleton, 1922.
48. Butler, Jarvis. "The General Board of the Navy," *U.S. Naval Institute Proceedings,* LVI (August, 1930), 700-705.
49. Buzanski, Peter M. "Admiral Mark L. Bristol and Turkish-American Relations, 1919-1922." Doctoral dissertation, University of California, 1960.
50. Byrd, Richard E. *Alone.* New York: G. P. Putnam's, 1938.
51. Byrd, Richard E. *Discovery: The Story of the Second Byrd Antarctic Expedition.* New York: G. P. Putnam's, 1935.
52. Byrd, Richard E. *Little America, Aerial Exploration in Antartica, the Flight to the South Pole.* New York: G. P. Putnam's, 1930.
53. Byrd, Richard E. *Skyward: Man's Mastery of the Air Shown by the Brilliant Flights of America's Leading Air Explorer.* New York: G. P. Putnam's, 1928.
54. Bywater, Hector. *The Great Pacific War: A History of the American-Japanese Campaign, 1931-1933.* Boston: Houghton-Mifflin, 1932.
55. Bywater, Hector. *Sea Power in the Pacific: A Study of the American-Japanese Naval Problem.* New York: Constable, 1934.
56. Cable, Frank T. *The Birth and Development of the American Submarine.* New York: Harper, 1924.
57. Capron, Walter C. *The U.S. Coast Guard.* New York: Franklin Watts, 1965.
58. Carter, Samuel. *The Incredible Great White Fleet.* New York: Crowell-Collier, 1970.
59. Catlin, Albertus W. *"With the Help of God and a Few Marines."* Garden City: Doubleday, Page, 1919.

60. Chadwick, French Ensor. *The Relations of the United States and Spain: The Spanish-American War.* New York: Charles Scribner's, 1911. 2 vols.

61. Challener, Richard D. *Admirals, Generals, and American Foreign Policy, 1898-1914.* Princeton: Princeton University Press, 1973.

62. Christian, Albert B. *History of the Naval Weapons Center, China Lake, California.* Volume I. *Sailors, Scientists, and Rockets: Origins of the Navy Rocket Program and the Naval Ordnance Test Station, Inyokern.* Washington: Naval History Division, 1971.

63. Clark, Charles E. *My Fifty Years in the Navy.* Boston: Little, Brown, 1917.

64. Clark, Joseph James. *Carrier Admiral.* New York: D. McKay, 1967.

65. Clark, William B. *When the U-Boats Came to America.* Boston: Little, Brown, 1929.

66. Clephane, Lewis P. *History of the Naval Overseas Transportation Service in World War I.* Washington: Naval History Division, 1969.

67. Clinard, Outten J. *Japan's Influence on American Naval Power, 1897-1917.* Berkeley: University of California Press, 1947.

68. Cline, Ray S. *Washington Command Post: The Operations Division.* Washington: Department of the Army, 1951.

69. Coady, Joseph W. "Franklin D. Roosevelt's Early Washington Years, 1913-1920." Doctoral dissertation, St. John's University, 1968.

70. Condit, Kenneth W., and Edwin T. Turnblat. *Hold High the Torch: A History of the 4th Marines.* Washington: Historical Branch G-3, Division Headquarters, U.S. Marine Corps, 1960.

71. Conn, Stetson, and Bryan Fairchild. *The Framework of Hemisphere Defense.* Washington: Department of the Army, 1960.

72. Connery, Robert H. *The Navy and the Industrial Mobilization in World War II.* Princeton: Princeton University Press, 1951.

73. Conroy, Robert. *The Battle of Manila Bay: The Spanish-American War in the Philippines.* New York: Macmillan, 1968.

74. Cooling, B. Franklin. *Benjamin Franklin Tracy: Father of the American Navy.* Hamden, Connecticut: Archon Books, 1973.

75. Coontz, Robert E. *From Mississippi to the Sea.* Philadelphia: Dorrance, 1930.

76. Costello, Daniel J. "Planning for War: A History of the General Board of the Navy, 1900-1914." Doctoral dissertation: Fletcher School of Law and Diplomacy, 1969.

77. Cronon, E. David, ed. *The Cabinet Diaries of Josephus Daniels, 1913-1921.* Lincon: University of Nebraska Press, 1963.

78. Cummings, Damon E. *Admiral Richard Wainwright and the United States Fleet.* Washington: G. P. O., 1962.

79. Cummins, Lejeune. *Quijote on a Burro: Sandino and the Marines, a Study of the Formulation of Foreign Policy.* Berkeley: The author, 1958.

80. Daniels, Jonathan. *The End of Innocence.* New York: J. B. Lippincott, 1954.

81. Daniels, Josephus. "Fuel Oil for the Navy," *Journal of the American Society of Naval Engineers*, XXXIII (February 1921), 60-63.

82. Daniels, Josephus. *Our Navy at War.* Washington: Pictorial Bureau, 1922.
83. Daniels, Josephus. *The Wilson Era: Years of Peace, 1910-1917.* Chapel Hill: University of North Carolina Press, 1944.
84. Daniels, Josephus. *The Wilson Era: Years of War and After, 1917-1921.* Chapel Hill: University of North Carolina Press, 1956.
85. Davidonis, Anthony C. *The American Naval Mission in the Adriatic, 1918-1921.* Washington: Navy Department, Administrative Reference Service Report No. 4. 1943.
86. Davis, George T. *A Navy Second to None: The Development of Modern American Naval Policy.* New York: Harcourt, Brace, 1940.
87. Davis, Vincent. *The Admirals' Lobby.* Chapel Hill: University of North Carolina Press, 1967.
88. De Novo, John A. "Petroleum in the United States Navy before World War I." *Mississippi Valley Historical Review,* XLI (July, 1956), 854-876.
89. Dewey, George. *The Autobiography of George Dewey, Admiral of the Navy.* New York: Charles Scribner's, 1913.
90. Dingman, Roger V. "Power in the Pacific: The Evolution of American and Japanese Naval Policies." Doctoral dissertation, Harvard University Press, 1969.
91. Douglas, Lawrence. "Submarine Disarmament, 1919-1935." Doctoral dissertation, Syracuse University, 1970.
92. Drury, Clifford M. *The History of the Chaplain Corps, United States Navy.* 6 vols. Washington: G. P. O., 1949-1960.
93. Duncan, Robert C. *American Use of Submarine Mines.* Silver Spring: United States Ordnance Laboratory, 1962.
94. Dyer, George C. *The Amphibians Came to Conquer: The Story of Admiral Richmond Kelley Turner.* Washington: G. P. O., 1972. 2 vols.
95. Ellinger, Werner B., and Herbert Rosinski. *Sea Power in the Pacific: A Bibliography.* Princeton: Princeton University Press, 1942.
96. Enders, Calvin W. "The Vinson Navy." Doctoral dissertation, Michigan State University, 1970.
97. Evans, Holden A. *One Man's Fight for a Better Navy.* New York: Dodd Mead, 1940.
98. Evans, Luther H. *The Virgin Islands from Naval Base to New Deal.* Ann Arbor: J. W. Edwards, 1945.
99. Evans, Robley D. *An Admiral's Log.* New York: D. Appleton, 1910.
100. Evans, Robley D. *A Sailor's Log: Recollections of Forty Years of Naval Life.* New York: D. Appleton, 1910.
101. Evans, Stephen H. *The United States Coast Guard, 1790-1915: A Definitive History.* Annapolis: United States Naval Institute, 1949.
102. Falk, Edwin. *Fighting Bob Evans.* New York: J. Cape and H. Smith, 1931.
103. Farago, Ladislas. *The Broken Seal: The Story of "Operation Magic" and the Pearl Harbor Disaster.* New York: Random House, 1970.
104. Fiske, Bradley A. *From Midshipman to Rear Admiral.* New York: Century, 1919.

105. Fiske, Bradley A. *The Navy as a Fighting Machine.* New York: Charles Scribner's, 1916.
106. Freidel, Frank B. *Franklin D. Roosevelt.* Boston: Little, Brown, 1952. 3 vols.
107. Freidel, Frank B. *The Splendid Little War.* Boston: Little, Brown, 1958.
108. Frost, Holloway H. *On a Destroyer's Bridge.* Annapolis: U.S. Naval Institute, 1930.
109. Frothingham, Thomas G. *The Naval History of the World War.* Cambridge: Harvard University Press, 1924-1926. 3 vols.
110. Fuller, Grace H. *A Selected List of References on the Expansion of the United States Navy, 1931-1939.* Washington: G. P. O., 1939.
111. Furer, Julius A. *Administrative History of the Navy Department in World War II.* Washington: G. P. O., 1959.
112. Garrett, Wendell D. "John D. Long, Secretary of the Navy, 1897-1902: A Study in Changing Political Alignments," *New England Quarterly*, XXXI (September, 1958), 291-311.
113. Gibson, Richard H., and Maurice Prendergast. *The German Submarine War, 1914-1918.* New York: Richard R. Smith, 1931.
114. Gilliam, Bates McC. "The World of Captain Mahan." Doctoral dissertation, Princeton University, 1961.
115. Gleaves, Albert L. *A History of the Transport Service: Adventures and Experiences of United States Transports and Cruisers in the World War.* New York: George H. Doran, 1921.
116. Gleaves, Albert L. *The Life of an American Sailor: Rear Admiral William Hemsley Emory.* New York: George H. Doran, 1923.
117. Gleaves, Albert L. *The Life and Letters of Stephen B. Luce, U.S. Navy, Founder of the Naval War College.* New York: G. P. Putnam's, 1925.
118. Goodhart, Philip. *Fifty Ships That Saved the World: The Foundation of the Anglo-American Alliance:* Garden City: Doubleday, 1965.
119. Goodrich, Casper F. *Rope Yarns from the Old Navy.* New York: Naval History Society, 1931.
120. Gray, J. A. C. *Amerika Samoa: A History of American Samoa and Its United States Naval Administration.* Annapolis: U.S. Naval Institute, 1960.
121. Grenville, John A. S. "Diplomacy and War Plans in the United States, 1890-1917." *Royal Historical Society, Transactions.* 5th Ser., II (1961), 1-21.
122. Grenville, John A. S. and George B. Young. *Politics, Strategy, and American Diplomacy: Studies in Foreign Policy.* New Haven: Yale University Press, 1966.
123. Groeling, Dorothy T. "Submarines, Disarmament and Naval Warfare." Doctoral dissertation, Columbia University, 1950.
124. Haight, John McV. "Franklin D. Roosevelt and a Naval Quarantine of Japan," *Pacific Historical Review*, XL (May, 1971), 203-226.
125. Halsey, William F., and J. Bryan. *Admiral Halsey's Story.* New York: McGraw Hill, 1947.
126. Hamer, Philip M. *Guide to Archives and Manuscripts in the United States.* New Haven: Yale University Press, 1961.

127. Hammett, Hugh B. "Hilary Abner Herbert: A Southerner Returns to the Union." Doctoral dissertation, University of Virginia, 1969.
128. Hammond, Paul. Y. *Organizing for Defense: The American Military Establishment in the Twentieth Century.* Princeton: Princeton University Press, 1961.
129. Hancock, Harry E. *Wireless at Sea: The First Fifty Years.* Chelmsford, England: Marconi International Marine Company, 1950.
130. Harris, Brayton. *The Age of the Battleship, 1890-1922: The Watts History of the United States Navy.* New York: Franklin Watts, 1965.
131. Hart, Caroline Brownson and Louise Powers Benesel. *From Frigate to Dreadnought: Willard Herbert Brownson, U.S.N.* Sharon, Connecticut: King House, 1973.
132. Hart, Robert A. *The Great White Fleet: Its Voyage Around the World, 1907-1909.* Boston: Little, Brown, 1956.
133. Hart, Thomas C. "Narrative of Events of Asiatic Fleet and Area Leading Up to World War II and Until 15 February 1942" (with "Supplement"). Unpublished manuscripts, 1942. In U.S. Naval History Division.
134. Hayes, John A. "Stephen B. Luce and the Beginning of the Naval War College," *Naval War College Review,* XXIII (January, 1971), 51-59.
135. Hayes, John D. "The Writings of Stephen B. Luce," *Military Affairs,* XIX (Winter 1955), 187-196.
136. Heffron, Paul T. "Secretary Moody and Naval Administrative Reform, 1902-1904," *American Neptune,* XXIX (January, 1969), 30-48.
137. Heinl, Robert D. *Soldiers of the Sea: The United States Marine Corps, 1775-1962.* Annapolis: U.S. Naval Institute, 1962.
138. Heinrichs, Waldo H., Jr. "The Role of the United States Navy," in Dorothy Borg and Shumpei Okamoto, *Pearl Harbor as History: Japanese-American Relations, 1931-1941.* New York: Columbia University Press, 1974.
139. Herrick, Walter R., Jr. *The American Naval Revolution.* Baton Rouge: Louisiana State University Press, 1966.
140. Herzog, James H. *Closing the Open Door: American Japanese Diplomatic Negotiations, 1936-1941.* Annapolis: U.S. Naval Institute, 1973.
141. Higham, Robin. *Armed Forces in Peacetime, Britain, 1918-1940: A Case Study.* Hamden, Connecticut: Archon Books, 1962.
142. Hilliard, Jack B. and Harold A. Bivins. *An Annotated Reading List of United States Marine Corps History.* Washington: U.S. Marine Historical Division, 1971.
143. Hoag, G. Leonard. *Preface to Preparedness: The Washington Conference and Public Opinion.* Washington: American Council on Public Affairs, 1941.
144. Hobbs, William H. *Peary.* New York: Macmillan, 1936.
145. Howe, M. A. De Wolfe. *George Von Lengerke Meyer.* New York: Dodd, Mead, 1922.
146. Howeth, Linwood S. *History of Communications-Electronics in the United States Navy.* Washington: G. P. O., 1963.

147. Hoyt, Edwin P. *The Last Explorer: The Adventures of Admiral Byrd.* New York: John Day, 1968.
148. Hughes, Thomas P. *Elmer Sperry: Inventor and Engineer.* Baltimore: Johns Hopkins Press, 1971.
149. Huntington, Samuel P. *The Soldier and the State: The Theory and Politics of Civil Military Relations.* Cambridge: Harvard University Press, 1957.
150. Icenhower, Joseph B. *The Panay Incident, December 12, 1937: The Sinking of an American Gunboat Worsens U.S. Japanese Relations.* New York: Franklin Watts, 1971.
151. Ichihashi, Yamato. *The Washington Conference and After.* Stanford University Press, 1928.
152. James, Henry J. *German Subs in Yankee Waters.* New York: Gotham House, 1940.
153. Jenkins, Innis L. "Josephus Daniels and the Navy Department, 1913-1916: A Study of Military Administration." Doctoral dissertation, University of Maryland, 1960.
154. Johnson, Alfred W. "A Brief History of the Organization of the Navy Department." Washington: Army Industrial College, 1933.
155. Johnson, Robert E. *Thence Round Cape Horn: The Story of United States Naval Forces on Pacific Station, 1818-1923.* Annapolis: U.S. Naval Institute, 1963.
156. Kahn, David. *The Codebreakers.* New York: Macmillan, 1967.
157. Karston, Peter. *The Naval Aristocracy: The Golden Age of Annapolis and the Emergence of Modern American Navalism.* New York: Free Press, 1972.
158. Keller, Allan. *The Spanish-American War: A Compact History.* New York: Hawthorn Books, 1969.
159. Kennedy, Thomas C. "Charles A. Beard and 'the Big Navy Boys,' " *Military Affairs*, XXXI (Summer 1967), 65-84.
160. King, Ernest J. and Walter Muir Whitehill. *Fleet Admiral King: A Naval Record.* New York: W. W. Norton, 1952.
161. Kitchans, Joseph H., Jr. "The Shearer Scandal and Its Origins: Big Navy Politics and Diplomacy in the 1920s." Doctoral dissertation, University of Georgia, 1969.
162. Kittredge, Tracy B. "Historical Monograph: U.S.-British Naval Cooperation, 1940-1945." Unpublished manuscript. In U.S. Naval History Division.
163. Kittredge, Tracy B. *Naval Lessons of the Great War.* Garden City: Doubleday, Page, 1921.
164. Knight, Austin M. and William D. Puleston. "History of the U.S. Naval War College." Unpublished manuscript. In Naval War College Library.
165. Knox, Dudley W. *The Eclipse of American Sea Power.* New York: Army and Navy Journal, 1922.
166. Knox, Dudley W. *A History of the United States Navy.* New York: G. P. Putnam's Sons, 1948.
167. Koginos, Maury T. *The Panay Incident: Prelude to War.* Lafayette, Indiana: Purdue University Studies, 1967.
168. Kreh, William R. *Citizen Sailors: The U.S. Naval Reserve in War and Peace.* New York: David McKay, 1969.

169. LaFeber, Walter. *The New American Empire: An Interpretation of American Expansion, 1860-1898.* Ithaca: Cornell University Press, 1963.
170. Laing, E. A. M. "Admiral Dewey and the Foreign Warships at Manila, 1898," *Mariner's Mirror*, LII (May, 1966), 167-171.
171. Lake, Simon. *The Submarine in War and Peace.* Philadelphia: J. B. Lippincott, 1918.
172. Lake, Simon. *Submarine: The Autobiography of Simon Lake, As Told to Herbert Corey.* New York: D. Appleton, 1938.
173. Land, Emory S. *Winning the War with Ships: Land, Sea and Air— Mostly Land.* New York: Robert M. McBride, 1958.
174. Langer, William L. and S. Everett Gleason. *The Challenge to Isolation, 1937-1940.* New York: Harper, 1937.
175. Langer, William L. and S. Everett Gleason. *The Undeclared War, 1940-1941.* London: Royal Institute of International Affairs, 1953.
176. Lanning, Harris. "An Admiral's Yarn." Typescript from Princeton University Library. 2 vols.
177. Lea, Homer. *The Valor of Ignorance.* New York: Harper, 1909.
178. Leech, Margaret. *In the Days of McKinley.* New York: Harper, 1959.
179. Leighton, John L. *Simsadus: London, The American Navy in Europe.* New York: H. Holt, 1920.
180. Lejeune, John A. *The Reminiscences of a Marine.* Philadelphia: Dorrance, 1930.
181. Leutze, James R. "If Britain Should Fall: Roosevelt and Churchill and Anglo-American Naval Relations, 1938-1940." Doctoral dissertation, Duke University, 1970.
182. Levine, Robert H. "The Politics of American Naval Rearmament, 1930-1938." Doctoral dissertation, Harvard University, 1972.
183. Lewis, David D. *The Fight for the Sea: The Past, Present, and Future of Submarine Warfare in the Atlantic.* Cleveland: World, 1966.
184. Lindley, Ernest K. *Franklin D. Roosevelt: A Career in Progressive Democracy.* Indianapolis: Bobbs-Merrill, 1931.
185. Link, Arthur S. *Woodrow Wilson.* Princeton: Princeton University Press, 1947- . 6 vols. to date.
186. Link, Arthur S. *Woodrow Wilson and the Progressive Era, 1910-1918.* New York: Harper, 1953.
187. Livermore, Seward W. "American Naval Development, 1898-1914, with Special Reference to Foreign Affairs." Doctoral dissertation: Harvard University, 1944.
188. Livermore, Seward W. "The American Navy as a Factor in World Politics, 1903-1913," *American Historical Review*, LXIII, (June 1958), 863-880.
189. Livermore, Seward W. "American Strategy Diplomacy in the South Pacific, 1890-1914," *Pacific Historical Review*, XII (February 1943), 33-51.
190. Livermore, Seward W. "Battleship Diplomacy in South America, 1905-1925," *Journal of Modern History*, XVI (March 1944), 31-48.
191. Livermore, Seward W. "Theodore Roosevelt, the American Navy, and the Venezuelan Crisis of 1902-1903," *American Historical Review*, LI (April, 1946), 452-471.

192. Livezey, William E. *Mahan on Sea Power*. Norman: University of Oklahoma Press, 1947.
193. Lockwood, Charles A. *Down to the Sea in Subs*. New York: Norton, 1967.
194. Lockwood, Charles A. and Hans C. Adamson. *The Tragedy at Honda*. Philadelphia: Chilton, 1960.
194. Long, John D. *The New American Navy*. New York: Outlook, 1903.
195. Long, John D. *Papers of John Davis Long, 1897-1904*. Edited by Gardner A. Allen. Boston: Massachusetts Historical Society, 1939.
197. Long, Margaret, ed. *The Journal of John D. Long*. Rindge, New Hampshire: Richard R. Smith, 1932.
198. Lott, Arnold S. *A Long Line of Ships: Mare Island's Centenary of Naval Activity in California*. Annapolis: U.S. Naval Institute, 1954.
199. Macaulay, Neill. *The Sandino Affair*. Chicago: Quadrangle Books, 1967.
200. McClellan, Edwin N. *The United States Marine Corps in the World War*. Washington: G. P. O., 1920.
201. McCrocklin, James H. *Garde D'Haiti: Twenty Years of Organization and Training by the U.S. Marine Corps*. Annapolis: U.S. Naval Institute, 1956.
202. MacDonald, Scot. *Evolution of Aircraft Carriers*. Washington: G. P. O., 1964.
203. McKenna, Richard. *The Sand Pebbles*. New York: Harper & Row, 1950.
204. Mahan, Alfred Thayer. *From Sail to Steam: Recollections of a Naval Life*. New York: Harper, 1907.
205. Mahan, Alfred Thayer. *The Influence of Sea Power Upon History, 1660-1783*. Boston: Little, Brown, 1890.
206. Mahan, Alfred Thayer. *Lessons of the War with Spain and Other Articles*. Boston: Little, Brown, 1899.
207. Mahan, Alfred Thayer. *Naval Administration and Warfare: Some General Principles with Other Essays*. Boston: Little, Brown, 1908.
208. Mahan, Alfred Thayer. *Naval Strategy, Compared and Contrasted with the Principles of Military Operations on Land*. Boston: Little, Brown, 1911.
209. Mahan, Alfred Thayer. *The Problem of Asia and Its Effect on International Policies*. Boston: Little, Brown, 1900.
210. Marder, Arthur J. *The Anatomy of British Sea Power*. New York: Alfred A. Knopf, 1940.
211. Marder, Arthur J. *From the Dreadnought to Scapa Flow*. London: Oxford University Press, 1961-1970. 5 vols.
212. Matloff, Maurice and Edwin M. Snell. *Strategic Planning for Coalition War, 1941-1942*. Washington: Department of the Army, 1953.
213. Matthews, Franklin. *Back to Hampton Roads: Cruise of the U.S. Atlantic Fleet from San Francisco to Hampton Roads, July 7, 1908-February 22, 1909*. New York: B. W. Huebsch, 1909.
214. Matthews, Franklin. *With the Battle Fleet: Cruise of the Sixteen Battleships of the United States Atlantic Fleet from Hampton Roads to the Golden Gate, December 1907-May 1908*. New York: B. W. Huebsch, 1908.

215. May, Ernest R. *The Ultimate Decision: The President as Commander-in-Chief.* New York: G. Brazillier, 1960.
216. Mayer-Oakes, Thomas Francis. *Fragile Victory: Prince Sainonji and the 1930 London Treaty Issue from the Memoirs of Baron Harada Kumao.* Detroit: Wayne University Press, 1968.
217. Megee, Vernon E. *United States Military Intervention in Nicaragua, 1909-1932.* Master's thesis, University of Texas at Austin, 1963.
218. Metcalf, Clyde H. *A History of the United States Marine Corps.* New York: G. P. Putnam's, 1939.
219. Millett, Allan R., and B. Franklin Cooling, III. *Doctoral Dissertations in Military Affairs: A Bibliography.* Manhattan: Kansas State University Library, 1973.
220. Millholland, Ray. *The Splinter Fleet at the Otranto Barrage.* New York: Bobbs-Merrill, 1936.
221. Millis, Walter. *Arms and Men: A Study in American Military History.* New York: G. P. Putnam's, 1956.
222. Millis, Walter. *The Martial Spirit: A Study of Our War with Spain.* Boston: Houghton Mifflin, 1936.
223. Mitchell, Donald W. *History of the Modern American Navy, from 1883 through Pearl Harbor.* New York: Alfred A. Knopf, 1946.
224. Moran, John B. *Creating a Legend: The Descriptive Catalog of Writing About the U.S. Marine Corps.* Chicago: Moran Andrews, 1973.
225. Morgan, H. Wayne. *William McKinley and His America.* Syracuse: Syracuse University Press, 1963.
226. Morison, Elting E. *Admiral Sims and the Modern American Navy.* Boston: Houghton Mifflin, 1942.
227. Morison, Elting E. "Naval Administration in the United States," *U.S. Naval Institute Proceedings,* LXXII (October 1946), 1303-1313.
228. Morison, Elting E. "Naval Administration: Selected Documents on Navy Department Organization, 1915-1940." Typescript, 1945. In Navy Department Library.
229. Morison, Elting E., ed. *The Letters of Theodore Roosevelt.* Cambridge: Harvard University Press, 1951-1954. 8 vols.
230. Morison, Samuel E. *History of United States Naval Operations in World War II.* Vol. I. *The Battle of the Atlantic, September 1939-May 1943.* Boston: Little, Brown, 1947.
231. Morison, Samuel E. *History of United States Naval Operations in World War II.* Vol. III. *The Rising Sun in the Pacific, 1931-April 1942.* Boston: Little, Brown, 1948.
232. Morris, Richard K. *John P. Holland, 1841-1941: Inventor of the Modern Submarine.* Annapolis: U.S. Naval Institute, 1966.
233. Morrison, Joseph L. *Josephus Daniels: The Small-d Democrat.* Chapel Hill: University of North Carolina Press, 1966.
234. Morton, Louis, "Army and Marines on the China Station: A Study of Military and Political Rivalry," *Pacific Historical Review,* XXIX (February 1960), 51-73.
235. Morton, Louis. *Strategy and Command: The First Two Years.* Washington: Department of the Army, 1962.
236. Morton, Louis. "War Plan Orange: Evolution of a Strategy," *World Politics.* XI (January 1959), 225-250.

237. Nalty, Bernard C. *The United States Marines in Nicaragua.* Marine Corps Historical Reference Series No. 21. Washington: Marine Historical Division Hq., 1962.
238. National Research Council. Committee on Undersea Warfare. *An Annotated Bibliography of Submarine Technical Literature, 1557-1953.* Washington: The Council, 1954.
239. Naval Historical Foundation. *Manuscript Collection: A Catalogue.* Washington: Library of Congress, 1974.
240. Neeser, Robert W. *Statistical and Chronological History of the United States Navy, 1775-1907.* New York: Macmillan, 1909. 2 vols.
241. Neu, Charles E. *An Uncertain Friendship: Theodore Roosevelt and Japan, 1906-1909.* Cambridge: Harvard University Press, 1967.
242. Neuhaus, Herbert M. "Fifty Years of Naval Engineering," *American Society of Naval Engineers Journal,* L (August 1938), 341-380.
243. Niblack, Albert P. "Operations of the Navy and the Marine Corps in the Philippine Archipelago, 1898-1902," *U.S. Naval Institute Proceedings,* XXX (December 1904), 745-753; XXXI (June 1905), 463-464, (September 1905), 698.
244. Nutting, William W. *The Cinderellas of the Fleet.* Jersey City: Standard Motor Construction Company, 1920.
245. O'Connor, Raymond G. *Perilous Equilibrium: The United States and the London Naval Conference of 1930.* Lawrence: University of Kansas Press, 1962.
246. O'Gara, Gordon C. *Theodore Roosevelt and the Rise of the Modern Navy.* Princeton: Princeton University Press, 1943.
247. Paine, Ralph D. *The First Yale Unit: A Story of Naval Aviation, 1916-1919.* Cambridge: Riverside, 1925. 2 vols.
248. Paine, Thomas O. *Submarining: Three Thousand Books and Articles.* Santa Barbara, California: General Electric Co.-TEMPO, Center for Advanced Studies, 1971.
249. Pater, Alan F. *United States Battleships: The History of America's Greatest Fighting Fleet.* Beverly Hills: Monitor, 1968.
250. Paullin, Charles Oscar. *Paullin's History of Naval Administration, 1775-1911: A Collection of Articles from the U.S. Naval Institute Proceedings.* Annapolis: U.S. Naval Institute, 1968.
251. Pawlowski, Gareth L. *Flat-Tops and Fledglings: A History of American Aircraft Carriers.* South Brunswick, New Jersey: A. S. Barnes, 1971.
252. Paxson, Frederic L. "The Naval Station at Alameda, 1916-1940: A Case Study in the Aptitude of Democracy for Defense," *Pacific Historical Review,* XIII (September 1944), 235-250.
253. Peary, Robert E. *The North Pole: Its Discovery in 1909 by the Peary Arctic Club.* New York: Frederick A. Stokes, 1910.
254. Peck, Taylor. *Round-Shot to Rockets: The Story of the Washington Navy Yard and Naval Gun Factory.* Annapolis: U.S. Naval Institute, 1949.
255. Pels, Stephen E. *The Race to Pearl Harbor.* Cambridge: Harvard University Press, 1974.
256. Perry, Hamilton D. *The Panay Incident: A Prelude to Pearl Harbor.* New York: Macmillan, 1969.

257. Polmar, Norman, Minoru Genda, Eric M. Brown, and Robert M. Langdon. *Aircraft Carriers: A Graphic History of Carrier Aviation.* Garden City: Doubleday, 1969.
258. Pomeroy, Earl S. *Pacific Outpost: American Strategy in Guam and Micronesia.* Stanford: Stanford University Press, 1951.
259. Potter, David. *Sailing the Sulu Seas: Belles and Bandits in the Philippines.* New York: E. P. Dutton, 1930.
260. Potter, Elmer B., and Chester W. Nimitz. *Sea Power: A Naval History.* Englewood Cliffs, New Jersey: Prentice-Hall, 1960.
261. Potter, John D. *Yamamoto: The Man Who Menaced America.* New York: Viking, 1965.
262. Pratt, Fletcher. *The Compact History of the United States Navy.* New York: Hawthorn Books, 1962.
263. Pratt, Julius W. *America's Colonial Experiment: How the United States Gained, Governed, and In Part Gave Away a Colonial Empire.* New York: Prentice-Hall, 1950.
264. Pratt, Julius W. *The Expansionists of 1898.* Baltimore: Johns Hopkins Press, 1925.
265. Pratt, Lawrence. "Anglo-American Naval Conversations on the Far East of January, 1938," *International Affairs,* XLVII (October 1972), 745-763.
266. Pringle, Henry F. *Theodore Roosevelt: A Biography.* New York: Harcourt, Brace, 1931.
267. Puleston, William D. *Mahan: The Life and Work of Captain Alfred Thayer Mahan.* New Haven: Yale University Press, 1939.
268. Pusey, Merlo J. *Charles Evans Hughes.* New York: Macmillan, 1951. 2 vols.
269. Quinlin, Robert J. "The United States Fleet: Diplomacy, Strategy and the Allocation of Ships (1940-1941)" in Harold Stein, *American Civil-Military Decisions: A Book of Case Studies.* Birmingham: University of Alabama Press, 1963.
270. Ragland, Reginald. *A History of the Naval Petroleum Reserves and of the Development of the Present National Policy Toward Them.* Los Angeles: The author, 1944.
271. Rappaport, Armin. *The Navy League of the United States.* Detroit: Wayne State University Press, 1962.
272. Rawlins, Dennis. "Peary and the North Pole: The Lingering Doubt," *U.S. Naval Institute Proceedings,* XCVI (June 1970), 32-41.
273. Ray, Thomas W. "The Bureaus Go On Forever," *U.S. Naval Institute Proceedings,* XCIV (January 1968), 50-63.
274. Reagen, Michael D. "The Far Eastern Crisis of 1931-1932: Stimson, Hoover and the Armed Services," in Harold Stein, *American Civil-Military Decisions: A Book of Case Studies.* Birmingham: University of Alabama Press, 1963.
275. Remey, George C. "Life and Letters of Rear Admiral George Collier Remey, United States Navy, 1841-1928." Edited by Charles M. Remey. Typescript. Washington, 1939. 10 vols.
276. Reynolds, Clark G. *The Fast Carriers: Forging of an Air Navy.* New York: McGraw-Hill, 1968.
277. Richardson, James O. *On the Treadmill to Pearl Harbor: The*

Memoirs of Admiral James O. Richardson, U.S.N. (Retired) as Told to Vice Admiral George C. Dyer, U.S.N. (Retired) Washington: Naval History Division, 1973.

278. Rodman, Hugh. Yarns of a Kentucky Admiral. Indianapolis: Bobbs-Merrill, 1928.

279. Roscoe, Theodore. On the Seas and in the Skies: A History of the U.S. Navy's Air Power. New York: Hawthorn Books, 1970.

280. Rose, Harold W. Brittany Patrol: The Story of the Suicide Fleet. New York: W. W. Norton, 1937.

281. Roseberry, Cecil R. Glenn Curtis: Pioneer of Flight. Garden City: Doubleday, 1972.

282. Rosendahl, Charles E. Up Ship! New York: Dodd, Mead, 1932.

283. Rosendahl, Charles E. What About the Airship? The Challenge to the United States. New York: Charles Scribner's, 1938.

284. Roskill, Stephen W. Naval Policy between the Wars. Vol. I. The Period of Anglo-American Antagonism, 1919-1929. London: Collins, 1968.

285. Sampson, William T. "The Atlantic Fleet in the Spanish-American War," Century Magazine, LVII (April 1899), 886-913.

286. Sargent, Nathan. Admiral Dewey and the Manila Campaign. Washington: Naval Historical Foundation, 1947.

287. Sawyer, Frederick L. Sons of Gunboats. Annapolis: U.S. Naval Institute, 1946.

288. Schilling, Warner R. "Admirals and Foreign Policy, 1913-1919." Doctoral dissertation, Yale University, 1953.

289. Schley, Winfield S. Fifty-Five Years Under the Flag. New York: D. Appleton, 1904.

290. Schofield, William G. Destroyers, 60 Years. New York: Rand McNally, 1962.

291. Schroeder, Peter B. Contact at Sea: A History of Maritime Radio Communications. Ridgewood, New Jersey: Gregg Press, 1967.

292. Schroeder, Seaton. A Half Century of Naval Service. New York: D. Appleton, 1922.

293. Scott, Lloyd N. Naval Consulting Board of the United States. Washington: G. P. O., 1920.

294. Seager, Robert. "Ten Years before Mahan: The Unofficial Case for the New Navy, 1880-1890," Mississippi Valley Historical Review, XL (December 1953), 491-512.

295. Sigsbee, Charles D. The "Maine": An Account of Her Destruction in Havana Harbor. New York: Century, 1899.

296. Silverstone, Paul H. U.S. Warships of World War I. Garden City: Doubleday, 1970.

297. Sims, William S. and Burton J. Hendrick. The Victory at Sea. New York: Doubleday, Page, 1920.

298. Smith, Richard K. The Airships Akron & Macon: Flying Aircraft Carriers of the United States Navy. Annapolis: U.S. Naval Institute, 1965.

299. Smith, Richard K. First Across! The U.S. Navy's Transatlantic Flight of 1919. Annapolis: U.S. Naval Institute, 1973.

300. Snowbarger, Willis E. "The Development of Pearl Harbor." Doctoral dissertation, University of California, Berkeley, 1950.

301. Society of Naval Architects and Marine Engineers. *Historical Transactions, 1893-1943.* New York: The Society, 1943.
302. Spector, Ronald H. *Admiral of the New Empire: A Study of the Life and Career of George Dewey.* Baton Rouge: Louisiana State University Press, 1974.
303. Spector, Ronald H. " 'Professors at War', the Naval War College and the Modern American Navy." Doctoral dissertation, Yale University, 1967.
304. Sprout, Harold and Margaret. *The Rise of American Naval Power, 1776-1918.* Princeton: Princeton University Press, 1946.
305. Sprout, Harold and Margaret. *Toward a New Order of Sea Power.* Princeton: Princeton University Press, 1946.
306. Sprout, Margaret. "Mahan: Evangelist of Sea Power," in Edward Mead Earle, *Makers of Modern Strategy.* Princeton: Princeton University Press, 1943.
307. Stafford, Edward P. *The Far and the Deep.* New York: G. P. Putnam's, 1967.
308. Standley, William H. and Arthur A. Ageton. *Admiral Ambassador to Russia.* Chicago: H. Regenery, 1955.
309. Stillson, Albert C. "The Development and Maintenance of the American Naval Establishment, 1901-1909." Ph.D. dissertation, Columbia University, 1959.
310. Stillson, Albert C. "Military Policy without Political Guidance: Theodore Roosevelt's Navy," *Military Affairs,* XXV (Spring 1961), 18-31.
311. Stirling, Yates. *Sea Duty.* New York: G. P. Putnam's, 1939.
312. Strobridge, Truman R. *United States Coast Guard: Annotated Bibliography.* Washington: U.S. Coast Guard, 1972.
313. Studer, Clara. *Sky Storming Yankee: The Life of Glenn Curtiss.* New York: Stackpole, 1937.
314. Sutphen, Harold J. "Anglo-American Destroyer Bases Agreement, September 1940." Doctoral dissertation, Fletcher School of Law and Diplomacy, 1967.
315. Swanborough, Gordon and Peter M. Bowers. *United States Navy Aircraft since 1911.* New York: Funk & Wagnalls, 1968.
316. Sweetman, Jack. *The Landing at Vera Cruz: 1914; The First Complete Chronicle of a Strange Encounter in April 1914, When the United States Navy Captured and Occupied the City of Vera Cruz, Mexico.* Annapolis: U.S. Naval Institute, 1968.
317. Taylor, Albert H. *The First Twenty-Five Years of the Naval Research Laboratory.* Washington: U.S. Navy Department, 1948.
318. Taylor, Charles C. *The Life of Alfred Thayer Mahan, Naval Philosopher, Rear Admiral United States Navy.* New York: George H. Doran, 1920.
319. Taylor, Theodore. *The Magnificent Mitscher.* New York: W. W. Norton, 1954.
320. Thomas Lowell. *Old Gimlet Eye: The Adventures of Smedley D. Butler.* New York: Farrar & Rhinehart, 1933.
321. Thorne, Christopher. *The Limits of Foreign Policy: The West and the Far Eastern Crisis of 1931-1933.* New York: G. P. Putnam's, 1973.

322. Tolley, Kemp. *Yangtze Patrol: The U.S. Navy in China.* Annapolis: U.S. Naval Institute, 1971.

323. Trask, David F. *Captains· and Cabinets: Anglo-American Naval Relations, 1917-1918.* Columbia: University of Missouri Press, 1972.

324. Tuleja, Thaddeus V. *Statesmen and Admirals: Quest for a Far Eastern Naval Policy.* New York: W. W. Norton, 1963.

325. Turk, Richard W. "United States Naval Policy in the Caribbean, 1865-1915." Doctoral dissertation, Fletcher School of Law and Diplomacy, 1968.

326. Turnbull, Archibald D., and Clifford L. Lord. *History of United States Naval Aviation.* New Haven: Yale University Press, 1949.

327. U.S. Adjutant General's Office. *Correspondence Relating to the War with Spain and Conditions Growing Out of Same, Including the Insurrection in the Philippines and the China Relief Expedition.* Washington: G. P. O., 1902. 2 vols.

328. U.S. Bureau of Construction and Repair. *Ships' Data, U.S. Naval Vessels.* Washington: G. P. O., 1911-1949.

329. U.S. Bureau of Navigation. *Appendix to the Report of the Chief of the Bureau of Navigation, 1898.* Washington: G. P. O., 1898.

330. U.S. Bureau of Navigation. *Navy Directory: Officers of the United States Navy and Marine Corps. Washington: G. P. O.*

331. U.S. Bureau of Navigation. *Register of Commissioned and Warrant Officers of the United States Navy and Marine Corps and Reserve Officers on Active Duty.* Washington: G. P. O. and various publishers, 1798- .

332. U.S. Bureau of Ordnance. *Navy Ordnance Activities: World War, 1917-1918.* Washington: G. P. O., 1920.

333. U.S. Bureau of Yards and Docks. *Activities of the Bureau of Yards and Docks, Navy Department: World War, 1917-1918.* Washington: G. P. O., 1920.

334. U.S. Congress. House of Representatives. *Bombardment of the Taku Forts in China.* House Rept. No. 645, 57th Cong., 1st Sess. Washington: G. P. O., 1902.

335. U.S. Congress. House of Representatives. *The Hepburn Report, 27 December 1937.* House Doc. No. 65, 76th Cong., 1st Sess. Washington: G. P. O., 1939.

336. U.S. Congress. House of Representatives. *Preliminary Report of the Navy Yard Commission.* House Doc. No. 1946, 64th Cong., 2nd Sess. Washington: G. P. O., 1917-1918.

337. U.S. Congress. Joint Committee on the Investigation of the Pearl Harbor Attack. *Pearl Harbor Attack.* Washington: G. P. O., 1946. 39 vols.

338. U.S. Congress. Senate. *Report of Policy Board.* Sen. Exec. Doc. No. 43, 51st Cong., 1st Sess. Washington: G. P. O., 1890.

339. U.S. Congress. Senate. *Report of the Naval Inquiry on the Destruction of the Maine.* Sen. Doc. No. 207, 55th Cong., 2d Sess. Washington: G. P. O., 1898.

340. U.S. Congress. Senate. Committee on Naval Affairs. *Naval Investigation: Hearings before the Subcommittee of the Committee on Naval Affairs.* 66th Cong., 2d Sess. Washington: G. P. O., 1921. 2 vols.

341. U.S. Department of State. *Froeign Relations of the United States, 1890-1941.* Washington: G. P. O., 1891-1962.
342. U.S. Laws, Statutes, etc. *Navy Yearbook: Compilation of Annual Appropriation Laws . . . Including Provisions for the Construction of All Vessels of the "New Navy", with Tables Showing Present Naval Strength.* Washington: G. P. O., 1906.
343. U.S. Library of Congress. *The National Union Catalogue of Manuscript Collections.* Various publishers, 1959- .
344. U.S. Library of Congress. Legislative Reference Service. *Checklist of Hearings before Congressional Committees through the 67th Congress.* Edited by Harold O. Thoman. Washington: G. P. O., 1942-1958. 9 vols.
345. U.S. Marine Corps. Division of Reserve. *The Marine Corps Reserve: A History.* Washington: G. P. O., 1966.
346. U.S. Marine Corps. Historical Division HQ. *Marine Corps Historical Bibliographies.* Washington: The Division, 1961- .
347. U.S. Marine Corps. Historical Division HQ. *Marine Corps Historical Reference Series.* Washington: The Division, 1961- .
348. U.S. National Archives. *Guide to the Records in the National Archives.* Washington: G. P. O., 1962.
349. U.S. Navy Department. *Annual Reports of the Navy Department.* Washington: G. P. O., 1890-1932. The Navy Department Library retains mimeographed copies of the reports for subsequent years.
350. U.S. Navy Department. *Annual Report of the Secretary of the Navy.* Washington: Various publishers, 1821-1948.
351. U.S. Navy Department. "U.S. Naval Administration in World War II." Unpublished manuscripts in U.S. Naval History Division. About 250 vols.
352. U.S. Navy Department. Schley Court of Inquiry. *Record of Proceedings of a Court of Inquiry in the Case of Rear Admiral Winfield S. Schley.* Washington: G. P. O., 1902. 3 vols.
353. U.S. Office of Naval Intelligence. *War Notes: Information from Abroad.* Washington: G. P. O., 1899. 8 nos.
354. U.S. Office of Naval Records and Library. *Monographs.* Washington: G. P. O., 1920-1923.
   No. 1. *German Submarine Activities on the Atlantic Coast of the United States and Canada.* 1920.
   No. 2. *The Northern Barrage and Other Mining Activities.* 1920.
   No. 3. *Digest Catalogue of Laws and Joint Resolutions, the Navy and the World War.* 1920.
   No. 4. *"The Northern Barrage" (Taking Up the Mines).* 1920.
   No. 5. *History of the Bureau of Engineering.* 1922.
   No. 6. *The United States Naval Railway Batteries in France.* 1922.
   No. 7. *The American Naval Planning Section London.* 1923.
   (Unnumbered) *American Ship Casualties of the World War.* 1923.
355. Van Deurs, George. *Wings of the Fleet.* Annapolis: U.S. Naval Institute, 1961.
356. Van Wyen, Adrian O. *The Aeronautical Board, 1916-1947.* Washington: G. P. O., 1949.

357. Van Wyen, Adrian O. *Naval Aviation in World War I.* Washington: G. P. O., 1969.

358. Van Wyen, Adrian O., and Lee M. Pearson. *United States Naval Aviation, 1910-1960.* Washington: G. P. O., 1961.

359. Vinson, John Chalmers. *The Parchment Peace: The United States Senate and the Washington Conference, 1921-1922.* Athens: University of Georgia Press, 1955.

360. Watson, Mark S. *Pre-War Plans and Preparations.* Washington: Historical Division, Department of the Army, 1950.

361. Weems, John E. *The Fate of the Maine.* New York: Henry Holt. 1958.

362. Weems, John E. *Peary, the Explorer and the Man, Based on His Personal Papers.* Boston: Houghton Mifflin, 1967.

363. Weigley, Russell F. *The American Way of War: A History of American Military Strategy and Policy.* New York: Macmillan, 1973.

364. West, James H. "A Short History of the New York Navy Yard." Mimeographed. 1941.

365. West, Richard S., Jr. *Admirals of American Empire: The Combined Story of George Dewey, Alfred Thayer Mahan, Winfield Scott Schley, and William Thomas Sampson.* Indianapolis: Bobbs-Merrill, 1948.

366. Westervelt, George C., Holden C. Richardson, and Albert C. Read. *The Triumph of the NC's.* Garden City: Doubleday, Page, 1920.

367. Wheeler, Gerald E. *Admiral William Veazie Pratt, U.S. Navy: A Sailor's Life.* Washington: G. P. O., 1974.

368. Wheeler, Gerald E. *Prelude to Pearl Harbor: The United States Navy and the Far East, 1921-1923.* Columbia: University of Missouri Press, 1963.

369. Wieand, Harold T. "The History of the Development of the United States Naval Reserves, 1899-1941." Doctoral dissertation, University of Pittsburgh, 1953.

370. Wiley, Henry A. *An Admiral from Texas.* Garden City: Doubleday, Doran, 1934.

371. Wilhelm, Maria. *The Man Who Watched the Rising Sun: The Story of Admiral Ellis M. Zacharias.* New York: Franklin Watts, 1967.

372. Willock, Roger. *Lone Star Marine: A Biography of the Late Colonel John W. Thomason, Jr., U.S.M.C.* Princeton: The author, 1961.

373. Wilson, Eugene E. *Slipstream: The Autobiography of an Air Craftsman.* New York: McGraw-Hill, 1950.

374. Wilson, Henry B. *An Account of Operations of the American Navy in France During the War with Germany.* U.S.S. Pennsylvania, 1919.

375. Wilson, John R. M. "Herbert Hoover and the Armed Forces: A Study of Presidential Attitudes and Policy." Doctoral dissertation, Northwestern University, 1971.

376. Wilson, John R. M. "The Quaker and the Sword: Herbert Hoover's Relations with the Military," *Military Affairs*, XXXVIII (April 1974), 41-47.

377. Wohlstetter, Roberta. *Pearl Harbor: Warning and Decision.* Stanford University Press, 1962.

378. Wood, Charles A., comp. *Marine Corps Personal Papers Collection Catalog.* Marine Corps Historical Reference Pamphlet. Washington: Marine Corps History and Museum Division Headquarters, 1974.
379. Yardley, Herbert O. *The American Black Chamber.* Indianapolis: Bobbs-Merrill, 1931.
380. Zacharias, Ellis M. *Secret Missions: The Story of an Intelligence Officer.* New York: G. P. Putnam's, 1946.

ARCHIVES.
381. Franklin D. Roosevelt Library, Albany Post Road, Hyde Park, New York, 12538.
382. Herbert Hoover Presidential Library, 284 S. Downey, West Branch, Iowa, 52358.
383. James Carson Breckinridge Library, Marine Corps Educational Center, Quantico, Virginia, 22134.
384. Library of Congress, Manuscript Division, Washington, D.C., 20540.
385. Marine Corps Historical Reference Library, HQ, U.S. Marine Corps, Washington, D.C., 20380.
386. National Archives, 8th St. and Pennsylvania Avenue, Washington, D.C., 20408.
387. Naval Historical Foundation, Building 220, Washington Navy Yard, Washington, D.C., 20374.
388. Naval History Division, Building 220, Washington Navy Yard, Washington, D.C., 20374.
389. Navy Department Library, Building 220, Washington Navy Yard, Washington, D.C., 20374.
390. Ohio Historical Society, 1982 Velma Street, Columbus, Ohio, 43211.
391. Submarine Library and Museum, Box 157, Groton, Connecticut, 06340.
392. U.S. Naval Academy Library, Naval Academy, Annapolis, Maryland, 21402.
393. U.S. Naval War College Library, Newport, Rhode Island, 02840.
394. Washington National Records Center, Archives Branch, Suitland, Maryland, 20233.
394. Harrod, Frederick J. "Enlisted Men in the United States Navy, 1899-1939." Ph.D. Dissertation: Northwestern University, 1973.

XIV

THE UNITED STATES ARMY IN WORLD WAR II

Robert W. Coakley

The history of the United States Army in World War II has certainly been recorded sooner, and probably more accurately, than has been the case in earlier American wars. In these earlier wars, there was little effort on the part of the Army itself or of the government to do more than at most publish a documentary record. In World War II special historical teams accompanied combat forces, and under a wartime directive issued by President Roosevelt a large number of histories were prepared to record the administrative experience of departments and agencies in directing the war effort. Once the war was over the Army's Historical Divison of the Special Staff (later the Office Chief of Military History and now the Center of Military History) launched a massive research effort, employing professional historians, to produce the *United States Army in World War II* series, finally projected at seventy-nine volumes, of which seventy-two have been published. Any bibliography covering the Army in World War II must therefore center around the histories produced as part of the official program, though certainly much that has been done outside that program merits consideration. Critics of official history will note that the series was produced under official Army auspices primarily for military use. Individual authors were, however, given access to all pertinent records and freedom in drawing their own conclusions therefrom. Kent Roberts Greenfield, who as the Army's Chief Historian was originally responsible for the technical direction of the effort, has provided interesting reflections on this experiment in historiography in *The Historian and the Army* (79).

The United States Army in World War II included the Army Air Forces. Since a separate chapter (XV) in this volume covers the Air Forces in the twentieth century, including World War II, the emphasis here will be on the ground army and its role in the global conflict. Any proper coverage of the ground army must include those general matters of strategy, policy, logistics, and combined operations which were the common concerns not only of the ground and air arms of the Army but of the Navy as well. The story of the Army Air Forces in World War II, told in a seven-volume series originally planned as part of the *United States Army in World War II* (47), therefore has much pertinence for ground operations. The Navy (155) and Marine Corps (180) official histories of the war are also of great value for those who would properly appreciate the role of the Army in the global conflict.

BIBLIOGRAPHIES. There are no comprehensive bibliographies devoted to secondary works on the U.S. Army in World War II. The listings in Janet Ziegler (240) include, *inter alia,* almost everything in print up to 1965; a supplement bringing the listings up to date is currently in process but not yet published. The U.S. Army Center of Military History regularly updates listings of its publications and the latest of these can be obtained from the agency. There are no published listings of its considerable holdings of manuscript histories. The *Readers Guide* (222) covers only the books in the *U.S. Army in World War II* series published through 1960. Higham's *Official Histories* (92) not only lists the volumes available to 1970 but also contains a historiographical essay.

MANUSCRIPT SOURCES. The most important manuscript sources for the study of the U.S. Army in World War II are the voluminous records created by the War Department and Army field units from theater headquarters to battalions and companies. These records are now in the custody of the National Archives and Records Service and are described in *Federal Records of World War II,* originally published in 1950 (226) and currently under revision. These papers are stored in a number of different depositories—records of the War Department staff agencies and of the Joint and Combined Chiefs of Staff, for instance, in the main National Archives building in Washington, D.C., most theater records including unit after-action reports at the Washington National Records Center at Suitland, Maryland, others in the records center at Kansas City, Missouri, and personnel records in the National Personnel Records Center in St. Louis, Missouri (where a considerable number were destroyed in a 1974 fire). Specific inquiries about Army records of World War II should be addressed to Modern Military Branch, Military Archives Division, National Archives and Records Service, Washington, D.C. 20408. The scholar would do well to consult footnotes and bibliographies of appropriate volumes of the *U.S. Army in World War II* Series for further description and helpful hints on the most useful of these voluminous sources.

Declassification of these records is proceeding at a rapid pace and in terms of volume at least the major portion of the Army's World War II records are now open to scholars. Where research does require consultation of classified files, access may be granted to qualified researchers subject to security clearance and review of notes by constituted authority. Applications for access to classified Army files should be addressed to Records Management Division, Administrative Management Directorate, Office of the Adjutant General, Department of the Army, Washington, D.C. 20314.

Other manuscript sources are to be found in various depositories throughout the country where participants have chosen to place their personal papers. These collections often contain generous portions of official files that have either been copied with official permission or allowed to remain in private hands. Indeed the dividing line between what is official and what personal is a thin one and this is particularly true of papers deposited in Presidential libraries. Of these the most important for the Army in World War II is the Dwight D. Eisenhower Library in Abilene, Kansas, where the papers of the supreme commander of the Allied invasion force in Europe rest along with those of a number of his principal associates. For the student of policy the papers in the Franklin D. Roosevelt Library at Hyde Park, New York, including as they do the papers of Harry L. Hopkins, are probably of greater import. Those in the Harry S. Truman Library at Independence, Missouri, are also of importance, particularly for the last months of the war.

Next to the Presidential libraries the most important repositories of World War II military papers are the special centers established for leading generals—notably the George C. Marshall Library and Research Center at Lexington, Virginia, and the MacArthur Memorial (Bureau of Archives) in Norfolk, Virginia. The papers in these centers supplement those in the official archives although many of them are duplicates. Like the Presidential libraries they have attracted the papers of lesser figures who were associated with the principals, Marshall and MacArthur, during the war.

The main manuscript holdings of the Center of Military History in Washington, D.C., consist of wartime monographs, agency and theater histories, foreign studies, and other types of unpublished products of the wartime and post-war historical programs. Most of these have been used in the preparation of the *U.S. Army in World War II* volumes but many contain greater detail or cover areas outside the pale of the official series. A developing repository of increasing significance is an adjunct of the center, the United States Army Military History Research Collection at Carlisle Barracks, Pennsylvania. The Research Collection was established to provide a single point within the Army for the collection of books and papers relating to the military history of the United States that do not belong in the official archives. The Collection has attracted the deposit of the papers of many officers of secondary rank during the war, and incidentally those of General Lewis B. Hershey, wartime director of Selective Service. The Collection put out a comprehensive listing and description of its manuscript holdings in 1972 (213). The Collection has also, since 1970, been conducting an oral history program, interviewing senior Army officers, concentrating on those who have retired in the last two decades. These oral interviews provide much personal testimony by figures who played important roles in World War II. Some of these interviews have already been opened to outside scholars; others will probably be as time passes.

Some of the papers of General of the Army Omar N. Bradley were deposited at the Military History Research Collection at Carlisle but the major portion have been donated to the Library of the U.S. Military Academy at West Point. This library has also been the beneficiary of donations of papers of other important World War II officers. The Library of Congress also has a number of useful collections, including the papers of General George S. Patton, Jr. Others are scattered around the country in various sorts of depositories. The papers of General Jacob Devers, for instance, wartime commander in the Mediterranean Theater, have been donated to the York County, Pennsylvania, Historical Society; those of General Mark Clark will eventually rest at the Citadel in South Carolina.

The restrictions that have been placed on the use of these collections of personal papers vary greatly; the only safe rule is to consult the director of the holding repository.

MILITARY PREPARATION AND THE OUTBREAK OF WAR. During the period 1939-41, the United States moved from a stance of strict neutrality to war. Military preparations and problems of this period vastly influenced the Army's posture and its later conduct of the war. Most of the topical volumes of the *U.S. Army in World War II* contain background material on this period. (See particularly 23, 42, 55, 65, 74, 77, 81, 94, 116, 137, 157, 158, 163, 172, 185, 196, 200). Mark Watson's *Chief of Staff: Pre-War Plans and Preparations* (231) is totally devoted to this period and provides a view from the highest Army level as does the second volume of Pogue's biography of Marshall (167). The two volumes in the *Western Hemisphere* sub-series (43, 44) devote at least half their coverage of the defense of the Americas to the pre-Pearl Harbor period. The voluminous record of the Congressional hearings and report on the Pearl Harbor attack (216) provides documents and oral testimony of the utmost value. These and other sources have been used effectively by Langer and Gleason (112), Millis (147), Morgenstern (153), and Butow (29), among others, to plot the American road to war 1939-41. Ladislas Farago (68) presents a detailed story of the breaking of the Japanese code and the Magic intercepts. Roberta Wohlstetter (238) has provided perhaps the best account of the reasons why the warnings received in the "Magic" intercepts went unheeded. And Walter Lord in *Day of Infamy* gives a graphic and detailed account of the actual Pearl Harbor attack (120).

STRATEGY AND THE HIGH COMMAND. Coalition strategy in World War II, which provided the guidelines for operations of British and American forces of all three services was determined by the Combined Chiefs of Staff (British and American) subject to the approval of the President and Prime Minister. On the American side the Joint Chiefs of Staff, during the war an *ad hoc* organization formed initially to provide an American counterpart to the British Chiefs, and responsible directly to the President, were the most important agency in determining strategy. The Operations Division of the War Department General Staff served, under General Marshall as Chief of Staff, as the Army's link with the joint and combined directing apparatus. Ray Cline's *Washington Command Post* (37), the story of the Operations Division, gives the best picture of the Washington planning and directional organization that has yet been published. Verne Davis' unpublished manuscript in the "History of the Joint Chiefs of Staff in World War II" (49a), available now in an unclassified version, describes the Joint Chiefs organization in greater detail.

The theme of much of the literature on strategy and high policy in World War II centers on the controversy between the British and Americans over strategy in the war against Germany. Hanson Baldwin (6) and Chester Wilmot (236), supported to some degree by J.F.C. Fuller (76), opened this controversy with contentions that the American strategy for direct cross-Channel invasion of Europe was a mistake, that the Americans, for political reasons, should have adopted the British design for invasion of the Balkans so as to put the western Allies in a better position *vis-à-vis* the Soviet Union at the end of the war. This argument, of course, assumed a British Balkan strategy, and the British official historians of strategy and policy have questioned its existence (56, 84, 95). Matloff's two volumes in the Army series (the first in collaboration with Snell) tell the story from the vantage point of the Army planners (137, 138) and stress the wisdom of the cross-Channel design that finally was followed after long debates with the British over a Mediterranean or Balkan strategy. Leighton and Coakley's two volumes in the same series (38 and 116) portray the relationships between strategic decisions and logistical realities and in so doing question some of the premises of the thesis that the final decision on a cross-Channel invasion represented a triumph of American over British strategic concepts.

Outside the official series, Trumbull Higgins has been the most vociferous on the American side in his attack on the British "Mediterranean" strategy (90, 91), which he identifies with the Prime Minister. Morison's *Strategy and Compromise* (156) takes the orthodox American view while Greenfield's second book *American Strategy in World War II: A Reconsideration* (80) is heavily influenced by the Leighton-Coakley viewpoint. Michael Howard, one of the authors of the British strategic volumes, has attempted to present a summary balanced view in *The Mediterranean Strategy in the Second World War* (95) but this has hardly ended the controversy. A recent work by Steele (192) on the decision to invade North Africa has thrown new light on Roosevelt's course in 1942 which started the train of events that led to the controversy.

The Army historian's collection of essays, *Command Decisions* (78) is revealing light on this and other major decisions of the war. In the broader field of politico-military relationships and the diplomacy of the war, Feis (72) and MacNeil (141a) are the most important works outside the realm of biography and memoir literature. In the accounts of grand strategy, the usual focus is on Europe with the strategy in the war against Japan a decidedly secondary issue. Morton's *Strategy and Command in the Pacific* (158) deals with this area up to the end of 1943 and is the standard work. No volume to cover the years 1944-45 in the war against Japan has been published in the Army series nor is one contemplated. The void is in part filled by Matloff (138), Coakley and Leighton (38), Pacific theater volumes (5, 30, 187), by an unpublished manuscript in the Center of Military History by Lt. Col. Henry Morgan (152), and by a Department of Defense release on American policy with regard to the entry of the USSR into the war against Japan (223).

Memoirs and biographies are most important in the treatment of the high command and most of the top figures of the U.S. Army in World War II have either written memoirs and/or have been the subject of biographies. Two of Pogue's three volumes on General George C. Marshall so far published (167, 168) cover the war years; the general never wrote his memoirs but did leave Pogue taped recollections. Stimson's memoirs (194) cover in some detail his term as Secretary of War during World War II and his unpublished diary at Yale University is a favorite source for historians of policy and strategy. Other American memoirs of importance for the study of strategy are those of Generals Eisenhower (59), John R. Deane (50), and Wedemeyer (232), and Admiral Leahy (113). On the

British side, Churchill's multivolume series (34), Lord Alanbrooke's story as told to Sir Arthur Bryant (24), Sir Frederick Morgan's *Overture to OVERLORD* (151), and Kennedy's *The Business of War* (106) illuminate many areas of the Anglo-American debate. Of the biographies of Roosevelt, only that of James MacGregor Burns (26) deserves serious consideration by the military student, and Burns' treatment of Roosevelt's military decisions leaves much to be desired. Sherwood's *Roosevelt and Hopkins* (181), more a source book than a secondary treatment, throws a great deal of light on both Roosevelt as Commander-in-Chief and on his relationship with Churchill and others.

OPERATIONS. The U.S. Army fought World War II on two broad fronts against the European Axis and Japan respectively, and it operated in theaters stretched around the globe each of which had its own characteristics and problems. The subject of operations can then best be approached by a theater breakdown. The main theaters in the war against Germany were the Mediterranean (first known as the North African) and the European; in the war against Japan they were the South, Central, and Southwest Pacific, and China-Burma-India. The basic works on operations in each theater are those produced as part of the U.S. Army in World War II; but some of the wartime work done on operations and published in the *Armed Forces in Action* series (227) still has value for the student of particular operations. The volume of work done by outside writers, and indeed by authors who worked on the World War II series publishing privately, is meanwhile growing.

THE MEDITERRANEAN THEATER. The World War II series on the Mediterranean Theater is complete except for a volume on the last phase of the Italian campaign, and one on the invasion of Southern France which also involves the European Theater. Both these works are currently in progress. The published works include Howe on the invasion of North Africa (97), Smyth and Garland on Sicily and the surrender of Italy (189), and Blumenson's *Salerno to Cassino* (15) on the first phase of the Italian campaign. There are also five pamphlets in the *Armed Forces in Action* series (227) dealing with Mediterranean operations. Chester G. Starr's *Salerno to the Alps: A History of Fifth Army* (191), written under official auspices though privately published, covers the Italian campaign. The British have produced a six-volume history of the operations of their own and allied armies in the Mediterranean and Middle East (165) that has much value for the study of U.S. Army operations in these areas. Blumenson has, in addition to his volume in the official series, contributed popular accounts of Kasserine Pass (18), the crossing of the Rapido (16), and the landing at Anzio (17). Two British writers, Charles Connell (45) and Fred Majdalany (130) have contributed accounts of the bloody fight at Cassino and Douglas Orgill one of the bitter mountain fighting along the Gothic line in the autumn of 1944 (162). W. G. Jackson's books on the *Battle for Rome* (101) and the *Battle for Italy* (102) constitute between them another history by a Britisher of the Italian campaign. Memoirs of particular interest for the Mediterranean campaign include those of Generals Mark Clark (34), Lucian Truscott (205), Bradley (22),

Patton (164), and Eisenhower (59). While a proposed logistical history of the Mediterranean Theater in the *U.S. Army in World War II* series was never completed, an outline logistical history was done in the theater that has some value (142).

The roles of the U.S. Army in the area east of Italy and Tunisia were mainly either air operations or logistical operations in support of allies. The most important was the operation of a supply line to the USSR through the Persian Gulf, the subject of T. H. Vail Motter's *Persian Corridor* (159).

THE EUROPEAN THEATER (NORTHWEST EUROPE). The official Army series on the European theater is now complete, save for the southern France volume mentioned earlier, and the writing on this theater published privately is greater than that on any other. The volumes in the *U.S. Army in World War II* are all top flight. Gordon Harrison's *Cross-Channel Attack* (86) covers the D-Day landings and the Normandy campaign up through the capture of Cherbourg; Martin Blumenson picks up the story in *Breakout and Pursuit* (14) and carries it through the advance to Paris and beyond. Charles B. MacDonald in the *Siegfried Line Campaign* (125) and Hugh Cole in *The Lorraine Campaign* (39) cover the fall and early winter campaigns as the drive ground to a halt just inside Germany. Hugh Cole's *Ardennes* (40) tells the graphic story of the Battle of the Bulge and MacDonald's *Last Offensive* (126) carries the armies all along the line to final victory in Europe. Pogue in his *Supreme Command* (166) deals with the planning and direction of the war by Eisenhower's headquarters, while Ruppenthal's two volumes on *Logistical Support of the Armies* (176) round out the theater's coverage with the story of rear-area support. Several pamphlets in the *Armed Forces in Action* series, notably those on *Omaha Beach* and *Utah Beach to Cherbourg,* prepared by wartime historical detachments, retain much value (227). MacDonald and Matthews have provided detail on several small unit actions in Italy and Northwest Europe in *Three Battles* (129).

Of the essentially popular accounts of actions in the European Theater the most notable are Cornelius Ryan's *Longest Day* (177), *A Bridge Too Far* (178), and *The Last Battle* (179), and John Toland's *Battle, The Story of the Bulge* (201) and *The Last Hundred Days* (202). Ryan and Toland have exploited personal recollections to an extent official historians could not do, but their works also suffer from some of the defects their methods engender, for fifteen to thirty-year old recollections are not always reliable. Blumenson has provided a popular version of his *Breakout and Pursuit* in *Duel for France* (19), and MacDonald has extracted and expanded a section of his *Siegfried Line Campaign* in *Battle for the Huertgen Forest* (128). MacDonald has also provided the only existing synthesis of the American military effort in the war against Germany in *The Mighty Endeavour* (127). Notable British accounts of the struggle in Northwest Europe are Belfield (12) and Essame (63).

Next to the D-Day landings, the Battle of the Bulge has attracted the most attention. S.L.A. Marshall, erstwhile Chief of the Army's Historical Section in Europe, published his detailed work on the first eight days in 1946 (134), and was followed in 1947 by one by Robert E. Merriam, who also based his account on work as an Army historian. Merriam published a more definitive book in 1958 (143), and Toland's account (201) followed in 1959. John Eisenhower ten years later used his father's papers to advantage in his account *The Bitter Woods* (70). Kenneth M. Hechler's *The Bridge at Remagen* (88) covers another dramatic incident of the European war and is also a product of work originally started with the Army's historical section in Europe under Col. Marshall's direction.

Of the memoirs, those of Generals Eisenhower (59), Bradley (22), Patton (164), Truscott (215), and Harmon (85) are most important for the European Theater operations. Additional light on Eisenhower's role is cast by General Walter B. Smith's *Eisenhower's Six Great Decisions* (188) and his naval aide, Commander Butcher's *Diary* (27). Eisenhower's papers edited by Chandler and Ambrose (31) are among the first collections of a leading military figure in World War II to be published. Based on them Ambrose has written the most authoritative biography of the wartime supreme commander yet to appear (3). Another recent biography of merit is by Peter Lyons (121). On the most flamboyant and successful of Eisenhower's lieutenants, General George Patton, Blumenson's two-volume *Patton Papers* (20), though a mixed source book and biography, does largely supplant the earlier lengthy biography by Ladislas Farago (69). On the British side, the memoirs of Field Marshal Montgomery (149, 150) and of his Chief of Staff de Guingand (51) are most important, while the British operational histories (61) necessarily treat of U.S. Army operations in western Europe.

THE PACIFIC THEATERS. The Army's operational histories of the Pacific theaters have been completed, but there is no companion piece to the Ruppenthal volumes in the European series on theater logistics. Louis Morton's *Fall of the Philippines* (157) is a graphic story of one of America's major military disasters. John Miller Jr. (144) and Samuel Milner (148) deal with the Guadalcanal and Papuan campaigns respectively in the South and Southwest Pacific, the beginnings of the American offensive. Miller's *CARTWHEEL* (145) tells of the convergence of the forces of the two theaters in the 1943-44 drive to neutralize Rabaul. Philip Crowl with Edmund Love (48) deals with the first campaign in the Central Pacific, that against the Gilberts and Marshalls, and Crowl alone (49) details the Army's role in the *Campaign in the Marianas*. Robert Ross Smith brings the advance along two lines in the Pacific nearly to its ultimate goal in *Approach to the Philippines* (186). M. Hamlin Cannon (30) and Smith (187) respectively deal with the campaigns on Leyte and Luzon. The last book in the Pacific series, actually the first to be published, prepared immediately after the war by Appleman, Gugeler, Burns, and Stevens covers *Okinawa: The Last Battle* (5).

These accounts in the *U.S. Army in World War II* series may be supplemented by four pamphlets in the Armed Forces in Action series (227) and by the so-called MacArthur history, *The Reports of General MacArthur* (217) prepared by his staff in Tokyo after the war and published by the Department of the Army. The MacArthur history contains an account of operations of the Japanese army; accounts prepared by Japanese participants under the auspices of the historical section of MacArthur's headquarters and used in the preparation of the World War II series have been described in a guide published by the Army (220).

The four-volume *History of Marine Corps Operations in World War II* (180) supplements the Army coverage and Morison's volumes on naval operations (155) are indispensable to the understanding of the Army's island campaigns. In the absence of a logistical volume in the Army's Pacific series, the reader should consult Leighton and Coakley (38, 116), technical service volumes on overseas operations (23a, 29, 51a, 141, 194a, 198, 199), combat volumes in the series, and a number of manuscript volumes in the Center of Military History (210, 211). The eight-volume *Engineers in the Southwest Pacific* (209), also an official Army history, is of great value in covering Engineer operations in MacArthur's theater.

There has been less writing by outside scholars on the Army in the Pacific War than on its operations in Europe. S.L.A. Marshall's *Island Victory* (133), a wartime work on the Tarawa campaign, has merit. Stanley Falk's two books, one on the Bataan Death March (67) and the other on the Leyte campaign (66) are the best on their subjects. Samuel B. Griffith (82) and Robert Leckie (114) have covered Army operations on Guadalcanal incidental to the Marine story. J.J. Beck has contributed a worthwhile study on the surrender in the Philippines (9), Lida Mayo one on the drive to Buna Mission in New Guinea (140), and the Belote brothers a study on Okinawa (13). General Heavey's story of the engineer amphibian brigades in the Southwest Pacific is a valuable account by a participant (87).

General Douglas B. MacArthur, of course, overshadows other Army commanders in the Pacific and he has found numerous biographers among them his staff officers Courtney Whitney (233) and Charles A. Willoughby (235). D. Clayton James' promising scholarly biography has not yet reached the wartime period. MacArthur's own story is told in *Reminiscences* (123) and *Public Papers* (122). Of other memoirs of Army leaders in the Pacific, those of Generals Wainwright (229), Eichelberger (58), including his edited letters to his wife (57), Kenny (107), and Krueger (111) are most significant.

CHINA, BURMA, AND INDIA. American operations in the China-Burma-India Theater during World War II were plagued by frustrations from beginning to end, and the central character in the American drama there, General Joseph W. Stilwell, was a highly controversial figure who has found his admirers and detractors in the post-war literature. The three volumes by Romanus and Sunderland in the official series (173) treat Stilwell quite sympathetically while presenting the fullest story of Army operations in the theater. Barbara Tuchman's celebrated biography (207), though written in her own inimitable style, has its factual base for the wartime period in the Romanus-Sunderland accounts. Of the anti-Stilwell faction, General Claire L. Chennault, the air commander who clashed continually with Stilwell, has published his own story (32), and Colonel Charles N. Hunter in *Galahad* (98), a personal account of the expedition against Myitkyina, leaves no question of his antipathy toward his old commander. A recent publication based on records of Chiang Kai-shek's government, Chin-tung Liang's *General Stilwell in China: The Full Story* (118) reflects the Generalissimo's dislike of the American commander.

A more balanced account by a Chinese-American scholar is Tsang Tsou's *America's Failure in China* (206) which accepts in essence the Romanus-Sunderland view of Chiang. Feis' *China Tangle* (70) fits the Stilwell story into the broader picture of Chinese-American relations during and after the war. Some of Stilwell's story in his own words may be found in the *Stilwell Papers,* edited by Theodore White (193), and published shortly after his death in 1946. One of his principal lieutenants, Frank Dorn, has written his own personal account in *Walkout with Stilwell in Burma* (52). Charlton Ogburn's *Marauders* (161) is a stirring account of the Myitkyina expedition. Some graphic first-hand medical material is to be found in the U.S. Army Medical Department publication *Crisis Fleeting* (194b).

LOGISTICS. The American victory in World War II was made possible by a logistical system that provided high quality support for troops deployed around the world, and the Army's logistical achievement was of monumental proportions. Indeed America's ability not only to produce the sinews of war but to deliver them to the battlefronts was probably the key to triumph over the Axis. The logistical effort, however, has attracted little detailed study outside the official Army series and works prepared under the auspices of other government agencies. The coverage in the *U.S. Army in World War II* is relatively complete except for certain technical service volumes still in process. Leighton and Coakley's two volumes (116, 38) provide a broad overall view of the problems of allocation of resources at the highest levels, R. Elberton Smith (185) deals with industrial mobilization and the massive Army procurement program during the war, and Fairchild and Grossman (65) treat of the Army's role in the use of industrial manpower. Army Service Forces was the agency charged with providing logistical support to the Army and John D. Millett (146) handles its organization and role.

The nuts and bolts of logistics are covered fully in the volumes on the technical services. Brophy, Miles, Cochran, Fisher, Kleber, and Birdsell have produced three volumes on the Chemical Warfare Service (23, 23a, 110); Wardlow, Bykofsky, and Larson three on the Transportation Corps (29, 230); Thomson, Mayo, Green, and Roots three on the Ordnance Department (77, 141, 200); Risch, Kieffer, Stauffer, Ross and Romanus four on the Quartermaster Corps (172, 174, 194a); Terrett, Thompson, and Harris three on the Signal Corps (196, 198, 199); Wiltse and Smith two on the Medical Department (184, 237) with two yet to be produced; and Remington, Fine, Dod, Keith, and Rosenthal three volumes on the Engineers with one yet to come (42, 51a, 74). These technical service volumes cover both zone of interior and overseas operations and in the ensemble present a detailed account of logistical operations unparalleled in any other American war.

In addition to the Army volumes, some of the administrative histories of other wartime agencies are of value, notably the Civilian Production Administration's *Industrial Mobilization for War* (35) and Frederic C. Lane's *Ships for Victory* (111a) which covers the massive shipbuilding effort of the Maritime Commission on which the Army was so dependent for support of its overseas operations.

TRAINING. The two volumes on the Army Ground Forces by Greenfield, Palmer, Wiley, and Keast (81, 163) provide an excellent analysis of the problems of training the ground army during World War II. The principal engineer of the training program, General Leslie McNair had his profile done in interesting fashion by Ely J. Kahn in 1945 (105).

SCIENCE AND TECHNOLOGY. Weapons development on the practical level is treated in the technical service volumes, most particularly those of the Ordnance Corps (77,200). Baxter in *Scientists against Time* (8) has provided almost a contemporary account of major problems in using science in the development of new weapons. The products of historical work in the Office of Scientific Research and Development (25, 197) are also valuable for the Army story. Kirk and Young in *Great Weapons of World War II* (109) deal at least in part with Army ordnance. The most important single scientific development in which the Army played a role was of course that of the atomic bomb. The Army's history of that role is still in process. However, General Groves has told his story (83), the Atomic Energy Commission has published an official history (89), and there are a number of other published works covering both the development of the bomb and the decision to use it (4, 72). See also chapters X and XII.

STATISTICS. There is no single reference on Army statistics in World War II and finding accurate statistics on certain aspects of Army operations is a difficult problem. The proposed statistical volume in the *U.S. Army in World War II* Series fell by the wayside when the Army statisticians became too involved in current operations during the Korean War. Some sections were completed and exist in pamphlet type form (219). The statistical review compiled by the Control Division, Army Service Forces, shortly after the war (215) is also very valuable in the absence of final compilations of statistics on the subjects covered. The Civilian Production Administration's statistics on procurement put out in 1947 also covers most major items of Army procurement (36). There are many useful statistics to be found in the various volumes of the *U.S. Army in World War II*.

MEDICAL HISTORY. The Historical Unit of the Army Medical Department has published, in addition to the administrative histories in the *U.S. Army in World War II*, a total of 32 volumes in a clinical series (218) prepared by medical specialists primarily for the medical profession. They are also useful to historians, however, as are volumes on battle casualties (10) and psychological tolerance (11) prepared independently by Beebe and DeBakey. (See chapter XII).

THE INDIVIDUAL SOLDIER. On the attitudes and psychology of the men in the ranks in World War II, the study by Stouffer *et al* (195) based on research conducted by the Adjutant General's Office in World War II, is outstanding. No similar study of the individual soldier exists for any other war. On the more popular side, Mauldin (139) and Pyle (169, 170) are the best sources for an interesting and accurate picture of the men in the ranks in the European war. There were no Pacific counterparts. S.L.A. Marshall's *Men Against Fire* (135) is a pioneering and influential study on the behaviour of infantrymen in combat. Audie Murphy's *To Hell and Back* (160), a personal account of experiences by the most decorated soldier of World War II, has its own distinct flavor. The Army magazine *Yank* (239) and the European and Pacific editions of *Stars and Stripes,* the soldiers' newspaper, are among the better sources for study of GI attitudes and behaviour. Charles B. MacDonald's *Company Commander* (124) was perhaps the best piece of writing to come out of World War II on the experiences of a young officer.

PHOTOGRAPHS AND MAPS. There are three photographic volumes in the *U.S. Army in World War II* series covering respectively the Mediterranean and European areas in the war against Germany, and the war against Japan in all theaters (221). The U.S. Army Audio-Visual Agency in the Pentagon maintains a comprehensive historical collection of still photographs covering the activities of the Army in World War II and afterward. Reproductions of unclassified photographs may be sold to the public under certain conditions. For information of the availability of Army photographs of World War II, contact the DA Still Photographic Library, US Army Audio-Visual Agency, ATTN: CEPA-POS-R, The Pentagon, Room 5A518, Washington, D.C. 20310.

The best military maps depicting U.S. ground operations in World War II are contained in the volumes in the *U.S. Army in World War II.* A selective grouping of considerable utility is in the *West Point Atlas of American Wars.* (62).

SPECIAL TOPICS. Volumes in the U.S. Army in World War II series also include a documentary on civil affairs operations (41), a history of the Women's Army Corps (203), a study of French Rearmament (228), one of procurement of aircraft materiel (94), a volume on employment of black troops (115), a chronology of the war (234), and a study of United States-Canadian military relations (55). Other works on special topics outside the series worth noting include treatments of psychological warfare by Lerner (117), Linebarger (119), and Margolian (131), of the early phases of military government in Germany by Friedrich (75) and Holborn (93), and Rundell's study of black marketing in the European theater (175).

OPPORTUNITIES FOR ADDITIONAL RESEARCH. Despite the great volume of writing on the U.S. Army in World War II there are still many areas which have not been covered, at least in published works. There are certain gaps in the World War II series. There are no logistical histories of either the Mediterranean or the Pacific theaters to match the Ruppenthal treatment (176) of the European theater. Nor is there any treatment of manpower problems and personnel management nor of tank procurement and doctrinal development. The strategy and command story of the war against Japan lacks a final volume covering the last year and eight months of the war. The whole puzzling question of the China-Burma-India theater could stand a dispassionate analysis based on all the sources now available. Certainly there are a plethora of battles, campaigns, and logistical problems that could stand a more detailed scholarly analysis than was possible in the Army series for all its bulk. Few of the generals of second rank during World War II have yet found biographers and here is perhaps one of the most fruitful areas of research as personal collections of papers become available. And perhaps the most fruitful field of all in a period when there is so much emphasis on the relationship of the Army to society lies in a sociological analysis of the mass conscripted army of World War II, the effects the Army had on the citizen soldier and in turn the effect the citizen soldier had on the Army.

BIBLIOGRAPHY

1. Allied Forces, Mediterranean Theater. *Report by the Supreme Allied Commander, Mediterranean Theater, Field Marshal the Viscount Alexander of Tunis to the Combined Chiefs of Staff on the Italian Campaign, 12th December 1944* to 2nd May 1945. London: H.M.S.O., 1951.
2. Allied Forces, Supreme Headquarters. *Eisenhower's Own Story of the War: the Complete Record by the Supreme Commander, General Dwight D. Eisenhower on the War in Europe from the Day of Invasion to the Day of Victory.* New York: Arco, 1946.
3. Ambrose, Stephen E. *The Supreme Commander: The War Years of General Dwight D. Eisenhower.* Garden City, New York, Doubleday & Co., 1970.
4. Amrine, Michael. *The Great Decision: The Secret History of the Atomic Bomb.* New York: Putnam, 1959.
5. Appleman, Roy E., James M. Burns, Russell A. Gugeler, and John Stevens. *Okinawa: The Last Battle,* U.S. Army in World War II Series, *Pacific Theater.* Washington: G.P.O., 1948.
6. Baldwin, Hanson W., *Great Mistakes of the War,* New York: Harper & Bros., 1950.
7. Ball, Edmund F. *Staff Officer with the Fifth Army: Sicily, Salerno, and Anzio.* New York: Exposition Press, 1958.
8. Baxter, James Phinney. *Scientists against Time.* Boston: Little, Brown & Co., 1946.
9. Beck, John Jacob. *MacArthur and Wainwright: Surrender of the Philippines.* Albuquerque: University of New Mexico Press, 1974.
10. Beebe, Gilbert W. and Michael E. DeBakey. *Battle Casualties: Incidence, Mortality and Logistic Considerations.* Springfield, Illinois: Thomas, 1952.
11. Beebe, Gilbert and John W. Apful, *Variations in Psychological Tolerance to Ground Combat in World War II.* Washington: National Academy of Sciences, 1958.
12. Belfield, Eversby M. and H. Essame. *The Battle for Normandy.* Chester Springs, Pennsylvania: Dufors, 1965.
13. Belote, James and William, *Typhoon of Steel: The Battle for Okinawa.* New York: Harper & Row, 1970.

14. Blumenson, Martin. *Breakout and Pursuit.* U.S. Army in World War II Series, *European Theater of Operations.* Washington: G.P.O., 1961.

15. Blumenson, Martin. *Salerno to Cassino*, U.S. Army in World War II Series, *Mediterranean Theater of Operations.* Washington: G.P.O. 1969.

16. Blumenson, Martin. *Bloody River: The Real Tragedy of the Rapido.* Boston: Houghton Mifflin Co., 1970.

17. Blemenson, Martin. *Anzio: The Gamble that Failed.* Philadelphia: Lippincott, 1963.

18. Blumenson, Martin. *Kasserine Pass.* Boston: Houghton Mifflin Co., 1967.

19. Blumenson, Martin. *The Duel for France, 1944.* Boston: Houghton Mifflin Co., 1963.

20. Blumenson, Martin. *The Patton Papers.* Boston: Houghton Mifflin Co., 1972-74. 2 vols.

21. Bowman, Waldo G. *American Military Engineering in Europe from Normandy to the Rhine.* New York: McGraw Hill, 1945.

22. Bradley, Omar N. *A Soldier's Story.* New York: Holt; London: Eyre & Spottiswoode, 1951.

23. Brophy, Leo P. and George J. B. Fisher, *The Chemical Warfare Service: Organizing for War*, US Army in World War II Series, *The Technical Services.* Washington: G.P.O., 1958.

23a. Brophy, Leo P., Wyndham D. Miles, and Rexmond C. Cochran. *The Chemical Warfare Service: From Laboratory to Field.* US Army in World War II Series, *The Technical Services.* Washington: G.P.O., 1959.

24. Bryant, Arthur. *The Turn of the Tide: A History of the War Years Based on the Diaries of Field Marshal Lord Alanbrooke, Chief of the Imperial General Staff.* London: William Collins & Sons, 1957. *Triumph in the West,* 1959.

25. Burchard, John E., ed. *Rockets, Guns and Targets: Rockets, Target Information, Erosion Information and Hypervelocity Guns developed during World War II by the Office of Scientific Research and Development. Science in World War II* Series of Office of Scientific Research and Development. Boston: Little, Brown, 1948.

26. Burns, James MacGregor. *Roosevelt: The Soldier of Freedom.* New York: Harcourt, Brace, Jovanovich, 1970.

27. Butcher, Harry C. *My Three Years with Eisenhower.* New York: Simon & Shuster, 1946.

28. Butow, Robert J. C. *Tojo and the Coming of the War.* Princeton: Princeton University Press, 1961.

29. Bykofsky, Joseph and Harold Larson. *The Transportation Corps: Operations Overseas*, US Army in World War II Series. *The Technical Services.* Washington: G.P.O., 1957.

30. Cannon, M. Hamlin. *Leyte: The Return to the Phillippines.* US Army in World War II Series, *The War in the Pacific.* Washington: G.P.O., 1954.

31. Chandler, Alfred D. Jr. and Stephen E. Ambrose, Eds. *The Papers*

of Dwight David Eisenhower, The War Years. Baltimore: Johns Hopkins Press, 1970. 5 vols.

32. Chennault, Claire L. *The Way of a Fighter: The Memoirs of Claire Lee Chennault.* Edited by Robert Hotz. New York: Putnam, 1949.

33. Churchill, Winston S. *The Second World War.* Boston: Houghton Mifflin, 1948-53. 6 vols.

34. Clark, Mark W. *Calculated Risk.* New York: Harper, 1950.

35. Civilian Production Administration. *Industrial Mobilization for War: Program and Administration.* Washington: G.P.O., 1947.

36. Civilian Production Administration. *Official Munitions Production of the United States by Months, July 1, 1940-August 31, 1945.* Washington: Civilian Production Administration Release, May 1, 1947.

37. Cline, Ray S. *Washington Command Post: The Operations Division,* US Army in World War II Series, *The War Depatment,* Washington: G.P.O., 1951.

38. Coakley, Robert W. and Richard M. Leighton. *Global Logistics and Strategy, 1943-1945.* US Army in World War II Series, *The War Department.* Washington: G.P.O., 1969.

39. Cole, Hugh M. *The Lorraine Campaign.* US Army in World War II Series, *European Theater of Operations.* Washington: G.P.O., 1950.

40. Cole, Hugh M. *The Ardennes: Battle of the Bulge.* US Army in World War II Series, *European Theater of Operations.* Washington: G.P.O., 1965.

41. Coles, Harry L. and Albert K. Weinberg. *Civil Affairs: Soldiers Become Governors.* US Army in World War II Series, *Special Studies.* Washington: G.P.O., 1964.

42. Coll, Blanche D., Jean E. Keith, and Herbert H. Rosenthal. *The Corps of Engineers, Troops and Equipment.* US Army in World War II Series, *The Technical Services.* Washington: G.P.O., 1958.

43. Conn, Stetson, Rose C. Engelman, and Byron Fairchild. *Guarding the United States and its Outposts.* US Army in World War II Series, *The Western Hemisphere.* Washington: G.P.O., 1964.

44. Conn, Stetson and Byron Fairchild. *The Framework of Hemisphere Defense.* US Army in World War II Series, *The Western Hemisphere.* Washington: G.P.O., 1960.

45. Connell, Charles. *Monte Cassino, The Historic Battle.* London: Elek, 1963.

46. Cooke, Elliot D. *All But Me and Thee: Psychiatry at the Foxhole Level.* Washington: Infantry Journal Press, 1946.

47. Craven, Wesley Frank and James Lea Cate, eds. *The Army Air Forces in World War II.* Chicago: University of Chicago Press, 1948-58. 7 vols.

48. Crowl, Philip A. and Edmund G. Love. *Seizure of the Gilberts and Marshalls.* US Army in World War II Series, *The War in the Pacific.* Washington: G.P.O., 1955.

49. Crowl, Philip A. *Campaign in the Marianas.* US Army in World War II Series, *The War in the Pacific.* Washington: G.P.O., 1955.

49a. Vernon E. Davis. "Organizational Development." In "History of the Joint Chiefs of Staff in World War II." MS, Historical Section, Joint Secretariat, Joint Chiefs of Staff. 2 vols.

50. Deane, Brig. Gen. John R. *The Strange Alliance: The Story of Our Efforts at Wartime Cooperation with Russia.* New York: Viking Press, 1947.
51. De Guingand, Sir Francis W. *Operation Victory.* London: Hodder & Stoughton, 1947.
51a. Dod, Karl C. *The Corps of Engineers: The War against Japan.* US Army in World War II Series, *The Technical Services.* Washington: G.P.O., 1966.
52. Dorn, Frank. *Walkout with Stilwell in Burma.* New York: Thomas Y. Crowell, 1971.
53. Dornbusch, C. E., compiler. *Histories of American Army Units World Wars I and II and Korean Conflict with some earlier Histories.* Washington: The Adjutant General, Department of the Army, Special Services Division, 1956.
54. Dornbusch, C. E. *Histories, Personal Narratives, United States Army, A Checklist.* Cornwallville, New York: Hope Farm Press, 1967.
55. Dziuban, Col. Stanley. *Military Relations Between the United States and Canada, 1939-1945.* US Army in World War II Series, *Special Studies.* Washington: G.P.O., 1959.
56. Ehrman, John. *Grand Strategy,* vol. V: *August 1943-September 1944, History of the Second World War,* UK Military Series. Edited by J. R. M. Butler. London: H.M.S.O., 1956.
57. Eichelberger, Robert L. *Dear Miss Em, General Eichelberger's War in the Pacific, 1942-1945.* Edited by Jay Luvaas. Westport, Connecticut: Greenwood Press, 1973.
58. Eichelberger, Lt. Gen. Robert L. *Our Jungle Road to Tokyo.* New York: Viking Press, 1950.
59. Eisenhower, Dwight D. *Crusade in Europe.* Garden City, New York: Doubleday, 1948.
60. Eisenhower, John. *The Bitter Woods.* New York: Putnam, 1969.
61. Ellis, Maj. L. F. and Lt. Col. A. E. Warhurst. *Victory in the West. History of the Second World War,* UK Military Series. Edited by J. R. M. Butler. London: H.M.S.O., 1962-68. 2 vols.
62. Esposito, Col. Vincent J., ed. *The West Point Atlas of American Wars.* New York: Praeger, 1959.
63. Essame, Hubert. *The Battle for Germany.* London: Batchford, 1969.
64. European Theater of Operations, United States Army. "Administrative and Logistical History of the European Theater of Operations." 11 studies, MS, US Army Center of Military History.
65. Fairchild, Byron and Jonathan Grossman. *The Army and Industrial Manpower,* US Army in World War II Series, *The War Department.* Washington: G.P.O., 1959.
66. Falk, Stanley L. *Decision at Leyte.* New York: W. W. Norton & Co., 1966.
67. Falk, Stanley L. *Bataan: The March of Death.* New York: W. W. Norton Co., 1962.
68. Farago, Ladislas. *The Broken Seal: The Story of "Operation Magic" and the Pearl Harbor Disaster.* New York: Random House, 1967.
69. Farage, Ladislas. *Patton: Ordeal and Triumph.* New York: Obolensky, 1964.

70. Feis, Herbert. *The Road to Pearl Harbor: The Coming of the War between the United States and Japan.* Princeton: Princeton University Press, 1950.
71. Feis, Herbert. *The China Tangle: The American Effort in China From Pearl Harbor to the Marshall Mission.* Princeton: Princeton University Press, 1953.
72. Feis, Herbert. *Churchill, Roosevelt, Stalin: The War They Waged and the Peace They Sought.* Princeton: Princeton University Press, 1957.
73. Feis, Herbert. *The Atomic Bomb and the End of World War II.* Princeton: Princeton University Press, 1966.
74. Fine, Lenore, and Jesse A. Remington, *The Corps of Engineers; Construction in the United States,* United States Army in World War II Series, *The Technical Services.* Washington: G.P.O., 1972.
75. Friedrich, Carl J. *American Experience in Military Government in World War II.* New York: Rhinehart, 1948.
76. Fuller, J. F. C. *The Second World War: A Strategical and Tactical History.* London: Eyre & Spottiswood, 1948.
77. Green, Constance McLaughlin, Harry C. Thomson and Peter C. Rootes. *The Ordnance Department: Planning Munitions for War.* US Army in World War II Series, *The Technical Services.* Washington: G.P.O., 1955.
78. Greenfield, Kent R., ed. *Command Decisions.* Washington: G.P.O., 1960.
79. Greenfield, Kent R. *The Historian and the Army.* New Brunswick, New Jersey: Rutgers University Press, 1954.
80. Greenfield, Kent R., *American Strategy in World War II: A Reconsideration.* Baltimore: Johns Hopkins Press, 1963.
81. Greenfield, Kent R., Robert R. Palmer, and Bell I. Wiley. *The Organization of Ground Combat Troops.* US Army in World War II Series, *Army Ground Forces.* Washington: G.P.O., 1947.
82. Griffith, Samuel B. *The Battle for Guadalcanal.* Philadelphia, Lippincott, 1963.
83. Groves, Leslie R. *Now it can be Told: The Story of the Manhattan Project.* New York: Harper, 1962.
84. Gwyer, J. M. A., and J. R. M. Butler, *Grand Strategy,* vol. III (2 parts), *June 1941-August 1942, History of the Second World War,* UK Military Series. Edited by J. R. M. Butler. London: H.M.S.O., 1972.
85. Harmon, Maj. Gen. Ernest R. with Milton Mackaye and William Russ Mackaye. *Combat Commander: Autobiography of a Soldier.* Englewood Cliffs, New Jersey: Prentice Hall, 1970.
86. Harrison, Gordon A. *Cross-Channel Attack.* US Army in World War II Series, *European Theater of Operations.* Washington: G.P.O., 1951
87. Heavey, Brig. Gen. William F. *Down Ramp! The Story of the Army Amphibious Engineers.* Washington: Infantry Journal Press, 1947.
88. Hechler, Kenneth W. *The Bridge at Remagen.* New York: Ballantine Books, 1957.
89. Hewett, Richard G., and Oscar E. Anderson. *The New World.*

University Park: Pennsylvania State University Press, 1962.
90. Higgins, Trumbull. *Winston Churchill and the Second Front, 1940-1943*. New York: Oxford University Press, 1957.
91. Higgins, Trumbull. *Soft Underbelly: The Anglo-American Controversy over the Italian Campaign, 1939-1945*. New York: Macmillan Co., 1968.
92. Higham, Robin. *Official Histories*. Manhattan: Kansas State University Library, 1970.
93. Holborn, Hajo. *American Military Government: Its Organization and Policies*. Washington: Infantry Journal Press, 1947.
94. Holley, Irving B. Jr. *Buying Aircraft: Materiel Procurement for the Army Air Forces*. US Army in World War II Series, *Special Studies*. Washington: G.P.O., 1964.
95. Howard, Michael. *Grand Strategy*, vol. IV, *August 1942-September 1943, History of the Second World War*, UK Military Series. Edited by J. R. M. Butler. London: H.M.S.O., 1972.
96. Howard, Michael. *The Mediterranean Strategy in the Second World War*. London: Weidenfield & Nicolson Ltd., 1968.
97. Howe, George F. *Northwest Africa: Seizing the Initiative in the West*. US Army in World War II Series, *Mediterranean Theater of Operations*. Washington: G.P.O., 1957.
98. Hunter, Col. Charles N. *Galahad*. San Antonio, Texas: Naylor, 1963.
99. Huston, James A. *Out of the Blue: U.S. Army Airborne Operations in World War II*. West Lafayette, Indiana: Purdue University Press, 1972.
100. Iseley, Jeter A., and Philip A. Crowl. *The U.S. Marines and Amphibious War: Its Theory and Its Practice in the Pacific*. Princeton: Princeton University Press, 1951.
101. Jackson, W. G. F. *The Battle for Rome*. London: William Clowes & Son, 1969.
102. Jackson, W. G. F. *The Battle for Italy*. New York and Evanston, Illinois: Harper & Row, 1967.
103. James, D. Clayton ed. *South to Bataan, North to Mukden; the Prison Diary of Brigadier General W. E. Brougher*. Atlanta: University of Georgia Press, 1971.
104. Janeway, Eliot. *The Struggle for Survival: A Chronicle of Economic Mobilization in World War II*. New Haven: Yale University Press, 1951.
105. Kahn, Ely J. *McNair, Educator of an Army*. Washington: Infantry Journal Press, 1945.
106. Kennedy, Sir John. *The Business of War*. Edited by Bernard Fergusson. London: Hutchinson, 1957.
107. Kenny, George C. *General Kenny Reports, A Personal History of the Pacific War*. New York: Duell, Sloan & Pierce, 1949.
108. Kirby, H. Woodburn et al. *The War against Japan. History of the Second World War*, UK Military Series. Edited by J. R. M. Butler. London: H.M.S.O., 1957-69. 5 vols.
109. Kirk, John, and Robert Young Jr. *Great Weapons of World War II*. New York: Walker, 1961.

110. Kleber, Brooks E., and Dale Birdsell. *The Chemical Warfare Service; Chemicals in Combat*. US Army in World War II Series, *The Technical Services*. Washington: G.P.O., 1965.

111. Krueger, General Walter. *From Down Under to Nippon; The Story of the Sixth Army in World War II*. Washington: Combat Forces Press, 1953.

111a. Lane, Frederic. *Ships for Victory: A History of Shipbuilding Under the U.S. Maritime Commission in World War II*. Baltimore: John Hopkins Press, 1951.

112. Langer, William S., and S. Everett Gleason. *The Challenge to Isolation, 1937-1940*. New York: Harper & Bros., 1952; *The Undeclared War, 1940-41*, 1953.

113. Leahy, Admiral William D. *I Was There*. New York: McGraw-Hill Book Co., 1950.

114. Leckie, Robert. *Challenge for the Pacfic: Guadalcanal, the Turning Point of the War*. Garden City, New York: Doubleday, 1965.

115. Lee, Ulysses. *The Employment of Negro Troops*. US Army in World War II Series, *Special Studies*. Washington: G.P.O., 1955.

116. Leighton, Richard M., and Robert W. Coakley. *Global Logistics and Strategy, 1940-1943*. US Army in World War II Series, *The War Department*. Washington: G.P.O., 1955.

117. Lerner, David. *Sykewar: Psychological Warfare Against Germany, D-Day to VE-Day*. New York: George W. Stewart Co., 1949.

118. Liang, Chin-Tung. *General Stilwell in China: The Full Story*. Jamaica, New York: St. John's University Press, 1973.

119. Linebarger, Paul M. A. *Psychological Warfare*. Washington: Infantry Journal Press, 1948.

120. Lord, Walter. *Day of Infamy*. New York, Holt, 1957.

121. Lyon, Peter. *Eisenhower: Portrait of the Hero*. Boston: Little Brown & Co., 1971.

122. MacArthur, Douglas. *A Soldier Speaks: Public Papers*. New York: Praeger, 1965.

123. MacArthur, Douglas. *Reminiscences*. New York: McGraw-Hill, 1964.

124. MacDonald, Charles B. *Company Commander*. Washington: Infantry Journal Press, 1947.

125. MacDonald, Charles B. *The Siegfried Line Campaign*. US Army in World War II Series, *European Theater of Operations*. Washington: G.P.O., 1963.

126. MacDonald, Charles B. *The Last Offensive*. US Army in World War II Series, *European Theater of Operations*. Washington: G.P.O., 1974.

127. MacDonald, Charles B. *The Mighty Endeavour: American Armed Forces in the European Theater in World War II*. New York: Oxford University Press, 1969.

128. MacDonald, Charles B. *The Battle of Huertgen Forest*, Philadelphia: Lippincott, 1963.

129. MacDonald, Charles B., and Sidney T. Matthews. *Three Battles: Arnaville, Altozzo, and Schmidt*. US Army in World War II Series, *Special Studies*. Washington: G.P.O., 1952.

130. Majdalany, Fred. *Cassino: Portrait of a Battle*. London: Longmans Green, 1957.
131. Margolian, Leo J. *Paper Bullets: A Brief Story of Psychological Warfare in World War II*. New York: Freben, 1946.
132. Marshall, George C., H. H. Arnold, and Ernest J. King. *The War Reports of General of the Army George C. Marshall, Chief of Staff, General of the Army H. H. Arnold, Commanding General, Army Air Forces, and Fleet Admiral Ernest J. King, Commander in Chief, United States Fleet, and Chief of Naval Operations*. Philadelphia: Lippincott, 1947.
133. Marshall, S. L. A. *Island Victory*. Washington and New York: Penguin Books by Infantry Journal Press, 1944.
134. Marshall, S. L. A. *Bastogne, The Story of the First Eight Days in Which the 101st Airborne Division Was Closed within the Ring of German Force*. Washington: Infantry Journal Press, 1944.
135. Marshall, S. L. A. *Men Against Fire*. Washington and New York: William Morrow Co., 1947.
136. Marshall, S. L. A. *Night Drop: The American Airborne Invasion of Normandy*. Boston: Little Brown & Co., 1962.
137. Matloff, Maurice and Edwin M. Snell. *Stragetic Planning for Coalition Warfare, 1941-1942*. US Army in World War II Series, *The War Department*. Washington: G.P.O., 1953.
138. Matloff, Maurice. *Strategic Planning for Coalition Warfare, 1943-1944*. US Army in World War II Series, *The War Department*. Washington: G.P.O., 1959.
139. Mauldin, William H. *Up Front*. Cleveland and New York: World Press, 1945.
140. Mayo, Lida. *Bloody Buna*. New York: Doubleday, 1974.
141. Mayo, Lida. *The Ordnance Department: On Beachhead and Battle Front*. US Army in World War II Series, *The Technical Services*. Washington: G.P.O., 1968.
141a. McNeill, William H. *America, Britain, and Russia: Their Co-operation and Conflict*. London: Oxford University Press, 1953.
142. Mediterranean Theater of Operations, United States Army, G-4 Section. *Logistical History of NATOUSA-MTOUSA*. Naples, Italy: G. Montanino, 1945. Available on film from the Photo-Duplication Service, Library of Congress, Washington 20540, for about $440.
143. Merriam, Robert E. *The Battle of the Ardennes*. London: Souvenir Press, 1958.
144. Miller, John Jr. *Guadalcanal: The First Offensive*. US Army in World War II Series, *The War in the Pacific*. Washington, G.P.O., 1949.
145. Miller, John Jr. *CARTWHEEL: The Reduction of Rabaul*. US Army in World War II Series, *The War in the Pacific*. Washington: G.P.O., 1959.
146. Millett, John D. *The Organization and Role of the Army Service Forces*. US Army in World War II Series, *The Army Service Forces*. Washington: G.P.O., 1954.
147. Millis, Walter. *This is Pearl! The United States and Japan*. New

York: William Morrow Co., 1947.

148. Milner, Samuel. *Victory in Papua*. US Army in World War II Series, *The War in the Pacific*. Washington: G.P.O., 1957.

149. Montgomery, Field Marshal Bernard L., *Normandy to the Baltic*. London: Hutchinson, 1947.

150. Montgomery, Field Marshal Bernard L. *The Memoirs of Field Marshal the Viscount Montgomery of Alamein, K. G.* Cleveland and New York, World Press, 1958.

151. Morgan, Sir Frederick. *Overture to OVERLORD*. Garden City, New York: Doubleday, 1950.

152. Morgan, Henry G., "Planning the Defeat of Japan: A Study of Total War Strategy." Unpublished MS, U.S. Army Center of Military History.

153. Morgenstern, George E. *Pearl Harbor: The Story of the Secret War.* New York: Devin-Adair, 1947.

154. Morison, Elting E. *Turmoil and Tradition: A Study of the Life and Times of Henry L. Stimson.* Boston: Houghton Mifflin, 1960.

155. Morison, Samuel Eliot. *History of U.S. Naval Operations in World War II.* Boston: Little Brown & Co., 1950-62. 15 vols.

156. Morison, Samuel Eliot. *Strategy and Compromise.* Boston: Little Brown, 1958.

157. Morton, Louis. *The Fall of the Philippines.* US Army in World War II, *The War in the Pacific.* Washington: G.P.O., 1953.

158. Morton, Louis. *Strategy and Command: The First Two Years.* US Army in World War II Series, *The War in the Pacific.* Washington: G.P.O., 1962.

159. Motter, T. H. Vail. *The Persian Corridor and Aid to Russia.* US Army in World War II Series, *The Middle East Theater.* Washington: G.P.O., 1952.

160. Murphy, Audie. *To Hell and Back.* New York: Henry Holt & Co., 1949.

161. Ogburn, Charlton Jr. *The Marauders.* New York: Harper & Bros., 1956.

162. Orgill, Douglas. *The Gothic Line: The Italian Campaign, Autumn, 1944.* New York: W. W. Norton, 1967.

163. Palmer, Robert R., Bell I. Wiley, and William R. Keast. *The Procurement and Training of Ground Combat Troops.* US Army in World War II Series, *Army Ground Forces.* Washington: G.P.O., 1948.

164. Patton, George S. *War as I Knew it.* Annotated by Paul D. Harkins, edited by Beatrice A. Patton. Boston: Houghton Mifflin, 1947.

165. Playfair, I. S. O., C. J. C. Molony, et al. *The Mediterranean and Middle East. History of the Second World War*, UK Military Series. Edited by J. R. M. Butler. London: H.M.S.O., 1954-73. 6 vols.

166. Pogue, Forrest C. *The Supreme Command.* US Army in World War II Series, *European Theater of Operations.* Washington: G.P.O., 1954.

167. Pogue, Forrest C. *George C. Marshall: Ordeal and Hope, 1939-1942.* New York: Viking Press, 1973.

168. Pogue, Forrest C. *George C. Marshall, Organizer of Victory 1943-1945.* New York: Viking Press, 1973.
169. Pyle, Ernest T. *Brave Men.* New York: Grosset & Dunlap, 1945.
170. Pyle, Ernest T. *Here is Your War.* New York: Henry Holt & Co., 1943.
171. Riegelman, Harold. *Caves of Biak: An American Officer's Experience in the Southwest Pacific.* New York: Dial Press, 1955.
172. Risch, Erna. *The Quartermaster Corps: Organization, Supply, and Services.* US Army in World War II Series, *The Technical Services.* Washington: G.P.O., 1953-55. (Vol. 2 with Chester L. Kieffer). 2 vols.
173. Romanus, Charles F., and Riley Sunderland. *Stilwell's Mission to China; Stilwell's Command Problems; Time Runs Out in the CBI.* US Army in World War II Series, *The China-Burma-India Theater.* Washington: G.P.O., 1953-59. 3 vols.
174. Ross, William F. and Charles F. Romanus. *The Quartermaster Corps: Operations in the War Against Germany.* US Army in World War II Series. Washington: G.P.O., 1965.
175. Rundell, Walter. *Black Market Money: The Collapse of U.S. Military Currency Control in World War II.* Baton Rouge: Louisiana State University Press, 1964.
176. Ruppenthal, Roland G. *Logistical Support of the Armies.* US Army in World War II Series, *European Theater of Operations.* Washington: G.P.O., 1953-59. 2 vols.
177. Ryan, Cornelius. *The Longest Day, June 6, 1944.* New York: Simon & Shuster, 1959.
178. Ryan, Cornelius. *The Last Battle.* New York: Simon & Shuster, 1966.
179. Ryan, Cornelius. *A Bridge Too Far.* New York: Simon & Shuster, 1974.
180. Shaw, Henry I. et al. *History of the United States Marine Corps Operations in World War II.* Washington: G.P.O., 1956-71. 4 vols.
181. Sherwood, Robert S. *Roosevelt and Hopkins: An Intimate History.* New York: Harpers, revised edition, 1950.
182. Sill, Van R. *American Miracle: The Story of War Construction around the World.* New York: Odyssey Press, 1947.
183. Silvera, John D. *The Negro in World War II.* New York: Arno Press, 1969.
184. Smith, Clarence M., *The Medical Department: Hospitalization and Evacuation, Zone of the Interior.* US Army in World War II Series, *The Technical Services.* Washington: G.P.O., 1956.
185. Smith, R. Elberton. *The Army and Economic Mobilization.* US Army in World War II Series, *The War Department.* Washington: G.P.O., 1959.
186. Smith, Robert Ross. *The Approach to the Philippines.* US Army in World War II Series, *The War in the Pacific.* Washington: G.P.O., 1953.
187. Smith, Robert Ross. *Triumph in the Philippines.* US Army in World War II Series, *The War in the Pacific.* Washington: G.P.O., 1963.

188. Smith, Lt. Gen. Walter B. *Eisenhower's Six Great Decisions.* New York, Longmans Green & Co., 1956.
189. Smyth, Howard McGaw and Lt. Col. Albert N. Garland. *Sicily and the Surrender of Italy.* US Army in World War II Series, *Mediterranean Theater of Operations.* Washington: G.P.O., 1965.
190. Stalin, Joseph. *Stalin's Correspondence with Churchill, Roosevelt, and Truman, 1941-1945.* New York: E. P. Dutton, 1958.
191. Starr, Lt. Col. Chester G., ed. *From Salerno to the Alps, A History of the Fifth Army, 1943-1945.* Washington: Infantry Journal Press, 1948.
192. Steele, Richard W. *The First Offensive, 1942.* Bloomington and London: Indiana University Press, 1973.
193. Stilwell, Joseph W. *The Stilwell Papers.* Arranged and edited by Theodore White, New York: Sloane, 1948.
194. Stimson, Henry L. and McGeorge Bundy. *On Active Service in Peace and War.* New York: Harpers, 1948.
194a. Stauffer, Alvin P. *The Quartermaster Corps: Operations in the War against Japan.* US Army in World War II Series, *The Technical Services.* Washington: G.P.O., 1956.
194b. Stone, James H., ed. *Crisis Fleeting: Original Reports on Military Medicine in India and Burma in the Second World War.* Washington: Office of the Surgeon General, 1969.
195. Stouffer, Samuel A. et al. *Studies in Social Psychology in World War II:* Vol. I, *The American Soldier: Adjustment during Army Life;* Vol. II, *The American Soldier: Combat and its Aftermath;* Vol. III, *Experiments in Mass Communication;* Vol. IV, *Measurement and Prediction.* Princeton: Princeton University Press, 1949. 4 vols.
196. Terrett, Dulany. *The Signal Corps: The Emergency.* US Army in World War II Series, *The Technical Services.* Washington: G.P.O., 1956.
197. Thiesmayer, Lincoln R. and John F. Burchard. *Combat Scientists.* Edited by Alan T. Waterman. *Science in World War II,* Office of Scientific Research and Development. Boston: Little Brown, 1947.
198. Thompson, George Raynor, Dixie R. Harris, Pauline M. Oakes, and Dulany Terrett. *The Signal Corps: The Test (December 1941 to July 1943).* US Army in World War II Series, *The Technical Services.* Washington: G.P.O., 1957.
199. Thompson, George Raynor and Dixie R. Harris. *The Signal Corps: The Outcome (July 1943 Through 1945).* US Army in World War II Series, *The Technical Services.* Washington: G.P.O., 1966.
200. Thomson, Harry C., and Lida Mayo. *The Ordnance Department: Procurement and Supply.* US Army in World War II Series. *The Technical Services.* Washington: G.P.O., 1960.
201. Toland, John. *Battle, The Story of the Bulge.* New York: Random House, 1959.
202. Toland, John. *The Last Hundred Days.* New York: Random House, 1966.
203. Treadwell, Mattie E. *The Women's Army Corps.* US Army in World War II, *Special Studies.* Washington: G.P.O., 1954.

204. Tregaskis, Richard W. *Guadalcanal Diary.* New York: Random House, 1955.
205. Truscott, Lucian K. *Command Missions: A Personal Story.* New York: Dutton, 1954.
206. Tsou, Tang. *America's Failure in China, 1941-1950.* Chicago: University of Chicago Press, 1963.
207. Tuchman, Barbara W. *Stilwell and the American Experience in China.* New York: Macmillan Co., 1971.
208. United States Army, Europe, Historical Division. *Guide to Foreign Military Studies.* Karlsruhe, Germany: 1954. Supplement issued in 1959.
209. United States Army Forces in the Pacific. *Engineers of the Southwest Pacific, 1942-45.* Washington: G.P.O., 1947-59. 8 vols.
210. United States Army Forces in the South Pacific, G-2 Historical Section. "History of United States Army Forces in the South Pacific During World War II from 30 March 1942 to 1 August 1944." MS, typescript, U.S. Army Center of Military History. 4 vols.
211. United States Army Forces in the Middle Pacific. "History of U.S. Army Forces, AFMIDPAC and Predecessor Commands." MS typescript, U.S. Army Center of Military History. 32 vols.
212. United States Army Military History Research Collection. *Special Bibliography of United States Army Unit Histories.* Carlisle Barracks, Pennsylvania: Sept., 1971.
213. United States Army Military History Research Collection. Special Bibliographic Series No. 6, *Manuscript Holdings of the Military History Research Collection.* Compiled by R. J. Sommers. Carlisle Barracks, Pennsylvania: August, 1972.
214. United States Army Service Forces, Information and Education Division. *Combat Divisions of World War II, Army of the United States.* Washington: 1946.
215. United States Army Service Forces, Control Division. *Statistical Review, World War II.* Washington, 1946.
216. United States Congress, *Hearings Before the Joint Committee on the Investigation of the Pearl Harbor Attack*, 79th Cong., 1st Sess. 38 parts. *Report* of Committee is Senate Document No. 244, 79th Cong., 2nd Sess., 1946.
217. United States Department of the Army. *The Reports of General MacArthur prepared by his General Staff.* Washington: G.P.O., 1966. 2 vols.
218. United States Department of the Army. *Medical Department United States Army in World War II, Clinical Series.* Washington: G.P.O., 1948-73. 32 vols. published.
219. United States Department of the Army, Office Chief of Military History. "Statistics." Prepared by R. H. Crawford, Lindsley F. Cook, George R. Powell, under the direction of Theodore E. Whiting. 9 sections: Military Personnel; Decorations and Awards; Civilian Personnel; Casualties; American Civilian Internees; Maintenance; Lend-Lease; Procurement.
220. United States Department of the Army, Office Chief of Military History. *Guide to Japanese Monographs and Japanese Studies on Manchuria.*

221. United States Department of the Army, Office Chief of Military History. *The War against Germany and Italy: Mediterranean and Adjacent Areas; The War against Germany: Europe and Adjacent Areas; The War against Japan.* US Army in World War II Series, *The Pictorial Record.* Washington: G.P.O., 1951-52, 3 vols.

222. United States Department of the Army, Office Chief of Military History. *Reader's Guide, United States Army in World War II.* Washington: G.P.O., 1960.

223. United States Department of Defense. *The Entry of the Soviet Union into the War against Japan, Military Plans 1941-45.* Washington: Special Release, 1955.

224. United States Forces European Theater, General Board. *General Board Reports.* 131 Studies. MS, U.S. Army Center of Military History.

225. United States Military Academy, Department of Military Art and Engineering. *A Military History of World War II.* Edited by T. Dodson Stamps and Vincent J. Esposito. West Point, New York: U.S. Military Academy, 1953-56. 2 vols.

226. United States National Archives. *Federal Records of World War II.* Washington: G.P.O., 1950. (Under revision in 1971). 2 vols.

227. United States War Department, Historical Division. *Armed Forces in Action.* Washington: G.P.O., 1943-46. 14 paperback volumes. *To Biserte with the II Corps (23 April-13 May 1943); Utah Beach to Cherbourg (6 June-27 June 1944); Salerno: American Operations from the Beaches to the Volturno (9 September-6 October 1943); Papuan Campaign: The Buna-Savanda Operation (16 November 1942-23 January 1943); From the Volturno to the Winter Line (6 October-15 November 1943); Omaha Beach to Cherbourg (6 June-13 June 1944); Anzio Beachhead, (22 January-25 May 1944); Merrill's Marauders (February-March 1944); The Admiralties: Operations of the 1st Cavalry Division (29 February-18 May 1944); Fifth Army at the Winter Line (15 November 1943-15 January 1944); The Capture of Makin (20 November-24 November 1943); Guam: Operations of the 77th Division (21 July-10 August 1944); Small Unit Actions; St. Lo (7 July-19 July 1944).*

228. Vigneras, Marcel. *Rearming the French.* US Army in World War II Series, *Special Studies. Washington: G.P.O., 1957.*

229. Wainwright, Jonathan M. *General Wainwright's Story.* Edited by Robert Considine. Garden City, New York: Doubleday, 1946.

230. Wardlow, Chester. *The Transportation Corps; Movements, Training, and Supply* and *Responsibilities, Organization, and Operations.* US Army in World War II Series, The Technical Services. Washington: G.P.O., 1951-56. 2 vols.

231. Watson, Mark S. *Chief of Staff: Prewar Plans and Preparations.* US Army in World War II Series, *The War Department.* Washington: G.P.O., 1950.

232. Wedemeyer, Albert C. *Wedemeyer Reports.* New York: Henry Holt, 1958.

233. Whitney, Courtney. *MacArthur: His Rendezvous with History.* New York: Knopf, 1956.

234. Williams, Mary A. *Chronology, 1941-1945*. US Army in World War II Series, *Special Studies*. Washington: G.P.O., 1950.
235. Willoughby, Charles A. and John Chamberlain. *MacArthur: 1941-1951: Victory in the Pacific*. London: Heineman, 1956.
236. Wilmot, Chester. *The Struggle for Europe*. New York: Harper, 1952.
237. Wiltse, Charles. *The Medical Department: Medical Service in the Mediteranean and Minor Theaters*. US Army in World War II Series, *The Technical Services*. Washington: G.P.O., 1966.
238. Wohlstetter, Roberta. *Pearl Harbor: Warning and Decision*. Stanford, California: Stanford University Press, 1962.
239. *Yank*, The Army Weekly. *YANK—The G. I. Story of the War*, By the Staff of *Yank*, the Army Weekly, selected and edited by Deb Myers and others. New York: Duell, Sloan & Pearce, 1947.
240. Ziegler, Janet. *World War II: Books in English, 1945-65*. Stanford, California: Hoover Institution Press, 1971.

XV

THE U.S. ARMY AIR CORPS
AND THE UNITED STATES
AIR FORCE, 1909-1973

Robert Frank Futrell

Even though the development of military aviation has had a major impact upon national life in the United States, relatively little scholarly attention has been given to anything approaching definitive histories of the U.S. Army Air Corps and the U.S. Air Force. For the first time during the years of World War II many professional historians worked in preparation of studies of wartime activity, but few of these professionals maintained any productive interest in air history after they returned to civilian life. Most went back to teaching and research in their original fields. After World War II, the continuing Air Force historical program—with a few notable exceptions—was mostly given to maintaining an internal Air Force institutional memory through the preparation of usually classified recurring historical reports and some special studies on subjects of Air Force interest. The mighty obstacle of security classifications denied civilian scholars free access to official source material, thus diminishing general interest in working in air history. In the mid-seventies the declassification of nearly all Department of Defense documents through 1945 and of Air Force documents through 1955 (314) may encourage scholarly research in military history, but it will be dificult. Historians must develop personal expertise necessary to work in air history and must be assured of reasonable prospects for publication of their histories. Especially in recent years, the market for military histories has been mainly for well-illustrated and popularly written "buff" narratives rather than for more substantial but inevitably less saleable efforts.

JOURNALS. Because of limited access to official sources, one of the principal sources for publishable air history has been official histories and periodical literature. In addition to standard military periodicals (196, 281) the principal Air Force journal—even though published by the unofficial Air Force Association—is *Air Force Magazine* (5). *The Airman* (7) is the official monthly magazine of the USAF, and the *Air University Review* (6) is published to stimulate professional thought. *Aviation Week and Space Technology* (13) provides a wide range of current information, chiefly technical. These journals are only incidentally concerned with air history, although it is perhaps significant that *Air Force Magazine* first published Goldberg's USAF history (105) and Schwiebert's history of missles (234), and articles from the *Air University Review* were assembled in three published books (64, 98, 245). The three important air historical journals are *Aerospace Historian* (4), the *American Aviation Historical Society Journal* (8), and *Cross and Cockade Journal* (57), the latter being concerned solely with World War I. The most detailed listing of articles of air interest appearing in military and aeronautical periodicals since 1949 is the quarterly *Air University Library Index to Military Periodicals* (267). Estep's bibliographies (76) are convenient screenings of pertinent articles as well as books, while articles and books of historical interest are also listed in the Cresswell-Berger bibliography of USAF history (56).

OFFICIAL HISTORIES AND GOVERNMENT DOCUMENTS. In the years between World Wars, the Army Air Corps had no official service histories independently of the U.S. Army, whose Historical Section functioned very slowly. The Army Historical Section's multivolume compendium of documents on World War I (275) was ultimately published in 1948 and includes some notice of Air Service activity. Under this circumstance, General Patrick's final report as chief, Air Service A E. F. (215) is perhaps the official Air Service history for World War I. As for logistics, the report of Benedict Crowell, assistant secretary of war and director of munitions, describes the procurement process and also the characteristics of aviation munitions (58). In addition, Colonel Edgar S. Gorrell superintended the preparation of individual Air Service unit histories. This so-called "Gorrell History" was collected in 286 manuscript volumes (58 microfilm rolls) in the National Archives and is the most substantial single collection of historical data relative to Air Service unit activities in World War I (107).

Under a directive from President Franklin D. Roosevelt that each agency would prepare an administrative record of its World War II activities, the U.S. Army Air Forces appointed an AAF Historian and established a Historical Division in 1942. A large number of historians was assembled for war service in Headquarters AAF, at commands and installations in the United States, and with combat air forces overseas. All AAF units were required to submit historical reports, and historians in Washington and at major headquarters prepared histories and historical monographs. The Air Historical Group was continued in the U.S. Air Force. But with much reduced personnel. It was moved from Washington to the Air University, Maxwell AFB, Alabama, in September 1949 and was renamed the USAF Historical Division. At this time, a small USAF Historical Division Liaison Office remained in Washington. In January 1969, the establishment was reversed when the Office of Air Force History (AFCHO) was opened under the USAF chief of staff in Washington, and the division at Maxwell AFB was redesignated the Albert F. Simpson Historical Research Center in memory of the first USAF Historian. The Historical Research Center retains the responsibility for assembling and maintaining the Air Force historical archives for both official and public research. The Office of Air Force History is in process of publishing an extensive chronology of air events in World War II and a pictorial history of the Air Force in Southeast Asia. A series of histories about the war in Southeast Asia is also projected for publication.

An incomplete list of the titles of AAF and USAF official histories and studies appears in Robin Higham's *Official Histories* (133, pp. 610-619), while additional volumes are noted here. All are available at the Historical Research Center, Maxwell AFB, Alabama. These official productions are based upon official papers, many of which have continued to be classified even after the histories were declassified. The greatest number of the histories was completed during World War II and was partly designed to support the preparation of more widely disseminated Air Force histories, these progressing through interim publication of a single AAF historical narrative (268) and a "Wings at War" series of popular histories (272) to the final official seven-volume *Army Air Forces in World War II* (55). Similarly, three originally classified USAF historical studies became the base for the official *United States Air Force in Korea, 1950-1953* (97). Other studies were drawn upon by the authors of *A History of the United States Air Force, 1907-1957*, edited by Alfred Goldberg (105). These service histories are important for their assembly and revelation of official sources, but each was prepared relatively close to the events described, and each was released with a recognition that additional sources would likely become available. Another part of the work of the USAF Historical Division was the preparation and publication —under direction of Maurer Maurer—of official studies on air victory credits (136, 191, 192) and two definitive lineage volumes on Air Force combat units (189) and combat squadrons (190) of World War II.

In addition to the formal historical program of World War II, AAF Commander General Henry H. Arnold wanted a portrayal of air activities in theaters of operations from the personal view of men in the field. In this program—conducted by an AAF Personnel Narratives Office—well-known authors were sponsored. Their production included innovative histories by Walter D. Edmonds (69), Vern Haugland (125), Harold B. Hinton (135), and Clive Howard and Joe Whitley (144), all of whom pioneered in oral historical techniques to provide popular but sound books. The wartime AAF medical history was also independently prepared by Link and Coleman (173) within the Office of the Air Surgeon.

Although the subject of government publications is addressed elsewhere (chapter XIX), any study of air history remains specifically dependent upon the many massive investigations undertaken by official agencies relative to air power, as well as upon published official reports. The catalogues and later monthly catalogues of the U.S. Superintendent of Documents (285) provide a general finding aid to aviation subjects. The U.S. Strategic Bombing Survey is a wide-ranging source for strategic air power evaluations of World War II, and its many reports are conveniently catalogued (284). It is less well known that U.S. World War II tactical air operations were separately evaluated by AAF Evaluation Boards in each major war theater (269). A complete file of these reports is in the Historical Research Center archives. Two of the many congressional hearings on air power are cited here as illustrations of valuable historical source material, namely the Senate Armed Services Committee's hearings in 1956-1957 entitled *Study on Airpower* (280) and in 1967 on *Air War Against North Vietnam* (279). The report of President Harry S. Truman's Air Policy Commission (the Finletter Commission) is cited as an illustration of a fact-finding report (283). A bibliography of all such hearings and official reports would be very handy but does not exist. In addition to these special publications, semiannual and annual reports of the secretary of defense (276, 277, 278, 282) contain useful, though much watered down, information about military matters, including the Air Force. Two Air Force submissions had been prepared when publication of the secretary of defense report was suspended in mid-1968 and have been put out by the Office of Air Force History (273, 274). Official statistics of the Army Air Forces in World War II were published in an *AAF Statistical Digest* (271).

In the years since 1948, the Research and Development (RAND) Corporation has conducted many semiofficial studies under the sponsorship of the Air Force. A number of these RAND studies are unclassified and are of historical importance (221).

PRIVATE PAPERS. The currently definitive catalogue of collections of private papers of significance to air history appears in Lawrence J. Paszek's, *A Guide to Documentary Sources* (214). Some collections are known to be mostly memorabilia (frequently photo albums), but others are rich in correspondence and diaries.

GENERAL HISTORIES. There is no single scholarly general history of the USAF and its predecessors although such a study is in preparation by Colonel Alfred E. Hurley (149). At present the closest approach to a general history is Goldberg's (105). In original conception, *A Quarter Century of Air Power, 1947-1972*, edited by Lieutenant Colonel John H. Scrivner, was expected to parallel and extend the Goldberg history, but it went wide of the mark and ended as a collection of chapters on recent uses of air power (237). Emme's *Impact of Air Power* (72) is a useful source of documentation on the development of air power and the USAF. Futrell's, *Ideas, Concepts, Doctrine: A History of Basic Thinking in the United States Air Force, 1907-1964* (96), traces the development of the Air Force as a manifestation of conceptual thought. Higham's, *Air Power: A Concise History*, offers a broad sweep of airpower experience (131). Hinton's, *Air History: The Men and the Machines* (135), encompasses the period from World War I to the end of World War II but is of course now dated. Other recent efforts at single volumes, such as General MacCloskey's, *The United States Air Force* (179), Richard's, *TAC: The Story of Tactical Air Command* (145), Hubler's *SAC: The Strategic Air Command* (145), and Vandergrift's, *A History of the Air Rescue Service* (286), tend to be illustrative and descriptive rather than straight history.

In the absence of a general Air Force history it is possible to put together something of a narrative of developing air organization by reference to the works of McClendon (177, 178), Harry Howe Ransom (223), Mooney and Layman (198, 199), and Edwin Williams (308). The dissertation by Tarr offers a still broader look at a century and a half of efforts toward U.S. defense unification (253). One of the problems encountered by neophyte AAF historians in World War II was lack of a background of events prior to 1939, and this inevitably required historical research to sketch backward. Thus Clauseen found it necessary to trace air materiel research and development from 1914 to get to 1945 (45, 47); Holley's monographs on liaison aircraft and gun turrets (138, 139) ran back to 1917; and Layman provided a separate study on air personnel and training programs between 1907-1939 (169) as

408 • A GUIDE TO THE SOURCES OF U.S. MILITARY HISTORY

background to her World War II study on the organization of AAF training (170). Similarly, Cohen covered the whole subject of the classification and assignment of air enlisted personnel from 1917 through 1945 (49).

Studies of the development of aerial technology and techniques necessarily demand and have received treatment over spans of years rather than in arbitrary time frames. Thus Monte Wright's excellent new history of aerial navigation (312) progresses from earliest beginnings to early World War II. Futrell's study of aeromedical transport is a full record up to 1960 (95). Infield's *Unarmed and Unafraid* (151) is a substantial record of aerial reconnaissance from the beginnings to the near present. Green Peyton (217) traces the history of aerospace medicine through fifty years, and Ryan (232) handles the long course of history of Scott Air Force Base. Prepared in the Office of Air Force History, Riley Sunderland's concise *Evolution of Command and Control Doctrine for Close Air Support* (247) follows the mechanics of close air support for ground operations from earliest beginnings through Indochina. Finally, Rae's survey of the development of the American aircraft industry in the years 1920-1960 (219) provides an excellent background for military considerations since the USAF has always depended upon private industry for most of its warplanes.

EARLY DAYS AND WORLD WAR I. The history of early military aeronautics in the United States was pioneered by Haydon (126) and was more fully developed by Juliette Hennesy (128), but·it is perhaps significant that more modern scholarship by Parkinson (212) has at last begun to show the real relationship between the adventurous early days and modern aeronautics. The more popular narrations by Colonel Sunderman (248), Tillman (259), and Harris (122) hold nostalgic interest.

American air experience during World War I has not been adequately addressed. Aside from the official sources already noted (107, 215, 275), Sweetser (252) and Toulmin (262) are useful but out of date, and both Generals Patrick (216) and Mitchell (206) offer recollections rather than history. The first modern scholarship on aviation in World War I was I. B. Holley's, *Ideas and Weapons* (140), followed by Lieutenant Colonel Flammer on the Lafayette Escadrille (84), Frank on Air Service aerial observation (90), and Hudson's able and complete combat history of the Air Service A. E. F. (146). Whitehouse's *Decisive Air Battles of the First World War* (307) is a good popular history by a World War I aviator.

BETWEEN THE WARS. The two decades from 1919-1939 were the major developmental period for American military aviation and were marked by emergence of strong American air leaders. Their struggle to provide an air power doctrine of war was first told in Earle's *Makers of Modern Strategy* (68) and is much more fully developed in Greer's *Development of Air Doctrine in the Army Air Arm, 1917-1941* (113). While Robert T. Finney's, *History of the Air Corps Tactical School, 1920-1940* (83), is only a brief summary, that little study should persuade some scholar to develop its full history as a seat of seminal air power thinking. The dissertations by Flugel (88) and Brune (34) offer information about air doctrinal developments, but Flugel's work was somewhat narrowly conceived. The late Mark S. Watson's *Chief of Staff: Prewar Plans and Preparations* (297) in the *United States Army in World War*

II series is a very mature account of General George C. Marshall's grasp of air power thinking at the end of the years between wars.

Such proving of air power in operations as there was between World Wars I and II is addressed by Hinkle (134), Horvat (143), and in Glines' story of the air mail fiasco (102), but a full development of the many pioneer flights and aerial military-civic action works of the period is not at hand, although Wesley Newton notes the significance of some of this between 1916-1929 (209). And Colonel Whiteley has recently published his memoirs (316). In the 1920s and 1930s there was a close and complementary relation between developing civil and military aviation. The dissertations of Downs (68), Bilstein (21), and Rutkowski (231) are significant to this subject.

WORLD WAR II. It is entirely probable that the official seven-volume *The Army Air Forces in World War II* prepared under the editorship of Professors W. Frank Craven and James Lea Cate (55) will always be the definitive narration of purely U.S. Army Air Forces experience in World War II, and the problem for future historical scholarship here is one of amending and extending this work—published too shortly after the events described—in terms of added and elaborative historical interpretations and evidence that were not available to Craven's and Cate's authors.

In presentations of strategy, especially in relation to strategic bombardment of Germany and Japan, Craven and Cate follows the views of wartime AAF commanders. Later historical scholarship—beginning with the monumental history of the Royal Air Force Bomber Command by Sir Charles Webster and Noble Frankland (304) and pursued by Emerson (70), Greenfield (112), Colonel Perry McCoy Smith (244), Higham (131, 132, 99), and by Frankland (91, 99)—has questioned the wisdom of the primacy accorded to strategic bombing, as well as the moral aspects of such bombing. The latter matter is dreadfully emphasized in Irving's *Destruction of Dresden* (154) and is only partly countered in Melden E. Smith's *The Bombing of Dresden Reconsidered* (243). On the other hand, General Hansell's, *The Air Plan that Defeated Hitler* (120), provides a sharper focus on strategic bombing theory from an American viewpoint than that in Craven and Cate, while Verrier's *Bomber Offensive* (287) shows a closer relationship between Anglo-American plans and operations than provided by either Craven and Cate or Webster and Frankland.

Although the seven volumes of *The Army Air Forces in World War II* are each of substantial length, individual chapters were tightly limited in space, with the result of forcing authors to display minimum detail. Only two of the seven volumes, moreover, deal with AAF support for combat operations, even though this was the predominant wartime activity. For this reason, AAF and USAF historical studies provide some of the needed elaboration often not included in the seven volume history. Among operational studies, those by Cate (38, 39), Coles (51, 52, 53), Ferguson (80, 81), George (100), Mayock (193, 194), Olson (210, 211), Ramsey (220), Frank Ransom (222), Taylor (254, 255, 256), Harris Warren (293), John C. Warren (294, 295), Watson (298, 299, 300), Weaver (302, 303), and Kathleen Williams (310, 311) are quite useful supplements. In regard to training, one should see Baldwin (17), Grant (110), Hollon (141), McNarney (185), Walters (292), White (306), and Howard Williams (309). Others studies elaborate logistical matters: Ackerman (1), Acomb (2), Claussen (46), Davis and Fenwick (59), Futrell (94), Russel and Claussen (229), and Toole and Ackerman (261). Other useful studies in the air historical series are Goldman on morale (106), England and Reither on women air force pilots (73), Futrell on command of observation aviation (93), Weathers on acquisition of AAF bases in Latin America (301), and Werrell's *Tactical Development of the Eighth Air Force Force in World War II.* (305).

At least two of the major histories of World War II air logistics grew out of service by their authors in the wartime AAF historical program. These are Holley's definitive *Buying Aircraft, Materiel Procurement for the Army Air Forces* (137), and Coleman's, *Development of Tactical Services in the Army Air Forces* (50). After duty as a wartime AAF journalist, Douglas J. Ingells provided a human-interest history of aeronautical development work at Wright Field (153). Oliver LaFarge, wartime historical officer of the Air Transport Command, prepared a history of ATC, confusingly titled *The Eagle in the Egg* (166). Another look at the ATC in war is by Reginald M. Cleveland (48).

The official histories of World War II leave more than adequate room for added historical studies. The personnel narrative approach of Edmonds (69), Haugland (125), and Howard and Whitley (144) has been noted. For the veteran who wants identification of his particular combat unit, the two best popular histories of World War II air forces are Roger Freeman's *Mighty Eighth* (92) and Ken Rust's *Ninth Air Force in World War II* (230). *No High Ground*, by Knebel and Bailey; reveals the once highly classified details of the atomic bombing of Japan that were denied to earlier historians (164). Thomas G. Miller reaccounts the trying experiences of Americans flying from Guadalcanal (197). Both Caidin (36) and Jablonski (155) have books on the Schweinfurt-Regensburg attacks, as have Glines (101) and Merrill (195) on the Doolittle raid against Tokyo, all benefiting from access to enemy sources. The best of the air battle narratives is Dugan and Stewart on the Ploesti air raid against the Rumanian oil refineries (65) Throne's *The Hump* retells the story of wartime air transport into China (258). Shores, *Highways in the Sky* (239), describes the wartime Army Airways Communications Service. Charles E. Francis introduces the greatly neglected history of Black aviators in World War II in *The Tuskegee Airmen* (89) but by no means exhausts the subject, which remains fruitful for research and interpretation, such as is being begun by Stanley Sandler. Works of independent scholarship on World War II air activities include S. L. A. Marshall's *Night Drop* (188) and Huston's detailed study of worldwide airborne operations (150); Jim Boyle on the XXI Bomber Command (29); Robert Boyle on photo reconnaissance in North Africa (30); Julian on AAF operations against Germany from Russian bases (162); Lukas on AAF lend-lease assistance to the Soviet Union (176); Erdmann on leaflet propaganda operations (75); Volan's history of the Ground Observer Corps (288); and David MacIsaac's highly significant dissertation on the United States Strategic Bombing Survey (184).

AFTER WORLD WAR II. For the years of nuclear weapons confrontation since 1945, U.S. State and Defense papers on strategy generally remain classified. Military historians therefore face great difficulties in any efforts to relate military operations to national strategy, although it has

THE U.S. ARMY AIR CORPS AND THE U.S. AIR FORCE, 1909-1973 • 411

been possible to record limited war experiences and to describe the development of new weapons in some generality.

In the absence of free access to official high-level U.S. papers on strategy, it has been necessary to place an often unsure reliance on official reports of the Department of Defense (273, 274, 276, 277, 278, 282) and on Congressional hearings (279, 280). Similarly, writings of influential Americans such as James Forrestal (86), Finletter (82), Bush (35), and Enthoven (74) provide "insider's" accounts to guide research. Broad descriptions of American strategic concerns are available in Brodie's *Strategy in the Missile Age* (32), General Dale O. Smith's *U.S. Military Doctrine* (242), and Lowe's *Age of Deterrence* (175). Samuel Huntington (147) and Schilling, Hammond, and Snyder (233) relate strategic programs to national politics. General Noel F. Parrish's *Behind the Sheltering Bomb* (213) is a penetrating historical analysis of U.S. politico-military decisions between 1945 and 1950, while Harland B. Moulton has addressed American strategic power between 1945 and 1965 (207). A significant portrayal of the USAF influence on German-American relations is given in Hickman's dissertation (130), and a similar study could well be done for Japan.

It will be no surprise to anyone that inter-Service relationships have continued to strain Department of Defense unification. This subject is handled in Murray Green's study on Stuart Symington (111), Bald's historical considerations of joint training exercises (15, 16), Grant's air historical study on the beginnings of continental air defense (109), and in two narrations of inter-Service disputes relative to missiles by Evans (77) and Armacost (11).

The relationship of scientific development and new missile technology to the postwar USAF is indicated in Ball (18), Baar and Howard (14), Downs (64), Gantz (98), Johns (160), and in the Wright-Paszek edition of the proceedings of the third USAF Academy historical symposium (313). Tom Sturm's history of the USAF scientific advisory board (246) will certainly stand the test of time, and Schwiebert's *History of U.S. Air Force Ballistic Missiles* (234) is useful pending the appearance of a definitive history that will be freely based upon still classified official papers.

The employment of the USAF in post-World War II cold- and limited-war operations began with the Berlin Airlift of 1948-1949, where W. Phillips Davison, *The Berlin Blockade* (60), is the standard over-all narration, and Donovan's *Bridge in the Sky* (61) provides an accurate popular story of the airlift. The best overall history of the Korean conflict is provided by David Rees (224). Futrell's, *United States Air Force in Korea, 1950-1953* (97), is the official USAF history, while Colonel Stewart's, *Airpower: The Decisive Force in Korea* (245), is a collection of articles on air activities, including General O. P. Weyland's personal summary of combat experience. Annis G. Thompson's *The Greatest Airlift* (257) is an authoritative though popularly written story of USAF air transport in Korea. The Scrivner edition, *A Quarter Century of Air Power* (237), includes chapters on the Taiwan, Lebanon, Congo, Cuban missile, and Dominican Republic crises and on USAF air operations in Southeast Asia. Pending release of Office of Air Force History publications on Southeast Asia that are in preparation, the official *Report* of Admiral U.S.G. Sharp and General W. C. Westmoreland (238) is the best single source of interpretation and information about activities in Southeast Asia. Air views are spelled out in the Senate hearings on *Air War Against North Vietnam* (279). Jack Broughton's *Thud Ridge* (33) is a stirring narrative by a combat colonel who fouled out on restrictions upon air operations, and Frank Harvey's *The Air War—Vietnam* (124) contains on-scene reports of an experienced aviation writer. Both Goulding (108) and Hoopes (142) are criticisms of U.S. policy and of air operations by former administration officials, Hoopes having served as Under-Secretary of the Air Force (1967-1969). The Littauer-Uphoff edition, *Air War in Indochina* (174) is an expressly hostile portrayal of U.S. air atrocities that are alleged to have occurred in Vietnam and Laos.

BIOGRAPHIES AND AUTOBIOGRAPHIES. The men attracted to service in the Army Air Corps and U.S. Air Force were generally of active rather than literary leanings, with the result that relatively few American air leaders have provided memoirs or autobiographies. In any approach to biographical matters, however, several works are handy references, notably Fogerty's compilation of data entries on Air Force general officers from 1918 to 1952 (85) and DuPre's USAF biographical dictionary which is current as of 1965 (67). Colonels Chandler and Lahm (40) included personal vignettes of early airmen, and Curt Anders, *Fighting Airmen* (9), traces the growth of the Air Force through the careers of leading air officers. The memoirs of General Benjamin Foulois encompass almost the entire span of air history (87), and General George W. Goddard's *Overview* (104) is the best existing history of the development of aerial photography. General Harbold's *Log of Air Navigation* (121) is a short book on the origins of this art by one of the pioneers in the field.

In the World War I period, General "Billy" Mitchell's *Memoirs* (206) are interesting and even exciting, but (even in the latest revised edition) they should be viewed with some reservations, as Colonel Hurley demonstrates in his *Billy Mitchell* (148). There are numerous other biographies of Mitchell, of which Levine's (172) is possibly still standard. Simpson's edition of the World War I combat diary of Colonel Frank Lahm represents meticulous editorial work (240). Two other autobiographies of note are those of the great fighter ace Eddie Rickenbacker (227) and the pioneer aviator Hiram Bingham (22).

For the period of World War II, General "Hap" Arnold's *Global Mission* (12) is the outstanding autobiography, although the memoirs of Generals Brereton (31), Kenney (163), and Chennault (43, 44), provide the views of major American theater air commanders. General Kuter's *Airman at Yalta* (165) is a reminiscence of a very important air planner and air commander. General Tunner's *Over the Hump* (263) tells the story of the airlift to China and of the officer who went on to command the Berlin and Korean airlifts. Colonel Scott's, *God is My Co-Pilot* (235), is surely more personal than historical in its recollection of early air combat in China. Contributions of World War II science are recalled in *Baxter's Scientists Against Time* (19), and the record of post-World War II science is narrated in the Von Karman memoir (289).

There are only a few biographical efforts of current interest to the post-World War II period. General Curtis E. LeMay's remarkable career both in

World War II and afterward is described in *Mission with LeMay* (171). General Thomas S. Power's *Design for Survival* (218) and General Nathan F. Twining's *Neither Liberty Nor Safety* (264) are autobiographical but both too frequently emphasize analyses of defense policy at the expense of the personal narratives. Lieutenant Colonel Scrivner's biography of General Orvil A. Anderson (236) is both a contribution to air history and an apt demonstration of the potential air biography as a fruitful field for additional scholarly effort.

PILOTS, PICTORIALS, PLANES, AND MISSILES. From the outpouring of copy it is quite apparent that there is a major public interest in stories of aerial combat, in illustrated air histories, and in often very detailed descriptions of historic aircraft types. These publications often appeal to nostalgia and to aviation buffs, but all contain historical information and the better ones are sound though light history.

The *American Heritage History of Flight* (161) is both handsomely illustrated and was based upon oral history interviews. Ulanoff's *Fighter Pilot* (265) has accounts of air fighting from World War II up through the Taiwan Straits crisis. Gurney (115), Sims (241), and Toliver (260) each offer narratives of American fighter aces, and in the USAF historical program Maurer has prepared official credits for air victories (136, 191, 192). Quite shortly after World War II, the AAF Historical Office sponsored an official pictorial history (270), and since then pictorial coverages have been expanded to include World War I (157) and World War II in great detail (42, 118, 119, 249, 250).

In the field of histories of aircraft and more lately missiles, DuBuque and Gleckner (66) is a somewhat dated scholarly effort to describe the development of the heavy bomber from 1918-1944, and Boylan's study of the problem of long-range fighter escort is well done, although again limited to World War II and the period immediately preceding it, whereas the problem of long-range fighter escort continued into the 1950s (28). *Jane's All the World's Aircraft* (159) is standard for its inclusion of U.S. aircraft in its annual volumes. Most useful of the books on aircraft are Wagner (290) and Swanborough (251), while Morgan's on bombers (204) and fighters (205) provide ready reference. Lamberton (167, 168) covers World War I. Fahey's old handbooks (78, 79) are unattractive but exceedingly thorough. Ulanoff (266) offers a guide to missiles and rockets. In addition to these compendiums, there are volumes dealing with Boeing aircraft in general (27) and with characteristics and combat histories of individual planes, notably the B-17 (24, 37, 156, 181), B-24 (25, 26), B-29 (20, 54, 116), B-58 (228), B-70 (225); the A-1 Skyraider (23, 158) and the AT-6 Harvard (200); the P-38 (117, 182, 186), P-40 (180), P-47 (3, 183, 203), P-51 (114, 129, 187, 202), F-86 (291), F-105 (10); the DC-3 and C-47 (103, 152, 201). The Atlas (41) and Thor (123) have descriptive volumes, as has the Minuteman missile (208).

One of the most useful services of the pictorial histories and the near surfeit of little books on specific aircraft is to provide a scholar with some perspective about the technology of earlier times. In a generation used to jet aircraft, it is difficult to think in terms of the propeller planes prevalent only a few years ago. In this regard, *Aerospace Historian* has volumes in progress by pilots describing how Air Corps and Air Force aircraft were flown. At least two other publications enhance perspective. Emme's National Aeronautics and Space Administration chronologies covering 1915 to the present (71) are valuable for orientation, and Heflin's *United States Air Force Dictionary* (127) offers historical word usages in air parlance.

BIBLIOGRAPHY

1. Ackerman, Robert F. *The Maintenance of Army Aircraft in the United States, 1939-1945 (General Development and Policies)*. AAF Historical Study No. 51, Aug. 1946.
2. Acomb, Frances. *Statistical Control in the Army Air Forces*. Air Historical Study No. 57, Jan. 1952.
3. Aero Publishers Aeronautical Staff. *Republic P-47 Thunderbolt*. Fallbrook, California: Aero, 1966.
4. *Aerospace Historian*. Quarterly publication of the Air Force Historical Foundation, Sept. 1954 to date. Title changes from *Air Power Historian* (July 1959) and from *Airpower Historian* (July 1965). Cumulative index, 1954-1973 (1974).
5. *Air Force Magazine*. Monthly publication, initially of U.S. Army air arm, given to Air Force Association effective July 1946, from Sept. 1918 to date. Title changes from *Air Service News Letter* (Apr. 1919), from *Air Corps News Letter* (Sept. 1941), from *Air Force* (June 1959), and from *Air Force and Space Digest* (Feb. 1971).
6. *Air University Review*. Air University, Maxwell AFB, Alabama, quarterly journal from Spring 1947 to Sept.-Oct. 1963 and bi-monthly afterward to date. Title changed from *Air University Quarterly Review*, Sept.-Oct. 1963.
7. *The Airmen*. Official monthly magazine of the U.S. Air Force, Aug. 1957 to date, now *Airman*.
8. *American Aviation Historical Society Journal*. Quarterly publication of the American Aviation Historical Society, Los Angeles. Spring 1956 to date.
9. Anders, Curt. *Fighting Airmen*. New York: Putnam's, 1966.
10. Archer, Robert D. *The Republic F-105*. Fallbrook, California: Aero, 1969.
11. Armacost, Michael H. *The Politics of Weapons Innovation: The Thor-Jupiter Controversy*. New York: Columbia University Press, 1969.
12. Arnold, [General of the Air Force] Henry H. *Global Mission*. New York: Harper, 1949.
13. *Aviation Week and Space Technology*. Weekly from Aug. 1, 1916 to date with title change from *Aviation and Aeronautical Engineering* (Nov. 1920), from *Aviation and Aircraft Journal* (Jan. 1922), from *Aviation* (July 1947), from *Aviation Week* (Mar. 1958), from *Aviation Week, Including Space Technology* (Jan. 1960).
14. Barr, James J., and William E. Howard. *Combat Missilemen*. New York: Harcourt, Brace, 1961.

15. Bald, Ralph D. *Air Force Participation in Joint Army-Air Force Training Exercises, 1946-1952.* USAF Historical Study No. 94, 1955.
16. Bald, Ralph D. *Air Force Participation in Joint Army-Air Force Training Exercises, 1947-1950.* USAF Historical Study No. 80, 1955.
17. Baldwin, Ben R. *Individual Training of Bombardiers.* AAF Historical Study No. 5, May 1944.
18. Ball, John D. *Edwards: Flight Test Center of the U.S.A.F.* New York: Duell, 1962.
19. Baxter, James Phinney, III. *Scientists Against Time.* Boston: Little, Brown, 1946. Paper, Cambridge: MIT Press, 1968.
20. Berger, Carl. *B-29—The Superfortress.* New York: Ballantine, 1970.
21. Bilstein, Roger E. *Prelude to the Air Age: Civil Aviation in the United States, 1919-1929.* Doctoral dissertation, Ohio State University, 1965.
22. Bingham, Hiram. *An Explorer in the Air Service.* New Haven: Yale, 1920.
23. Birdsall, Steve. *The A-1 Skyraider.* New York: Arco, 1970.
24. Birdsall, Steve. *The B-17 Flying Fortress.* New York: Arco, 1965.
25. Birdsall, Steve. *The B-24 Liberator.* New York: Arco, 1968.
26. Birdsall, Steve. *Log of the Liberators: An Illustrated History of the B-24.* Garden City: Doubleday, 1973.
27. Bowers, Peter M. *Boeing Air-Craft Series 1926.* 2 ed. New York: Funk and Wagnalls, 1968.
28. Boylan, Bernard L. *The Development of the American Long-Range Escort Fighter.* Doctoral dissertation, Missouri, 1955.
29. Boyle, [Lieutenant Colonel] James M. *The XXI Bomber Command: Primary Factor in the Defeat of Japan.* Doctoral dissertation, St. Louis University, 1964.
30. Boyle, Robert D. *History of Photo Reconnaissance in North Africa including My Experience with the 3rd Photo Group.* Doctoral dissertation, University of Texas, 1949.
31. Brereton, [Lieutenant General] Lewis H. *The Brereton Diaries: The War in the Air in the Pacific, Middle East and Europe, 30 October 1941-8 May 1945.* New York: Morrow, 1945.
32. Brodie, Bernard. *Strategy in the Missile Age.* Princeton: Princeton University Press, 1959.
33. Broughton, [Colonel] Jack. *Thud Ridge.* Philadelphia: J. B. Lippincott, 1969.
34. Brune, Lester H. *The Foundations of American Air Power Doctrine—Aviation and National Defense, 1919-1933.* Doctoral dissertation, University of Rochester, 1959.
35. Bush, Vannevar. *Modern Arms and Free Men: A Discussion of the Role of Science in Preserving Democracy.* New York: Simon and Schuster, 1949.
36. Caidin, Martin. *Black Thursday.* New York: Dutton, 1960.
37. Caidin, Martin. *Flying Forts.* New York: Meredith, 1968.
38. Cate, James L. *History of the Twentieth Air Force: Genesis.* AAF Historical Study No. 112, 1945.
39. Cate, James L. *Origins of the Eighth Air Force: Plans, Organization, Doctrines to 17 August 1942.* AAF Historical Study No. 102, Oct. 1944.

40. Chandler, [Colonel] Charles DeF., and [Colonel] Frank P. Lahm. *How Our Army Grew Wings: Airmen and Aircraft Before 1914*. New York: Ronald, 1943.

41. Chapman, John. *Atlas: The Story of a Missile*. New York: Harper, 1960.

42. Charleton, [Air Commodore] L. E. O. *The Royal Air Force and the U.S.A.A.F.: A Complete Record in Text and Pictures, Sept. 1939/ Dec. 1940-Oct. 1944/Sept. 1945*. London: Hutchinson, 1939-1945. 5 vols.

43. Chennault, Anna. *Chennault and the Flying Tigers*. New York: Eriksson, 1963.

44. Chennault, [Major General] Claire L. *Way of a Fighter: The Memoirs of Claire Lee Chennault*. New York: Putnam's, 1949.

45. Claussen, Martin P. *Comparative History of Research and Development Policies Affecting Air Materiel, 1915-1944*. AAF Historical Study No. 20, June 1945.

46. Claussen, Martin P. *Distribution of Air Materiel to the Allies, 1939-1944: Controls, Procedures, and Policies*. AAF Historical Study No. 106, July 1944.

47. Claussen, Martin P. *Materiel Research and Development in the Army Air Arm, 1914-1945*. AAF Historical Study No. 50, Nov. 1946.

48. Cleveland, Reginald M. *Air Transport at War*. New York: Harper, 1964.

49. Cohen, Victor H. *Classification and Assignment of Englisted Men in the Army Air Arm, 1917-1945*. USAF Historical Study No. 76, 1953.

50. Coleman, John M. *The Development of Tactical Services in the Army Air Forces*. New York: Columbia University Press, 1950.

51. Coles, Harry L. *AAF in Amphibious Landings in World War II*. USAF Historical Study No. 96, 1953.

52. Coles, Harry L. *Ninth Air Force in the Western Desert Campaign to 23 January 1943*. AAF Historical Study No. 30, 1945.

53. Coles, Harry L. *Participation of the Ninth and Twelfth Air Forces in the Sicilian Campaign*. AAF Historical Study No. 37, 1945.

54. Collison, Thomas. *The Superfortress is Born: The Story of the Boeing B-29*. New York: Duell, 1945.

55. Craven, Wesley F., and James L. Cate, eds. *The Army Air Forces in World War II*. Chicago: University of Chicago Press, 1948-1958. 7 vols. 1. *Plans and Early Operations, January 1939 to August 1942* (1948). 2. *Europe—Torch to Pointblank, August 1942 to December 1943* (1949). 3. *Europe: Argument to V-E Day, January 1944 to May 1945* (1951). 4. *The Pacific—Guadalcanal to Saipan, August 1942 to July 1944* (1950). 5. *The Pacific—Matterhorn to Nagasaki, June 1944 to August 1945* (1953). 6. *Men and Planes* (155). 7. *Services Around the World* (1958).

56. Cresswell, Mary Ann, and Carl Berger. *United States Air Force History, An Annotated Bibliography*. Washington: Office of Air Force History, 1971.

57. *Cross and Cockade Journal*. Quarterly publication of the Society of World War I Aero Historians, Santa Ana, California, from Spring 1960 to date.

58. Crowell, Benedict. *America's Munitions, 1917-1918.* Washington: G.P.O., 1919.
59. Davis, Paul M., and Amy C. Fenwick. *Development and Procurement of Gliders in the Army Air Forces, 1941-1944.* AAF Historical Study No. 47, Mar. 1946.
60. Davison, W. Phillips. *The Berlin Blockade: A Study in Cold War Politics.* Princeton: Princeton University Press, 1958.
61. Donovan, Frank R. *Bridge in the Sky.* New York: McKay, 1968.
62. Dornbusch, Charles E., comp. *Unit Histories of the United States Air Force, Including Privately Printed Personal Narratives.* Hampton Bays, New York: Hampton Books, 1958.
63. Downs, [Colonel] Eldon W. *Contributions of U.S. Army Aviation to Uses and Operation of Aircraft.* Doctoral dissertation, University of Wisconsin, 1959.
64. Downs, [Colonel] Eldon W., ed. *The U.S. Air Force in Space.* New York: Praeger, 1966.
65. Dugan, James, and Carroll Stewart. *Ploesti: The Great Ground- Air Battle of 1 August 1943.* New York: Random House, 1962.
66. DuBuque, Jean H., and Robert F. Gleckner. *The Development of the Heavy Bomber, 1918-1944.* Air Historical Study No. 6, Aug. 1951.
67. DuPre, Flint O. *U.S. Air Force Biographical Dictionary.* New York: Watts, 1965.
68. Earle, Edward M., ed. *Makers of Modern Strategy: Military Thought from Machiavelli to Hitler.* Princeton: Princeton University Press, 1944. Reprinted 1972.
69. Edmonds, Walter D. *They Fought With What They Had: The Story of the Army Air Forces in the Southwest Pacific, 1941-1942.* Boston: Little, Brown, 1951.
70. Emerson, William. *Operation Pointblank: A Tale of Bombers and Fighters. The Fourth Harmon Memorial Lecture.* Colorado Springs: U.S. Air Force Academy, 1962.
71. Emme, Eugene M. *Aeronautics and Astronautics: An American Chronology of Science and Technology in the Exploration of Space, 1915-1960.* Washington: G.P.O., 1961. Continued by annual National Aeronautics and Space Administration chronologies, *Astronautics and Aeronautics,* 1962-   .
72. Emme, Eugene M., ed. *The Impact of Air Power: National Security and World Politics.* Princeton: Van Nostrand, 1959.
73. England, J. Merton, and Joseph C. Reither. *Women Pilots with the AAF, 1941-1944.* AAF Historical Study No. 55, Mar. 1946.
74. Enthoven, Alain C., and K. Wayne Smith. *How Much is Enough? Shaping the Defense Program, 1961-1969.* New York: Harper, 1971.
75. Erdmann, James M. *Leaflet Operations in the Second World War.* Denver: Denver Instant Printing for author, 1969.
76. Estep, Raymond. *An Air Power Bibliography.* Maxwell AFB: Air University, 1956. Continued by *An Air Power Bibliography, 1955-1956* (1957), *A Space Bibliography through 1958* (1959), *An Aerospace Bibliography, 1962* (1962), *An Aerospace Bibliography, 1965* (1965), *An Aerospace Bibliography, 1967* (1967).
77. Evans, Eugene E. *Dispute Settlement and Hierarchy: The Guided*

Missile Controversy, 1955-1960. Doctoral dissertation, University of Illinois, 1963.

78. Fahey, James C., ed. *U.S. Army Aircraft (Heavier-than-air), 1908-1946.* New York: Ships and Aircraft, 1946.

79. Fahey, James C., ed. *United States Air Force and United States Army Aircraft, 1947-1956.* Falls Church, Virginia: Ships and Aircraft, 1956.

80. Ferguson, Arthur B. *The Antisubmarine Command.* AAF Historical Study No. 107, 1945.

81. Ferguson, Arthur B. *The Early Operations of the Eighth Air Force and the Origins of the Combined Bomber Offensive, 17 August 1942-10 June 1943.* AAF Historical Study No. 118, 1946.

82. Finletter, Thomas K. *Power and Policy: U.S. Foreign Policy and Military Power in the Hydrogen Age.* New York: Harcourt-Brace, 1954.

83. Finney Robert T. *History of the Air Corps Tactical School, 1920-1940.* USAF Historical Study No. 100, Mar. 1955.

84. Flammer, [Lieutenant Colonel] Philip M. *Primus Inter Pares: A History of Lafayette Escadrille.* Doctoral dissertation, Yale University, 1963.

85. Fogerty, Robert P. *Biographical Data on Air Force General Officers, 1918-1952.* USAF Historical Study No. 91, 1953. 2 vols.

86. Forrestal, James. *The Forrestal Diaries.* Walter Millis, ed. New York: Viking, 1951.

87. Foulois, [Major General] Benjamin D., and Carroll V. Glines. *From the Wright Brothers to the Astronauts: The Memoirs of Benjamin D. Foulois.* New York: McGraw, 1968.

88. Flugel, Raymond R. *United States Air Power Doctrine: A Study of the Influence of William Mitchell and Guilio Douhet at the Air Corps Tactical School, 1921-1935.* Doctoral dissertation, University of Oklahoma, 1965.

89. Francis, Charles E. *The Tuskegee Airmen: The Story of the Negro in the U.S. Air Force.* Boston: Bruce Humphries, 1956.

90. Frank, Sam H. *American Air Service Observation in World War I.* Doctoral dissertation, University of Florida, 1961.

91. Frankland, Noble. *The Bomber Offensive: The Devastation of Europe.* New York: Ballantine, 1970.

92. Freeman, Roger A. *The Mighty Eighth: Units, Men, and Machines. A History of the U.S. Eighth Air Force.* Garden City: Doubleday, 1970.

93. Futrell, Robert F. *Command of Observation Aviation: A Study in Control of Tactical Air Power.* USAF Historical Study No. 24, 1952.

94. Futrell, Robert F. *Development of AAF Base Facilities in the United States, 1939-1945.* USAF Historical Study No. 69, July 1947.

95. Futrell, Robert F. *Development of USAF Aeromedical Evacuation.* USAF Historical Study No. 23, 1961.

96. Futrell, Robert F. *Ideas, Concepts, Doctrine: A History of Basic Thinking in the United States Air Force, 1907-1964.* Maxwell AFB, Alabama: Air University, 1971. 2 vols.

97. Futrell, Robert F. *The United States Air Force in Korea, 1950-1953.* New York: Duell, 1961. Reprinted, New York: Arno, 1971.

98. Gantz, [Lieutenant Colonel] Kenneth F., ed. *The United States Air Force Report on the Ballistic Missile: Its Technology, Logistics, and Strategy*. Garden City: Doubleday, 1958.

99. Geffen, [Colonel] William, ed. *Command and Commanders in Modern Warfare. The Proceedings of the Second Military History Symposium, U.S. Air Force Academy*. Washington: Office of Air Force History and USAF Academy, 1971.

100. George, Robert H. *Ninth Air Force, April-November 1944*. AAF Historical Study No. 36, 1945.

101. Glines, Carroll V. *Doolittle's Tokyo Raiders*. Princeton: Van Nostrand, 1964.

102. Glines, Carroll V. *The Saga of the Airmail*. Princeton: Van Nostrand, 1968.

103. Glines, Carroll V., and Wendell F. Moseley. *The DC-3: The Story of a Fabulous Airplane*. Philadelphia: J. B. Lippincott, 1966.

104. Goddard, [Brigadier General] George W. *Overview: A Life-long Adventure in Aerial Photography*. Garden City: Doubleday, 1969.

105. Goldberg, Alfred, ed. *A History of the United States Air Force, 1907-1957*. Princeton: Van Nostrand, 1957.

106. Goldman, Martin R. *Morale in the AAF in World War II*. USAF Historical Study No. 78, 1953.

107. Gorrell, [Colonel] Edgar S., comp. "History of the U.S. Army Air Services." Unpublished manuscript in National Archives. 286 vols. (58 microfilm rolls).

108. Goulding, Phil G. *Confirm or Deny: Informing the People on National Security*. New York: Harper, 1970.

109. Grant, Clement L. *Development of Continental Air Defense to 1 September 1954*. USAF Historical Study No. 126, 1957.

110. Grant, Clement L. *The Development and Functions of AAF OCS and OTS*. USAF Historical Study No. 97, 1954.

111. Green, Murray. *Stuart Symington and the B-36*. Doctoral dissertation, American University, 1960.

112. Greenfield, Kent Roberts. *American Strategy in World War II: A Reconsideration*. Baltimore: Johns Hopkins, 1963.

113. Greer, Thomas H. *Development of Air Doctrine in the Army Air Arm, 1917-1941*. USAF Historical Study No. 89, June 1953.

114. Gruenhagen, Robert W. *Mustang: The Story of the P-51 Fighter*. New York: Genesis Press, 1969.

115. Gurney, [Colonel] Gene. *Five Down and Glory: A History of the American Ace*. New York: Putnam's, 1958.

116. Gurney, [Colonel] Gene. *Journey of the Giants*. New York: Coward-McCann, 1961.

117. Gurney, [Colonel] Gene. *The P-38 Lightning*. New York: Arco, 1969.

118. Gurney, [Colonel] Gene. *The War in the Air: A Pictorial History of World War II Air Forces in Combat*. New York: Crown, 1962.

119. Haggerty, James J., and Warren R. Smith. *The U.S. Air Forces: A Pictorial History in Art*. New York: Books, Inc., 1966.

120. Hansell, [Major General] Haywood S., Jr. *The Air Plan that Defeated Hitler*. Atlanta, Georgia: Higgins-McArthur/Longino & Porter, 1972.

121. Harbold, [Major General] Norris B. *The Log of Air Navigation*. San Antonio: Naylor Co., 1970.

122. Harris, Sherwood. *The First to Fly: Aviation's Pioneer Days*. New York: Simon and Schuster, 1970.
123. Hartt, Julian. *The Mighty Thor: Missile in Readiness*. New York: Duell, 1961.
124. Harvey, Frank. *The Air War—Vietnam*. New York: Bantam, 1967.
125. Haugland, Vern. *The AAF Against Japan*. New York: Harper, 1948.
126. Haydon, Frederick S. *Aeronautics in the Union and Confederate Armies*. Baltimore: Johns Hopkins University Press, 1941.
127. Heflin, Woodford, A., ed. *The United States Air Force Dictionary*. Washington: G.P.O., 1956.
128. Hennesy, Juliette A. *The United States Army Air Arm, April 1861 to April 1917*. USAF Historical Study No. 98, May 1958.
129. Hess, William N. *Fighting Mustang: The Chronicle of the P-51*. Garden City: Doubleday, 1970.
130. Hickman, Thomas J. *The United States Air Force: German-American Relations, 1945-1955*. Doctoral dissertation, Fordham University, 1959.
131. Higham, Robin. *Air Power: A Concise History*. New York: St. Martin's, 1973.
132. Higham, Robin. *The Military Intellectuals in Britain, 1918-1940*. New Brunswick, New Jersey: Rutgers, 1966.
133. Higham, Robin, ed. *Official Histories: Essays and Bibliographies from Around the World*. Manhattan: Kansas State University Library, 1970.
134. Hinkle, Stacy C. *Wings and Saddles: The Air and Cavalry Punitive Expedition of 1919*. El Paso: Texas Western Press, 1967.
135. Hinton, Harold B. *Air History: The Men and the Machines*. New York: Harper, 1948.
136. Historical Research Division, Aerospace Studies Institute, Air University. *U.S. Air Service Victory Credits: World War I*. USAF Historical Study No. 133, June 1969. (See also Nos. 189-192).
137. Holley, Irving B., Jr. *Buying Aircraft: Materiel Procurement for the Army Air Forces. United States Army in World War II*. Washington: Office of Chief of Military History, 1964.
138. Holley, Irving B., Jr. *Development of Aircraft Gun Turrets in the AAF, 1917-1944*. AAF Historical Study No. 54, June 1947.
139. Holley, Irving B., Jr. *Evolution of the Liaison-Type Airplane, 1917-1944*. AAF Historical Study No. 44, April 1946.
140. Holley, Irving B., Jr. *Ideas and Weapons: Exploitation of the Aerial Weapon by the United States During World War I*. New Haven: Yale, 1953. Reprinted, Hamden, Connecticut: Archon, 1971.
141. Hollon, W. Eugene. *History of Preflight Training in the AAF, 1941-1953*. USAF Historical Study No. 90, June 1953.
142. Hoopes, Townsend. *The Limits of Intervention*. New York: David McKay, 1969.
143. Horvat, William J. *Above the Pacific*. Fallbrook, California: Aero, 1966.
144. Howard, Clive, and Joe Whitley. *One Damned Island After Another*. Chapel Hill, North Carolina: University of North Carolina Press, 1946.
145. Hubler, Richard G. *SAC: The Strategic Air Command*. New York: Duell, 1958.

146. Hudson, James J. *The Hostile Skies: A Combat History of the American Air Service.* Syracuse: Syracuse University Press, 1968.
147. Huntington, Samuel P. *The Common Defense, Strategic Programs in National Politics.* New York: Columbia, 1961.
148. Hurley, [Colonel] Alfred E. *Billy Mitchell: Crusader for Air Power.* New York: Watts, 1964.
149. Hurley, [Colonel] Alfred E. *History of the United States Air Force.* New York: Macmillan, 197-   .
150. Huston, James A. *Out of the Blue: U.S. Army Airborne Operations in World War II.* West Lafayette, Indiana: Purdue Studies, 1972.
151. Infield, Glenn B. *Unarmed and Unafraid.* New York: Macmillan, 1970.
152. Ingells, Douglas J. *The Plane that Changed the World: A Biography of DC-3.* Fallbrook, California: Aero, 1966.
153. Ingells, Douglas J. *They Tamed the Sky: The Triumph of American Aviation.* New York: Appleton, 1947.
154. Irving, David. *The Destruction of Dresden.* Rev. ed. London: Transworld, 1966.
155. Jablonski, Edward. *Double Strike: The Epic Air Raids on Regensburg-Schweinfurt, August 17, 1943.* Garden City: Doubleday, 1974.
156. Jablonski, Edward. *Flying Fortress: The Illustrated Biography of the B-17s and the Men Who Flew Them.* Garden City: Doubleday, 1965.
157. Jablonski, Edward. *The Knighted Skies: A Pictorial History of World War I in the Air.* New York: Putnam's, 1964.
158. Jackson, B. R. *Douglas Skyraider.* Fallbrook, California: Aero, 1969.
159. *Jane's All the World's Aircraft.* London: Sampson, Low, 1909- and New York: McGraw-Hill, 1953-   .
160. Johns, Claude, Jr. *The United States Air Force Intercontinental Ballistic Missile Program, 1954-1959: Technological Change and Organizational Innovation.* Doctoral dissertation, University of North Carolina, 1964.
161. Josephy, Alvan M., Jr., ed. *The American Heritage History of Flight.* New York: American Heritage Publishing Co., 1962.
162. Julian, [Colonel] Thomas A. *Operation Frantic and the Search for American-Soviet Collaboration.* Doctoral dissertation, Syracuse University, 1968.
163. Kenney, [General] George C. *General Kenney Reports: A Personal History of the Pacific War.* New York: Duell, 1949.
164. Knebel, Fletcher, and Charles W. Bailey. *No High Ground.* New York: Harper, 1960.
165. Kuter, [General] Laurence S. *Airman at Yalta.* New York: Duell, 1955.
166. LaFarge, Oliver. *The Eagle in the Egg.* Boston: Houghton-Mifflin, 1949.
167. Lamberton, W. M., comp. *Fighter Aircraft of the 1914-1918 War.* E. F. Cheesman, ed. Letchworth, England: Harleyford, 1960.
168. Lamberton, W. M., comp. *Reconnaissance & Bomber Aircraft of the 1914-1918 War.* E. F. Chessman, ed. Los Angeles, California: Aero, 1962.
169. Layman, Martha E. *Legislation Relating to the Air Corps Personnel and Training Programs, 1907-1939.* AAF Historical Study No. 39, Dec. 1945.

170. Layman, Martha E. *Organization of AAF Training Activities, 1939-1945.* AAF Historical Study No. 53, June 1946.
171. LeMay, [General] Curtis E., and Mackinlay Kantor. *Mission With LeMay: My Story.* Garden City: Doubleday, 1965.
172. Levine, Isaac D. *Mitchell, Pioneer of Air Power.* Rev. ed., New York: Duell, 1958.
173. Link, Mae M., and Hubert A. Coleman. *Medical Support of the Army Air Forces in World War II.* Washington: G.P.O., 1954.
174. Littauer, Raphael, and Norman Uphoff, eds. *The Air War in Indochina.* Rev. ed. Boston: Beacon, 1972.
175. Lowe, George E. *The Age of Deterrence.* Boston: Little, Brown, 1964.
176. Lukas, Richard C. *Eagles East: The Army Air Forces and the Soviet Union, 1941-1945.* Tallahassee: Florida State University Press, 1970.
177. McClendon, R. Earl. *Autonomy of the Air Arm.* Rev. ed. Maxwell AFB, Alabama: Air University, 1954.
178. McClendon, R. Earl. *Unification of the Armed Forces.* Maxwell AFB, Alabama: Air University, 1952.
179. MacCloskey, [Brigadier General] Monro. *The United States Air Force.* New York: Praeger, 1967.
180. McDowell, Ernest R. *The P-40 Kittyhawk.* New York: Arco, 1968.
181. McDowell, Ernest R., and Richard Ward. *Boeing B-17B-H Flying Fortress.* New York: Arco, 1970.
182. McDowell, Ernest R., and Richard Ward. *Lockheed P-38 Lightning.* New York: Arco, 1969.
183. McDowell, Ernest R., and Richard Ward. *Republic P-47 Thunderbolt.* New York: Arco, 1968.
184. MacIsaac, [Lieutenant Colonel] David. *The United States Strategic Bombing Survey, 1944-1947.* Doctoral dissertation, Duke University, 1970.
185. McNarney, Betty J. *The Glider Pilot Training Program, 1941 to 1943.* AAF Historical Study No. 1, Sept. 1943.
186. Maloney, Edward T. *Lockheed P-38 "Lightning."* Fallbrook, California: Aero, 1968.
187. Maloney, Edward T. *North American P-51 Mustang.* Fallbrook, California: Aero, 1967.
188. Marshall, S. L. A. *Night Drop: The American Airborne Invasion of Normandy.* Boston: Little, Brown, 1962.
189. Maurer, Maurer, ed. *Air Force Combat Units of World War II.* Washington: G.P.O., 1961. Reprinted, New York: Watts, 1963.
190. Maurer, Maurer, ed. *Combat Squadrons of the Air Force, World War II.* Washington: G.P.O., 1969.
191. Maurer, Maurer, ed. *A Preliminary List of U.S. Air Force Aces, 1917-1953.* USAF Historical Study No. 73, 1962.
192. Maurer, Maurer. *USAF Credits for Destruction of Enemy Aircraft, Korean War.* USAF Historical Study No. 81, 1963.
193. Mayock, Thomas J. *Air Phase of the North African Invasion, November 1942.* AAF Historical Study No. 105, 1944.
194. Mayock, Thomas J. *The Twelfth Air Force in the North African Winter Campaign, 11 November 1942 to the Reorganization of 10 February 1943.* AAF Historical Study No. 114, 1946.

195. Merrill, James M. *Target Tokyo: The Halsey-Doolittle Raid.* Chicago: Rand-McNally, 1964.
196. *Military Affairs.* Quarterly journal of the Amercan Military Institute from April 1937 to date, with title changes from *Journal of the American Military History Foundation* (1939) and from *Journal of the American Military Institute* (1941).
197. Miller, Thomas G., Jr. *The Cactus Air Force.* New York: Harper, 1969.
198. Mooney, Chase C. *Organization of Military Aeronautics, 1935-1945 (Executive, Congressional, and War Department Action).* AAF Historical Study No. 46, Apr. 1946.
199. Mooney, Chase C., and Martha E. Layman. *Orgnization of Military Aeronautics, 1907-1935 (Congressional and War Department Action.)* AAF Historical Study No. 25, Dec. 1944.
200. Morgan, Len. *The AT-6 Harvard.* New York: Arco, 1965.
201. Morgan, Len. *The Douglas DC-3.* New York: Arco, 1964.
202. Morgan, Len. *The P-51 Mustang.* New York: Arco, 1964.
203. Morgan, Len. *The P-47 Thunderbolt.* New York: Arco, 1963.
204. Morgan, Terry. *Bomber Aircraft of the United States.* New York: Arco, 1967.
205. Morgan, Terry. *Fighter Aircraft of the United States.* New York: Arco, 1967.
206. Mitchell, [Brigadier General] William. *Memoirs of World War I: "From Start to Finish of Our Greatest War."* New York: Random House, 1960.
207. Moulton, Harland B. *American Strategic Power: Two Decades of Nuclear Strategy and Weapon Systems, 1945-1965.* Doctoral dissertation, University of Minnesota, 1969.
208. Neal, Roy. *Ace in the Hole: The Story of the Minuteman Missile.* Garden City: Doubleday, 1962.
209. Newton, Wesley P. *Aviation in the Relations of the United States and Latin America, 1916-1929.* Doctoral dissertation, University of Alabama, 1964.
210. Olson, James C. *Operational History of the Seventh Air Force, 7 December 1941-6 November 1943.* AAF Historical Study No. 41, 1945.
211. Olson, James C. *Operational History of the Seventh Air Force, 6 November 1943-31 July 1944.* AAF Historical Study No. 38, 1945.
212. Parkinson, Russell J. *Politics, Patents and Planes: Military Aeronautics in the United States, 1863-1907.* Doctoral dissertation, Duke University, 1963.
213. Parrish, [Brigadier General] Noel F. *Behind the Sheltering Bomb: Military Indecision from Alamogordo to Korea.* Doctoral dissertation, Rice University, 1968.
214. Paszek, Lawrence. *United States Air Force History. A Guide to Documentary Sources.* Washington: Office of Air Force History, 1973.
215. Patrick, [Major General] Mason M. *Final Report of Chief of Air Service, A.E.F. (Air Service Information Circular* II, No. 180). Washington: G.P.O., 1921.

216. Patrick, [Major General] Mason M. *The United States in the Air.* Garden City: Doubleday, 1928.

217. Peyton, Green. *50 Years of Aerospace Medicine.* Brooks AFB, Texas: Aerospace Medical Division, 1968.

218. Power, [General] Thomas S., and Albert A. Arnhym. *Design for Survival.* New York: Coward-McCann, 1965.

219. Rae, John B. *Climb to Greatness: The American Aircraft Industry, 1920-1960.* Cambridge: The MIT Press, 1968.

220. Ramsey, John. *The War Against the Luftwaffe: AAF Counter-Air Force Operations, April 1943-June 1944.* AAF Historical Study No. 110, 1945.

221. RAND Corporation Bibliographies. To obtain copies of RAND bibliographies one should write to Communications Department, RAND, 1700 Main Street, Santa Monica, California 90406.

222. Ransom, Frank E. *Air-Sea Rescue, 1941-1952.* USAF Historical Study No. 95, 1953.

223. Ransom, Harry Howe. *The Air Corps Act of 1926: A Study of the Legislative Process.* Doctoral dissertation, Princeton University, 1954.

224. Rees, David. *Korea: The Limited War.* New York: St. Martin's, 1964.

225. Rees, Ed. *Manned Missile: The Story of the B-70.* New York: Duell, 1960.

226. Richards, Leverett G. *TAC: The Story of Tactical Air Command.* New York: John Day, 1961.

227. Rickenbacker, Edward V. *Rickenbacker.* Englewood Cliffs: Prentice Hall, 1967.

228. Robinson, Douglas H. *The B-58 Hustler.* New York: Arco, 1967.

229. Russel, Robert R., and Martin P. Claussen. *Expansion of Industrial Facilities Under Army Air Forces Auspices, 1940-1945.* AAF Historical Study No. 40, 1946.

230. Rust, Ken C. *The Ninth Air Force in World War II.* Fallbrook, California: Aero, 1967.

231. Rutkowski, Edwin. *The Politics of Military Aviation Procurement, 1926-1934: A Study in the Political Assertion of Consensual Values.* Columbus: Ohio State University Press, 1966.

232. Ryan, Carl W. *Modern Scott: A History of Scott Air Force Base.* Doctoral dissertation, St. Louis University, 1969.

233. Schilling, Warner R., Paul Y. Hammond, and Glenn H. Snyder. *Strategy, Politics, and Defense Budgets.* New York: Columbia University Press, 1962.

234. Schwiebert, Ernest G. *A History of the U.S. Air Force Ballistic Missiles.* New York: Praeger, 1965.

235. Scott, Colonel Robert Lee. *God is My Co-Pilot.* New York: Scribner's, 1943.

236. Scrivner, [Lieutenant Colonel] John H., Jr. *Pioneer into Space: A Biography of Major General Orvil Arson Anderson.* Doctoral dissertation, University of Oklahoma, 1971.

237. Scrivner, [Lieutenant Colonel] John H., Jr., ed. *A Quarter Century of Air Power, Studies in the Employment of Air Power, 1947-1972.* Maxwell AFB, Alabama: Air Force ROTC, 1973.

238. Sharp, Adm. U.S.G., and Gen. W. C. Westmoreland. *Report on the War in Vietnam (As of 30 June 1968)*. Washington: G. P. O., 1968.

239. Shores, Louis. *Highways in the Sky: The Story of the AACS*. New York: Barnes, 1947.

240. Simpson, Albert F., ed. *The World War I Diary of Col. Frank P. Lahm, Air Service, A.E.F.* Maxwell AFB, Alabama: Air University, 1970.

241. Sims, Edward H. *American Aces in Great Fighter Battles of World War II*. New York: Harper, 1958.

242. Smith, [Major General] Dale O. *U.S. Military Doctrine*. New York: Duell, 1955.

243. Smith, Melden E., Jr. *The Bombing of Dresden Reconsidered*. Doctoral dissertation, Boston University, 1971.

244. Smith, [Colonel] Perry McCoy. *The Air Force Plans for Peace, 1943-1945*. Baltimore: Johns Hopkins University Press, 1970.

245. Stewart, [Colonel] James T., ed. *Airpower: The Decisive Force in Korea*. Princeton: Van Nostrand, 1957.

246. Sturm, Thomas A. *The USAF Scientific Advisory Board: Its First Twenty Years, 1944-1964*. Washington: G. P. O., 1967.

247. Sunderland, Riley. *Evolution of Command and Control Doctrine for Close Air Support*. Washington: Office of Air Force History, 1973.

248. Sunderman, [Colonel] James F., ed. *Early Air Pioneers, 1862-1935*. New York: Watts, 1961.

249. Sunderman, [Colonel] James F., ed. *World War II in the Air: Europe*. New York: Crown, 1963.

250. · Sunderman, [Colonel] James F., ed. *World War II in the Air: The Pacific*. New York: Bramhall House, 1962.

251. Swanborough, [F.] Gordon, and Peter Bowers. *United States Military Aircraft Since 1909*. New York: Putnam's, 1963.

252. Sweetser, Arthur. *The American Air Service: A Record of Its Problems, Its Difficulties, Its Failures, and Its Achievements*. New York: Appleton, 1919.

253. Tarr, Curtis W. *Unification of America's Armed Forces: A Century and a Half a Conflict, 1798-1947*. Doctoral dissertation, Stanford, Stanford University, 1962.

254. Taylor, Joe G. *Air Supply in the Burma Campaigns*. USAF Historical Study No. 75, 1957.

255. Taylor, Joe G. *Close Air Support Operations in the War against Japan*. USAF Historical Study No. 86, 1955.

256. Taylor, Joe G. *Development of Night Air Operations*. USAF Historical Study No. 92, 1953.

257. Thompson, [Captain] Annis G. *The Greatest Airlift: The Story of Combat Cargo*. Tokyo: Dai-Nippon Printing Co., 1954.

258. Throne, Bliss K. *The Hump: The Great Military Airlift of World War II*. New York: Lippincott, 1965.

259. Tillman, Stephen F. *Man Unafraid: The Miracle of Military Aviation*. Washington: Army Times, 1958.

260. Toliver, Raymond F., and Trevor J. Constable. *Fighter Aces*. New York: Macmillan, 1965.

261. Toole, Virginia G., and Robert W. Ackerman. *The Modification of Army Aircraft in the United States, 1939-1945.* AAF Historical Study No. 62, Aug. 1947.

262. Toulmin, Harry Aubrey. *Air Service: American Expeditionary Force, 1918.* New York: Van Nostrand, 1927.

263. Tunner, [General] William H. *Over the Hump.* New York: Duell, 1964.

264. Twining, [General] Nathan F. *Neither Liberty Nor Safety: A Hard Look at U.S. Military Policy and Strategy.* New York: Holt, 1966.

265. Ulanoff, Stanley M., ed. *Fighter Pilot.* Garden City: Doubleday, 1962.

266. Ulanoff, Stan. *Illustrated Guide to U.S. Missiles and Rockets.* Rev. ed. Garden City: Doubleday, 1962.

267. U.S. Air Force. *Air University Library Index to Military Periodicals.* Maxwell AFB, Alabama: Air University, Oct.-Dec. 1949-   . Quarterly.

268. U.S. Army Air Forces. *Army Air Forces in the War Against Japan, 1941-1942.* AAF Historical Narratives. Washington: G. P. O., 1945.

269. U.S. Army Air Forces. *Air Evaluation Board Reports, World War II, 1944-1947.* Copies at Historical Research Center, Maxwell AFB, Alabama.

270. U.S. Army Air Forces. Historical Office. *The Official Pictorial History of the AAF.* New York: Duell, 1947.

271. U.S. Army Air Forces. *Statistical Digest: World War II.* Washington: Office of Statistical Control, 1945.

272. U.S. Army Air Forces. *Wings at War Series: An Interim Report.* Washington: G. P. O., 1945. 6 vols.: 1. *The AAF in the Invasion of Southern France.* 2. *Sunday Punch in Normandy. The Tactical Use of Heavy Bombardment in the Normandy Invasion.* 3. *Pacific Counterblow. The 11th Bombardment Group and the 67th Fighter Squadron in the Battle for Guadalcanal.* 4. *Airborne Assault on Holland.* 5. *Air-Ground Teamwork on the Western Front. The Role of the XIX Tactical Air Command during August 1944.* 6. *The AAF in Northwest Africa. An Account of the Twelfth Air Force in the Northwest African Landings and Battle for Tunisia.*

273. U.S. Department of the Air Force. *Historical Summary, July 1, 1968 to June 30, 1969.* Washington: Office of Air Force History, 1973.

274. U.S. Department of the Air Force. *Historical Summary, July 1, 1969 to June 30, 1970.* Washington: Office of Air Force History, 1973.

275. U.S. Department of the Army. Historical Division. *United States Army in World War, 1917-1919.* Washington: G. P. O., 1948. 17 vols.

276. U.S. Department of Defense. *Annual Report of the Secretary of Defense and the Annual Reports of the Secretary of the Army, Secretary of the Navy, Secretary of the Air Force,* July 1, 1958 through 30 June 1968. Washington: G. P. O., 1960-1971.

277. U.S. Department of Defense. *Second Report of the Secretary of Defense and the Annual Reports of the Secretary of the Army,*

Secretary of the Navy, Secretary of the Air Force for the Fiscal Year 1949. Washington: G. P. O., 1950. (See also No. 282)

278. U.S. Department of Defense. *Semiannual Report of the Secretary of Defense and the Semiannual Reports of the Secretary of the Army, Secretary of the Navy, and Secretary of the Air Force, July 1, 1949 to December 31, 1949* through *January 1, 1958 to June 30, 1958.* Washington: G. P. O., 1950-1959.

279. U.S. Congress. Senate Committee on Armed Services, 90th Cong. 1st Sess. *Air War Against North Vietnam.* Washington: G. P. O., 1967. 5 pts.

280. U.S. Congress. Senate Committee on Armed Services, 84th Cong. 2d Sess. *Study on Airpower.* Washington: G. P. O., 1956-1957. 24 pts.

281. *United States Naval Institute Proceedings.* Annapolis, Maryland, published with varied frequency from 1874 and monthly from 1917 to date.

282. U.S. National Military Establishment. *First Report of the Secretary of Defense, 1948.* Washington: G. P. O., 1948.

283. U.S. President's Air Policy Commission. *Survival in the Air Age.* Washington: G. P. O., 1948. (The Finletter Commission report.)

284. U.S. Strategic Bombing Survey. *Index to Records of the United States Strategic Bombing Survey.* Washington: G.P.O., 1947.

285. U.S. Superintendent of Documents. *Catalogue of the Public Documents of Congress and of All Departments of the Government of the United States.* Washington: G. P. O., 1893-1940. Issued monthly after 1941 under title *Monthly Catalogue of United States Government Publications.* Washington: G. P. O., 1941-

286. Vandergrift, John L., ed. *A History of the Air Rescue Service.* Orlando AFB, Florida: Hq. Air Rescue Service, 1959.

287. Verrier, Anthony. *The Bomber Offensive.* New York: Macmillan, 1969.

288. Volan, Denys. *A History of the Ground Observer Corps, 1940-1959.* Doctoral dissertation, University of Colorado, 1969.

289. Von Karman, Theodore, with Lee Edson. *The Wind and Beyond: Theodore von Karman. Pioneer in Aviation and Pathfinder in Space.* Boston: Little, Brown, 1967.

290. Wagner, Ray. *American Combat Planes.* Rev. ed. Garden City: Doubleday, 1968.

291. Wagner, Ray. *The North American Sabre.* Garden City: Doubleday, 1963.

292. Walter, Raymond. *Weather Training in the AAF, 1937-1945.* USAF Historical Study No. 56, 1952.

293. Warren, Harris G. *Special Operations: AAF Aid to European Resistance Movement, 1943-1945.* Air Historical Study No. 121, 1947.

294. Warren, John C. *Airborne Missions in the Mediterranean, 1942-1945.* USAF Historical Study No. 74, Sept. 1955.

295. Warren, John C. *Airborne Operations in World War II, European Theater.* USAF Historical Study No. 97, Sept. 1956.

296. *The War Reports of General of the Army George C. Marshall,*

Chief of Staff; General of the Army H. H. Arnold, Commanding General, Army Air Forces; and Fleet Admiral Ernest J. King, Commander-in-Chief, United States Fleet and Chief of Naval Operations. Philadelphia: Lippincott, 1947. (This is a convenient assembly of separately published reports.)

297. Watson, Mark S. *Chief of Staff: Prewar Plans and Preparations. United States Army in World War II.* Washington: Office of Chief of Military History, 1950.

298. Watson, Richard L. *Air Action in the Papuan Campaign, 21 July 1942-23 January 1943.* AAF Historical Study No. 17, Aug. 1944.

299. Watson, Richard L. *The Fifth Air Force in the Huon Peninsula Campaign, January-October 1943.* AAF Historical Study No. 113, 1946.

300. Watson, Richard L. *The Fifth Air Force in the Huon Peninsula Campaign, October 1943-February 1944.* AAF Historical Study No. 116, 1947.

301. Weather, [Major] Bynum E., Jr. *Acquisition of AAF Bases in Latin America, June 1939-June 1943.* USAF Historical Study No. 63, 1960.

302. Weaver, Herbert. The Fourteenth Air Force to 1 October 1943. AAF Historical Study No. 109, 1945.

303. Weaver, Herbert. *The Tenth Air Force, 1943.* AAF Historical Study No. 117, 1946.

304. Webster, Sir Charles [K.,] and Noble Frankland. *The Strategic Air Offensive Against Germany, 1939-1945. History of the Second World War.* London: H.M.S.O., 1961. 4 vols.

305. Werrell, Kenneth P. *The Tactical Development of the Eighth Air Force in the World War II.* Doctoral dissertation, Duke University, 1969.

306. White, Gerald T. *Training of Foreign Nationals by the AAF, 1939-1945.* Air Historical Study No. 64, 1947.

307. Whitehouse, Arch. *Decisive Air Battles of the First World War.* New York: Duel, 1963.

308. Williams, Edwin L., Jr. *Legislative History of the AAF and USAF, 1941-1951.* USAF Historical Study No. 84, Aug. 1954.

309. Williams, Howard D. *Basic Military Training in the AAF, 1939-1944.* AAF Historical Study No. 49, Nov. 1946.

310. Williams, Kathleen. *The AAF in Australia to the Summer of 1942.* AAF Historical Study No. 9, July 1944.

311. Williams, Kathleen. *Air Defense of the Panama Canal, 1 January 1939- 7 December 1941.* AAF Historical Study No. 42, 1946.

312. Wright, [Lieutenant Colonel] Monte Duane. *Most Probable Position.* Lawrence: The University Press of Kansas, 1972.

313. Wright, [Lieutenant Colonel] Monte D., and Lawrence J. Paszek, eds. *Science, Technology, and Warfare. The Proceedings of the Third Military History Symposium, United States Air Force Academy.* Washington: Office of Air Force History and USAF Academy, 1971.

314. Access to Official Records. Throughout the U.S. Department of Defense security restrictions have generally been removed from U.S.

military records through the end of World War II. In addition, the USAF is removing most security restrictions from Air Force documents originated through 1955. In the declassification categories a few Defense and Air Force documents will currently remain classified for specific causes such as cryptographic security. For access to Air Force records, U.S. citizens should write to the Office of Information, Office of the Secretary of the Air Force (SAF/OIP), Washington, D.C. 20330. Foreign nationals should submit research requests through their Embassy in Washington to the Foreign Liaison Division (AF-CVF), Headquarters USAF, Washington, D.C. 20330.

315. The two principal Air Force photographic depositories are the USAF Central Audio-Visual Depository, Aerospace Audio-Visual Service (MAC), Norton AFB, California 92405 for motion picture film and the USAF Central Still Photographic Depository, 1361st Photographic Squadron, Aerospace Audio-Visual Service, 1221 S. Fern Street, Arlington, Virginia 22205 for current and historical still photographs. These collections are identified and catalogued for retrieval, and reproductions from film can be provided to private individuals with approval from the Director of Information Services, Office of the Secretary of the Air Force, Washington, D.C. 20330.

316. Whiteley, John F. *Early Army Aviation: The Engineering Air Force.* Manhattan, Ks.: Military Affairs/Aerospace Historian, 1974.

XVI

THE DEPARTMENT OF DEFENSE, DEFENSE POLICY AND DIPLOMACY, 1945-1973

Calvin L. Christman

Any researcher using the sources available for the study of postwar national security policy is struck with the vastness of the literature—a veritable mountain of printed matter. And this despite the fact that most official records on the period have yet to be opened. Probably at no other time in American history has contemporary interest in military affairs been so great, emotional feeling so keen, and opinion so polarized. Thus even emotional and cliché-ridden works cannot be ignored completely by the researcher, for they vividly exemplify the times. In studying the postwar period, the researcher must use energy and judiciousness.

GENERAL SOURCES. John Greenwood's bibliography, *American Defense Policy since 1945* (625), provides a fine take-off point for any researcher in this period. Organized around subject headings, this bibliography is particularly helpful in the area of government publications and periodical articles. It lacks, however, an author or title index. Two shorter and contrasting bibliographic surveys are found in the books edited by Huntington (219) and Rodberg and Shearer (399). Huntington is a scholar generally favorable to the military, while the latter authors are strongly critical of the growth of the military establishment since World War II. *Military Affairs* (670) and *Foreign Affairs* (658) list current material published in their respective areas. The RAND Corporation, a private research institution or "think tank" that has delved largely into defense-related topics, has published a guide to its publications (635), and updates this list with quarterly announcements (707).

A handy guide to books on foreign affairs is the series put out by the Council on Foreign Relations (620). This has recently been completely redone (621). The Council also has been producing an annual documents collection (619) since 1939 and an annual survey of *The United States in World Affairs* (622) since 1932. The State Department published a helpful and extensive collection of documents covering the 1950-1955 period (606). Its regular documents series, *Foreign Relations of the United States: Diplo-*

matic Papers (608, 631), had in 1974 only reached the year 1948. The State Department publishes current documents in its weekly *Bulletin* (691).

The United States government puts out a massive number of publications, many of them dealing with national security matters; in the decade from January 1961 to December 1971, the *Monthly Catalog of United States Government Publications* (see chapter XIX) listed over 200,000 items. Unfortunately, however, this material has been difficult to mine effectively, for the catalog has lacked an easy-to-use subject index. This will hopefully be remedied with a forthcoming privately published subject guide (733) to the catalogs of this century. For congressional material since 1971, the Congressional Information Service provides a monthly *Index* (699) and *Annual* (728). The first part of the *Annual* furnishes abstracts of congressional publications and legislative histories, while the second part gives an index to congressional publications and public laws. These CIS publications are particularly useful for their abstracts of all congressional hearings, documents, prints, and other related materials that are sometimes difficult for the researcher to locate and use.

Additional material on both defense and foreign policy can be found in the *Weekly Compilation of Presidential Documents* (695) and in the *Public Papers of the Presidents of the United States* (610). The latter series began in 1958 with the publication of the papers of President Truman. A last general source for the period, and one that is particularly helpful in viewing the reaction of the American public to the various security-related issues that swept over them after World War II, is the three-volume summary of *The Gallup Poll* (155).

MANUSCRIPT COLLECTIONS. The most important collections for this period are housed in the various presidential libraries (see Introduction), established for all of the presidents since World War II. Researchers should address inquiries to the director of the individual library, being as specific as possible concerning their research needs. The greater the information provided in the request, the easier it will be for the library staff to find available material. Since presidential files are often kept by the name of the correspondent rather than by subject heading, names as well as subjects should be provided in the letter of inquiry whenever possible. Along with documentary materials, these libraries often have valuable oral history sources. Given the proper information by researchers, the staff can photocopy needed material or, if the bulk makes this impractical, give the researcher an indication of the extent of material dealing with his subject. The director can also provide information on access, which is especially important in this recent period, since many records will be closed for some years to come.

Along with the papers of the presidents, many key advisors and policymakers have deposited their personal papers or oral memoirs in presidential or private libraries. Princeton University Library provides a particularly rich source for scholars, for it houses the papers of James Forrestal (717), Bernard Baruch (710), and John Foster Dulles (716). Some of the other collections that may be of interest to researchers of this period are those of Dean Acheson (709), McGeorge Bundy (712), James Byrnes (713), Clark Clifford (714), Henry Cabot Lodge (718), Robert Patterson (721), W. W.

Rostow (723), and Henry Stimson (724). In the field of congressional foreign policy, papers of Senator Robert Taft (725) and Senator Arthur Vandenberg (727) may be helpful. Some of these papers will not be deposited until the death of the owner, while access is still limited on other material; inquiry should first be made as to the availability of specific papers. Other officials, such as Robert McNamara and Henry Kissinger, have not yet made decisions as to future placement of their papers.

Some government officials, such as Thomas Gates, Robert Lovett, and Dean Rusk, left all papers in the files of their agency when they left office. Official records of an agency are ultimately housed in the National Archives, where availability can be ascertained by writing the relevant Branch, either Modern Military or Diplomatic. There is a general 30-year restriction rule on material, though this may vary with circumstances.

Papers of military leaders that may be valuable are those of Omar Bradley (711), Lawton Collins (715), Douglas MacArthur (719), George C. Marshall (720), Matthew Ridgway (722), and Maxwell Taylor (726). The same warning on access pertains to these collections.

The above is obviously not an exhaustive list. Other collections are currently open and of importance, while more will be available in the future. Hamer provides *A Guide to Archives and Manuscripts in the United States* (626), while listings of new acquisitions can be found in *The National Union Catalog of Manuscript Collections* (634). With the decline of written correspondence, oral history material has become increasingly important, and Mason and Starr furnish an index to one of the most important sources of personal recollections, *The Oral History Collection of Columbia University* (632). The Military has also shown an increased interest in this form of preserving historical material (224), with a new program starting at Ft. Leavenworth.

NEWSPAPERS AND PERIODICALS. A number of newspapers give substantial coverage to defense and foreign policy, with the efforts of the *New York Times* and *Washington Post* being the most extensive. Both of these newspapers have indexes (704, 703). Beyond the field of newspapers lies a vast number of periodicals available to the researcher.

A feeling for the environment of the period can be found in some of the magazines of commentary: *Nation* (672), *National Review* (674), *New Republic* (678), *Harper's* (661), and *Atlantic Monthly* (648). Articles often critical of defense policy and diplomacy appear in *I. F. Stone's Weekly* (663) and *Human Events* (662). The former criticism comes from the political left, the latter from the right. *Fortune* (660) often contains fine articles on the Department of Defense (DOD) and defense economics, while *Aviation Week and Space Technology* (649), an important trade journal, is an excellent source for aerospace developments, current weapons technology, and budgetary considerations. Weapons technology also receives occasional but important review in *Scientific American* (688).

There exists a large number of scholarly publications that often contain material treating national security affairs. Among those with which a researcher might wish to have some familiarity are the *American Political Science Review* (644); *Annals of the American Academy of Political and Social Science* (645), which centers the entire issue on a single topic; *Foreign*

Affairs (658), published by the influential Council on Foreign Relations; *Foreign Policy* (659); *Journal of Conflict Resolution* (667); *Orbis* (681); *Political Science Quarterly* (684); *Survival* (689); and *World Politics* (696). Issues and questions revolving around nuclear weaponry receive attention in *Science and Public Affairs* (687), which was formerly the *Bulletin of the Atomic Scientists*.

Among the journals specifically devoted to military topics, *Aerospace Historian* (639), *Air University Review* (643), *Military Affairs* (670), *Military Review* (671), and *United States Naval Institute Proceedings* (692) give a wide-ranging coverage, with considerable emphasis on history and defense thought. Information on defense management can be found in *Perspectives in Defense Management* (683), *Common Defense* (651), *Armed Forces Management* (647), and *Defense Industry Bulletin* (655). The first of these is put out by the Industrial College of the Armed Forces (ICAF), while the last originated in the DOD.

Most of the articles from these periodicals are listed or abstracted in at least one of the various published indexes; of these, the researcher will probably find the *Air University Library Index to Military Periodicals* (698), *Reader's Guide to Periodical Literature* (706), and *Social Science and Humanities Index* (708) the most helpful starting place.

AUTOBIOGRAPHICAL AND BIOGRAPHICAL MATERIALS. There are at present no scholarly biographies of any of the postwar presidents, though there are some important studies of specific aspects of their administrations. These studies will be mentioned elsewhere. Of the various presidential memoirs, that of Truman (479) stands out as the best and most rewarding to the researcher, although those of Eisenhower (127) and Johnson (235) should not be ignored.

For studies of the secretaries of state, Ferrell and Bemis are editors of the continuing series, *The American Secretaries of State and Their Diplomacy* (144). To date, volumes have appeared on Stettinius and Byrnes (492), Marshall (143), Acheson (440), Dulles (160), and Herter (351). In addition, Byrnes (67, 68) and Acheson (2) left first-hand accounts of their service. Acheson's *Present at the Creation*, while strongly partisan, gives a wealth of detail to accompany his sharply-etched vignettes; it is perhaps the outstanding political memoir of this entire period. To Acheson, one of the great heroes of the immediate postwar years was George C. Marshall, whose biographer, Forrest Pogue (372), has not yet reached this period of the general's life. Pogue expects to cover Marshall's China trip in volume four and his service as secretary of state and secretary of defense in the fifth and concluding volume.

The foreign policy of most of the 1950s is strongly identified with Eisenhower's secretary of state, John Foster Dulles. Along with the Gerson (160) volume, there are studies of Dulles's secretaryship by Hoopes (209) and Guhin (174). The latter attempts to dispel the earlier view that Dulles was hindered by the rigidity of his moral and ideological beliefs, stressing instead the secretary's pragmatic statesmanship. As yet, there has been no general study of Dean Rusk, though early attempts to sketch the personality and thinking of Henry Kissinger have already appeared (168, 280).

The only secretary of defense who has inspired full-scale biographical treatment has been James V. Forrestal. Rogow (400) covers Forrestal's entire life in a psychological study, while Albion and Connery (7) limit themselves to the secretary's earlier service in the Navy Department. In his various papers and memoranda that were later edited and published (326), Forrestal provided one of the basic sources on events and thought within the Truman administration during the crystallization of the Cold War. There is an abundance of material on Robert McNamara and various aspects of his thought and work (245, 401), but there is no scholarly political biography as yet. Journalists and scholars have generally ignored the other secretaries, though Borklund (48) gives brief sketches of all the secretaries up through McNamara.

Important military leaders have not been shy about presenting their recollection of events, although they have couched them in varying degrees of frankness. Generals Ridgway (394), Taylor (471), LeMay (288), and MacArthur (306) have all left memoirs, with General Westmoreland's on the way. Of these men, MacArthur was far and away the most controversial. Studies of the general either love the man—and that clearly includes his own memoir—or hate him; there is no middle ground. Clayton James is currently preparing the main attempt at an objective treatment in *The Years of MacArthur* (729); the third and concluding volume will deal with the general's role in the occupation of Japan and in the Korean War.

A researcher will also find a large number of civilian memoirs from which to choose. Sherman Adams (5), Eisenhower's presidential chief of staff, and Allen Dulles (121), Eisenhower's director of the CIA, published recollections. Arthur Krock, one of Washington's most astute political reporters, presents much background material to the postwar period in his *Sixty Years on the Firing Line* (276), while three men closely concerned with early atomic matters--Lewis Strauss, David Lilienthal, and Bernard Baruch—each left memoirs (462, 295, 28). Patterson presents a major biographical study of Senator Robert A. Taft (361), who was the main Republican critic of early postwar foreign policy. The papers of Senator Arthur Vandenberg (486), one of the key Republican supporters of foreign policy during that same period, have been edited and published.

Diplomats of the postwar period who published recollections include Robert Murphy (342), Henry Cabot Lodge (300), Charles Bohlen (46), and George F. Kennan (250); the last named is usually credited with being the main architect of the postwar "containment" policy. Gardner, an historian who is usually critical of the development of postwar American foreign policy, examines the role of eleven key policy-makers in *Architects of Illusion* (156), while Paterson has edited a volume (360) on the contemporary critics of the Truman administration's efforts in this field.

As any researcher soon discovers, memoirs and biographies need to be used with a degree of caution. Memoirs are only one person's recollection of events and too often tend to be self-serving, while biographers sometimes overestimate the importance of their subject, having the entire world revolve around this one figure. Despite these problems, a researcher should not ignore such materials, for they can provide insights and information available nowhere else.

DEFENSE ORGANIZATION AND OPERATION. The researcher

should be familiar with a number of important government sources, starting with the annual report of the Secretary of Defense (602); the title and format have changed slightly since 1971 (604). Probably the most comprehensive study of the development of the DOD and the various defense-related agencies are the materials compiled by the Senate subcommittee headed by Henry Jackson. Along with a three-volume undertaking (591), the Jackson subcommittee also collected bibliographies (592, 589) and selected materials (593). In following the formation and evolution of the DOD, there exist also the hearings held during its creation as part of the National Security Act of 1947 (575), as well as its various modifications in 1949 (557), 1953 (565), and 1958 (571). The Senate Armed Services Committee print of the *National Security Act of 1947, as Amended through December 31, 1969* (576) may also be of interest. As part of any study of the creative and evolutionary process, a researcher needs also to be aware of the assorted published special studies on defense organization, including the Eberstadt Report (596), which influenced the structure as created in 1947, the Hoover Commission (541, 542), the Rockefeller Committee (543), and the Blue Ribbon Report (538).

Demetrois Caraley (71) furnishes the best study of the politics of the unification process and the components—many of them irrational and self-serving—that produced the National Security Act of 1947, while Paul Hammond (186) provides a comprehensive history of American efforts at defense organization since the turn of this century. Studies of the DOD are available by Kintner (259) and Borklund (47), the latter's book serving as a concise laymen's guide to its history and organization. Defense management is stressed by Ries (395), while broad studies of national security organization are available from Powers (375) and Stanley (455). The ICAF provides fine volumes in *Organization for National Security* (529), *The National Security Structure* (135), *The Environment of National Security* (133), and *Defense Organization and Management* (29); emphasis of the last volume is on the period since 1961.

The best sources for information on the National Security Council (NSC) are the materials put out by Senator Jackson's subcommittee: *Organizing for National Security* (591), *Organizational History of the National Security Council* (590), and the commercially published volume on *The National Security Council* (226). May's article (312) contributes historical background on the NSC, while Falk (134) and Sander (410) give short studies of individual presidential use of the Council. There is considerable material on both the NSC and the Joint Chiefs of Staff in the previously mentioned studies by Hammond, Stanley, and the ICAF.

Harry Howe Ransom's *The Intelligence Establishment* (385) delivers the best historical and functional examination of the subject, covering both the CIA and other U.S. intelligence agencies. The value of this standard work is enhanced by an excellent annotated bibliography. Other useful volumes include those by Zlotnick (532), Platt (371), Kirkpatrick (262, 263), Kent (254), Hilsman (203), and Dulles (121). The CIA and decision-making is the subject of a recent article by Cooper (98), while Kahn's study of cryptology (240) contains the best available discussion of the National Security Agency.

DEFENSE PROBLEMS. A basic concern for any armed force is manpower, and this question has nagged the United States since World War II. In the immediate postwar period, President Truman took an interest in the possibility of Universal Military Training, appointing the Compton Committee (612) to report on its feasibility. Contemporary views on the subject are also found in the September 1945 issue of the *Annals* (14), which devoted its entire issue to the subject. The nation, however, failed to accept the concept of UMT and returned instead to the draft in 1948. A case study of this action is furnished by Jacobs and Gallaher (227), while the actual operation of the Selective Service System and its effect on the draft-age population is outlined by Davis and Dolbeare (106). With the escalation of the Vietnamese War, the draft became unacceptable to an increasing number of people. By the end of the 1960s, a large number of critiques of the system had appeared, with many of them being uneven and emotional. President Nixon appointed the Gates Commission to study the possibility of an all-volunteer army. The Commission's report (614) and its supplementary studies (615) furnish basic sources on the subject, as do various congressional materials (551, 553, 578, 570). Daniel (624) contributes an annotated bibliography covering the all-volunteer concept. Concise arguments for and against this concept, written in laymen's terms, come from Miller (324) and Marmion (310). Janowitz provides recent studies (232, 233) on the all-volunteer force, while Goldman (165) explores the utilization of women. For an historical overview of the manpower policies and problems since 1945, Gerhardt's fine volume (159) is the best available; Canby's *Military Manpower Procurement* (70) adds a recent discussion.

The major study of congressional policy-making for the armed forces reserve components is William Levantrosser's *Congress and the Citizen-Soldier* (289), while Brayton (54) furnishes a short summary of reserve policies since the close of World War II. Though Dupuy (125), Hill (201), and Riker (396) have written general histories of the National Guard, a full scholarly study still needs to be done. Derthick's *The National Guard in Politics* (113) centers on the lobbying activities of the National Guard Association rather than on the Guard itself.

Another aspect of the manpower question concerns the decision made during the Truman administration to end segregation in the armed forces. Richard Dalfiume (103) contributes the standard treatment of military desegregation, covering the period from 1939-1953 and demonstrating the key part played by the Fahy Committee (617). An additional summary is found in Stillman's book (460), while Moskos furnishes a concise picture of "Race in the Armed Forces" (335). This latter study provides helpful tabular and bibliographical material.

Manpower clearly has not been the only problem facing the defense establishment in the postwar period. Defense spending has at different times been criticized as too low—during the latter years of the Eisenhower administration—and too high—during the latter 1960s and early 1970s. In the 1970s it climbed past the $80 billion mark, though any researcher should view spending not solely in terms of total dollars, but also in terms of constant dollars, percentage of gross national product, and percentage of total budget.

The best studies of defense economics are by Hitch and McKean (206) and by Schlesinger (427). The latter volume, written by Nixon's secretary of defense, gives an especially comprehensive treatment of the disparate factors comprising the subject and their interrelationship to national security as a whole. Further material can be located in the volume by Lincoln, Stone, and Harvey (296), which was the first postwar study of the subject, as well as in the works by Clark (79) and McKean (317). For coverage of defense economics during specific periods, Charles J. V. Murphy's articles (341) in *Fortune* throughout the years of the Eisenhower administration are excellent, while Baldwin's book examines *The Structure of the Defense Market, 1955-1964* (24). This decade covered the period when the defense market had finished its adjustment to the terminiation of the Korean War but had not yet begun its build-up for Vietnam.

The various congressional materials on defense spending represent one of the most important sources for any study of the defense establishment. Especially valuable are the budget hearings by the House and Senate Committees on Appropriations (546, 548, 549, 566, 568, 569). This voluminous material includes budget justification throughout and discusses a very wide range of defense problems, weapons, and strategies. Defense budget-related materials can also be found in hearings of other committees. Additional budget information is summarized in a volume by the Bureau of the Budget (539) and in an *Appendix* (540), the latter containing a large amount of tabular material on defense spending. The Brookings Institution has given heavy emphasis to defense spending in its very useful budget studies, *Setting National Priorities* (431), started in 1970.

The link between policy-making and defense spending has been examined by Warner Schilling, Paul Hammond, and Glen Snyder (424) in their important case studies of "The Politics of National Defense: Fiscal 1950," "NSC-68: Prologue to Rearmament," and "The 'New Look' of 1953." The relationship of Congress to the defense budget has been the subject of studies by Huzar (223) and Kolodziej (274); the former covers the period 1933-1950, the latter 1945-1963. Both conclude that Congress has not fully exercised the legal control that it possesses. That conclusion is partially questioned by Kanter (242).

Criticism of defense spending has been part of the broader-based attack on the entire military structure, and almost all volumes with the military-industrial complex as a subject devote at least part of their space to defense spending. Centering specifically on this topic is Melman's *Pentagon Capitalism* (322). The same author has investigated the problems of converting industry from a military to a civilian purpose (321, 323), as have Udis (484) and the U.S. Arms Control and Disarmament Agency (ACDA) (534).

In the attack on the defense budget, most of the criticism has centered on the acquisition of and the need for certain weapons systems. The Department of Defense modified its management and decision-making approach to new weapons and strategies during the 1960s, partially as a result of changes outlined in the Defense Reorganization Act of 1958 and partially from ideas brought into the Pentagon by Secretary of Defense Robert McNamara. The new concepts, revolving around an intensive, broadly conceived analysis of needs and programs, formed McNamara's Planning-Programming-Budgeting System (PPBS); this approach is often referred to by the name of one of its components, systems analysis. The best major introduction to and support of defense analysis comes from Enthoven and Smith (130). Enthoven served as Assistant Secretary of Defense for Systems Analysis under McNamara, and his volume includes valuable discussions of such specific weapons-systems decisions as the B-70, the Skybolt, and the TFX. A shorter but no less helpful treatment is Hitch's *Decision-Making for Defense* (205). Hitch was one of the major forces behind the PPBS approach. Further information is found in Quade and Boucher (379), and in the volumes published by the ICAF: *Requirements for National Defense* (30), which places emphasis on the concepts and practices developed since 1961; *Defense Weapon Systems Management* (465); and *Case Studies in Military Systems Analysis* (448). Two articles should also be noted: Paul Hammond (185) discusses McNamara's PPBS concept; Schlesinger (428) questions whether the efficiency of analysis will always lead to the right decision. The Greenwood bibliography (625) gives a further listing of material on this subject.

For discussion of the weapons acquisition process, the researcher should turn to the congressional hearings (579) on this subject, as well as to the volumes by Scherer (419) and Peck and Scherer (363). Kurth (278) contributes both a criticism of weapons procurement and an attempt to distinguish the major competing explanations—strategic, technocratic, bureaucratic, democratic, and economic—for weapons policy. Probably the clearest and most concise discussion of the research and development programs that stand behind a weapons system are in the volumes by Powers (375) and the ICAF (411).

An outstanding general source for the development of nuclear weaponry and nuclear policy is the detailed official history (196, 197) of the Atomic Energy Commission (AEC); the two volumes published thus far cover the period through 1952 and the detonation of the first H-bomb. The decision to develop this weapon has been examined in an article by Schilling (422), while an additional source of information is the AEC hearing, *In the Matter of J. Robert Oppenheimer* (537). Moss (339) contributes a well-researched, journalistic account of the H-bomb's conception and development, with emphasis on the men involved in the project. The memoirs of Baruch (28), Strauss (462), and Lilienthal (295) supply additional sources on nuclear policy.

Concerning specific weaponry, Paul Hammond's discussion of the "Super Carriers and B-36 Bombers" in Stein's volume (459) is the best and most concise treatment of that controversy of the late 1940's, with additional information being found in Huntington's article (221) on interservice competition and in Davis' studies (107, 108, 109) of Navy policy. Two sets of congressional hearings, *Study of Airpower* (577) and *Inquiry into Satellite and Missile Programs* (573), not only provide information on weapons development and policy but also furnish some of the most valuable sources for the study of defense policy during the Eisenhower administration. Articles by Licklider (290), Dick (114), and Gray (169) consider the possible factors which produced speculation in the late 1950's that a lag in U.S. missile technology and deployment would result in a dangerous "missile gap" with the Soviet Union. Lasby (284) gives a very well-researched discussion of U.S. importation of German rocket scientists in the years following World War II, while Emme's edited essays on *The History of Rocket Technology* (129) provide helpful early studies of specific rocket programs. The two best scholarly analyses of specific missile programs are Armacost's volume (16) on the Thor-Jupiter controversy, which stresses the essentially political nature of the weapons innovation process, and Sapolsky's treatment (413) of the Polaris development, which provides a case study of a highly successful program.

Among the manned aircraft systems, the TFX or F-111 became the most controversial in its contractual, developmental, and operational stages. Major sources for the researcher are the lengthy congressional hearings and report (594, 595) on the aircraft, though the article by Smith (446) at the time of the TFX development and the later volume by Art (17) should be noted. The problem with another aircraft, the gigantic C-5A transport, is covered by Rice (391) and Fitzgerald (146).

An additional major weapons issue centered on the decision to deploy antiballistic missiles (ABM). Halperin (179) discusses the original decision of the Johnson administration for deployment, while Rathjens (386) gives a concise outline of the essential problems that have to be met by any effective ABM system. Basic sources on the subject are the hearings on the Safeguard ABM system (550), while Adams (4) gives a technical and informative discussion of ABM development and policy. There exists a number of volumes which argue the pros and cons of the ABM; among the more valuable are those by Rabinowitch and Adams (381), Holst and Schneider (208), Kinter (260), Wiesner (507), and the Center for the Study of Democratic Institutions (74). Finally, two very different views of the entire subject of weapons technology and what it holds for the future are contained in York's *Race to Oblivion* (528) and Possony and Pournelle's *The Strategy of Technology* (373). Both York and Wiesner held important positions on various Presidential Scientific Advisory Committees.

One defense consideration that has been somewhat ignored in recent popular discussion has been civil defense. For the researcher who wishes to delve into this subject, the Department of Army's *Civil Defense* bibliography (597) is a useful starting point, while the ICAF volume (329) on the subject is the most concise and complete treatment available. Additional studies completed during the last decade are available by Wigner (509, 510), Weaver (498), and Heer (192). At the present time, no scholarly history exists on civil defense planning during the last three decades.

One possible solution to both massive defense expenditures and the protection of population lies in disarmament and arms control, though there exists no guarantee of success in the difficult, complex, and time-consuming process of agreement. Since 1961, the ACDA has published an annual collection of *Documents on Disarmament* (535), while the Department of State published a two-volume collection (607) in 1960 that covered the years since 1945. For bibliographical guides, the researcher can turn to the volume (601) produced by the Department of Army and the *Complete Handbook on Weapons Control* (637) by Walch.

Probably the best overall analysis of the complexities of arms control is Hedley Bull's *The Control of the Arms Race* (63). In a field often mired in jargon, this volume has the added benefit of being expressed in laymen's terms. Another basic treatment of the subject is by Schelling and Halperin (417), who delineate the vital relationship between arms control and military strategy; these considerations are not mutually exclusive. Other useful treatments of the issue are by Brennan (55, 56) and York (526). The latter book contributes an excellent collection of articles from the *Scientific*

American. Wainhouse (491) discusses the tremendous technical and political problems involved in arms-control verification, while Feld (142) and York (527) demonstrate the impact of new technology on the arms race, with the last article discussing both the history of the multiple independently targeted re-entry vehicle (MIRV) and the complications its development introduced into the arms control equation.

Chalmers Roberts provides a concise, journalistic survey of the arms race and arms control since 1945 in his *Nuclear Years* (397), while Bernhard Bechhoefer, a State Department specialist in arms control, does somewhat the same in his more substantial and lengthy *Postwar Negotiations for Arms Control* (32). The gamesmanship and propaganda that accompany negotiations form the theme of the study by Spanier and Nogee (453). Two views of individuals involved in arms negotiations are found in short volumes by Dean (112) and Wadsworth (490).

The Nuclear Test Ban Treaty and the Strategic Arms Limitation Talks (SALT) emerged as the two major negotiated agreements of the postwar period. Major sources for the history of the first agreement come from agency publications (609, 536) and congressional hearings (585); the latter (581, 574, 586, 556, 558) provide the same for the second agreement. John Newhouse gives a dramatic and carefully-researched history of the first round of SALT in *Cold Dawn* (348), while early examinations of the problems and prospects of SALT come from Kaplan (243) and Kintner and Pfaltzgraff (261).

CIVIL-MILITARY RELATIONS AND THE MILITARY ESTAB-LISHMENT. The best bibliographical guide in this area is Arthur Larson's *Civil Military Relations and Militarism* (630), which devotes a major portion of its coverage to the United States. Other guides are those by the Social Science Research Council (636), which covers 1940-1952, and by Lang (629).

Samuel P. Huntington's *The Soldier and the State* (222) delivers both a history of U.S. civil-military relations and a vigorous defense of the military ethic. It contains an excellent section of notes and bibliography. Both Smith (444) and Kerwin (255) published studies in the early postwar period, while Lasswell (285) and Ransom (384) have attempted to gauge what increased national security needs will mean for traditional American values and institutions. Nelson (344) and Clayton (83) do somewhat the same in a collection of sources and readings. General Dale O. Smith presents a military view of what the civil-military equation should be in his *Eagles Talons* (441), while the British historian Michael Howard (214) gives a comparative sketch of civil-military relations in Britain and the United States from 1945-1958.

Adam Yarmolinsky has contributed a major treatment of *The Military Establishment* (523), as well as editing a valuable issue of the *Annals* (522) which centers on "The Military and American Society." Other important studies are by the sociologists Morris Janowitz (234, 231, 230) and C. Wright Mills (328), with additional material by Just (237), Ackley (3), Moskos (338), Oppenheimer (353), and Little (299). Major examinations of military education and of ROTC are contained respectively in the studies by Masland and Radway (311) and Lyons and Masland (304), while *The*

American Enlisted Man (336) is the subject of the recent study by Moskos. Attempts to portray and diagnose the problems besetting the post-Vietnam military come in books by Hauser (189), Loory (301), King (257), Lovell and Kronenberg (302), and in a short article by Yarmolinsky (524).

For a significant segment of the American population, a major casualty of the Vietnamese War was their trust in the American military. As the American role in the war increased, so too did the criticism of what became known as the military-industrial complex. Though much of the resultant outcry was uneven and emotional, there can be little doubt as to the sincerity and concern of most of the critics. The earliest attacks, such as by Cook (96), Coffin (86), and Swomley (466), appeared before major United States involvement occurred in Vietnam. As the American commitment grew, the commentary on the military-industrial complex and militarism reached floodtide proportions, so no attempt can be made to survey it completely. Among the better argued presentations, however, are those by Rodberg and Shearer (399), Barnet (25), Kaufman (244), Lapp (281, 282), Russett (409), and Donovan (118), the last author being a military officer. A defense of the military-industrial complex is found in Baumgartner's *Lonely Warriors* (31). Attempts at a broad assessment of the military-industrial complex are contained in the edited volumes by Schiller and Phillips (421), Pursell (378), Sarkesian (414), and Rosen (404).

DEFENSE POLICY. A most helpful guide to this subject is the exhaustive bibliographical set prepared by Charles Donnelly. His first volume, *United States Defense Policies since World War II* (544), appeared in 1957. He followed his original survey with annual volumes (545) up to 1966, when he retired. Since the bibliographies were published as House Documents, it is much easier for a researcher to retrieve the volumes if he uses the document numbers, which are respectively for the year of publication: 1958, No. 436; 1959, No. 227; 1960, No. 432; 1961, No. 207; 1962, No. 502; 1963, No. 155; 1964, No. 335; 1965, No. 285; and 1966, No. 344. In addition, there is the bibliography (561) put out by the House Committee on Foreign Affairs, as well as guides published by the Department of the Army (600, 598). Valuable summaries of policy during a specific administration appear in *Congress and the Nation* (92), published every four years.

Samuel P. Huntington gives the most thorough history of defense policy from the end of World War II until 1960 in *The Common Defense* (220). This important study focuses on strategic programs, always keeping in view the political bargaining that determines policy. A very concise treatment of policy since 1945 is contained in Halperin's *Defense Strategies for the Seventies* (180), while Millis (327) surveys policy from 1930-1957, with an emphasis on the postwar period. In addition, the Millis volume is supported by Stein's superb case studies (459) of specific decisions. Weigley also gives considerable coverage to the postwar period in *The American Way of War* (499). The critical—and too often ignored—link between national policy and military strategy is the subject of Brodie's *War and Politics* (61), a study giving considerable discussion to the Korean and Vietnamese Wars.

A survey of the postwar nuclear environment, with a stress on developing inventories of strategic weapons, is found in George Quester's *Nuclear Diplomacy* (380), with additional works on the subject by Moulton (340) and Bottome (49). Particularly fine sets of readings on United States defense policy come from Trager and Kronenberg (477), Kissinger (266), Head and Rokke (191), and Halperin and Kanter (183), with the last concentrating on the bureaucratic environment. Some useful information on United States defense policy can also be gained in the study of her close allies. Snyder (449), Rosecrance (403), and Pierre (370) provide studies of British defense policy in the postwar period, Conant (91) and McLin (318) do the same for Canada, while Weinstein discusses Japan (500).

The role of various presidents in military affairs is found in Ernest May's *The Ultimate Decision* (314). Hassler's short book (188) surveys the same territory, while Clark and Legere (80) present a fuller study of the presidential role in decision-making for defense. Halperin's article on "The President and the Military" (182) can also be useful. Smith and Cotter cover the *Powers of the President during Crises* (443), a subject that has received increasing interest in congress since Vietnam, as witnessed by hearings and documents (559, 584, 588, 564).

No secretary of defense has provoked more discussion or has affected defense policy as greatly as Robert McNamara. His short book, *The Essence of Security* (319), gives few insights into the man himself, being composed mainly of slightly-revised statements he made while in office. The only early effort at a complete survey of the secretary's defense career is by Trewhitt (478). Roherty's (401) more narrowly conceived volume, centering on two case studies, builds a theoretical picture of both McNamara and the earlier secretaries and provides an extensive treatment of McNamara's approach to defense management. Kaufmann gives the best early portrait of *The McNamara Strategy* (245), but he deals only with the first four years of the secretary's tenure and rarely penetrates beneath the level of McNamara's public statements. One may also wish to check Brodie's review (59) of the Kaufmann book. Among the numerous other writings about McNamara, the books or articles by Tucker (482), Bower (50), Baldwin (22), and Seligman (433) can be useful.

In the period following World War II, academicians rather than military men have produced the major discussions and critiques of defense policy. Within a rather sparse military field are books by Generals Twining (483), Power (374), LeMay (287), and Gavin (157), but the only publication to have a major influence was General Maxwell Taylor's *The Uncertain Trumpet* (472); it argued that the United States must give as much attention to the problem of and response to limited wars as it had been devoting to nuclear deterrence.

The scientific-academic professionals have not been nearly so reticent as the military, and their full-fledged involvement in military policy and research has been one of the important phenomena of the past few decades. Though somewhat dated, the major portrayal and assessment of this interest in military thought comes in Lyons and Morton's *Schools for Strategy* (305). One university's reaction to scientific-military research is pictured by Nelkin (343). The RAND Corporation, the first of the "think tanks" to develop in the Cold War environment, published a quick summary (383) of its history. Smith (439) gives a much fuller organizational and operational picture, but his very favorable judgment of RAND is challenged by Green (171). Dickson furnishes a journalist's view of the whole subject in *Think Tanks* (115).

Two broad explorations of the scientist's role are by Vannevar Bush (65) and Sir Solly Zuckerman (533); Bush held a key advisory position in the United States, while Zuckerman did the same in Britain. Schilling (423) and Skolnikoff (436) provide historical coverage of the scientist's developing policy participation since 1945. The latter author also evaluates existing policy machinery and sketches needs for the future. Additional information comes from Gilpin (162), Wiesner (508), Nieburg (350), and Jacobson and Stein (228), with the focus of the last authors on the role of the scientist-technologist in the Nuclear Test Ban negotiations. Gilpin and Wright have edited a group of essays, *Scientists and National Policy-Making* (163), as have Mansfield (309) and Grodzins and Rabinowitch (173).

As mentioned, American strategic theorists of the postwar period have sprung largely from academic rather than military ranks. Introductions to postwar strategic thought can be found in Harry Coles' helpful "Strategic Studies since 1945" (87), Michael Howard's "The Classical Strategists" (215), and Urs Schwarz's concise *American Strategy* (432). As a sampling of strategic thought, the researcher should be acquainted with the works by Brodie (57, 60, 58), Green (170), Kahn (241), Kaufmann (246), Kissinger (264, 265), Morgenstern (333), Osgood (354), Schelling (416, 418), Strausz-Hupé (463, 464), and Wohlstetter (517). Licklider's *The Private Nuclear Strategists* (291) attempts a portrait of such thinkers.

DIPLOMACY AND THE COLD WAR. Although the conduct of foreign policy is separated from defense policy for reasons of chapter organization, it is an artificial division; in actuality they need to be interrelated closely, if not inseparably, especially for a period that saw neither clear-cut war nor peace. A good concise introduction is Radway's *Foreign Policy and National Defense* (382), backed by an excellent bibliographical essay. Hilsman's *The Politics of Policy Making in Defense and Foreign Affairs* (202) serves something of a similar purpose, with emphasis on the president. Almond discusses *The American People and Foreign Policy* (10), while Wilcox (511), Robinson (398), and Dahl (102) cover Congress and foreign policy. Sapin and Snyder give a general treatment of *The Role of the Military in American Foreign Policy* (412). Among the articles and books that treat the relationship between foreign policy and domestic politics are the studies by Westerfield (501), Caridi (72), Theoharis (474), Graebner (167), and Divine (117). Knorr (270) explores the problem of using contemporary military power to further diplomatic aims, while Allison (9) tries to gauge the link between American military capabilities and resultant foreign policy. A solid general assessment for the future can be found in Owen's *The Next Phase in Foreign Policy* (356).

For coverage of military and foreign policy in the Truman administration, researchers should be familiar with McLellan and Reuss' excellent chapter in *The Truman Period as a Research Field* (633). Unfortunately, no similar volumes have appeared on the other postwar presidents. There exists no scholarly history of Truman or his presidency, the only general survey being the rather uncritical journalistic treatment by Phillips (369). Bernstein and Matusow (37) are more critical in their documentary history, with much of their selection treating foreign affairs. A study by Haynes (190) examines Truman's role as commander in chief.

Most of the early books covering the Eisenhower administration tend to be critical of the general as a president. An example is the treatment by Hughes (217), one of Eisenhower's ex-staff members. The more recent judgment by Parmet (359) is far more favorable. Both devote sizeable coverage to foreign affairs. There is also a moderately helpful documentary history by Branyan and Larsen (53).

A starting point for material on Kennedy is Crown's bibliographical essay (623). Sorenson (450) and Schlesinger (426), both of whom were in the administration, have produced lengthy history-memoirs of Kennedy's presidency; the latter is particularly critical of the inertia of the State Department. Insights into a number of the foreign crises of the Kennedy administration are furnished by Hilsman (204), a Kennedy foreign affairs specialist. Rostow's *The Diffusion of Power* (405) serves partially as a memoir; in addition, it helps to exemplify the view of many of Kennedy's advisors toward Vietnam. The early favorable assessments of Kennedy are now being questioned, as in Walton's *Cold War and Counterrevolution* (495), which claims that Kennedy's legacy is one of miscalculations and world tensions.

Geyelin (161) gives an early appraisal of Johnson's foreign policy, while Hoopes (210) delivers an inside account of the Johnson administration's shift in policy toward Vietnam in early 1968. For a discussion of the same period by the incoming secretary of defense, see the personal recollection by Clark Clifford (84). A source for the foreign policy of Richard Nixon is his set of reports on *U.S. Foreign Policy for the 1970's* (611). Henry Brandon, a British journalist, gives an early favorable judgment of the Nixon-Kissinger efforts in *The Retreat of American Power* (52). The researcher should also remember the previously mentioned memoirs and biographies that relate to the various administrations.

Broad efforts to assess the traditions and needs of American foreign policy in light of the Cold War are found in Tannenbaum (468), Thompson (475), Morgenthau (334), Kennan (249), and Tucker (480). There exists an extensive literature on the origins and developments of the cold war; among the better general treatments are those of Brown (62), Feis (141), Halle (178), Hammond (184), Lukacs (303), Rostow (406), Schlesinger (425), Spanier (451), and Ulam (485). Generally, their works sketch the war in terms either of the brave and essential response of the United States to the military and ideological expansion of the Soviet Union at the close of World War II or of the inevitability of conflict brought on by the destruction of Germany, the resultant power vacuum, and the need to reestablish a balance of power. Early critics of such interpretations generally came from the political right, arguing that the United States was far too slow in recognizing the Soviet threat and far too naive in allowing pro-communist elements within the government. Such attacks, however, generally received little credence within the academic community.

A much more vigorous critique made itself felt in the 1960s. Pushed by a group of scholars and journalists who were often young and politically active, the new interpretation saw the Cold War not in terms of Soviet aggression—for her actions had always been essentially defensive—but in terms of United States military and economic imperialism. For this "New Left" school of history, it was American capitalism, not Soviet communism, that caused the misery of the postwar world. William A. Williams, often called the father of the "New Left," first presented the outline of this view in *The Tragedy of American Diplomacy* (515), which appeared in 1959. This was soon followed by Fleming's massive treatment, *The Cold War and Its Origins* (147), which also placed major blame on the United States. At first, these two studies were largely ignored. With the events of the mid-1960s, however, they received increased attention and stimulated a flood of books, for American capitalism was seen as the ultimate source of the Vietnamese War. Examples of this economic interpretation are furnished by Alperovitz (11), Barnet (26, 27), Chomsky (78), Horowitz (212), Kolko (271, 272, 273), Magdoff (308), and, to a somewhat lesser extent, by La-Feber (279) and Steel (458). LaFeber (279) and Spanier (451) both have excellent bibliographies of Cold War literature. With the withdrawal of American troops from Vietnam, there is some indication that "New Left" views may have peaked. Originally, they were criticized for their simplistic and often conspiratorial view of American foreign policy. More recently, Tucker (481) has questioned their theoretical base, while Maddox (307) has vigorously accused them of faulty and dishonest scholarship. Recent Cold War histories, such as those of Gaddis (152) and Rose (402), downplay economic motives, pointing instead to institutional factors and human errors on both sides of the Iron Curtain.

PROBLEMS AND CRISES. In the remaining part of this survey, it would be impossible to discuss the very extensive literature on various postwar events and issues. Hopefully, a rapid overview will point to basic materials. And, of course, many of the works listed have bibliographies of their own.

Problems of peace-making with Germany and Japan are covered in books by Feis (138, 140) and Dunn (124). Backer (18), Rundell (408), and Gimbel (164) provide information on the American occupation of Germany, while General Lucius D. Clay (82) discusses events from his perspective. Material on the occupation of Japan is found in books by Wildes (512), Kawai (247), and Yoshida (435).

Xydis (521), Jones (236), and Price (376) cover the events of 1947 that led to the Truman Doctrine and the Marshall Plan. The decision to rearm Germany is sketched in Martin's essay in the set of case studies by Stein (459) and treated more extensively by McGeehan (315), while the American policy toward German reparations is criticized by Kuklick (277). Treatments of the various Berlin crises come from Davison (110), Smith (442), and Schick (420). A European participant's overview of this whole period is presented by van der Beugel (487). Whitaker (502) contributes the major examination of American policy toward Franco's Spain. Basic to an understanding of American postwar actions in Europe is Kennan's famous and influential article, "The Sources of Soviet Conduct" (252). Lippman (297) delivered a contemporary refutation of Kennan's arguments, while Kennan himself largely modified his views in *Russia, the Atom and the West* (251). Kennan's recent article (248) gives his views for the 1970s.

Tang Tsou presents the standard discussion of *America's Failure in China* (467); Feis (139) covers much of the same ground. Foster Rhea Dulles surveys *American Foreign Policy toward Communist China* (123), while the Congressional Quarterly (77) has published useful background material on the same subject.

For coverage of the Korean War, researchers should be familiar with Blanchard's *Korean War Bibliography* (618) and the MacArthur Hearings (580); the latter is a basic source for both the war and the Truman-MacArthur controversy. Standard histories of the war are by Rees (387) and Leckie (286), while Paige (358) provides the major examination of the American decision to respond to the North Korean invasion. Air and naval operations are covered respectively by Futrell (see Chapter XV) and by Cagle (see Chapter XVIII). Memoirs of the war include those of Generals Ridgway (393), Collins (89), and Clark (81). Halperin's *Limited War in the Nuclear Age* (181) includes both a penetrating chapter on the war and an excellent annotated bibliography on limited war.

The main scholarly study of the clash between President Truman and General MacArthur is by Spanier (452), with additional material in works by Higgins (198), Neustadt (347), and Rovere and Schlesinger (407), as well as in the memoirs of the participants. A sharp attack on both the United States role in Korea and the political action of MacArthur is mounted by I. F. Stone (461).

Material on the Cuban missile crisis is numerous and growing. General treatments of the crisis are found in books by Abel (1), Pachter (357), and Allison (8); the last volume is probably the best of these, analyzing the events through the building of theoretical models and providing an extensive bibliography. The president's brother, Robert Kennedy (253), has written his recollection of events. Larson (283) contributes a documentary collection of the events of the fall of 1962, while Divine (116) has edited a volume of both documents and essays. Valuable material on the events and interpretations of the crisis is provided by Crane (101), Horelick (211), Kahan and Long (238), Knorr (268), and Wohlstetter (518). A criticism of Kennedy's handling of the crisis can be found in Hagan's article (176).

Coverage of American involvement in Vietnam has already achieved gargantuan proportions. A starting place for a researcher is the bibliography by Leitenberg and Burns (730), with other helpful sources being congressional hearings (582, 731, 583, 555) and the various editions of *The Pentagon Papers* (605, 364, 365, 366). Cooper (99) gives what is perhaps the best examination of American policy-making toward Vietnam; it includes an extensive bibliography. Halberstam's *The Best and the Brightest* (177) brilliantly etches personality portraits of policy-makers, but makes no effort at objective history; it should be balanced by Hanson Baldwin's review (19). Kahin and Lewis (239) provide a history of *The United States in Vietnam*, while Gurtov (175) covers United States policy during the end of the French rule in 1953-1954. Edited essays and materials can be found in books by Fall and Raskin (137) and by Pfeffer (368); the latter is particularly valuable for showing the full spectrum of American thought on the war. Recent examinations of American policy, with major parts devoted to Vietnam, are in George, Hall, and Simons' *The Limits of Coercive Diplomacy* (158) and in May's *"Lessons" of the Past* (313).

Recent sources for NATO information are the Department of the Army bibliography (599) and the congressional hearings (563, 554) on American relations with Europe. Volumes by Knorr (269) and Wolfers (519) provide examples of American thought in the late 1950s, while Cottrell and Dougherty (100) provide a compact history of NATO and a useful review of its extensive literature. Other important examinations of NATO and American policy toward Europe are by Fox (148), Fox and Schilling (149), Hoffmann (207), Jackson (225), Kissinger (267), Osgood (355), and Slessor (438). Such specific alliance problems as the Skybolt missile and the commitment of United States troops abroad are covered respectively by Neustadt (346) and Williams (514) and by Newhouse (349), Stambuck (454), and Paul (362). Explorations of the possibilities for detente are covered by Dulles and Crane (122) and Stanley and Whitt (457).

The major treatment of American policy for the Middle East is by Campbell (69), with additional coverage in the issue of the *Annals* edited by Hart (187). Policy considerations for Asia are examined by Greene (172), Fifield (145), and Reischauer (389, 390). Little exists on SEATO other than the works by Modelski (330, 331).

RESEARCH NEEDED. Despite the amount of material already published, much of this work has been produced without recourse to official records of the Department of Defense, the Department of State, or the Office of the President, for most government material is currently closed for the years beyond 1947. Records are or should be available in the near future to study areas that have been ignored previously. For example, the role of General Omar Bradley and the Joint Chiefs of Staff in the Truman administration deserves study, as do such administration advisors as Averell Harriman. Another example is the need to amend the general neglect of some early secretaries of defense; little or nothing exists on Louis Johnson and Robert Lovett or on Eisenhower's first secretary of defense, Charles E. Wilson. Detailed studies of specific procurement programs and the relationships of hardware to policy and strategy are and will be fruitful fields. These are just a few of the topics that need treatment; many of the others have been mentioned in related portions of the essay. And, still lying beyond such specific topics, is the essential question of whether America's perceived security needs can be reconciled fully and harmoniously with traditional American values and institutions. The answer to that query remains in the future.

BIBLIOGRAPHY

ARTICLES AND BOOKS
1. Abel, Elie. *The Missile Crisis*. Philadelphia: Lippincott, 1966.
2. Acheson, Dean. *Present at the Creation: My Years in the State Department*. New York: Norton, 1969.
3. Ackley, Charles Walton. *The Modern Military in American Society: A Study in the Nature of Military Power*. Philadelphia: Westminster Press, 1972.
4. Adams, Benson D. *Ballistic Missile Defense*. New York: American Elsevier, 1971.

5. Adams, Sherman. *Firsthand Report: The Story of the Eisenhower Administration*. New York: Harper & Brothers, 1961.
6. Agapos, A. M., and Lowell E. Galloway. "Defense Profits and the Renegotiation Board in the Aerospace Industry." *Journal of Political Economy*, September-October 1970.
7. Albion, Robert G., and Robert H. Connery. *Forrestal and the Navy*. New York: Columbia University Press, 1962.
8. Allison, Graham T. *Essence of Decision: Explaining the Cuban Missile Crisis*. Boston: Little, Brown, 1971.
9. Allison, Graham T. "Military Capabilities and American Foreign Policy." *Annals*, March 1973.
10. Almond, Gabriel. *The American People and Foreign Policy*. New York: Praeger, 1961.
11. Alperovitz, Gar. *Atomic Diplomacy: Hiroshima and Potsdam*. New York: Simon and Schuster, 1965.
12. Alsop, Stewart. *The Center: People and Power in Political Washington*. New York: Harper & Row, 1968.
13. Ambrose, Stephen E., and James Alden Barber, eds. *The Military and American Society*. New York: Free Press, 1972.
14. Anderson, Paul Russell, ed. "Universal Military Training and National Security." *Annals*, September 1945. Issue devoted to this subject.
15. Appleman, Roy E. *South to the Naktong, North to the Yalu (June-November, 1950). United States Army in the Korean War*. Washington: Office of the Chief of Military History, 1961.
16. Armacost, Michael H. *The Politics of Weapons Innovation: The Thor-Jupiter Controversy*. New York: Columbia University Press, 1969.
17. Art, Robert J. *The TFX Decision: McNamara and the Military*. Boston: Little, Brown, 1968.
18. Backer, John H. *Priming the German Economy: American Occupational Policies, 1945-1948*. Durham, North Carolina: Duke University Press, 1971.
19. Baldwin, Hanson W. "The Best and Brightest?" Review of *The Best and the Brightest*, by David Halberstam. *Intercollegiate Review*, Winter 1973-1974.
20. Baldwin, Hanson W. *The Great Arms Race: A Comparison of U.S. and Soviet Power Today*. New York: Praeger, 1958.
21. Baldwin, Hanson W. "Limited War." *Atlantic Monthly*, May 1959.
22. Baldwin, Hanson W. "The McNamara Monarchy." *Saturday Evening Post*, 9 March 1963.
23. Baldwin, Hanson W. *Strategy for Tomorrow*. New York: Harper & Row, 1970.
24. Baldwin, William L. *The Structure of the Defense Market, 1955-1964*. Durham: Duke University Press, 1967.
25. Barnet, Richard J. *The Economy of Death*. New York: Atheneum, 1970.
26. Barnet, Richard J. *Intervention and Revolution: America's Confrontation with Insurgent Movements around the World*. New York: World, 1968.

27. Barnet, Richard J. *Roots of War: The Men and Institutions behind United States Foreign Policy.* New York: Atheneum, 1972.
28. Baruch, Bernard. *Baruch: The Public Years.* New York: Holt, Rinehart and Winston, 1960.
29. Bauer, Theodore W., and Harry B. Yoshpe. *Defense Organization and Management.* Washington: Industrial College of the Armed Forces, 1971.
30. Bauer, Theodore W. *Requirements for National Defense.* Washington: Industrial College of the Armed Forces, 1970.
31. Baumgartner, John Stanley. *The Lonely Warriors: Case for the Military-Industrial Complex.* Los Angeles: Nash Publishing, 1970.
32. Bechhoefer, Bernhard G. *Postwar Negotiations for Arms Control.* Washington: Brookings Institution, 1961.
33. Beishline, Colonel John Robert. *Military Management for National Defense.* New York: Prentice Hall, 1950.
34. Bell, James A. "Defense Secretary Louis Johnson." *American Mercury*, June 1950.
35. Benoit, Emile. "Cutting Back Military Spending: The Vietnam Withdrawal and the Recession." *Annals*, March 1973.
36. Benson, Robert S. "The Military on Capitol Hill: Prospects in the Quest for Funds." *Annals*, March 1973.
37. Bernstein, Barton J., and Allen J. Matusow, eds. *The Truman Administration: A Documentary History.* New York: Harper & Row, 1966.
38. Biderman, Albert D. *March to Calumny: The Story of American POW's in the Korean War.* New York: Macmillan, 1963.
39. Biderman, Albert D. "Where Do They Go from Here?—Retired Military in America." *Annals*, March 1973.
40. Blackman, John L. *Presidential Seizure in Labor Disputes.* Cambridge: Harvard University Press, 1967.
41. Bleicken, Gerhard D. "The Role of Nonmilitary Defense in American Foreign Policy and Defense Policy." *Political Science Quarterly*, December 1959.
42. Blum, Albert A. *Drafted or Deferred: Practices Past and Present.* Ann Arbor: University of Michigan Press, 1967.
43. Bobrow, Davis B. "Military Research and Development: Implications for the Civil Sector." *Annals*, March 1973.
44. Bobrow, Davis B., ed. *Weapons Systems Decisions: Political and Psychological Perspectives on Continental Defense.* New York: Praeger, 1969.
45. Bogart, Leo. *Social Research and the Desegregation of the U.S. Army.* Chicago: Markham, 1969.
46. Bohlen, Charles E. *Witness to History, 1929-1969.* New York: Norton, 1973.
47. Borklund, Carl W. *The Department of Defense.* New York: Praeger, 1968.
48. Borklund, Carl W. *Men of the Pentagon: From Forrestal to McNamara.* New York: Praeger, 1966.
49. Bottome, Edgar. *The Balance of Terror: A Guide to the Arms Race.* Boston: Beacon, 1972.

50. Bower, Brock. "McNamara Seen Now, Full Length." *Life*, 10 May 1968.
51. Brandon, Henry. *Anatomy of Error: The Inside Story of the Asian War on the Potomac, 1954-1969*. Boston: Gambit, 1969.
52. Brandon, Henry. *The Retreat of American Power*. Garden City: Doubleday, 1973.
53. Branyan, Robert L., and Lawrence H. Larsen, eds. *The Eisenhower Administration, 1953-1961: A Documentary History*. New York: Random House, 1971. 2 vols.
54. Brayton, Abbott A. "American Reserve Policies since World War II." *Military Affairs*, December 1972.
55. Brennan, Donald G., ed. *Arms Control and Civil Defense*. Harmon-on-Hudson, New York: Hudson Institute, 1963.
56. Brennan, Donald G., ed. *Arms Control, Disarmament, and National Security*. New York: George Braziller, 1961.
57. Brodie, Bernard, ed. *The Absolute Weapon: Atomic Power and World Order*. New York: Harcourt, Brace, 1946.
58. Brodie, Bernard. *Escalation and the Nuclear Option*. Princeton: Princeton University Press, 1966.
59. Brodie, Bernard. "The McNamara Phenomenon." *World Politics*, July 1965.
60. Brodie, Bernard. *Strategy in the Missile Age*. Princeton: Princeton University Press, 1959.
61. Brodie, Bernard. *War and Politics*. New York: Macmillan, 1973.
62. Brown, Seyom. *The Faces of Power: Constancy and Change in United States Foreign Policy from Truman to Johnson*. New York: Columbia University Press, 1968.
63. Bull, Hedley. *The Control of the Arms Race*. 2nd ed. New York: Praeger, 1965.
64. Burns, Arthur E. "Aerospace Profits and Renegotiation: A Comment." *Journal of Political Economy*, July-August 1972.
65. Bush, Vannevar. *Modern Arms and Free Men: A Discussion of the Role of Science in Preserving Democracy*. New York: Simon and Schuster, 1949.
66. Buzzard, A., J. Slessor, and R. Lowenthal. "The H-Bomb, Massive Retaliation, and Graduated Deterrence." *International Affairs*, April 1956.
67. Byrnes, James F. *All in One Lifetime*. New York: Harper & Brothers, 1958.
68. Byrnes, James F. *Speaking Frankly*. New York: Harper & Brothers, 1947.
69. Campbell, John C. *Defense of the Middle East: Problems of American Policy*. 2nd ed. New York: Harper & Brothers, 1960.
70. Canby, Steven L. *Military Manpower Procurement: A Policy Analysis*. Lexington, Massachusetts: D. C. Heath, 1972.
71. Caraley, Demetrios. *The Politics of Military Unification: A Study of Conflict and the Policy Process*. New York: Columbia University Press, 1966.
72. Caridi, Ronald J. *The Korean War and American Politics: The*

Republican Party as a Case Study. Philadelphia: University of Pennsylvania Press, 1968.

73. Center for Strategic Studies, Georgetown University. *Economic Impact of the Vietnam War.* New York: Renaissance Editions, 1967.

74. Center for the Study of Democratic Institutions. *Anti-Ballistic Missile: Yes or No?* New York: Hill and Wang, 1969.

75. Chapman, James L. *Atlas: The Story of a Missile.* New York: Harper & Brothers, 1960.

76. Chayes, Abram, and Jerome B. Wiesner, eds. *ABM: An Evaluation of the Decision To Deploy an Antiballistic Missile System.* New York: Harper & Row, 1969.

77. *China and U.S. Far East Policy, 1945-1967.* Washington: Congressional Quarterly, 1967.

78. Chomsky, Noam. *American Power and the New Mandarins.* New York: Pantheon Books, 1969.

79. Clark, John J. *The New Economics of National Defense.* New York: Random House, 1966.

80. Clark, Keith C., and Laurence J. Legere, eds. *The President and the Management of National Security.* New York: Praeger, 1969.

81. Clark, General Mark W. *From the Danube to the Yalu.* New York: Harper & Brothers, 1954.

82. Clay, General Lucius D. *Decision in Germany.* Garden City: Doubleday, 1950.

83. Clayton, James L., ed. *The Economic Impact of the Cold War.* New York: Harcourt, Brace & World, 1970.

84. Clifford, Clark M. "A Viet Nam Reappraisal: The Personal History of One Man's View and How It Evolved." *Foreign Affairs,* July 1969.

85. Cline, Ray S., and Maurice Matloff. "Development of War Department Views on Unification." *Military Affairs,* Summer 1949.

86. Coffin, Tristram. *The Passion of the Hawks: Militarism in Modern America.* New York: Macmillan, 1964.

87. Coles, Harry L. "Strategic Studies since 1945: The Era of Overthink." *Military Review,* April 1973.

88. Coles, Harry L., ed. *Total War and Cold War: Problems in Civilian Control of the Military.* Columbus: Ohio State University Press, 1962.

89. Collins, General J. Lawton. *War in Peacetime: The History and Lessons of Korea.* Boston: Houghton Mifflin, 1969.

90. Commager, Henry Steele. "The Perilous Folly of Senator Bricker." *Reporter,* 13 October 1953.

91. Conant, Melvin. *The Long Polar Watch: Canada and the Defense of North America.* New York: Harper & Brothers, 1962.

92. *Congress and the Nation.* Washington: Congressional Quarterly Service, 1965-   . Published every four years.

93. Conn, Stetson. "Changing Concepts of National Defense in the United States, 1937-1947." *Military Affairs,* Spring 1964.

94. Connery, Robert H. "Unification of the Armed Services—The First Year." *American Political Science Review,* February 1949.

95. Connor, Commander Sidney, and Carl J. Friedrich, eds. "Military Government." *Annals*, January 1950. Issue devoted to this subject.
96. Cook, Fred J. *The Warfare State*. New York: Macmillan, 1962.
97. Cooling, B. Franklin. "Civil Defense and the Army: The Quest for Responsibility, 1946-1948." *Military Affairs*, February 1972.
98. Cooper, Chester L. "The CIA and Decision-Making." *Foreign Affairs*, January 1972.
99. Cooper, Chester L. *The Lost Crusade: America in Vietnam*. New York: Dodd, Mead, 1970.
100. Cottrell, Alvin J., and James E. Dougherty. *The Politics of the Atlantic Alliance*. New York: Praeger, 1964.
101. Crane, Robert D. "The Cuban Crisis: A Strategic Analysis of American and Soviet Policy." *Orbis*, Winter 1963.
102. Dahl, Robert A. *Congress and Foreign Policy*. New York: Harcourt, Brace, 1950.
103. Dalfiume, Richard M. *Desegregation of the U.S. Armed Forces: Fighting on Two Fronts, 1939-1953*. Columbia: University of Missouri Press, 1969.
104. Davidson, Eugene. *The Death and Life of Germany: An Account of the American Occupation*. New York: Knopf, 1959.
105. Davis, Franklin M., Jr. *Come as a Conqueror: The United States Army's Occupation of Germany, 1945-1949*. New York: Macmillan, 1967.
106. Davis, James W., Jr., and Kenneth M. Dolbeare. *Little Groups of Neighbors: The Selective Service System*. Chicago: Markham, 1968.
107. Davis, Vincent. *The Admirals Lobby*. Chapel Hill: University of North Carolina Press, 1967.
108. Davis, Vincent. *The Politics of Innovation: Patterns in Navy Cases*. Denver: University of Denver, 1967.
109. Davis, Vincent. *Postwar Defense Policy and the U.S. Navy, 1943-1946*. Chapel Hill: University of North Carolina Press, 1966.
110. Davison, W. Phillips. *The Berlin Blockade: A Study in Cold War Politics*. Princeton: Princeton University Press, 1958.
111. Deagle, Edwin A., Jr. "Contemporary Professionalism and Future Military Leadership." *Annals*, March 1973.
112. Dean, Arthur H. *Test Ban and Disarmament: The Path of Negotiation*. New York: Harper & Row, 1966.
113. Derthick, Martha. *The National Guard in Politics*. Cambridge: Harvard University Press, 1965.
114. Dick, James C. "The Strategic Arms Race, 1957-61: Who Opened a Missile Gap?" *Journal of Politics*, November 1972.
115. Dickson, Paul. *Think Tanks*. New York: Atheneum, 1971.
116. Divine, Robert A., ed. *The Cuban Missile Crisis*. Chicago: Quadrangle, 1971.
117. Divine, Robert A. *Foreign Policy and U.S. Presidential Elections, 1940-1960*. New York: Franklin Watts, 1974.
118. Donovan, James A. *Militarism, USA*. New York: Scribner's, 1970.
119. Dorn, Walter L. "The Debate over American Occupation Policy in Germany in 1944-1945." *Political Science Quarterly*, December 1957.

120. Draper, Theodore. "The Dominican Intervention Reconsidered." *Political Science Quarterly*, March 1971.
121. Dulles, Allen. *The Craft of Intelligence*. New York: Harper & Row, 1963.
122. Dulles, Eleanor Lansing, and Robert Dickinson Crane, eds. *Detente: Cold War Strategies in Transition*. New York: Praeger, 1965.
123. Dulles, Foster Rhea. *American Foreign Policy toward Communist China, 1949-1969*. New York: Thomas Y. Crowell, 1972.
124. Dunn, Frederick S. *Peace-Making and the Settlement with Japan*. Princeton: Princeton University Press, 1963.
125. Dupuy, R. Ernest. *The National Guard: A Compact History*. New York: Hawthorne, 1971.
126. Eads, George, and Richard P. Nelson. "Government Support of Advanced Civilian Technology: Power Reactors and the Supersonic Transport." *Public Policy*, Summer 1971.
127. Eisenhower, Dwight D. *The White House Years*. Vol. I: *Mandate for Change, 1953-1956*; Vol. II: *Waging Peace, 1956-1961*. Garden City: Doubleday, 1963-1965. 2 vols.
128. Ellsberg, Daniel, *Papers on the War*. New York: Simon and Schuster, 1972.
129. Emme, Eugene M., ed. *The History of Rocket Technology: Essays on Research, Development, and Utility*. Detroit: Wayne State University Press, 1964.
130. Enthoven, Alain C., and K. Wayne Smith. *How Much Is Enough? Shaping the Defense Program, 1961-1969*. New York: Harper & Row, 1971.
131. Enthoven, Alain C., and K. Wayne Smith. "What Forces for NATO? And from Whom?" *Foreign Affairs*, October 1969.
132. Erickson, John, ed. *The Military-Technical Revolution: Its Impact on Strategy and Foreign Policy*. New York: Praeger, 1966.
133. Falk, Stanley L. *The Environment of National Security*. Washington: Industrial College of the Armed Forces, 1968.
134. Falk, Stanley L. "The National Security Council under Truman, Eisenhower, and Kennedy." *Political Science Quarterly*, September 1964.
135. Falk, Stanley L., and Theodore W. Bauer. *The National Security Structure*. Revised ed. Washington, D.C.: Industrial College of the Armed Forces, 1972.
136. Fall, Bernard B. *Last Reflections on a War*. New York: Schocken, 1972.
137. Fall, Bernard B., and Marcus G. Raskin, eds. *The Viet-Nam Reader*. Revised ed. New York: Vintage Books, 1967.
138. Feis, Herbert. *Between War and Peace: The Potsdam Conference*. Princeton: Princeton University Press, 1960.
139. Feis, Herbert. *The China Tangle: The American Effort in China from Pearl Harbor to the Marshall Mission*. Princeton: Princeton University Press, 1953.
140. Feis, Herbert. *Contest over Japan*. New York: Norton, 1967.
141. Feis, Herbert. *From Trust to Terror: The Onset of the Cold War, 1945-1950*. New York: Norton, 1970.

142. Feld, Bernard T., *et. al. Impact of New Technologies on the Arms Race.* Cambridge, Massachusetts: M.I.T. Press, 1971.

143. Ferrell, Robert H. *George C. Marshall.* New York: Cooper Square, 1966.

144. Ferrell, Robert H., and Samuel Flagg Bemis, eds. *The American Secretaries of State and Their Diplomacy.* New York: Cooper Square, 1963- .

145. Fifield, Russell H. *Southeast Asia in United States Policy.* New York: Praeger, 1963.

146. Fitzgerald, A. Ernest. *The High Priests of Waste.* New York: Norton, 1972.

147. Fleming, D. F. *The Cold War and Its Origins.* Vol. I: *1917-1950;* Vol. II: *1950-1960.* Garden City: Doubleday, 1961. 2 vols.

148. Fox, William T. R., and Annette Baker Fox. *NATO and the Range of American Choice.* New York: Columbia University Press, 1967.

149. Fox, William T. R., and Warner R. Schilling, eds. *European Security and the Atlantic System.* New York: Columbia University Press, 1973.

150. Freeland, Richard M. *The Truman Doctrine and the Origins of McCarthyism: Foreign Policy, Domestic Politics, and Internal Security, 1946-1948.* New York: Knopf, 1972.

151. Fulbright, Senator J. W. *The Pentagon Propaganda Machine.* New York: Liveright, 1970.

152. Gaddis, John Lewis. *The United States and the Origins of the Cold War, 1941-1947.* New York: Columbia University Press, 1972.

153. Galbraith, John Kenneth. *How to Control the Military.* Garden City: Doubleday, 1969.

154. Galloway, Eilene. *History of the United States Military Policy on Reserve Forces, 1775-1957.* Prepared for the House Committee on Armed Services by U.S. Library of Congress, Legislative Reference Service. Washington: G. P. O., 1957.

155. Gallup, George H. *The Gallup Poll: Public Opinion, 1935-1971.* New York: Random House, 1972. 3 vols.

156. Gardner, Lloyd C. *Architects of Illusion: Men and Ideas in American Foreign Policy, 1941-1949.* Chicago: Quadrangle, 1970.

157. Gavin, General James M. *War and Peace in the Space Age.* New York: Harper & Brothers, 1958.

158. George, Alexander L., David K. Hall, and Colonel William E. Simons. *The Limits of Coercive Diplomacy: Laos, Cuba, Vietnam.* Boston: Little, Brown, 1971.

159. Gerhardt, James M. *The Draft and Public Policy: Issues in Military Manpower Procurement, 1945-1970.* Columbus: Ohio State University Press, 1971.

160. Gerson, Louis L. *John Foster Dulles.* New York: Cooper Square, 1967.

161. Geyelin, Philip. *Lyndon B. Johnson and the World.* New York: Praeger, 1966.

162. Gilpin, Robert. *American Scientists and Nuclear Weapons Policy.* Princeton: Princeton University Press, 1962.

163. Gilpin, Robert, and Christopher Wright, eds. *Scientists and National Policy-Making.* New York: Columbia University Press, 1964.
164. Gimbel, John. *The American Occupation of Germany: Politics and the Military, 1945-1949.* Stanford, California: Stanford University Press, 1968.
165. Goldman, Nancy. "The Utilization of Women in the Military." *Annals,* March 1973.
166. Goulding, Phil G. *Confirm or Deny: Informing the People on National Security.* New York: Harper & Row, 1970.
167. Graebner, Norman A. *The New Isolationism: A Study in Politics and Foreign Policy since 1950.* New York: Ronald Press, 1956.
168. Graubard, Stephen R. *Kissinger: Portrait of a Mind.* New York: Norton, 1973.
169. Gray, Colin S. " 'Gap' Prediction and America's Defense Arms Race Behavior in the Eisenhower Years." *Orbis,* Spring 1972.
170. Green, Philip. *Deadly Logic: The Theory of Nuclear Deterrence.* Columbus: Ohio State University Press, 1966.
171. Green, Philip. "Science, Government and the Case of RAND: A Singular Pluralism." *World Politics,* January 1968.
172. Greene, Fred. *U.S. Policy and the Security of Asia.* New York: McGraw-Hill, 1968.
173. Grodzins, Morton, and Eugene Rabinowitch, eds. *The Atomic Age: Scientists in National and World Affairs.* New York: Basic Books, 1963.
174. Guhin, Michael A. *John Foster Dulles: A Statesman and His Times.* New York: Columbia University Press, 1972.
175. Gurtov, Melvin. *The First Vietnam Crisis: Chinese Communist Strategy and United States Involvement, 1953-1954.* New York: Columbia University Press, 1967.
176. Hagan, Roger. "Triumph or Tragedy," *Dissent,* Winter 1963.
177. Halberstam, David. *The Best and the Brightest.* New York: Random House, 1972.
178. Halle, Louis J. *The Cold War as History.* New York: Harper & Row, 1967.
179. Halperin, Morton H. "The Decision To Deploy the ABM: Bureaucratic and Domestic Politics in the Johnson Administration." *World Politics,* October 1972.
180. Halperin, Morton H. *Defense Strategies for the Seventies.* Boston: Little, Brown, 1971.
181. Halperin, Morton H. *Limited War in the Nuclear Age.* New York: John Wiley, 1963.
182. Halperin, Morton H. "The President and the Military." *Foreign Affairs,* January 1972.
183. Halperin, Morton H., and Arnold Kanter, eds. *Readings in American Foreign Policy: A Bureaucratic Perspective.* Boston: Little, Brown, 1973.
184. Hammond, Paul Y. *The Cold War Years: American Foreign Policy since 1945.* New York: Harcourt, Brace & World, 1969.
185. Hammond, Paul Y. "A Functional Analysis of Defense Department

Decision-Making in the McNamara Administration." *American Political Science Review*, March 1968.

186. Hammond, Paul Y. *Organizing for Defense: The American Military Establishment in the Twentieth Century.* Princeton: Princeton University Press, 1961.

187. Hart, Parker T., ed. "America and the Middle East." *Annals*, May 1972. Issue devoted to this subject.

188. Hassler, Warren W., Jr. *The President as Commander in Chief.* Reading, Massachusetts: Addison-Wesley, 1971.

189. Hauser, Colonel William L. *America's Army in Crisis: A Study in Civil-Military Relations.* Baltimore: Johns Hopkins Press, 1973.

190. Haynes, Richard F. *The Awesome Power: Harry S. Truman as Commander in Chief.* Baton Rouge: Louisiana State University Press, 1973.

191. Head, Richard G., and Ervin J. Rokke, eds. *American Defense Policy.* 3rd ed. Baltimore: Johns Hopkins Press, 1973.

192. Heer, David M. *After Nuclear Attack: A Demographic Inquiry.* New York: Praeger, 1965.

193. Heise, J. Arthur. *The Brass Factories: A Frank Appraisal of West Point, Annapolis, and the Air Force Academy.* Washington: Public Affairs Press, 1969.

194. Henry, John B., II. "February, 1968." *Foreign Policy*, Fall 1971.

195. Hersh, Seymour M. *Chemical and Biological Warfare: America's Hidden Arsenal.* Indianapolis: Bobbs-Merrill, 1968.

196. Hewlett, Richard G., and Oscar E. Anderson, Jr. *A History of the United States Atomic Energy Commission.* Vol. I: *The New World, 1939-1946.* University Park: Pennsylvania State University Press, 1962.

197 Hewlett, Richard G., and Francis Duncan. *A History of the United States Atomic Energy Commission.* Vol. II: *Atomic Shield, 1947-1952.* University Park: Pennsylvania State University Press, 1969.

198. Higgins, Trumbull. *Korea and the Fall of MacArthur: A Precis in Limited War.* New York: Oxford University Press, 1960.

199. Higham, Robin, ed. *Bayonets in the Streets: The Use of Troops in Civil Disturbances.* Lawrence: University Press of Kansas, 1969.

200. Higham, Robin, ed. *Intervention or Abstention.* Lexington: University Press of Kentucky, 1975.

201. Hill, Jim Dan. *The Minute Man in Peace and War: A History of the National Guard.* Harrisburg: Stackpole, 1964.

202. Hilsman, Roger. *The Politics of Policy Making in Defense and Foreign Affairs.* New York: Harper & Row, 1971.

203. Hilsman, Roger. *Strategic Intelligence and National Decisions.* Glencoe, Illinois: Free Press, 1956.

204. Hilsman, Roger. *To Move a Nation: The Politics of Foreign Policy in the Administration of John F. Kennedy.* Garden City: Doubleday, 1967.

205. Hitch, Charles J. *Decision-Making for Defense.* Berkeley: University of California Press, 1965.

206. Hitch, Charles J., and Roland N. McKean. *The Economics of Defense in the Nuclear Age.* Cambridge: Harvard University Press, 1960.

207. Hoffmann, Stanley. *Gulliver's Troubles, or the Setting of American Foreign Policy.* New York: McGraw-Hill, 1968.
208. Holst, John J., and William Schneider, Jr., eds. *Why ABM? Policy Issues in the Missile Defense Controversy.* Elmsford, New York: Pergamon Press, 1969.
209. Hoopes, Townsend. *The Devil and John Foster Dulles: The Diplomacy of the Eisenhower Era.* Boston: Atlantic Monthly Press, 1973.
210. Hoopes, Townsend. *The Limits of Intervention: An Inside Account of How the Johnson Policy of Escalation in Vietnam Was Reversed.* New York: David McKay, 1969.
211. Horelick, Arnold. "The Cuban Missile Crisis: An Analysis of Soviet Calculations and Behavior." *World Politics,* April 1964.
212. Horowitz, David. *The Free World Colossus: A Critique of American Foreign Policy in the Cold War.* Revised ed. New York: Hill and Wang, 1971.
213. Hovey, Harold A. *United States Military Assistance: A Study of Policies and Practices.* New York: Praeger, 1965.
214. Howard, Michael. "Civil-Military Relations in Great Britain and the United States, 1945-1958." *Political Science Quarterly,* March 1960.
215. Howard, Michael. *Studies in War and Peace.* New York: Viking, 1972.
216. Hoyt, Edwin C. "The United States Reaction to the Korean Attack." *American Journal of International Law,* January 1961.
217. Hughes, Emmet John. *The Ordeal of Power: A Political Memoir of the Eisenhower Years.* New York: Atheneum, 1963.
218. Hunter, Major Robert W. "Social Sciences, the Armed Forces, and Society: Interview with Dr. Morris Janowitz." *Air Force,* July 1973.
219. Huntington, Samuel P., ed. *Changing Patterns of Military Politics.* [*International Yearbook of Political Behavior Research,* Vol. 3.] New York: Free Press of Glencoe, 1962.
220. Huntington, Samuel P. *The Common Defense: Strategic Programs in National Politics.* New York: Columbia University Press, 1961.
221. Huntington, Samuel P. "Interservice Competition and the Political Roles of the Armed Services." *American Political Science Review,* March 1961.
222. Huntington, Samuel P. *The Soldier and the State: The Theory and Politics of Civil-Military Relations.* Cambridge: Belknap Press of Harvard University Press, 1957.
223. Huzar, Elias. *The Purse and the Sword: Control of the Army by Congress through Military Appropriations, 1933-1950.* Ithaca, New York: Cornell University Press, 1950.
224. "An Interview with John T. Mason, Jr., Director of Oral History at the U.S. Naval Institute," *United States Naval Institute Proceedings,* July 1973.
225. Jackson, Senator Henry M., ed. *The Atlantic Alliance: Jackson Subcommittee Hearings and Findings.* New York: Praeger, 1967.
226. Jackson, Senator Henry M., ed. *The National Security Council: Jackson Subcommittee Papers on Policy-Making at the Presidential Level.* New York: Praeger, 1965.
227. Jacobs, Clyde E., and John F. Gallagher. *The Selective Service*

Act: A Case Study of the Governmental Process. New York: Dodd, Mead, 1967.

228. Jacobson, Harold Karan, and Eric Stein. Diplomats, Scientists, and Politicians: The United States and the Nuclear Test Ban Negotiations. Ann Arbor: University of Michigan Press, 1966.

229. Janeway, Eliot. The Economics of Crisis: War, Politics, and the Dollar. New York: Weybright & Talley, 1968.

230. Janowtiz, Morris, ed. The New Military: Changing Patterns of Organization. New York: Russell Sage Foundation, 1964.

231. Janowitz, Morris. The Professional Soldier: A Social and Political Portrait. Glencoe, Illinois: Free Press, 1960.

232. Janowitz, Morris. "The Social Demography of the All-Volunteer Armed Forces." Annals, March 1973.

233. Janowitz, Morris. "Volunteer Armed Forces and Military Purpose." Foreign Affairs, April 1972.

234. Janowitz, Morris, and Colonel Roger Little. Sociology and the Military Establishment. Revised ed. New York: Russell Sage Foundation, 1965.

235. Johnson, Lyndon B. The Vantage Point: Perspectives of the Presidency, 1963-1969. New York: Holt, Rinehart and Winston, 1971.

236. Jones, Joseph M. The Fifteen Weeks (February 21-June 5, 1947). New York: Viking, 1955.

237. Just, Ward. Military Men. New York: Knopf, 1970.

238. Kahan, Jerome H., and Anne K. Long. "The Cuban Missile Crisis: A Study of Its Strategic Context." Political Science Quarterly, December 1972.

239. Kahin, George McTurnan, and John W. Lewis. The United States in Vietnam. Revised ed. New York: Dell, 1969.

240. Kahn, David. The Codebreakers: History of Secret Writing. New York: Macmillan, 1967.

241. Kahn, Herman. On Thermonuclear War. Princeton: Princeton University Press, 1960.

242. Kanter, Arnold. "Congress and the Defense Budget, 1960-70." American Political Science Review, March 1972.

243. Kaplan, Morton A., ed. SALT: Problems and Prospects. Morristown, New Jersey: General Learning, 1973.

244. Kaufman, Richard F. The War Profiteers. Indianapolis: Bobbs-Merrill, 1970.

245. Kaufmann, William W. The McNamara Strategy. New York: Harper & Row, 1964.

246. Kaufmann, William W., ed. Military Policy and National Security. Princeton: Princeton University Press, 1956.

247. Kazuo Kawai. Japan's American Interlude. Chicago: University of Chicago Press, 1960.

248. Kennan, George F. "After the Cold War: American Foreign Policy in the 1970's," Foreign Affairs, October 1972.

249. Kennan, George F. American Diplomacy, 1900-1950. Chicago: University of Chicago Press, 1951.

250. Kennan, George F. Memoirs. Vol. I: 1925-1950; Vol. II: 1950-1963. Boston: Little, Brown, 1967-1972. 2 vols.

251. Kennan, George F. *Russia, the Atom and the West*. New York: Harper & Brothers, 1957.
252. [Kennan, George F.] "The Sources of Soviet Conduct." *Foreign Affairs*, July 1947.
253. Kennedy, Robert F. *Thirteen Days: A Memoir of the Cuban Missile Crisis*. New York: Norton, 1969.
254. Kent, Sherman. *Strategic Intelligence for American World Policy*. Princeton: Princeton University Press, 1949.
255. Kerwin, Jerome G., ed. *Civil-Military Relationships in American Life*. Chicago: University of Chicago Press, 1948.
256. Kim, K. H., Susan Farrell, and Ewan Clague. *The All-Volunteer Army: An Analysis of Demand and Supply*. New York: Praeger, 1971.
257. King, Colonel Edward L. *The Death of the Army: A Pre-Mortem*. New York: Saturday Review Press, 1972.
258. Kinkead, Eugene. *In Every War But One*. New York: Norton, 1959.
259. Kintner, William R. *Forging a New Sword: A Study of the Department of Defense*. New York: Harper & Brothers, 1958.
260. Kintner, William R., ed. *SAFEGUARD: Why the ABM Makes Sense*. New York: Hawthorne, 1969.
261. Kintner, William R., and Robert L. Pfaltzgraff, Jr., eds. *SALT: Implications for Arms Control in the 1970's*. Pittsburgh: University of Pittsburgh Press, 1973.
262. Kirkpatrick, Lyman B., Jr. *The Real CIA*. New York: Macmillan, 1968.
263. Kirkpatrick, Lyman B., Jr. *The U.S. Intelligence Community: Foreign Policy and Domestic Activities*. New York: Hill and Wang, 1973.
264. Kissinger, Henry A. *The Necessity for Choice: Prospects of American Foreign Policy*. New York: Harper & Brothers, 1961.
265. Kissinger, Henry A. *Nuclear Weapons and Foreign Policy*. New York: Harper and Brothers, 1957.
266. Kissinger, Henry A., ed. *Problems of National Strategy: A Book of Readings*. New York: Praeger, 1965.
267. Kissinger, Henry A. *The Troubled Partnership: A Re-Appraisal of the Atlantic Alliance*. New York: McGraw-Hill, 1965.
268. Knorr, Klaus. "Failure in National Intelligence Estimates: The Case of the Cuban Missiles." *World Politics*, April 1964.
269. Knorr, Klaus, ed. *NATO and American Security*. Princeton: Princeton University Press, 1959.
270. Knorr, Klaus. *On the Uses of Military Power in the Nuclear Age*. Princeton: Princeton University Press, 1966.
271. Kolko, Gabriel. *The Politics of War: The World and United States Foreign Policy, 1943-1945*. New York: Random House, 1968.
272. Kolko, Gabriel. *The Roots of American Foreign Policy: An Analysis of Power and Purpose*. Boston: Beacon, 1969.
273. Kolko, Joyce, and Gabriel Kolko. *The Limits of Power: The World and United States Foreign Policy, 1945-1954*. New York: Harper & Row, 1972.
274. Kolodziej, Edward A. *The Uncommon Defense and Congress, 1945-1963*. Columbus: Ohio State University Press, 1966.

275. Korb, Lawrence J. "Robert McNamara's Impact on the Budget Strategies of the Joint Chiefs of Staff." *Aerospace Historian*, December 1970.

276. Krock, Arthur. *Memoirs: Sixty Years on the Firing Line.* New York: Funk & Wagnalls, 1968.

277. Kuklick, Bruce. *American Policy and the Division of Germany: The Clash with Russia over Reparations.* Ithaca, New York: Cornell University Press, 1972.

278. Kurth, James R. "A Widening Gyre: The Logic of American Weapons Procurement." *Public Policy*, Summer 1971.

279. LaFeber, Walter. *America, Russia, and the Cold War, 1945-1971.* 2nd ed. New York: John Wiley, 1972.

280. Landau, David. *Kissinger: The Uses of Power.* Boston: Houghton Mifflin, 1972.

281. Lapp, Ralph E. *Arms beyond Doubt: The Tyranny of Weapons Technology.* New York: Cowles Book Company, 1970.

282. Lapp, Ralph E. *The Weapons Culture.* New York: Norton, 1968.

283. Larson, David, ed. *The "Cuban Crisis" of 1962: Selected Documents and Chronology.* Boston: Houghton Mifflin, 1963.

284. Lasby, Clarence G. *Project Paperclip: German Scientists and the Cold War.* New York: Atheneum, 1971.

285. Lasswell, Harold D. *National Security and Individual Freedom.* New York: McGraw-Hill, 1950.

286. Leckie, Robert. *Conflict: The History of the Korean War.* New York: Putnam's, 1962.

287. LeMay, General Curtis E. *America Is in Danger.* New York: Funk & Wagnalls, 1968.

288. LeMay, General Curtis E., with MacKinlay Kantor. *Mission with LeMay: My Story.* Garden City: Doubleday, 1965.

289. Levantrosser, William F. *Congress and the Citizen-Soldier.* Columbus: Ohio State University Press, 1967.

290. Licklider, Roy E. "The Missile Gap Controversy." *Political Science Quarterly*, December 1970.

291. Licklider, Roy E. *The Private Nuclear Strategists.* Columbus: Ohio State University Press, 1971.

292. Liddell Hart, B. H. *Defense of the West.* New York: William Morrow, 1950.

293. Liddell Hart, B. H. *Deterrent or Defense: A Fresh Look at the West's Military Position.* New York: Praeger, 1960.

294. Lieberson, Stanley. "An Empirical Study of Military-Industrial Linkages." *American Journal of Sociology*, January and July 1971.

295. Lilienthal, David E. *The Journals of David E. Lilienthal.* Vol. II: *The Atomic Energy Years, 1945-1950.* New York: Harper & Row, 1964-1969.

296. Lincoln, George A., William S. Stone, and Thomas H. Harvey, eds. *Economics of National Security.* New York: Prentice-Hall, 1950.

297. Lippman, Walter. *The Cold War: A Study in U.S. Foreign Policy.* New York: Harper & Brothers, 1947.

298. Littauer, Raphael, and Norman Uphoff, eds. *The Air War in Indochina.* Revised ed. Boston: Beacon, 1972.

299. Little, Roger W., ed. *Handbook of Military Institutions.* Beverly Hills, California: Sage, 1971.
300. Lodge, Henry Cabot. *The Storm Has Many Eyes: A Personal Narrative.* New York: Norton, 1973.
301. Loory, Stuart H. *Defeated: Inside America's Military Machine.* New York: Random House, 1973.
302. Lovell, John P., and Philip S. Kronenberg. *New Civil-Military Relations: The Agonies of Adjustment to Post-Vietnam Realities.* New York: E. P. Dutton, 1974.
303. Lukacs, John. *A History of the Cold War.* Garden City: Doubleday, 1961.
304. Lyons, Gene M., and John W. Masland. *Education and Military Leadership: A Study of the ROTC.* Princeton: Princeton University Press, 1959.
305. Lyons, Gene M., and Louis Morton. *Schools for Strategy: Education and Research in National Security Affairs.* New York: Praeger, 1965.
306. MacArthur, General of the Army Douglas. *Reminiscences.* New York: McGraw-Hill, 1964.
307. Maddox, Robert James. *The New Left and the Origins of the Cold War.* Princeton: Princeton University Press, 1973.
308. Magdoff, Harry. "Militarism and Imperialism." *American Economic Review*, May 1970.
309. Mansfield, Edwin, ed. *Defense, Science, and Public Policy.* New York: Norton, 1968.
310. Marmion, Harry A. *The Case against a Volunteer Army.* Chicago: Quadrangle, 1971.
311. Masland, John W., and Laurence I. Radway. *Soldiers and Scholars: Military Education and National Policy.* Princeton: Princeton University Press, 1957.
312. May, Ernest R. "The Development of Political-Military Consultation in the United States." *Political Science Quarterly*, June 1955.
313. May, Ernest R. *"Lessons" of the Past: The Use and Misuse of History in American Foreign Policy.* New York: Oxford University Press, 1973.
314. May, Ernest R., ed. *The Ultimate Decision: The President as Commander in Chief.* New York: George Braziller, 1960.
315. McGeehan, Robert. *The German Rearmament Question: American Diplomacy and European Defense after World War II.* Urbana: University of Illinois Press, 1971.
316. McGuire, Martin C. *Secrecy and the Arms Race: A Theory of the Accumulation of Strategic Weapons and How Secrecy Affects It.* Cambridge: Harvard University Press, 1965.
317. McKean, Ronald N., ed. *Issues in Defense Economics.* New York: National Bureau of Economic Research, Distributed by Columbia University Press, 1967.
318. McLin, Jon B. *Canada's Changing Defense Policy, 1957-1963: The Problems of a Middle Power in Alliance.* Baltimore: Johns Hopkins Press, 1967.
319. McNamara, Robert S. *The Essence of Security: Reflections in Office.* New York: Harper & Row, 1968.

320. McNeill, William Hardy. *Greece: American Aid in Action, 1947-1956.* New York: Twentieth Century Fund, 1957.
321. Melman, Seymour, ed. *The Defense Economy: Conversion of Industries and Occupations to Civilian Needs.* New York: Praeger, 1970.
322. Melman, Seymour. *Pentagon Capitalism: The Political Economy of War.* New York: McGraw-Hill, 1970.
323. Melman, Seymour, ed. *The War Economy of the United States: Readings on Military Industry and Economy.* New York: St. Martin's, 1971.
324. Miller, James C., III, ed. *Why the Draft? The Case for a Volunteer Army.* Baltimore: Penguin, 1968.
325. Millis, Walter. *Arms and Men: A Study in American Military History.* New York: Putnam's, 1956.
326. Millis, Walter, ed. *The Forrestal Diaries.* New York: Viking, 1951.
327. Millis, Walter, with Harvey C. Mansfield and Harold Stein. *Arms and the State: Civil-Military Elements in National Policy.* New York: Twentieth Century Fund, 1958.
328. Mills, C. Wright. *The Power Elite.* New York: Oxford University Press, 1956.
329. Mitchell, Donald W. *Civil Defense: Planning for Survival and Recovery.* Washington: Industrial College of the Armed Forces, 1966.
330. Modelski, George. *SEATO.* Vancouver: University of British Columbia, 1962.
331. Modelski, George, ed. *SEATO: Six Studies.* Melbourne: F. W. Cheshire, 1962.
332. Mollenhoff, Clark W. *The Pentagon: Politics, Profits, and Plunder.* New York: Putnam's, 1967.
333. Morgenstern, Oskar. *The Question of a National Defense.* New York: Random House, 1959.
334. Morgenthau, Hans J. *A New Foreign Policy for the United States.* New York: Praeger, 1969.
335. Moskos, Charles C., Jr. "The American Dilemma in Uniform: Race in the Armed Forces." *Annals,* March 1973.
336. Moskos, Charles C., Jr. *The American Enlisted Man: The Rank and File in Today's Military.* New York: Russell Sage, 1970.
337. Moskos, Charles C., Jr. "Minority Groups in Military Organization." *Handbook of Military Institutions.* Edited by Roger W. Little. Beverly Hills, California: Sage, 1971.
338. Moskos, Charles C., Jr., ed. *Public Opinion and the Military Establishment.* Beverly Hills, California: Sage, 1971.
339. Moss, Norman. *Men Who Play God: The Story of the Hydrogen Bomb.* Revised ed. Baltimore: Penguin, 1972.
340. Moulton, Harland B. *From Superiority to Parity: The United States and the Strategic Arms Race, 1961-1971.* Westport, Connecticut: Greenwood Press, 1973.
341. Murphy, Charles J. V. *Fortune,* 1953-1959. Numerous articles on defense.
342. Murphy, Robert. *Diplomat among Warriors.* Garden City: Doubleday. 1964.

343. Nelkin, Dorothy. *The University and Military Research: Moral Politics at M.I.T.* Ithaca, New York. Cornell University Press, 1972.

344. Nelson, Keith L., ed. *The Impact of War on American Life: The Twentieth-Century Experience.* New York: Holt, Rinehart and Winston, 1971.

345. Nelson, Richard R., Merton J. Peck, and Edward D. Kalachek. *Technology, Economic Growth, and Public Policy.* Washington: Brookings Institution, 1967.

346. Neustadt, Richard E. *Alliance Politics.* New York: Columbia University Press, 1970.

347. Neustadt, Richard E. *Presidential Power: The Politics of Leadership.* Revised ed. New York: John Wiley, 1969.

348. Newhouse, John. *Cold Dawn: The Story of SALT.* New York: Holt, Rinehart and Winston, 1973.

349. Newhouse, John. *U.S. Troops in Europe: Issues, Costs, and Choices.* Washington: Brookings Institution, 1971.

350. Nieburg, Harold L. *In the Name of Science.* Revised ed. Chicago: Quadrangle, 1970.

351. Noble, G. Bernard. *Christian A. Herter.* New York: Cooper Square, 1970.

352. Norman, John. "MacArthur's Blockade Proposals against Red China." *Pacific Historical Review,* May 1957.

353. Oppenheimer, Martin, ed. *The American Military.* 2nd edition. New York: E. P. Dutton, 1973.

354. Osgood, Robert E. *Limited War: The Challenge to American Strategy.* Chicago: University of Chicago Press, 1957.

355. Osgood, Robert E. *NATO: The Entangling Alliance.* Chicago: University of Chicago Press, 1962.

356. Owen, Henry, ed. *The Next Phase in Foreign Policy.* Washington: Brookings Institution, 1973.

357. Pachter, Henry M. *Collision Course: The Cuban Missile Crisis and Coexistence.* New York: Praeger, 1963.

358. Paige, Glenn D. *The Korean Decision: June 24-30, 1950.* New York: Free Press, 1968.

359. Parmet, Herbert S. *Eisenhower and the American Crusades.* New York: Macmillan, 1972.

360. Paterson, Thomas G., ed. *Cold War Critics: Alternatives to American Foreign Policy in the Truman Years.* Chicago: Quadrangle, 1971.

361. Patterson, James T. *Mr. Republican: A Biography of Robert A. Taft.* Boston: Houghton Mifflin, 1972.

362. Paul, Roland A. *American Military Commitments Abroad.* New Brunswick, New Jersey: Rutgers University Press, 1973.

363. Peck, Merton J., and Frederic M. Scherer. *The Weapons Acquisition Process: An Economic Analysis.* Boston: Graduate School of Business Administration, Harvard University, 1962.

364. *The Pentagon Papers.* New York Times edition. New York: Bantam, 1971.

365. *The Pentagon Papers: The Defense Department History of United States Decision-Making on Vietnam.* Senator Gravel edition. Boston: Beacon, 1971. 4 vols.

366. *The Pentagon Papers.* Vol. V: *Critical Essays Edited by Noam Chomsky and Howard Zinn and an Index to Volumes One-Four.* Boston: Beacon, 1972.

367. See the official government set, number 605.

368. Pfeffer, Richard M., ed. *No More Vietnams? The War and the Future of American Foreign Policy.* New York: Harper & Row, 1968.

369. Phillips, Cabell. *The Truman Presidency: The History of a Triumphant Succession.* New York: Macmillan, 1966.

370. Pierre, Andrew J. *Nuclear Politics: The British Experience with an Independent Strategic Force, 1939-1970.* New York: Oxford University Press, 1972.

371. Platt, General Washington. *Strategic Intelligence Production: Basic Principles.* New York: Praeger, 1957.

372. Pogue, Forrest C. *George C. Marshall.* New York: Viking, 1963-   . 3 vols. to date.

373. Possony, Stefan E., and J. E. Pournelle. *The Strategy of Technology: Winning the Decisive War.* New York: Dunellen, 1971.

374. Power, General Thomas S. *Design for Survival.* New York: Coward-McCann, 1965.

375. Powers, Colonel Patrick W. *A Guide to National Defense: The Organization and Operations of the U.S. Military Establishment.* New York: Praeger, 1964.

376. Price, Harry Bayard. *The Marshall Plan and Its Meaning.* Ithaca, New York: Cornell University Press, 1955.

377. Proxmire, Senator William. *Report from Wasteland: America's Military-Industrial Complex.* New York: Praeger, 1970.

378. Pursell, Carroll W., Jr. ed. *The Military-Industrial Complex.* New York: Harper & Row, 1972.

379. Quade, E. S., and W. I. Boucher, eds. *Systems Analysis and Policy Planning: Applications in Defense.* New York: American Elsevier Publishing, 1968.

380. Quester, George H. *Nuclear Diplomacy: The First Twenty-Five Years.* New York: Dunellen, 1970.

381. Rabinowitch, Eugene, and Ruth Adams, eds. *Debate the Antiballistic Missile.* Chicago: Bulletin of the Atomic Scientists, 1967.

382. Radway, Laurence I. *Foreign Policy and National Defense.* Glenview, Illinois: Scott, Foresman, 1969.

383. RAND Corporation. *The First Fifteen Years.* Santa Monica, California: November 1963.

384. Ransom, Harry Howe. *Can American Democracy Survive Cold War?* Garden City: Doubleday, 1963.

385. Ransom, Harry Howe. *The Intelligence Establishment.* Revised and enlarged ed. of *Central Intelligence.* Cambridge: Harvard University Press, 1970.

386. Rathjens, George W. "The ABCs of ABMs." *Science and Public Affairs,* March 1971.

387. Rees, David. *Korea: The Limited War.* New York: St. Martin's, 1964.

388. Reeves, Thomas, and Karl Hess. *The End of the Draft.* New York: Vintage Books, 1970.

389. Reischauer, Edwin O. *Beyond Vietnam: The United States and Asia.* New York: Vintage Books, 1967.
390. Reischauer, Edwin O. *The United States and Japan.* 3rd ed. Cambridge: Harvard University Press, 1965.
391. Rice, Berkeley. *The C-5A Scandal: An Inside Story of the Military-Industrial Complex.* Boston: Houghton Mifflin, 1971.
392. Rich, Bennett M., and Philip H. Burch, Jr. "The Changing Role of the National Guard." *American Political Science Review*, September 1956.
393. Ridgway, General Matthew B. *The Korean War.* Garden City: Doubleday, 1967.
394. Ridgway, General Matthew B. *Soldier: The Memoirs of Matthew B. Ridgway.* New York: Harper & Brothers, 1956.
395. Ries, John C. *The Management of Defense: Organization and Control of the U.S. Armed Services.* Baltimore: Johns Hopkins Press, 1964.
396. Riker, William H. *Soldiers of the States: The Role of the National Guard in American Democracy.* Washington: Public Affairs Press, 1958.
397. Roberts, Chalmers M. *The Nuclear Years: The Arms Race and Arms Control, 1945-1970.* New York: Praeger, 1970.
398. Robinson, James A. *Congress and Foreign Policy Making: A Study in Legislative Influence and Initiative.* Revised ed. Homewood, Illinois: Dorsey Press, 1967.
399. Rodberg, Leonard S., and Derek Shearer, eds. *The Pentagon Watchers: Students Report on the National Security State.* Garden City: Doubleday, 1970.
400. Rogow, Arnold A. *James Forrestal: A Study of Personality, Politics, and Policy.* New York: Macmillan, 1963.
401. Roherty, James Michael. *Decisions of Robert S. McNamara: A Study of the Role of the Secretary of Defense.* Coral Gables, Florida: University of Miami Press, 1970.
402. Rose, Lisle A. *After Yalta.* New York: Scribner's, 1973.
403. Rosecrance, R. N. *Defense of the Realm: British Strategy in the Nuclear Epoch.* New York: Columbia University Press, 1968.
404. Rosen, Steven, ed. *Testing the Theory of the Military-Industrial Complex.* Lexington, Massachusetts: D. C. Heath, 1973.
405. Rostow, W. W. *The Diffusion of Power: An Essay in Recent History.* New York: Macmillan, 1972.
406. Rostow, W. W. *The United States in the World Arena: An Essay in Recent History.* New York: Harper & Brothers, 1960.
407. Rovere, Richard H., and Arthur M. Schlesinger, Jr. *The General and the President and the Future of American Foreign Policy.* New York: Farrar, Straus & Young, 1951.
408. Rundell, Walter, Jr. *Black-Market Money: The Collapse of U.S. Military Currency in World War II.* Baton Rouge: Louisiana State University Press, 1964.
409. Russett, Bruce M. *What Price Vigilance? The Burdens of National Defense.* New Haven: Yale University Press, 1970.
410. Sander, Alfred D. "Truman and the National Security Council: 1945-1947." *Journal of American History*, September 1972.

411. Sanders, Ralph, ed. *Defense Research and Development*. Washington: Industrial College of the Armed Forces, 1968.
412. Sapin, Burton M., and Richard C. Snyder. *The Role of the Military in American Foreign Policy*. Garden City: Doubleday, 1954.
413. Sapolsky, Harvey M. *The Polaris System Development: Bureaucratic and Programmatic Success in Government*. Cambridge: Harvard University Press, 1972.
414. Sarkesian, Sam C., ed. *The Military Industrial Complex: A Reassessment*. Beverly Hills, California: Sage, 1972.
415. Sawyer, Major Robert K. *Military Advisors in Korea: KMAG in Peace and War*. United States Army Historical Series. Washington: Office of the Chief of Military History, 1962.
416. Schelling, Thomas C. *Arms and Influence*. New Haven: Yale University Press, 1966.
417. Schelling, Thomas C., and Morton H. Halperin. *Strategy and Arms Control*. New York: Twentieth Century Fund, 1961.
418. Schelling, Thomas C. *The Strategy of Conflict*. Cambridge: Harvard University Press, 1960.
419. Scherer, Frederic M. *The Weapons Acquisition Process: Economic Incentives*. Boston: Graduate School of Business Administration, Harvard University, 1964.
420. Schick, Jack M. *The Berlin Crisis, 1958-1962*. Philadelphia: University of Pennsylvania Press, 1971.
421. Schiller, Herbert I., and Joseph D. Phillips, eds. *Super-State: Readings in the Military-Industrial Complex*. Urbana: University of Illinois Press, 1970.
422. Schilling, Warner R. "The H-Bomb Decision: How To Decide without Actually Choosing." *Political Science Quarterly*, March 1961.
423. Schilling, Warner R. "Scientists, Foreign Policy, and Politics." *American Political Science Review*, June 1962.
424. Schilling, Warner R., Paul Y. Hammond, and Glen H. Snyder. *Strategy, Politics, and Defense Budgets*. New York: Columbia University Press, 1962.
425. Schlesinger, Arthur M., Jr. "Origins of the Cold War." *Foreign Affairs*, October 1967.
426. Schlesinger, Arthur M., Jr. *A Thousand Days: John F. Kennedy in the White House*. Boston: Houghton Mifflin, 1965.
427. Schlesinger, James R. *The Political Economy of National Security: A Study of the Economic Aspects of the Contemporary Power Struggle*. New York: Praeger, 1960.
428. Schlesinger, James R. "Quantitative Analysis and National Security." *World Politics*, January 1963.
429. Schubert, Glendon A. "Politics and the Constitution: The Bricker Amendment during 1953." *Journal of Politics*, May 1954.
430. Schug, Willis E., ed. *United States Law and the Armed Forces*. New York: Praeger, 1972.
431. Schultze, Charles L., et. al. *Setting National Priorities: The 19— Budget*. Washington, D.C.: Brookings Institution, 1970-   . Annual.
432. Schwarz, Urs. *American Strategy: A New Perspective: The Growth*

of Politico-Military Thinking in the United States. Garden City: Doubleday, 1966.

433. Seligman, Daniel. "McNamara's Management Revolution." *Fortune*, July 1965.

434. Sheldon, Walt. *The Honorable Conquerors: The Occupation of Japan, 1945-1952.* New York: Macmillan, 1965.

435. Shigeru Yoshida. *The Yoshida Memoirs: The Story of Japan in Crisis.* Boston: Houghton Mifflin, 1962.

436. Skolnikoff, Eugene B. *Science, Technology, and American Foreign Policy.* Cambridge: M.I.T. Press, 1967.

437. Slessor, Sir John. *The Great Deterrent.* New York: Praeger, 1957.

438. Slessor, Sir John. *What Price Coexistence? A Policy for the Western Alliance.* New York: Praeger, 1961.

439. Smith, Bruce L. R. *The RAND Corporation: A Case Study.* Cambridge: Harvard University Press, 1966.

440. Smith, Gaddis. *Dean Acheson.* New York: Cooper Square, 1972.

441. Smith, General Dale O. *The Eagles Talons.* Washington: Spartan Books, 1966.

442. Smith, Jean Edward. *The Defense of Berlin.* Baltimore: Johns Hopkins Press, 1963.

443. Smith, J. Malcolm, and Cornelius P. Cotter. *Powers of the President during Crises.* Washington: Public Affairs Press, 1960.

444. Smith, Louis. *American Democracy and Military Power: A Study of Civil Control of the Military Power in the United States.* Chicago: University of Chicago Press, 1951.

445. Smith, Perry M. *The Air Force Plans for Peace, 1943-1945.* Baltimore: Johns Hopkins Press, 1970.

446. Smith, Richard Austin. "The $7-Billion Contract that Changed the Rules [TFX]." *Fortune*, March-April 1963.

447. Snyder, Glen H. *Deterrence and Defense: Toward a Theory of National Security.* Princeton: Princeton University Press, 1961.

448. Snyder, William P. *Case Studies in Military Systems Analysis.* Washington: Industrial College of the Armed Forces, 1967.

449. Snyder, William P. *The Politics of British Defense Policy, 1945-1962.* Columbus: Ohio State University Press, 1964.

450. Sorenson, Theodore C. *Kennedy.* New York: Harper & Row, 1965.

451. Spanier, John W. *American Foreign Policy since World War II.* 6th ed. New York: Praeger, 1973.

452. Spanier, John W. *The Truman-MacArthur Controversy and the Korean War.* Cambridge: Belknap Press of Harvard University Press, 1959.

453. Spanier, John W., and Joseph L. Nogee. *The Politics of Disarmament: A Study in Soviet-American Gamesmanship.* New York: Praeger, 1962.

454. Stambuk, George. *American Military Forces Abroad: Their Impact on the Western State System.* Columbus: Ohio State University Press, 1963.

455. Stanley, Timothy W. *American Defense and National Security.* Washington: Public Affairs Press, 1956.

456. Stanley, Timothy W. *NATO in Transition: The Future of the Atlantic Alliance.* New York: Praeger, 1965.

457. Stanley, Timothy W., and Darnell M. Whitt. *Detente Diplomacy: United States and European Security in the 1970's.* New York: Dunellen, 1970.
458. Steel, Ronald. *Pax Americana.* Revised ed. New York: Viking, 1970.
459. Stein, Harold, ed. *American Civil-Military Decisions: A Book of Case Studies.* Twentieth Century Fund Study. University, Alabama: University of Alabama Press, 1963.
460. Stillman, Richard J., II. *Integration of the Negro in the U.S. Armed Forces.* New York: Praeger, 1968.
461. Stone, I. F. *The Hidden History of the Korean War.* New York: Monthly Review Press, 1952.
462. Strauss, Lewis L. *Men and Decisions.* Garden City, New York: Doubleday, 1962.
463. Strausz-Hupé, Robert, et. al. *Protracted Conflict.* New York: Harper & Brothers, 1959.
464. Strausz-Hupé, Robert, William R. Kintner, and Stefan T. Possony. *A Forward Strategy for America.* New York: Harper & Brothers, 1961.
465. Strohlein, John. *Defense Weapon Systems Management.* Washington, D.C.: Industrial College of the Armed Forces, 1968.
466. Swomley, John M., Jr. *The Military Establishment.* Boston: Beacon, 1964.
467. Tang Tsou. *America's Failure in China, 1941-1950.* Chicago: University of Chicago Press, 1963.
468. Tannenbaum, Frank. *The American Tradition in Foreign Policy.* Norman: University of Oklahoma Press, 1955.
469. Tatum, Lawrence B. "The Joint Chiefs of Staff and Defense Policy Formulation." *Air University Review,* May-June and July-August, 1966.
470. Tax, Sol, ed. *The Draft: A Handbook of Facts and Alternatives.* Chicago: University of Chicago Press, 1967.
471. Taylor, General Maxwell D. *Swords and Plowshares.* New York: Norton, 1972.
472. Taylor, General Maxwell D. *The Uncertain Trumpet.* New York: Harper & Brothers, 1960.
473. Taylor, Telford. *Nuremberg and Vietnam: An American Tragedy.* Chicago: Quadrangle, 1970.
474. Theoharis, Athan G. *The Yalta Myths: An Issue in U.S. Politics, 1945-1955.* Columbia: University of Missouri Press, 1970.
475. Thompson, Kenneth W. *Political Realism and the Crisis of World Politics: An American Approach to Foreign Policy.* Princeton: Princeton University Press, 1960.
476. Thompson, Sir Robert. *Revolutionary War in World Strategy, 1945-1969.* New York: Taplinger, 1970.
477. Trager, Frank N., and Philip S. Kronenberg. *National Security and American Society: Theory, Process, and Policy.* Lawrence: University Press of Kansas, 1973.
478. Trewhitt, Henry L. *McNamara: His Ordeal in the Pentagon.* New York: Harper & Row, 1971.
479. Truman, Harry S. *Memoirs.* Vol. I: *Year of Decisions;* Vol. II: *Years of Trial and Hope.* Garden City: Doubleday, 1955-1956. 2 vols.

480. Tucker, Robert W. *The Just War: A Study in Contemporary American Doctrine.* Baltimore: Johns Hopkins Press, 1960.

481. Tucker, Robert W. *The Radical Left and American Foreign Policy.* Baltimore: Johns Hopkins Press, 1971.

482. Tucker, Samuel A., ed. *A Modern Design for Defense Decision: A McNamara-Hitch-Enthoven Anthology.* Washington: Industrial College of the Armed Forces, 1966.

483. Twining, General Nathan F. *Neither Liberty Nor Safety: A Hard Look at U.S. Military Policy and Strategy.* New York: Holt, Rinehart and Winston, 1966.

484. Udis, Bernard, ed. *The Economic Consequences of Reduced Military Spending.* Lexington, Massachusetts: D. C. Heath, 1973.

485. Ulam, Adam B. *The Rivals: America and Russia since World War II.* New York: Viking, 1971.

486. Vandenberg, Arthur, Jr. *The Private Papers of Senator Vandenberg.* Boston: Houghton Mifflin, 1952.

487. van der Beugel, Ernest H. *From Marshall Plan to Atlantic Partnership: European Integration as a Concern of American Foreign Policy.* New York: American Elsevier, 1966.

488. Van Riper, Paul P., and Darab B. Unwalla. "Voting Patterns among High-Ranking Military Officers." *Political Science Quarterly*, March 1965.

489. Vansant, Carl. *Strategic Energy Supply and National Security.* New York: Praeger, 1971.

490. Wadsworth, James J. *The Price of Peace.* New York: Praeger, 1962.

491. Wainhouse, David W. *Arms-Control Agreements: Designs for Verification and Organization.* Baltimore: Johns Hopkins Press, 1968.

492. Walker, Richard L., and George Curry. *E. R. Stettinius, Jr. [and] James F. Byrnes.* New York: Cooper Square, 1965.

493. Wallace, Don, Jr. "The War-Making Powers: A Constitutional Flaw?" *Cornell Law Review*, May 1972.

494. Walt, General Lewis W. *Strange War, Strange Strategy: A General's Report on Vietnam.* New York: Funk & Wagnalls, 1970.

495. Walton, Richard J. *Cold War and Counterrevolution: The Foreign Policy of John F. Kennedy.* New York: Viking, 1972.

496. Warner, W. Lloyd, *et. al. The American Federal Executive: A Study of the Social and Personal Characteristics of the Civilian and Military Leaders of the United States Federal Government.* New Haven: Yale University Press, 1963.

497. Watson, Mark S. "Two Years of Unification." *Military Affairs*, Winter 1949.

498. Weaver, Leon. *The Civil Defense Debate: Differing Perceptions of a Persistent Issue in National Security Policy.* East Lansing: Michigan State University, 1967.

499. Weigley, Russell F. *The American Way of War: A History of United States Military Strategy and Policy.* New York: Macmillan, 1973.

500. Weinstein, Martin E. *Japan's Postwar Defense Policy, 1947-1968.* New York: Columbia University Press, 1971.

501. Westerfield, H. Bradford. *Foreign Policy and Party Politics: Pearl Harbor to Korea.* New Haven: Yale University Press, 1955.
502. Whitaker, Arthur P. *Spain and Defense of the West: Ally and Liability.* New York: Harper & Brothers, 1961.
503. White, Ralph K. *Nobody Wanted War: Misperception in Vietnam and Other Wars.* Garden City: Doubleday, 1968.
504. White, General Thomas D. "Strategy and Defense Intellectuals." *Saturday Evening Post,* 4 May 1963.
505. Whiting, Allen S. *China Crosses the Yalu: The Decision To Enter the Korean War.* New York: Macmillan, 1960.
506. Whitney, Courtney. *MacArthur: His Rendezvous with Destiny.* New York: Knopf, 1956.
507. Wiesner, Jerome B., ed. *ABM: An Evaluation of the Decision To Deploy an Anti-Ballistic Missile System.* New York: New American Library, 1969.
508. Wiesner, Jerome B. *Where Science and Politics Meet.* New York: McGraw-Hill, 1965.
509. Wigner, Eugene P., ed. *Survival and the Bomb: Methods of Civil Defense.* Bloomington: University of Indiana Press, 1969.
510. Wigner, Eugene P., ed. *Who Speaks for Civil Defense?* New York: Scribner's, 1968.
511. Wilcox, Francis O. *Congress, the Executive, and Foreign Policy.* New York: Harper & Row, 1971.
512. Wildes, Harry Emerson. *Typhoon in Tokyo: The Occupation and Its Aftermath.* New York: Macmillan, 1954.
513. Williams, Justin. "Completing Japan's Political Reorientation, 1947-1952." *American Historical Review,* June 1968.
514. Williams, Raymond C. "Skybolt and American Foreign Policy." *Military Affairs,* Fall 1966.
515. Williams, William A. *The Tragedy of American Diplomacy.* 2nd revised and enlarged ed. New York: Dell, 1972.
516. Wise, David, and Thomas B. Ross. *The U-2 Affair.* New York: Random House, 1962.
517. Wohlstetter, Albert. "The Delicate Balance of Terror." *Foreign Affairs,* January 1959.
518. Wohlstetter, Roberta. "Cuba and Pearl Harbor: Hindsight and Foresight." *Foreign Affairs,* July 1965.
519. Wolfers, Arnold, ed. *Alliance Policy in the Cold War.* Baltimore: Johns Hopkins Press, 1959.
520. Wool, Harold. *The Military Specialist: Skilled Manpower for the Armed Forces.* Baltimore: Johns Hopkins Press, 1968.
521. Xydis, Stephen G. *Greece and the Great Powers, 1944-1947: Prelude to the 'Truman Doctrine'.* Salonika: Institute for Balkan Affairs, 1963.
522. Yarmolinsky, Adam, ed. "The Military and American Society." *Annals,* March 1973. Issue devoted to this subject.
523. Yarmolinsky, Adam. *The Military Establishment: Its Impact on American Society.* Twentieth Century Fund Study. New York: Harper & Row, 1971.
524. Yarmolinsky, Adam. "Picking Up the Pieces: The Impact of Vietnam on the Military Establishment." *Yale Review,* Summer 1972.

525. York, Herbert F. "ABM, MIRV, and the Arms Race." *Science*, July 1970.
526. York, Herbert F., ed. *Arms Control*, San Francisco: W. H. Freeman, 1973.
527. York, Herbert F. "Multiple-Warhead Missiles." *Scientific American*, November 1973.
528. York, Herbert F. *Race to Oblivion: A Participant's View of the Arms Race*. New York: Simon & Schuster, 1970.
529. Yosphe, Harry B., and Stanley Falk. *Organization for National Security*. Washington: Industrial College of the Armed Forces, 1963.
530. Young, Oran R. *The Politics of Force: Bargaining during International Crises*. Princeton: Princeton University Press, 1969.
531. Zink, Harold. *The United States in Germany, 1944-1955*. Princeton: D. Van Nostrand, 1957.
532. Zlotnick, Jack. *National Intelligence*. Washington: Industrial College of the Armed Forces, 1964.
533. Zuckerman, Sir Solly. *Scientists and War: The Impact of Science on Military and Civil Affairs*. New York: Harper & Row, 1967.

GOVERNMENT MATERIALS

534. U.S. Arms Control and Disarmament Agency. *Defense Industry Diversification: An Analysis with 12 Case Studies*. Publication No. 30. Washington: G. P. O., 1966.
535. U.S. Arms Control and Disarmament Agency. *Documents on Disarmament*. Washington: G. P. O., 1961-   . Annual.
536. U.S. Arms Control and Disarmament Agency. *International Negotiations on Ending Nuclear Weapon Tests, September 1961-September 1962*. Publication No. 9. Washington: G. P. O., 1962.
537. U.S. Atomic Energy Committee. *In the Matter of J. Robert Oppenheimer: Transcript of Hearing before Personnel Security Board*. 12 April-6 May 1954. Washington: G. P. O., 1954.
538. U.S. Blue Ribbon Defense Panel. *Report to The President and the Secretary of Defense on the Department of Defense by the Blue Ribbon Defense Panel, 1 July 1970*. [Gilbert Fitzhugh Report] Washington: G. P. O., 1970.
539. U.S. Bureau of the Budget. *Budget for the Military Function of the Department of Defense, ...* [House Document Number varies with Congress] Washington: G. P. O., -   . Annual.
540. U.S. Bureau of the Budget. *The Budget of the United States Government . . . —Appendix*. Washington: G. P. O., -   . Annual.
541. U.S. Commission on Organization of the Executive Branch of the Government. *Report to the Congress on the National Security Organization*. [Herbert Hoover Commission] Washington: G. P. O., 1949.
542. U.S. Commission on Organization of the Executive Branch of the Government. Committee on the National Security Organization. *Task Force Report on National Security Organization (Appendix G) for the Commission on Organization of the Executive Branch of the Government*. [Ferdinand Eberstadt, chairman] Washington: G. P. O., 1949.

543. U.S. Committee on Department of Defense Organization. *Report of the Rockefeller Committee on Department of Defense Organization.* [Rockefeller Report] Washington: G. P. O., 1953.

544. U.S. Congress. House of Representatives. *United States Defense Policies since World War II.* Prepared by Charles H. Donnelly. House Doc. 100. 85th Cong., 1st Sess. Washington: G. P. O., 1957.

545. U.S. Congress. House of Representatives. *United States Defense Policies in 19—.* Prepared by Charles H. Donnelly. [House Document Number varies with Congress] Washington: G. P. O., 1958-1966.

546. U.S. Congress. House. Committee on Appropriations. *Department of Defense Appropriations. Hearings.* Washington: G. P. O., 1949- . Annual.

547. U.S. Congress. House. Committee on Appropriations. Subcommittee on Department of Defense. *Department of Defense Apropriations for 1973. Hearings.* 9 parts. 92nd Cong., 2nd Sess. January-July 1972.

548. U.S. Congress. House. Committee on Appropriations. Subcommittee on Foreign Operations and Related Agencies. *Foreign Assistance and Related Agencies Appropriations for 1973. Hearings.* 2 parts. 92nd Cong., 2nd Sess. February-May 1972. Annual.

549. U.S. Congress. House. Committee on Appropriations. Subcommittee on Military Construction. *Military Construction Appropriations for 1973. Hearings.* 5 parts. 92nd Cong., 2nd Sess. March-April 1972. Annual.

550. U.S. Congress. House. Committee on Appropriations. *Safeguard Antiballistic Missile System. Hearings.* 91st Cong., 1st Sess. 1969.

551. U.S. Congress. House. Committee on Armed Services. *Draft Deferments, Message from the President.* House Doc. No. 324. 91st Cong., 2nd Sess. 23 April 1970.

552. U.S. Congress. House. Committee on Armed Services. Special subcommittee on Drug Abuse in the Armed Services. *Drug Abuse in the Armed Services. Hearings.* 92nd Cong., 1st and 2nd Sess. October 1971-January 1972.

553. U.S. Congress. House. Committee on Armed Services. *Extension of the Draft and Bills Related to the Voluntary Force Concept and Authorization of Strength Levels. Hearings.* 92nd Cong., 1st Sess. February-March 1971.

554. U.S. Congress. House. Committee on Armed Services. Special subcommittee on North Atlantic Treaty Organization Commitments. *Hearings.* 92nd Cong., 1st and 2nd Sess. October 1971-March 1972.

555. U.S. Congress. House. Committee on Armed Services. *Investigation of the My Lai Incident. Print.* 91st Cong., 2nd Sess. 15 July 1970.

556. U.S. Congress. House. Committee on Armed Services. *Military Implications of the Strategic Arms Limitation Talks Agreements. Hearings.* 92nd Cong., 2nd Sess. 25-27 July 1972.

557. U.S. Congress. House. Committee on Armed Services. *To Convert the National Military Establishment into . . . the Department of Defense. Hearings.* 81st Cong., 1st Sess. 1949.

558. U.S. Congress. House. Committee on Foreign Affairs. *Agreement*

on *Limitation of Strategic Offensive Weapons. Hearings.* 92nd Cong., 2nd Sess. July-August 1972.

559. U.S. Congress. House. Committee on Foreign Affairs. Subcommittee on National Security Policy and Scientific Developments. *Congress, the President, and the War Powers. Hearings.* 91st Cong., 2nd Sess. June-August 1970.

560. U.S. Congress. House. Committee on Foreign Affairs. Subcommittee on National Security Policy and Scientific Developments. *National Security Policy and Scientific Developments. National Security Policy and the Changing World Power Alignment. Hearings.* 92nd Cong., 2nd Sess. May-August 1972.

561. U.S. Congress. House. Committee on Foreign Affairs. Subcommittee on National Security Policy and Scientific Developments. *National Security Policy and the Changing World Power Alignment: Outline and Bibliography. Print.* 92nd Cong., 2nd Sess. 1972.

562. U.S. Congress. House. Committee on Foreign Affairs. *Strategy and Science: Toward a National Security Policy for the 1970's. Hearings.* 91st Cong., 1st Sess. 1969.

563. U.S. Congress. House. Committee on Foreign Affairs. Subcommittee on Europe. *United States Relations with Europe in the Decade of the 1970's. Hearings.* 91st Cong., 2nd Sess. February-April 1970.

564. U.S. Congress. House. Committee on Foreign Affairs. Subcommittee on National Security Policy and Scientific Developments. *War Powers. Hearings.* 93rd Cong., 1st Sess. 7-20 March 1973.

565. U.S. Congress. House. Committee on Government Operations. *Reorganization Plan No. 6 of 1953: Department of Defense. Hearings.* 83rd Cong., 1st Sess. 1953.

566. U.S. Congress. Senate. Committee on Appropriations. *Department of Defense Appropriations. Hearings.* Washington: G. P. O., 1949- . Annual.

567. U.S. Congress. Senate. Committee on Appropriations. Subcommittee on the Department of Defense. *Department of Defense Appropriations for FY73. Hearings.* 5 parts. 92nd Cong., 2nd Sess. February-September 1972.

568. U.S. Congress. Senate. Committee on Appropriations. Subcommittee on Foreign Operations and Related Agencies. *Foreign Assistance and Related Programs Appropriations, FY73. Hearings.* 92nd Cong., 2nd Sess. February-June 1972. Annual.

569. U.S. Congress. Senate. Committee on Appropriations. Subcommittee on Military Construction. *Military Construction Appropriations, FY73. Hearings.* 92nd Cong., 2nd Sess. May-September 1972. Annual.

570. U.S. Congress. Senate. Committee on Armed Services. *All-Volunteer Armed Forces: Progress, Problems, and Prospects. Report.* 93rd Cong., 1st Sess. 1973.

571. U.S. Congress. Senate. Committee on Armed Services. *Department of Defense Reorganization Act of 1958. Hearings.* Washington: G. P. O., 1958.

572. U.S. Congress. Senate. Committee on Armed Services. *FY73 Authorization for Military Procurement, Research and Development, Con-*

struction Authorization for Safeguard ABM, and Active Duty and Selected Reserve Strengths. Hearings. 6 Parts. 92nd Cong., 2nd Sess. February-April 1972.

573. U.S. Congress. Senate. Committee on Armed Services. Subcommittee on Preparedness Investigating. *Inquiry into Satellite and Missile Programs. Hearings.* 3 vols. 85th Cong., 1st and 2nd Sess. November 1957-January 1958.

574. U.S. Congress. Senate. Committee on Armed Services. *Military Implications of the Treaty on the Limitations of Anti-Ballistic Missile Systems . . . and Strategic Offensive Arms. Hearings.* 92nd Cong., 2nd Sess. June-July 1972.

575. U.S. Congress. Senate. Committee on Armed Services. *National Defense Establishment. . . . Hearings.* 3 parts. 80th Cong., 1st Sess. 1947.

576. U.S. Congress. Senate. Committee on Armed Services. *National Security Act of 1947, as Amended through December 31, 1969. Print.* 91st Cong., 2nd Sess. 1970.

577. U.S. Congress. Senate. Committee on Armed Services. Subcommittee on the Air Force. *Study of Airpower. Hearings.* [Symington Hearings] 84th Cong., 2nd Sess. April-July 1956.

578. U.S. Congress. Senate. Committee on Armed Services. Subcommittee on Volunteer Armed Force and Selective Service. *Volunteer Armed Force and Selective Service. Hearings.* 92nd Cong., 2nd Sess. 10-13 March 1972.

579. U.S. Congress. Senate. Committee on Armed Services. *Weapon Systems Acquisition Process. Hearings.* 92nd Cong., 1st Sess. 3-9 December 1971.

580. U.S. Congress. Senate. Committees on Armed Services and Foreign Relations. *Military Situation in the Far East. Hearings* [MacArthur Hearings] 5 parts. 82nd Cong., 1st Sess. May-August 1951.

581. U.S. Congress. Senate. Committee on Foreign Relations. Submittee on Arms Control, International Law and Organization. *ABM, MIRV, SALT, and the Nuclear Arms Race. Hearings.* 91st Cong., 2nd Sess. April-June 1970.

582. U.S. Congress. Senate. Committee on Foreign Relations. *Background Information Relating to Southeast Asia and Vietnam. Print.* 91st Cong., 2nd Sess. June 1970.

583. U.S. Congress. Senate. Committee on Foreign Relations. *Causes, Origins, and Lessons of the Vietnam War. Hearings.* 92nd Cong., 2nd Sess. 9-11 May 1972.

584. U.S. Congress. Senate. Committee on Foreign Relations. *Documents Relating to the War Power of Congress, the President's Authority as Commander-in-Chief, and the War in Indochina. Print.* 91st Cong., 2nd Sess. July 1970.

585. U.S. Congress. Senate. Committee on Foreign Relations. *Nuclear Test Ban Treaty. Hearings.* 88th Cong., 1st Sess. 12-27 August 1963.

586. U.S. Congress. Senate. Committee on Foreign Relations. *Strategic Arms Limitation Agreements. Hearings.* 92nd Cong., 2nd Sess. June-July 1972.

587. U.S. Congress. Senate. Committee on Foreign Relations. *United States Strategy. . . . Print.* 86th Cong., 1st Sess. December 1959.

588. U.S. Congress. Senate. Committee on Foreign Relations. *War Powers Legislation. Hearings.* 92nd Cong., 1st Sess. March-October 1971.

589. U.S. Congress. Senate. Committee on Government Operations. Subcommittee on National Security Staffing and Operations. *Administration of National Security: A Bibliography. Print.* 87th Cong., 2nd Sess. 1962.

590. U.S. Congress. Senate. Committee on Government Operations. Subcommittee on National Policy Machinery. *Organizational History of the National Security Council. Print.* [Jackson Subcommittee] 86th Cong., 2nd Sess. 1960.

591. U.S. Congress. Senate. Committee on Government Operations. Subcommittee on National Policy Machinery. *Organizing for National Security* [Jackson Subcommittee] Washington: G. P. O., 1961. 3 vols.

592. U.S. Congress. Senate. Committee on Government Operations. Subcommittee on National Policy Machinery. *Organizing for National Security: A Bibliography. Print.* [Jackson Subcommittee] 86th Cong., 1st Sess. 1959.

593. U.S. Congress. Senate. Committee on Government Operations. Subcommittee on National Policy Machinery. *Organizing for National Security: Selected Materials. Print.* [Jackson Subcommittee] 86th Cong., 2nd Sess. 1960.

594. U.S. Congress. Senate. Committee on Government Operations. Permanent Subcommittee on Investigations. *TFX Contract Investigation. Hearings.* 10 vols. 88th Cong., 1st Sess. 1963.

595. U.S. Congress. Senate Committee on Government Operations. Permanent Subcommittee on Investigations. *TFX Contract Investigation. Report.* 91st Cong., 2nd Sess. 1970.

596. U.S. Congress. Senate. Committee on Naval Affairs. *Report to Hon. James Forrestal, Secretary of the Navy, on Unification of the War and Navy Departments and Postwar Organization for National Security.* [Ferdinand Eberstadt Report] 79th Cong., 1st Sess. 22 October 1945.

597. U.S. Department of the Army. Army Library. *Civil Defense: 1960-1967. A Bibliographic Survey.* D. A. Pamphlet 500-3. Washington: G. P. O., 1967.

598. U.S. Department of Army. Army Library. *Military Power and National Objectives: A Selected List of Titles.* Special Bibliography No. 15. Washington, 19 August 1957.

599. U.S. Department of the Army. *Nuclear Weapons and NATO: Analytical Survey of Literature.* D. A. Pamphlet 50-1. Washington: G. P. O., 1970.

600. U.S. Department of the Army. *United States National Security: A Bibliography.* Special Bibliography, No. 7. Washington: G. P. O., 1956.

601. U.S. Department of the Army. Army Library. U.S. *Security, Arms Control, and Disarmament.* Washington, D.C.: Office of the

Deputy Assistant Secretary for Arms Control & Department of Defense, 1960-1965.

602. U.S. Department of Defense. *Annual Report Including Reports of the Secretary of Defense, Secretary of the Army, Secretary of the Navy, Secretary of the Air Force, for the Fiscal Year 19--.* [various titles] Washington: G.P.O., 1946-1970.

603. U.S. Department of Defense. *Dictionary of United States Military Terms for Joint Usage.* Washington: G.P.O., 1968.

604. U.S. Department of Defense. *Statement of Secretary of Defense Melvin R. Laird . . . on the FY 1973 Defense Budget and FY 1973-1977 Program, February 15, 1972.* [Outside cover: *National Security: Strategy of Realistic Deterrence*] Washington: G.P.O., 1972. Title varies, 1971- . Annual.

605. U.S. Department of Defense. *United States-Vietnam Relations, 1945-1967: Study* [*Pentagon Papers.*] Washington: G.P.O., 1971. 12 vols.

606. U.S. Department of State. *American Foreign Policy, 1950-1955: Basic Documents.* Washington: G.P.O., 1957. 2 vols.

607. U.S. Department of State. Bureau of Public Affairs. *Documents on Disarmament, 1945-1959.* Washington: G.P.O., 1960. 2 vols.

608. U.S. Department of State. *Foreign Relations of the United States: Diplomatic Papers.* Washington: G.P.O., 1862- .

609. U.S. Department of State. United States Disarmament Administration. *Geneva Conference on the Discontinuance of Nuclear Weapon Tests: History and Analysis of Negotiations.* Publication 7258. Washington: G.P.O., 1961.

610. U.S. President. *Public Papers of the Presidents of the United States.* Washington: G.P.O., 1958- .

611. U.S. President. *U.S. Foreign Policy for the 1970's:* [various subtitles] *A Report to the Congress by Richard Nixon, President of the United States.* [various dates] Washington: G.P.O., 1970- .

612. U.S. President's Advisory Commission on Universal Training. *A Program for National Security, May 29, 1947. Report* [Karl T. Compton Report] Washington: G.P.O., 1947.

613. U.S. President's Air Policy Commission. *Survival in the Air Age: A Report.* [Thomas K. Finletter Report] Washington: G.P.O., 1948.

614. U.S. President's Commission on an All-Volunteer Armed Force. *Report* [Thomas S. Gates Report] Washington: G.P.O., 1970.

615. U.S. President's Commission on an All-Volunteer Armed Force. *Studies Prepared for the President's Commission on an All-Volunteer Armed Force.* Washington: G.P.O., 1970. 2 vols.

616. U.S. President's Commission on Campus Unrest. *Report.* [William Scranton Report] Washington: G.P.O., 1970.

617. U.S. President's Committee on Equality of Treatment and Opportunity in the Armed Services. *Freedom To Serve, . . . : A Report.* [Charles Fahy Report] Washington: G.P.O., 1950.

BIBLIOGRAPHIES AND REFERENCE BOOKS

618. Blanchard, Carroll Henry. *Korean War Bibliography and Maps of*

Korea. Albany, New York: Korean Conflict Research Foundation, 1964.

619. Council on Foreign Affairs. *Documents on American Foreign Relations.* New York: 1939-   . Annual.

620. Council on Foreign Relations. *Foreign Affairs Bibliography* (1919-1962). New York, 1933-1964. 4 vols.

621. Council on Foreign Relations. *Foreign Affairs 50-Year Bibliography: New Evaluations of Significant Books on International Relations, 1920-1970.* New York: R. R. Bowker, 1972.

622. Council on Foreign Relations. *The United States in World Affairs.* New York: 1932-   . Annual.

623. Crown, James Tracy. *The Kennedy Literature: A Bibliographical Essay on John F. Kennedy.* New York: New York University Press, 1968.

624. Daniel, Steven F. *A Volunteer Military for the United States: An Annotated Bibliography.* Kensington, Maryland: American Institute for Research, Information Systems Branch, 1972.

625. Greenwood, John, comp. *American Defense Policy since 1945: A Preliminary Bibliography.* Kansas State University Library Bibliography Series, No. 11. Lawrence: University Press of Kansas, 1973.

626. Hamer, Philip M., ed. *A Guide to Archives and Manuscripts in the United States.* New Haven: Yale University Press, 1961.

627. Huntington, Samuel P. "Recent Writing in Military Politics—Foci and Corpora." *Changing Patterns of Military Politics.* Edited by Samuel P. Huntington. New York: Free Press of Glencoe, 1962. See number 219.

628. Kirkendall, Richard S., ed. *The Truman Period as a Research Field.* Columbia: University of Missouri Press, 1967.

629. Lang, Kurt. *Military Institutions and the Sociology of War: A Review of the Literature with Annotated Bibliography.* Beverly Hills, California: Sage, 1972.

630. Larson, Arthur D., comp. *Civil-Military Relations and Militarism: A Classified Bibliography Covering the United States and Other Nations of the World.* Bibliography Series, No. 9. Manhattan: Kansas State University Library, 1971.

631. Leopold, Richard W. "The 'Foreign Relations' Series Revisited: One Hundred Plus Ten." *Journal of American History.* March 1973.

632. Mason, Elizabeth B., and Louis M. Starr. *The Oral History Collection of Columbia University.* 3rd ed. New York: Microfilm Corporation of America, 1973.

633. McLellan, David S., and John W. Reuss. "Foreign and Military Policies." *The Truman Period as a Research Field.* Edited by Richard S. Kirkendall. Columbia: University of Missouri Press, 1967.

634. *The National Union Catalog of Manuscript Collections.* Ann Arbor, Michigan: J. W. Edwards, 1962-   . Annual.

635. RAND Corporation. *Index of Selected Publications of the RAND Corporation, 1946-1962.* Santa Monica, California, 1962.

636. Social Science Research Council, Committee on Civil-Military Relations Research. *Civil-Military Relations: An Annotated Bibliography, 1940-1952.* New York: Columbia University Press, 1954.
637. Walch, J. Weston. *Complete Handbook on Weapons Control.* Portland, Maine: Published by author, 1964. *Supplement* published in 1965. 2 vols.

PERIODICALS

638. *Adelphi Papers.* London, 1963- . Irregular.
639. *Aerospace Historian* (formerly *Airpower Historian*). Manhattan, Kansas, 1954- . Index. Cum. index, *1954-1973.*
640. *Aerospace International.* Washington, 1965- .
641. *Aerospace Management.* Philadelphia, 1966- . Indexed: Eng. Ind.
642. *Air Force Magazine* (formerly *Air Force and Space Digest*). Washington, 1946- . Indexed: Air Un. Lib. Ind.
643. *Air University Review* (formerly *Air University Quarterly Review*). Maxwell Field, Alabama, 1947- . Indexed: Air Un. Lib. Ind.; Eng. Ind.; P.A.I.S.
644. *American Political Science Review.* Washington, 1906- . Index. Cum. index. Indexed: Int. Polit. Sci. Abstr.; Soc. Sci. & Hum. Ind.; P.A.I.S.
645. *Annals of the American Academy of Political and Social Science.* Philadelphia, 1891- . Cum. index. Indexed: Bk. Rev. Ind.; Curr. Cont.; P.A.I.S.; R.G.
646. *Armed Forces Journal* (formerly *Journal of the Armed Forces).* Washington, 1863- . Indexed: Air Un. Lib. Ind.
647. *Armed Forces Management.* Washington, 1954-1970. Indexed: Air Un. Lib. Ind.
648. *Atlantic Monthly.* Boston, 1857- . Indexed: R.G.
649. *Aviation Week and Space Technology.* New York, 1916- . Indexed: R.G.; B.P.I.
650. *Collier's.* Springfield, Ohio, 1888-1957. Indexed: R.G.
651. *Common Defense.* Washington, 1945- .
652. *Congressional Digest.* Washington, 1921- . Index. Indexed: P.A.I.S.; R.G.
653. *Congressional Quarterly Service. Weekly Report.* Washington, 1945- . Index. Indexed: P.A.I.S.
654. *Current Biography.* New York, 1940- . Index. Cum. index every 10 years.
655. *Defense Industry Bulletin.* Washington, 1965- . Index.
656. *Defense Management Journal* (formerly *Cost Reduction Journal*). Washington, 1963-1971. Merged with *Defense Industry Bulletin* in December 1971.
657. *Defense Manager* (formerly *AFMA Bulletin*). Washington, 1967-
658. *Foreign Affairs.* New York, 1922- . Index *1922-1972.* Indexed: P.A.I.S.; R.G.; Soc. Sci. & Hum. Ind.
659. *Foreign Policy.* New York, 1971- .
660. *Fortune.* New York, 1930- . Indexed: B.P.I.; P.A.I.S.; R.G.
661. Harper's. New York, 1850- . Index. Indexed: R.G.

662. *Human Events*. Washington, 1944-   . Index. Cum. index.
663. *I.F. Stone's Weekly*. Washington, 1953-1971. Index.
664. *Interavia*. Geneva, Switzerland, 1946-   . Index.
665. *International Affairs*. London, 1922-   . Index. Indexed: Br. Hum. Ind.; P.A.I.S.; Soc. Sci. & Hum. Ind.
666. *International Defense Review*. Geneva, Switzerland, 1968-   . Index.
667. *Journal of Conflict Resolution* (formerly *Conflict Resolution*). Ann Arbor, Michigan, 1957-   . Indexed: P.A.I.S.; Psychol. Abstr.; Soc. Sci. & Hum. Ind.
668. *Life*. Chicago, 1936-1972. Indexed: R.G.
669. *Look*. Des Moines, Iowa, 1937-1971. Indexed: R.G.
670. *Military Affairs*. Washington, 1937-1968. Manhattan, Kansas, 1968-   . Index. Cum. index *1937-1968*. Indexed: Air Un. Lib. Ind.; Hist. Abstr.
671. *Military Review*. Fort Leavenworth, Kansas, 1922-   . Index *1922-1965*. Indexed: Air Un. Lib. Ind.; P.A.I.S.
672. *Nation*. New York, 1865-   . Index. Indexed: R.G.
673. *National Guardsman*. Washington, 1947-   . Indexed: Air Un. Lib. Ind.
674. *National Review* (published alternately with *National Review Bulletin*). New York, 1955-   . Index. Indexed: R.G.
675. *NATO's Fifteen Nations*. Amsterdam, 1956-   . Indexed: Air Un. Lib. Ind.
676. *NATO Review* (formerly *NATO Letter*). Brussels, 1953-   .
677. *Naval War College Review*. Newport, Rhode Island, 1948-   . Cum. index.
678. *New Republic*. Washington, 1914-   . Indexed: R.G.
679. *Newsweek*. New York, 1933-   . Indexed: R.G.
680. *Officer*. Washington, 1924-   . Indexed. Air Un. Lib. Ind.
681. *Orbis*. Philadelphia, 1957-   . Index. Indexed: Amer. Hist. & Life: Curr. Cont.; Hist. Abstr.; Int. Polit. Sci. Abstr.; P.A.I.S.; Soc. Sci. & Hum. Ind.
682. *Parameters*. Carlisle Barracks, Pennsylvania, 1971-   .
683. *Perspectives in Defense Management*. Washington, 1967-   .
684. *Political Science Quarterly*. New York, 1886-   . Index. Indexed: Ind.
685. *Royal United Service Institution Journal*. London, 1857-   . Index. Indexed: Air Un. Lib. Ind.; Br. Hum. Ind.; P.A.I.S.
686. *Saturday Evening Post*. Philadelphia, 1821-1969. 1973-   . Index: R.G.
687. *Science and Public Affairs* (formerly *Bulletin of the Atomic Scientists*). Chicago, 1945-   . Index. Indexed: Biol. Abstr.; P.A.I.S.; Psychol. Abstr.; R.G.
688. *Scientific American*. New York, 1845-   . Index. Indexed: R.G.
689. *Survival*. London, 1959-   .
690. *Time*. Chicago, 1923-   . Indexed: R.G.
691. *U.S. Department of State. Bulletin*. Washington, 1939-   . Indexed: R.G.; P.A.I.S.
692. *United States Naval Institute Proceedings*. Annapolis, Maryland,

1873-   . Index *1874-1956*. Indexed: Air Un. Lib. Ind.; Chem. Abstr.; P.A.I.S.
693. *U.S. News and World Report*. Washington, 1933-   . Indexed: R.G.; P.A.I.S.
694. *Vital Speeches of the Day*. Southold, Long Island, New York, 1934-   . Index *1934-1959*. Indexed: R.G.
695. *Weekly Compilation of Presidential Documents*. Washington, 1965-   . Index.
696. *World Politics*. Princeton, New Jersey, 1948-   . Index. Indexed: P.A.I.S.

INDEXES
697. *ABC Pol Sci*. Santa Barbara, California, 1969-   .
698. *Air University Library Index to Military Periodicals*. Maxwell Field, Alabama, 1949-   .
699. *CIS Index*. Washington, 1970-   . Index.
700. *Engineering Index*. New York, 1884-   .
701. *Historical Abstracts: Bibliography of the World's Periodical Literature*. Part A: *Modern History Abstracts*, 1450-1914; Part B: *Twentieth Century Abstracts*, 1914 to present. Santa Barbara, California, 1955-
702. *International Political Science Abstracts*. Oxford, England, 1951-.
703. *Newspaper Index*. Wooster, Ohio, 1972-   . Covers *Chicago Tribune, Los Angeles Times, New Orleans Times-Picayune*, and *Washington Post*.
704. *The New York Times Index*. New York, 1851-   .
705. *Public Affairs Information Service Bulletin*. New York, 1915-   .
706. *Reader's Guide to Periodical Literature*. New York, 1900-   .
707. *Selected RAND Abstracts*. Santa Monica, California, 1963-   .
708. *Social Science and Humanities Index*. New York, 1907-   . Titles have changed: *International Index to Periodicals*, 1907-1955; *International Index*, 1955-1965.

MANUSCRIPT COLLECTIONS
709. Acheson, Dean G. Truman Library.
710. Baruch, Bernard M. Princeton University Library, Princeton, New Jersey.
711. Bradley, General Omar N. Omar N. Bradley Museum, Carlisle Barracks, Carlisle, Pennsylvania, and United States Military Academy Library, West Point, New York.
712. Bundy, McGeorge. Kennedy and Truman Libraries.
713. Byrnes, James F. Clemson University Library, Clemson, South Carolina.
714. Clifford, Clark M. Johnson and Truman Libraries.
715. Collins, General J. Lawton. Eisenhower Library.
716. Dulles, John Foster. Princeton University Library, Princeton, New Jersey.
717. Forrestal, James V. Princeton University Library, Princeton, New Jersey.
718. Lodge, Henry Cabot. Massachusetts Historical Society, Boston, Massachusetts.

719. MacArthur, General Douglas. MacArthur Memorial, Norfolk, Virginia.
720. Marshall, General George C. George C. Marshall Research Library, Lexington, Virginia.
721. Patterson, Robert P. Library of Congress, Washington, D.C.
722. Ridgway, General Matthew B. United States Army Military History Research Collections, Carlisle Barracks, Carlisle, Pennsylvania.
723. Rostow, W. W. Johnson Library.
724. Stimson, Henry L. Yale University Library, New Haven, Connecticut.
725. Taft, Robert A. Library of Congress, Washington, D.C.
726. Taylor, General Maxwell D. National War College, Washington, D.C.
727. Vandenberg, Arthur H. University of Michigan Library, Ann Arbor, Michigan.

ADDITIONS TO BIBLIOGRAPHY

728. *CIS/Annual.* Washington, D.C.: Congressional Information Service, 1971- . Annual.
729. James, D. Clayton. *The Years of MacArthur.* One vol. to date. Boston: Houghton Mifflin, 1970- .
730. Leitenberg, Milton, and Richard Dean Burns, eds. *The Vietnam Conflict: Its Geographical Dimensions, Political Traumas, and Military Developments. [War-Peace Bibliography Series.]* Santa Barbara, California: Clio Press, 1973.
731. U.S. Congress. Senate. Committee on Foreign Relations. *Supplemental Foreign Assistance Fiscal Year 1966- Vietnam. Hearings.* [Vietnam Hearings] 89th Cong., 2nd Sess., 1966. See number 732.
732. Fulbright, Senator J. William, introd. *The Vietnam Hearings.* New York: Random House, 1966. See number 731.
733. *Cumulative Subject Index to the Monthly Catalog of United States Government Publications, 1900-1971.* 14 vols. Washington, D.C.: Carrollton Press, forthcoming publication.

XVII

THE ARMY, 1945-1973

B. Franklin Cooling III

Russell F. Weigley begins the final post-World War II portion of his *History of the United States Army* with the Thucydidean conclusion that the course of war by itself contrives most things upon the occasion and that he who complies with it in the most balanced and even-tempered fashion stands the firmest, while he who displays the greatest ardor and passion often miscarries. The United States Army has been cast as a servant of postwar American policy which often has displayed little wisdom but much ardor. Accordingly, the Army has suffered the agonizing readjustment from principal architect of total victory in World War II to mere copartner (and often a very junior one at that), in a deterrent national strategy where total victory belongs to no one, and total war can only mean total annihilation.

The period 1945-1973 has been one of both feast and famine for the U.S. Army. Both the traditional tranquility and isolation of the United States and its army evaporated as the Second World War forced the nation to expand its political and military commitments around the globe. Yet, the Army demobilized at the very time when peace turned to something styled "cold war." The new position in the world had its impact upon military policy and organization. Air power and the atomic bomb seemed to render large land forces obsolete, while the organizational developments within and among the armed services from 1945 to 1950 were perhaps the most significant in the history of the U.S. military establishment. The National Security Act of 1947 (and its amendment in 1949), partially unified the military services for the first time, and caused anguished hand-wringing by a budget-conscious, doctrineless Army in the late forties. Then came Korea.

Neither the Army nor the nation were ready for the Korean conflict. It differed markedly from previous American wars of the twentieth century since it was fought for limited political and military objectives. The use of the Army to obtain them was hardly a unique phenomenon in American history. But, the fact that this war was conducted in a new atmosphere of global ideological tension, especially after the end of a total war which had terminated in the unconditional surrender of the enemy, made the limited war policy very difficult to execute and onerous to many professional soldiers as well as countless civilians. Moreover, new tactics, weapons, and technology were introduced as the U.S. Army's system based on mechanization and firepower confronted an Asian system of high fluidity, flexibility, and mass infantry attacks with complete disregard for resultant casualties. It was the Army's initial confrontation with the Maoist philosophy of the ability of mobilized masses to overwhelm an enemy armed and equipped in a superior manner. Similarly, the Army learned that limited war in the nuclear age necessarily required increased civilian involvement in traditional military affairs since the amount of force employed had to be closely attuned to political objectives. The aim was no longer destruction of the enemy's power and will to resist, but rather to cause him to return to the *status quo ante*. War became less of a crusade and more of a tool of diplomatic persuasion. Many senior military commanders in Korea, such as Douglas MacArthur, chafed under such restrictions.

American military policy after Korea retired under the convenient nuclear air umbrella of "Massive Retaliation." The Army once more found itself defending its very existence; preoccupied in the later fifties with implementation of a strong Reserve force, and the Pentagon infighting for a larger slice of the Defense budget. Continued tension between the Soviet Union, China, and the western democracies resulted in the American military playing a far larger role in formulation of national policy than heretofore. Then too, the increased momentum of technology dictated that the military professional become less a heroic combat leader and more a manager of systems and organizations. Even the traditional antipathy between business and military communities broke down with an increasingly important role played by the military in the American economy. Some would call it "the military-industrial complex," and the Army was to have its own share of the equation.

But the increasingly implausible doctrine of "Massive Retaliation" spawned a school of critics, including many in Army green. They argued for alternative strategies to total war. They envisioned limited conflicts requiring conventional forces—particularly tailored land forces. With the outbreak of Communist insurgencies in the 1960s, the Army caught favor with Washington politicians and statesmen, thus leading to an ever-increasing involvement in Latin America and Southeast Asia. The turbulent decade witnessed an Army deeply enmeshed in an unwinnable war in Vietnam; utilized as an instrument of intervention against Latin American dissidents in Panama and the Dominican Republic; and employed in suppression of domestic unrest and riots in the cities of the continental United States. It became largely alienated from the nation's citizenry; yet, at the same time, forced to cope with new organization, managerial, and technological responsibilities such as development and operation of the controversial and expensive anti-ballistic missile system, all of which required great public trust and understanding. Just as the understrength, harried legions of the Roman empire were forced to counter violence on the frontiers and disintegration at home, so the American army found it necessary to muster a high degree of professionalism, discipline, and efficiency for its mission as unprotesting guardian of American security.

PROBLEMS OF SOURCES. Despite the importance of the Army in the years since 1945, there are few original sources immediately available to the historian. The element of secrecy remains omnipresent in current defense planning. Still, the rate of political, technological, and conceptual change renders it plausible that the time has arrived for opening Army records, at least for the immediate postwar years, if not through the 1950s. The dedicated researcher would do well to consult, and periodically to prod, the principal repositories for such materials. The climate of secrecy is under severe assault in America today. Agencies such as the Army's Adjutant General's Office; the National Archives and Records Service (and its field branches); the Truman, Eisenhower, Kennedy, and Johnson presidential libraries; the repositories at the U.S. Military Academy, U.S. Army Command and General Staff College, the Army War College, Center of Military History, and the Military History Research Collection (Carlisle), must periodically reexamine and reassess policies and procedures so as to free information for professional use while at the same time maintaining a proper balance with demands of national security. Material will surface eventually, especially since the study of contemporary American defense problems has increased apace in the past three decades along with the general rise of interest in military affairs. Of the published works, the general quality may be considered good, subject to understanding of personal prejudices, lack of detachment and perspective, and chronological proximity to the events themselves. Even the periodicals (listed in the introduction), must be viewed with the forbearance demanded of all journalism in the United States today. Certainly any of these published materials contain far more useful clues and leads than any one essay of this type can provide by itself.

ARCHIVAL SOURCES. The more patient researcher should not fail to consult such official Army repositories as the Center of Military History in Washington, D.C., the Military History Research Collection at Carlisle Barracks, Pa., and the Institute of Heraldry in Alexandria, Va. for such materials as unit histories, manuscripts, research monographs, oral history collections, unit insignia, battle streamers, lineage and honors data, and the hidden resource—dedicated professional historians, archivists, librarians, and artists whose storehouse of knowledge will save countless hours of work in blind alleys. Although these institutions are somewhat imperfectly organized to handle a large volume of non-official traffic, their service function to taxpayers both in uniform and mufti forms part of their mission. Likewise, one should not overlook the document or "authority file" collections of the Army Library in the Pentagon, West Point and Leavenworth libraries, the various post library facilities, as well as other public and private repositories. Among those indispensable document files are general orders, administrative publications such as Army regulations, special regulations, circulars, pamphlets, DOD directives, DA memoranda, Logistics staff memoranda and directives, supply manuals, blank forms, Chief of Staff memoranda, international standardization agreements, Army personnel tests and measures, guides to Army audiovisual materials, indices to major and Continental Army Command documents, technical manuals and tables of organization and equipment, supply manuals, doctrinal, training, and organizational publications, as well as National Guard and Army Reserve publications, i.e. all of the paper impedimenta without which the modern American army would seem to be unable to function, are being accumulated in repositories. One might also consult the Center of Military History concerning the various annual historical summaries and special studies published by historical offices of the major Army commands. The CMH annual program summary (350) can be extremely helpful here.

POLICY AND STRATEGY. If research on the contemporary Army is to be anything more than narrowly parochial it must measure American land forces against a changing world environment as well as the mainstream of general American security policy and organization. Background for American foreign policies can be effectively traced in the somewhat traditionalist Feis, *From Trust to Terror* (90); Osgood, et. al., *America and the World* (259), and revisionist work of Joyce and Gabriel Kolko, *The Limits of Power* (191), as well as the newer works by Raymond Aron, *The Imperial Republic* (15), and Ronald Steel, *Pax Americana* (314). Among standard works on postwar American defense policy are Huntington, *The Common Defense* (156); Stanley, *American Defense and National Security* (310); Schilling, Hammond, and Snyder, *Strategy, Politics and Defense Budgets* (295), and Brodie, *Strategy in the Missile Age* (33). Kolodziez, *Uncommon Defense* (192), examines the role of Congress while Kaufmann, "Limited War" (173); Osgood, *Limited War* (260); Diechtman, *Limited War* (69), Akerman, *Limited War* (6), Taylor, *Uncertain Trumpet* (332), and Yale, White, and Manteuffel, *Alternative to Armageddon* (383), all point toward limited war as an alternative to nuclear holocaust, with a correspondingly larger role for the U.S. Army. Akerman reflects upon this concept as of 1972 (6), while George, Hall, and Simons (110) suggests limits to all manner of coercive diplomacy. Naturally, such works found high favor on the reading lists recommended for consumption by aspiring Army personnel.

The Army's continued impact (or even lack thereof, in some cases) upon strategic policies may be followed in Abshire and Allen, *National Security* (2): the American Security Council committee observations on the antiballistic missile and strategic balance (11); the defense policy readings of Furniss (99); Head and Rooke (135a); Smith and Johns (303); Martin, *Arms and Strategy* (226); and Paul (269) on American commitments abroad. Osanka (258); Paret and Shy (264); and Taber (326) all treat guerrilla warfare which captivated everyone in the sixties. Michael Klare studied future war planning in the wake of Vietnam (183) with the Bradford and Brown, *The United States Army in Transition* (30), suggesting the usual post hoc preoccupation with "lessons learned." Amos Jordan and colleagues in 1967 (167) suggested certain issues of national security which would hallmark the seventies, and it should prove stimulating to evaluate their validity today, something which Rosenberg does in *Beyond Containment* (289). Kirkpatrick's book on the intelligence community must be investigated for Army activities in that field (182).

When it comes to viewing the Army from the White House, see Haynes's (135) and Kirkendall's (181) works on Truman as Commander in Chief, Weaver's (365), Parmet's (265), and Larson's (195) similar studies for Eisenhower as well as that president's own *Mandate for Change* (79), and *Waging Peace* (80). Similarly, one should consult Schlesinger, *A Thousand Days* (296); FitzSimons, *Kennedy Doctrine* (95); Walton, *Cold War and Counterrevolution* (360); and Sorensen, *Kennedy* (305), for those halcyon days when the Army returned to temporary favor. Lyndon Johnson's perspectives on his presidency (165); Kaufmann's treatment of Robert

McNamara's strategy (172); and Lawrence Martin's essay on military issues during the first Nixon administration (227) fall into this same category. Urs Schwarz, *Confrontations and Intervention in the Modern World* (299), as well as the Mydans, *Violent Peace* (245), should precede any attempt to analyze the Army's role in such areas as Lebanon, Berlin, the Cuban missile crisis, the Dominican Republic, as well as Korea and Vietnam. Specific crises and Army involvement may be discerned in Abel, *The Cuban Missile Crisis* (1); Allison, *Essence of Decision* (9); Divine, *The Cuban Missile Crisis* (73); and Robert Kennedy, *Thirteen Days* (174), for that major Russo-American confrontation. Szulc, *Dominican Diary* (325); Lowenthal, *Dominican Intervention* (205); and the Georgetown Center for Strategic Studies work (111) provide insight into that Latin American imbroglio in which the U.S. Army played an even more active role. Perhaps Bletz, *Role of the Military Professional in U.S. Foreign Policy* (25), and Hovey's study of military assistance (152) will provide grist for some future historian probing the blur that has become the traditional separation of military and diplomatic sectors of the American system.

ORGANIZATION AND DOCTRINE. Much of Weigley's attention focused upon organization and administrative development of the Army as an institution. The post-World War II scene should prove no less fascinating in light of the National Security Act of 1947 which pointed toward unification. Millis's edition of the *Forrestal Diaries* (236) and Caraley, *Politics of Unification* (43), are indispensable for comprehending the army in the late forties with Watson, "Two Years of Unification" (364), offering an early commentary on the effect of the move. Powers, *Guide* (274), while dated, is clear-cut in leading us through the labyrinth of national defense organization; Borklund, *Department of Defense* (28), will also prove useful here. Perhaps the best work comes with Hammond's overall study of organizing for defense in the twentieth century (132) while Clark and Legere look at the president and management of national security (48). Janowitz (161) offers sagacious comments on the pattern of organization in what he styles "the New Military," while Blumenson's official historical study (26) and other Army Project-80 reports (353-354) address specific Army reorganization in the early sixties. Ries, *The Management of Defense* (283); Knoll and McFadden, *American Militarism 1970* (186); as well as Enthoven and Smith, *How Much Is Enough?* (84), all tend to reflect the thinking of many Americans in the last decade when they approach the question of control over the military establishment as Huzar first did in *Purse and Sword* (159). Fulbright, *The Pentagon Propaganda Machine* (98); Goulding, *Confirm or Deny* (120); and Moskos's study of public opinion and the military (242) all cite the need for greater public awareness of Pentagon power, which was the title of Jack Raymond's 1964 study on the subject (278). Tactical organizational developments can be traced with such phenomenon as the ROAD division in various periodical articles like Chamberlin (44); Hollis (149); Kleinman (185); Wermuth (369) and Winfree (379). Several fine pieces show the Army's attempt to enunciate a doctrine by integration of sophisticated organization, weaponry, and personnel via air mobility—Galvin and (103) and Olson (255); and Special

Forces which find discussion in Department of the Army official tracts (351); and Robin Moore's superb fictional *The Green Berets* (238).

OPERATIONS. Operational history of the Army will undoubtedly remain of greatest interest for some time to come. From the postwar occupational activities in Europe and the Far East to the Southeast Asian crusade in the last decade, the Army's deterrent role has been often as active as it has been latent. Postwar demobilization can best be appreciated through the Senate hearings on the subject (348). The German occupation should be studied through Coles and Weinberg, *Soldiers Become Governors* (54); Davis, *Come as A Conqueror* (65); monthly reports of the military governor (233); Meade's general treatment of American military government (230); Lucius Clay's *Decision in Germany* (51); Montgomery, *Forced to Be Free* (237); and Tim, *Bremen Under U.S. Military Occupation* (335). The U.S. European Command, *Occupation Forces,* in Europe series (356), covers such diverse subjects as administration, refugee care, currencies, communications, POW repatriation, political and press reorientation, and law and order. Bader, *Austria* (16), and Allied Forces, Supreme Headquarters handbook for military government in Austria (8) are essential. Likewise, Beech, *Tokyo and Points East* (21); Brines, *MacArthur's Japan* (32); Martin, *The Allied Occupation* (225); Feary, *Occupation of Japan, Second Phase* (88); and USCAP's history (323) do the same for the Army in occupied Japan. Kang (171) treats American military government in Korea, while Morris (240) and Watanabe (362) bring the Okinawan problem down to the very recent past. Blakeslee covers the international Far Eastern commission from 1945 to 1952 (24), while the continued American army presence beyond our territorial boundaries is examined by Newhouse, *U.S. Troops in Europe* (249); Stambuk, *American Military Forces Abroad* (309); and Wolf, *Garrison Community* (380).

The cold war turned hot on several occasions necessitating the army's employment as an arm of American policy, with Korea and Southeast Asia as the preeminent examples. General accounts of Korea provide the appropriate starting point and they are numerous. Truman's memoirs (338), Acheson, (3), Senate armed services and foreign relations committees' reports (349), as well as the journalist observations of Marguerite Higgins (145) and Kahn, *The Peculiar War* (170), will be useful, while Gardner, (106) offers revisionist perspective. Berger, *The Korean Knot* (22) studies the troublesome military-political implications of the first of the limited wars in the period; Generals Ridgway (281) and Collins (55) give the commanders' viewpoints; and Trumbull Higgins, *Korea and the Fall of MacArthur* (146); Leckie, *Conflict* (196); Miller et. al. *Korea 1951-1953* (234) Rees, *Korea; The Limited War* (279); and Dille, *Substitute For Victory* (70), all provide more or less sound general accounts of the fighting. Paige studied the six-day decision to intervene (261) and Fehrenbach, *This Kind of War* (89) treated the affair as a study in unpreparedness.

Three volumes of the official U.S. Army history of Korea merit special attention if only as the preliminary advance into the cumbersome maze of records and the whole thorny "official history" question. Appleman, *South to the Naktong* (13), adequately deals with the period June-November 1950;

Schnabel (298) covers policy and direction during the first year of the war; and Hermes, *Truce Tent and Fighting Front* (138), probes the final period of truce negotiations. A former Chief of Military History contributed an early analysis of Korea in 1950 (361) while the Army medical people added a detailed series encompassing the battle casualties, blood program, and advances in medicine and surgery as a result of the war (153, 342, 343).

Combat action, particularly with reference to the U.S. Army should be approached first with Gugeler, *Combat Actions in Korea* (125), and then with the superb, in-depth analyses of S.L.A. Marshall (221, 222, 223). More specialized works include Sheldon, *Hell or High Water* (300), on the Inchon landings; McGovern, *To the Yalu* (211), treating the Chinese intervention; and Westover (371) covering combat support in the Land of the Morning Calm. Spanier (306) provides the best work on the Truman-MacArthur controversy. Side issues of great moment include the POW question with White's general account (374) as the logical beginning. The American POWs receive attention from Biderman, *March to Calumny* (23); Kinkead, *In Every War But One* (178); Pasley, *21 Stayed* (266); and Pate, *Reactionary* (268). The U.S. Army's questionable administration of the Koje Island compound for Communist prisoners can be followed in Vetter (358). Bill Mauldin's contribution to Morale can be discerned (229); Sawyer critically analyzed the Korean Military Assistance Group contributions prior to the war (292); Skaggs (302), has made a fine first effort to evaluate the "KATUSA" experiment which integrated Korean nationals into the U.S. Army from 1950 to 1965; and Kriebel (193) gives us a good idea about the continuing frustrations of the Korean Military Armistice Commission down to 1970.

America's second land war in Asia, Vietnam, has produced an even greater amount of writing, controversy, and ill-feeling. Since all the results will not be determined for sometime, one can only surmise the depths to which the nation and its military institutions have been affected. The U.S. Army which bore the brunt of the bloody conflict has not yet escaped from the implications of the disaster. While a survey conducted in the fall of 1973 by the Institute for Social Research at the University of Michigan disclosed that Americans rated the military above fifteen other American institutions in how well they were performing their job, there remained an undercurrent that many citizens would prefer to see the military return to some form of traditional peacetime isolation and exile from the mainstream of society. Certainly the continuing agony over the nation's recent Asian experience can best be felt in such works as David Halberstam's brilliant account of the Byzantine antics of American policymakers during the sixties, *The Best and the Brightest* (130), some of whom wore the Army green. Bernard Fall's various works (86, 87) remain the traditional starting point for evaluating U.S. participation; closely followed by Fitzgerald's prize winner, *Fire in the Lake* (94), and Buttinger, *Vietnam* (40, 41); Thompson's observations as a British player both in Malaya and Vietnam (333, 334); with Adams and McCoy (5) and Stevenson, *The End of Nowhere* (337) on Laos. The so-called Pentagon Papers (121, 250, 355); and the work of the Committee of Concerned Asian Scholars (56) as well as Browne (36) on the early days in Vietnam are useful background. Anyone failing to utilize Vo Nguyen

Giap's published works, *Great Victory* and *Peoples War* (115, 116); Pike's study of the Vietcong (271) or Mallin's edition of Communist documents on guerrilla warfare (214) as well as Andrews, *The Village War* (12) eschews a chance to subtly analyze American reaction through the eyes of the opposition. Gettleman, *Vietnam: History, Documents, and Opinions* (114); Greene, *U.S. Policy* (123), as well as Manning and Janeway, *Who We Are* (215) add to the useful background studies of the war, while Robinson and Kemp, *Report* (287) put the Senate hearings on Vietnam in better perspective. Cooper, *The Lost Crusade* (61) suggests that Vietnam was the first defeat in U.S. history as does Corson, *Consequences of Failure* (62) while Flood (96) simply terms the whole affair a "war of innocents," thereby falling in with Halberstam and company on suggestions of American strategic and tactical naivete. The spate of unfriendly accounts of American participation can be only partially offset by President Johnson's memoirs and Taylor's observations in *Responsibility and Response* (330). To understand the U.S. Army's opposition on the homefront, one should consult Menzel, *Moral Argument* (231); Schlesinger, *The Bitter Heritage* (297); Stavins, et. al., *Washington Plans an Aggressive War* (313); and O'Neill's conclusion (256) that Vietnam was one example of America's coming apart in the sixties. Even Murray Polner's study of returning Vietnam veterans, *No Victory Parades* (273) or Starr, Henry, and Bonner, *The Discarded Army* (312), clearly indicate why Vietnam is likely to remain the most controversial of America's wars for some years to come.

Likewise, official histories of the U.S. Army in Southeast Asia will likely incur some criticism, mainly because of production time and inability to present the full picture of decision-making and policy formulation in a war of this type. Still, useful introductory work on the problems, techniques, and direction of the effort may be discerned in Charles P. MacDonald's essay on official history and Vietnam in Paret, "Contemporary History and War" (263); as well as Spector, "Getting Down To the Nitty-Gritty" (307). From there the trail leads to Westmoreland's official report on operations in South Vietnam, 1964-1968 (370); and the first of a series of Army Vietnam Studies, of uneven quality, done by general officer participants including Dunn (77) on base development; Eckhardt (78) on command and control; Fulton (389) on riverine operations; Hay (387), on tactical and materiel innovations; Heiser (385) on logistics; Neel (247) on medical support; Ploger (386) on Army Engineers; Rienzi on communications electronics (390); and Tolson (336) on airmobility.

Slowly the official tactical accounts will emerge with the superb Center of Military History study by Albright, Cash, and Sandstrom, *Seven Firefights* (7) as merely the vanguard. The Adjutant General report on "lessons learned" by brigade commanders (352)—where available—is also a must. McCuen, *The Art of Counter-Revolutionary War* (210), is a good, unofficial primer while Weller (368) on "bargain-basement warfare"; Bashore, "Search and Destroy" (19); Galvin, "Three Innovations" (104); Stillwell, "Evolution in Tactics," (320); Neilands, *Harvest of Death* (248); and Weisberg (367) on chemical and biological warfare; Race (277) on revolutionary war in one Vietnamese province; and Nighswonger (252) on rural pacification and Tanham (327) offer penetrating comments on how actual operations emerged. As in his Korean pieces, S.L.A. Marshall (218, 219,

220, 224) retains his touch in recounting specific formal Army maneuvers; closely followed by Kinnard (179) on Ia Drang; Oberdorfer (253) on the Tet offensive in 1968; and Mertel (232) on 1st Cavalry activities in the highlands. The staff of *Infantry* magazine (308) and Colonel A.N. Garland (107) have contributed panegyrics to the role of the footslogger; Galloway (101) treats engineer contributions; while Duncan (76) and Jury (168) provide illustrated works which show how this war was carried so well by the media into the very living rooms of American suburbia.

Both Korea and Vietnam witnessed little outpouring of personal accounts in the traditional sense of other American wars. Nevertheless, for action in Southeast Asia, Fain, *Brown Letters* (86); Rowe, *Five Years to Freedom (290);* Hughes, *You Can See a Lot* (154); Vance, *Courageous and Proud* (357); and Williams, *Just Before the Dawn* (377), fill the void, while Lee, *No U.S. Personnel* (197), provides some much needed humor for a distinctly humorless war. One participant's case will remain before the public eye for all time—Lieutenant William Calley, accused of war crimes at My Lai. This controversial case illuminates much about the involvement of the nation and its land forces in Vietnam and can be followed in Citizens Commission of Inquiry, *War Crimes* (47); Gershen, *Destroy or Die* (113); Greenhaw, *Making of A Hero* (124); Hammer, *Court Martial* (131); Hersh, *Cover-Up (*139); Knoll and McFadden, *War Crimes* (187); and Sack, *Lieutenant Calley* (291). But if the Calley case represents many of the agonies and frustrations of America with its Vietnamese albatross, nothing so aptly suggests the Army's own dilemmas as a result of Southeast Asia as Bunting's controversial novel, *The Lionheads* (38).

CIVIL-MILITARY RELATIONS. The Army has been employed in other critical operations since World War II, and the unpopularity of Korea and Vietnam may have overshadowed employment of U.S. military forces against citizens in American cities. The use of troops in so-called "civil disturbances" forms the subject of an official Army study by Coakley, et. al. (53), while Scheips (293) discusses the Oxford, Mississippi, and Coakley (52) the Little Rock, Arkansas, civil rights problems and the U.S. Army. Higham, *Bayonets in the Streets* (147), in addition to its catchy title, contains essays on both historical and on recent episodes of this type. The full ramifications of these domestic involvements plus the various overseas crusades of the American military have yet to find ultimate synthesis, although the greater role of the military in American life since World War II generally has led to increased scrutiny and analysis. Ekirch, *Civilians and the Military* (81); Huntington, *Soldier and The State* (157); Janowitz, *The Professional Soldier* (162); Millis, *Arms and the State* (235); and Glick, *Soldiers, Scholars, and Society* (118), have emerged at the forefront of such study. Likewise the works of Ackley, *Modern Military* (4); Donovan and Shoup, *Militarism, USA* (75); Hickman, *The Military and American Society* (144); Oppenheimer, *The American Military* (257); and Yarmolinsky, *The Military Establishment* (384), all point to a well-plowed field exploring the sociological side of military institutions. More specifically oriented to the U.S. Army are *Army in Crisis* (134) by Hauser, himself a bright, professional officer; Mylander, *The Generals* (246), whose balanced and perceptive analysis of Army officer career patterns and environment is refreshingly different from the usual hand-wringing; and Moskos (241) on enlisted men will provide good benchmarks for measuring trends and remedies. The peaceful employment of military forces by Hanning (133) and Glick (117) are vital, while Cooling (58, 60) explores the Army's reluctant involvement with civil defense and disaster relief, which, with the possible exception of such pieces as Alaskan Earthquake analyses (57) remains obscure and unappreciated by both civilian and military professionals.

INSTITUTIONAL HISTORY. Indeed, one of the critical areas of traditional concern to the Army as an institution has been its manpower policies—brought into sharp, critical focus by the extremes of the turbulent sixties. Southeast Asia, My Lai, student protests, antiwar feelings, "ticket-punching" by the West Point club; corruption among senior noncoms and the provost marshal, drugs, and the draft are all indigenous to recent Army history. Whether it be friendly accounts by Hicken, *Fighting Man* (143); or Just, *Military Men* (169); or the critically sensitive works by Herbert and Wooten, *Soldier* (137); King, *Death of the Army* (177); Loory, *Defeated* (204); Kerry et. al., *New Soldier* (175); or Walton, *Tarnished Shield* (359)—all are essential for understanding the evolution of the Army in this period. On basic manpower policy questions, see Canby, *Military Manpower* (42); and Wool, *The Military Specialist* (381). For discussions of selective service, the Director of the Selective Service (72); Gerhardt, *Draft and Public Policy* (112); Liston, *Greeting* (201); Chapman, *The Wrong Man* (45); and Little, *Selective Service* (202) are quite useful. The All-Volunteer Forces (which by necessity means mainly the army), receives preliminary scrutiny in Gates's official report (108); Janowitz, *"Decline"* and *"Volunteer Armed Forces"* (160, 163); Kim et. al., *The All-Volunteer Army* (176); Kohn, *Too High A Price* (190); Marmion, *Case* (216); Reeves and Hess, *End of the Draft* (280); as well as the Army's various PIO pieces such as (340). The results are certainly unclear as the early years of the all-volunteer idea have produced anything but the requisite numbers envisioned by military planners. The reserves receive good coverage in Brayton, *Reserve Policies* (31); Eliot, *Reserve Forces* (82); Hill, *Minute Man* (148); Levantrosser, *Reserve Merger* (199); Derthick, *National Guard in Politics* (68); and the dated work of Riker, *Soldiers of the States* (285). Stapp, *Up Against the Brass* (311) provides a lively and interesting account of the fight to unionize the U.S. Army. The general topic of military training and education should be approached via Lyons and Masland, *Education* (206); Masland and Radway, *Soldiers and Scholars* (228); and Tauber, *Sunshine Soldiers* (329) on basic training. The extremely sensitive problems of command, discipline, and military justice gain attention through Finn, *Conscience and Command* (92); Gardner, *Unlawful Concert* (105); Sherrill, *Military Justice* (301); Ulmer, *Military Justice* (339); Waterhouse and Wizard, *Turning the Guns Around* (363); Di Mona, *Great Court-Martial Cases* (71), as well as the Brodsky and Eggleston premier study of the military prison (34). Integration and the Army is discussed in Bogart, *Social Research* (27); Paszeck, *Negroes and the Air Force 1939-1949* (267); Dalfiume, *Desegregation of the Armed Forces* (63); and Stillman, *Integration* (318). The intriguing subject of state funerals including those of Army figures such as Generals Craig, Pershing, March, Summerall, Marshall, Bedell Smith, MacArthur, and President Eisenhower, as well as Secretary of War Patterson and the Unknown Soldiers of World War II and Korea, are described in Mossman and Stark, *Last Salute* (243). The thinly treated subject of disposition of war dead finds Steere and Boardman (315) standing almost alone in rather ironic fashion to the memories and postmortem caterwaulings of many generals and GIs.

ARMS AND BRANCHES. Certain aspects of Army history will always, it seems, receive somewhat partisan attention, i.e. West Point, the Army educational system in general, and various component arms and branches. Still, they provide integral parts of the Army story, especially in the recent period where so many policy and organizational changes have tended to blur long traditions of service pride and professionalism. One should consult the extensive unit history collections of the Center of Military History and Military History Research Collection for specific unit traditions. The infantry receives treatment in Stillman (319); with Mahon and Danysh (213) supplying official lineage information. Armor lineage is in the Stubbs, McKinney, and Connor studies (321, 322); and field artillery developments can be followed tentatively in Stevens, *Artillery Through the Ages* (316). The medics story is told somewhat by Lee and McDaniel, *Army Medical Specialist Corps* (198); Engle, *Medic* (83); and White, *Back Down The Ridge* (373); while Barnard's official study (18) should be consulted on air defense artillery; Honeywell on the Chaplains (151); Marshall on the Signal Corps (217); and Morgan (239) as well as Davis and Jones (66) on the Engineers. U.S. Army Aviation can begin with Cooling's brief overflight (59); Butterworth's more detailed volume, *Flying Army* (39); with the Goldberg (119) and MacClosky (209) studies of the Air Force for the immediate post-World War II story; Weinert's official history through 1962 (366); and Politella's treatment (272) of Army aviation in Korea. Scrutiny of the Army school system should include Wilkins survey (376); Ambrose, *Duty, Honor, Country* (10), Heise, *The Brass Factories* (136), and Galloway and Johnson, *West Point* (102), on the military academy; Pappas, *Prudens Futuri* (262) for the inadequately studied War College; and Emma-Jo Davis on the Transportation School (64).

WEAPONS, TECHNOLOGY, LOGISTICS. The Army's involvement with the complexities of modern weaponry cuts across the full spectrum from atomic warfare to hand guns. Useful background can be gained if related to the sensitive yet timely question of a military-industrial complex (MIC) which has mesmerized scholars, politicians, and laymen in the Vietnam era. Baumgartner, *Lonely Warriors* (20); Galbraith, *New Industrial State* (100); Lapp, *Arms Beyond Doubt* (194); Proxmire, *Report From Wasteland* (275); and Schiller and Phillips, *Super State* (294) provide sagacious comments on that phenomenon, although Lincoln and Jordan (200) succinctly present the case for technology and the changing nature of general war in a manner but calculated to illustrate why the MIC might be considered inevitable. The Army's contribution to atomic energy is nicely conveyed by official AEC historians in Hewlett and Duncan, *Atomic Shield* (141), as well as Hewlett and Anderson, *New World* (142).

Another area of Army involvement with large weapons systems concerns missiles, both offensive and defensive. The antiballistic missile (whose implications for air defense mean Army responsibility) provided a controversial, open-ended debate which may be followed in Barnaby and Boserup, *Implications* (17); Chayes, *ABM* (46); Holst and Schneider, *Why ABM?* (150); Kintner, *Safeguard* (180); as well as Rabinowitch and Adams, *Debate* (276). Army contributions to other missile programs are best covered by NASA historians such as Green and Lomack, *Vanguard* (122); Swenson, Grimwood, and Alexander, *This New Ocean* (324); as well as Armacost on Thor-Jupiter (14), Bullard on *Redstone* (37); and Hunnicutt on *Pershing* (155). Chemical-biological-radiological warfare finds extensive attention in Brown, *Chemical Warfare* (35); Clarke, *Silent Weapons* (50); Hersh, *Hidden Arsenal* (140); McCarthy, *Ultimate Folly* (208); and Whiteside, *Withering Rain* (375); especially in light of the highly criticized use of such agents in Southeast Asia. Smaller weapons systems should be studied through WE Inc., *Tank Data* (328); Dolvin, *Main Battle Tank* (74); Foss, *Armoured Fighting Vehicles* (97); and Jarrett and Icks, *Portrait of Power* (164), for armored vehicles; Smith and Smith (304) on small arms; and Worley, *Digest* (382), as well as Fisher, *Weapons and Equipment* (93), for syntheses of developments in Army weapons, tactics, organization, and equipment down to the eve of Vietnam. Virgil Nye provides a suggestive study of the evolution of field manuals from Valley Forge to Vietnam (251) while histories of Redstone, Rock Island, and Watervliet arsenals (166, 345, 347) serve as models for that neglected subject. In fact, technology, weaponry, and production as they interface with the Army after World War II are a neglected field and quite open for scholarly exploitation.

Equally important, and equally neglected, are matters of supply and logistics with respect to the U.S. Army. Preeminent stands Huston's overall study of Army logistics, which ends with the Korean truce (158), although Army Materiel Command historians have contributed *Arsenal For The Brave* (341). Otherwise, we possess only highly specialized studies, often hard to retrieve for further research. These include official Quartermaster Corps historical monographs like Haggard's on manufacture of clothing (127); procurement of clothing and textiles (128); and quartermaster inspection (129); for the period 1945-53. Similarly, the QMC historical studies by Koehler on coffee (188); and special rations (189); Peifer on airborne QM supply (270); Rifkind on the QM market system (284); and Erna Risch on demobilization planning and operations at the end of World War II)286) stand as lone sentinels in this field. The interested researcher must turn (when he can), to such official historical summaries as the Seventh Army report on its support command (346), dated 1958.

MEN AND EVENTS. Biographies and memoirs remain one of the more stimulating measurements of history. Subtle nuances and perspectives from the top can be gleaned from Truman's, Eisenhower's, and Johnson's memoirs (338, 79, 80, 165). Borklund (29) investigates the secretaries of defense and their policies while Roherty (228), Trewhitt (337), and McNamara himself (212) try to explain the latter's place in the era. On Douglas MacArthur, see Gunther (126), Long (203), Whan (372),

Willoughby and Chamberlin (378), as well as MacArthur himself (207). Mark Clark (49), William F. Dean (67), James Gavin (109), Matthew Ridgway (282), Maxwell Taylor (331) and Ferguson on Westmoreland (91) have all added their comments on men and events. Most enticing is the continuing official oral history project for retired general officers conducted by the Military History Research Collection in conjunction with the Army War College and the Command and General Staff College. To date, material has been gathered on tape from Generals Besson, Betts, Bolte, Bonesteel, Boyle, Carraway, Chesarek, Clark, Clay, J. Lawton Collins, Decker, Eaker, Freeman, Handy, Harrell, Hodson, Hoge, Howze, Johnson, Lasher, Lemnitzer, Magruder, Mather, Palmer, Polk, Reckord, Ridgway, Seaman, Taylor, Trudeau, Woolnough, Wedemeyer, Van Fleet, Wood, Wheeler, which will become available in varying degrees in the future.

SUGGESTIONS FOR FURTHER RESEARCH. The history of the United States Army since World War II then, offers a wide-range of opportunities for studying peaks and troughs; conflicts and consensus; personalities and philosophies; as well as changing techniques and programs as electronics and science constantly changed the rules and conduct of land warfare. Domestic civic action vied with combat operations abroad, and the picture is by no means clear as to the full impact of such programs as Reserve Forces Act of 1955 (RFA), Volunteer Army Program (VOLAR), Special Forces, Strategic Hamlets, Main Battle Tank-70 (MBT-70), and SENTINEL/SAFEGUARD antiballistic missile systems. Even the question of why the search for a doctrinal counterpart to "airpower," or "seapower," has eluded the Army down to the present time remains unanswered. Both sister services have long enjoyed such philosophical underpinnings while the Army has never clearly enunciated anything meaningful for the term "landpower," Thus, the postwar Army will provide material for countless studies of men and conflict as well as the ecological ramifications of a military institution. For a time the problem will be less that of concepts, topics, and research proposals, and more one of techniques, mechanics, and procedure.

A great need exists for a balanced, nonpolemical history of the U.S. Army since 1945. In its absence, however, various individual topics suggest themselves for further research. As yet we know all too little about top Army commanders, with the absence of a definitive biography of General Omar Bradley standing in stark relief. Similarly we do not fully comprehend Army power and position on the Joint Chiefs of Staff for the period. Barred access to the records, the researcher can still hope to contribute solid, contemporary studies of the branches and components of the Army such as armor, finance, JAG, and field artillery. We are missing anything definitive on the noncommissioned officer corps, and on the whole maze of enlisted ranks and specialties, notwithstanding the continued overkill accorded the commissioned grades. Technology and weaponry has not been attacked through studies of managerial, budgetary, and R&D factors vis-à-vis the U.S. Army. The field is open for studies of military posts and their impact upon surrounding communities—studies similar to the wealth of knowledge we possess for nineteenth-century counterparts. Then too, do we really know very much about the influence of Army personnel and their families on local politics, school systems, churches, and other American institutions in this period? Do we understand not only civilian distrust of the military, but the extreme sensitivity of the military vis-à-vis civilians since 1945? Naturally the final chapters have not been written on Korea, Vietnam, the smaller uses of force in Latin America or Lebanon, nor Army participation in disaster relief, and these opportunities seem too obvious to require further mention.

While the U.S. Army approaches its own Bicentennial by agonizing over its recent past (and greater attention to history in general—see Kleber, 184), we have been told that the late John F. Kennedy was fond of suggesting his own version of the Kiplingesque Tommy Atkins in modern U.S. Army garb:

> God and the soldier all men adore,
>   In time of danger and no more,
> For when the danger is past and all things righted,
>   God is forgotten and the old soldier slighted.

One suspects that for future historians, at least, this will no longer be applicable for the U.S. Army, 1945-1973.

BIBLIOGRAPHY

1. Abel, Elie. *The Missile Crisis*. Philadelphia: Lippincott, 1966.
2. Abshire, David M. and Richard V. Allen. Editors. *National Security: Political, Military, and Economic Strategies in the Decade Ahead.* New York: Praeger and Hoover Institution, 1963.
3. Acheson, Dean. *The Korean War*. New York: Norton, 1971.
4. Ackley, Charles Walton. *The Modern Military In American Society: A Study in the Nature of Military Power.* Philadelphia: Westminster, 1972.
5. Adams, Nina S. and Alfred W. McCoy. Editors. *Laos: War and Revolution*. New York: Harper and Row, 1970.
6. Akerman, Nordal. *On the Doctrine of Limited War*. Lund, Sweden: Berlingska Boktryckeriet, 1972.
7. Albright, John, John A. Cook and Allan W. Sandstrum. *Seven Firefights in Vietnam*. Washington: Office, Chief of Military History, 1970.
8. Allied Forces, Supreme Headquarters. *Provisional Handbook For Military Government in Austria*. n.p., April 1945.
9. Allison, Graham T. *Essence of Decision; Explaining The Cuban Missile Crisis*. Boston: Little, Brown, 1971.
10. Ambrose, Stephen E. *Duty, Honor, Country: A History of West Point*. Baltimore; Johns Hopkins Press, 1966.
11. American Security Council Committee. *The ABM and The Changed Strategic Military Balance*. Washington: Acropolis Books, 1969.

12. Andrews, William R. *The Village War:Vietnamese Communist Revolutionary Activities in Dink Tuong Province, 1960-1964.* Columbia: University of Missouri Press, 1973.
13. Appleman, Roy E. *South To The Naktong, North To The Yalu*; (June-November 1950) [U.S. Army in the Korean War]. Washington: Office, Chief of Military History, 1961.
14. Armacost, Michael H. *The Politics of Weapons Innovation: The Thor-Jupiter Controversy.* New York: Columbia University Press, 1969.
15. Aron, Raymond, *The Imperial Republic; The United States and the World 1945-1973.* Englewood Cliffs, New Jersey: Prentice Hall, 1974.
16. Bader, William B. *Austria Between East and West, 1945-1955.* Stanford: Stanford University Press, 1966.
17. Barnaby, C. R. and A. Boserup. Editors. *Implications of Anti-Ballistic Missile Systems.* New York: Humanities, 1969.
18. Barnard, Roy S. *The History of ARADCOM; Volume I, The Gun Era 1950-1955.* [Historical Project ARAD 5M-I]. Colorado Springs: Headquarters U.S. Army Air Defense Command, n.d.
19. Bashore, Boyd. "The Name of the Game is 'Search and Destroy' " *Army* 17, February 1967. 56-60.
20. Baumgartner, John S. *The Lonely Warriors: Case for the Military-Industrial Complex.* Los Angeles: Nash, 1970.
21. Beech, Keyes. *Tokyo and Points East.* Garden City: Doubleday, 1954.
22. Berger, Carl. *The Korea Knot; A Military-Political Knot.* Philadelphia: University of Pennsylvania Press, 1957.
23. Biderman, Albert D. *March to Calumny; The Story of American POW's in the Korean War.* New York: Macmillan, 1963.
24. Blakeslee, George H. *The Far Eastern Commission:A Study in International Cooperation 1945 to 1952* [U.S. Department of State Pub. 5138]. Washington: G.P.O., 1953.
25. Bletz, Donald F. *The Role of the Military Professional in U.S. Foreign Policy.* New York: Praeger, 1972.
26. Blumenson, Martin. *Reorganization of the Army, 1962.* Washington: Office, Chief of Military History, 1965.
27. Bogart, Leo, ed. *Social Research and the Desegregation of the U.S. Army.* Chicago: Markham, 1969.
28. Borklund, C. W. *The Department of Defense* [Praeger Library of U.S. Government Departments and Agencies]. New York: Praeger, 1968.
29. Borklund, Carl W. *Men of the Pentagon, From Forrestal to McNamara.* New York: Praeger, 1966.
30. Bradford, Zeb B., Jr. and Frederick J. Brown. *The United States Army in Transition.* Beverly Hills/London: Sage Publications, 1973.
31. Brayton, Abbott A. "American Reserve Policies Since World War II." *Military Affairs* XXXVI (December 1972) 139-142.
32. Brines, Russell. *MacArthur's Japan.* Philadelphia: J. B. Lippincott, 1948.

33. Brodie, Bernard, *Strategy in The Missile Age*. Princeton: Princeton University Press, 1959.

34. Brodsky, Stanley L. and Norman E. Eggleston. *The Military Prison, Theory, Research, & Practice*. Carbondale: Southern Illinois University Press, 1970.

35. Brown, Frederick J. *Chemical Warfare, A Study in Restraints*. Princeton: Princeton University Press, 1968.

36. Browne, Malcom W. *The New Face of War*. Indianapolis: Bobbs-Merrill, 1965.

37. Bullard, John W. *History of the Redstone Missile System* [AMC Historical Monograph 23M]. Redstone Arsenal, Alabama: U.S. Army Missile Command Historical Division, 1965.

38. Bunting, Josiah. *The Lionheads*. New York: George Braziller, 1972.

39. Butterworth, W. E. *Flying Army; The Modern Air Arm of the U.S. Army*. Garden City, New York: Doubleday, 1974.

40. Buttinger, Joseph. *Vietnam: A Dragon Embattled*. 2 vol. New York: Praeger, 1967.

41. Buttinger, Joseph. *Vietnam: A Political History*. New York: Praeger, 1968.

42. Canby, Steven L. *Military Manpower Procurement; A Policy Analysis*. Lexington, Massachusetts: D. C. Heath, 1972.

43. Caraley, Demetrios. *The Politics of Military Unification: A Study of Conflict and the Policy Process*. New York: Columbia University Press, 1966.

44. Chamberlain, Edwin W. "The Hidden Versatility of Our New Divisions." *Army*, XIV, April 1964, 61-63.

45. Chapman, Bruce K. *The Wrong Man in Uniform, Our Unfair and Obsolete Draft—and How We Can Replan It*. New York: Trident, 1967.

46. Chayes, Abram. Editor. *ABM; An Evaluation of the Decision to Deploy an Antiballistic Missile System*. New York: Harper & Row, 1969.

47. Citizens Commission of Inquiry. *The Dellums Committee Hearings on War Crimes in Vietnam; An Inquiry into Command Responsibility in Southeast Asia*. New York: Vintage, 1972.

48. Clark Keith C. and Laurence J. Legere, ed. *The President and The Management of National Security: A Report by the Institute for Defense Analysis*. New York: Praeger, 1969.

49. Clark, Mark W. *From The Danube to The Yalu*. New York: Harper, 1954.

50. Clarke, Robin. *The Silent Weapons: The Realities of Chemical and Biological Warfare*. New York: David McKay, 1968.

51. Clay, Lucius D. *Decision in Germany*. Garden City, New York: Doubleday, 1950.

52. Coakley, Robert W. *Operation Arkansas*. Washington: Office, Chief of Military History, 1957-58.

53. Coakley, Robert W., Paul J. Scheips, and Vincent H. Demma. *Use of Troops in Civil Disturbances Since World War II*. Washington: Office, Chief of Military History, 1965; as well as Paul Scheips and

Warner Stark. *Supplement II*. Washington: Office, Chief of Military History, 1969.

54. Coles, Harry L. and Albert K. Weinberg. *Civil Affairs: Soldiers Become Governors*. [United States Army in World War II; Special Studies]. Washington: Department of the Army, 1964.

55. Collins, J. Lawton. *War in Peacetime; The History and Lessons of Korea*. Boston: Houghton Mifflin, 1969.

56. Committee of Concerned Asian Scholars. *The Indochina Story; A Fully Documented Account*. New York: Pantheon, 1970.

57. Committee on the Alaska Earthquake of the Division of Earth Sciences National Research Council. *The Great Alaska Earthquake of 1964; Summary and Recommendations*. Washington: National Academy of Sciences, 1973.

58. Cooling, B. Franklin. "Civil Defense and the Army: The Quest for Responsibility, 1946-48." *Military Affairs*, XXXVI, February, 1972, 11-14.

59. Cooling, B. Franklin. "A History of U.S. Army Aviation." *Aerospace Historian*, v. 21, Summer 1974, 102-109.

60. Cooling, B. Franklin. "U.S. Army Support of Civil Defense: The Formative Years." *Military Affairs*, XXXV, February 1971, 7-11.

61. Cooper, Chester L. *The Lost Crusade; America in Vietnam*. New York: Dodd, Mead, 1970.

62. Corson, William R. *Consequences of Failure*. New York: Norton, 1974.

63. Dalfiume, Richard M. *Desegregation of the U.S. Armed Forces: Fighting on Two Fronts, 1939-1953*. Columbia: University of Missouri, 1969.

64. Davis, Emma-Jo L. *History of the United States Army Transportation School, 1942-1962*. Fort Eustis: Office of Historian, U.S. Army Transportation School, October 1967.

65. Davis, Franklin M. *Come as a Conqueror; The United States' Army's Occupation of Germany 1945-1949*. New York: Macmillan, 1967.

66. Davis, Franklin M. and Thomas T. Jones. Editors. *The U.S. Army Engineers: Fighting Elite*. New York: Franklin Watts, 1967.

67. Dean, William F. and William L. Worden. *General Dean's Story*. New York: Viking, 1954.

68. Derthick, Martha. *The National Guard in Politics*. Cambridge: Harvard University Press, 1965.

69. Dietchman, Seymour J. *Limited War and American Defense Policy*. Cambridge: M.I.T. Press, 1964.

70. Dille, John. *Substitute For Victory*. Garden City, New York: Doubleday, 1954.

71. Di Mona, Joseph. *Great Court-Martial Cases*. New York: Grosset & Dunlap, 1972.

72. Director, Selective Service System. *Outline of Historical Background of Selective Service*. n.p., 1965 edition.

73. Divine, Robert A., ed. *The Cuban Missile Crisis*. Chicago: Quadrangle, 1971.

74. Dolvin, Wilborn F. *Lessons Learned: Joint International Program*

Management For The US/FAG Main Battle Tank. Rock Island: U.S. Army Management Training Agency, 1966.

75. Donovan, James A. and David M. Shoup. *Militarism, U.S.A.* New York: Scribners, 1970.

76. Duncan, David Douglas. *War Without Heroes*. [Pictorial-Viet Nam]. New York: Harper & Row, 1970.

77. Dunn, Carroll H. *Base Development in South Vietnam 1965-1970*. [Vietnam Studies]. Washington: Deparment of the Army, 1972.

78. Eckhardt, George S. *Command and Control 1950-1969*. [Vietnam Studies]. Washington: Department of the Army, 1974.

79. Eisenhower, Dwight D. *Mandate For Change, 1953-1956; The White House Years*. Garden City: Doubleday, 1963.

80. Eisenhower, Dwight D. *Waging Peace, 1956-1961; The White House Years*. Garden City, New York: Doubleday, 1965.

81. Ekirch, Arthur A., Jr. *The Civilian and The Military*. New York: Oxford University Press, 1956.

82. Eliot, George Fielding. *Reserve Forces and the Kennedy Strategy*. Harrisburg: Stackpole, 1962.

83. Engle, Eloise. *Medic; America's Medical Soldiers, Sailors and Airmen in Peace and War*. New York: John Day, 1967.

84. Enthoven, Alain C., and K. Wayne Smith. *How Much Is Enough? Shaping The Defense Program 1961-1969*. New York: Harper & Row, 1971.

85. Fain, Monte, ed. *A Collection of Letters and Writings by Captain Gerald Austin Brown* [to] *Grace Spaulding* (mother). Fort Worth: Branch-Smith, 1973.

86. Fall, Bernard B. *Last Reflections On A War*. Garden City: Doubleday, 1967.

87. Fall, Bernard B. *The Two Viet Nams; A Political and Military Analysis*. New York: Praeger, 1964.

88. Fearey, Robert A. *The Occupation of Japan Second Phase, 1948-50*. New York: Macmillan, 1950.

89. Fehrenbach, T. R. *This Kind of War; A Study in Unpreparedness*. New York: Macmillan, 1963.

90. Feis, Herbert. *From Trust to Terror: The Onset of the Cold War, 1945-1950*. New York: Norton, 1970.

91. Ferguson, Ernest B. *Westmoreland: The Inevitable General*. Boston: Little, Brown, 1968,

92. Finn, James. Editor. *Conscience and Command; Justice and Discipline in the Military*. New York: Random House, 1971.

93. Fisher, Ernest F. *Weapons and Equipment Evolution and Its Influence Upon Organization and Tactics in the American Army from 1775 to 1963*. Washington: Office, Chief of Military History, 1963.

94. FitzGerald, Frances: *Fire in the Lake; The Vietnamese and the Americans in Vietnam*. Boston: Little, Brown, 1972.

95. FitzSimons, Louise, *The Kennedy Doctrine*. New York: Random House, 1972.

96. Flood, Charles B. *The War of the Innocents*. New York: McGraw Hill, 1970.

97. Foss, Christopher F. *Armoured Fighting Vehicles of the World.* New York: Scribners, 1971.
98. Fulbright, J. W. *The Pentagon Propaganda Machine.* New York: Liveright, 1970.
99. Furniss, Edgar S., Jr. *American Military Policy; Strategic Aspects of World Political Geography.* New York: Rinehart & Co., 1951.
100. Galbraith, John Kenneth. *The New Industrial State.* Boston: Houghton-Miffflin, 1967.
101. Galloway, G. E. *A Historical Study of United States Army Engineer Operations in the Republic of Vietnam January 1965-November 1967.* Fort Leavenworth: U.S. Army Command and General Staff College, 1968.
102. Galloway, Bruce and Robert Bowie Johnson, Jr. *West Point: America's Power Fraternity.* New York: Simon & Schuster, 1973.
103. Galvin, John R. *Air Assault: The Development of Airmobile Warfare.* New York: Hawthorn, 1969.
104. Galvin, John R. "Three Innovations: Prime Tactical Lessons of the Vietnam War." *Arms,* 22, March 1972, 16-24.
105. Gardner, Fred. *The Unlawful Concert: An Account of the Presidio Meeting Case.* New York: Viking, 1970.
106. Gardner, Lloyd C. *The Korean War.* New York: Quadrangle, 1972.
107. Garland, Albert N. Editor. *Infantry in Vietnam.* Fort Benning, Georgia: Infantry Magazine, 1967.
108. Gates, Thomas S. *The Report of the President's Commission on an All-Volunteer Armed Force.* New York: Macmillan, 1970.
109. Gavin, James M. *War and Peace in the Space Age.* New York: Harper & Brothers, 1958.
110. George, Alexander L., David K. Hall and William R. Simons. *The Limits of Coercive Diplomacy: Laos; Cuba, Vietnam.* Boston: Little, Brown, 1971.
111. Georgetown University, Center for Strategic Studies. *Dominican Action, 1965: Intervention or Cooperation.* Washington: Georgetown University, Center for Strategic Studies, 1966.
112. Gerhardt, James M. *The Draft and Public Policy; Issues in Military Manpower Procurement 1945-1970.* Columbus: Ohio State University Press, 1971.
113. Gershen, Martin. *Destroy or Die; The True Story of Mylai.* New Rochelle, New York: Arlington House, 1971.
114. Gettleman, Marvin E., ed. *Vietnam; History, Documents and Opinions on a Major World Crisis.* Greenwich: Fawcett, 1965.
115. Giap, Vo Nguyen. *Great Victory, Great Task.* New York: Praeger, 1968.
116. Giap, Vo Nguyen. *Peoples War, People's Army.* New York: Praeger, 1962.
117. Glick, Edward Bernard. *Peaceful Conflict. The Non-Military Use of the Military.* Harrisburg: Stackpole, 1967.
118. Glick, Edward Bernard. *Soldiers, Scholars, and Society; The Social Impact of the American Military.* Pacific Palisades, California: Goodyear, 1971.
119. Goldberg, Alfred, ed. *A History of the United States Air Force 1907-1957.* Princeton: D. Van Nostrand, 1957.

120. Goulding, Phil G. *Confirm or Deny; Informing the People on National Security.* New York: Harper & Row, 1970.

121. Gravel, Mike, ed. *The Pentagon Papers; The Defense Department History of United States Decision-making on Vietnam.* Boston: Beacon Press, 1971.

122. Green, Constance Mc. L. and Milton Lomack. *Vanguard: A History.* Washington: National Aeronautics and Space Administration, 1970.

123. Greene, Fred. *U.S. Policy and the Security of Asia.* New York: McGraw Hill, 1968.

124. Greenhaw, Wayne. *The Making of A Hero; A Behind-The-Scenes View of the Lt. William Calley Affair.* Louisville: Touchstone, 1971.

125. Gugeler, Russell A. *Combat Actions in Korea; Infantry, Artillery, Armor.* Washington: Combat Forces Press, 1954 and Office, Chief of Military History, 1970.

126. Gunther, John. *The Riddle of MacArthur.* New York: Harper & Brothers, 1950.

127. Haggard, John V. *Manufacture of Clothing 1945-53.* [QMC Historical Series II, #1]. Washington: Office of Quartermaster General, 1956.

128. Haggard, John V. *Procurement of Clothing and Textiles 1945-53.* [QMC Historical Studies, Series II, #3]. Washington: Historical Branch, Office of Quartermaster General, 1957.

129. Haggard, John V. *Quartermaster Corps Inspection 1946-1956.* [QMC Historical Studies, Series II, #7]. Washington: Office of Quartermaster General, Historical Office, 1962.

130. Halberstam, David. *The Best and the Brightest.* New York: Random House, 1972.

131. Hammer, Richard. *The Court-Martial of Lt. Calley.* New York: Coward, McCann and Geoghegan, 1971.

132. Hammond, Paul Y. *Organizing for Defense: The American Military Establishment in the Twentieth Century.* Princeton: Princeton University Press, 1961.

133. Hanning, Hugh. *The Peaceful Uses of Military Forces.* New York: Praeger, 1967.

134. Hauser, William L. *America's Army in Crisis: A Study in Civil-Military Relations.* Baltimore: Johns Hopkins Press, 1973.

135. Haynes, Richard F. *The Awesome Power: Harry S. Truman as Commander-in-Chief.* Baton Rouge: Louisiana State University Press, 1973.

135a. Heard, Richard G. and Ervin J. Rokke. *American Defense Policy.* 3d edition. Baltimore and London: Johns Hopkins Press, 1973.

136. Heise, J. Arthur. *The Brass Factories: A Frank Reappraisal of West Point, Annapolis, and The Air Force Academy.* Washington: Public Affairs Press, 1969.

137. Herbert, Anthony B. and James T. Wooten. *Soldier.* New York: Holt, Rinehart and Winston, 1973.

138. Hermes, Walter G. *Truce Tent and Fighting Front.* [U.S. Army in Korean War Series]. Washington: G. P. O., 1966.

139. Hersh, Seymour M. *Chemical and Biological Warfare; America's Hidden Arsenal.* Indianapolis: Bobbs-Merrill, 1968.

140. Hersh, Seymour M. *Cover-Up.* New York: Random House, 1972.

141. Hewlett, Richard G. and Francis Duncan. *Atomic Shield, 1947/1952.* [A History of the United States Atomic Energy Commission. Volume II]. University Park: Pennsylvania State University Press, 1969. 1969.

142. Hewlett, Richard G. and Oscar E. Anderson, Jr. *The New World, 1939/46.*[A History of the United States Atomic Energy Commission. Volume I.] University Park: Pennsylvania State University Press, 1963.

143. Hicken, Victor. *The American Fighting Man.* New York: Macmillan, 1969.

144. Hickman, Martin B. *The Military and American Society.* Beverly Hills, California: Glencoe Press, 1971.

145. Higgins, Marguerite. *War in Korea; The Report of A Woman Combat Correspondent.* Garden City: Time Inc., 1951.

146. Higgins, Trumbull. *Korea and the Fall of MacArthur; A Precis in Limited War.* New York: Oxford University Press, 1969.

147. Higham, Robin, ed. *Bayonets in the Streets: The Use of Troops in Civil Disturbances.* Lawrence: University Press of Kansas, 1969.

148. Hill, Jim Dan. *The Minute Man in Peace and War: A History of the National Guard.* Harrisburg: Stackpole, 1963.

149. Hollis, Charles H. "This Is a ROAD Brigade. *Army,* XIII, April 1963, 31-35.

150. Holst, John J. and William Schneider, Jr., ed. *Why ABM? Policy Issues in the Missile Defense Controversy.* New York: Pergamon, 1969.

151. Honeywell, Roy J. *Chaplains of the United States Army.* Washington: Department of the Army, Office of Chief of Chaplains, 1958.

152. Hovey, Harold A. *United States Military Assistance.* New York: Praeger, 1965.

153. Howard, John M., editor in chief. *Battle Casualties in Korea: Studies of the Surgical Research Team;* v.I *The Systematic Response to Injury;* v.II *Tools for Resuscitation;* v.III *The Battle Wound: Clinical Experiences;* v.IV *Post Traumatic Renal Insufficiency.* Washington: Walter Reed Medical Center, 1954.

154. Hughes, Larry. *You Can See a Lot Standing Under a Flare in the Republic of Vietnam: My Year at War.* New York: William Morrow, 1969.

155. Hunnicutt, R. P. *Pershing: A History of the Medium Tank T20 Series.* Berkeley: Feist, 1971.

156. Huntington, Samuel P. *The Common Defense: Strategic Programs in National Politics.* New York: Columbia University Press, 1961.

157. Huntington, Samuel P. *The Soldier and the State: The Theory and Politics of Civil-Military Relations.* New York: Random House, 1964.

158. Huston, James A. *The Sinews of War: Army Logistics 1775-1953.* [Army Historical Series]. Washington: G. P. O., 1966.

159. Huzar, Elias. *The Purse and Sword; Control of the Army by Congress Through Military Appropriations 1933-1950.* Ithaca: Cornell University Press, 1950.

160. Janowitz, Morris. "The Decline of the Mass Army." *Military Review,* LII, February 1972, 10-16.

161. Janowitz, Morris, ed. *The New Military; Changing Pattern of Organization*. New York: Norton, 1964.
162. Janowitz, Morris. *The Professional Soldier; A Social and Political Portrait*. New York: Free Press, 1960.
163. Janowitz, Morris. "Volunteer Armed Forces and Military Purposes." *Foreign Affairs*, V. 50, April 1972, 427-433.
164. Jarrett, George B. and Robert J. Icks. *Portrait of Power; A Photo-History of United States Tanks and Self-Propelled Artillery*. Wickenburg, Arizona: Normount Technical Publications, 1971.
165. Johnson, Lyndon Baines. *The Vantage Point; Perspectives of the Presidency 1963-1969*. New York: Holt, Rinehart & Winston, 1971.
166. Joiner, Helen Brents. *The Redstone Arsenal Complex in the Pre-Missile Era. (A History of Huntsville Arsenal, Gulf Chemical Warfare Depot, and Redstone Arsenal, 1941-1949). Redstone Arsenal, 1941-1949*. Redstone Arsenal, Alabama: U.S. Army Missile Command Historical Division, 1966.
167. Jordan, Amos A., Jr., ed. *Issues of National Security in the 1970's (Essays Presented to Colonel George A. Lincoln on His Sixtieth Birthday)*. New York: Praeger, 1967.
168. Jury, Mark. *The Vietnam Photo Book*. New York: Grossman, 1971.
169. Just, Ward. *Military Men*. New York: Knopf, 1970.
170. Kahn, E. J., Jr. *The Peculiar War; Impressions of a Reporter in Korea*. New York: Random House, 1952.
171. Kang, Han Mu. *The United States Military Government in Korea 1945-1948: An Analysis and Evaluation of Its Policy*. Ann Arbor: University Microfilms, 1970.
172. Kaufmann, William W. *The McNamara Strategy*. New York: Harper & Row, 1964.
173. Kaufmann, William W., ed. *Military, Policy and National Security*. Princeton: Princeton University Press, 1956.
174. Kennedy, Robert F. *Thirteen Days: A Memoir of the Cuban Missile Crisis*. New York: Norton, 1969.
175. Kerry, John and Vietnam Veterans Against the War; David Thorne and George Butler, ed. *The New Soldier*. New York: Macmillan, 1971.
176. Kim, K. H., Susan Farrell and Ewan Clogue. *The All-Volunteer Army; An Analysis of Demand and Supply*. New York: Praeger, 1971.
177. King, Edward L. *The Death of the Army; A Pre-Mortem*. New York: Saturday Review Press, 1972.
178. Kinkead, Eugene. *In Every War But One*. New York: Norton, 1959.
179. Kinnard, Harry. W. O. "A Victory in the Ia Drang: The Triumph of a Concept." *Army* 17, September 1967, 71-91.
180. Kintner, William R. Editor. *Safeguard: Why the ABM Makes Sense*. New York: Hawthorn, 1969.
181. Kirkendall, Richard S. *The Truman Period As a Research Field*. Columbia: University of Missouri Press, 1967.
182. Kirkpatrick, Lyman B., Jr. *The U.S. Intelligence Community: Foreign Policy and Domestic Activities*. New York: Hill & Wang, 1973.
183. Klare, Michael T. *War Without End: American Planning For The Next Vietnams*. New York: Knopf, 1972.

184. Kleber, Brooks E. "The Army Looks At Its Need For Military History." *Military Affairs,* XXXVII, April 1973, 47-48.
185. Kleinman, Forrest K. "ROAD Sign for Big Sixties," and "On the Road to ROAD." *Army,* XII, July 1962, 62-66.
186. Knoll, Erwin and Judith Nies McFadden. *American Militarism 1970.* New York: Viking, 1969.
187. Knoll, Edwin and Judith Nies McFadden. *War Crimes and The American Conscience.* New York: Holt, Rinehart and Winston, 1970.
188. Koehler, Franz A. *Coffee For The Armed Forces: Military Development and Conversion to Industry Supply.* [QMC Historical Studies, Series II, #5]. Washington: Office of the Quartermaster General, Historical Branch, 1958.
189. Koehler, Franz A. *Special Rations For The Armed Forces 1946-53.* [QMC Historical Studies, Series II, #6]. Washington: Office of the Quartermaster General Historical Branch, 1958.
190. Kohn, Richard H. "The All-Volunteer Army: Too High a Price?" *United States Naval Institute Proceedings,* 100, March 1974, 35-43.
191. Kolko, Joyce and Gabriel. *The Limits of Power: The World and United States Foreign Policy, 1945-1954.* New York: Harper & Row, 1972.
192. Kolodziez, Edward A. *The Uncommon Defense and Congress, 1945-1963.* Columbus: Ohio State University Press, 1966.
193. Kriebel, P. Wesley. "Korea: The Military Armistice Commission, 1965-1970." *Military Affairs,* XXXVI, October 1972, 96-99.
194. Lapp, Ralph E. *Arms Beyond Doubt; The Tyranny of Weapons Technology.* New York: Cowles, 1970.
195. Larson, Arthur. *Eisenhower; The President Nobody Knew.* New York: Scribner, 1968.
196. Leckie, Robert. *Conflict: The History of the Korean War, 1950-53.* New York: G. P. Putnams, 1962.
197. Lee, Bill, ed. *Absolutely No U.S. Personnel Permitted Beyond This Point.* New York: Dell, 1972.
198. Lee, Harriet S. and Myra L. McDaniel. *Army Medical Specialist Corps.* Washington: Department of the Army, Office of Surgeon General, 1968.
199. Levantrosser, William. "The Army Reserve Merger Proposal." [1964-65]. *Military Affairs,* XXX, Fall 1966, 135-148.
200. Lincoln, George H. and Amos A. Jordan, Jr. "Technology and the Changing Nature of General War." *Military Review,* XXVI, May 1957, 1-13.
201. Liston, Robert. *Greeting: You Are Hereby Ordered For Induction . . . The Draft in America.* New York: McGraw-Hill, 1970.
202. Little, Roger W., ed. *Selective Service and American Society.* New York: Russell Sage Foundation, 1969.
203. Long, Gavin, *MacArthur as Military Commander.* New York: Van Nostrand Reinhold, 1969.
204. Loory, Stuart. *Defeated; Inside America's Military Machine.* New York: Random House, 1973.
205. Lowenthal, Abraham F. *The Dominican Intervention.* Cambridge: Harvard University Press, 1972.

206. Lyons, Gene M. and John W. Masland. *Education and Military Leadership*. Princeton: Princeton University Press, 1959.

207. MacArthur, Douglas. *Reminiscences*. New York: McGraw-Hill, 1964.

208. McCarthy, Richard D. *The Ultimate Folly; War By Pestilence, Asphyxiation, and Defoliation*. New York: Knopf, 1969.

209. MacCloskey, Monro. *The United States Air Force*. New York: Praeger, 1967.

210. McCuen, John J. *The Art of Counter-revolutionary War; The Strategy of Counter-insurgency*. Harrisburg: Stackpole, 1966.

211. McGovern, James. *To The Yalu: From The Chinese Invasion of Korea To MacArthur's Dismissal*. New York: Morrow, 1972.

212. McNamara, Robert S. *The Essence of Security; Reflections in Office*. New York: Harper & Row, 1968.

213. Mahon, John K. and Romana Danysh. *Infantry Part I: Regular Army*. [Army Lineage Series]. Washington: Office, Chief of Military History, 1953.

214. Mallin, Jay, ed. *Strategy For Conquest; Communist Documents on Guerrilla Warfare*. Coral Gables, Florida: University of Miami Press, 1970.

215. Manning, Robert, and Michael Janeway. Editors. *Who We Are; An Atlantic Chronicle of the United States and Vietnam*. Boston: Atlantic Monthly Press, 1969 edition.

216. Marmion, Harry A. *The Case Against A Volunteer Army*. Chicago: Quadrangle Books, 1971.

217. Marshall, Max L., ed. *The Story of the U.S. Army Signal Corps*. New York: Franklin Watts, 1965.

218. Marshall, S.L.A. *Ambush: The Battle of Dan Tieng, Also Called The Battle of Dong Minh Chau, Was Zone C, Operation Attleboro, and Other Deadfalls in South Vietnam*. New York: Cowles, 1969.

219. Marshall, S.L.A. *Battles in The Monsoon; Campaigning in the Central Highlands, South Vietnam, Summer 1966*. New York: Morrow, 1967.

220. Marshall, S.L.A. *Bird; The Christmastide Battle*. New York: Cowles, 1968.

221. Marshall, S.L.A. *Notes on Infantry Tactics in Korea*. Baltimore: Operations Research Office, Johns Hopkins University, Far East Command, 1951.

222. Marshall, S.L.A. *Pork Chop Hill: The American Fighting Man in Action in Korea, Spring 1953*. New York: Morrow, 1956.

223. Marshall, S.L.A. *The River and The Gauntlet; Defeat of the Eighth Army By The Chinese Communist Forces November, 1950 in the Battle of the Chongchon River, Korea*. New York: Morrow, 1953.

224. Marshall, S.L.A. *West To Cambodia*. New York: Cowles, 1968.

225. Martin, Edwin M. *The Allied Occupation of Japan*. New York: American Institute of Pacific Relations, 1948.

226. Martin, Laurence. *Arms and Strategy: The World Power Structure Today*. New York: David McKay, 1973.

227. Martin, Lawrence W. "Military Issues: Strategic Parity and Its Implications." in Robert E. Osgood, et.al. *Retreat From Empire?*

The First Nixon Administration. Baltimore: Johns Hopkins Press, 1973.

228. Masland, John W., and Laurence I. Radway. *Soldiers and Scholars; Military Education and National Policy.* Princeton: Princeton University Press, 1957.

229. Masland, John W., and Lawrence I. Radway. *Bill Mauldin in Korea.* New York: W. W. Norton, 1952.

230. Meade, Grant E. *American Military Government.* New York: Columbia University Press, 1951.

231. Menzel, Paul T. *Moral Argument and The War in Vietnam; A Collection of Essays.* Nashville: Aurora, 1971.

232. Mertel, Kenneth D. *Year of the Horse—Vietnam, 1st Air Cavalry in the Highlands.* New York: Exposition, 1968.

233. Military Government of Germany, U.S. Zone. *Monthly Reports.* Office of Military Government for Germany (U.S.), 1945-1949.

234. Miller, John, Jr., Owen J. Carroll, and Margaret E. Tackley. *Korea, 1951-1953.* Washington: Department of the Army, 1956.

235. Millis, Walter. *Arms and the State: Civil-Military Elements in National Policy.* New York: Twentieth Century Fund, 1958.

236. Millis, Walter R., ed. *The Forrestal Diaries.* New York: Viking, 1951.

237. Montgomery, John D. *Forced To Be Free: The Artificial Revolution in Germany and Japan.* Chicago: University of Chicago Press, 1957.

238. Moore, Robin. *The Green Berets.* New York: Crown, 1965.

239. Morgan, Arthur E. *Dams and Other Disasters; A Century of the Army Corps of Engineers in Civil Works.* Boston: Porter Sargent, 1971.

240. Morris, M. D. *Okinawa: A Tiger By The Tail.* New York: Hawthorn, 1968.

241. Moskos, Charles C., Jr. *The American Enlisted Man; The Rank and File in Today's Military.* New York: Russell Sage Foundation, 1970.

242. Moskos, Charles C., Jr., ed. *Public Opinion and the Military Establishment.* Beverly Hills, California: Sage Publications, 1971.

243. Mossman, B. C. and M. W. Stark. *The Last Salute: Civil and Military Funerals 1921-1969.* Washington: Department of the Army, 1971.

244. Murdock, Clark. *Defense Policy Formation: A Comparative Analysis of the McNamara Era.* Albany: New York State University Press, 1974.

245. Mydan, Carl and Shelley Mydan. *The Violent Peace.* New York: Time Inc., 1968 edition.

246. Mylander, Maureen. *The Generals.* New York: Dial, 1974.

247. Neel, Spurgeon. *Medical Support of the U.S. Army in Vietnam, 1965-1970.* Washington: G. P. O., 1973.

248. Neilands, J. B. et. al. *Harvest of Death; Chemical Warfare in Vietnam and Cambodia.* New York: Free Press, 1972.

249. Newhouse, John. *U.S. Troops in Europe; Issues, Costs, and Choices. Washington: The Brookings Institution, 1971.*

250. New York Times, eds. *The Pentagon Papers.* New York: Bantam Books, 1971.

251. Ney, Virgil. *Evolution of the United States Army Field Manual, Valley Forge to Vietnam.* Combat Operations Research Group, CORG Memorandum, CORG-M-244 prepared by Technical Operations, Inc. Combat Operations Research Group for Headquarters, United States Army Combat Developments Command, Fort Belvoir, Virginia, 1966.
252. Nighswonger, William A. *Rural Pacification in Vietnam.* New York: Praeger, 1967.
253. Oberdorfer, Don. *Tet!* New York: Doubleday, 1971.
254. O'Connor, Raymond G. *Force and Diplomacy; Essays Military and Diplomatic.* Coral Gables, Florida: University of Miami, 1972.
255. Olson, Robert A. "Air Mobility For the Army; A Case Study of Policy Evolution in Relation To Changing Strategy." *Military Affairs,* XXVIII, Winter 1964/65, 163-173.
256. O'Neill, William L. *Coming Apart; An Informal History of America in the 1960's.* Chicago: Quadrangle, 1971.
257. Oppenheimer, Martin, ed. *The American Military.* Chicago: Aldine, 1971.
258. Osanka, Franklin Mark. *Modern Guerrilla Warfare; Fighting Communist Guerrilla Movements, 1941-1961.* New York: The Free Press, 1962.
259. Osgood, Robert E. et. al. *America and the World; From The Truman Doctrine to Vietnam.* Baltimore: Johns Hopkins Press, 1970.
260. Osgood, Robert E. *Limited War; The Challenge to American Strategy.* Chicago: University of Chicago Press, 1957 edition.
261. Paige, Glenn D. *The Korean Decision.* [June 24-30, 1950]. New York: Free Press, 1968.
262. Pappas, George S. *Prudens Futuri: The U.S. Army War College 1901-1967.* Carlisle Barracks: Alumni Association of U.S. Army War College, 1967.
263. Paret, Peter, et. al. "Contemporary History and War." *Military Affairs,* XXXII, Spring 1968, 1-19.
264. Paret, Peter and John Shy. *Guerrillas in the 1960's.* New York: Praeger, 1962.
265. Parmet, Herbert S. *Eisenhower and The America Crusades.* New York: Macmillan, 1972.
266. Pasley, Virginia. *21 Stayed; The Story of the American GI's Who Chose Communist China—Who They Were and Why They Stayed.* New York: Farrar, Strauss, Cudahy, 1955.
267. Paszeck, Lawrence J. "Negroes and the Air Force, 1939-1949." *Military Affairs,* XXI, Spring 1967, 1-10.
268. Pate, Lloyd W. *Reactionary!* New York: Harper & Bros, 1955.
269. Paul, Roland A. *American Military Commitments Abroad.* New Brunswick: Rutgers University Press, 1973.
270. Peifer, William H. *Supply By Sky: The Quartermaster Airborne Development, 1950-53.* [QMC Historical Studies Series II, #2]. Washington: Office of the Quartermaster General Historical Branch, 1957.
271. Pike, Douglas. *Viet Cong: The Organization and Techniques of the National Liberation Front of South Vietnam.* Cambridge: MIT Press, 1966.

272. Politella, Dario. *Operation Grasshopper.* [The Story of Army Aviation in Korea]. Tyler, Texas: Robert R. Lango, 1958.

273. Polner, Murray. *No Victory Parades; The Return of the Vietnam Veteran.* New York: Holt, Rinehart, & Winston, 1971.

274. Powers, Patrick W. *A Guide To National Defense: The Organization and Operations of the U.S. Military Establishment.* New York: Praeger, 1964.

275. Proxmire, William. *Report from Wasteland: America's Military-Industrial Complex.* New York: Praeger, 1970.

276. Rabinowitch, Eugene and Ruth Adams. Editors. *Debate the Antiballistic Missile.* Chicago: Bulletin of the Atomic Scientist, 1967.

277. Race, Jeffrey. *War Comes to Long An; Revolutionary Conflict in a Vietnamese Province.* Berkeley: University of California, 1972.

278. Raymond, Jack. *Power At The Pentagon.* New York: Harper & Row, 1964.

279. Rees, David. *Korea: The Limited War.* New York: St. Martins, 1964.

280. Reeves, Thomas and Karl Hess. *The End of the Draft.* New York: Random House, 1970.

281. Ridgway, Matthew B. *The Korea War.* Garden City, New York: Doubleday, 1967.

282. Ridgway, Matthew B. *Soldier: The Memoirs of Matthew B. Ridgway.* New York: Harper, 1956.

283. Ries, John C. *The Management of Defense; Organization and Control of the U.S. Armed Services.* Baltimore: Johns Hopkins Press, 1964.

284. Rifkind, Herbert R. *Fresh Foods For The Armed Forces; The Quartermaster Market Center System, 1941-1948.* [QMC Historical Series I, #20]. Quartermaster General, Historical Section, 1951.

285. Riker, William H. *Soldiers of the States: The Role of The National Guard in American Democracy.* Washington: Public Affairs Press, 1957.

286. Risch, Erna. *Demobilization Planning and Operation in the Quartermaster Corps.* [QMC Historical Studies Series I, #19]. Washington: Office of the Quartermaster General, 1948.

287. Robinson, Frank M and Earl Kemp. *Report on the U.S. Senate Hearings—The Truth About Vietnam.* San Diego: Greenleaf Classics Inc., 1966.

288. Roherty, James M. *Decisions of Robert S. McNamara; A Study of the Role of The Secretary of Defense.* Coral Gables: University of Miami Press, 1970.

289. Rosenberg, Milton J., ed. *Beyond Conflict and Containment; Critical Studies of Military and Foreign Policy.* New Brunswick, New Jersey: Transaction Books, 1972.

290. Rowe, James N. *Five Years To Freedom.* Boston: Little, Brown, 1971.

291. Sack, John. *Lieutenant Calley; His Own Story.* New York: Viking, 1971 edition.

292. Sawyer, Robert K. *Military Advisors in Korea: KMAG in Peace and War.* [Army Historical Series]. Washington: G. P. O., 1962.

293. Scheips, Paul J. *The Role of the Army in The Oxford, Mississippi,*

Incident, 1962-1963. Washington: Office, Chief of Military History, 1965.

294. Schiller, Herbert I. and Joseph D. Phillips, eds. *Super State: Readings in the Military-Industrial Complex.* Urbana: University of Illinois Press, 1970.

295. Schilling, Warner B., Paul Y. Hammond, and Glenn H. Snyder. *Strategy, Politics, and Defense Budgets.* New York: Columbia University Press, 1962.

296. Schlesinger, Arthur M., Jr. *A Thousand Days; John F. Kennedy in the White House.* Boston: Houghton Mifflin, 1965.

297. Schlesinger, Arthur M. *The Bitter Heritage; Vietnam and American Democracy, 1941-1966.* Boston: Houghton Mifflin, 1967.

298. Schnabel, James. *Policy and Direction: The First Year.* [U.S. Army in the Korean War Series]. Washington: Department of the Army, 1972.

299. Schwarz, Urs. *Confrontation and Intervention In the Modern World.* Dobbs Ferry, New York: Oceana Publications Inc., 1970.

300. Sheldon, Walt. *Hell or High Water; MacArthur's Landing at Inchon.* New York: Macmillan, 1968.

301. Sherrill, Robert. *Military Justice Is to Justice as, Military Music Is to Music.* New York: Harper & Row, 1969.

302. Skaggs, David Curtis. "The KATUSA Experiment; The Integration of Korean Nationals Into the U.S. Army, 1950-1965." *Military Affairs,* XXXVIII April 1974, 53-58.

303. Smith, Mark E., III. and Claude J. Johns, Jr., eds. *American Defense Policy.* Baltimore: Johns Hopkins Press, 1968 edition.

304. Smith, W. H. B. and Joseph E. Smith. *Small Arms of the World.* Harrisburg: Stackpole, 1973, edition.

305. Sorensen, Theodore C. *Kennedy.* New York: Harper & Row, 1965.

306. Spanier, John W. *The Truman-MacArthur Controversy and the Korean War.* New York: Norton, 1965.

307. Spector, Ronald. "Getting Down To The Nitty-Gritty: Military History, Official History and The American Experience in Vietnam." *Military Affairs,* XXXVIII, February 1974, 11-12.

308. Staff of Infantry Magazine. Editors. *A Distant Challenge: The U.S. Infantryman in Vietnam, 1967-70.* Birmingham: Birmingham Publishing Co., 1971.

309. Stambuk, George. *American Military Forces Abroad; Their Impact on The Western State System.* Columbus: Ohio State University Press, 1963.

310. Stanley, Timothy W. *American Defense and National Security.* Washington: Public Affairs Press, 1956.

311. Stapp, Andy. *Up Against the Brass.* New York: Simon & Schuster, 1970.

312. Starr, Paul, James Henry, and Raymond Bonner. *The Discarded Army: The Nader Report on Vietnam Veterans and the Veterans Administration.* New York: Charterhouse Books, 1973.

313. Stavins, Ralph L., Richard J. Barnet, and Marcus G. Raskin. *Washington Plans An Aggressive War.* New York: Vantage, 1971.

314. Steel, Ronald. *Pax Americana.* New York: Viking, 1967.

315. Steere, Edward and Thayer M. Boardman. *Final Disposition of World War II Dead 1945-57.* [QMC Historical Studies, Series II, #4]. Washington: Office of the Quartermaster General, Historical Branch, 1957.

316. Stevens, Philip H. *Artillery Through The Ages.* New York: Franklin Watts, 1965.

317. Stevenson, Charles A. *The End of Nowhere: American Policy Toward Laos Since 1954.* Boston: Beacon, 1972.

318. Stillman, Richard J. *Integration of the Negro in the U.S. Armed Forces.* New York: Praeger, 1968.

319. Stillman, Richard J., ed. *The U.S. Infantry: Queen of Battle.* New York: Franklin Watts, 1965.

320. Stillwell, Richard G. "An Evolution in Tactics: The Vietnam Experience." *Army* 20, February 1970, 15-23.

321. Stubbs, Mary Lee and Stanley Russell Connor. *Armor-Cavalry.* Part I. Washington: Office, Chief of Military History, 1969.

322. Stubbs, Mary Lee and Janice R. McKinney. *Armor-Cavalry, Part II.* Washington: Office, Chief of Military History, 1972.

323. Supreme Commander of Allied Powers. *Organization and Activities of General Headquarters, Supreme Commander for the Allied Powers and Far East Command.* Tokyo: ?, 1950.

324. Swenson, Loyd S., Jr., James M. Grimwood, and Charles C. Alexander. *This New Ocean; A History of Project Mercury.* Washington: National Aeronautics and Space Administration, 1966.

325. Szulc, Tad. *Dominican Diary.* New York: Delacorte, 1965.

326. Taber, Robert. *The War of the Flea: A Study of Guerrilla Warfare Theory and Practise.* New York: Lyle Stuart, 1965.

327. Tanham, George K. et. al. *War Without Guns: American Civilians in Rural Vietnam.* New York: Praeger, 1966.

328. Tanham, George K. et. al. *Tank Data: Aberdeen Proving Grounds Series.* Old Greenwich, Connecticut: WE Inc., 1969.

329. Tauber, Peter. *The Sunshine Soldiers.* New York: Simon and Schuster, 1971.

330. Taylor, Maxwell D. *Responsibility and Response.* New York: Harper & Row, 1967.

331. Taylor, Maxwell D. *Swords and Plowshares.* New York: Norton, 1972.

332. Taylor, Maxwell D. *The Uncertain Trumpet.* New York: Harper & Brothers, 1959.

333. Thompson, Robert G. K. *Defeating Communist Insurgency: The Lesson of Malaya and Vietnam.* New York: Praeger, 1966.

334. Thompson, Sir Robert. *No Exit From Vietnam.* New York: David McKay, 1969.

335. Tim, Clifton Daniel. *Bremen Under U.S. Military Occupation, 1945-1949: The Reform of Education.* Ann Arbor: University Microfilms, 1974. 74-8722.

336. Tolson, John J. *Airmobility 1961-1971.* [Vietnam Studies]. Washington: Department of the Army, 1973.

337. Trewhitt, Henry L. *McNamara; His Ordeal in the Pentagon.* New York: Harper & Row, 1971.

338. Truman, Harry S. *Memoirs; Volume I, Year of Decisions; Volume II, Years of Trial and Hope.* Garden City: Doubleday, 1955-1956.

339. Ulmer, S. Sidney. *Military Justice and The Right To Counsel.* Lexington: University Press of Kentucky, 1970.

340. U.S. Army. *The Army's Master Program for the Modern Volunteer Army; A Program for Professionals.* n.p., n.d.

341. U.S. Army Materiel Command, Historical Office. *Arsenal For The Brave: A History of the United States Army Materiel Command 1962-1968.* Washington: U.S. Army Materiel Command Historical Office, 1969.

342. U.S. Army Medical Service. *Blood Program in World War II.* Washington: Department of the Army, Office of the Surgeon General, 1964.

343. U.S. Army Medical Service Graduate School. *Recent Advances in Medicine and Surgery; Based on Professional Medical Experiences in Japan and Korea 1950-1953.* Washington: Walter Reed Army Medical Center, 1954.

345. U.S. Army, Rock Island Arsenal, Historical Branch. *U.S. Army Rock Island Arsenal; A History of Rock Island Arsenal From Earliest Times to 1954;* plus Supplement *A Snyopsis of Events on Rock Island From 1954 to 1965.* Rock Island, Illinois: Historical Office, Rock Island Arsenal, 1965.

346. U.S. Army Seventh Army. *History of Seventh U.S. Army Support Command.* Mannheim Germany: U.S. Army Seventh Army Support Command, 1958.

347. U.S. Army, Watervliet Arsenal. *A History of Watervliet Arsenal 1813-1968.* Watervliet, New York: U.S. Army, Watervliet Arsenal, 1969.

348. U.S. Congress, 79th, Senate, 1st. Session, S. 1358. *Hearings on S. 1358; Demobilization of the Armed Forces.* Washington: G.P.O., 1945.

349. U.S. Congress, 82d Senate, 1st Sesstion, Committee on Armed Services and the Committee on Foreign Relations. *Hearings-Military Situation in the Far East.* Washington: G.P.O., 1951.

350. U.S. Department of the Army. *Army Historical Program, FY 1974.* Washington: Department of the Army, 1973.

351. U.S. Department of the Army. *Guerrilla Warfare and Special Forces Operations.* Washington: G.P.O., 1958.

352. U.S. Department of the Army, Office of the Adjutant General. *Operations Report—Lessons Learned '66-67—"Observations of a Brigade Commander."* Washington: Department of the Army, 1969.

353. U.S. Department of the Army. *Report on the Reorganization of the Department of the Army* (December 1961). Washington: Department of the Army, 1961.

354. U.S. Department of the Army. *Study of the Functions; Organization and Procedures of the Department of the Army (OSD Project 80—Army).* Washington: Department of the Army, 1961.

355. U.S. Department of Defense. *United States Vietnam Relations, 1945-1967; Study Proposed by the Department of Defense* [Vietnam Task Force, Leslie H. Gelb, chairman]. Washington: G.P.O., 1971.

356. U.S. European Command, Historical Division. *Occupation Forces in Europe Series*. Frankfurt-am-Main, 1947.

357. Vance, Samuel. *The Courageous and The Proud*. New York: Norton, 1970.

358. Vetter, Hal. *Mutiny on Koje Island*. Rutland, Vermont: Charles E. Tuttle, 1965.

359. Walton, George H. *The Tarnished Shield; A Report on Today's Army*. New York: Dodd, Mead, 1973.

360. Walton, Richard J. *Cold War and Counterrevolution; The Foreign Policy of John F. Kennedy*. New York: Viking, 1972.

361. Ward, Orlando. *Korea, 1950*. Washington: Department of the Army, 1952.

362. Watanabe, Akio. *The Okinawa Problem: A Chapter in Japan-U.S. Relations*. Melbourne: Melbourne University Press, 1970.

363. Waterhouse, Larry G. and Mariann G. Wizard. *Turning the Guns Around; Notes on the G.I. Movement*. New York: Praeger, 1971.

364. Watson, Mark S. "Two Years of Unification." *Military Affairs*, XIII, Winter 1949, 193-194.

365. Weaver, James D. *The Commander in Chief, Civilian Supremacy, Command and Control; Civil-Military Relations in the Eisenhower Presidency, 1972*. Ann Arbor: University Microfilms, 1973.

366. Weinert, Richard P. *A History of Army Aviation 1950-1962, Phase 1: 1950-1954*. Fort Monroe, Virginia: U.S. Continental Army Command Historical Office, 1971.

367. Weisberg, Barry. *Ecocide in Indochina; The Ecology of War*. San Francisco: Canfield Press, 1970.

368. Weller, Jac. *Fire and Movement: Bargain-Basement Warfare in the Far East*. New York: Thomas Y. Crowell, 1967.

369. Wermuth, Anthony L. "High on the ROAD: Some Observations on the Role of the Brigade." *Army*. XIV, November 1963, 39-43.

370. Westmoreland, William C. *Report on Operations in South Vietnam January 1964-June 1968*; with U. S. G. Sharp. *Report on the War in Vietnam* (as of 30 June 1968). Washington: G.P.O., 1968.

371. Westover, John G. *Combat Support in Korea*. Washington: Combat Forces Press, 1955.

372. Whan, Vorin E., ed. *A Soldier Speaks: Public Papers and Speeches of General of the Army Douglas MacArthur*. New York: Frederick A. Praeger, 1965.

373. White, William L. *Back Down The Ridge*. New York: Harcourt Brace, 1953.

374. White, William Lindsay. *The Captives of Korea; An Unofficial White Paper on the Treatment of War Prisoners; Our Treatment of Theirs; Their Treatment of Ours*. New York: Scribners, 1957.

375. Whiteside, Thomas. *The Withering Rain: America's Herbicidal Folly*. New York: Dutton, 1971.

376. Wilkins, Thurman S. "The Postwar Military School System." *Military Affairs*, X, Summer 1946, 42-49.

377. Williams, Fenton A. *Just Before The Dawn; A Doctor's Experiences in Vietnam*. New York: Exposition, 1971.

378. Willoughby, Charles A. and John Chamberlain. *MacArthur 1941-1951*. New York: McGraw-Hill, 1954.

379. Winfree, Robert T. "ROAD Can Be Geared to the Needs of the Nuclear Battlefield." *Army,* XII, December 1961, 62-63.
380. Wolf, Charlotte. *Garrison Community: A Study of an Overseas Military Community.* Westport, Connecticut: Greenwood, 1969.
381. Wool, Harold, *The Military Specialist: Skilled Manpower for the Armed Forces.* Baltimore: Johns Hopkins Press, 1968.
382. Worley, Marvin L. *A Digest of New Developments in Army Weapons, Tactics, Organization and Equipment.* Harrisburg: Military Service Publishing Co., 1958.
383. Yale, Wesley W., I.D. White and Hasso E. van Manteuffel. *Alternative To Armageddon; The Peace Potential of Lightning War.* New Brunswick: Rutgers University Press, 1970.
384. Yarmolinsky, Adam. *The Military Establishment: Its Impacts on American Society.* New York: Harper & Row, 1971.
385. Heiser, Joseph. *Logistic Support* [Vietnam Studies] Washington: Department of the Army, 1974.
386. Ploger, Robert R. *U.S. Army Engineers 1965-1970* [Vietnam Studies] Washington: Department of the Army, 1974.
387. Hay, John H. Jr. *Tactical and Materiel Innovations* [Vietnam Studies] Washington: Department of the Army, 1974.
388. Kelly, Francis J. *U.S. Army Special Forces 1961-1971* [Vietnam Studies] Washington: Department of the Army, 1973.
389. Fulton, William B. *Riverine Operations 1966-1969* [Vietnam Studies] Washington: Department of the Army, 1973.
390. Rienzi, Thomas M. *Communications-Electronics 1962-1970* [Vietnam Studies] Washington: Department of the Army, 1972.

XVIII

THE NAVY 1941-1973

Dean C. Allard

The large body of literature on World War II, originated by participants, scholars, and popular writers, contrasts with the more limited coverage available for the postwar period. For the latter era, greater dependence needs to be placed on periodical articles and specialized works.

REFERENCE WORKS. Smith's multivolume *World War II Naval Bibliography* (307) is the most comprehensive work in its field. Two selective and overall bibliographies, the Naval History Division's *United States Naval History* (365) and Albion's *Naval and Maritime History* (5), include the 1941-1973 period. The Air University's *Index to Military Periodicals* (4) and Schultz's more recent *Bibliography of Naval and Maritime History* (292) cover the postwar periodical literature. Specialized bibliographies on the Marine Corps and Coast Guard are Hilliard's and Bivins's *Annotated Reading List* (134), Moran's *Creating a Legend* (226), and Strobridge's *United States Coast Guard Annotated Bibliography* (323). Ziegler's *World War II: Books in English* (392) and Blanchard's *Korean War Bibliography* (27) cover military as well as nonmilitary aspects.

Unpublished or processed materials are identified in Millett and Cooling, *Doctoral Dissertations in Military Affairs* (223), which is updated annually in *Military Affairs* (221). The numerous oral histories of senior naval officials, notably those undertaken by John T. Mason at Columbia University and the U.S. Naval Institute, are identified in Mason and Starr, *The Oral History Collection of Columbia University* (202), and in an article by Mason (203). Other special materials are described in the Naval History Division's *World War II Histories and Historical Reports* (362), Dornbusch's *Unit Histories of World War II* (81), and Frank's *Marine Corps Oral History Collection Catalog* (101a).

The large volume of naval archival and manuscript resources in the Washington area is summarized in Allard and Bern, *U.S. Naval History Sources* (7), the Naval Historical Foundation's *Manuscript Collection: A Catalog* (237), and Wood's *Marine Corps Personal Papers Collection Catalog* (388a). For such holdings outside the national capital region, see *The National Union Catalog of Manuscript Collections* (234) and Hamer's *Guide to Archives and Manuscripts in the United States* (120).

Biographical accounts of senior officers appear in such standard sources as the *Supplements* to the *Dictionary of American Biography, Who's Who in America, National Cyclopedia of American Biography,* and *Current Biography.* More popular coverage of other naval personnel appears in Schuon's *U.S. Navy Biographical Dictionary* (293) and Tunney's *Biographical Dictionary of World War II* (335). Information regarding exceptional naval and Marine heroes is in the Senate Committee on Veterans' Affairs, *Medal of Honor Winners, 1863-1973* (348). Standard registers of Naval (340), Marine (353), and Coast Guard officers (343) appeared throughout the 1941-1973 period. Brief, mimeographed biographies for recent senior naval officers are available from the Navy's Office of Information.

Numerous publication give details on ship and airctaft characteristics. *Jane's Fighting Ships* (158), *Jane's All the World's Aircraft* (157), *Ships' Data* (340a), and *The Ships and Aircraft of the U.S. Fleet* (278), published periodically during this period, are standard sources. More specialized treatment appears in such sources as Lenton's *Navies of the Second World War* (186), Silverstone's *U.S. Warships in World War II* (302), and *United States Naval Aircraft Since 1911* by Swanborough and Bowers (325). Ship characteristics and brief histories of individual ships are in the Naval History Division's *Dictionary of American Naval Fighting Ships* (359).

Chronologies represent another basic reference. An overall chronicle of Allied and Axis naval operations in World War II is by Rohwer and Hummelchen (270). U.S. operations are covered in the Naval History Division's *United States Naval Chronology, World War II* (364) and in volume two of the Marine Corps History Division's *Chronology of United States Marine Corps* (354). For postwar events, readers can consult volumes three and four of the Marine Corps *Chronology* (354), Cooney's *Chronology of the U.S. Navy, 1775-1965* (63), and the Naval Institute's *Naval and Maritime Chronology, 1961-1971* (235). The latter work is updated in the annual *Naval Review* (238). An excellent specialized chronology of naval aviation, including valuable statistical appendices, is the official *United States Naval Aviation, 1910-1970* (351).

Several glossaries define the formidable array of naval abbreviations, acronyms, and code words. Two publications of the Naval History Division, *Glossary of U.S. Naval Code Words* (361) and *Glossary of U.S. Naval Abbreviations* (360), relate to the World War II period. For the postwar era, see Wedertz's *Dictionary of Naval Abbreviations* (380), and *Naval Terms Dictionary* (243) compiled by Noel and Beach.

PERIODICALS. There is no journal devoted exclusively to naval history. As an aspect of military history, contributions appear in the basic American journal, *Military Affairs* (221). Insofar as the field is part of maritime history, it is covered in *American Neptune* (8) and the British *Mariner's Mirror* (201). Some historical articles appear in general naval periodicals, including *U.S. Naval Institute Proceedings* (367), *[U.S.] Naval Review* (238), *Naval War College Review* (239), *Marine Corps Gazette* (200), *Shipmate* (300), and *Naval Aviation News* (236). The *Pacific Historical Review* (247) carries more naval articles than most general historical journals.

I. 1941-1945

GENERAL NAVAL ACCOUNTS OF WORLD WAR II. Samuel Eliot Morison's 15-volume *History of United States Naval Operations in World War II* (227) and his one-volume *The Two Ocean War* (229) are the standard operational accounts. These volumes, initiated while Morison served in the Navy during World War II, were completed under a contractual arrangement with the Naval History Division. The five-volume official *History of U.S. Marine Corps Operations in World War II* (355) is a counterpart to the Morison volumes. Overall coverage of the Coast Guard is in Willoughby's *The U. S. Coast Guard in World War II* (384).

Other full-scale works are Furer's *Administration of the Navy Department in World War II* (105); the *Annual Reports* of the Secretary of the Navy (369); Fleet Admiral King's memoirs (172) and his reports as Commander in Chief, U.S. Fleet (17); two extensive anthologies of writings on naval and Marine aspects of the conflict, edited by Stanley E. Smith (308) (309); and the five-volume *Battle Report* (165) by Walter Karig and others.

U.S. naval historians are fortunate to have extensive writings in English on allied and enemy navies. Through the use of these volumes, it is possible to appreciate the interaction of the United States maritime forces with both friend and foe. Two histories containing an overview of all navies are Creswell's *Sea Warfare* (66) and Potter's and Nimitz's *The Great Sea War* (255). A distinguished history of the U.S. Navy's chief ally is Stephen W. Roskill's official four-volume *The War at Sea* (275) and his one-volume *White Ensign* (276). Kemp's bibliographic survey of the Royal Navy (167) identifies many other titles. The roles of Commonwealth navies are chronicled by Gill (111, 111a), Waters (379), Schull (291), and Turner and others (336). One-volume histories of the French and Italian Navies in World War II are by Auphan and Mordal (15) and Bragadin (32). Mitchell's overall history of Russian seapower (224) includes World War II.

As for America's maritime enemies, a standard account of the German Navy has been written by Friedrich Ruge (280). A less satisfactory history of the Japanese Navy is Andrieu d'Albas's (11), which may be supplemented by O'Connor's anthology of articles by Japanese personnel (245). Valuable special materials are the numerous processed volumes, known as *Japanese Monographs* (159), and the extensive *Record* of the International Military Tribunal for the Far East (154). Potter's *Yamamoto* (256) is basic for Japan's preeminent naval leader.

Strategic Policy During World War II: Morison's short study, *Strategy and Compromise* (228), is a concise appreciation. The memoirs of Fleet Admirals Leahy (181) and King (172), an article by Admiral Spruance (313), and an assessment by Puleston (258) also are significant. The best volume presently available on the Commander of the Pacific Ocean area is Hoyt's *Nimitz and His Admirals* (147). Secretary of the Navy Forrestal is assessed by Albion and Connery (6) and in a more controversial study by Rogow (268). Documentary sources include the *Forrestal Diaries* (100) and the World War II volumes of *The Foreign Relations of the United States* (350). The latter series includes separate volumes for the major international conferences at which Allied naval officers developed the war's basic strategy in cooperation with political and military leaders. A specialized documentary title is Volume II of *The Papers of Adlai E. Stevenson* (318). Stevenson served as a special assistant to the Secretary of the Navy.

Studies by Joint Chiefs of Staff historians throw light upon U.S. Naval strategic thinking. Kittredge's *Global Strategy* (174) and Hayes' detailed assessment of Pacific strategy (126) deserve particular notice. Craven's and Cate's official history of the Army Air Force (65) and the Army's historical volumes provide some insight into the Navy's role. In the latter series, pertinent volumes are by Matloff and Snell (205), Matloff (204), Conn and Fairchild (60), Conn, Engleman, and Fairchild (59), Leigton and Coakley (185), Coakley and Leighton (56), and Morton (230).

Weigley's recent *American Way of War* (381) interprets overall military and naval strategic thinking. Emerson's assessment of Franklin D. Roosevelt as commander in chief (89) is another overview of interest to naval historians.

OVERALL SOURCES ON ATLANTIC OPERATIONS IN WORLD WAR II. U.S. naval operations in this theatre included antisubmarine campaigns in the North Atlantic, Caribbean, and South Atlantic regions; other operations to control and use the critical maritime lines of supply; and amphibious assaults in North Africa, Southern Europe, and Normandy. Morison's history (227) provides the only overview of these diverse activities. A more personal summary is in Admiral King's memoirs (172). Due to the combined nature of most Atlantic campaigns, Roskill's history of the Royal Navy (275) also is basic. For the enemy's side, Ruge's overall account (280) is deepened by the memoirs of Admiral Doenitz (78), architect of the German U-boat campaign and later Germany's overall naval commander.

Accounts of Atlantic Campaigns. Aside from Morison's accounts, the critical campaign to control the Atlantic is covered in a number of specialized works. Royal E. Ingersoll, the Atlantic Fleet commander, prepared an oral history as part of the Columbia University series (202). Lewis's *Fight For the Sea* (187) places Atlantic operations in the context of pre- and postwar Atlantic strategy. Farago's *Tenth Fleet* (95) primarily recounts the direction of antisubmarine operations by senior naval officials in Washington, but needs to be used critically. Operations by U.S. destroyers and Coast Guard units are covered by Roscoe (274), Abbazia (1), and Willoughby (384), while the antisubmarine scientific measures developed by the U.S. and the Allies are assessed by Sternhell and Thorndike (317) and Baxter (20). Two general accounts of the U.S. merchant marine and merchant shipbuilding, by Land (177) and Lane (178), are related to the German assault on Allied mercantile tonnage. Personnel accounts are by Taylor (328), Schofield (288), Lederer (183), and Doris (81a). Also useful are Bunker's study of Liberty Ships (38) and Carse's general history of the U.S. Merchant Marine (49). An incisive article by a German scholar is Rohwer's "The U-Boat War Against the Allied Supply Lines" (271). Rohwer also prepared an indispensable statistical summary (269) indicating the results of each torpedo and gunfire attack by U-boats.

A number of sources provide details on specific operations. Daniel

Gallery, commander of one of the carrier hunter-killer forces that achieved notable success against the U-boats, wrote *Twenty-Million Tons Under the Sea* (108). An account of the ordeal of North Atlantic convoys in the winter of 1942-1943 was written by Waters (378), a Coast Guard officer. The Allied convoys to North Russia, including the famous PQ-17, are the subject of accounts by Campbell and Macintyre (46) and Carse (48), among others. A more controversial volume covering PQ-17 is David Irving's (155). The ordeal of one Army convoy of small craft is depicted in Gibson's study of Convoy NY-119 (110). McCann's overall work on U.S.-Brazilian operations (207) includes data on the U.S. South Atlantic Force whose mission was to control the South Atlantic narrows.

Morison's depiction of offensive amphibious operations against the European and North African land masses can be supplemented by Roskill's history of the Royal Navy (275) and the official accounts of the U.S. Army (371). A perceptive history of amphibious operations, written by a British officer, is Brigadier Fergusson's *Watery Maze* (97). The diary of Harry Butcher (41), General Eisenhower's naval aide, provides insight into the naval aspects of Ike's thinking. The *Mighty Endeavor*, by MacDonald (198), includes coverage of maritime as well as U.S. ground and air forces in the European theatre. One aspect of the activities of the Navy's senior commander in Europe, Admiral Harold G. Stark, is assessed in Simpson's dissertation on U.S.-French naval relations (303).

In the absence of a published biography of Admiral H. Kent Hewitt, the senior U.S. Naval Commander in the landings at Northern Africa, Sicily, Italy, and Southern France, historians may consult his series of articles (129a, 129b, 129c) and the Admiral's oral history (202). The operations of U.S. PT boats in the Mediterranean are recounted by Bulkley (37). Blumenson's *The Gamble That Failed* (28) covers the controversial Anzio landing. A damaging German air attack on U.S. shipping at Bari, Italy, is described by Infield (152).

In the case of the Normandy landings, the standard accounts by Morison (227) and Roskill (275) are accompanied by an article by Elsey (88), a popular volume by Ryan (283), and Harrison's study (124) in the Army's historical series. Unpublished oral histories exist for two senior U.S. Naval commander, Alan G. Kirk and J. L. Hall (202).

An overview of naval air operations in the Atlantic theatre is included in Buchanan's work (34). One famous episode, the loss of Joseph P. Kennedy, Jr., during a special mission against German rocket installations in Europe, is recounted by Searls (294) and Olsen (246).

Carter and Duvall (51) trace the contributions of naval logistics ships and salvage units operating in the Atlantic. Also pertinent is a Bureau of Ships history (341) of the Navy's Salvage Service.

GENERAL ACCOUNTS OF PACIFIC OPERATIONS. Overviews of the Pacific war appear in Morison's multivolume and single volume accounts (227) (229) and the other general works listed above. Additional reference can be made to the excellent reports of the U.S. Strategic Bombing Survey (374), assessing the effect of both naval and air actions on the Japanese, and two volumes containing detailed assessments of Japanese ship losses (151) (161). The memoirs of Leahy (181) and King (172) and Hoyt's *Nimitz* (148) are useful.

Nimitz's counterpart as a unified commander in the Southwest Pacific Area was Douglas MacArthur. Some coverage of the naval operations in that theatre is included in MacArthur's reports (324) and in the extensive official and unofficial literature on this leader. The overall naval commander in the Southwest Pacific during 1943-1945, Thomas C. Kinkaid, prepared an oral history (202). Daniel E. Barbey, another naval officer in the Southwest Pacific, published his reminiscences (18).

Among the major operational commanders in Nimitz's Pacific Ocean Area who wrote memoirs were the colorful William F. Halsey (119); Charles Lockwood, the Pacific submarine commander (189); the carrier task force commanders Frederick Sherman (297) and Joseph J. Clark (55); and two commanding officers of aircraft carriers, Cato D. Glover (113) and Rufus Zogbaum (393). Two key Marine commanders, Generals Holland M. Smith and A. A. Vandergrift (306) (375), also prepared reminiscences.

Numerous other senior officers have recorded their recollections in unpublished oral histories (202) (203). General reminiscences by junior officers and enlisted personnel serving in the Pacific include titles by Fahey (91), Lee (184), and Dorris (81a).

In addition to Hoyt's study of Nimitz, biographical accounts for Pacific commanders are included in studies by Buell and Forrestal of the diffident but highly successful Raymond A. Spruance (36), 101); Taylor's book on Marc A. Mitscher (329); Dyer's comprehensive work on Kelly Turner (86); and Murphy's biography of Admiral Callaghan (232).

A number of sources summarize specific categories of naval warfare. Air operations are assessed in Buchanan's *Naval Air War* (34), Reynolds' *Fast Carriers* (262), and Roscoe's *On the Sea and in the Skies* (272). More specialized titles include Stafford's history of carrier *Enterprise* (314), Sims's account of naval and marine air aces (304, Sherrod's history of Marine aviation (298), and a volume by Winton (387) relating to the British carrier force operating with the U.S. Navy after 1944. Bryan's diary (33) as a junior officer serving in carriers is published. Operational and other details of U.S. carriers appear in works by Pawlowski (249), MacDonald (199), and Polmar (252).

The equally successful operations of U.S. submarines against Japanese lines of communication are recounted by Charles Lockwood, the commander of this force (190). A standard title is Roscoe's *United States Submarine Operations in World War II* (274). Additional general accounts are authored by Holmes (138), Stafford (315), and Beach (22). Among specialized sources are the Naval History Division's edition of *United States Submarine Losses* (366), Dissette and Adamson's account of submarine support of the Philippine Guerrilla movement (77), and reminiscences by two petty officers, Sterling (316) and McDonald (214).

Two key titles for amphibious operations are Iseley and Crowl's *U.S. Marines and Amphibious War* (156) and Dyer's study of Admiral Turner (86). Mining operations are recounted in writings by Lott (196), Duncan (84), Johnson and Katcher (160), and Meacham (217).

Other categories of naval warfare also are covered in the literature. The operations of destroyers in surface engagements, as carrier task force escorts, and in anti-submarine warfare are described in detail by Roscoe (273). The indispensable logistical support ships are chronicled by Carter (50). Memoirs by Houston (142), a reserve officer who served in small amphibious units, are available. A standard source on PT operations is Bulkley's *At Close Quarters* (37). Among the accounts of underwater demolition teams are those of Fane and Moore (93) and the reminiscences of Higgins (133). Karneke has recorded his experience as a Navy diver (166).

Accounts of Pacific Campaigns. The dramatic events of the first six months of the Pacific War are recounted by Morison (227) and Toland (332). Extensive source material on the Pearl Harbor attack appears in the 40 volumes of documents and testimony published by the Congressional committee of inquiry (346). Other titles bearing on the complex issue of responsibility for Pearl Harbor include Wohlstetter's judicious *Pearl Harbor: Warning and Decision* (388). More controversial works are the account of the senior naval commander on the scene, *Admiral Kimmel's Story* (170); the reminiscences of Admiral Richardson (265), who was Kimmel's predecessor; Admiral Theobold's *Final Secret of Pearl Harbor* (330); Admiral Zacharias' *Secret Missions* (391); and Farago's *The Broken Seal* (94). Walter Lord's *Day of Infamy* (192) is a dramatic account of the attack. Wallin's *Pearl Harbor* (376) is especially useful for the author's post-attack achievements as chief salvage officer.

Naval events in the Asiatic Defense Campaign, in which Allied forces fought a gradual retreat to Australia, are described in an unpublished narrative (125) and oral history (202) by Thomas C. Hart, the Asiatic Fleet commander. Also pertinent are the Belotes's *Corregidor* (23), Thomas's study of the Battle of Java Sea (331), Underbrink's *Destination Corregidor* (337), Tolley's *Cruise of the Lanikai* (333), and Winslow's account of USS *Houston* (386).

For the Japanese capture of Wake Island, readers may balance the earlier account of Devereux (76), the Marine commander, with the volume by Cunningham (68), the senior officer on the island.

Japanese submarine operations off the West Coast of the United States, early in the war, are discussed by Reynolds (263). One of the earliest offensive operations by U.S. forces, the 1942 Halsey-Doolittle raid on Tokyo, is assessed by Merrill (219) and Glines (122).

The Battle of the Coral Sea, the first of the classic carrier task force duels of the war, has been analyzed by the Naval War College (368). Hoehling (137) treats *Lexington's* loss at Coral Sea.

The Battle of Midway, which closed the initial phases of the Pacific conflict by checking Japanese expansion, is possibly the most famous naval engagement of the war. Historical assessments include accounts by Lord (193), Tuleja (334), and Hough (141). A Naval War College tactical analysis also is available for this action (368). One U.S. Naval participant, William W. Smith, prepared a volume (310) that can be read in conjunction with an account prepared by two Japanese officers, Fuchida and Okumiya (103).

Starting with the Guadalcanal landings of August 1942, the bitterly contested Solomon's campaign initiated the American Pacific offensive. Overviews of the strategic background and the numerous engagements in the Solomons appear in Dyer's study of Turner (86), Griffith's *Battle for Guadalcanal* (117), and a volume by Leckie (182), in addition to the standard histories by Morison (227), the Marine Corps official historians

(355), and the Vandegrift (375) and Halsey memoirs (119). Appropriate volumes in the official U.S. Army historical series (371) and the *Army Air Forces in World War II* (65) show the interaction of the Navy with the non-sea services. More specialized titles on naval actions include analyses of the Japanese tactical victory at the Battle of Savo Island by the Naval War College (368) and of the U.S. success at the Battle of Cape Esperance by Cook (62). The role of naval and Marine aviators at Guadalcanal is covered by Miller (222). Accounts of two famous combat commanders— one a naval officer and the other a Marine—are presented in Jones's book on Arleigh "31-Knot" Burke (162) and Davis's study of Lewis B. "Chesty" Puller (72). One celebrated incident of the South Pacific campaign, the loss of John F. Kennedy's PT-109, is recounted by Donovan (79). Davis has a detailed account of the joint Navy-Army Air Force operation in the South Pacific resulting in the death of Admiral Yamamoto (71).

The long series of amphibious assaults in the Gilberts, Marshalls, Marianas, Philippines, Iwo Jima, and Okinawa, during 1943-1945, brought the United States to the doorway of the Japanese home islands. The history of these operations is developed in the Morison series (227), the official histories of the Marines (355), Army (371), and Army Air Force (65), and in the biographies or autobiographies of Admirals Nimitz (148), Halsey (119), Spruance (36, 101) and Turner (86), and General Holland M. Smith (306).

There also are volumes covering specific engagements. The Tarawa operation is recounted by Sherrod (299). Two major naval fleet actions, the Battle of the Philippine Sea in May 1944 and the Battle of Leyte Gulf in October 1944, are the subjects of several studies. In the case of the Philippine Sea engagement, Lockwood's volume (191) is a full account. It may be supplemented by Admiral Clark's reminiscences (55) and Reynolds' study of the fast carriers (262). Leyte Gulf has been treated from the U.S. point of view by a Naval War College Tactical Analysis (368), Woodward (389), Falk (92), and Hoyt (147), while Field has contributed *The Japanese at Leyte Gulf* (98).

Admiral Halsey's experiences with western Pacific typhoons, are described by Adamson and Kosco (3). Other specialized titles bearing on the Pacific offensive of 1943-1945 are Newcomb's *Iwo Jima* (242) and the Belotes's assessment of the battle of Okinawa (24). A dramatic volume on one of the many U.S. Naval ships that faced the Kamkikaze corps off Okinawa, USS *Aaron Ward*, is Lott's *Brave Ship, Brave Men* (195). A Japanese history of the Kamikaze was prepared by Inoguchi and Nakajima (153). Newcomb (241) and Helm (129) have somewhat sensational accounts of the sinking of cruiser *Indianapolis* late in the war.

A joint article by Bauer and Coox (19) assesses U.S. plans and Japanese preparations for the unexecuted invasion of the Japanese home islands.

Aside from operations in the major Pacific regions, U.S. Naval forces were committed to other theatres. Naval activities in the North Pacific region, including the Aleutians and Alaska, are included in Garfield's *The Thousand Mile War* (109). In Asia, a unique naval command, Naval Group China, trained Chinese guerrillas and maintained an extensive intelligence net. The commander of that force, Milton E. Miles, wrote *A Different Kind of War* (220).

Other Aspects of World War II. A detailed assessment of the administrative history of Navy Department offices in Washington has been written by Julius A. Furer (105). This may be supplemented by the numerous unpublished administrative histories of naval organizations (370) and the study of Forrestal by Albion and Connery (6). Specialized organizational histories cover the Bureau of Ordnance (279), the Bureau of Medicine and Surgery (338), the Bureau of Yards and Docks (342), the Chaplain Corps (82), and the Navy's Office of Information (175). A useful reminiscence by a Navy surgeon has been written by Pugh (257).

Furer's volume also covers procurement and other national logistical programs of the Navy Department. Additional accounts of these aspects include Connery's *The Navy and Industrial Mobilization* (61), Ballantine's *U.S. Naval Logistics in World War II* (17), and the memoirs of Lewis L. Strauss (322). Shipbuilding programs are covered by Fassett (96) and in the *Historical Transactions* of the Society of Naval Architects and Marine Engineers (311). Hunsaker prepared a short biography (150) of Admiral Cochrane, Chief of the Bureau of Ships during World War II. The World War II activities of the Navy Yard at Mare Island are included in a history by Lott (194).

Some coverage of naval research and development programs appears in the Office of Scientific Research and Development historical volumes by Stewart (319), Boyce (31), and Burchard (39), as well as in Baxter's *Scientists Against Time* (20). The best general account from the Navy's perspective appears is an unpublished study sponsored by the Office of Naval Research (251). In the area of ordnance, there are volumes by Rowland and Boyd (279), Christman (53), and Peck (250). Advances in radar and other aspects of electronics are covered by Howeth (146), Schroeder (290), and Page (248). Taylor's account of the Naval Research Laboratory (327) includes the World War II years. Admiral Bowen, a prominent scientific leader, has published his reminiscences (30). A useful thesis on ship battle damage is Ross's "The Best Way to Destroy a Ship" (277).

Intelligence activities are among the least documented aspects of the war. An unpublished administrative history of the Office of Naval Intelligence (370) provides essential background. Among the volumes on communications intelligence, Kahn's (164) and Farago's (94) are best known. A participant's account of British naval intelligence, McLachlan's *Room 39* (216), throws some light on U.S.-British intelligence cooperation in the Atlantic. Admiral Zacharias's *Secret Missions* (391) and a biography of that officer by Wilhelm (383a) discuss intelligence and psychological warfare programs in which Zacharias participated.

The roles of black personnel in the Navy is discussed by Nelson (240) and in a more specialized account by Purdon (259). For the role of women in the Navy, there is a useful memoir by Joy Bright Hancock (123).

The Navy's civil government in the Central Pacific region is recounted in in volume I of Richard's study of the Trust Territory (264). Gray covers naval government in Samoa (115), which was outside the Trust Territory.

Two unusual reminiscences by naval personnel assigned to the White House during World War II are by Rigdon (267) and McIntire (215), the president's physician.

II. 1945-1973

GENERAL ACCOUNTS OF POSTWAR NAVAL EVENTS. In contrast to the dramatic World War II years, there are no overall accounts of U.S. naval history covering this period. However, *Annual Reports of the Secretary of the Navy* (369) were submitted through 1968. Extensive information is contained in printed government documents, and notably those resulting from the Navy's contacts with the House and Senate Armed Services Committees. Further, there are general volumes for the Korean War, including accounts by Field (99), Cagle and Manson (43) and Karig (165). Marine operations are covered in detail in an official five-volume *History of U.S. Marine Corps Operations in Korea* (358). Official histories are under preparation by the Navy and Marine historical divisions for the Vietnam conflict, but these volumes have not appeared as of 1974.

Postwar Navy to the Outbreak of the Korean War: A key source for naval strategic thinking is Forrestal's diary as secretary of the navy and (after 1947) first secretary of defense (100). Leahy's memoirs (181) and those of Cato Glover (113), as well as the oral histories of a number of other senior naval officers (202) (203), also are useful. Davis's *Post-War Defense Policy and the U.S. Navy* (75) covers a specialized aspect. Hoare's essay on Truman as commander in chief (135) provides useful background. Weigley's overall study of U.S. military thinking (381) is pertinent to this era.

Postwar Navy roles in the Far East and in European waters are reflected in *The Foreign Relations of the United States* (350). A discussion of the Marine presence in China appears in volume V of the Corps history of World War II (355). The little-known trials of lesser Japanese war criminals, conducted by the Navy, are covered by Erickson (90).

The perceived Soviet threat in the Mediterranean, and U.S. Navy reactions, are documented in Forrestal's diary (100) and a special work by Xydis on Greece (390). U.S. negotiations with Spain for naval and air bases in the Mediterranean region, extending through the early 1950s, are recounted by Lowi (197).

Technological and scientific developments involving the Navy in the immediate post-war period are discussed in the reminiscences of Admiral Bowen (30), the first chief of Naval Research; Lasby's study of the role of former German scientists (180); an article by Hall on early naval research in satellites (118); and a comprehensive history of the nuclear submarine program by Hewlett and Duncan (132). Volumes by Pawlowski (249), MacDonald (198), and Polmar (252) cover post-World War II aircraft carriers.

The history of unification, including the 1949 debate on the Air Force's B-36 bomber versus the Navy carriers, and other events of strategic significance, are covered in writings by Hammond (121, 122), Ries (266), Caraley (47), and Schilling and others (286). A key source is the B-36 hearings of the House Armed Services Committee (345). Field's Korean War history (99) includes a perceptive chapter on unification. The reminiscences of Admiral Gallery (106) contain his reactions to these events.

Korean War. In addition to the general histories mentioned previously, an important specialized source is the extensive series of *Interim Evaluation Reports* prepared at the Pacific Fleet headquarters during the conflict (373). Two volumes by Heinl (128) and Sheldon (296) cover the significant Inchon landings. Admiral Joy has recounted his experiences as a truce negotiator (163). Writings by Lott (196), Meacham (217), and Karneke (166) cover mine warfare aspects. An overall policy volume by General J. Lawton Collins (58), written from the perspective of the Joint Chiefs of Staff, and Schnabel's study in the Army's official history series (287), include some insight into naval thinking.

International Crises and the Navy. Two unpublished studies by Howe (143) (144) give overall assessments of the operations of the Sixth and Seventh Fleets, with particular reference to their influence on Soviet foreign policy.

Among more specialized accounts, Admiral Glover's memoirs (113) and an unpublished manuscript by Smelser (305) recount the U.S. Navy's neutral role in the Suez Crisis of 1956. Howe's *Multicrises* (145) includes an excellent analysis of the Navy's commitment to the Quemoy-Matsu operation of 1958. Admiral Burke, chief of Naval Operations in 1958, has contributed an essay on the strategic background to the Lebanon landings (40), McClintock, the American ambassador in Lebanon, describes the operation (210), and a separate monograph covers Marine operations in Lebanon (356). General background for the 1953-1961 period is provided by May's essay on Eisenhower as commander in chief (206).

The 1962 Cuban missile crisis is recalled in an essay by Admiral Anderson, who then was chief of Naval Operations (9). The international law aspects of the Cuban blockade are discussed by Christol and Davis (54). Useful general background on all aspects of the crisis appears in a documentary volume edited by Larson (179) and Abel's account (1a). Of the large volume of literature on the Kennedy family's role in the crisis, Attorney General Robert Kennedy's *Thirteen Days* (169) is of particular note.

Naval and Marine operations in the Dominican Republic during 1965 are discussed by Dare (70). Howe's *Multicrises* (145) includes excellent coverage of naval operations during the Mid-East War of 1967.

The 1967 capture of USS *Pueblo* by North Korea is documented in a Congressional report (344). Among several survivor accounts is one by Bucher (35), the ship's commanding officer. Bucher's actions are evaluated critically by Gallery (107). One overall study is by Armbrister (13).

The forcible Soviet removal of a defector from a Coast Guard cutter, during a 1970 incident off the American coast, is described by Ruksenas (281). McConnell and Kelly (211) assess U.S. naval operations during the Indo-Pakistani War of 1972.

Vietnam Conflict. Despite the absence of overall naval histories of the Vietnam war, a number of special accounts provide insight. The twelve-volume Department of Defense edition of the so-called "Pentagon Papers" is a valuable source on naval and national policy in Southeast Asia from 1945 to 1967 (349). The Pacific Command prepared an overall history of the war to 1968 (372), while Schreadley has a long article (289) summarizing the

Navy's participation in Vietnam from 1950 to 1970. Marine operations are summarized in an anthology, *The Marines in Vietnam* (357) that includes a series of excellent overall articles by Simmons and an annotated bibliography. Lewis Walt, an early Marine commander in Vietnam, prepared an assessment of the conflict (377). The achievements of Coast Guard patrol craft in the Gulf of Thailand are described by Hodgman (136).

Among sources discussing the Navy's role in transporting North Vietnamese refugees to South Vietnam in 1954-1955, at the close of the French-Viet Minh War, are books by Dooley (80) and an official history of the Bureau of Medicine and Surgery (339). An early journalistic account of the naval aspects of the Southeast Asian conflict is Chapelle's "Water War in Viet Nam" (52). The Tonkin Incident of 1964, is documented in Secretary McNamara's testimony to the Senate Foreign Relations Committee (347). Journalistic accounts by Goulden (114) and Windchey (385) also cover this famous episode. An official history of Navy Chaplains in Vietnam, during the 1954-1964 decade, is available (225).

Specialized aspects of naval and Marine operations during the period of direct U.S. participation in the Vietnam War (1965-1973) are recounted in books or articles on carrier and Marine aviation by Cagle (42) and McCutcheon (212); on riverine and amphibious operations by Mumford (231), Swartzrauber (326) and Wells (382); and by Shore (301) and West (383) relating to Marine combat actions. A Naval History Division anthology (363) bears on riverine campaigns. Kreh's popular account of naval reservists (176) includes a section on their experiences in Vietnam. Oberdorfer's *Tet!* (244) covers some of the naval aspects of that famous Viet Cong offensive. Sheehan's journalistic account (295) describes the controversial relief of Lieutenant Commander Arnheiter as commander of a ship operating off Vietnam.

Admiral Hooper (139), the Pacific Service Force commander, assesses operational logistics in Vietnam during 1965-1968. National logistics during the conflict are covered in a comprehensive report by the Joint Logistics Review Board (352). More specialized aspects of naval and Marine logistics are in articles by Collins (57), Hooper (140), Huff (149), Kendall (168), King (173), Merdinger (218), and Soper (312). McClendon (209) handles naval medical aspects.

One important post-hostilities event, the clearing of U.S. mines from the Haiphong area in 1973, is described by Admiral McCauley (208), the commander of the operation. A former U.S. Naval prisoner of war, Rutledge, has published his reminiscences (282).

An ongoing series of monographs by Army commanders includes two titles of interest to naval historians: Fulton's discussion of riverine operations (104) and Dunn's assessment of base construction (85), a program that was under the overall supervision of the U.S. Navy. Nalty's study (233) for the Air Force of the Khe Sanh siege includes naval and Marine aspects.

OTHER ASPECTS OF POST-WORLD WAR II NAVAL HISTORY. The Navy's extensive experience in the Arctic and Antarctic regions are recorded in the *Antarctic Journal* (12), Dufek's account of the Deepfreeze operations (83), Betrand's *Americans in Antarctica* (25), and a National Archives conference on Polar Exploration (102).•A history of the Navy's

Arctic Laboratory at Point Barrow, Alaska, is available (261). The commanders of two submarines that cruised to the North Pole, William R. Anderson (10) and James F. Calvert (45), have accounts.

Some aspects of the Navy's assistance programs to allied navies are covered in Auer's study of Japanese maritime rearmament (14), Blair's assessment of the U.S. military presence in Morocco (26), Moore's history of Navy Chaplains in Vietnam (225), and an account by Croizat, a Marine advisor, of the formation of an independent South Vietnamese Navy (67).

Volumes II and III of Richard's comprehensive account of the Navy's civil administration of the Pacific Trust Territory, prior to 1951, cover an important chapter in the history of civil affairs (264).

The Navy's relations with Congress and the public are covered in part in a dissertation by Craft (64), Davis's *The Admiral's Lobby* (73), and Rappaport's study of the Navy League (260). An article by Stockstill (321) discusses Carl Vinson, a dominant congressional figure in naval affairs during and after World War II.

The Bureau of Medicine and Surgery (339) and the Navy's Chaplain Corps (82) have contributed organizational histories covering portions of the postwar period. The reminiscences of Pugh (257), a Navy surgeon, include the post-war years.

Social historians will be interested in commentaries on the Navy appearing in works by Ackley (2), Calvert (44), and Davis (73). The integration of black personnel in the postwar period is covered in volumes by Stillman (320) and Dalfiume (69). Joy Bright Hancock, who headed the Waves after World War II, published her reminiscences (123). Three additional memoirs by naval personnel with specialized post-war experience are by Bosworth (29), Karneke (166), and Rigdon (267).

In the technological area, Davis (74) presents a theoretical analysis of several innovative projects. The nuclear submarine program through 1959 has been recounted by Hewlett and Duncan (132). Other pertinent titles are by Beach (21), Polmar (253), and Gimpel (111b). Sapolsky conducted a study of the Navy's management of the Polaris missile submarine programs (284), while a popular account of that highly successful project is by Baar and Howard (16). Polmar contributed a volume on the loss of nuclear submarine *Thresher* (254), while the journalist Flora Lewis recounts the Navy's recovery of a nuclear weapon lost by the Air Force off the coast of Spain in 1966 (188). The official history of the Atomic Energy Commission by Hewlett and others (130) (131), and a NASA study of the Vanguard satellite program (116) include some information on Navy roles.

In more recent years, extensive attention has been given to the Soviet naval threat. Series of articles on sea power by John D. Hayes place this subject in its broad, strategic setting (127). Among the many titles relating to the implications of the Soviet Navy for the United States are Eller's *Soviet Sea Challenge* (87), McGwire's *Soviet Naval Developments* (213), Mitchell's *History of Russian and Soviet Sea Power* (224), and Saunders' *The Soviet Navy* (285).

SUGGESTIONS FOR FURTHER RESEARCH. Overall or specialized accounts of the Navy's role in formulating strategy and policy during World War II are an obvious need. Major biographical studies of the many senior naval leaders that are not covered in the existing literature represent another opportunity. Despite the numerous operational histories of World War II, there is a need for more coverage of a number of aspects, including antisubmarine warfare by air and surface units in the Western Atlantic, operations in the Mediterranean, and campaigns in the Southwest Pacific.

Few naval historians have assessed post-World War II fleet operations, which offer numerous research opportunities. For example, the interaction of overseas naval operations and foreign policy, during the first post-war decade, remains to be addressed in detail. Studies of a number of specific international crises would be valuable, as would accounts of selected naval campaigns during the Korean and Vietnam conflicts.

Institutional aspects of the Navy are among the most neglected areas. Profitable work can be done on overall naval policy, the evolution of specific categories of tactics, or postwar fleet construction programs and research and development projects. Other examples are assessments of the training and attitudes of officer and enlisted personnel and the experience of minority groups. Accounts of major fleet commands and shore facilities, or such Navy Department components as the Office of Naval Intelligence, both in the World War II and postwar periods, would be profitable subjects.

The Navy's external relations with Congress, with the urban economies surrounding major naval bases, with industry, the other services, or the Office of the Secretary of Defense, represent examples of another broad research category.

Allard's and Bern's *U.S. Naval History Sources* (7) list several hundred illustrative research topics in naval history.

BIBLIOGRAPHY

1. Abbazia, Patrick. "Mr. Roosevelt's Navy: The Little War of the United States Atlantic Fleet, 1939-1942." Doctoral dissertation, Columbia University, 1972.

1a. Abel, Elie. *The Missile Crisis*. Philadephia: Lippincott, 1966.

2. Ackley, Charles Walton. *The Modern Military in American Society*. Philadelphia: Westminster Press, 1972.

3. Adamson, Hans C. and George F. Kosco. *Halsey's Typhoons*. New York: Crown, 1967.

4. *Air University Library Index to Military Periodicals*. Maxwell Air Force Base, Alabama, 1949-   .

5. Albion, Robert G. *Naval and Maritime History: An Annotated Bibliography*. 4th ed. Mystic Seaport, Connecticut: Marine Historical Association, 1972.

6. Albion, Robert G. and Robert H. Connery. *Forrestal and the Navy*. New York: Columbia University Press, 1962.

7. Allard, Dean C. and Betty Bern, eds. *U.S. Naval History Sources in the Washington Area and Suggested Research Subjects*. Washington: G.P.O., 1970.

8. *American Neptune*. (Peabody Museum of Salem). Salem, Massachusetts, 1941-

9. Anderson, George W., Jr. "The Cuban Crisis." In U.S. Naval Academy, History Department. *Proceedings: Naval History Symposium.* Annapolis: U.S. Naval Academy, 1973.
10. Anderson, William R. and Clay Blair. *Nautilus 90 North.* Cleveland: World, 1959.
11. Andrieu d'Albas, Emmanuel M. *Death of a Navy: Japanese Naval Action in World War II.* New York: Devin-Adair, 1957.
12. *Antarctic Journal of the United States.* (U.S. National Science Foundation). Washington, D.C., 1966-
13. Armbrister, Trevor. *A Matter of Accountability.* New York: Coward-McCann, 1970.
14. Auer, James E. *The Postwar Rearmament of Japanese Maritime Forces, 1945-1971.* New York: Praeger, 1973.
15. Auphan, Paul and Jacques Mordal. *The French Navy in World War II.* Annapolis: U.S. Naval Institute, 1959.
16. Baar, James and William E. Howard. *Polaris!* New York: Harcourt Brace, 1960.
17. Ballantine, Duncan S. *U.S. Naval Logistics in the Second World War.* Princeton: Princeton University Press, 1947.
18. Barbey, Daniel E. *MacArthur's Amphibious Navy: Seventh Amphibious Force Operations, 1943-1945.* Annapolis: U.S. Naval Institute, 1969.
19. Bauer, K. Jack and Alvin C. Coox. "Olympic vs Ketsu-Go," *Marine Corps Gazette,* Aug. 1965, pp. 32-44.
20. Baxter, James Phinney. *Scientists Against Time.* Boston: Little, Brown, 1946.
21. Beach, Edward L. *Around the World Submerged.* New York: Holt, Rinehart and Winston, 1962.
22. Beach, Edward L. *Submarine!* New York: Holt, 1952.
23. Belote, James H. and William M. Belote. *Corregidor: The Saga of a Fortress.* New York: Harper and Row, 1967.
24. Belote, James H. and William M. Belote. *Typhoon of Steel: The Battle of Okinawa.* New York: Harper and Row, 1970.
25. Bertrand, Kenneth J. *Americans in Antarctica, 1775-1948.* New York: American Geographical Society, 1971.
26. Blair, Leon B. *Western Window in the Arab World.* Austin: University of Texas Press, 1970.
27. Blanchard, Carroll H. *Korean War Bibliography and Maps of Korea.* Albany, New York: Korean Conflict Research Foundation, 1964.
28. Blumenson, M. *Anzio: The Gamble That Failed.* Philadelphia: Lippincott, 1963.
29. Bosworth, Allen R. *My Love Affair with the Navy.* New York: Norton, 1969.
30. Bowen, Harold G. *Ships, Machinery and Mossbacks: the Autobiography of a Naval Engineer.* Princeton: Princeton University Press, 1954.
31. Boyce, Joseph C., ed. *New Weapons for Air Warfare.* Boston: Little, Brown, 1947.
32. Bragadin, Marc Antonio. *The Italian Navy in World War II.* Annapolis: U.S. Naval Institute, 1957.

33. Bryan, Joseph. *Aircraft Carrier*. New York: Ballantine, 1954.
34. Buchanan, Albert R., ed. *The Navy's Air War*. New York: Harper, 1946.
35. Bucher, Lloyd M. with Mark Rascovich. *Bucher: My Story*. Garden City: Doubleday, 1970.
36. Buell, Thomas B. *The Quiet Warrior: A Biography of Admiral Raymond A. Spruance*. Boston: Little, Brown, 1974.
37. Bulkley, Robert J. *At Close Quarters: PT Boats in the United States Navy*. Washington: G.P.O., 1962.
38. Bunker, John. *Liberty Ships, the Ugly Ducklings of World War II*. Annapolis: U.S. Naval Institute, 1972.
39. Burchard, John E., ed. *Rockets, Guns, and Targets*. Boston: Little, Brown, 1947.
40. Burke, Arleigh. "The Lebanon Crisis." In U.S. Naval Academy, History Department. *Proceedings: Naval History Symposium*. Annapolis: U.S. Naval Academy, 1973.
41. Butcher, Harry C. *My Three Years with Eisenhower*. New York: Simon and Schuster, 1946.
42. Cagle, Malcolm W. "Task Force 77 in Action Off Vietnam." In *Naval Review, 1972*. Annapolis: U.S. Naval Institute, 1972. pp. 66-109.
43. Cagle, Malcolm W. and Frank A. Manson. *The Sea War in Korea*. Annapolis: U.S. Naval Institute, 1957.
44. Calvert, James F. *The Naval Profession*. New York: McGraw-Hill, 1971.
45. Calvert, James F. *Surface at the Pole: The Extraordinary Voyages of the USS Skate*. New York: McGraw-Hill, 1960.
46. Campbell, Ian and Donald G. Macintyre. *The Kola Run: A Record of Arctic Convoys, 1941-1945*. London: Muller, 1958.
47. Caraley, Demetrios. *The Politics of Military Unification*. New York: Columbia University Press, 1966.
48. Carse, R. *The Long Haul: The United States Merchant Service in World War II*. New York: Norton, 1965.
49. Carse, Robert. *A Cold Corner of Hell*. New York: Doubleday, 1969.
50. Carter, Worrall R. *Beans, Bullets and Black Oil: The Story of Fleet Logistics Afloat in the Pacific During World War II*. Washington: G.P.O., 1953.
51. Carter, Worrall R. and Elmer E. Duvall. *Ships, Salvage, and Sinews of War: The Story of Fleet Logistics Afloat in Atlantic and Mediterranean Waters During World War II*. Washington: G.P.O., 1954.
52. Chapelle, Georgette L. "Water War in Viet Nam," *National Geographic Magazine*, Feb., 1966, pp. 272-96.
53. Christman, Albert B. *Sailors, Scientists, and Rockets: Origins of the Navy Rocket Program and of the Naval Ordnance Test Station, Inyokern*. Washington: G.P.O., 1971.
54. Christol, C. Q. and C. R. Davis. "Maritime Quarantine: The Naval Interdiction of Offensive Weapons and Associated Materiel to Cuba, 1962," *American Journal of International Law*, July 1963, pp. 525-45.
55. Clark, Joseph J. and Clark G. Reynolds. *Carrier Admiral*. New York: McKay, 1967.
56. Coakley, Robert W. and Richard M. Leighton. *Global Logistics and Strategy, 1943-1945*. Washington: G.P.O., 1968.

57. Collins, Frank C., Jr. "Maritime Support of the Campaign in I Corps." In *Naval Review, 1971*. Annapolis: U.S. Naval Institute, 1971, pp. 156-79.

58. Collins, J. Lawton. *War In Peacetime: The History and Lessons of Korea*. Boston: Houghton Mifflin, 1969.

59. Conn, Stetson, Rose C. Engleman, and Byron Fairchild. *Guarding the United States and Its Outposts*. Washington: G.P.O., 1964.

60. Conn, Stetson and Byron Fairchild. *The Framework of Hemispheric Defense*. Washington: G.P.O., 1960.

61. Connery, Robert H. *The Navy and Industrial Mobilization in World War II*. Princeton: Princeton University Press, 1951.

62. Cook, Charles. *The Battle of Cape Esperance: Strategic Encounter at Guadalcanal*. New York: Crowell, 1968.

63. Cooney, David M. *A Chronology of the U.S. Navy: 1775-1965*. New York: Watts, 1965.

64. Craft, James P. "The Role of Congress with Determination of Naval Strategy in Support of United States Foreign Policy, 1956-1966." Doctoral dissertation, University of Pittsburgh, 1969.

65. Craven, Wesley Frank and James Lea Cate, eds. *The Army Air Forces in World War II*. Chicago: University of Chicago Press, 1948-55. 6 vols.

66. Creswell, John. *Sea Warfare, 1939-1945*. Berkeley: University of California Press, 1967.

67. Croizat, Victor J. "Vietnamese Naval Forces: Origin of the Species," *U.S. Naval Institute Proceedings*, Feb. 1973, pp. 49-58.

68. Cunningham, Winfield S. *Wake Island Command*. Boston: Little, Brown, 1961.

69. Dalfiume, R. M. *Desegregation of the United States Armed Forces, 1939-1953*. Columbia: University of Missouri Press, 1969.

70. Dare, James A. "Dominican Diary," *U.S. Naval Institute Proceedings*, Dec. 1965, pp. 36-45.

71. Davis, Burke. *Get Yamamoto*. New York: Random House, 1969.

72. Davis, Burke. *Marine! The Life of Lt. Gen. Lewis B. (Chesty) Puller, USMC (ret)*. Boston: Little, Brown, 1962.

73. Davis, Vincent. *The Admirals Lobby*. Chapel Hill: University of North Carolina Press, 1967.

74. Davis, Vincent. *The Politics of Innovation: Patterns in Navy Cases*. Denver: University of Denver Press, 1967.

75. Davis, Vincent. *Post-War Defense Policy and the U.S. Navy, 1943-1946*. Chapel Hill: University of North Carolina Press, 1966.

76. Devereux, James P. S. *The Story of Wake Island*. Philadelphia: Lippincott, 1947.

77. Dissette, Edward and Hans C. Adamson. *Guerrilla Submarines*. New York: Ballantine, 1972.

78. Doenitz, Karl. *Memoirs: Ten Years and Twenty Days*. Tr. by R. H. Stevens. Cleveland: World Press, 1959.

79. Donovan, Robert J. *PT-109: John F. Kennedy in World War II*. New York: McGraw-Hill, 1961.

80. Dooley, Thomas A. *Deliver Us from Evil: The Story of Viet Nam's Flight to Freedom*. New York: Farrar, Strauss, 1956.

81. Dornbusch, C. E. *Unit Histories of World War II.* N.p.: Office of the Chief of Military History and New York Public Library, 1950-1953.
81a. Dorris, Donald Hugh. *A Log of the Vincennes.* Louisville: Standard Printing Co., 1947.
82. Drury, Clifford M. *The History of the Chaplain Corps, United States Navy.* Washington: G.P.O., 1949-1960. 6 vols.
83. Dufek, George J. *Operation Deepfreeze.* New York: Harcourt Brace, 1957.
84. Duncan, Robert C. *America's Use of Sea Mines.* Silver Spring, Maryland: U.S. Naval Ordnance Laboratory, 1962.
85. Dunn, Carroll H. *Base Development in South Vietnam, 1965-1970.* Washington: G.P.O., 1972.
86. Dyer, George C. *The Amphibians Came to Conquer: The Story of Richmond Kelly Turner.* Washington: G.P.O., 1971. 2 vols.
87. Eller, Ernest M. *The Soviet Sea Challenge.* New York: Cowles, 1972.
88. Elsey, George M. "Naval Aspects of Normandy in Retrospect." In The Eisenhower Foundation. *D-Day: The Normandy Invasion in Retrospect.* Lawrence: University Press of Kansas, 1971. p. 170-97.
89. Emerson, William R. "F. D. R. (1941-1945)." In May, Ernest R., ed. *The Ultimate Decision.* New York: Braziller, 1960. pp. 133-78.
90. Erickson, George E., Jr. "United States Navy War Crimes Trials (1945-1949)," *Washburn Law Journal,* Winter 1965, pp. 89-111.
91. Fahey, James J. *Pacific War Diary, 1942-1945.* Boston: Houghton Mifflin, 1963.
92. Falk, Stanley L. *Decision at Leyte.* New York: Norton, 1966.
93. Fane, Francis D. and Don Moore. *The Naked Warriors.* New York: Appleton Century-Crofts, 1956.
94. Farago, Ladislas. *The Broken Seal: The Story of "Operation Magic" and the Pearl Harbor Disaster.* New York: Random House, 1967.
95. Farago, Ladislas. *The Tenth Fleet.* New York: Obolensky, 1962.
96. Fassett, Frederick G., ed. *The Shipbuilding Business of the United States of America.* New York: Society of Naval Architects and Marine Engineers, 1948. 2 vols.
97. Fergusson, Bernard. *The Watery Maze: The Story of Combined Operations.* New York: Holt, Rinehart and Winston, 1961.
98. Field, James A., Jr. *The Japanese at Leyte Gulf: The Sho Operation.* Princeton: Princeton University Press, 1947.
99. Field, James A., Jr. *United States Naval Operations: Korea.* Washington: G.P.O., 1962.
100. Forrestal, James V. *The Forrestal Diaries.* Ed. by Walter Millis. New York: The Viking Press, 1951.
101. Forrestel, Emmet P. *Admiral Raymond A. Spruance, USN: A Study in Command.* Washington: G.P.O., 1966.
101a. Frank, Benis M. *Marine Corps Oral History Collection Catalog.* Washington: U.S. Marine History and Museums Division, 1973.
102. Friis, Herman R. and Shelby G. Bale, Jr., eds. *Conference on United States Polar Exploration.* Athens: Ohio University Press, 1970.
103. Fuchida, Mitsuo and Masatake Okumiya. *Midway, The Battle that Doomed Japan: The Japanese Navy's Story.* Annapolis: U.S. Naval Institute, 1955.

104. Fulton, William B. *Riverine Operations, 1966-1969.* Washington: G.P.O., 1973.
105. Furer, Julius A. *Administration of the Navy Department in World War II.* Washington: G.P.O., 1959.
106. Gallery, Daniel V. *Eight Bells and All's Well.* New York: Norton, 1965.
107. Gallery, Daniel V. *The Pueblo Incident.* Garden City: Doubleday, 1970.
108. Gallery, Daniel V. *Twenty Million Tons Under the Sea: The Submarine War in the Atlantic and the Daring Capture of the U-505.* Chicago: Regnery, 1956.
109. Garfield, Brian W. *The Thousand-Mile War: World War II in Alaska and the Aleutians.* Garden City: Doubleday, 1969.
110. Gibson, Charles Dana, II. *Ordeal of Convoy N.Y. 119.* New York: South Street Seaport Museum, 1973.
111. Gill, George H. *Royal Australian Navy, 1939-1942.* Canberra: Australian War Memorial, 1957.
111a. Gill, George H. *Royal Australian Navy, 1942-1945.* Canberra:Australian War Memorial, 1968.
111b. Gimpel, Herbert J. *The United States Nuclear Navy.* New York: Franklin Watts, 1965.
112. Glines, Carroll V. *Doolittle's Tokyo Raiders.* Princeton: Van Nostrand, 1964.
113. Glover, Cato D. *Command Performance—With Guts.* New York: Greenwich Book Publishing, 1969.
114. Goulden, Joseph C. *Truth is the First Casualty.* Chicago: Rand McNally, 1969.
115. Gray, J. A. C. *Amerika Samoa: A History of American Samoa and Its United States Naval Administration.* Annapolis: U.S. Naval Institute, 1960.
116. Green, Constance M. and Milton Lomask. *Vanguard: A History.* Washington: G.P.O., 1970.
117. Griffith, Samuel B. *The Battle for Guadalcanal.* New York: Lippincott, 1963.
118. Hall, R. Cargill. "Early Satellites, A First Look by the United States Navy in the 1940's." Unpublished manuscript, Jet Propulsion Laboratory, California Institute of Technology, 1970. In U.S. Naval History Division.
119. Halsey, William F. and Joseph Bryan. *Admiral Halsey's Story.* New York: Whittlesey House, 1947.
120. Hamer, Philip M. *A Guide to Archives and Manuscripts in the United States.* New Haven: Yale University Press, 1961.
121. Hammond, Paul Y. *Organizing for Defense.* New York: Columbia University Press, 1959.
122. Hammond, Paul Y. "Super Carriers and B-36 Bombers: Appropriations, Strategy and Politics." In Stein,Harold, ed. *American Civil-Military Decisions.* Birmingham: University of Alabama Press, 1963. pp. 465-567.
123. Hancock, Joy Bright. *Lady in the Navy.* Annapolis: U.S. Naval Institute, 1972.
124. Harrison, Gordon A. *Cross-Channel Attack.* Washington: G.P.O., 1951.

125. Hart, Thomas C. "Narrative of Events of Asiatic Fleet and Area Leading up to World War II and Until 15 February 1942" (with "Supplement"). Unpublished manuscripts, 1942. In U.S. Naval History Division.

126. Hayes, Grace P. *The History of the Joint Chiefs of Staff in World War II: The War Against Japan.* Washington: JCS, 1954. 2 vols.

127. Hayes, John D. "Sea Power: A Commentary." In *Naval Review, 1969-1971.* Annapolis: U.S. Naval Institute, 1969-71.

128. Heinl, Robert D. *Victory at High Tide: The Inchon-Seoul Campaign.* Philadelphia: Lippincott, 1968.

129. Helm, Thomas. *Ordeal by Sea: The Tragedy of the USS Indianapolis.* New York: Dodd Mead, 1963.

129a. Hewitt, H. Kent. "The Allied Navies at Salerno," *U.S. Naval Institute Proceedings,* Sept. 1953, pp. 959-76.

129b. Hewitt, H. Kent. "Naval Aspects of the Sicilian Campaign," *U.S. Naval Institute Proceedings,* July 1953, pp. 705-23.

129c. Hewitt, H. Kent. "Planning Operation Anvil-Dragoon," *U.S.. Naval Institute Proceedings,* July 1954, pp. 731-45.

130. Hewlett, Richard G. and Oscar E. Anderson, Jr. *The New World, 1939-1946.* University Park: Pennsylvania State University Press, 1962.

131. Hewlett, Richard G. and Francis Duncan. *Atomic Shield, 1947-1952.* University Park: Pennsylvania State University Press, 1969.

132. Hewlett, Richard G. and Francis Duncan. *The Nuclear Navy: An Historical Study of the Strategy and Tactics of Technological Innovation.* Chicago: University of Chicago Press, 1974.

133. Higgins, Edward T. *Web-Footed Warriors.* New York: Exposition Press, 1955.

134. Hilliard, Jack B. and Harold A. Bivins. *An Annotated Reading List of United States Marine Corps History.* Washington: U.S. Marine History and Museums Division, 1971.

135. Hoare, Wilber W., Jr. "Truman (1945-1953)." In May, Ernest R., ed. *The Ultimate Decision.* New York: Braziller, 1960. pp. 179-210.

136. Hodgman, James A. "Market Time in the Gulf of Thailand." In *Naval Review, 1968.* Annapolis: U.S. Naval Institute, 1968. pp. 36-67.

137. Hoehling, Adolph A. *The Lexington Goes Down.* Englewood Cliffs, New Jersey: Prentice-Hall, 1971.

138. Holmes, Wilfred Jay. *Underseas Victory: The Influence of Submarine Operations on the War in the Pacific.* Garden City: Doubleday, 1966.

139. Hooper, Edwin B. *Mobility, Support, Endurance: A Story of Naval Operational Logistics in the Vietnam War, 1965-1968.* Washington: G.P.O., 1972.

140. Hooper, Edwin B. "The Service Force, Pacific Fleet, in Action." In *Naval Review, 1968.* Annapolis: U.S. Naval Institute, 1968. pp. 114-27.

141. Hough, Richard A. *The Battle of Midway.* New York: Macmillan, 1969.

142. Houston, H. N. *The Holligan Navy.* New York: Vantage Press, 1971.

143. Howe, Jonathan T. "The Influence of the Seventh Fleet on Soviet Foreign Policy." Unpublished manuscript, 1968. In U.S. Naval History Division.

144. Howe, Johnathan T. "The Influence of the Sixth Fleet on Soviet Foreign Policy." Unpublished manuscript, 1963. In U.S. Naval History Division.

145. Howe, Johnathan T. *Multicrises: Sea Power and Global Politics in the Missile Age*. Cambridge: M.I.T. Press, 1971.

146. Howeth, L. S. *History of Communications-Electronics in the United States Navy*. Washington: G.P.O., 1963.

147. Hoyt, Edwin P. *The Battle of Leyte Gulf: The Death Knell of the Japanese Fleet*. New York: Weybright and Talley, 1972.

148. Hoyt, Edwin P. *How They Won the War in the Pacific: Nimitz and His Admirals*. New York: Weybright and Talley, 1970.

149. Huff, K. P. "Building the Advanced Base at Da Nang." In *Naval Review, 1968*. Annapolis: U.S. Naval Institute, 1968. pp. 88-113.

150. Hunsaker, Jerome C. *Edward Lull Cochrane, 1892-1959: A Biographical Memoir*. New York: Columbia University Press, 1961.

151. *The Imperial Japanese Navy in World War II*. [Tokyo]: General Headquarters, Far East Command, 1952.

152. Infield, Glen B. *Disaster at Bari*. New York: Macmillan, 1971.

153. Inoguchi, Rikihei and Tadashi Nakajima, with Roger Pineau. *The Divine Wind: Japan's Kamikaze Force in World War II*. Annapolis: U.S. Naval Institute, 1958.

154. International Military Tribunal for the Far East. *Record of the Proceedings, Documents, Exhibits, Judgements, Dissenting Judgements, Interrogations, etc.* Tokyo: n.p., 1946-1949.

155. Irving, David. *The Destruction of Convoy PQ-17*. New York: Simon and Schuster, 1968.

156. Isely, Jeter A. and Philip A. Crowl. *The U.S. Marines and Amphibious War: Its Theory and Its Practice in the Pacific*. Princeton: Princeton University Press, 1951.

157. *Jane's All the World's Aircraft*. New York: Various Publishers, 1909- .

158. *Jane's Fighting Ships*. New York: Various Publishers. 1898- .

159. *Japanese Monographs*. [Tokyo]: General Headquarters, Far East Command, 1945-1960. 135 vols.

160. Johnson, Ellis A. and David A. Katcher. *Mines Against Japan*. Silver Spring, Maryland: Naval Ordnance Laboratory, 1974.

161. Joint Army-Navy Assessment Committee. *Japanese Naval and Merchant Shipping Losses During World War II By All Causes*. Washington: G.P.O., 1947.

162. Jones, Ken. *Destroyer Squadron 23: Combat Exploits of Arleigh Burke's Gallant Force*. Philadelphia: Chilton, 1959.

163. Joy, Charles T. *How Communists Negotiate*. New York: Macmillan, 1955.

164. Kahn, David. *The Codebreakers*. New York: Macmillan, 1967.

165. Karig, Walter and others. *Battle Report*. New York: Farrar and Rinehart, 1944-1952. 6 vols.

166. Karneke, Joseph S. as told to Victor Boesen. *Navy Diver*. New York: G. P. Putnam's, 1959.

167. Kemp, Peter K. "Royal Navy, 1939-45." In Higham, Robin, ed. *A*

Guide to the Sources of British Military History. Berkeley: University of California Press, 1971. pp. 470-86.

168. Kendall, Lane C. "U.S. Merchant Shipping and Vietnam." In *Naval Review, 1968.* Annapolis: U.S. Naval Institute, 1968. pp. 128-47.

169. Kennedy, Robert F. *Thirteen Days: A Memoir of the Cuban Missile Crisis.* New York: Norton, 1969.

170. Kimmel, Husband E. *Admiral Kimmel's Story.* Chicago: Regnery, 1955.

171. King, Ernest J. *The United States Navy at War, 1941-1945: Official Reports to the Secretary of the Navy.* Washington: G.P.O., 1946.

172. King, Ernest J. and Walter M. Whitehill. *Fleet Admiral King: A Naval Record.* New York: Norton, 1952.

173. King, Herbert T. "Naval Logistic Support, Qui Nhon to Phu Quoc." In *Naval Review, 1969.* Annapolis: U.S. Naval Institute, 1969. pp. 84-111.

174. Kittredge, Tracy B. "The Evolution of Global Strategy." Unpublished manuscript, Joint Chiefs of Staff, no date. In U.S. National Archives.

175. Klinkerman, R. Dale. "From Blackout at Pearl Harbor to Spotlight on Tokyo Bay: A Study of the Evolution in U.S. Navy Public Relations." Master's thesis, University of Wisconsin, 1972.

176. Kreh, William R. *Citizen Sailors: The U.S. Naval Reserve in War and Peace.* New York: McKay, 1969.

177. Land, Emory Scott. *Winning the War With Ships: Land, Sea and Air—Mostly Land.* New York: McBride, 1958.

178. Lane, Frederick C. and others. *Ships for Victory: A History of Shipbuilding Under the U.S. Maritime Commission in World War II.* Baltimore: Johns Hopkins Press, 1951.

179. Larson, David L., ed. *The "Cuban Crisis" of 1962: Selected Documents and Chronology.* Boston: Houghton Mifflin Co., 1963.

180. Lasby, Clarence C. *Project Paperclip: German Scientists and the Cold War.* New York: Atheneum, 1971.

181. Leahy, William D. *I Was There.* New York: Whittlesey House, 1950.

182. Leckie, Robert. *Challenge for the Pacific: Guadalcanal, the Turning Point of the War.* Garden City: Doubleday, 1965.

183. Lederer, William J. *All the Ships At Sea.* New York: Norton, 1970.

184. Lee, Robert E. *To The War.* New York: Knopf, 1968.

185. Leighton, Richard M. and Robert W. Coakley. *Global Logistics and Strategy, 1940-1943.* Washington: G.P.O., 1955.

186. Lenton, Henry T. *Navies of the Second World War.* Garden City: Doubleday, 1965-   .

187. Lewis, David D. *The Fight for the Sea.* Cleveland: World Publishing Co., 1961.

188. Lewis, Flora. *One of Our H-Bombs is Missing.* New York: McGraw-Hill, 1967.

189. Lockwood, Charles A. *Down to the Sea in Subs.* New York: Norton, 1967.

190. Lockwood, Charles A. *Sink 'em All: Submarine Warfare in the Pacific.* New York: Dutton, 1951.

191. Lockwood, Charles A. and Hans C. Adamson. *Battles of the Philippine Sea.* New York: Crowell, 1967.

192. Lord, Walter. *Day of Infamy.* New York: Holt, 1957.
193. Lord, Walter. *Incredible Victory.* New York: Harper and Row, 1967.
194. Lott, Arnold S. *A Long Line of Ships: Mare Island's Century of Naval Activity in California.* Annapolis: U.S. Naval Institute, 1954.
195. Lott, Arnold S. *Brave Ship, Brave Men.* Indianapolis: Bobbs-Merrill, 1964.
196. Lott, Arnold S. *Most Dangerous Sea: A History of Mine Warfare Operations in World War II and Korea.* Annapolis: U.S. Naval Institute, 1959.
197. Lowi, Theodore J. "Bases in Spain." In Stein, Harold, ed. *American Civil-Military Decisions.* Birmingham: University of Alabama Press, 1963. pp. 667-702.
198. MacDonald, Charles B. *The Mighty Endeavor: American Armed Forces in the European Theatre in World War II.* New York: Oxford University Press, 1969.
199. MacDonald, Scot. *Evolution of Aircraft Carriers.* Washington: Office of the Chief of Naval Operations, 1964.
200. *Marine Corps Gazette.* (Marine Corps Association). Quantico, Virginia, 1916-
201. *Mariner's Mirror.* (Society for Nautical Research). Greenwich, England, 1911-
202. Mason, Elizabeth and Louis M. Starr. *The Oral History Collection of Columbia University.* New York: Columbia University Press, 1973.
203. Mason, John T., Jr. "An Interview with John T. Mason, Jr., Director of Oral History," *U.S. Naval Institute Proceedings,* July 1973, pp. 42-47.
204. Matloff, Maurice. *Strategic Planning for Coalition Warfare.* Washington: G.P.O., 1959.
205. Matloff, Maurice and Edwin M. Snell. *Strategic Planning for Coalition Warfare, 1941-1942.* Washington: G.P.O., 1953.
206. May, Ernest R., "Eisenhower and After (1953-   )." In May, Ernest R., ed. *The Ultimate Decision.* New York: Braziller, 1960. pp. 211-36.
207. McGann, Frank D., Jr. *The Brazilian-American Alliance in World War II, 1937-1945.* Princeton: Princeton University Press, 1973.
208. McCauley, Brian. "Operation End Sweep," *U.S. Naval Institute Proceedings,* Mar. 1974, pp. 18-25.
209. McClendon, F. O. "Doctors and Dentists, Nurses and Corpsmen in Vietnam." In *Naval Review, 1970.* Annapolis: U.S. Naval Institute, 1970. pp. 276-89.
210. McClintock, Robert. "The American Landing in Lebanon," *U.S. Naval Institute Proceedings,* Oct. 1962. pp. 65-79.
211. McConnell, James M. and Anne M. Kelly. "Superpower Naval Diplomacy in the Indo-Pakistani Crisis." In McGwire, Michael, ed. *Soviet Naval Developments: Capability and Context.* New York: Praeger, 1973. pp. 442-55.
212. McCutcheon, Keith B. "Marine Aviation in Vietnam, 1962-1970." In *Naval Review, 1971.* Annapolis: U.S. Naval Institute, 1971. pp. 122-2.
213. McGwire, Michael, ed. *Soviet Naval Developments: Capability and Context.* New York: Praeger, 1973.
214. McDonald, Jack. *Navy Retread.* New York: Vantage Press, 1969.

215. McIntire, Ross T. *White House Physician.* New York: G. P. Putnam's, 1946.

216. McLachlan, Donald. *Room 39.* New York: Atheneum, 1968.

217. Meacham, James A. "Four Mining Campaigns," *Naval War College Review,* June 1967, pp. 75-129.

218. Merdinger, Charles J. "Civil Engineers, Seabees, and Bases in Vietnam." In *Naval Review, 1970.* Annapolis: U.S. Naval Institute, 1970. pp. 254-75.

219. Merrill, James M. *Target Tokyo, the Halsey-Doolittle Raid.* Chicago: Rand-McNally, 1964.

220. Miles, Milton E. *A Different Kind of War: The Little-Known Story of the Combined Guerrilla Forces Created in China by the U.S. Navy and the Chinese During World War II.* Garden City: Doubleday, 1967.

221. *Military Affairs.* (American Military Institute). Various places, 1937-

222. Miller, Thomas G. *The Cactus Air Force.* New York: Harper and Row, 1969.

223. Millett, Allan R. and B. Franklin Cooling, III. *Doctoral Dissertations in Military Affairs.* Manhattan: Kansas State University Library, 1972.

224. Mitchell, Donald W. *A History of Russian and Soviet Sea Power.* New York: Macmillan, 1974.

225. Moore, Withers M. *Navy Chaplains in Vietnam, 1954-1964.* Washington: Chief of Chaplains, U.S. Navy Department, 1968.

226. Moran, J. B. *Creating a Legend: The Descriptive Catalog of Writing About the U.S. Marine Corps.* Chicago: Moran Andrews, 1973.

227. Morison, Samuel E. *History of United States Naval Operations in World War II.* Boston: Little, Brown, 1947-1962. 15 vols.

228. Morison, Samuel E. *Strategy and Compromise.* Boston: Little, Brown, 1958.

229. Morison, Samuel E. *The Two Ocean War: A Short History of the United States Navy in the Second World War.* Boston: Little, Brown, 1963.

230. Morton, Louis. *Strategy and Command: The First Two Years.* Washington: G.P.O., 1962.

231. Mumford, Robert E., Jr. "Jackstay: New Dimensions in Amphibious Warfare." In *Naval Review, 1968.* Annapolis: U.S. Naval Institute, 1968. pp. 68-87.

232. Murphy, Francis. *Fighting Admiral: The Story of Dan Callaghan.* New York: Vantage Press, 1952.

233. Nalty, Bernard C. *Air Power and the Fight for Khe Sanh.* Washington: Office of Air Force History, 1973.

234. *The National Union Catalog of Manuscript Collections.* Various publishers, 1959-

235. *Naval and Maritime Chronology, 1961-1971.* Annapolis: U.S. Naval Institute, 1973.

236. *Naval Avaition News.* (U.S. Office of Naval Operations). Washington, 1919-

237. Naval Historical Foundation. *Manuscript Collection, A Catalog.* Washington: Library of Congress, 1974.

238. *Naval Review.* Annapolis: U.S. Naval Institute, 1962-   .

239. *Naval War College Review.* (U.S. Naval War College). Newport, Rhode Island: 1948-   .

240. Nelson, Dennis D. *The Integration of the Negro into the U.S. Navy.* New York: Farrar, Strauss and Young, 1951.

241. Newcomb, Richard F. *Abandon Ship! Death of the USS Indianapolis.* New York: Holt, 1958.

242. Newcomb, Richard F. *Iwo Jima.* New York: Holt, Rinehart and Winston, 1965.

243. Noel, John V., Jr. and Edward L. Beach. *Naval Terms Dictionary.* Annapolis: U.S. Naval Institute, 1971.

244. Oberdorfer, Don. *Tet!* Garden City: Doubleday, 1971.

245. O'Connor, Raymond G., ed. *The Japanese Navy in World War II.* Annapolis: U.S. Naval Institute, 1969.

246. Olsen, Jack. *Aphrodite: Desperate Mission.* New York: G. P. Putnam's, 1970.

247. *Pacific Historical Review.* (American Historical Association, West Coast Branch). Berkeley, California, 1932-   .

248. Page, Robert M. *The Origin of Radar.* Garden City: Anchor Books, 1962.

249. Pawlowski, Gareth L. *Flat-Tops and Fledglings: A History of American Aircraft Carriers.* South Brunswick, New Jersey: A. S. Barnes, 1971.

250. Peck, Taylor. *Round-Shot to Rockets: The Story of the Washington Navy Yard.* Annapolis: U.S. Naval Institute, 1949.

251. Pittsburgh University Historical Staff, Office of Naval Research. "The History of United States Naval Research and Development in World War II." Unpublished manuscript, 1950. In U.S. Naval History Division.

252. Polmar, Norman. *Aircraft Carriers: A Graphic History of Carrier Aviation and Its Influence on World Events.* Garden City: Doubleday, 1969.

253. Polmar, Norman. *Atomic Submarines.* Princeton: Van Nostrand, 1963.

254. Polmar, Norman. *Death of Thresher.* Philadelphia: Chilton, 1964.

255. Potter, E. B. and C. W. Nimitz, eds. *The Great Sea War: The Story of Naval Action in World War II.* Englewood Cliffs, New Jersey: Prentice-Hall, 1960.

256. Potter, John D. *Yamamoto: The Man Who Menaced America.* New York: Viking, 1965.

257. Pugh, Herbert L. *Navy Surgeon.* Philadelphia: Lippincott, 1959.

258. Puleston, William D. *The Influence of Sea Power in World War II.* New Haven: Yale University Press, 1947.

259. Purdon, Eric. *Black Company: The Story of Sub Chaser 1264.* Washington: R. B. Luce, 1972.

260. Rappaport, Armin. *The Navy League of the United States.* Detroit: Wayne State University Press, 1962.

261. Reed, John C. and Andreas G. Ronhovde. *Arctic Laboratory: A History (1947-1966) of the Naval Arctic Research Laboratory at Point Barrow, Alaska.* Washington: Arctic Institute of North America, 1971.

262. Reynolds, Clark G. *The Fast Carriers: The Forging of an Air Navy.* New York: McGraw-Hill, 1968.

263. Reynolds, Clark G. "Submarine Attacks on the Pacific Coast, 1942." *Pacific Historical Review*, May 1964, pp. 183-93.

264. Richard, Dorothy E. *United States Naval Administration of the Trust Territory of the Pacific Islands.* Washington: G. P. O., 1957-1963. 3 vols.

265. Richardson, James O. *On the Treadmill to Pearl Harbor: The Memoirs of Admiral James O. Richardson.* Washington: G. P. O., 1973.

266. Ries, John C. *The Management of Defense: Organization and Control of the U.S. Armed Services.* Baltimore: Johns Hopkins Press, 1964.

267. Rigdon, William M. with James Derieux. *White House Sailor.* Garden City: Doubleday, 1962.

268. Rogow, Arnold A. *James Forrestal: A Study of Personality, Politics, and Policy.* New York: Macmillan, 1963.

269. Rohwer, Jurgen. *Die U-Boot-Erfolge Der Achsenmachte, 1939-1945.* Munich: J. F. Lehmanns, 1968.

270. Rohwer, Jurgen and G. Hummelchen. *Chronology of the War at Sea, 1939-1945.* New York: Arco, 1974.

271. Rohwer, Jurgen. "The U-Boat War Against the Allied Supply Lines." In H. A. Jacobsen and J. Rohwers, eds. *Decisive Battles of World War II: The German View.* New York: Putnam, 1965. pp. 259-315.

272. Roscoe, Theodore. *On the Seas and in the Skies: A History of the U.S. Navy's Air Power.* New York: Hawthorn Books, 1970.

273. Roscoe, Theodore. *United States Destroyer Operations in World War II.* Annapolis: U.S. Naval Institute, 1953.

274. Roscoe, Theodore. *United States Submarine Operations in World War II.* Annapolis: U.S. Naval Institute, 1949.

275. Roskill, Stephen W. *The War at Sea, 1939-1945.* London: H. M. S. O., 1954-1961. 4 vols.

276. Roskill, Stephen W. *White Ensign.* Annapolis: U.S. Naval Institute, 1960.

277. Ross, Tweed W. "The Best Way to Destroy a Ship: The Evidence of European Naval Operations in World War II." Master's thesis, Kansas State University, 1967.

278. Rowe, John S. and Samuel L. Morison. *The Ships and Aircraft of the U.S. Fleet.* Annapolis: U.S. Naval Institute, 1972. (eight earlier editions compiled by James C. Fahey).

279. Rowland, Buford and William Boyd. *U.S. Navy Bureau of Ordnance in World War II.* Washington: G. P. O., 1953.

280. Ruge, Friedrich. *Der Seekrieg: The German Navy's Story, 1939-1945.* Annapolis: U.S. Naval Institute, 1957.

281. Ruksenas, Algis. *Day of Shame.* New York: McKay, 1973.

282. Rutledge, Howard and Phyllis Rutledge, with Mel and Lyla White. *In the Presence of Mine Enemies, 1965-1973: A Prisoner of War.* Old Tappan, New Jersey: Fleming H. Revell Co., 1973.

283. Ryan, Cornelius. *The Longest Day.* New York: Simon and Schuster, 1959.

284. Sapolsky, Harvey M. *The Polaris System Development*. Cambridge: Harvard University Press, 1972.
285. Saunders, M. G., ed. *The Soviet Navy*. New York: Praeger, 1958.
286. Schilling, Warner R., Paul Y. Hammond, and Glenn H. Snyder. *Strategy, Politics, and Defense Budgets*. New York: Columbia University Press, 1962.
287. Schnabel, James F. *Policy and Direction: The First Year*. Washington: G. P. O., 1972.
288. Schofield, W. G. *Eastward the Convoys*. Chicago: Rand McNally, 1965.
289. Schreadley, R. L. "Naval War in Vietnam, 1950-1970." In *Naval Review, 1971*. Annapolis: U.S. Naval Institute, 1971. pp. 180-209.
290. Schroeder, Peter B. *Contact at Sea: A History of Maritime Radio Communications*. Ridgewood, New Jersey: Gregg Press, 1967.
291. Schull, J. *The Far Distant Ships: An Official Account of Canadian Naval Operations in the Second World War*. Ottawa: Edmond Cloutier, 1950.
292. Schultz, Charles R., comp. *Bibliography of Naval and Maritime History: Periodical Articles*. Mystic Seaport, Connecticut: Marine Historical Association, 1971-
293. Schuon, Karl. *U.S. Navy Biographical Dictionary*. New York: Watts, 1965.
294. Searls, Henry. *The Lost Prince: Young Joe, The Forgotten Kennedy*. New York: World Publishing, 1969.
295. Sheehan, Neil. *The Arnheiter Affair*. New York: Random House, 1971.
296. Sheldon, Walter J. *Hell or High Water: MacArthur's Landing at Inchon*. New York: Macmillan, 1968.
297. Sherman, Frederick C. *Combat Command: The American Aircraft Carriers in the Pacific War*. New York: Dutton, 1950.
298. Sherrod, Robert L. *History of Marine Corps Aviation in World War II*. Washington: Combat Forces Press, 1952.
299. Sherrod, Robert L. *Tarawa: The Story of a Battle*. New York: Duell, Sloan, and Pearce, 1954.
300. *Shipmate*. (U.S. Naval Academy Alumni Association). Annapolis, Maryland, 1938-
301. Shore, Moyers S. *The Battle for Khe Sanh*. Washington: G. P. O., 1969.
302. Silverstone. Paul H. *U.S. Warships of World War II*. Garden City: Doubleday, 1965.
303. Simpson, Benjamin M., III. "The Navy and United States-French Relations, 1942-1944." Doctoral dissertation, Fletcher School of Law and Diplomacy, 1968.
304. Sims, Edward H. *Greatest Fighter Missions of the Top Navy and Marine Aces of World War II*. New York: Harper, 1962.
305. Smelser, Marshall. "The Amiable Armada: Operations of the United States Sixth Fleet During the Suez War." Unpublished manuscript, no date. In the U.S. Naval History Division.
306. Smith, Holland M. and Percy Finch. *Coral and Brass*. New York: Scribner, 1949.

307. Smith, Myron J., Jr. *The Naval Bibliography of World War II.* Metuchen, New Jersey: Scarecrow Press, 1975- .

308. Smith, Stanley E. *The United States Marine Corps in World War II: The One-Volume History, from Wake to Tsingtao, by the Men Who Fought in the Pacific and by Distinguished Marine Experts, Authors, and Newspapermen.* New York: Random House, 1969.

309. Smith, Stanley E. *The United States Navy in World War II: The One-Volume History, from Pearl Harbor to Tokyo Bay, by Men Who Fought in the Atlantic and the Pacific and by Distinguished Naval Experts, Authors and Newspapermen.* New York: Morrow, 1966.

310. Smith, William W. *Midway: Turning Point of the Pacific.* New York: Crowell, 1966.

311. Society of Naval Architects and Marine Engineers. *Historical Transactions, 1893-1943.* New York: The Society, 1945.

312. Soper, James B. "A View From FMF Pac of Logistics in the Western Pacific, 1965-1971." In *Naval Review, 1972.* Annapolis: U.S. Naval Institute, 1972. pp. 222-39.

313. Spruance, Raymond A. "The Victory in the Pacific," *Journal of the Royal United Services Institute*, Nov. 1946. pp. 539-55.

314. Stafford, Edward Perry. *The Big E: The Story of the USS Enterprise.* New York: Random House, 1962.

315. Stafford, Edward Perry. *The Far and the Deep.* New York: Putnam, 1967.

316. Sterling, Forest J. *Wake of the Wahoo.* Philadelphia: Chilton, 1960.

317. Sternhell, C. M. and A. M. Thorndike. *Antisubmarine Warfare in World War II.* Washington: Operations Evaluation Group, 1946.

318. Stevenson, Adlai E. *The Papers of Adlai E. Stevenson.* Ed. by Walter Johnson and Carol Evans. Boston: Little, Brown, 1972-

319. Stewart, Irving. *Organizing Scientific Research for War: The Administrative History of the Office of Scientific Research and Development.* Boston: Little, Brown, 1948.

320. Stillman, Richard J. *Integration of the Negro in the U.S. Armed Forces.* New York: Praeger, 1968.

321. Stockstill, Louis R. "Uncle Carl Vinson: Backstage Boss of the Pentagon," *Army-Navy-Air Force Journal*, 18 February 1961, pp. 1, 22-28.

322. Strauss, L. L. *Men and Decisions.* Garden City: Doubleday, 1962.

323. Strobridge, Truman R. *United States Coast Guard Annotated Bibliography.* Washington: G. P. O., 1972.

324. Supreme Commander for the Allied Powers. *Reports of General MacArthur, Prepared by his General Staff.* Ed. by Charles A. Willoughby. Washington: G. P. O., 1966-1967. 4 vols.

325. Swanborough, Gordon and Peter M. Bowers. *United States Navy Aircraft Since 1911.* New York: Funk and Wagnalls, 1968.

326. Swartzrauber, S. A. "River Patrol Relearned." In *Naval Review, 1970.* Annapolis: U.S. Naval Institute, 1970. pp. 120-57.

327. Taylor, Albert H. *The First Twenty-Five Years of the Naval Research Laboratory.* Washington: U.S. Navy Department, 1948.

328. Taylor, Theodore. *Fire on the Beaches*. New York: Norton, 1958.
329. Taylor, Theodore. *The Magnificent Mitscher*. New York: Norton, 1954.
330. Theobold, Robert A. *The Final Secret of Pearl Harbor*. New York: Devin-Adair, 1954.
331. Thomas, David A. *Battle of the Java Sea*. London: Deutsch, 1968.
332. Toland, John. *But Not in Shame: The Six Months After Pearl Harbor*. New York: Random House, 1961.
333. Tolley, Kemp. *The Cruise of the Lanikai*. Annapolis: U.S. Naval Institute, 1973.
334. Tuleja, Thaddeus V. *Climax at Midway*. New York: Norton, 1960.
335. Tunney, Christopher. *Biographical Dictionary of World War II*. New York: St. Martin's, 1972.
336. Turner, L. C., H. R. Gordon-Cumming, and J. E. Betzler. *War in the Southern Oceans, 1939-1945*. Capetown and New York: Oxford University Press, 1961.
337. Underbrink, Robert L. *Destination Corregidor*. Annapolis: U.S. Naval Institute, 1971.
338. U.S. Bureau of Medicine and Surgery. *History of the Medical Department of the United States Navy in World War II*. Washington: G. P. O., 1950-1953. 3 vols.
339. U.S. Bureau of Medicine and Surgery. *History of the Medical Department of the United States Navy, 1945-1955*. Washington: G. P. O., 1958.
340. U.S. Bureau of Naval Personnel. *Register of Commissioned and Warrant Officers of the United States Navy*. Washington: G. P. O., 1941- .
340a. U.S. Bureau of Ships. *Ships' Data, U.S. Naval Vessels*. Washington: G. P. O., 1938-1949.
341. U.S. Bureau of Ships. *A Short History of the Navy Salvage Service*. Washington: U.S. Navy Department, 1949.
342. U.S. Bureau of Yards and Docks. *Building the Navy's Bases in World War II: History of the Bureau of Yards and Docks and the Civil Engineering Corps, 1940-1946*. Washington: G. P. O., 1947. 2 vols.
343. U.S. Coast Guard. *Register of Officers and Cadets of the United States Coast Guard in Order of Precedence*. Washington: G. P. O., 1941- .
344. U.S. Congress. House. Committee on Armed Services. *Inquiry Into the USS Pueblo and EC-121 Plane Incidents*. Washington: G. P. O., 1969.
345. U.S. Congress. House. Committee on Armed Services. *The National Defense Programs: Unification and Strategy*. Washington: G. P. O., 1949.
346. U.S. Congress. Joint Committee on the Investigation of the Pearl Harbor Attacks. *Hearings* and *Report*. Washington: G. P. O., 1946. 40 vols.
347. U.S. Congress. Senate. Committee on Foreign Relations. *The Gulf of Tonkin, the 1964 Incidents*. Washington: G. P. O., 1968.
348. U.S. Congress. Senate. Committee on Veterans' Affairs. *Medal of Honor Recipients, 1863-1973*. Washington: G. P. O., 1973.

349. U.S. Department of Defense. *United States-Vietnam Relations, 1945-1967.* Washington: G. P. O., 1971. 12 vols.

350. U.S. Department of State. *The Foreign Relations of the United States, 1942-1948.* Washington: G. P. O., 1956- .

351. U.S. Deputy Chief of Naval Operations (Air) and Commander, Naval Air Systems Command. *United States Naval Aviation, 1910-1970.* Washington: G. P. O., 1970.

352. U.S. Joint Logistics Review Board. *Logistic Support in the Vietnam Era: A Report.* Washington: The Board, 1970.

353. U.S. Marine Corps. *Combined Lineal List of Officers on Active Duty in the Marine Corps.* Washington: G. P. O., 1943- .

354. U.S. Marine History and Museums Division. *A Chronology of the United States Marine Corps.* Washington: U.S. Marine Corps, 1965- . 4 vols.

355. U.S. Marine History and Museums Division. *History of U.S. Marine Corps Operations in World War II.* Washington: G. P. O., 1958-1971. 5 vols.

356. U.S. Marine History and Museums Division. *Marines in Lebanon.* Washington: U.S. Marine Corps, 1968.

357. U.S. Marine History and Museums Division. *The Marines in Vietnam, 1954-1973: An Anthology and Annotated Bibliography.* Washington: U.S. Marine Corps, 1974.

358. U.S. Marine History and Museums Division. *U.S. Marine Operations in Korea, 1950-1953.* Washington: G. P. O., 1954.

359. U.S. Naval History Division. *Dictionary of American Naval Fighting Ships:* Washington: G. P. O., 1959- . 5 vols.

360. U.S. Naval History Division. *Glossary of U.S. Naval Abbreviations.* 5th ed. Washington: G. P. O., 1949.

361. U.S. Naval History Division. *Glossary of U.S. Naval Code Words.* Washington: G. P. O., 1947.

362. U.S. Naval History Division. *Partial Checklist: World War II Histories and Historical Reports in the U.S. Naval History Division.* Washington: U.S. Naval History Division, 1973.

363. U.S. Naval History Division: *Riverine Warfare: Vietnam.* Washington: G.P.O., 1972.

364. U.S. Naval History Division. *United States Naval Chronology, World War II.* Washington: G.P.O., 1955.

365. U.S. Naval History Division. *United States Naval History: A Bibliography.* 6th ed. Washington: G.P.O., 1972.

366. U.S. Naval History Division. *United States Submarine Losses, World War II.* Washington: G.P.O., 1964.

367. *U.S. Naval Institute Proceedings.* (U.S. Naval Institute). Annapolis, Maryland, 1874- .

368. U.S. Naval War College. *Strategic and Tactical Analyses* [for Battles of Coral Sea, Midway, Savo Island, and Leyte Gulf]. Newport, Rhode Island: Naval War College, 1947-1958. 4 reports.

369. U.S. Navy Department. *Annual Report of the Secretary of the Navy, 1941-1968.* Washington: various publishers, 1941- . (After 1948, these appear in *Annual Report of the Secretary of Defense).*

370. U.S. Navy Department. "U.S. Naval Administration in World War II." Unpublished manuscripts. In U.S. Naval History Division. About 250 vols.

371. U.S. Office of the Chief of Military History. *United States Army in World War II.* Washington: G.P.O., 1947-

372. U.S. Pacific Command. *Report on the War in Vietnam As of 30 June 1968.* Washington: G.P.O., 1969.

373. U.S. Pacific Fleet. *Korean War, U.S. Pacific Fleet Operations: Interim Evaluation Reports, 25, June 1950-27 July 1953.* 6 Reports. Processed documents, 1951-1954. In the U.S. Naval History Division.

374. U.S. Strategic Bombing Survey. *Reports: European and Pacific Wars.* Washington: G.P.O., 1945-47. 319 vols.

375. Vandegrift, Alexander A. as told to Robert B. Asprey. *Once A Marine: The Memoirs of General A. A. Vandegrift, U.S. Marine Corps.* New York: Norton, 1964.

376. Wallin, Homer N. *Pearl Harbor: Why, How, Fleet Salvage and Final Appraisal.* Washington: G.P.O., 1968.

377. Walt, Lewis W. *Strange War, Strange Strategy: A General's Report on Vietnam.* New York: Funk and Wagnalls, 1970.

378. Waters, John M. *Bloody Winter.* Princeton: Van Nostrand, 1967.

379. Waters, Sydney D. *The Royal New Zealand Navy.* Wellington: War History Branch, Department of Internal Affairs, 1956.

380. Wedertz, Bill. *Dictionary of Naval Abbreviations.* Annapolis: U.S. Naval Institute, 1970.

381. Weigley, Russell F. *The American Way of War.* New York: Macmillan, 1973.

382. Wells, W. C. "The Riverine Force in Action, 1966-1967." In *Naval Review, 1969.* Annapolis: U.S. Naval Institute, 1960. pp. 46-83.

383. West, Francis J. *Small Unit Action in Vietnam, Summer 1966.* Washington: U.S. Marine History Division, 1967.

383a. Wilhelm, Maria. *The Man Who Watched the Rising Sun: The Story of Admiral Ellis M. Zacharias.* New York: Franklin Watts, 1967.

384. Willoughby, Malcom F. *The U.S. Coast Guard in World War II.* Annapolis: U.S. Naval Institute, 1957.

385. Windchey, Eugene. *Tonkin Gulf.* Garden City: Doubleday, 1971.

386. Winslow, Walter G. *USS Houston: The Ghost of the Java Coast.* Bethesda, Maryland: Winslow Books, 1971.

387. Winton, John. *The Forgotten Fleet: The British Navy in the Pacific, 1944-1945.* New York: Crown-McCann, 1969.

388. Wohlsetter, Roberta. *Peal Harbor: Warning and Decision.* Stanford: Stanford University Press, 1962.

388a. Wood, Charles Anthony. *Marine Corps Personal Papers Collection Catalog.* Washington: U.S. Marine History and Museums Division, 1974.

389. Woodward, C. Vann. *The Battle for Leyte Gulf.* New York: Macmillan, 1947.

390. Xydis, Stephen G. *Greece and the Great Powers, 1944-1947: Prelude to the Truman Doctrine.* Chicago: Argonaut, 1963.

391. Zacharias, Ellis M. *Secret Missions.* New York: G.P. Putnam's, 1946.
392. Ziegler, Janet. *World War II: Books in English, 1945-1965.* Stanford: Hoover Institution Press, 1971.
393. Zogbaum, Rufus Fairchild. *From Sail to Saratoga.* Rome: privately printed, 1961.

PRINCIPAL ARCHIVES AND MANUSCRIPT REPOSITORIES

394. Dwight D. Eisenhower Library, Abilene, Kansas 67410. In addition to Presidential papers, the Eisenhower Library has files of certain Naval Aides to the President (Evan P. Aurand, Edward L. Beach) and personal papers of other naval officers associated with Eisenhower, including William W. Outerbridge and Harry C. Butcher.

395. Franklin D. Roosevelt Library, Hyde Park, New York 12538. The President's papers include much material of interest to naval historians. Among naval personal papers at the Library are those of Admiral Ross T. McIntire.

396. Harry S. Truman Library, Independence, Missouri 64050. In addition to Presidential papers relating to naval affairs, the Truman Library has the files of former naval aide Robert L. Dennison and Secretaries of the Navy Francis P. Matthews and Dan A. Kimball.

397. Historical Officer, U.S. Naval Facilities Engineering Command, Port Hueneme, California 93043. This activity has official records of Navy Construction Battalions and personal papers of Admiral Ben Moreell.

398. Hoover Institution of War, Revolution, and Peace, Palo Alto, California 92605. Among the Institution's personal papers are groups from Admirals Charles M. Cooke, Milton E. Miles, and Raymond A. Spruance.

399. Manuscript Division, Library of Congress, Washington, D.C. 20540. In addition to holding most of the collections of the Naval Historical Foundation, the Manuscript Division has a number of other personal papers from naval officials and officers.

400. Naval Historical Collection, U.S. Naval War College, Newport, Rhode Island 02840. This activity has the official archives of the War College, as well as the personal papers of certain officers associated with the College, including a group from Admiral Spruance.

401. Naval Historical Foundation, Building 220, Washington Navy Yard, Washington, D.C. 20374. The Foundation has the largest single group of naval officer personal papers. Most collections are deposited in the Library of Congress. Some are retained in the Foundation's repository in the Washington Navy Yard.

402. Operational Archives, U.S. Naval History Division, Building 210, Washington Navy Yard, Washington, D.C. 20374. This activity holds the Navy's basic operational records since 1941, as well as sources documenting strategy, policy, and tactics as developed by the Office of the Chief of Naval Operations and other senior headquarters. The papers of some senior naval officers are held, as are

materials from the Japanese and German navies of World War II and transcripts of oral histories with senior naval officers.

403. U.S. Marine History and Museums Division, Arlington, Virginia 22214. In addition to collections of operational records, this Division has a number of personal papers from Marine senior officers and extensive oral history material on Marine Corps History.

404. U.S. National Archives, 8th and Pennsylvania Avenues, NW, Washington, D.C. 20408. This agency has the basic groups of general naval and Marine records for the post-1941 period, including materials from the Office of the Secretary of the Navy, Bureaus, fleet commands, and other major offices and organizations.

XIX

MUSEUMS AS HISTORICAL
RESOURCES

Philip K. Lundeberg

Increasing numbers of historians have become aware of the wide range
of documentation available for the refinement of their research in museums and art galleries in North America and overseas. A noteworthy
influx of historians into the museum profession since World War II has
made it highly probable that those scholars who venture beyond library
and archival repositories relevant to their particular studies will discover
that national, regional, local, and topical museums hold not only significant three-dimensional and photographic collections pertinent to their
themes but also an increasing depth of documentation and range of curatorial knowledge relating to technical fields represented by the artifacts
bearing on those same themes. Documentation indeed represents the
vital though generally unrecognized bond between the academic historian
and his museum counterpart, for the methodical collection and evaluation
of reliable data, based on primary sources (frequently epitomized by the
correspondence of donors), constitutes a preoccupation for the museum
curator in no sense secondary to the collecting of artifacts themselves.
Without such documentation, museum specimens remain essentially
suspect, subject to varied forms of testing to determine the authenticity of
such attributions as they may initially possess (37).

Recently the National Museum of History and Technology received on
exchange from the Peabody Museum of Harvard University a venerable
butter firkin, fitted with a lockplate from a flintlock musket attached beneath its cover and accompanied by a sketchy provenance indicating that
it was a Revolutionary War sea mine. Held earlier by the Boston Museum
and previously thereto by the Peale Museum of Philadelphia, this keg,
although bearing consecutive Roman numerals on its staves (a characteristic feature of eighteenth-century wood craftsmanship), lacked contemporary documentation to confirm the possibility that it was indeed one of
those rude infernal devices eulogized by Francis Hopkinson in his mock-
heroic ballad, "The Battle of the Kegs." Happily, however, an ensuing
search of the Charles Willson Peale Papers in the Historical Society of
Pennsylvania revealed that the manuscript catalogue or "Memoranda
of the Philadelphia Museum" included an arresting accession entry for

May 10, 1797: "One of the Kegs, celebrated in time of the Revolution," accompanied by notation of the donor, one Major George Fleming, a veteran of the 2nd Continental Artillery, providing a highly plausible link to those dimly remembered events at Philadelphia early in 1778. Further confirmation of this mine's authentic character was provided by discovery of the name "Galton" on the Brown Bess lockplate installed to ignite its powder charge. With the assistance of the veteran curator of firearms and edge weapons at the Smithsonian Institution, Craddock Goins, it was possible to establish the fabrication of this lockplate between 1750 and 1792 by Thomas Galton of London and Birmingham. Through such cumulative documentation not only had a curious relic achieved substantial authentication, but a seminal and generally overlooked episode in the emergence of undersea warfare had now moved beyond the ken of the literary historian to serious consideration by students of the history of American military technology (34, 36).

Such curious and occasionally important artifacts will continue to surface, at times requiring careful considerations by historians of a specific era. Existing guidebooks and detailed catalogues of major military and naval museum collections provide substantial, though not complete, indication of the variety of artifacts that survive as material evidence of some three hundred years of military history in North America. The early obsolescence of such publications, occasioned by the addition of substantial numbers of new accessions or major transfers to other repositories—a grim fact of life in the precarious evolution of many military museums—will be recognised by the researcher. Put more directly, the thorough scholar invariably moves beyond the static printed catalogue to avail himself personally of the knowledge of museum specialists, including those who have for some time been retired. In the area of early American naval and maritime history, for instance, knowledgeable students have drawn extensively on such classic treatises as Howard I. Chapelle's *The History of American Sailing Ships* (15), *The History of the American Sailing Navy* (16), *The National Watercraft Collection* (17), and *The Search for Speed under Sail* (18) as well as Marion V. Brewington's *Chesapeake Bay: A Pictorial Maritime History* (8), *Shipcarvers of North America* (9) and his collaborative *The Marine Paintings and Drawings in the Peabody Museum of Salem* (10). As opportunity permitted, they have additionally corresponded with and visited these notable authorities on American naval construction in the age of sail, thereby drawing upon their exceptional command of relevant plans, specifications, paintings and journals that document the careers of individual vessels, shipbuilders and naval architects.

Through personal association with such internationally recognized authorities the scholar gains access to specialized information extant not only in individual American museums but also in related institutions abroad. The range of such curatorial expertise, founded on years of exposure to and study of major national collections, as well as extensive research overseas, has been greatly enhanced in recent years through closer trans-Atlantic collaboration, generated by the emergence of two major museum associations, the International Association of Museums of Arms and Military History, whose secretary general is seated at the new National Army Museum in Chelsea, London, and the International Congress of

Maritime Museums, currently based at the National Maritime Museum in Greenwich. A concise guide to the resources of the former Association, which was founded in 1957, is provided in the *Directory of Museums of Arms and Military History* (3), an invaluable record of the location, staff, collections, archives, publications and business hours of more than two hundred of the world's principal military and naval museums. Additional insight into the history, collections, facilities, organization, exhibition techniques, public services and museum philosophy of more than a score of Europe's leading military repositories is afforded in J. Lee Westrat's *European Military Museums* (55), a perspective study undertaken in 1958 by President Dwight D. Eisenhower's Committee on the American Armed Forces Museum. For the military and naval historian seriously interested in securing an adequate perspective of "the other side of the hill," these publications provide vital guideposts to fruitful trans-Atlantic study. Evidence of research interests in the maritime area is afforded in *The Proceedings of the First International Congress of Maritime Museums* (5), as well well as periodic notices in P. K. Lundeburg's "Museum Perspective" contribution to *Military Affairs* (37).

MILITARY MUSEUMS. An important guide to military museum prospecting in North America is found in the *Directory of U.S. Army Museums* (23). Herein are described, by army area, no fewer than sixty-seven establishments, ranging from overseas divisional exhibit centers to the venerable West Point Museum at the U.S. Military Academy, that constitute the U.S. Army Museum System. To these notices are appended data on seventeen non-Army museums including the U.S. Air Force Museum at Wright-Patterson Air Force Base, Dayton, Ohio, 45433; the Medical Museum of the Armed Forces Institute of Pathology at the National Bureau of Standards, Washington, D.C. 20234; some 279 museums, battlefield sites and historic houses in the National Park Service system; and such private establishments as the War Memorial Museum of Virginia at Newport News and the John Woodman Higgins Armory at Worcester, Massachusetts.

Under the direction of Joseph H. Ewing, Head of the Historical Properties Office in the Center for Military History, the Army is currently compiling an automated master inventory of artifacts in these numerous official repositories, some of which have prepared concise guides to their resources. Of particular importance is Lloyd J. Kirtland's *Catalogue of the United States Military Academy Museum* (28), reflecting the impressive holdings in that institution for students of American ordnance, small arms and uniform development. Attention may be drawn to the unique collection of Confederate mines and torpedoes donated to the West Point Museum by Captain Peter S. Michie and illustrated in Milton F. Perry's *Infernal Machines: The Story of Confederate Submarine and Mine Warfare* (44). A particularly important collection of small arms is displayed at the Springfield Armory Museum in Springfield, Massachusetts, a private, nonprofit establishment that exhibits this major collection on loan arrangement with the Army's Historical Properties Office. Together with the National Park Service's Harper's Ferry Arsenal Museum in Maryland; the John W. Higgins Armory at Worcester, Massachusetts; the Smithsonian Institution's National Museum of History and Technology; and four Army-operated establishments in the Frankford Arsenal Museum at Philadelphia, the Picatinny Arsenal Ammunition Museum at Dover, New Jersey, the Watervliet Arsenal Museum in New York, and the John M. Browning Museum at Rock Island, Illinois; the venerable Springfield institution affords students of ninteenth-century American enterprise and weapons development valuable materiel and documentary resources on the evolution of military procurement in the United States. The Army has systematically developed the history of its numerous special corps at such centers as the Field Artillery Museum at Fort Sill, Oklahoma; the U.S. Army Medical Museum at Fort Sam Houston, Texas; the U.S. Army Intelligence Museum at Fort Huachuca, Arizona; the U.S. Cavalry Museum at Fort Riley, Kansas; the U.S. Army Finance Corps Museum at Indianpolis, Indiana; the Special Warfare Museum at Fort Bragg, North Carolina; the U.S. Army Ordnance Museum at the Aberdeen Proving Ground, Maryland; the U.S. Army Engineer Museum at Fort Belvoir, Virginia; the George S. Patton Museum of Cavalry and Armor, Fort Knox, Kentucky; the U.S. Army Quartermaster and Transportation Museums at Fort Eustis, Virginia; the National Infantry Museum at Fort Benning, Georgia; the U.S. Army Aviation Museum at Fort Rucker, Alabama; the U.S. Army Chaplain Museum at Fort Hamilton, New York; the U.S. Army Military Police Corps Museum at Fort Gordon, Georgia; the U.S. Army Communications Electronics Museum at Fort Monmouth, New Jersey; and the U.S. Army Air Defense Artillery Museum at Fort Bliss, Texas. Students of World War II will profitably explore the resources not only of the Patton Museum and the Omar N. Bradley Museum at Carlisle Barracks, Pennsylvania, but also of the National Archives' Dwight D. Eisenhower Library and Museum at Abilene, Kansas; the Douglas MacArthur Memorial at Norfolk, Virginia; the George C. Marshall Research Library and Museum at Lexington, Virginia; and the Citadel Memorial Military Museum and Archives at Charleston, South Carolina (23). The relationship between the Office of the Chief of Military History and the broad range of aforementioned military museums is effectively displayed in the proceedings of two Annual Army Museum Conferences, held at Fort Sheridan in 1973 and Fort Lee in 1974 and recorded in the useful *Army Museum Newsletter,* Numbers 9 (November 1973) and 11 (October 1974).

NAVAL MUSEUMS. The museum resources of the United States Army are somewhat more compactly organized, being substantially clustered in the national capital area and administered respectively by the Naval History Division of the Navy Department, located in the Washington Navy Yard; and by the Historical Division, Headquarters, United States Marine Corps, Washington, D.C. Information on Marine Corps museum and historical programs is provided in *Fortitudine,* the quarterly newsletter of that well-organized program, which includes not only the central Marine Corps Museum at Quantico but also developing exhibit centers at Parris Island and Camp Lejeune (22). Plans are currently developing to relocate the collections presently exhibited at Quantico, which are notably strong on uniform and automatic weapon development, in a more accessible site in the venerable Marine Corps Barracks within the Washington Navy Yard. Supported by the photographic archives, extensive reference library and combat art resources of the Marine Corps Historical Program, the Museum has developed a Manuscript Register Series that affords ample introduction to its growing collection of manuscripts illuminating the careers of representative Marines. Of special interest is the second in this series, compiled by Charles A. Wood and Jack B. Hilliard, *Register of the McLane Tilton Papers, 1861-1914* (58), which provides insight into a critical era in the Corps' development.

Located on the waterfront of the Washington Navy Yard is the U.S. Naval Memorial Museum, the possessor of an outstanding collection of American naval ordnance dating from the mid-nineteenth century that is particularly rich in captured heavy Confederate armament. Housed within one of the large gun-turning sheds of the former Naval Gun Factory, this Museum draws upon the extensive historical collections of the Navy Department to depict the chronological development of American sea power. Within the Museum is located the curator's office of the Naval History Center, which is currently embarked on a major program to incorporate the Navy's historical holdings in a central data bank. At present, these holdings are being increased by inclusion of numerous models, personal memorabilia and archival items found in the Submarine Force Library and Museum maintained at the U.S. Submarine Base in Groton, Connecticut. This latter institution, currently seriously understaffed, affords students of United States undersea warfare development a wide range of photographic and technical data, owing to this Museum's earlier close association with the Electric Boat Company. Similarly related to the Washington-based Naval History Center is the U.S. Naval Aviation Museum, located at the Naval Aviation School in Pensacola, Florida, an establishment that has recently developed an important collection of historic American naval aircraft (4). A useful guide to American warship exhibits, ranging from the Continental Gondola *Philadelphia* and Frigate *Constitution* to the World War II battleships *Massachusetts* and *North Carolina* is provided in an appendix to Volume III of the Naval History Division's *Dictionary of American Naval Fighting Ships* (51).

Of major significance to naval historians are the pictorial, documentary and three-dimensional collections of the Naval Historical Foundation, which offers topical exhibitions from these and related holdings in its Truxtun-Decatur Naval Museum located west of Jackson Place in Washington. Numerous printed registers of the Foundation's archival holdings in the Library of Congress Manuscripts Division have been consolidated in *The Naval Historical Foundation Manuscripts Collection: A Catalogue* (42). Employed in conjunction with the Foundation's impressive print collections, these manuscript holdings constitute important resources for the biographer and social historian. They may be profitably supplemented by the extensive photographic archives of the Naval History Center located in the Naval Memorial Museum, and by the nearby holdings, particularly impressive for the period since 1941, of the U.S. Navy Combat Art Center.

At nearby Annapolis are found the extensive collections, archives and library of the U.S. Naval Academy Museum, reflecting the careers of that institution's notable graduates. Still useful is Herman F. Kraft's *Catalogue of Historic Objects at the United States Naval Academy* (29), reflecting the existence of important artifacts in other parts of the Yard. Incorporating the earlier collections of the Brooklyn Naval Lyceum and the Boston Naval Library and Institute, the Naval Academy Museum also possesses two significant foreign holdings of interest to students of naval architecture. Long overlooked but rich in association with the bicentennials of the American and French Revolutions is the small but striking Vattemare Collection of French naval models, some of which were originally fashioned at St. Malo for the unfortunate Louis XVI. Including a rigged model of the Comte de Grasse's flagship *Ville de Paris,* this collection has survived extraordinary vicissitudes, having been unsuccessfully offered to Napoleon Bonaparte and Tsar Alexander I, and after suffering years of neglect at the Ministry of Marine in Paris, having been finally donated to the young Naval Academy on the Severn in 1854 through the good offices of John Quincy Adams. Scarcely less remarkable has been the career of the magnificent Henry Huddleston Rogers Collection at Annapolis, a holding of original British warship models that is comparable in historical associations and research value to the rich Admiralty model collections in the National Maritime Museum at Greenwich and the Science Museum at London. The second edition of its catalogue, *The Henry Huddleston Rogers Collection of Ship Models* (50), provides excellent photographic coverage of such superb works as the *Royal William* (1692) and *Duke* (1776) models but presents unchanged several attributions challenged two decades ago by Howard I. Chapelle. Students of the American Revolution will find the Naval Academy's holdings of John Paul Jones material particularly rewarding, including the John L. Senior Collection of Jones manuscripts. Researchers will also profit from careful perusal of the *Catalogue of the Beverley R. Robinson Collection of Naval Battle Prints* (49), which provides entree to a collection of over 1200 items.

In addition to the resources of the aforementioned naval museums, extensive pictorial, library and artifact collections are found in the Mariners' Museum at Newport News, Virginia; the Peabody Museum of Salem, Massachusetts; and the new National Museum of History and Technology of the Smithsonian Institution. A comprehensive introduction to the Newport News establishment is provided in *The Mariners' Museum: A History and Guide* (40), reflecting its notable holdings in ship figureheads, ship models, marine prints and perhaps the nation's finest maritime library. The latter resource is thoroughly displayed in the Museum's *Dictionary Catalogue of the Library* (39), a publication that identifies one of the prime motives for the recent establishment of a joint program in American maritime and naval history sponsored by the Mariners' Museum and Christopher Newport College of Newport News. In addition to its wide-ranging coverage of the maritime history of Chesapeake Bay, the Mariners' Museum affords notable facilities for students of the history of American naval architecture, including the Crabtree collection of ship models and a gallery devoted to the career of William Francis Gibbs, one of the nation's foremost modern naval architects and marine engineers.

The evolution of a unique New England maritime institution is delineated in Walter M. Whitehill's *The East India Marine Society and the Peabody Museum of Salem* (56), whose history is intertwined with early American trade and overseas exploration. More specifically naval resources at Salem include the papers of Josiah Fox, an important link in the transmission of British shipbuilding technology to the infant United States, and the venerable model of the frigate *Constitution,* presented to the East India Marine Society by Captain Isaac Hull at the height of her fighting career. The pictorial treasures of the Peabody Museum, frequently revealed in the *American Neptune,* have been handsomely reproduced in Marion V. and Dorothy Brewington's *The Marine Paintings and Drawings in the Peabody Museum of Salem* (10), as well as in John Wilmerding's *A History of American Marine Painting* (57). The latter work provides an important guide to significant collections of marine art, private as well as institutional, throughout the United States, suggesting to students the particular strengths of the Boston Museum of Fine Arts; the Essex Institute of Salem, Massachusetts; the Brooklyn Museum; the Metropolitan Museum; the New York Historical Society; the National Gallery of Art; and the National Portrait Gallery. Similarly, by reference to the Catalogue of American Portraits being banked by the National Portrait Gallery, the researcher will avail himself of an increasingly useful guide to historical portraits throughout the nation. Before concluding this survey of naval resources at the Salem institution, one should cite also Marion V. Brewington's *The Peabody Museum Collection of Navigation Instruments* (11), another facet of seafaring that has proved of increasing significance to naval historians.

Through the Smithsonian Studies in History and Technology and other serial publications, the National Museum of History and Technology has undertaken not only to survey major national military collections in that institution but, in accordance with the tradition of scientific inquiry at the Smithsonian, to explore areas in the history of military technology that have hitherto been substantially neglected in the United States. The extensive uniform collections of its Division of Military History, founded upon early and substantial accessions from the Quartermaster Corps collections at Philadelphia, have been surveyed in part in J. Duncan Campbell and Edgar M. Howell's well-documented *American Military Insignia, 1800-1851* (13) and Edgar M. Howell and Donald E. Kloster's *United States Army Headgear to 1854* (25), the latter work shortly to be followed by a second volume on that theme rounding out the century. The Museum's extensive firearms collections are initially represented in Berkeley R. Lewis's *Small Arms and Ammunition in the United States Service* (31). A remarkable example of in-depth probing of museum artifacts and related archival material is Chauncey C. Loomis's *Weird and Tragic Shores: The Story of Charles Francis Hall, Explorer* (33) which utilizes the extensive Charles Francis Hall Collection in the Division of Naval History. The technique of verifying the age of military colors through fabric and fiber analysis is exhaustively described in Grace Rogers Cooper's *Thirteen-Star Flags: Keys to Identification* (21), which has proven a veritable blockbuster during the Bicentennial of the American Revolution. The social history of the United States Navy, long neglected, is reflected in Mendel L. Peterson's *The Journals of Daniel Noble Johnson (1822-1863), United States Navy* (47), affording evidence in microcosm from surviving naval journals on those themes dealt with in Harold D. Langley's trailblazing *Social Reform in the United States Navy, 1798-1862* (30), a work which provides the basis for more broadly interpretive exhibits on the American naval service.

Representative of a second category of Smithsonian publications in military history is Emmanuel Raymond Lewis's *Seacoast Fortifications of the United States: An Introductory History* (32), which provides a succinct, illustrated survey of the evolution of American coastal defense systems since the colonial era. Hitherto neglected, save in National Park Service monographs and guides to individual sites such as Fort McHenry, Fort Pulaski and Fort Sumpter, Lewis's preliminary outline suggests the need for a multivolume treatment of this classic theme, based on archival holdings in Europe as well as the United States. Graphic insight into ordnance technology during the era of the American Revolution is provided in Melvin H. Jackson and Charles de Beer's *Eighteenth Century Gunfounding* (27), which carefully documents an exceptional series of fifty pencil and watercolor drawings on the art of gunfounding as practiced by Jan and Pieter Verbruggen in the Royal Brass Foundry at Woolwich. An enigmatic chapter in the evolution of sea mine technology in the United States is explored by Philip K. Lundeberg in *Samuel Colt's Submarine Battery* (34), a study that reflects the interaction of early telegraphy, marine salvage, and galvanic mine warfare. Representative of growing Smithsonian attention to peripheral modes of warfare is Melvin H. Jackson's *Privateer's in Charleston, 1793-1796* (26), which provides an intriguing case study in the spontaneous generation of that form of economic warfare.

Striking episodes in the evolution of American naval architecture that are embodied in models exhibited in the Hall of the Armed Forces have also received extensive documentation in recent publications. Howard I. Chapelle and Leon D. Polland's *The Constellation Question* (19), a veritable head-on collision within two covers, thoroughly ventilates the continuing controversy as to whether the *Constellation* presently exhibited at Baltimore is indeed the original 36-gun frigate launched at that Maryland entrepot in 1797 or a classic example of an "administrative rebuilding" of the type occasionally carried out by the Navy in the nineteenth century, in this instance at the Norfolk Navy Yard during 1853-55.

The extensive collection of American warship models developed at the National Museum of History and Technology during the past two decades, ranging from a modern model of the 50-gun H.M.S. *Falkland*, constructed in the Province of Maine in 1695, to a sleek model of the nuclear, ballistic missile submarine *George Washington,* includes some 180 original builders' half models as well as two score fully-rigged models on long-term loan from the total official warship model holdings of the Navy Department. The half models, dating from the War of 1812, cover much of the nineteenth century, while the full-hulled official specimens were first undertaken by the Bureau of Construction and Repair for the Columbian Exposition in 1893. The vital importance of adequate archival resources for museum research is embodied in some thirty fully-rigged warship models created for the collection to illustrate two centuries of American naval construction prior to the Columbian Exposition. Admiralty draughts in the National Maritime Museum at Greenwich provide the technical basis for those models representing the colonial and Revolutionary War eras. The importance of European archives for the evolution of 19th century warship construction in the United

States is strikingly illustrated in a model of the world's first steam warship, described in Howard I. Chapelle's *Fulton's "Steam Battery": Blockship and Catamaran* (14), which is based on detailed analysis of a rare set of French draughts for that vessel discovered by Chapelle in 1960 at the Rigsarkivet in Copenhagen. Conversely, many of the original half models at the Smithsonian are irreplacable primary sources on nineteenth century American naval construction, for, in the absence of surviving contemporary building draughts, they provide the basis for reconstructing the exact lines on which these vessels were constructed. A detailed description of one technique utilized by the Division of Naval History in taking the hull lines from a half model is contained in Dana Wegner's "An Experiment in Taking off Lines" (54).

Archaeological sites on land and under water promise to provide important technical data for students of military technology and social history during the ensuing decade, particularly at sites currently being excavated by the National Park Service in conjunction with the Bicentennial of the American Revolution. An important contribution already available is Harold L. Peterson's *Arms and Armor in Colonial America, 1526-1783* (45), based on archaeological finds as well as major arms collections in Europe and North America. A particularly valuable supplement emanating from one of the nation's most remarkable restored fortresses is *The Bulletin of the Fort Ticonderoga Museum* (12). Promising underwater exploration is currently under way in Narragansett Bay and the Penobscot River, strongly indicating that the era of the American Revolution is indeed ripe for major archaeological programing. Of great practical value in such enterprises is Mendel L. Peterson's *History under the Sea: A Manual for Underwater Exploration* (46), a pioneer work that may usefully be supplemented by George F. Bass, editor, *A History of Seafaring Based on Underwater Archaeology* (6), which deals succinctly with a number of important underwater sites in North America.

Presently the only intact man-of-war from the era of the American Revolution exhibited on this continent, the Continental Gondola *Philadelphia* on display in the National Museum of History and Technology constitutes an exceptional time capsule from Benedict Arnold's Northern Campaign of 1776, having been recovered from the depths of Valcour Bay in 1935 with its main battery and much of its crew's equipage in identifiable condition. With the recent discovery of the *Philadelphia* crew's payroll, which opens up the long obscure human dimension of her brief career on Lake Champlain, this venerable gunboat demonstrates that such a national treasure may become susceptible of virtually unending documentation.

In concluding this survey of museum resources for United States military history, the point should be reemphasized that an exceptional amount of important documentation survives in both European and North American archives and museums. The importance of the holdings at the National Archives of Canada and the Canadian War Museum at Ottawa is well recognized, but scholars may be unfamiliar with the extent of military pictorial material at the New Brunswick Museum, which is impressively documented in the *Catalogue of the John Clarence Webster Canadiana Collection, New Brunswick Museum* (53). From R. C. Anderson's *Catalogue of Ship Models* (2); A. H. Waite and A. L. Tucker's *Ships' Plans: A Select*

List from the Collection of the National Maritime Museum (52); and the multivolume Catalogue of the Library (41) of the National Maritime Museum at Greenwich to G. S. Laird Clowes' earlier classic, Sailing Ships: Their History and Development, as Illustrated by the Collection of Ship-Models in the Science Museum (20), the researcher in the history of naval technology in the age of sail finds exceptional resources in the London area. A superb reflection of comparable museum resources in France is afforded in Jean Boudriot's brillantly illustrated Le Vaisseau de 74 Canons (7), whose four volumes will provide unparalleled insight into the technology and management of French naval power during the era of the American Revolution. Additional bibliographic leads might be detailed regarding holdings of militaria overseas that may fruitfully be researched by students of American military and air power history, yet the fundamental principle holds that their most accessible and reliable guides will be knowledgeable curators at military and naval museums in the United States.

BIBLIOGRAPHY

1. The American Neptune. The Peabody Museum of Salem, Massachusetts.
2. Anderson, R. C. Catalogue of Ship Models. London: H.M.S.O., 1952.
3. Anon. Directory of Museums of Arms and Military History. Second edition, Copenhagen: Tojhusmuseum, 1970. Compiled by Arne Hoff.
4. Anon. "The New Naval Aviation Museum." Naval Aviation News (September 1974).
5. Anon. The Proceedings of the First International Congress of Maritime Museums. Greenwich, England: National Maritime Museum, 1974. Edited by David Proctor.
6. Bass, George, editor. A History of Seafaring Based on Underwater Archaeology. New York: Walker, 1972.
7. Boudriot, Jean. Le Vaisseau de 74 Canons. 4 vols., Grenoble, France: Editions de 4 Seigneurs, 1973-1975.
8. Brewington, Marion V. Chesapeake Bay: A Pictorial Maritime History. Cambridge, Md.: Cornell Maritime Press, 1956.
9. Brewington, Marion V. Shipcarvers of North America. Barre, Mass.: Barre Publishing Co., 1962.
10. Brewington, Marion V. and Dorothy. The Marine Paintings and Drawings in the Peabody Museum of Salem. Salem, Mass.: Peabody Museum, 1968.
11. Brewington, Marion V. The Peabody Museum Collection of Navigation Instruments. Salem, Mass.: Peabody Museum, 1963.
12. Bulletin of the Fort Ticonderoga Museum. Ticonderoga, N.Y.
13. Campbell, J. Duncan, and Edgar M. Howell. American Military Insignia, 1800-1851. Washington: Smithsonian Institution Press, 1963.

14. Chapelle, Howard I. *Fulton's "Steam Battery": Blockship and Cata-maran.* Washington: Smithsonian Institution Press, 1964.
15. Chapelle, Howard I. *The History of American Sailing Ships.* New York: Norton, 1935.
16. Chapelle, Howard I. *The History of the American Sailing Navy.* New York: Norton, 1949.
17. Chapelle, Howard I. *The National Watercraft Collection.* Washington: Smithsonian Institution Press, 1960.
18. Chapelle, Howard I. *The Search for Speed under Sail.* New York: Norton, 1967.
19. Chapelle, Howard I., and Leon D. Polland. *The "Constellation" Question.* Washington: Smithsonian Institution Press, 1970.
20. Clowes, G. S. Laird. *Sailing Ships: Their History and Development, as Illustrated by the Collection of Ship-Models in the Science Museum.* 2 vols., London: H.M.S.O., 1930-1948.
21. Cooper, Grace Rogers. *Thirteen-Star Flags: Keys to Identification.* Washington: Smithsonian Institution Press, 1973.
22. *Fortitudine.* History and Museums Division, Headquarters, U.S.M.C.
23. *Directory of Museums of Arms and Military History.* Second edition. Copenhagen: Tojhusmuseum, 1970.
24. Historical Properties Branch, U.S. Army. *Directory of U.S. Army Museums.* Washington: Office of the Chief of Military History, 1968.
25. Howell, Edgar M., and Donald E. Kloster. *United States Army Headgear to 1854.* Washington: Smithsonian Institution Press, 1969.
26. Jackson, Melvin H. *Privateers in Charleston, 1793-1796: An Account of a French Palatinate in South Carolina.* Washington: Smithsonian Institution Press, 1969.
27. Jackson, Melvin H., and Charles de Beer, *Eighteenth Century Gunfounding.* Newton Abbot, England: David and Charles, 1974.
28. Kirtland, Lloyd J. *Catalogue of the United States Military Academy Museum.* West Point, N.Y.: U.S.M.A. Printing Office, 1944.
29. Kraft, Herman F. *Catalogue of Historic Objects at the United States Naval Academy.* Annapolis: U.S. Naval Institute, 1925.
30. Langley, Harold D. *Social Reform in the United States Navy, 1798-1862.* Urbana: University of Illinois Press, 1967.
31. Lewis, Berkeley R. *Small Arms and Ammunition in the United States Service.* Washington: Smithsonian Institution Press, 1960.
32. Lewis, E. Raymond. *Seacoast Fortifications of the United States: An Introductory History.* Washington: Smithsonian Institution Press, 1970.
33. Loomis, Chauncey C. *Weird and Tragic Shores: The Story of Charles Francis Hall, Explorer.* New York: Knopf, 1971.
34. Lundeberg, Philip K. *Samuel Colt's Submarine Battery: The Secret and the Enigma.* Washington: Smithsonian Institution Press, 1974.
35. Lundeberg, Philip K. *The Continental Gondola "Philadelphia".* Washington: Smithsonian Institution Press, 1966.
36. Lundeberg, Philip K. "The Challenge of the Museum Dimension,"

Military Affairs, XXXVII (October 1973), pp. 105-107.

37. Lundeberg, Philip K. "The Museum Perspective." *Military Affairs*, 1968-1975.

38. *The Mariners' Mirror*. The Society for Nautical Research, National Maritime Museum, Greenwich, England.

39. The Mariners Museum. *Dictionary Catalogue of the Library*. 9 vols., Boston: G. K. Hall, 1964.

40. The Mariners Museum. *The Mariners Museum: A History and Guide*. Newport News, Va.: Mariners Museum, 1950.

41. National Maritime Museum. *Catalogue of the Library*. Multivolume edition, London: H.M.S.O., 1968 to date.

42. Naval Historical Foundation. *The Naval Historical Foundation Manuscripts Collection*. Washington: G.P.O., 1975.

43. New Brunswick Museum. *Catalogue of the John Clarence Webster Canadiana Collection, New Brunswick Museum*. St. John: New Brunswick Museum, 1939-1949. 3 vols.

44. Perry, Milton F. *Infernal Machines: The Story of Confederate Submarine and Mine Warfare*. Baton Rouge, La.: Louisiana University Press, 1965.

45. Peterson, Harold. *Arms and Armor in Colonial America, 1526-1783*. Harrisburg: Stackpole, 1956.

46. Peterson, Mendel L. *History Under the Sea: A Manual for Underwater Exploration*. Washington: Smithsonian Institution Press, 1965, 1969.

47. Peterson, Mendel L. *The Journals of Daniel Noble Johnson (1822-1863), United States Navy*. Washington: Smithsonian Institution Press, 1959.

48. Pineau, Roger, editor. *The Japan Expedition, 1852-1854: The Personal Journal of Commodore Matthew C. Perry*. Washington: Smithsonian Institution Press, 1968.

49. United States Naval Academy Museum. *Catalogue of the Beverley R. Robinson Collection of Naval Battle Prints*. Annapolis: U.S. Naval Academy Museum, 1953.

50. United States Naval Academy Museum. *The Henry Huddleston Rogers Collection of Ship Models*. Annapolis: U.S. Naval Academy Museum, 1972.

51. United States Navy Naval History Division. *Dictionary of American Naval Fighting Ships*. Multivolume edition, Washington, Naval History Division, 1959 to date. Volume III includes an appendix on "Historic Ship Exhibits in the United States."

52. Waite, A. H., and A. L. Tucker. *Ships' Plans: A Select List from the Collection of the National Maritime Museum*. Greenwich, England: National Maritime Museum, 1959.

53. Webster, John Clarence. *Catalogue of the John Clarence Webster Canadiana Collection, New Brunswick Museum*. 3 vols., St. John: New Brunswick Museum, 1939-1949.

54. Wegner, Dana. "An Experiment in Taking Off Lines." *Nautical Research Journal*, XX (April 1974), pp. 149-155.

55. Westrate, J. Lee. *European Military Museums: A Survey of Their Philosophy, Facilities, Programs, and Management*. Washington: Smithsonian Institution Press, 1961.

56. Whitehill, Walter M. *The East India Society and the Peabody Museum of Salem*. Salem, Mass.: Peabody Museum, 1949.
57. Wilmerding, John. *A History of American Marine Painting*. Boston: Little, Brown, 1968.
58. Wood, Charles A., and Jack B. Hilliard. *Register of the McLane Tilton Papers, 1861-1914*. Quantico, Va.: Marine Corps Museum, no date.